W9-CIA-297

THE SHAH AND I

THE SHAH AND I :

The Confidential Diary of Iran's Royal Court, 1969–1977

Asadollah Alam

Introduced and Edited by
Alinaghi Alikhani

Translated into English by
Alinaghi Alikhani and
Nicholas Vincent

St. Martin's Press
New York

Library of Congress Cataloging-in-Publication Data

Alam, Asadollah, 1919–1977.
    The Shah and I : the confidential diary of Iran's royal court, 1969–1977 /
Asadollah Alam ; introduced and edited by A. Alikhani.
        p.   cm.
    Abridged translation from the Persian manuscript.
    Includes bibliographical references.
    ISBN 0-312-07133-7
        1. Alam, Asadollah, 1919–1977—Diaries. 2. Statesmen—Iran—Diaries.
3. Mohammed Reza Pahlavi, Shah of Iran, 1919-   .   4. Iran—Politics and
    government—1941–1979.   I. Alikhani, A. (Alinaghi)   II. Title.
    DS316.9.A35A3   1992
955.05'3'092—dc20
[B]   91-33221
                                                                      CIP

First published in Great Britain by I.B. Tauris & Company Limited.

First U.S. Edition: February 1992
10   9   8   7   6   5   4   3   2   1

Preface

The diaries of prominent people contribute greatly to our understanding of history. They possess that warm, human dimension often lacking in official records. Those published here form a daily commentary on the habits and the philosophy of Mohammad Reza Shah Pahlavi. They begin in 1969 with the Shah approaching the zenith of his political power, intervening with increasing regularity in the day-to-day concerns of government. To his command of the army he had added personal control over the nation's oil policy and foreign relations. It was to the Shah himself that foreign leaders were referred in their dealings with Iran. His too was the ultimate authority in matters of social or economic policy. To handle such a weight of business the Shah required the services of a first-rate politician, capable of relaying orders and of ensuring that they were obeyed. In Amir Asadollah Alam he found precisely the man he was after. Appointed Minister of Court in December 1966, Alam combined experience, loyalty and shrewd efficiency. By virtue of his office he ranked as one of the two or three most powerful men at court, but of these no one was closer to the Shah or more trusted by him.

Hardly a day went by without Alam and the Shah spending an hour or more alone in audience, besides the constant stream of telephone conversations and memoranda that passed between them. Often they lunched or dined together. No one else enjoyed such access at court, often for as much as five or six hours a day.

The diaries themselves begin in 1969 and continue with various interruptions until Alam's retirement as Court Minister in the summer of 1977. His death and the first stirring of revolution occurred only a few months later. Generally he wrote late at night, using his diary not only for personal impressions but to file copies of letters and memoranda that he considered worth preserving. As might be expected his workload forced him to write in considerable haste. In addition to his daily encounters with the Shah, he was at pains to record meetings with foreign ambassadors and officials,

Iranian politicians, government ministers and a wealth of others. As an observer, he was acute and possessed of a great sense of humour.

Since 1979 there has been a flood of books and articles on pre-revolutionary Iran, most of them handicapped by a shortage of documentary evidence, above all of evidence from within the Shah's regime. For example it has been assumed that the Shah was aware of the cancer that eventually killed him; others have suggested that his half-hearted attempts to widen political debate during his final years heralded a liberalization of Iran, a desire to bequeath a more stable, democratic nation to his son. In fact, Alam's diary reveals that the Shah went in ignorance of the true nature of his illness right up to the revolution. By the same token, he remained convinced of the faultlessness of his conduct of government, wishing it to continue entirely unchanged under his successor. In this and countless other ways, the diaries rank as an historical source of the first magnitude.

In general, Alam adhered to the same format day by day; recording first local and then international events. He usually begins each entry with an account of the meetings held at his house over breakfast, followed by his regular, daily audiences with the Shah, and whatever other discussions occurred later. For palace lunches and dinners he records titbits of conversation, political or light-hearted. He then provides a candid résumé of his own and the Shah's outings. Only then does he pass on to international affairs, reporting news from around the world, often in repetitive detail, accompanied by comments which reflect his own, or more probably the Shah's, personal view. Interspersed amongst these entries are various letters exchanged between the Shah and other world leaders, private correspondence, reports and various miscellaneous jottings.

To begin with Alam used hard-backed notebooks, resorting to loose sheets as security came to concern him more. Regular instalments were dispatched to Switzerland for safe-keeping. Of these there is incontrovertible evidence that the earliest notebook, preceding that which now begins the diary, has gone missing; it was never deposited in Geneva. No diary at all was kept for the Iranian calendar year 1350 (21 March 1971–21 March 1972), due to Alam's involvement in organizing celebrations to mark 2500 years of monarchy in Iran. Despite these gaps, the archive of diaries, letters and memoranda stands at well in excess of five thousand pages.

For the purposes of this English edition it has been thought best to delete or radically reduce the following classes of entry, significant deletions being marked by dots in the printed text:

Alam's breakfast time discussions, save in a few instances where these were sufficiently interesting to merit their preservation.

The routine pleasantries that begin virtually every audience with the Shah; remarks about the weather, above all the Iranian *idée fixe* concerning lack of rain.

The final sentence to most entries which records the time of writing, generally after midnight.

The names of a few individuals still living in Iran – concealed here for reasons that are all too obvious.

Various ruthless and derogatory remarks concerning friends whom the Alam family has no desire to offend.

What might be termed affairs, not necessarily of the heart; repetitive in effect and excluded here save where they contribute to the general atmosphere or shed an amusing light.

World news reported at great length by Alam, included here only where he records some personal remark by himself or the Shah.

Issues that can have little or no meaning to non-Iranian readers; obscure personalities, topographical details.

In addition, the editor has corrected a few obvious errors in names and dates. Marginalia and misplaced entries have been inserted in the main text in logical sequence.

In the final months of his life Alam grew increasingly pessimistic about the prospects for Iran and her monarchy. He asked that his wife delay disclosure or publication of his diaries until such time as the Pahlavi dynasty no longer ruled Iran. Accordingly it was not until June 1987, nearly a decade after the revolution, that Mrs Alam and her daughters, Roudabeh and Naz, considered the time had come to carry out Alam's wishes. I was approached as editor, and allowed complete freedom in selecting material for inclusion or deletion. Beyond this process of selection, outlined above, I have added footnotes, brief explanatory passages at the start of each year and as an introduction, sketches of Alam and the Shah, all of them intended to make these diaries more approachable to non-specialist readers.

Among those many people who have helped in the preparation of this book I should particularly like to thank Mrs Alam, Roudabeh and Naz Alam, who during the course of several extended interviews discussed their lives with Alam and their memories of the Imperial Court. Mrs Fatemeh Khozeymeh Alam and her husband Mr Amir Hossein Khozeymeh Alam, the diarist's sister and brother-in-law, provided much valuable information on the Alam family and their centuries old association with Birjand. I am also indebted to many other friends, especially to Majid A'alam, Manoutchehr Agah, Ali Naqi Assadi, Sadeq Azimi, Mohammad Ja'far Behbehanian, Paul H. Broughal Woods, Cyrus Ghani, Ebrahim Golestan, Said Goudarznia, Manouchehr Hashemi, Amir Parviz Khozeymeh Alam, Pirouz Mojtahedzadeh, Reza Moqaddam, Farrokh Najmabadi, Said Rezvani and Mohammed Yeganeh.

The present edition is an abridgement of the Persian original. English is my third language. I would never have been able to write this edition without the help of Nicholas Vincent – of Peterhouse, Cambridge, who transliterated virtually every word from my original draft. Although he is a historian by profession, Nicholas is also a poet and this gave us the opportunity to include various literal translations of Persian poetry jotted down by Alam.

Finally, I should like to thank my wife Suzanne. Besides providing encouragement and support, she single-handedly typed out this translation not once, nor twice, but in at least three complete revisions, a feat of tact and endurance whose true extent is known only to herself.

Introduction

There are two principal actors in these diaries; Alam, the author who believed himself to be witnessing one of the greatest periods in Iranian history; and the Shah, who was convinced that his dreams had been realized and that he ruled as the hero of his nation, loved and venerated by the Iranian people. Paradoxically it was Alam, the admirer, who was sprung from the old Persian aristocracy; his hero, the Shah, was born the son of a humble soldier, albeit a soldier who was later to ascend the throne. Amidst the turbulence and vicissitudes of post-war Iran a bond of friendship had been forged beween the two men. The Shah could rely on Alam's unfailing loyalty and opened his heart to him more readily than to any other individual at Court. To appreciate the full historical and human significance of their relationship we need to know more of both men.

Amir Asadollah Alam

For more than a thousand years the name Alam has been associated with what now forms Iran's eastern frontier. The second Abbasid Caliph, al-Mansour (AD 754–775) dispatched one of his commanders, Khazem bin Khozeymeh, to quell a revolt in the province of Khorassan. Having successfully completed their mission Khazem and his Khozeymeh clan settled in Qohestan, the southern part of the province, from where he and his descendants ruled the semi-desert surrounding the present city of Birjand. In the late eighteenth century three heads of the clan in succession took the name Amir Alam Khan, giving rise to a branch of the family named Alam, sprung from the main root which retained the name Khozeymeh.

Amir Asadollah Alam's father, Mohammad Ebrahim (1881–1944) succeeded a brother far older than himself and was granted the governorship of Birjand and the title *Showkat al-Molk* by Mozaffareddin Shah Qajar. Mohammad Ebrahim was a remarkable man who in his youth witnessed the Iranian constitutional revolution (1905–7), an experience that was to live with him for the rest of his life. He

1

established contacts with the leading constitutionalists, and their liberal ideas prompted him to attempt various radical departures within Birjand, his great ambition being to introduce modern schooling to the region.

All three of Mohammad Ebrahim's daughters and his only son, Amir Asadollah, were born in Birjand and educated at the school established by their father. In addition, they received private coaching in the Persian classics and in French – the fashionable language of the day. Alam's familiarity with the classics shines through in his diaries. Although writing late at night, overworked and, towards the end, in the throes of a fatal illness, he none the less makes frequent quotations from Persian poetry; everything from the greatest masterpieces down to simple proverbs.

Alam was born in August 1919, only two months before the Shah. His school days were passed exclusively in Birjand – a pleasant but a frugal existence. Sport, especially riding, shooting and tennis, were the order of the day; and his father had a particular fondness for family picnics. All these activities were to remain dear to Alam who subsequently became a leading patron of Iran's Equestrian Society. It was during his childhood that the Qajar dynasty was driven from the throne (1925), to be supplanted by Reza Shah, founder of a new dynasty, the Pahlavis. Reza Shah attempted a vast programme of modernization accompanied by nationalistic propaganda glorifying the country's pre-Islamic past. Such policies had a special appeal to the young such as Alam, who enjoyed the additional spur of a forward-looking father, himself a supporter of Reza Shah. It was in response to the Shah's notorious fear of provincial conspiracy that Alam's father took up residence in Tehran, leaving the management of his vast estates to his son. Mohammad Ebrahim's loyalty was rewarded with his appointment as Governor of Fars, in the south of the country, and subsequently as Minister of Posts and Telecommunications. More important than his official position, as a member of Reza Shah's inner court, he enjoyed direct access to his sovereign.

Twice Reza Shah was to make decisive interventions in the life of the young Alam. First when Alam's father proposed sending the boy to Europe to study agriculture, the Shah insisted instead on his own newly established Tehran University, with its school of agriculture at Karaj, 40 km. west of the city. Secondly it was the Shah who

2

suggested Alam marry Malektaj, daughter of Ebrahim Qavam (Qavam al-Molk). It was a match intended to strengthen the links between the royal family and the non-Qajar aristocracy, since Qavam's son Ali was already married to Princess Ashraf, Reza Shah's daughter. Alam and Malektaj were betrothed on their fathers' instructions and married in the autumn of 1939. Soon after they set out for Karaj where Alam obtained his degree in agronomy. Via her network of relations his wife had already been introduced to Court, spending most weekends with the royal family. Alam now joined her, leading to his earliest, fleeting encounters with the Crown Prince, Mohammad Reza Pahlavi.

Reza Shah had long been accused of pro-German sentiments. In September 1941 Iran was invaded by British and Russian armies. The Shah was forced to abdicate in favour of his son, and to go into exile abroad. Princess Ashraf seized her opportunity. Resenting her arranged marriage, and now free from the domestic tyranny of her father, she obtained a divorce from Ali Qavam. Alam's occasional visits to Court thus ceased abruptly. It was not until four years later and in very different circumstances that he once again made contact with the young Shah. The allied army of occupation had undertaken to evacuate Iran within six months of hostilities ending in Europe. But in the event, the USSR delayed withdrawal, actively encouraging a separatist movement in Azerbaijan which seized power there, declaring an autonomous republic, independent of Tehran. With problems such as these on his northern frontier, Prime Minister Ahmad Qavam,* a shrewd man, wished to ensure strict order elsewhere in the country. Knowing the Alam family and the great influence they exerted in the south-east and eastern provinces, he appointed Alam, still only in his mid-twenties, as Governor of Sistan and Baluchistan. Hence it was that early in 1945 Alam renewed his acquaintance at Court.

Despite his youth and inexperience, Alam acquitted himself well. He was careful to cultivate the Shah's friendship at a time when the Shah himself cut little ice in Iranian politics. The Shah's ambition was none the less fierce. It first expressed itself in an attempt to replace various of the ministerial old guard, men who regarded him with something not far short of contempt, with younger politicians.

---

* Qavam Saltaneh, no relation of Ebrahim Qavam.

3

In this way, in 1950 Alam found himself appointed Minister of the Interior, and subsequently Minister of Agriculture. But the assassination of the new prime minister, General Razmara, in March 1951, brought his promotion to an end. A movement favouring the nationalization of the oil industry seized power, headed by Dr Mosaddeq, leader of the National Front. Once again the Shah was relegated to the political wilderness where only a few loyal friends, Alam amongst them, cared to join him.

Only with Mosaddeq's fall in August 1953 could the Shah attempt that style of personal government that had long been his ambition. Henceforth he accumulated ever more power, surrounding himself with those who preached the advantages of strong monarchy, where the king both reigned and ruled. This was a view shared by Alam who already ranked as one of the most influential figures at Court. Between 1953 and 1962 he held a variety of appointments both at Court and as a government minister. At the Shah's bidding, he founded the Mardom (People) party, which, in Iran's travesty of democracy, was intended to perform the function of an official opposition.

From the late 1950s the Shah faced burgeoning problems both at home and abroad. Relations with Soviet Russia deteriorated rapidly after March 1959 and the signing of a bilateral defence agreement with the USA. Economic mismanagement produced a worsening balance of payments deficit, inflation and popular outcry. Events elsewhere in the region, the military coup of July 1958 which brought down Iraq's monarchy, the mounting tensions within Turkey, convinced the US government that Iran was close to collapse. The Shah was persuaded to seek aid from the International Monetary Fund and to adopt a programme of economic stabilization which, though essential, provoked yet further public criticism of his regime. Meanwhile the USA pressed him to appoint an administration capable of social reform, their favoured candidate to head it being the former Finance Minister and one time ambassador to Washington, Ali Amini.

The Shah distrusted Amini's independence and it was only with reluctance that he was persuaded to appoint him prime minister. For his part, Amini was determined to combat corruption and to introduce the sort of land reforms which had for long been advocated by the Iranian government but stifled by great landowners and their allies who dominated Parliament. At Amini's bidding the Shah dissolved both Houses of Parliament. Henceforth the government was to rule by decree, an innovation at odds with the Iranian Constitution, but considered essential by Amini. Apart from the Foreign and Defence Ministers whose nomination continued to rest with the Shah, all other ministerial posts were thrown open to Amini's appointees. Outstanding amongst these was the Minister of Agriculture, Hassan Arsanjani, a successful lawyer and journalist with leanings towards social democracy. Besides forging a straight-forward, practical approach to land reform, it was Arsanjani who managed to stir up support by the emotional force of his speeches, both amongst intellectuals and the rural masses.

Yet the Shah continued to be wary both of Amini and Arsanjani. His intervention in day-to-day policy was curtailed by Amini, whilst Arsanjani seemed to be growing too popular in the country at large. After only fourteen months in power Amini was forced to resign the premiership, prompted by a row with the Shah over the budget for the armed services. The next day (21 July 1962) Alam found himself appointed prime minister. He was given two principal objectives: to quell the mounting opposition to land reform and at the same time to subsume it within the so-called White Revolution or the Revolution of Shah and People. Arsanjani was retained as Minister of Agriculture at the Shah's command; a decision intended to brand him as the Shah's man and to transfer popular support for his policies away from Arsanjani to the Shah. As a step in this direction, various additional reforms were introduced; the formation of education corps, whose conscripts undertook basic military training followed by far longer spells teaching in rural schools; the granting of political rights to women; the establishment of profit sharing amongst sections of the industrial work force; all of which helped create the desired impression that Arsanjani and his reforms were merely one aspect of a far wider design, the Shah's mighty plan for his nation. Following a moving speech in which the Shah put forward a six-point pro-gramme of social reform, the government called a national ref-erendum for 26 January 1963. It proved a tremendous success for the regime, despite concerted opposition from the National Front (a party drawing its inspiration from Mosaddeq), the clergy and the greater landowners.

Alam's first assignment had been successfully fulfilled; to promote the concept of a White Revolution under the sole leadership of the Shah. The time was now ripe to dispense with Arsanjani. Completely outmanoeuvred by the Shah, within a matter of a few weeks, he was persuaded to step down from government, taking up an appointment as Iran's ambassador to Italy. In notifying the press of these changes, Alam spoke merely of disagreements with his former Minister of Agriculture over economic policy. At the same time he reminded the reporters that 'Land reform has been one of the important schemes brought to fruition by His Imperial Majesty. As you are all no doubt well aware, it was His Imperial Majesty who first initiated the scheme by his redistribution of the imperial estates ...'[1]

Having secured himself against rivalry within the regime, in the spring of 1963 Alam moved to crush the opposition beyond. A rebellion by the tribal chieftains of Fars was decisively suppressed by the army, one of the rebel leaders being killed, the others arrested. They were later tried by military tribunal and the death sentence pronounced. Meanwhile, Alam realized the necessity of undermining tribal loyalties by reforms intended to improve the lot of ordinary tribesmen. It was he who launched the regional development programme which swept away the archaic traditions of tribalism. But in the cities far more serious opposition was developing both to reform and to the Shah's dreams of personal rule. Protest was especially strident in Tehran and in the holy city of Qom, egged on by a teacher in the renowned local theological seminary, Rouhollah Khomeini, the future Ayatollah. Alam urged the need for firm resistance; should demonstrations break out the government must hit back as hard as possible. 'But how?', the Shah is said to have asked. 'With bullets, Your Majesty', Alam replied, adding that he himself would assume all the blame should their efforts fail.[2] The Shah, who was all too prone to shy away at critical moments, lost no delay in placing the security forces under Alam's personal command. The show-down came on 5 June 1963. Riots broke out, but were quelled by a violent counterattack within a matter of a few hours.

Alam's determined reaction saved the day, more or less silencing any form of organized opposition for several years to come. With the Shah's approval a new party, *Iran Novin* (New Iran), was created and allowed to contest the customary, rigged elections. This in turn paved the way for the Shah's dreams of autocracy; with the Shah cast in the role of reforming monarch, patron of a new party and a revitalized Parliament in which women, intellectuals and the working classes were for the first time allotted a place. It is a measure of the Shah's trust in him that Alam was briefed in unusual detail on the changes about to take place. Hassan Ali Mansour, leader of the new party, was to be made prime minister; an event that duly took place on 7 March 1964.

Less than a fortnight later Alam was appointed president of the Pahlavi University at Shiraz; a body urgently in need of firm management, and one for which the Shah had great ambitions, hoping that it might rival or even surpass the University of Tehran, founded by his father. In the two years of Alam's appointment, Shiraz began to be recognized as one of the country's most important centres of learning. Even so, Alam continued to devote a substantial part of his time to political and diplomatic affairs, as and when called for by the Shah. It was therefore no surprise that late in 1966 he returned to Tehran as Minister of Court. The years following this appointment form the subject of these diaries. In 1968, his doctors diagnosed the leukaemia which was gradually to weaken him and to sap his strength. However, he remained in office. Only in August 1977 did the Shah reluctantly and with much misgiving ask for his resignation. He died less than a year later, in April 1978.

The Shah

In the late 1960s the Shah stood at the very pinnacle of success. His dreams had been more or less realized. As he had always wished, he towered supreme over Iranian politics. The younger generation whom he had introduced to government looked to him as their mainstay and patron. Iran enjoyed an economic buoyancy virtually unparalleled in the third world. The future of the monarchy was guaranteed following the birth of the Crown Prince and his younger brother. A decade earlier, when chaos seemed about to engulf her, few could have anticipated that Iran would be set so securely on the highway to success. In no small part this impression of well-being stemmed from the social reforms implemented after 1963. For the first time the Shah felt himself to be at the head of his nation, portrayed as a progressive egalitarian, propelled ever onwards and upwards by the affectionate loyalty of his people. The people themselves seemed unconcerned by developments backstage. The impact of the Kennedy administration in forcing change upon Iran, the role played by Amini and his cabinet, the outstanding influence of Arsanjani, none of these things clouded public confidence in the Shah who alone was regarded as the author of reform. The Shah himself discovered a new talent in himself; the ability to deliver moving speeches, music to the ears of the masses.

To consolidate his position it was necessary for him to maintain momentum in socio-political reform. To begin with he was successful in this. The civil service was overhauled according to new, merito-cratic principles. New ministries and government agencies were set up and under the premiership of Hassan Ali Mansour and Amir Abbas Hoveyda a group of young and previously unknown men promoted to high office. As was to be expected such ministers were far more capable than their ageing predecessors of appreciating the need for dynamic, technological and social advance. Backed by the Shah they were able for a while to introduce real efficiency to the machinery of government. Free debate was encouraged, except on the issues of foreign policy, security and the armed services which were considered sacrosanct by the Shah. In the meetings he chaired, the Economic Council for example, the Shah attempted to reach consensus; even in private audiences he avoided imposing his own views on his ministers.

As government changed so did society; educational opportunities expanded almost as rapidly as the teeming cities. A generation of innovative entrepreneurs stepped in to turn the country's new-found dynamism to advantage, making use of Iran's political stability, the relative efficiency of her government and the great wealth of her natural resources. Government, funded mainly by oil income, allo-cated a substantial share of this revenue towards developing the infrastructure and assisting the private sector. Here again the Shah was influential, serving as an inspiration to the business community through his whole-hearted encouragement of local entrepreneurs.

Quite naturally people came to regard social reform as the first stage in a movement towards greater individual freedom, political participation and the rule of law. Yet the same spirit of optimism encouraged quite contrary perceptions in the Shah. Henceforth, his own, increasingly megalomaniac, dreams began to shear away ever more dangerously from the hopes and expectations of his people. Pessimism sprang up, followed swiftly by anger. Dreams of a golden future evaporated.

The trend towards autocracy

A secretive man by nature, the Shah could however be disarmingly candid. Once, during a meeting of the Economic Council, he declared that he grabbed at each new success, each new burst of popular approval, as an opportunity to consolidate his personal power.[3] It was in this way that jubilation over the freeing of Azerbaijan (1946) and the subsequent reaction to the attempt on his life (1949) enabled him to call the Constituent Assembly which increased his own personal authority. It was in this spirit and in light of the referendum of 1963 that he convinced himself that he had rendered such great service to his nation that he could dispense with even grudging obedience to the Constitution. The nation had been led into the path of greater happiness and prosperity by him and should, by definition, always endorse his decisions.

After twenty-two eventful years on the throne, the Shah reached the crossroads of his reign. Rather than respond to the spiritual and material needs of his people, a course which would have immortalized him as a great reformer, he chose to pursue a personal, fleeting glory. A system that might have been capable of rescuing Iran from backwardness and misery was allowed to collapse. The Shah could not bear the idea of democratic participation in the political decision-making process, nor could he tolerate the prospect that someone else might gain a degree of popularity. Herein lay his tragedy. He saw any successful or respected personality as a potential opponent. To counter this threat he took great care not to allow anyone else a power-base. In the Shah's opinion it was success over oil that had enabled Dr Mosaddeq to usurp the people's affections. Hence the oil industry had to be reshaped so as to avoid giving any one man overall control. When, despite these precautions, the Finance Minister, Jamshid Amouzegar, pulled off a personal triumph in negotations between OPEC and the oil companies, the Shah transferred him to the Ministry of the Interior. A few years earlier when Arsanjani demonstrated that even the humble Ministry of Agriculture could serve as a springboard to power, he was hived off to an ambassadorial position far away. Subsequently the functions of the Ministry of Agriculture were carved up between five other ministries, eliminating the threat once and for all.

Given the Shah's sensitivity to the success of his own appointees, it is hardly surprising that he regarded the prospect of popular, and possibly successful, leaders elected through democratic processes as intolerable. As the years went by, so the mere word 'democracy' came to produce an allergic response in him. Once, to mark Constitution Day the two main evening newspapers published leaders, proclaiming that Iran 'Will gradually develop western-style democracy, as the people grow accustomed to political participation at the level of village, county and province.' The Shah's response was to order Alam to call in the papers' editors and insist that they print new articles, stressing that Iran 'has no desire to pursue western-style democracy so long as in practice it merely encourages treachery and leads to tyranny by a minority.' (Diaries, 9 August 1972) Superficially between 1963 and 1975 the country boasted a pluralist political system, with a government answerable to Parliament. But in practice Parliament was carefully packed with government supporters and was forbidden by the Shah from uttering any whisper of complaint. When the official opposition leader, A. Kani, stated quite correctly that the government had rigged local elections, the Shah was furious at the slight against his country's supposed political freedoms (Diaries, 22 July 1972) and Kani was forced to resign. Yet in interviews with the press, the Shah continued to feign belief in a multi-party system, declaring that 'As a single-party system leads to dictatorship, so there must needs be an alternative party, perhaps several ... although the scope of such alternatives must be limited since our overall ideology set out in the Shah and People programme commands such popular support that there can be very little room for dissent.'[4] Convinced that the people shared his political beliefs, the Shah could see little point in an opposition party.

Throughout these years it was fashionable for the government to disclaim adherence to any political 'ism', be it communism, socialism or liberalism. As Hoveyda put it, 'Our society, our traditions and our culture differ from those of other societies, where the inability of prevailing programmes even to solve their own problems provides us with no sort of model for Iran ... Foreign ideologies are like ready-made suits, inadequate for our shape or size.'[5] In the Shah's view the people should continue to look for inspiration to the Shah and People revolution, its six main points accepted in the referendum of 1963 and since supplemented by a further thirteen. In reality these propositions carried no ideological weight, but comprised a rag-bag of slogans, of varying degrees of rationality or significance.[6]

In the autumn of 1973, the price of crude oil rose sharply, pushed upwards by OPEC resolutions and above all by the Arab–Israeli war. Iranian propagandists heralded the price rise as a great national 'victory', coining the overblown catchphrase that Iran had reached 'The Gates of the Great Civilization'. Optimism pervaded the government, most of whose ministers assumed the tremendous influx of wealth would solve every difficulty; in no time at all Iran would join the ranks of the world's most privileged nations. The Shah, who had made an undeniable contribution to OPEC's success, believed the time ripe for yet further steps towards autocracy. In March 1975 he proclaimed a single-party state, abolishing all political groups save the newly formed Rastakhiz (Resurgence) party. At the same time, in addition to the usual rhetoric about his role as the 'Guardian of the Constitution' and the Revolution of Shah and People, he introduced the idea of an 'Imperial Order', in the hierarchy of slogans and shibboleths judged equal or even superior to the Constitution. Later, attempting to justify his changes, he claimed that 'a pluralistic system only deprives the opposition of political activity'.[7]

The Shah was equally prompt to deny suggestions that his reforms heralded a transition to democracy and the limitation of his personal power. The fashionable jargon of the day spoke of both 'Imperial Order' and 'Imperial Command'. The Shah hinted to government officials that bills approved by him had legal status and could be acted upon even before their submission to Parliament. This was to slight the Constitution and the legislature to such an extent that in practice no government official ever heeded it.

The restriction of personal and political freedom implied by the new order caused the Shah no great concern. In his opinion, material well-being was the only goal for which the masses strove; hence the popularity of slogans extolling 'economic democracy' or 'democratic economics'. In the Shah's view land reform and profit-sharing had secured contentment amongst the newly-enriched work-force. In 1973, to mark the tenth anniversary of the 'White Revolution', he announced yet further reforms by which up to 49 per cent of shares in industrial corporations would be offered first to industry's own employees, and afterwards to the public. Following the declaration of the single-party state, he commanded the government to provide workers and civil servants with interest-free loans for share purchases. A month later, as the country rejoiced at the spectacular prospects for oil income, he proclaimed nationwide free education and free health care. As always, he fancied that to issue grandiloquent commands was to have those commands instantly and universally obeyed. Henceforth he genuinely believed himself the ruler of a country whose people lacked for no material comfort; peasants owned their own land, workers their own shares; from kindergarten to university and from cradle to grave the state supplied schooling and health care entirely free of charge; and all thanks to the Shah's own magnanimous endeavour. With such convictions, popular unrest could only reflect ignorance or malice. A commentator on the BBC once announced that Iran's huge arms purchases would enable her army to suppress any threat of revolution. The Shah reacted angrily, denying that contented farmers and workers could ever be tempted by revolution (Diaries, 7 October 1973). The happy farmer and the contented worker were stock figures in the Shah's pantheon, characters who tumbled from the lips of his entourage at each and every opportunity. The repetition of such catchphrases convinced the Shah of their validity. He had not a shred of doubt that his personal rule served the best interests of the country, and that it was acknowledged as such by the majority of the people.

The Shah's methods and priorities in government

The problems of his early years, his natural inclination towards intervention in government and his sense of personal destiny contributed to the make-up of a knowledgeable, some might say a brilliant, personality. Few could rival the Shah's experience. He had visited virtually every corner of Iran and travelled extensively abroad. He knew all of the more important world leaders and was at home in the hurly-burly of international politics. In private audience he exhibited the most exquisite manners and a touching shyness. It was in these, the more intimate encounters, that he was most impressive, his apparent modesty combined with a natural aura of distinction and intelligence. Lacking deep expertise in any particular field, his vast general knowledge still ranked him high amongst the world's heads of state.

Throughout, he had one fatal flaw; he wished to raise Iran to the level of the developed nations but he could not understand that to succeed Iran must first respect the rule of law, and permit some degree of popular political participation. He had always been contemptuous of the Iranian Constitution, despite his oath to uphold it. Until 1949 when he was voted additional powers, he openly declared the Constitution to be a document written 'against the King'.[8] Any code or regulation which limited his freedom of action he inevitably regarded with distaste. He could not bear to be dictated to in the administration of the state. Yet, increasingly, his personal intervention in government resulted in contradictory orders, confusion and ultimate frustration. Where foreign heads of state relied upon special advisers, the Shah refused to contemplate such practices in Iran. It was a necessity regularly urged on him by Alam, as was the advisability of allowing those in titular authority actually to make decisions. Prime Minister Hoveyda spoke of himself as a mere deputy, pointing to the Shah as the real prime minister. Hoveyda, who never once resisted the Shah's command or willingly assumed responsibility for any decision, was allowed to continue in office for thirteen, fateful years.

There were four principal areas in which the Shah intervened: the army, foreign policy, economic and social affairs, and propaganda.

The army

Following the introduction of regular five-year development plans in the 1950s, the government was supposed to devote most of its oil revenue to economic development. In practice, in maximizing oil income, the Shah had an altogether different ambition, to devote ever greater resources to the army. In the wake of every 'oil victory', and before the government could muster its own list of development projects, the Shah invariably presented a catalogue of military needs. For the fiscal year 1973–4, capital investment in the armed services increased by 300 per cent and current military expenditure more than doubled – yet still no one dared challenge the priorities of such spending. It was the Shah in person who determined the nature and quantity of any hardware to be bought, often without consulting his own commanders. News that the Shah had placed orders with foreign defence suppliers could arrive by complete surprise at staff headquarters, precipitating a mad rush to allocate funds and ensure that troops were trained and logistic arrangements made to receive such new equipment.

In his obsession with military expansion, two factors worked to the Shah's advantage. First there was President Nixon's decision to authorize the sale of unlimited conventional military hardware to Iran, without the prior approval of the State and Defense Departments. Secondly, the remarkable rise in oil prices encouraged the Shah's dreams of an army a million strong, equipped with the most advanced types of weapon. By the late 1970s military spending had risen to quite incredible levels, absorbing 10.6 per cent of gross national product, by comparison to 3.9 per cent in France or 8.7 per cent in Iran's poorer rival, Iraq. Such extravagance devoured the vast majority of oil revenue in addition to a disproportionate share of skilled labour and local commodities such as building materials, already in short supply. The country's overworked ports and harbours were clogged by the influx of imported military goods.

So long as the border dispute with Iraq grumbled on, the Shah could justify his schemes. But the Algiers agreement of 1975 effectively ended hostilities with Baghdad. Henceforth the Shah turned to more grandiose ambitions, principally in respect to the Indian Ocean, stressing the need for his navy to contribute to the protection of shipping throughout the region. Political developments in East Africa began to interest him and Iran engaged in military and economic support for Somalia in her war with Ethiopia. Close relations were established with the island of Mauritius in the hope of securing an Iranian naval base. As was repeatedly pointed out to him, the western powers considered themselves perfectly capable of policing the Indian Ocean, but the Shah continued with grandiose military designs, totally incompatible with the capabilities or needs of Iran. Prior to the Algiers agreement Iran's army might have been considered an instrument of foreign policy. Thereafter diplomacy became subordinate to the armed forces, directed almost entirely towards justifying the Shah's grandiose military ambitions.

Foreign policy
Always keen to control foreign policy, from the late 1950s the Shah's interventions became increasingly frequent until he and not the government became sole arbiter in diplomatic affairs. In the spring of 1969, for example, Iran came close to war with Iraq, yet the Shah notified his Prime Minister and the national defence council of these developments only after the army had been fully mobilized. The oil boom after 1973 only accentuated these problems, encouraging the Shah's desire for autocracy. The Ministry of Foreign Affairs, like

the army, was trea: :d as an instrument of imperial will. Iran's ambassadors were forbidden direct access to the Prime Minister even on affairs of state (Diaries, 6 March 1974).

Paramount amongst the Shah's objectives were the maintenance of close relations with his western allies, especially the United States, and the containment of threats posed by Arab nationalism and communist infiltration. This was by no means an entirely negative programme. In the Persian Gulf, the Shah achieved great success, combining perseverance with flexibility. Iran dropped her claims over Bahrain, thus ridding herself of a long-standing source of tension that had adversely affected her relations in the Persian Gulf. At the same time she stood fast over Tunbs and Abu Musa, strategically important islands which were duly recovered. By supporting rebellion amongst the Kurds and maintaining pressure along the Iraqi border, the Shah managed to force concessions from Baghdad: above all the demarcation of the Iran–Iraq border along the Shatt al-Arab waterway in accordance with Iran's most cherished hopes.

In his final decade the Shah occupied a prominent position in international politics, with innumerable contacts throughout the world. Trusted by his western allies, the Shah himself was never able to reciprocate that trust. Suspicion dogged his every move, most often his fear that the superpowers would reach some sort of bilateral understanding, with Iran caught inexorably between them. These fears grew particularly acute during oil negotiations; the Shah wary lest the Americans and the British attempt to intervene, much as they had once brought down Dr Mosaddeq prior to restoring the Shah. His feelings towards the British bordered on outright paranoia, blaming them for the hostile attitude of various Arab states, especially Iraq. In reality the western allies were far keener to undermine Iraq as an obvious Soviet satellite than they were in any way to embarrass the Shah. Even his assessment of the political systems of these countries contained its share of fantasy. Although he was familiar with the United States and had a first-hand knowledge of the func-tioning of American democracy, he once confided in Alam that the USA was guided by some sort of hidden force; an organization working in secrecy (Diaries, 9 September 1970). Never were his imaginings more fevered than when the British press printed articles even vaguely critical of Iran. Barring such misconceptions, his views on international and regional developments were mostly pertinent and realistic, and his achievement here was undeniably positive.

Economic and social policy
From the start of Iran's impressive economic development in the 1960s, the Shah's three main objectives were to be rapid economic growth, price stability and social reform. To achieve these ends, he used oil income and five-year development plans. As far as he was able, the Shah attempted to raise output and hence income from oil. The government was not altogether frustrated by the Shah's obsession with military expenditure. Great strides were made in developing the national infrastructure, promoting rapid, though unbalanced, economic growth. Paradoxically, economic performance before the oil boom of the mid-1970s was superior to that of later years.

Virtually every economist working with the Plan Organization urged caution in the aftermath of the sudden oil price increase of 1973. Before such vast new wealth could be absorbed it was clear that the system had to be rid of serious bottlenecks; training of labour, transport, and port handling were all woefully inadequate. Rather than overload the system, any surplus revenue could be deposited with international financial institutions. But the Shah ignored this advice, accusing the men who offered it of lacking vision. He was especially delighted with the witticism, coined by Franklin Roosevelt but repeated time and again by Prime Minister Hoveyda, that the one-armed economist was best, immune from the besetting sin of his species, the temptation to confuse matters by hedging his bets 'on the one hand ... but then again on the other hand'. Over-riding every principle of sound planning, an expansionist programme was put in place, made up of large-scale projects, many of them economically unjustified.

The results of such grandiose folly soon became apparent. A flood of imports, especially foodstuffs and military hardware, choked the ports. Ships waited months to be unloaded. The shortage of labour, warehousing or transport facilities forced up costs. Wages rose steeply amongst skilled workers who in turn fuelled new demands for housing and foodstuffs already in short supply. Inflation soared to unprecedented levels increasing unrest amongst the masses, particularly those with fixed incomes. Rather than cut back on its reckless expansion of the public sector, the root cause of the problem, the government chose to fight only the symptoms, loading the blame for its plight upon 'hoarders and profiteers'. A number of such men were severely penalized. Likewise, responsibility for housing shortages was offloaded upon a 'small group of speculators' rather than upon the government whose neglect was originally to blame. Such unjustified hostility towards the private sector coincided with imperial decrees requiring industrialists to distribute up to 49 per cent of the shares in their companies to the public and their own work-force. No wonder that the business community, crucial to the country's economic success, grew disheartened. Private capital began to flee Iran for safer havens abroad.

From 1975 onwards the volume of Iran's oil exports declined, squeezing government revenue. Despite this the Shah continued to press for the implementation of his favoured projects, many of which were peripheral or of low priority. The result was to starve priority projects of cash. The five-year plan was over-ridden time and time again in favour of the Shah's personal preferences. Glossing over its loss of direction the government spoke of a switch from five-yearly to annual planning, which made no economic sense.

Public money was squandered; fickle military and economic objectives took priority over discipline or sense. The result was chaos. During the last two years of the regime there were power-cuts on a near daily basis; inflation and housing shortages brought the mass of city dwellers to the brink of rebellion. Yet the Shah appeared oblivious to such developments, confiding in the then head of the Plan Organization that although he understood his schemes were causing problems, he needed only another ten years to realize his dreams; thereafter he would do whatever his economists advised.[9] Even after the revolution his opinion remained unchanged. In exile he repeated that he had been fighting 'a race against time ... If only I had been able to surmount the short-term problems, Iran would have basked in unparalleled power and prosperity. I'll admit; we should have fought harder, on behalf of the nation, against back stabbing and enemy propaganda ... But I was so sure of myself that I simply ignored the attacks, the slanders and insults. That was why malice and subversion took root in so many people's hearts, especially amongst the younger generation ...'[10]

In reality the Shah's final years were spent denying and undermining the very policies which had earlier made for his success.

Long-term economic planning was replaced by whim and wishful thinking; the private sector was outrageously abused; inflation was permitted to spiral. Popular expectations rose to meet the boom in oil prices and the government's bombastic claims. As reality began to dawn, so the violence of the people's disillusionment matched the desperation of their plight.

Propaganda
The Shah had an obsessive desire to be ranked amongst the immortals of Iranian history; above every past statesman or hero stretching back into the mists of time. Every achievement had to be credited to him alone. Should his subordinates show flair or success it could only be as a reflection of his own guiding genius. As a young man his abilities were doubted by his father; at least so he himself believed.[11] Certainly in his earliest years as Shah he had been scorned by the political establishment; condescended to, both by the old guard at home, and abroad by the great powers. Such insults lingered even after his rise to autocracy and his elimination of every rival. He knew himself to be an exceptional man and was determined to have that status pandered to by his entourage. Sycophancy became the order of the day. In letters to the Shah, Alam invariably addressed him as 'My mighty leader'; Hoveyda, a devotee of yoga, referred to him as 'My guru'. Never exactly attuned to mass politics, the Shah ended up incapable of distinguishing popular devotion to his own person from love of nation itself. He assumed the masses possessed a single purpose, loyalty to their Shah. In return it was the Shah's sole duty to pursue the good of his people; an objective he believed identical with his own sense of destiny.

In this atmosphere of sycophancy and egomania, the media were expected to guide the people. State radio and television adhered to a system much appreciated by the Shah, whereby items of news were inserted according to the seniority of the personalities involved, regardless of their actual priority as news. Invariably such broadcasts began with the activities of the Shah and his family and only then passed on to reports from Iran and around the world. Even these reports were carefully selected, to reflect glory upon the Shah and his great achievements. Iran was portrayed as a haven of peace and prosperity, its people entirely satisfied with their lot, immune from the stormy events reported on the international stage. As a result the official media lacked credibility; anyone seriously interested came to rely upon foreign broadcasts.*

As for Iran's newspapers – they too led a precarious existence. Proprietors and editors risked severe reprimand for causing the Shah even the least annoyance. They were expected to be little short of clairvoyant; able to anticipate exactly which news items to play up and which to ignore in accordance with the Shah's own preferences. Such heavy-handedness turned many against the press; indeed it ensured that the Shah's genuine triumphs met with scepticism within Iran. It was a problem of which the Shah was not unaware. Discussing the latest oil agreement, undoubtedly a great sucess, he expressed surprise at the level of the public's indifference; remarking that this might be the fault of earlier failures to keep the masses informed or to give them any sense of participation in current affairs (Diaries 24 May 1973).

As for the foreign media, here too the Shah expected nothing but praise. Objective reports that so much as mentioned his shortcomings were anathema. From early in his reign he developed an obsession with such articles, personally reading the reports filed by every foreign correspondent. The favourable ones he allowed to be quoted or syndicated amongst the Iranian press; for the rest, Alam and his colleagues would be required to drag in the ambassador concerned for a thorough grilling. Throughout, he found it impossible to believe that the media in democratic countries could be truly independent of state control. Told that an interview with *Newsweek* remained unpublished, he suggested to Alam that the US government had forbidden its appearance, 'since I state my conviction that the Russians no longer pose us any threat' (Diaries 3 November 1969). When it came to the British, suspicion gave place to outright paranoia. The hand of the British government, he believed, lay behind every criticism of Iran. This obsession with the British press was the source of many hours' work for Alam, forced to summon Britain's diplomatic representatives, none of whom succeeded in ridding the Shah of his delusions.

During his final years, the Shah was fatally isolated from the truth. No one dared brave his wrath to bring home to him the reality of

---

* This helps to explain the major role played by the BBC Persian Service during the revolution of 1978–9.

his situation. He heard only what he wanted to hear: praise of his heroic services to the nation; glowing reports of the public's prosperity and contentment. Wanting proof of the benefits of autocracy he turned to myths when the truth became too bitter to bear. Paradoxically he remained convinced that his government and his various intelligence-gathering agencies kept him well informed, both of events and public opinion. In fact, it was these same sources which tried hardest to shield him from reality. Prime Minister Hoveyda was a master of the art of concealment; subordinates he silenced by threatening to force them to repeat their allegations in front of the Shah; those wanting to remain in office had no alternative but to retract. Government ministers soon learned the requisite techniques: how to advance an argument leaving freedom for retreat should the Shah prove unresponsive. Occasionally the odd or exceptional character would inflict a dose of cold fact on the Shah; but such men were always rare at Court and towards the end became virtually extinct. Only Queen Farah behaved irreproachably. As far as her knowledge and her experience allowed she strove to keep her husband in touch with reality. Alam wrote of her as 'a valuable safeguard against the abuse of power. She alone has the ability to open HIM's eyes to the truth. In this respect I run her a very poor second, but I do at least try my best to be truthful, which is more than can be said for anyone else at Court.' (Diaries 28 September 1970)

The Shah believed himself the ruler of a contented, grateful people. Amidst the surrounding quagmire of myth and self-delusion there was at least some basis for his claims. Women's right were promoted with considerable success. Land reform and industrial profit-sharing were both noble ambitions. Yet land reform should have been consolidated by the encouragement of village councils, of genuine peasant co-operatives. Instead the government reserved investment for a few spectacular projects, ignoring the vast new class of peasant landowners. Likewise profit-sharing came to bear no relation to productivity or real profit, merely adding a month or so's salary to the annual wage-packet. By launching the sale of shares when he did, up to 49 per cent in the great corporations, the Shah ensured that any real enthusiasm or benefit would be wiped out by the effects of inflation. Meanwhile the workers continued to be denied the right to genuine free trades unions; those that existed enjoyed an even lower reputation than the official political parties.

Even in the large cities health and educational services were poor; the Shah's decision to make them free to the consumer increased access and hence popular awareness of these deficiencies. By 1975, 50 per cent of the population was illiterate set against only 40 per cent in Turkey or 34 per cent in Tanzania. One in every four children had no access whatsoever to primary education even though classes of seventy or eighty were common, schooled in three daily shifts, even in Tehran. By the same token, average life expectancy stood at a mere fifty-two years, more or less identical to the fifty-one years of countries such as India and considerably below the sixty years of Turkey. Iran's relatively high per capita income failed to raise her above the levels of health or education experienced in less prosperous countries.

The land reforms, which took in religious agricultural endowments, were undeniably a bold step forward. Women's political rights and the 'Family Law' – which in practice put an end to polygamy and the repudiation of wives at the husband's will – were progressive measures. But they antagonized the clergy which previously, for the most part, had found little fault with the Shah. To fill the gap caused by the elimination of great landowners and the increasingly hostile clergy, the Shah might have permitted farmers, women, the burgeoning middle classes and even the intellectuals some say in managing the country. Instead, his increasingly autocratic rule allowed for no dissent nor any possibility for the people to vent their grievances. As free political gatherings were prohibited so university campuses, literary venues and mosques became the meeting place for the opposition. The new generation of technocrats advanced since the 1960s lacked weight or a political power-base. The old guard had been gagged for years and had slipped from public memory. The only viable opposition lay in the hands of radical groups composed for the most part of idealistic university students and reactionary clerics, enraged by the social reforms. The growing mass of the disaffected turned towards religion, not from piety, but for the lack of any alternative refuge. By refusing to share power with the more dynamic elements within society, the Shah forced them into a desperate alliance with radical and reactionary extremists.

With hindsight various commentators have sought to attribute the Iranian revolution to the accelerated pace of western-style modernization previously imposed by the Shah. Set against this must be the fact that the Shah neither understood nor showed any sympathy for the basic tenets of western modernity. True, he dreamed of material advances for Iran that would place her on a par with the developed western nations. Yet in tandem with this material advance he hoped to impose an archaic, authoritarian political system, rejected long before by his competitors in the west. Whilst encouraging millions to attend school and tens of thousands to graduate each year from Iran's universities, he could never tolerate the prospect of such people participating in the nation's political decisions. To a large extent he was a romantic, wishing immediate fulfilment for each of a wide range of contradictory dreams. A vast army was to be financed at the same time as rapid economic growth; the people themselves were to live contented lives, yet to enjoy absolutely no control over their own political destinies.

Mundane realities bored the Shah; it was the future that inspired him. In many ways devoted to his country, most fanatically hard-working, he was a visionary whose imagination failed him in certain crucial respects. Above all, he simply failed to credit popular scepticism towards his own noble intentions. As the chasm between illusion and reality widened, so the Shah retreated ever further into make-believe. Publicity or even the public itself was to blame, never imperial policy. Never once, not even in exile, did he wake from these dreams to the nightmare that had engulfed Iran.

The relationship between the Shah and Alam

Of the same age and almost identical build, the Shah and Alam had much in common. The Shah was a gifted sportsman but Alam, thanks to a tough upbringing, could match him in horse riding and prove a worthy partner in tennis. Both possessed physical courage, but it was Alam's ability to assume responsibility at critical moments, added to his loyalty, that most impressed the Shah.

In the wilderness years of his youth, the Shah once asked friends at a party what profession each of them wished they could pursue. The replies were ribald and amusing until it came to the Shah's turn. Had he not been a king, he said, he would have liked to be a public servant, earning enough money to indulge his passion for sport. He then went on to make a significant remark, one that runs true to form: he would prefer a job that spared him the burden of decision-making.[12]

Whenever political prospects seemed grim, the Shah could be relied upon to prevaricate. In his earlier years he relied upon veterans such as Ahmad Qavam or strong soldiers like Generals Razmara and Zahedi, all of them suspected, rightly or wrongly, of entertaining personal ambitions. Later the Shah brought forward his own men – people like Dr Eqbal and Sharif Emami. But none of them enjoyed the same degree of intimacy with the Shah as Alam. Both in troubled times and as a companion and confidant Alam could be relied upon. The Shah's entourage could be divided into two groups: friends with no particular official position; and reliable officials with whom he had no particular friendship. Alam was unique in belonging to both groups. His absolute loyalty to the Shah derived from his personal friendship and his upbringing. His father had been totally devoted to Reza Shah. But there was more to it than simply keeping up tradition. Alam was fascinated by the Shah's outlook on the world. Although he confided misgivings to his friends and was not always happy with his master's decisions, he believed the Shah to be a man of great wisdom and intellectual ability. In particular he admired the Shah's memory, which allowed him to reel off military and economic statistics, his handling of foreign affairs and his negotiations over oil.

In all of these fields he overestimated the Shah's mastery. But he did not always blindly follow in his master's footsteps. When Alam was Prime Minister at the time of Kennedy's assassination, the Shah wrote to Lyndon Johnson, congratulating him on his appointment as President and criticizing Kennedy who, he claimed, had never understood Iran's problems. The Shah dictated the letter in person to Abbas Aram, the Foreign Minister, ordering him to dispatch it without anybody's knowledge – meaning without Alam's. Loyalty and modesty never ranked amongst President Johnson's greatest virtues, but none the less Aram realized that such a letter coming at such a tragic time would be regarded as an insult by many Americans. He showed the letter to Alam who stopped it from being sent and requested that he and Aram be granted an audience. The Shah was furious and told Alam that as he claimed to be a better judge of national interests, he could do as he chose. For a few weeks the two men were not on speaking terms, Alam restricting their meetings to the bare minimum required to discharge official duties. The Shah probably came to realize his friend's good sense. In any event their quarrel was patched up, the Shah making light of it with a display of good humour towards Alam.

Those were the days when it was still possible to argue with the Shah. Later things changed for the worse. Everybody, including Alam, had to tread more cautiously. But their friendship remained unaffected to the very end. The Shah realized the seriousness of Alam's illness and was genuinely concerned by it. He did what he could to reduce his workload so that during his last months in office Alam was more or less excused all official outings. Over the same period the Shah asked Alam's opinion of certain government ministers. It was uncharacteristic of him to talk about matters of this sort, a fact that Alam fully appreciated although he chose to ignore the implication: that he must prepare himself for retirement. In the summer of 1977, while Alam was convalescing in southern France, the Shah telephoned personally to ask for his resignation on grounds of ill health. He confided that he intended making major changes in the government. Two days later Jamshid Amouzegar was appointed Prime Minister and, to Alam's consternation, Hoveyda became Minister of Court. It was Hoveyda that Alam blamed for Iran's deteriorating situation. In the final entry to his diaries he wrote: 'People showed no enthusiasm for Hoveyda's appointment. It's a vital role he's been given ... but it's said the Shah chose badly. If Hoveyda's government was to blame for the present chaos, why promote him still further?' (9 September 1977).

At the end even he, the lifelong friend and the most loyal servant of his beloved Shah, failed to grasp the complexity of his master's mind.

NOTES

1. *Ettela'at*, 12 March 1963.
2. As related to the Editor by Mr Sadeq Azimi, a friend of Alam.
3. The Editor was himself present at this meeting.
4. Interview with the Shah; *Ettela'at*, 18 June 1973.
5. *Ettela'at*, 9 January 1973.
6. The first six points concerned land reform, nationalization of forests, sale of state-owned enterprises, industrial workers' profit-sharing arrangements,

women's political rights and the creation of the education corps. Additional points such as 'the administrative and educational revolution' lacked substance while others, such as 'fight inflation and overcharging' and 'fight corruption', were mere slogans.

7. See the Shah's statement during an audience given to the members of the Association of Scholars and Intellectuals, *Ettela'at*, 7 June 1975.

8. E. A. Bayne, *Kingship in Transition* (USA 1968), p. 143.

9. As related to the Editor by Mr A. M. Majidi, then head of the Plan Organization.

10. Mohammad Reza Shah, *Answer to History* (Persian edition not dated), p. 231. The paragraph in question is deleted from the final English version.

11. 'I asked [my father] what he considered the purpose of his reign, and his response hurt my feelings dreadfully. He said simply that it was to create a government organization to carry on the state after he had left. I considered this a slap at me at the time – as though I wasn't intelligent enough to carry on the monarchy as he had – but now I very much understand what he meant ... We must build a government that can carry on, whether a King is successful or not.' Bayne, *Kingship in Transition*, p. 58. This incident haunted the Shah who reminisced about it on several occasions.

12. As related to the Editor by Mr Majid A'alam, a childhood friend of the Shah, unrelated to the diarist.

1969

The diaries start at the end of a decade which witnessed Iran's social and economic transformation. In spite of all shortcomings, spectacular changes had made people optimistic about their future. Without any irony, many inside and outside the country spoke of an 'economic miracle', seeing Iran as a 'second Japan'. The Arabs reeled under the shock of their defeat by Israel in 1967. Turkey suffered from military intervention in her political system, and Pakistan tottered on the verge of collapse. By contrast, Iran stood out as a haven of stability and initiative.

In 1967 after twenty-six years on the throne, the Shah crowned himself. He enjoyed great popularity among the masses. His populist rhetoric continued to attract support. Many still hoped he would acquiesce in some degree of democratic or popular sovereignty. What dissent there was concentrated upon the universities, attributed by the Shah and his government to the turbulence of youth, the irresponsibility of academics and various subversive, leftist elements. Alam by contrast had direct experience of the Pahlavi University at Shiraz and already felt unease, not helped by his low opinion of Prime Minister Hoveyda.

But this was the time of the Vietnam war and of Soviet rapprochement with the Arab nations of the Middle East. Containment of the communist threat through a military build-up and a pattern of regional alliances took precedence over western concerns about the authoritarian nature of the regimes in many third world countries. In Iran rapid economic development was presented as a means of achieving social harmony and material well-being. Little was said about democracy or human rights. The government was complacent. So long as the Shah lived, his rule of iron and his immense authority appeared to guarantee political stability.

As was customary, the Shah spent his winter holidays in St Moritz, Switzerland, preceded by a consultation with Professor Fellinger of Vienna. He then went on to Zurich to meet representatives of the

Oil Consortium, the co-operative venture established in 1954 to exploit Iran's major oil fields – at the time concentrated in the southwest and designated the Agreement Area. The Shah hoped to pressure the Consortium into a 10 per cent increase in production, but the meeting proved inconclusive. He then threatened to legislate a reduction of the Agreement Area. For many years Iran had complained of the inadequacy of her oil revenues and of the Consortium's reluctance to increase output. This reluctance stemmed in part from the peculiar make-up of the Consortium, whose principal members possessed even greater interests in neighbouring countries, as shown in the following table:

Members of the Iranian Oil Consortium	Share %	Shares in Kuwait Oil Company %	Shares in Aramco %
British Petroleum	40	50	
Royal Dutch-Shell	14		
Compagnie Française des Pétroles	6		
Standard Oil (Exxon)	7	—	30
Socony Mobil Oil	7	—	10
Standard Oil (California)	7	—	30
Gulf Oil	7	50	
Texas Oil Company (Texaco)	7	—	30
Iricom*	5		

Since Saudi and Kuwaiti oil reserves were enormous and their production costs lower, the major oil companies had no obvious incentive to raise Iranian output above that of neighbouring countries. However, they were forced to bear in mind Iran's geopolitical status, and her disproportionate need for revenue to supply a population far larger than that of the other Persian Gulf states. In turn, the Shah hoped to use a higher income to sustain the rapid growth of the Iranian economy, and above all to finance his expansion of Iran's armed forces, in the Persian Gulf and on the frontier with Iraq.

Alam's diaries for 1969 deal extensively with the future of the Persian Gulf and Iran's relations with Iraq. In January 1968 the

---

* An agency made up of nine separate American companies, each holding between 0.4 per cent and 1.25 per cent of the Consortium's shares.

British government announced its intention to withdraw from the Persian Gulf by the end of 1971. The Shah considered it imperative that he devise a new settlement to fill the vacuum created by the collapse of the British Empire. Bahrain and the seven Trucial Emirates of the southern Persian Gulf ranked as British protectorates under the terms of nineteenth-century treaties. Before she could grant independence to these states, Britain had first to untangle their relations with Iran and Saudi Arabia. For over a century Iran had pursued a hotly contested and increasingly unrealistic claim to sovereignty over Bahrain. As the diaries show, the Shah was concerned that the settlement of Iran's claims should not be interpreted as a betrayal of the national interest (Diaries, 13 August). To enable Iran to withdraw her objections to Bahrain's independence, Iran and Britain agreed to submit their differences to the Secretary-General of the United Nations, U Thant, who sent a personal representative to Bahrain to discover the will of the local population. Coincidentally Iran laid claim to the islands of Greater and Lesser Tunbs, which according to Britain belonged to the Sheikh of Ras al-Khaimah. The islands were no more than barren outcrops visited infrequently by passing fishermen. Iran asserted that the only means to establish their status was by considering their position in relation to the Persian Gulf's median line; in which respect they lay far closer to the Iranian than to the Arabian coast. However to the southwest of Tunbs was yet another island, Abu Musa. Abu Musa lay on the Arabian side of the Persian Gulf but was nevertheless claimed by Iran. The British asserted that it belonged to the Sheikh of Sharjah.

Far more serious than these problems was Iran's border dispute with Iraq. The land border dividing the two countries was poorly defined, and rival claims led to armed conflict. The issues were even more complicated in the case of the Shatt al-Arab waterway, serving as the border-line to the south. Virtually all international rivers are divided according to the Thalweg line – a theoretical median running along a river's deepest channel dividing the two banks. By contrast, all the waters of the Shatt al-Arab had been awarded to the Ottoman Empire by the terms of treaties drawn up with Anglo-Russian co-operation before 1914. The Ottoman claim had later been transferred to Iraq. In 1937, it was agreed that sections of the waterway opposite Abadan and Khorramshahr be divided equally with Iran. But Iraq consistently refused to implement the terms of the 1937 treaty, leading in April 1969 to the treaty's complete abrogation by Iran — a move which very nearly resulted in war. Relations continued to deteriorate, marked by sporadic border clashes between 1969 and 1975.

1969

[The Shah, the Queen and Prince Ali Reza[1] are
in St Moritz, Switzerland; Alam returns to Tehran]

Thursday, 13 February
At ten this evening I arrived back in Tehran. Hurried to kiss my mother's
hand. Was delighted to find her well.

Friday, 14 February
A restful day. Saw a few friends. Since I missed her son's wedding I felt
obliged to accept an invitation to dinner with Princess Shams.[2] The Queen
Mother[3] and the Prime Minister[4] were there. It's been a month since I've
listened to Iranian music, but tonight we had singers and a band; it was
all most enjoyable.

Saturday, 15 February
'... Called in the evening at the Niavaran Palace[5] where HRH the Crown
Prince[6] was dining with Princess Farahnaz.[7] I was brought a whisky and
sat with them. I am fond of them both and they seem to return my affection.
They're gifted and intelligent children. May God grant them happiness.
Prince Ali Reza is not at school, but in St Moritz with HIM [His Imperial
Majesty].

Monday, 17 February
... This afternoon, the British ambassador, Sir Denis Wright, came to see
me. He is upset by the goings-on in Zurich where the representatives of
the Oil Consortium have had a tense audience with HIM and refused to
guarantee us an oil income of $1 billion. As for Bahrain, negotiations are
already under way with a view to implementing HIM's wishes.

[1] Third son of the Shah and Queen Farah (1966–).
[2] The Shah's sister (1917–): President of the Iran Red Lion and Sun Society – equivalent
to the Red Cross. Unlike her younger sister, Ashraf, she was uninvolved in politics, and led a
quiet, family life.
[3] Queen Taj ol Molouk (1891–1981): married Reza Shah (then Colonel Reza Khan), 1916. Her
memory failed her in later years and she was never to appreciate the tragic developments in Iran
or the death of her son, the Shah, a few months before her own death in California where she
lived with her favourite daughter, Princess Shams.
[4] Amir Abbas Hoveyda: a man of great political talent and considerable culture; Prime Minister
1965–77; Minister of Court, 1977–8. He was executed in 1979.
[5] A palace complex situated in the north-eastern suburbs of Tehran. Consisted of an old Qajar
palace, Jahan Nama, where the Shah usually worked, and a new palace, the main winter residence
of the royal family.
[6] Prince Reza Pahlavi (1960–): son of the Shah and Queen Farah.
[7] Daughter of the Shah and Queen Farah (1963–)..

In strict confidence he told me that the Islands of Tunbs are certain to be handed over to Iran. The British have warned the Sheikh of Ras al-Khaimah that the islands lie on our side of the median line and that, unless he comes to some sort of understanding with us, we shall simply take them, legally or if needs be by force. The Sheikh is prepared to make a deal. I then asked about the island of Abu Musa. The ambassador replied that it lies below the median line. I told him that we are sufficiently powerful to disregard the line. We joked for a while. More seriously he expressed concern that our policy in the Gulf may lead to trouble with the Arabs. 'To hell with it', I said. 'What have the Arabs ever done for us? If only they would stop all this nonsense, agree to pay for the defence of the Gulf, and let us get on with the work.' The ambassador questioned the extent to which the Arabs will allow us a free hand. After all they persist in describing it as the 'Arabian' Gulf.[1] I replied that we are prepared to draw up a fifty years defence agreement with them, and that all in all it will be much the same as the agreement they once had with the British ...

Tuesday, 18 February

... The American ambassador, Armin Meyer, came to see me. He is alarmed by the oil discussions in Zurich[2] and afraid, if Iran takes any unilateral action, that all the Middle Eastern countries will follow suit. Even so he agreed with our stand and admitted that the Consortium's proposal of $900 million for next year, an increase of only 4.5 per cent on our current income, is simply inadequate. But this is his personal opinion and he asked that I keep it to myself. I've been reliably informed that he is to be transferred to a more prestigious posting but didn't mention it for fear that he would guess my source.

We briefly discussed some wider issues. The situation in Pakistan is extremely tense – disorder is spreading right across the country. Worse still, President Ayub Khan has lost his nerve and agreed to negotiate with the opposition. Tomorrow he is to meet with representatives of eight of their political parties, Bhutto's amongst them. Previously Foreign Minister, Bhutto was released from gaol only a few days ago amidst the most incredible scenes of jubilation. I know him well. He is a *bon-vivant*, a heavy drinker and above all an extraordinarily ambitious demagogue. Despite

[1] In the fifties Arab nationalists chose to rename the Persian Gulf the Arabian Gulf. Ever since, this has been a bone of contention between Iran and her Arab neighbours.
[2] See introductory note 1969.

being one of the richest men in Pakistan he's as thick as thieves with communist China.

Thursday, 20 February

... Another humiliating blow to Ayub Khan – the opposition parties have refused to meet him[1] ...

Saturday, 22 February

... Dinner at the palace of HM the Queen Mother. Iskandar Mirza,[2] ex-President of Pakistan, was there, greatly aged but retaining all his former wit. His wife is the daughter of Amir Teymour Kalali.[3] Returning home I found a long telegram from Houshang Ansari, our ambassador in Washington.[4] He is pessimistic over the oil talks. I sent it on to HIM with a covering note to the effect that everyone here supports us and that the British ambassador has cabled London on our behalf. Moreover the oil companies are concerned that HIM will bring forward legislation to seize half of their output, an initiative which could easily be taken up by other countries. I begged HIM to return as soon as possible, though I doubt he will appreciate my advice. He's been absent too long ...

Tuesday, 25 February

O'Brien, head of the Oil Consortium, called this morning, full of gloom about the future. I told him, 'There are two courses of action open to you; either you fall in with HIM's wishes and save yourself a lot of worry, or else you disobey him, in which case I shall not envy you your situation. If it comes to a fight neither of us stands to win, but your losses will be greater than ours. We can tighten our belts, and if we bring forward legislation to seize control of oil production, many others will follow our example. You can kiss goodbye to thousands of millions of dollars.' He agreed with this, but at heart I was gravely troubled and still am troubled that our present financial difficulties[5] will make further retrenchment

---

[1] President Ayub Khan's position had been shaken by Pakistan's near defeat in the war against India of 1965. Mounting opposition and street violence were eventually to force his resignation.
[2] Ousted by Ayub Khan.
[3] Mohammad Ebrahim Kalali: a highly respected politician who, as a close friend of Dr Mosaddeq, retired from politics in 1953.
[4] A shrewd businessman who succeeded in attracting the Shah's attention; successively ambassador to Washington, Minister of Economics, Minister of Finance and, just before the revolution, head of the National Iranian Oil Company (NIOC).
[5] The large military outlay insisted upon by the Shah for the fiscal year 21 March 1969–21 March 1970 put great pressure on the government's budget. Although it was decided to increase indirect taxes, the deficit could only be made good by generating higher revenues from oil.

impossible. I have tried to emphasize this point in writing to HIM.

Later I called at the Saudi Arabian embassy to present my condolences on the death of the late King Saud, exiled to Athens following a coup led by his brother, the present King Faisal. He was a sot and a fool ...

I've sent a long letter to HIM detailing my discussions with O'Brien. Once again I stressed that HIM should return before *Eyd-e Ghadir.*[1]

Wednesday, 26 February

... At the insistence of Prince Gholam Reza,[2] I have been obliged to summon a meeting of the Regency Council, made up of the Shah's two brothers, Gholam Reza and Abdul Reza,[3] the Prime Minister, the two Speakers of Parliament[4] and myself. But, why convene a discussion which has nothing to discuss? Despite my reluctance, we got together for an hour at the Niavaran Palace. What nonsense was talked! I sat in silence, not bothering to waste my breath.

I have sent further detailed bulletins to HIM. A private letter has arrived from President Nixon; I forwarded it without any idea as to its contents.

Levi Eshkol, the Prime Minister of Israel, has died. I've arranged for HIM to offer discreet condolences to the Israeli President, without risking trouble from the Arabs ...

Invited to dinner by General Hashemi Nejad, Commander of the Imperial Guard. Dinner not bad, but the company dull. Mrs Diba,[5] the mother of the Queen, was expected but hadn't shown up by midnight when I left. Apparently she was preoccupied with rallies to celebrate the sixth anniversary of the granting of women's suffrage.

Thursday, 27 February

... Dinner at my father-in-law's. A gaggle of women, some of them beauties in their day but now sadly incapable of growing old gracefully.

---

[1] One of the most important religious festivals in Shiite Islam, its date is determined by the lunar calendar.

[2] Third son of Reza Shah, and only child of his third wife, a Qajar princess. A general, he held the mainly honorary position of Inspector-General of the Army.

[3] The Harvard-educated fourth son of Reza Shah. A huntsman of international renown, he was Chairman of the Trustees of the Organization for the Protection of the Environment, besides heading the boards of several institutions of higher education.

[4] Parliament was composed of two Houses: the *Majlis* (Lower House) whose members were elected by universal suffrage; and the Senate where half the members were appointed by the Shah and the rest elected by a two-tier system.

[5] Mrs Farideh Diba (née Qotbi): married Sohrab Diba, father of Queen Farah, in 1932. He died in 1943. A modest and well respected woman, she maintained a sense of proportion and hence considerable dignity after her daughter became Queen.

Many of them as old as I am, yet still swanning about like tipsy débutantes.

Friday, 28 February
Went riding with my love again this morning. The rain was still falling but spring's rain and spring's flowers are sweet.

In the afternoon, the British ambassador came to tell me that the Consortium has tired of our threats and refuses to meet our demand for an additional $100 million. I told him that we are just as sick of their endless discussions as they are fed up with our threats. We shall now take whatever steps appear necessary, even at the risk of considerable hardship. The ambassador protested that I knew the trouble he had been to on our behalf, putting pressure on London. He is an honest man and I believe him, but even so I feel sure that neither the British nor the American government has made any effort to sway the oil companies.

After his departure I turned to thinking about our present financial situation and the impossibility of pressuring the oil men. It will take at least a year or two to get anything from them. What are we to do in the meantime? I have long complained that our government, the Central Bank, the Plan Organization and several of our ministries are riddled with placemen of one or other foreign power. For all his intelligence, HIM fails to appreciate this fact. It is we, not our opponents, who are under pressure. How can we wage economic warfare when the treasury is empty? HIM with his wisdom and foresight may none the less find a way.[1]

This evening I called on the Imperial children and we joked and horsed about. Farahnaz has written me a few lines which I shall keep here as a memento. She's a delightful girl . . .

Sunday, 2 March
. . . In the afternoon Dr Fallah[2] came to brief me on his discussions with the oil companies. They still reject our proposals. The only solution is for the British and the Americans to persuade Abu Dhabi, Qatar and Saudi Arabia to reduce their output, allowing us room for an increase. As things stand, Iran carries the full burden of defending the Gulf while the Arabs reap all the benefits . . .

---

[1] Whenever Alam criticizes policy, he hastens thereafter to praise the Shah; a sensible precaution lest his diaries fell into the wrong hands.
[2] Reza Fallah: Deputy Manager of NIOC, in charge of international relations and marketing. A shrewd man of affairs, the Shah used him as a behind-the-scenes negotiator with the oil companies.

Monday, 3 March

... The King Hassan of Morocco's birthday, so I paid my respects at the embassy. King Hassan was instrumental in reconciling us to King Faisal.[1]

The Lebanese ambassador tells me that General Bakhtiar[2] is certain to be extradited to Iran. To accomplish this we have been reluctantly forced to accept the advice of the Turkish ambassador ...

Thursday, 6 March

... HIM returned from Europe this evening in a grim mood. We went directly from the airport to dinner at the Queen Mother's and I had an opportunity for a brief conversation. HIM was sombre throughout the meal, downcast by the government's financial predicament and by the attitude of the Oil Consortium ... He has a slight cold and wished to cancel his attendance at the *Salaam*[3] of *Eyd-e Ghadir*, but I insisted that he should go. Pray God that his cold and his nervousness don't get worse or we shall all be in trouble ...

Friday, 7 March

HIM attended the *Salaam*, much to my relief. He coughed a little but otherwise seemed in reasonable shape, though very tired and a touch fidgety. Evidently the oil negotiations and the precarious state of the treasury are preying on his mind. In an audience with the Board of the NIOC, he allowed himself one outburst against the Consortium, but was wise enough to mingle threats with blandishments. As Sa'adi[4] says:

> Before drawing your weapons for battle take care
> That the pathway to peace is discreetly cleared.

---

[1] A few months earlier the Saudis had welcomed the Sheikh of Bahrain to Riyadh as head of state, only a week before the Shah's own proposed official visit to their country. As a result the Shah cancelled his trip in protest and for a while relations between the two countries became frosty.

[2] General Teymour Bakhtiar: head of Savak, the Iranian Intelligence and Security Agency, 1956–61. Once one of the staunchest supporters of the Shah, he was subsequently banished and became an active opponent of the regime. The present entry refers to a trip he made to Lebanon where the Iranian authorities applied for his extradition. On the advice of the Turkish ambassador considerable amounts of money were distributed amongst Lebanese politicians. But the Iraqis secured his release and gave him refuge in Baghdad.

[3] *Salaam*: royal public audience, of which there were two kinds: grand *Salaams* on the Iranian New Year (21 March) and on the Shah's birthday, attended by government officials, members of Parliament, the diplomatic corps and various other organizations; and special *Salaams* for important religious festivals such as *Eyd-e Ghadir* or the birth of the Prophet Mohammad, at which attendance was more restricted.

[4] Iranian poet (*c*. AD 1184–*c*. 1280).

Attended Lunch and Dinner.[1] HIM felt a little better this evening. I've been notified in confidence that the Kurds have sabotaged Iraqi pipelines around Mosul and Kirkuk. The oil companies will use this as a pretext to criticize Iraq's poor security and switch their production targets to Iran. I told HIM that nothing is definite as yet, but that something along these lines remains a distinct possibility ...

Saturday, 8 March
Audience ... Briefed HIM on recent developments and raised a few points which upset him. I told him that the country is disturbed by the sudden doubling of water prices, that the asphalt in the streets is falling apart, that corruption by the Customs men is on the increase, that bank credits are being squeezed and that various businesses are heading towards bankruptcy. Finally I warned him of the financial crisis in the universities.

HIM lost his temper and snapped at me, 'What can we do when there's no money coming in?' For my part I replied that whenever I have drawn His Majesty's attention to our lack of funds, his response has been that the government is well provided for and that my reports are misinformed. But only yesterday HIM spoke out against NIOC for over-expenditure on various petrochemical projects; for presenting an initial costing of $100 million and then spending two and a half times that amount; for allowing the gas pipeline to devour $650 million set against an original estimate of only $350 million. I have long cautioned His Majesty on the gravity of our situation, only to be met by the sort of angry denial he gave me this morning. 'Again', I said, 'I must warn you that it is unreasonable to deny the legitimate expectations of the people. I am Your Majesty's loyal servant and desire only to work to your greater glory, but there are many others at court who would soothe you with fine words merely to retain their positions and to profit from Your Majesty's false sense of security.' I am confident that he will see the truth of this; he knows how utterly devoted to him I am.

Sunday, 9 March
This morning's audience again centred on the universities and the financial crisis. HIM repeated 'What can I do without money? Every project has exceeded its estimate.' ...

He asked whether I had met the British and American ambassadors or

---

[1] Throughout, 'Attended Dinner' or 'Lunch' implies that Alam sat at the Shah's table.

heard their reaction to his remarks of yesterday. If I see them I am to stress the seriousness of our intent. I promised to do this, but what response can I hope for if they already know our plight? One cannot wage economic warfare without money. HIM said 'We are not yet quite so poor as you like to make out.' In any event I replied that we can only do our best and await developments ...

Tuesday, 11 March

Audience. Reported at length on last night's discussions with the US ambassador. He says that Iran can expect no more than $900 million so long as the increase in Middle East oil production is set at below 6.5 per cent. I told the ambassador that this was bound to lead to confrontation. He expressed his alarm and cautioned patience, but I fear that in our present financial situation my words must sound like simple bluff. I repeated that any move on Iran's part will be copied by our neighbours but this failed to convince him. Nevertheless this morning HIM said, 'He can think what he likes, but the Russians will come to our assistance and then the whole region will be thrown into even greater turmoil.' God help us if there really is to be a show-down ...

In three days time I leave for Kabul at the invitation of the Afghan Minister of Court. HIM has instructed me to raise our differences over the Hirmand river[1] and to express our deep concern about recent disorders in Pakistan. Afghanistan must not try to make political capital out of the situation there or precipitate a crisis by reasserting her claims to Pashtunistan.[2] They should consider closer links to Tehran; if Pakistan goes red then we may be the only guarantee of Afghanistan's survival.

The telephone rang during our discussions – Dr Eqbal[3] reporting that the Consortium now requires extra time before announcing its decisions. Just as I suggested to the American ambassador, it's better for them to drag their feet than to issue a categorical negative. Apparently they now consider guaranteeing us an income of $950 million, with an interest-free loan to bring us up to our target of $1 billion. So far I have followed HIM's instructions and cold-shouldered all approaches from the Consortium's

---

[1] A river in the south-west of Afghanistan, flowing into the Iranian province of Sistan. The division of its waters had long been disputed between the two countries.
[2] North-western frontier province of Pakistan, claimed by the Afghans.
[3] Manouchehr Eqbal, ex-Prime Minister: head of the National Iranian Oil Company; he was regarded for the most part as a distinguished figurehead and hence excluded from the nitty gritty of oil policy or negotiations.

representatives. At the same time he now wants me to step up pressure via the British and American embassies.

I then brought up a question relating to Iraq which I prefer not to record in writing, save to say that its gist was:

> No man can truly be elated
> Until his rivals die frustrated.

HIM agreed with this and confirmed that he has issued the necessary instructions. If only their impact can be felt before too long[1] ...

Sunday, 16 March

I've been in Kabul from the 12th until today. On my return went directly to the palace to put in an appearance.

I had three assignments in Afghanistan, none of which went altogether smoothly. I was to discuss Pakistan, air our differences over the Hirmand river and invite the King to Iran. But King Mohammad Zaher pleads that elections and a tense situation with his parliament oblige him to remain in Afghanistan for most of the coming year. I urged the Afghans to remain aloof from Pakistan's internal problems but in any event they themselves had already decided against intervention. With regard to the Hirmand, I pressed our need for more water or at least a better seasonal distribution of what water there is. All to no avail ...

Monday, 17 March

Audience to report my trip to Kabul ... I said that the Afghans are casting about for friends; clearly they can't rely on Pakistan, still less on the Russians. Many factors incline them towards closer relations with Iran, but they are greedy and will only supply us with more water, beyond the agreed concessions, on a commercial basis. Even if we accept this and set about building up confidence, it will be but the first step on a very long road. We shall have to grant them credit facilities, assist their development programme downstream along the Hirmand river, and grant them access to our ports. We must also co-operate in matters of security if we are to transform them from a potential rival into a dependant of Iran ... HIM was most interested and instructed me to talk things over with the PM and various ministers ...

---

[1] This refers to the sabotage of Iraqi pipelines by the Kurdish dissidents of northern Iraq.

Tuesday, 18 March

Audience ... HIM very put out by his daughter Shahnaz[1] who has left her fiancé Zanganeh.[2] 'Either she's mad', he said, 'or she's heading that way. She's full of crazy ideas.' I replied that she strikes me as being remarkably intelligent. 'Madness and intelligence often go together', he said, which greatly annoyed me.

Again I brought up the question of the rise in water prices. HIM said, 'How long do you suppose that the public can have something for nothing? Progress costs money.' I replied that a 70 per cent price increase is not progress; it's simply an injustice. We should remember Mansour,[3] who raised the price of domestic oil products. It cost him his life. HIM chose to ignore this. His indifference hurt me, and I shall raise the subject again tomorrow. How long can we overlook the people and their needs? Four years ago Mansour's death came as a blessing from God, but today it is my beloved sovereign who will pay for the follies of an incompetent administration, too short-sighted to heed the lessons of the past.

HIM says he will not go on holiday to the Caspian Sea this summer as it has always made him ill. He then asked me when the facilities on Kish Island are due to be completed. 'God willing, by next March', I said, 'in time for the *Now Rouz*.'[4]

Wednesday, 19 March

Again I took the opportunity to raise the subject of water prices, despite which HIM claims that the cost of living is increasing by less than 1 per cent a year. Why put the people under such strain? In contrast to yesterday, HIM accepted my criticism and will now seek a revision of the government's proposals.

We discussed Shahnaz. HIM told me that on her return I am to warn her to mend her ways or he will disown her. I said that I'm well aware she's mixed up in an undesirable life-style but it's the result of poor upbringing, the loss of her mother's love and supervision. The child herself

[1] Born in 1940 to the Shah's first wife Fawzia, sister of King Farouk of Egypt. Her parents divorced a few years later and she was sent to school in Switzerland. Married Ardeshir Zahedi, 1957. Divorced him, 1964. In the seventies married Khosrow Jahanbani whose activities are the subject of much speculation in these diaries.

[2] Mahmoud Zanganeh: from a prominent Kurdish family; businessman, well-known in Court circles as a *bon vivant*.

[3] Hassan Ali Mansour: Prime Minister, March 1964 – assassinated January 1965. His government doubled the domestic price of gasoline and kerosene, but, confronted with mass protests and strikes, backed down after only a few weeks.

[4] The Iranian New Year falls on 21 March, although the festivities start at the exact moment of the vernal equinox.

is not to be blamed. She needs understanding, at least that's the line I intend taking with her. We talked it over at length and HIM eventually came round to my way of seeing things.

Pakistan was mentioned, and Ayub's deteriorating position. Disorder is spreading in the cities. Like HIM, I believe that Ayub must react with determination if he's to re-establish law and order. 'Poor Ayub', I said, 'he's so unpopular amongst his fellow countrymen. Bear that in mind and you will appreciate why, for all Your Majesty's achievements, I am anxious lest a similar situation develop here.' Both HIM and I are tempted to believe that Ayub has deliberately let his people off the leash. The army seems still to be behind him. Encourage a little chaos and it might provide an excuse for firmer repression later on.

The British ambassador met me in the afternoon. We discussed Bahrain and the Gulf islands which he was keen to present as two distinct issues. He told me that Tunbs will be easy for us to recover but not Abu Musa, which lies too close to the Arabian peninsula.[1] I replied that this didn't alter Iran's rights nor entitle the Arabs to hold on to Iranian territory; territory which HIM will never abandon. The ambassador suggested that a solution to the problem of Bahrain will almost certainly encourage the establishment of a Federation of Arab Emirates, at which stage Iran might well occupy Abu Musa in the interests of joint security in the Gulf. We can depend on support from the British, should this happen.

Attended Dinner and passed on the ambassador's various suggestions. HIM asked me to tell the ambassador that with friends like him, Iran has no need of enemies. I refused to rise to this and said that in my view it is much more important to guarantee the interests of the Iranian minorities in Bahrain and the Gulf. HIM was pensive but said nothing . . .

Thursday, 20 March
Now Rouz fell at a quarter to eleven this evening. My wife, my children and I were with my mother. Later I had the honour of offering my best wishes to HIM who presented me with a few gold coins. The entire Imperial family was in attendance . . .

Friday, 21 March
HMQ attended this morning's *Salaam* as she did last year . . . The Crown Prince delivered his first broadcast message to the nation; he read it quite beautifully.

---

[1] See introductory note, 1969.

Because today was the second day of *Moharram*, various people suggested to HIM that the *Salaam* should have been cancelled in deference to the mourning of *Ashura*.[1] I was consulted and advised him to ignore such quibbling: national traditions must not be sacrificed for the sake of non-sensical gestures.[2] HIM agreed. We went ahead and invited the clergy, who arrived early and seemed as keen as anyone to offer HIM their new year's greetings ... When there is authority most such problems are easily solved. Without it you'll be taken for a ride by every villain under the sun and life really won't be worth living.

For example when I was Prime Minister we granted equal political rights to women. For a whole year I was besieged by complaints from the clergy, but then the Shah took a hand and they were soon put in their place. I had some of them arrested, others we banished[3] and a couple of particularly troublesome thugs ended up on the gallows. In that way we put paid to the problem once and for all. Now women sit in both Houses of Parliament and one of them has even been appointed Minister of Education[4] ...

... Attended Dinner. HIM was downcast. He told me of his frustration with the Oil Consortium and his disappointment at the British attitude towards the islands, especially Abu Musa which he was sure he'd bagged after his declaration on Bahrain. He is also concerned by the state of the treasury. We talked for an hour and I have been instructed to pursue further discussions with the British ambassador.

... The situation in Pakistan is very grave. Chaos erupting ...

Sunday, 23 March

... The British ambassador called. I told him we can reach no settlement in respect to Bahrain until we know the fate of Tunbs and Abu Musa. In that case, he declared, we have all been wasting our time. 'So be it', I said. He then suggested we approach the Sheikh of Sharjah[5] as we did the

---

[1] On the tenth (*Ashura*) of the month of *Moharram* (lunar calendar), Hossein, grandson of the Prophet and third Imam of the Shi'as, was killed along with several members of his family, in a battle against the Umayyads.

[2] For Iranians in general, unlike the Arabs, Islam is not the sole source of their culture. Since the Muslims of Iran – overwhelmingly Shi'a – do not understand Arabic, the language of the Koran and daily prayers, Shiite Islam focuses chiefly on rituals, timed by the lunar calendar. Occasionally such rituals clash with Iran's traditional festivities, governed by the solar calendar.

[3] One of those banished was Ayatollah Khomeini.

[4] Mrs Farrokhrou Parsa: educationalist and one of the leaders of the women's rights movement; she was among those executed in 1979, following Ayatollah Khomeini's return to Iran and the success of the revolution.

[5] Khalid bin Mohammad al-Qasimi: in 1965 succeeded his cousin, Sheikh Saqr, who had been deposed as ruler. Following accusations of collaboration with Iran occasioned by the settlement over Abu Musa, Sheikh Khalid was to be assassinated by rebels led by his cousin in January 1972.

Sheikh of Ras al-Khaimah. A deal might be struck and the British would back us. I said I would pass this on to HIM but was in no position to comment myself.

The ambassador seemed more inclined than he was the other day to link any solution for Bahrain to proposals over the islands. He hinted that if Iran were to back the creation of an Arab Federation in the Emirates, then we might well be called upon to occupy the islands on the Federation's behalf, without any fear of a backlash from the Arabs. I told him: 'Quite frankly I have lost any confidence in your forecasts ... Six years ago ... you yourself, Mr Ambassador ... told me that for at least another twenty years you were bound to the Sheikhs by the firmest of commitments, and that any outside intervention in their territory would be regarded as a direct attack upon British interests. Yet it has taken only five years since then for Britain to announce her complete withdrawal from the Persian Gulf. You, and the western countries in general, are obsessed solely with protecting your oil interests, interests which Iran is perfectly capable of assuming on your behalf.' He made no comment, but I believe deep down the western powers are apprehensive of Iran, reluctant to see us dominate the Persian Gulf. Now I can only wait and see what happens.

I explained this point at my audience this evening. HIM was absolutely furious with me. The trouble is that I'm utterly frank with him. The others tell him only what he wants to hear, but I have no such scruples ...

At the end of this evening's audience HIM announced that unless he hears definite news of his projected trip to America or of Nixon's visit here, he will write to Nixon spelling out our position on the oil negotiations and over Britain's attitude to the Persian Gulf.

Tuesday, 25 March
... The radio has broadcast Ayub Khan's resignation ... It has upset us both ... HIM enquired as to the popular reaction to his New Year message. I said that HIM's proclamations always have a calming effect. This is true enough, since it's well known that the Shah wants nothing for himself but is dedicated to the common good. He asked me whether there had been any signs of disappointment after his message, since it mentioned the over-expenditure and the mistakes made by various of our foreign allies with respect to particular development schemes. I told him that there was undoubtedly a degree of popular bewilderment and an expectation that HIM will name the guilty parties. He made no comment.

Ayub Khan's resignation has left me greatly troubled this evening. It bodes ill for us all. Some time ago the American ambassador asked my opinion on Pakistan. I told him that, to begin with, we should expect the rise of some form of democratic regime, accompanied by general disorder. Then the military would intervene to quell the chaos. My predictions have come true rather more quickly than I expected, since Ayub has resigned in favour of Yahya Khan, the former Chief of Staff. He in turn has appointed the commanders of the Navy and the Air Force as his deputies and imposed martial law in both East and West Pakistan. The situation in the East is particularly grave; the mob have set up people's tribunals in imitation of communist China and lynched those they hold responsible for the situation. Here I must pay tribute to Ayub. He at least realized that the game was up and resigned for the sake of the country. It had begun to look as if his half-hearted attempts at restoring order would lose him all credibility amongst the army.

I am deeply worried by the attitude shown in official circles here, their indifference to the basic needs of the people. It's now midnight and I go to bed sick at heart.

Wednesday, 26 March

This is the first morning I've been back to my office since the start of the New Year. Only a few meetings. Towards noon I joined their Majesties, the Crown Prince and Princess Farahnaz, and flew with them by helicopter to Shahdasht[1] where we attended lunch with HM the Queen Mother.

At Shahdasht I made my report and mentioned complaints I have received from the American ambassador. HIM has given an interview to the *New York Times* in which he announced his determination to prevent the American Navy, who have a temporary base at Bahrain, from replacing the British as Bahrain's protectors. Moreover, he declared that if America fails to come up with the arms he has asked for, Iran will turn to the Soviets for assistance. When I mentioned the ambassador's objections to these remarks, HIM replied that he had meant exactly what he said and that the Americans should take careful note of our opposition to foreign intervention in the Gulf. America must be made to realize that we are an independent sovereign power and will make way for no one ...

The government's severe economic measures, the imposition of high import tariffs, all these things alarm me. Life will become harder, prices will rise and a fear of inflation will compel the government to place further

[1] A village 60km. south-west of Tehran, the principal residence of the Queen Mother.

restrictions on credit, leading to unemployment, hardship and popular unrest. It's a harsh world, but why so burden the people and frustrate their desires? Next Friday, when I have more time, I shall bring all this to HIM's attention ...

Thursday, 27 March
HIM in high spirits at this morning's audience. His first order to me was to commission articles in the press, pointing out that if it had accomplished even a thousandth of what our regime has done for the people, the government of Pakistan would have had no need to fear riots. Of course HIM is quite right. We have carried out a unique revolution in Iran and because of it both our regime and the Iranian people can sleep soundly in their beds. But recently new policies have begun to threaten this stability, whether intentionally or not. HIM's instructions gave me an opportunity to open my heart. I told him that the new import tariffs have brought only hardship and extra expense; the roads are in a dreadful state and even when they're mended the work brings traffic to a standstill. It is difficult to obtain fresh meat and the price of water has soared. All this causes unnecessary suffering. HIM replied that whatever is done this year to restrict imports is done for the future happiness of the people. I admitted this might be so, but added that people have yet to be convinced; it is difficult for them to equate happiness with so many painful sacrifices. I don't know whether this angered him but he personally telephoned Javad Mansour, the Minister of Information, and asked him to convey the instructions to the press which he had originally asked me to deliver ...

I have been ordered to meet the British ambassador as soon as possible, to clarify his country's position. I suggested that the British may secretly be in awe of us and are deliberately creating difficulties. HIM replied that this was probably so; that the British have no desire to see the entire Gulf dominated by Iran.

This evening I attended various religious meetings in remembrance of Imam Hossein,[1] third Imam of the Shi'as whose anniversary it is. Falsafi[2] was preaching at one of them, brilliantly as always. He has a remarkable memory and a fine, strident voice but all the same he is ... not exactly a model of Islamic virtue! Thirteen years ago, when I was Minister of the Interior, he was busily pushing himself into the limelight, aiming to be the

[1] See note p. 42.
[2] Mohammad Taqi Falsafi; a prominent Mullah and preacher who came into his own after the revolution, although his life-style continued to be dogged by controversy.

Tehran representative of the late Ayatollah Boroujerdi.[1] In fact Falsafi gave all the orders and the poor Ayatollah was simply too bewildered to expose him. He managed to dupe both HIM and the military authorities and started up a campaign against the Baha'is which brought this country to the brink of disaster. It was Ramadan[2] and his noon-day speeches were broadcast to all the provinces, stirring up violence and spreading panic. City mobs slaughtered a few Baha'is here and there. Falsafi justified it all on the grounds that it would boost the prestige of HIM. I had no choice but to react with my own kind of rashness and forbade him to preach until order had been re-established. Later, during my time as Prime Minister, he rose to become one of the chief clerics supporting the feudalists against HIM's social reforms. Following a riot in Tehran in June 1963 I had him locked up. From prison the only request he sent me was for alcohol and opium which I duly supplied. Tonight he was raving against a talented young playwright whose latest, highly successful play pokes fun at the clergy. I was concerned that he might get his revenge on me by inciting his audience to violence but fortunately he didn't get very far ...

Saturday, 29 March–5 April
Saturday was *Ashura*, the anniversary of Imam Hossein's death, and I had meant to remain at home until the afternoon when traditionally I should accompany HIM to the mosque. I was still asleep in bed when the telephone rang. It was the American ambassador with a telegram on behalf of General Eisenhower's family inviting HIM to the great man's funeral. Via the American government they have approached only those few heads of states with whom Eisenhower had particularly close dealings. If HIM decides to go he must somehow arrange to be in Washington by tomorrow afternoon. I dressed hurriedly and went to let him know that De Gaulle had already accepted the invitation. HIM was still at breakfast but asked me to find out if the Queen of England was to be there. I said that the British are so entangled by protocol that there could be no possibility of her attending. Since it was time for the news on the BBC World Service, I turned on the radio which confirmed precisely what I had just said, although it's clear that many other heads of state will be present. HIM made up his mind to attend. I pointed out that it will provide an ideal opportunity to meet the

---

[1] Ayatollah Mohammad Hossein Tabatabai Boroujerdi (1876–1961): the most prominent Ayatollah of the 1950s. He was a conservative who effectively opposed several attempts at land reform.
[2] Month of fasting.

new American administration and he agreed. We decided to leave following the ceremony at the mosque. I had great difficulty arranging things at such short notice, particularly since everything had closed down for the public holiday. At six we took an Iranair charter flight to London and early the next morning flew Pan-Am to Washington. In our full ceremonial dress, at precisely 2 p.m., a helicopter landed us in front of the church where the funeral was held.

HIM attended the church service and the ceremony at Arlington cemetery. Nixon and Johnson were also there. Despite De Gaulle's presence the first seat was reserved for HIM. Nixon held a dinner party at the White House in honour of the visiting dignitaries and between them HIM and De Gaulle stole the show. None of the others got a look in.

As anticipated our trip allowed HIM to meet the new administration and to see some old acquaintances. He met the President, Secretary of State William Rogers, Melvin Laird the Defense Secretary and Laird's predecessor Robert McNamara, who is now president of the World Bank, Pierre-Paul Schweitzer, head of the IMF, and Henry Kissinger who has replaced Walt Rostow as National Security Adviser to Nixon. Both Rostow and his brother were very friendly to us. Nixon was to have received each head of state for between five and fifteen minutes, but De Gaulle was in there for an hour, and the meeting with HIM lasted an hour and a quarter. Likewise the session between HIM and the Vice-President overran by a full three quarters of an hour. Habib Bourguiba, the President of Tunisia, was kept waiting outside, poor man!

HIM explained our differences with the Oil Consortium. He stressed the dangers inherent in boosting output from Kuwait and Abu Dhabi; they will become so rich that the West may find itself fashioning a pair of monsters. Even now Kuwait could paralyse the British economy by a sudden withdrawal of its deposits from British banks. Likewise Abu Dhabi, which has an oil income of half a billion dollars set against a population of twenty thousand, or Libya where an oil income of $1.2 billion supports a population of only two million. The oil companies think solely of max-imizing their profits and count every cent; they pay no attention to the logical needs of the various oil-producing countries. HIM elaborated these arguments with both Nixon and Secretary of State Rogers. They expressed their agreement but disclaimed any influence over the oil companies.

The Americans have a quota for oil imports equivalent to 12.5 per cent of their domestic production. For several years we have been keen to sell them oil beyond this quota, even if it means bartering our oil for American goods and services. So far we have had no success, but HIM insisted on reiterating our proposals and suggested that the Americans stockpile Iranian oil in salt mines[1] and suchlike places, ready for use in an emergency. He mentioned the names of several leading American companies, General Electric, Bethlehem Steel, and so on, that might partner us in such a deal ... He also asked the Americans to consider the advantages they receive from their friendship with us. He stressed that Iran is not an American stooge but that we nevertheless prefer to remain independent of Soviet influence. Iran is a friend of the West sufficiently powerful to maintain her own sovereignty, able to defend her own interests and by implication capable of defending the interests of her western friends.

Various other problems were discussed, commercial matters and the training of pilots and technicians. With regard to the Gulf, HIM declared that it was in America's own interest to pull out as soon as the British have withdrawn; this, he claimed, was the most logical way of preventing the Russians from acquiring influence. But here I'm not at all sure about HIM's logic. Obviously such a withdrawal makes sense from our point of view, but it's pretty debatable for the Gulf as a whole. I advised him to commission a study of this but he ignored my advice. HIM despises anything that goes by the name of 'study', and in the modern world such an attitude is dangerous. The head of state, as in other countries, should be guided by policy studies in which every aspect of a problem is carefully analysed and considered. For example we should bear in mind that the presence of the American fleet is an important factor in keeping the Russian navy out of the Gulf. Provided the Americans stay outside our territorial waters we have no right to insist that they leave the Gulf altogether. In any event it is my duty to convince HIM that every problem must be properly studied before he makes decisions. Naturally both the Ministry of Foreign Affairs and our Intelligence Agency draw up reports but I have seen them and know how shallow and misleading they can be. They'd be much better written by those with no axe to grind ...

Many dignitaries came to our embassy without prior notice to pay their respects to HIM. It was a time-consuming business receiving them, and it occupied us night and day. I never had more than three or four hours sleep. HIM was also exhausted. Although I was absent from his discussions, he generally gave me a full briefing. I was, however, present at his meeting with Vice-President Spiro Agnew, at which HIM spoke out strongly in

[1] The idea was originally promoted in Iran by Dr Reza Fallah.

support of King Constantine of Greece who has been ousted by the military.

The American ambassador accompanied us throughout, and attended dinner on the evening of our return to London. Amongst other things we discussed the prospects for Iran in the event, God forbid, of something happening to the Shah. The ambassador believes that for a year or two the country will maintain its momentum. Later things might begin to break down. I gained the impression that HIM was more than a little hurt by these remarks. In London the following day he asked me to explain them; did they reveal some plot by the Americans which the ambassador had accidentally let slip? I replied that they will undoubtedly have made some preliminary studies of the likely succession to His Majesty: the appointment of HMQ as Regent[1] with strong majority support. But personally I believe them to be misguided. There is no viable replacement for HIM. HMQ is an angel of purity but she is inexperienced and rather impulsive. Like the Crown Prince she is simply too young to assume power. The majority party will have no influence with the army and I foresee a very troubled road ahead; disorder and collapse with no certain solution.

HIM suffered from toothache in Washington and decided to stop off at Zurich for a couple of days to visit his dentist. And in Zurich, in spite of the dentist, a good time was had by all . . .

Saturday, 12 April

. . . In the evening, on HIM's instructions, I received Barran, the President of Shell Oil. Officially he is on a simple fact-finding mission to Iran, but behind the scenes he hopes to obtain a solution to the Iranian demand for higher oil production. We talked for nearly two hours. Apparently the Consortium is keen to find some way of meeting our demand for an increase of $100 million. It is also prepared to see us increase production by an annual rate of 10 per cent, which, even so, is still less than the 15 per cent we have asked for. It is the future that concerns them most, since $50 million of our increase this year is intended as credit advanced against next year's production. But if they accept our target of a net 15 per cent increase in next year's output, we shall in effect require a total output increase of 20 per cent to amortize the credits they intend to advance this year. This will be unacceptable to our competitors. I replied that we're only asking

---

[1] On 7 September 1967 the constitution was amended to allow the Queen to be appointed Regent should the Shah die or be incapacitated before the Crown Prince reached his twentieth birthday.

for what is ours by right, and one way or another we intend to get it. Two years ago, during the Arab–Israeli war we deliberately maintained the flow of oil as a sign that we are not to be classed with the Arabs.

Monday, 14 April

... Invited Barran to breakfast. I suggested that some sort of guarantee over this year's income will make life easier for them when we come to discuss future rates of production. But following HIM's orders I also brought up the threat of legislation forcing the oil companies to accept our demands. The oil men fear that any action we take will quickly spread to our neighbours, although the American ambassador is unconvinced by this. The Consortium feels that our demands for increased production are quite out of the question.

Audience to report my discussions with Barran. The Consortium will find a way to guarantee our demand for an additional income of $100 million, even if this means paying some advance, but fear we shall demand similar arrangements in future. Were we to do so, the oil companies could end up with unpaid debts of half a billion dollars, a crippling burden. HIM grinned maliciously at this and said that, so burdened, they would have no alternative but to increase our production targets. HIM's shrewdness delights me.

Lunch as a guest of the British ambassador. Barran was present as was Patrick Gordon-Walker, former British Foreign Secretary.

Afterwards ... went to report our discussions ... HIM flies to Tunisia tomorrow. I have sought his permission to spend a couple of days in Birjand.

Thursday, 17 April

Last Tuesday, before leaving for his trip, HIM ordered me to pass on a message to the American ambassador, Armin Meyer, who is to inform President Nixon that HIM had discussed 'the matter' with the Russians and has received a favourable response. This is meaningless to all save HIM and Nixon.[1]

Flew with my love to Birjand, intending to stay four days ... but this morning, before I could begin my proposed inspection of the earthquake

---

[1] The Shah and the USA were both disturbed by events in Pakistan. In all likelihood they cautioned India against taking advantage of the situation. Whatever the exact nature of their joint initiative, its significance lies in the extent to which the Americans now regarded the Shah as a reliable friend and ally.

sites, General Nassiri,[1] head of Savak, telephoned from Tehran to request my immediate return. In spite of the bad weather, I found a plane that could take me, and invited the General to come round the moment I landed. He was in a dreadful state, literally begging me to help him. Our Minister of Foreign Affairs Ardeshir Zahedi has made a complete cock-up and landed us on a war-footing with Iraq. HIM has ordered the army to stand by on red-alert. I had no idea of how far our relations had deteriorated and the magnitude of this latest crisis comes as an appalling shock ...[2]

... I have cabled HIM and am gravely concerned. Is this really an appropriate moment for us to resort to force, in the midst of vital nego-tiations with the oil companies and just as we are approaching an under-standing with the Arabs of the Gulf? It makes my blood boil. I'm all too familiar with the Iranian character – the merest whisper of defeat could bring down the regime ... Never underestimate your opponents; even if the Iraqis avoid a war, they can still paralyse our economy by denying us use of the Shatt al-Arab. We have no internationally accredited sea-pilots and depend on the Iraqis to guide our ships ...

Friday, 18 April

A restless night, slept badly. At home most of the day with no inclination to go riding or see my beloved. Switched on the world news nearly every hour but there are no fresh developments. Went briefly to see HIM's children. To add to my troubles Farahnaz and Ali Reza are both unwell. Ali Reza's nanny thinks he may have swallowed a needle. I love the Shah's children as my own ...

Received HIM's reply to my cable.[3] Who can argue with him? But I have done my best and can only pray that my fears are unfounded. God willing everything may still turn out in our favour.

Sunday, 20 April

The American ambassador called this afternoon, anxious to know what's going on with Iraq. I told him as little as I thought expedient. Beforehand

---

[1] Executed after the revolution.
[2] The Shah had decided to abrogate the treaty with Iraq over the Shatt al-Arab waterway. It was planned that a ship flying the Iranian flag would sail through the waterway – still legally under Iraqi sovereignty. The army was put on red alert, ordered to intervene should the Iraqi authorities attempt to stop the vessel. All these measures were taken in secret, unbeknown to Alam and the entire government.
[3] The Shah's brief reply reads as follows: 'They [the Iraqis] were getting exceedingly arrogant; they needed putting in their place.'

General Nassiri had come to my office with encouraging news; the internal situation in Iraq is close to breakdown and their army has come under attack from the Kurds. In these circumstances Al-Takriti,[1] their Defence Minister, has assured the Savak representative in Baghdad that there can be no question of war. What's more, the Iraqi shore of the Shatt al-Arab has flooded and brought their army to a stand-still. Merely to save face, they have repeated their claim to possess inalienable rights in the Shatt al-Arab. Tomorrow the *Abu Sina* will sail under an Iranian flag from Abadan to the Gulf. If the Iraqis open fire on her then we'll know to fear the worst.

Monday, 21 April

... HMQ has gone to Paris to open the *Maison de l'Iran*[2] and so HIM returned alone from Tunisia, going straight from the airport to the headquarters of the Joint Chiefs of Staff for a briefing on the military situation and the state of our defences. He was met off the plane by the head of Savak who brought news that General Bakhtiar has obtained Iraqi citizenship. This is disgraceful. Now he's sure to team up against us with the Kurdish leader, Talebani.[3]

The *Abu Sina* was unable to sail today but several merchant vessels entered our ports without harassment from the Iraqis.

Tuesday, 22 April

Saw HIM for a few minutes this morning ... He was expecting Omar Saqqaf, the Saudi Foreign Minister, who called in at my office for half an hour before his audience. Amongst the Arabs he passes as something of a sage. He is critical of America's failure to tell friend from foe ...

... The ship *Abu Sina* sailed today without any reaction from Iraq.

Wednesday, 23 April

Some interesting meetings this morning. Winston Churchill, grandson of the great Prime Minister, came to see me. He is currently working as a journalist with *The Times* and his eye-witness accounts have roused British public opinion against the civil war in Nigeria where his government sells

[1] General Hardan al-Takriti – no relation of Saddam Hussein, but from the same town, Takrit; he was sacked from the government in October 1970 and banished, dying at the hands of an assassin in Kuwait in March 1971.
[2] Sited in the Avenue des Champs-Elysées, it was intended as a cultural and promotional centre, but ended up doing little more than sell carpets and caviar
[3] Jalal Talebani; a prominent leftist Iraqi Kurdish leader, sometime rebel against the Baghdad regime; a rival of Mustafa Barzani.

arms to the federal regime for use against Biafra . . . Next Armand Hammer, President of Occidental Petroleum, called prior to his audience with HIM. His company is active in Libya and has achieved a great deal in recent years. Amongst several interesting points he declared a willingness to market at cost any quantity of oil we can obtain from the Consortium. In addition he is prepared to operate on our behalf any part of the agreement area Iran may take back from the Consortium. He's a lively old man and his proposals have greatly cheered me. They provide us with a valuable bargaining counter in our forthcoming discussions with the Consortium – due to meet here on 10 May . . .

Thursday, 24 April
At this morning's audience I handed over a coded letter which Ansari has sent by courier from Washington. HIM's reply was also coded and so I am left entirely in the dark. There is nothing to be done; the Shah is entitled to keep certain secrets to himself. Sooner or later I'm sure he will let me in on the details.

Dr Fallah of NIOC has returned from America and called to see me, pessimistic over our prospects of penetrating the domestic US oil market which is heavily protected by import quotas. The oil companies are dead against it and we're faced with the new problem of Alaskan oil which sells at a higher price than that charged for our own exports to America. Fallah now suggests that we stockpile surplus Iranian oil in America on our own initiative. In an emergency the Americans would be entitled to draw on these reserves simply by increasing our quota. We might even barter them against American goods and services. So great would be the profit that we could afford to put half of the stockpile at America's disposal free of charge. Iran is unique in the Middle East in her potential consumption of American goods and services and so we alone could make such a deal. It is an attractive proposal but, as far as I'm concerned, divorced from all reality.

Relations with Iraq are steadily improving.

This evening the American ambassador came to tell me that he is shortly to be transferred to another posting. I had already sensed that such a change was in the air.

Saturday, 26 April
Marvellous spring weather, but sadly I was too busy to enjoy it. The usual early morning briefings followed by an audience with HIM. He has lent me the manuscript autobiography of Ardeshirji, a foreigner who died over

thirty years ago. His son[1] now works for British Intelligence and hopes to publish his father's memoirs which deal in part with Reza Shah.[2] I said what an interesting idea this seemed, but HIM shrewdly observed, 'Provided they're not some attempt by the son to pass off his own work under Ardeshirji's name.' Nevertheless I am convinced that they are genuine. As I pointed out to HIM, there is nobody these days capable of inventing so much authentic detail.

Attended Dinner. Some uproarious teasing by HIM of his mother, the rest of us barely able to stifle our giggles and HIM himself having a whale of a time. Later he told me he'd seen the Soviet ambassador who made a discreet effort to mediate between us and Iraq. I said that he would be a welcome go-between so long as he refrained from exaggerating the problem out of all proportion. I also brought up the subject of the press. They have been most unfair in claiming that the Shatt al-Arab treaty of 1937 was forced on the Shah's late father when in fact he used it to obtain several valuable concessions. HIM agreed and instructed me to ensure that the Ministry of Information corrects this attempt to mislead the public ...

Sunday, 27 April

Audience ... HIM instructed me to invite King Faisal to visit Iran next autumn. Imelda Marcos, the wife of the Philippine President, has expressed a desire to visit us and we should make arrangements for her trip. There is also the Tehran meeting of CENTO Foreign Ministers[3] to be arranged for 15 May.

The Ministry of Foreign Affairs has issued a highly judicious statement on our differences with Iraq over the Shatt al-Arab, clearly acting under orders from HIM. On their own they could never have shown such intelligence.

---

[1] Sir Shapour Reporter (Ardeshirji): according to his own account, his father – a Parsee – was also in the service of British Intelligence. Reporter himself became an important figure in the promotion of British commercial and military exports to Iran.

[2] Father of the Shah (1878–1944): a powerful and fascinating autocrat who rose from a lowly military rank to crown himself Shah in 1925. He was forced to abdicate by the British in 1941 after the Anglo-Soviet invasion of Iran.

[3] The Central Treaty Organization, a military and political alliance, was set up in 1959 between Iran, Pakistan, Turkey and Great Britain. It never functioned very effectively, chiefly because of Pakistan's dissatisfaction with US policy towards India, and Iran's disappointment that the USA participated only as an observer. The USA had a separate Mutual Defence Agreement with Iran.

Monday, 28 April

De Gaulle has resigned following his defeat in the referendum. He will go down in history as one of the truly great. As for his nation and the world at large, I am unsure of the future. Clearly France is set for chaos. What a pity that De Gaulle is too old to make yet another come-back. But a third return to power is beyond him. When I last saw him, at the White House, he was nearly blind. Only when he heard my name did he show any sign of recognition. Today we have witnessed a turning point in French history and who knows, maybe even the history of the world. I admire his honesty and the confidence he has shown in the French people by permitting completely free elections.

... Audience this afternoon. I began by enquiring whether HIM had ridden out after lunch as planned. 'How could I?', he said, 'It's Prince Ali Reza's birthday.' I also asked him why he works so late into the evening. He smiled meaningfully and said, 'I'm a man like any other. Since I'm allowed to say and do so little at home I'd much rather stay at my desk.' In my opinion there's not a woman in this country, from the most humble to the Queen herself, who fully appreciates the burden on man's shoulders or the means to lighten it. Rather they're keen only to add to our load.

A cable from Ansari about the oil negotiations which are faring badly. HIM said, 'What does it matter? If we fail to reach a settlement with the companies we shall simply legislate to obtain our own share in their production or to take over part of the agreement area. The oil companies can be sure that the Arabs will follow our example. What else are they expected to do when it was they that proposed such legislation to OPEC in the first place?'

According to HIM, the Queen's entourage has blocked work on a new hotel at Isfahan, complaining that it spoils a view of the Si-o-Seh Pol.[1] I am to investigate this nonsense and report my findings ...

Tuesday, 29 April

... The British ambassador came to see me this afternoon. On HIM's orders I protested against certain articles in the British press which accuse us of operating gun-boat diplomacy against Iraq. Such a description would be justified if Iran were seeking to impose unjust terms on the Iraqis but on the contrary, in this instance it is we who are attempting to protect our legitimate interests against injustice ... In reply the ambassador pointed

---

[1] 'The Bridge of thirty-three Arches'; a magnificent early seventeenth-century structure.

out that with few exceptions the British press has taken the side of Iran, which is true enough. He was exceedingly pessimistic about the oil talks and I felt obliged to let him know that we fully contemplate legislation to give us a direct share in production ...

Wednesday, 30 April

At this morning's audience HIM gave me a handwritten letter for dispatch to General De Gaulle. I reported the comments of the British ambassador, who tells me that the delay in negotiations with Bahrain springs from the Sheikh's reluctance to allow the UN Secretary-General U Thant to send a fact-finding mission to the island at the invitation of Britain and Iran. This has come as a real surprise. According to HIM, 'We shall accept no compromise on Bahrain until the status of Abu Musa and Tunbs has been clarified.' I told him that I had already made this point clear to the ambassador, but HIM instructed me to make it doubly clear.

A visit from François Charles-Roux, the French ambassador, at noon – a fine man, very close to De Gaulle and amongst the first to join him in London on the formation of his Free French Government. He informed me that De Gaulle's advisers all warned him against the complexity of the reforms proposed in the referendum; the people would not be able to grasp their meaning; they were not an urgent priority and the general had no need to link his own future to their outcome. But De Gaulle was adamant. Pride comes before a fall, though such absolute self-confidence is surely a sign of genius.

In the afternoon HIM opened the new Arj factory, manufacturing a whole range of domestic appliances. It began as a small workshop set up by a handful of entrepreneurs but in the past few years has developed into a major industrial complex. HIM enjoys these sorts of visits. I did not accompany him but went for a stroll with my beloved, up in the Lavizan hills.[1] They've been planted with trees at HIM's instructions. The weather was fine, and every moment of the walk was worth treasuring. A light shower of rain only added to our enjoyment. Altogether it reminds me of the lines of Khayyam:

> Clouds swept and wept over the meadow
> What would life be without the rose-hued wine?
> For the meadow that delights us today, who knows,
> May tomorrow give delight to others as it covers our grave.

[1] East of Tehran.

After a few drinks we laughed at the futility of life. I prayed for the Shah with his love for planting forests. It is God's will that moves him in this way.

Attended Dinner. A report arrived stating that Iraq has finally taken her complaints against us to the UN Security Council. HIM enraged, gave me various instructions which I passed on to our representative at the UN. An hour later the news came back that Iraq has issued no formal complaint, but merely submitted her own version of events.

Thursday, 1 May
Before my audience HIM received the military top brass: the Supreme Commander's Chief of Staff, General Ariana; Generals Zarghami, Khatami,[1] Admiral Rassa'i, Commanders of the Army, Air Force and Navy; and General Azimi, Adjutant-General to HIM. Yesterday HIM was vocal in his condemnation of military preparations against Iraq so I knew the military were in for a hard time. Only the Air Force has come up to scratch. HIM had clearly not minced his words since I entered to find him red in the face with anger.

Audience later for the Head of the Diwan of the Emir of Kuwait – a sort of Minister of Court, though as he ranks no higher than our own Grand Chamberlain I did not welcome him in person but sent a member of our Protocol Department. Prior to his meeting with HIM he came to see me, soliciting my support for Kuwait as mediator in our dispute with Iraq ...

Friday, 2 May
... At noon the American ambassador called with an official invitation to HIM to visit the USA this autumn. Previously we had anticipated that no such invitation would be issued until next year. Attended Lunch and explained the situation to HIM who has accepted the American offer and asked me to arrange a suitable set of dates. The new administration is clearly anxious for him to travel to America far sooner than was expected. For the first time I saw clear signs that HIM is alarmed by our confrontation with Iraq. He declared that our military commanders were caught day-

---

[1] General Mohammad Khatami: Commander of the Air Force, 1957–75; husband of the Shah's younger sister, Princess Fatemeh. Liked by the Shah and respected for his professional competence; popular among his fellow officers in the air force.

dreaming, hence his decision to sack most of them. The Air Force alone has performed well but is short of aircraft. The full consignment of Phantoms will not be delivered until 1971 although we're already in need of them. In an emergency we might buy a few of the inferior F5s. Iraq has a force of 250 planes, although not all of them as good as their Mig 25s.

General Ariana and General Zarghami have both been replaced. General Djam[1] takes over as Supreme Commander's Chief of Staff and General Minbashian[2] as Commander of Land Forces. Minbashian was previously in charge of the Third Army based in Fars, Khuzistan and Kerman. I believe him to be totally useless, but General Djam is good.

HIM is outraged that, in his speech to the Security Council, Mehdi Vakil, our ambassador to the UN, failed to mention Iraq's lowering of the national flag on Iranian shipping. Another of HIM's remarks came as a grave disappointment. I had told him that my office has no record of his response to the Emir of Kuwait which was prepared and dispatched via the Ministry of Foreign Affairs. To this he replied that the Ministry of Court should have no concern with political correspondence of this sort. His words came as a shock; the judgment of my dear sovereign sometimes amazes me. I am ready to sacrifice anything on his behalf, yet he feels obliged to offer all of us these cutting reminders of who is boss ... I suppose I must accept that there's nothing to be done; ingratitude is all part of the job.

Monday, 5–Saturday, 10 May

Travelled to Shiraz with HIM ... He showed his customary pleasure with the progress of Pahlavi University[3] and had many kind words to say to me on this subject. There he attended the national conference of Iranian Universities. Once again Pahlavi came out top of the league. However HIM was less than delighted with the poor showing of the University of Tehran and finished by demanding that the Court send him regular reports on the progress of each university.

Articles favourable to Iran and critical of the oil companies have appeared

---

[1] General Fereidoun Djam: Chief of Staff, 1969–71; first husband of the Shah's elder sister, Princess Shams. Later fell out of favour with the Shah, after which he was sent as Ambassador to Spain.

[2] General Fathollah Minbashian: Commander of Land Forces, 1969–72; brother of Mehrdad Pahlbod (formerly Minbashian), second husband of Princess Shams; a classmate of the Shah at the Tehran Military Academy.

[3] The Shah was particularly fond of this university, his own creation, which he hoped would come to rival or even surpass the University of Tehran, founded by his father. His appointment of Alam as President in 1964 was intended to symbolize the importance he attached to it.

in American and British newspapers, including the conservative *Daily Telegraph*.

Ansari has cabled that the US government would prefer Iran to borrow from the American private banking system rather than the public sector for future military procurement. HIM greatly annoyed. We fired off several robust messages to Washington and I telephoned the American ambassador for an explanation of this mess.

From Shiraz we went on to Isfahan where we spent two nights in the Shah Abbas Hotel ... Toured the Shah Abbas dam[1] and the site of the new steel-mill, both of which have raised my spirits ... It must be nearly twenty years ago that the Shah flew to a small diversion dam up this same river. On his way back his plane developed engine trouble and he was forced into a crash landing in the foothills, not far from the site of today's project. HIM emerged unhurt:

> In God I put my trust
> For he guards the delicate crystal
> inviolate amongst the rocks

God has assigned his work to the Shahanshah, striving on behalf of the people of Iran. As I told him, 'God is obliged to preserve you for at least another thirty years. Provided only that the interests of our nation remain unchanged and that you never cease, which God forbid, to serve the common good.'

Monday, 12 May

This morning HIM told me that the Consortium proposed guaranteeing us an annual income of $930 million besides paying us a month of this income as an advance. In this way we can expect a total oil-income of around $1.01 billion, which is actually an increase on our original demand. The only snag will arise if we're called upon to repay the month's advance from next year's allocation ...

The American ambassador telephoned with a farewell message. He is off to America for a few days and will then proceed directly from Tehran to Tokyo where he takes up his new embassy. He has been told by the representatives of the Consortium here of their decision to give way to Iran's demands for the coming year – just as HIM told me. However they insist on the idiotic proviso that 'Iran's demands over the next three years

---

[1] On the river Zayandeh Roud, near Isfahan.

are most unlikely to be met.' I suggested to the ambassador that the companies carry over our month's advance until the last year of our present agreement. He begged me to do all I can to ensure that our last moment rapprochement with the Consortium is maintained.

Attended Dinner and briefed HIM on my conversation with the ambassador. HIM says that he came close to agreeing to the Consortium's proposals but, 'There's no point in trusting their promises. Last year we anticipated an income of $865 million but in practice received only $846 million. If they agreed to compensate us for this shortfall we might put some faith in their guarantees for the future. Moreover they should amend their rules; if one member of the Consortium is prepared to market oil beyond its quota, the others should refrain from opposing it.' He instructed me to telephone these points to the ambassador. I woke the poor man up at midnight and told him to arrange a crash briefing of the Consortium's delegates.

Wednesday, 14 May
A much better day, since the Consortium has met our demands ... HIM elated but still not satisfied. He confided his desire that we take oil production into our own hands and then sell our output to the companies. In this way future confrontation will be avoided. This seems thoroughly reasonable; the companies will buy from us according to their needs and we can offload any surplus via the market. I'm convinced that this will come about sooner or later ...

As I was leaving I bumped into Dr Eqbal, President of the NIOC, on his way to an audience with HIM. He was puffed-up like a peacock, positively oozing self-importance, as if our success in the oil negotiations were entirely his responsibility. He's well intentioned but stupid.

In the evening the Nuncio of the Holy See presented me with a papal decoration. Our recent relations with the Vatican have been far from happy. The Ministry of Foreign Affairs warned HIM against the activities of the Maronite Archbishop of the Lebanon who intervened on behalf of General Bakhtiar. When the Pope made no effort to rebuke him we recalled our ambassador from the papal court. Any attempt by the Pope to disclaim the Archbishop (after all the poor Pope has no authority over the Maronites) met with a stony silence from our Foreign Ministry. Eventually I arranged an audience for the Nuncio to explain the situation and put an end to the bad blood that had been allowed to develop. Today's decoration was sent to me long before all this business with the Maronites, but until now I had put off accepting it. However yesterday's meeting between the Nuncio and HIM was followed by instructions for me to accept my decoration and for our ambassador to return to the Vatican ...

Thursday, 15 May

Rather surprised this morning to find HIM deep in thought. He asked me, 'Do you suppose we might have obtained an even higher income had we raised the pressure still further?' I said, half-mockingly, that it all depended on the timing and what sort of pressure he considered applying. This raised a laugh but he remained lost in thought. I pointed out that we would have been ill-advised to push for any further concessions given the state of our relations with Iraq. Besides, there have been major discoveries of oil in Nigeria, a country where various members of the Consortium, Shell and BP amongst them, have established interests, and far closer than us to the European market. How could we bring any more pressure to bear with our finances in such a mess? Any such attempt would have cost us dear. HIM appeared less than appreciative of this last remark.

... This evening accompanied HIM on a pretty remarkable spree[1] ... Late at night, after the party, HIM repeated that I must insist to the British and American ambassadors that they persuade the smaller shareholders in the Consortium to sell their shares to Iran. I'm sure that he's been told by a well-informed source, probably Armand Hammer, that we could have obtained a better deal. May God grant him many more years. Even at two in the morning he remains obsessed by the national interest.

Friday, 16 May

... This morning went with HIM to lunch in the Jajroud[2] valley ... During the meal he returned to the subject of oil production, saying that he believes the Russians to be in need of imports and willing to obtain them from the Gulf. He would like to open negotiations with them for the construction of a pipeline; 200 million tons of Arab oil each year, pumped from the Gulf to Russia across Iran. A company could be established in which we would participate but the Arabs would hold the majority of shares. In this way we should kill several birds with one stone; the Russians would be encouraged to protect the security of the Gulf whilst at the same time having less reason to covet a personal foothold in the region. They

---

[1] The Queen was away water-skiing in southern Iran.
[2] A river east of Tehran.

would obtain access to the Gulf's resources, but since the pipeline would lie within Iran, we should have a permanent lever to use against both Russia and the Arabs. Eventually too we could expect a substantial income from royalties. I praised the Shahanshah's idea and reminded him that, as Prime Minister, I suggested to him that any interest shown by Russia in Middle Eastern oil was likely to enhance our security. At the time he declared the idea was premature. 'True enough', he said, 'but now the time is right. Russia and America have no desire for a show-down in the Middle East.'

I am reminded of the time, four years ago, when HIM and I paid an official visit to the Soviet Union. We were walking along the sea-front at Yalta and to prevent the Russians from bugging our conversation we both of us switched on our pocket radios. He confided in me that at that evening's dinner, a tête-à-tête with the Deputy Chairman of the Praesidium, he intended proposing a 25-year non-aggression pact between Russia and Iran. Asked for my opinion I replied that such a pact would be a superb diplomatic coup, but might be a bit too much, coming on top of our planned agreements over the purchase of a steel-mill and the sale of natural gas. The western powers, especially the Americans, would be highly alarmed. America supplies us with weapons solely that we may stand as a bulwark against Soviet influence, not for us to fall swooning into the arms of Moscow. Perhaps we should wait and see how things go with the steel-mill. Better to take things one step at a time. And now, having followed that advice, we have at last become masters of our own destiny.

We returned this evening and I attended Dinner. HIM ordered me to inform the British ambassador that if the London newspapers and the Foreign Office continue to support Iraq, they must prepare for whatever reaction we deem necessary ...

Saturday, 17 and Sunday, 18 May

On Saturday morning I accompanied HIM to Mashad. It was the anniversary of Imam Reza's death and the courtyard of the mausoleum was packed with mourners. The Shahanshah took up his place and suddenly the throng became a crowd 60,000 strong, no longer in mourning but cheering their Shah. A remarkable sight. I recalled how in 1935 this same courtyard was the scene of a demonstration against Reza Shah's reforms, a mob angered by his prohibition against women wearing the veil. His soldiers fired on the crowd and nearly 200 were killed. But today all this is put behind us. Reza Shah's strong measures have been forgiven now that the people can see that they were undertaken not for personal gain but for the good of the country. They would have been justified even if 2,000 had died. Likewise I myself, as Prime Minister, ordered the dispersal of a protest against social reforms on 5 June 1963. Nearly ninety people lost their lives, but the number was immaterial. I was determined to make a stand since the very survival of our country was at stake.

On Sunday morning rain prevented HIM from flying to inspect the recent development schemes around Sarakhs.[1] As it was the eve of my daughter's wedding I sought leave to return to Tehran ...

Monday, 19 May
Early this afternoon I went to the airport to greet HIM's return. I passed on a cable from Ansari who states that reports filed by Mehdi Vakil, our ambassador to the UN, are wrong to suggest that America is supporting Iraq. This enraged HIM.

Later I attended the marriage of my daughter Roudi to Askar Ghaffari. An enjoyable occasion followed by an excellent dinner party thrown by Naz, my younger daughter.

In the course of this morning's audience I transmitted a message from the unofficial Israeli ambassador to Tehran.[2] He suggests that if Israeli policy is recognized as being beneficial to Iran's interests we should talk seriously to Rogers, US Secretary of State, on his forthcoming visit, and ask him why his own government keeps switching direction in the Middle East. HIM smiled and said, 'We may be delighted to see Israel putting the Arabs in their place, but we have repeatedly condemned their occupation of Arab territory. Really we can't be expected to become Israel's wet-nurse.' The Shah is a realist and is only seldom taken in ...

Saw HIM again this afternoon ... He was concerned by the progress of a German ship sailing in the Shatt al-Arab under the Iranian flag, which is being shadowed by two Iraqi launches. I was instructed to contact the headquarters of the armed forces to ensure that we are sent regular bulletins. Much to my relief at half past four I was told by the Supreme Commander's Chief of Staff that the ship is nearing Abadan and has shaken off its

---

[1] Sarakhs, on the border between north-eastern Iran and the USSR. A large agricultural and urban development programme was implemented there. Substantial deposits of gas were discovered by NIOC.

[2] In view of Arab sensitivity, Iran only extended *de facto* recognition to the state of Israel. The heads of the respective missions in Tehran and Tel Aviv – theoretically on a consular level – were in practice treated as ambassadors. The two countries maintained very close relations and co-operated in many fields ranging from tourism to the exchange of intellignece and military resources.

pursuers. HIM greatly relaxed. At five the vessel made port safely at Khorramshahr.

... To mark my daughter's wedding Their Majesties paid us the signal compliment of a personal visit to our home. A most enjoyable occasion. HIM left at 2 a.m. but HMQ and a few others stayed on for another three hours. It's now past dawn and I must go to bed – I've had no sleep in twenty-four hours. Today promises to be very busy.

Thursday, 22 May

Audience. Discussed HIM's autumn trip to the USA and the invitation to King Faisal to visit Iran ... King Hussein of Jordan has sent a message, declaring that he has successfully foiled an attempt by the Iraqis who hoped to convene a summit of Arab Foreign Ministers with a view to issuing a joint resolution against Iran. Hussein now wants to visit HIM in Tehran. It was decided to invite him from 30 May to 1 June.

I was present when the Crown Prince of Dubai lunched with HIM. Dubai will shortly open up oil production, set, to begin with, at 50,000 barrels a day – hardly in the same league as Iran's 3.5 million barrels a day, but then such differentials are only fair; look at the greed of a country like Abu Dhabi; half a million barrels a day to maintain a population of barely 50,000.

My daughter has set out on her honeymoon. Later she will spend a year in the UK with her husband who is being trained as a technician ... My younger daughter, married with her own household, this evening accompanies HMQ to the south of the country. The lights in my house have all been extinguished.

Saturday, 24 May

... Lunch with an American Middle East specialist who is shortly to have an audience with HIM. It becomes increasingly obvious why the oil question was solved in our favour. America can count on only one stable country in the entire region: Iran. Even Turkey is too volatile to trust. Saving a miracle, there is bound to be another Arab–Israeli war. Last time it was Egypt, next it will be Syria's turn to suffer humiliation. The export of Middle Eastern oil is sure to be interrupted again, and Iran will once more be the only reliable country to maintain the flow. Now that we have a pipeline under joint Israeli–Iranian ownership,[1] pumping oil from Eilath

[1] In 1959 a joint venture company, Transasiatic, designed for the transportation of Iranian oil, was agreed between NIOC and a group of Israeli oil-distribution companies (Paz-Delek ...). A

to the Mediterranean, we are looked upon with even greater favour by the West.

Sunday, 25 May

Audience. I passed on a personal reply from De Gaulle to HIM. The General writes in very amicable terms ...

I did my best to intercede on behalf of a number of people who are in trouble. One of these cases moved the Shahanshah and he telephoned the PM for further details. However the response must have been unfavourable, since the Shah had changed his mind by the time he put down the receiver. This incident has made me question the whole nature of autocracy, its fickleness and injustice. The Shah is truly a man of God, but his mind can still be altered by a biased judgment. I fully realize my own responsibility; I see him every morning and have the power to influence him for either good or evil. Pray God that I never abuse this power by turning him against the public interest. One false suggestion from me and the whole country could be affected ...

US Secretary of State Rogers arrived this evening and dined with HIM ... Our discussions were varied and carried on after dinner. The Americans are fully behind our stand against Iraq. HIM announced that the Iraqi Foreign Minister recently received our ambassador to Baghdad and warned him: 'Iran is strong today, but bear in mind that tomorrow Iraq may be stronger. Think of this and try to reach an understanding with us now, before it is too late.' HIM said this implied the Russians have given Iraq missiles which could be turned against us. The American Secretary of State dismissed the suggestion.

The Americans approve our assumption of greater responsibility in the Gulf, but nothing was said as to details or as to who will bear the cost ... In my opinion America should prevail upon the Arabs to contribute to our military expenditure in the interests of common security. But I was given no opportunity to express this view; the discussion was limited to HIM and the Secretary of State. HIM brought up the possible sale of oil to the Soviets and expounded the advantages of his scheme for a trans-Iranian pipeline ...

Their discussions returned to the Gulf and opposition to the withdrawal of British troops from the region. Edward Heath,[1] leader of the British

---

10-inch pipeline laid in 1959 between Eilath and the Haifa refinery was later supplemented by a second 16-inch pipeline. In 1968 a 42-inch pipeline was built between Eilath and Ashkelon.

[1] Leader of the opposition; Prime Minister, 1970–74.

Conservative party, has announced that the Shahanshah is personally in favour of a continued British presence. This is nonsense; HIM is adamant that he told Heath no such thing, but on the contrary advised an immediate withdrawal. He says that for all his tomfoolery he prefers doing business with Harold Wilson, the Prime Minister, who at least admits the inevitability of a withdrawal, albeit that this is the one and only sensible comment Wilson has made to date. Rogers remarked, 'I get the impression that Your Majesty and Harold Wilson are not exactly the best of friends.'

Nothing was said over dinner about the prospects of an Arab–Israeli conflict but it must surely have been discussed later on. The Israeli representative in Tehran has contacted HIM via me, begging him to dissuade Rogers from ever again supporting Nasser. How many times has that bastard accepted outside aid only to bite the hand that feeds him? HIM replied that whilst in principle objecting to Israel's policy towards the Arabs, he will certainly raise their anxiety over Nasser.

Rogers was highly optimistic over the war in Vietnam and declared that, but for support from China, the North Vietnamese and the Vietcong would long ago have sued for peace, so crippling have their losses been. The Russians are reluctant to see Hanoi pushing southward with Chinese support, but have no choice but to mask their indignation. He said, 'If nothing comes of the peace talks we shall push on to certain victory.' HIM enquired about reaction on the American home front, to which Rogers replied that, 'Things at home are not as bad as they're painted in the press. We're gradually getting the message across to people that the war is going well.' He himself is proud that his own son has experienced front line combat on the Mekong delta.

The American ambassador, Armin Meyer, made another lame effort to extol the virtues of the British. HIM's only comment was that their ambassador, Sir Denis Wright, seems a well-intentioned man.

With regard to Pakistan, HIM stressed his favourable opinion of the new regime which he believes would like to foster close links with both Tehran and Washington. The US government should encourage their attempt to resume purchases of American military hardware. Rogers' response to this last point was quite astonishing. He said that America is in a tough position. Faced with the rival expectations of India and Pakistan, Israel and the Arabs, she is unsure whether to supply both sides or steer clear of involvement altogether. Many would prefer the neutral option, in which event, the Shahanshah replied, the Russians will have no hesitation in occupying the vacuum.

HIM was critical of the corruption that flourished under Ayub and said that he has since advised the new regime to root out this evil. By which, of course, he meant to imply that we ourselves are entirely free of such things. But to me this seemed an underhand way for HIM to make his point, by blackening the reputation of a defeated regime. I am sure that my sovereign's conscience is as good a guide in such matters as anything I might say. Incidentally, he appears deeply hurt that Ayub's recent book should have lavished praise on Nasser.

Rogers said, 'The Afghans tell us how much they appreciate our presence now that they're more anxious about Chinese influence over Pakistan.' HIM, with his customary quick-wittedness, replied 'Ah, so the closer the Afghans get to the Russians the more shy they become of admitting it. Hence their eagerness to complain against Chinese infiltration.' There is a great deal of truth in this remark.

After dinner, whilst HIM held private discussions with Rogers, I led the other guests on a tour of the Palace. Joseph Sisco, US Assistant Secretary of State, took me to one side to make a point which he was concerned that Rogers would forget to mention to the Shah. America has told the Russians quite bluntly that they believe the Egyptian President Nasser to be totally oblivious to the prospects of a peaceful solution in the Middle East. The Russians were asked to inform Nasser that so long as this situation prevails, Washington will bring no pressure to bear on Israel. Hence Sisco's optimism; he feels certain that the Russians will put pressure on Nasser and that we can look forward to peace in the near future.

Monday, 26 May
... A group of young colonels have staged a successful *coup d'état* in the Sudan and established a leftist regime. Such news depresses me and makes me wonder how much we really know of our own situation here in Tehran.

Tuesday, 27 May
Today it was the turn of the British Foreign Secretary and his party to be received. As before, I attended the lunch but not the audience. Discussion centred on the French elections and the possible devaluation of the franc. Foreign Secretary Michael Stewart said quite rightly that De Gaulle opposed British entry to the EEC not for any economic reason, but because in the absence of the UK he hoped to make France the dominant power in Europe.

This was the first time I'd met Stewart face to face. I had pictured him as a crusty old history professor and was pleasantly surprised instead to meet a man of quick wit, enterprise and determination. Apparently his delegation had been subjected to some pretty blunt speaking before lunch, but at the meal itself HIM was the soul of courtesy, listening to them sympathetically and at the end, much to everyone's surprise, personally conducting them out of the room.

King Hussein arrived at 5.30 this evening accompanied by his Prime Minister. Outwardly he has come to mediate between us and Iraq, but I believe his real purpose is to make contact with both the Americans and the Israelis whose Air Force Commander is presently in Tehran.

I missed the dinner thrown in Hussein's honour, and on HIM's instructions dined at the British embassy to brief Michael Stewart on a number of important issues. To begin with I asked him and his colleagues what they made of their audience with HIM. They said it had been protracted and difficult but that they hoped the end results were worthwhile. Stewart then asked me if I could explain HIM's viewpoint in greater detail. I replied that HIM's chief grievance against the British is their inability to tell friend from foe. Worse, they sometimes sacrifice an ally to appease an enemy. For example, Iran was the only Middle Eastern oil producer which maintained the flow of oil during the last Arab–Israeli war, and yet when it came to our expressed requirement of $1 billion for the coming year, we were faced by endless British arguments that we were seeking to increase our output at the expense of the Arabs; such a tiresome and frustrating claim, when the Arabs neither need so much money nor have any idea how to spend their already inflated income. Similarly faced with HIM's magnanimity and vision in negotiations over Bahrain and the creation of a Federation of Arab Emirates, the British continue to drag their feet in respect to restoring our islands of Tunbs and Abu Musa. As I told him, he must be well aware that Britain had gained unlawful possession of these islands and handed them as a blighted inheritance to the Sheikhs of Sharjah and Ras al-Khaimah whom his government now supports against Iran. We can see no sense in this policy, since Iran is set to become the Emirates' sole protector once the British withdraw.

He thought for a while before delivering the following reply. Its wisdom disarms me: 'You are absolutely correct in all you say. Britain cannot simply disregard the concerns of the Arab world, but I tell you in all good faith that I consider it our duty to ensure that the islands are restored to Iran.' 'Six years ago', I said, 'I suggested to your ambassador that the British government turn a blind eye if we packed the islands with our own nationals to secure them for Iran. The ambassador's reply was that Britain would remain in the Persian Gulf for another twenty years and had no intention of reneging on her agreements with the Sheikhs. This was said only six years ago and already you've announced your complete withdrawal from the region. This, I suppose, is a demonstration of the timeless profundity of British diplomacy which one hears so much about?' He smiled and said, 'Our policy has changed in step with our change of government.' In that case, I enquired, what was one to make of the claim that British foreign policy is bi-partisan and unchanging?

With regard to our dispute with Iraq I told him: 'Outwardly you support us but we have doubts as to your underlying commitment.' He assured me that Britain's support is earnest and genuine. One of his aides expressed optimism about the future Federation of Arab Emirates, saying that the administrative framework had already been agreed. I replied that the spirit of the union was what should concern him, rather than any question of constitutional tinkering. If the Sheikhs choose to ignore present realities and continue to rule like medieval chieftains, the federation will be wrecked by conflict between feudalists and progressives, the latter manipulated by outside influences. Stewart much appreciated these remarks.

Wednesday, 28 May
This morning reported my discussions to HIM. He ordered me to let the British know that a satisfactory response to our demands over the islands remains a pre-condition of any future settlement over Bahrain ...

Thursday, 29 May
... In the evening a reception thrown by Amir Khosrow Afshar, our Deputy Foreign Minister, in honour of the British Foreign Secretary. Our Prime Minister and Foreign Minister also present ... Stewart had been deeply impressed by a tour of Persepolis and said: 'Your Empire was founded by Cyrus. Xerxes extended it and Darius preserved it. Your present ruler seems to me to possess something of the qualities of all three of these mighty kings.' Clearly HIM has made a considerable impression.

Friday, 30 May
This morning accompanied HIM to Jajroud ... He enjoyed his trip. Returned after lunch to the Niavaran Palace and walked for an hour in the gardens until Her Majesty's return from water-skiing. We discussed a broad range of topics, amongst them HIM's concern about the murmuring

in the diplomatic corps against the Minister of Foreign Affairs ... He has asked me to pass on the advice that Zahedi[1] take greater care before opening his mouth ...

Saturday, 31 May

The death has been announced of Hassan Arsanjani,[2] former Minister of Agriculture, powerful, dogged and well-informed. In his twenties he was appointed assistant to the then Prime Minister Qavam.[3] Amini[4] promoted him to the Ministry of Agriculture where he remained on my own appointment as Prime Minister. He had already embarked on land reform and I would brook no changes whilst the scheme was under way. Besides which he was a personal friend. His only great weakness was a burning conviction that whatever he said was automatically correct and that whatever suited him must be good for others. For the most part his qualities as a public servant far outweighed his defects. But towards the end he came to see himself as the hero of land reform and created problems by his intransigence towards official policy. HIM instructed me to sack him but then appointed him ambassador in Rome. Under Mansour's regime he was recalled to Tehran and gradually forfeited HIM's regard despite my best endeavours. His death is to be followed by official mourning at court and this has been well received amongst the nation's youth and intelligentsia. A heart attack carried him off at the age of only forty-seven.

Tuesday, 3 June

The Shah's personal dentist arrived from Switzerland last night. HIM visited him in the dispensary of the Niavaran Palace and rang me early this morning to cancel all his other appointments. I thought his check-up might last for an hour or two, but he called me after only thirty minutes having emerged with flying colours. I asked him why so short a visit and he replied: 'My tooth had become a nuisance so the dentist pulled it. Now

[1] Ardeshir Zahedi: an exuberant figure who was one of the Shah's closest friends and for a while his son-in-law; Ambassador to the USA and the UK; Foreign Minister, 1967–71. He introduced the Shah to the young Farah Diba, then a student at the Paris School of Architecture holidaying in Tehran.
[2] Hassan Arsanjani: Minister of Agriculture in the Amini and Alam governments. See the main introduction.
[3] Ahmad Qavam (1872–1955): several times Prime Minister of Iran. The present entry refers to his premiership 1946–7. An aristocrat and a politician of the old school with exceptional diplomatic ability, he persuaded the Soviets to withdraw their forces from Iran at the end of the Second World War.
[4] Ali Amini: ambassador to the USA, and later Prime Minister. Alam succeeded him in July 1962. See the main introduction.

you can bring me up to date on all the news.' This I proceeded to do for the next two hours.

Meanwhile Her Majesty paid her own visit to the dentist. An hour later when she returned to find us still hard at work she expressed her surprise at such a lengthy audience, but as I told her, we had an immense backlog of work to go through. She stayed to chat with HIM and amongst other things told him of a dream she'd had the night before which had convinced her that they will have a fourth child, another boy. HIM said: 'But I thought you wanted a girl?' 'Yes', she said, 'but in my dream it was a boy and I was happy.'

Wednesday, 4 June

Audience. I brought up the matter of General Jahanbani's son[1] and his imprisonment. He and Princess Shahnaz are in love. HIM ... and, as soon as the young man went off on his military service, had him court-martialled and sentenced to three years in prison for some trifling misdemeanour. Since then Shahnaz has refused to take anyone else as her husband and the boy for his part continues to profess his love. As I said to HIM: 'This is an impossible situation. As things stand it's better to have the boy released and allow him to marry the Princess.' HIM asked me to find out whether conviction by a military court will affect his civilian rights.

I showed him a letter I had received from Amini and said, 'I haven't seen the fellow for a couple of years but from the moment he caught sight of me at Arsanjani's funeral, he's been plaguing me and now writes this admittedly rather charming letter seeking Your Majesty's permission to travel abroad.' HIM asked me to look into Amini's request which may be difficult to grant as the prosecution is being handled by the Ministry of Justice.[2]

---

[1] Khosrow Jahanbani (1942–), the youngest son of a respected general who had served under Reza Shah. Khosrow was eventually to marry Princess Shahnaz. Before the revolution, he and the princess became devout Muslims under the influence of a man known as Ayatollah Malayeri – to whom he was introduced by Prince Ali Patrick, the Shah's nephew. After 1979 the princess insisted on being addressed as Hajar Alavi, devoutly Islamic names, far removed from the tainted Pahlavi name. The couple now live in Switzerland with their two children.

[2] The Shah never forgave Amini's independent attitude as Prime Minister or the fact that he had been openly supported by the Americans. After his resignation, and at the Shah's instigation, he was several times questioned before magistrates and prevented from leaving the country. This harassment ended after a few years.

Saturday, 7 June
This afternoon Alikhani, the Minister of Economics, came to see me following his audience with HIM. They had disagreed over the price rises for steel products. Alikhani feels that, having failed to please HIM, he is duty bound to resign. I cautioned patience. HIM may have been upset, but when he has had a chance to think it over he will actually be quite pleased to know that at least one person in the government has the courage to speak plainly without glossing over unpleasant realities ... Poor Alikhani says that he finds the present PM and his entourage quite impossible and that resignation is his only option ...

Tuesday, 10 June
Audience. Discussed Princess Shahnaz. HIM has abandoned all hope for her. I became greatly upset and said, 'Were she a cripple, think how much you would suffer and how you would move heaven and earth to nurse her. We cannot simply abandon her to her fate. She is as much your child and flesh of your flesh as the Crown Prince or Princess Farahnaz. If she suffers now for Your Majesty's past neglect, whose fault is that?' HIM was deeply moved by this and said: 'Her fate is in your hands. You have my blessing to do whatever you deem necessary. From now on you should consider yourself the girl's tutor.' His words touched me profoundly; I consider it a sacred trust. With God's help I shall do all I can to secure her happiness.

Wednesday, 11 June
At this morning's audience HIM announced that the Russians have made known to our ambassador in Moscow that they will never abandon Iran for the sake of Iraq. Their arms sales to the Arabs, and to Egypt in particular, are merely for security, not to facilitate any new offensive. I agreed that this seemed plausible ...

Saw HIM this evening and submitted a cable from Aram, our ambassador in London. He has been told that the Sultan of Muscat is interested in visiting Iran en route to London. HIM has ordered the Foreign Ministry to look into this. Such a visit promises little benefit to us and might seriously jeopardize our relations with King Faisal. The Sultan is a usurper in Oman where the previous ruler continues to enjoy King Faisal's support. Moreover he is said to be a bit of a monster; for the past ten years he's locked himself away in his palace and refused any contact with the people. Diehard reactionaries like this are doomed – and good riddance, say I.

Saturday, 14 June

This morning I showed HIM an encouraging article in *The Times*. Written by Winston Churchill, it provides an excellent summary of Iran's situation. There were two errors in the draft which were corrected on HIM's orders.

... Princess Shahnaz cannot read my letters if I write to her in Persian, so I sent her a long letter in English, assuring her of how much we all love her and admire her beauty and intelligence. Even so, I am baffled by the life she has chosen to lead. We must simply wait and see what she does next.

Sunday, 16 June

Audience. Passed on several personal letters to HIM. He likes such things to be preserved as souvenirs and so handed them back to me for safe-keeping.[1] I told him that I entrust them all to Mr X who looks after them at his home and who has my absolute confidence. He knows that if I die suddenly or am killed, he should destroy all the letters. 'No need for that', said HIM. 'He can simply return them to me.' I took note of his indifference to the thought of my death, but said nothing. We then joked for a while whilst the unfortunate PM was kept waiting outside.

Alikhani called before dinner to say that he personally tendered his resignation this afternoon and had openly criticized administrative short-comings ...

Sunday, 22 June

For the past few days I have been unable to refer to this diary, and must now seek to record recent events from memory. HIM accepted Alikhani's resignation and offered him the alternative of our Paris embassy or the Presidency of Tehran University. Alikhani would not go to France, saying that he wished his children to grow up in Iran – a patriotic stand which I salute from the bottom of my heart.

Amini came to see me, once again seeking permission to travel abroad. He is not to be trusted. I've several times fallen victim to his political duplicity, but all the same I forwarded his request to HIM who has approved it. I must now arrange matters with the Justice Ministry, to ensure that after seven years of restriction he is once again free to go where he pleases. For the moment he is full of gratitude, but given a change in

---

[1] Various of the Shah's female friends liked to think of themselves as his correspondents – although he of course never wrote back.

circumstances I have no doubt that he would turn against all of us, the Shah included. But HIM remains magnanimous. As he said to me, 'Amini may be cunning but he's no more of a fox than Teymour Bakhtiar, and Bakhtiar was much more courageous.'

Bakhtiar himself has been granted nationality by the regime in Baghdad. He has written an open letter to the Iraqi President Hassan al-Bakr, expressing concern for the future of the Iranian people. A disgraceful thing to do, especially since it comes from a man who has become a millionaire by extorting money from the very nation he claims to represent ... I told HIM that we might take the opportunity afforded by Iraqi persecution of the children of Ayatollah Hakim,[1] a prominent Shi'a leader, and arrange for them to flee Iraq in protest. Apparently this came as a new idea to HIM, who thought for a while but made no comment. I am fairly sure that he will attempt to get things moving on this, but who will implement his orders? It strikes me that the Foreign Ministry could mess it up in just the same way they messed up the business over Bakhtiar.

The King of Morocco has used me to convey a desire that his heir take his holidays in St Moritz and so become the childhood friend of our own Crown Prince.

... I read HIM an article from the *Daily Telegraph*, which asserts that the British government has adopted a more cautious policy towards the Gulf, speaking now of only military and not full political withdrawal. I suggested we appoint a steering committee to monitor developments and supervise policy proposals, but HIM replied, 'I myself am monitor enough.' I refrained from pointing out to my dear master that the only monitoring he does is of reports prepared by the Ministry of Foreign Affairs not worth the paper they're written on. Even so I have a national duty and must remind HIM of our deficiencies whenever the opportunity arises.

Monday, 23 June

... Ansari, our ambassador to Washington, is currently in Tehran. He says that once the Apollo 11 mission and the moon landings are successfully completed, President Nixon intends to make a tour of friends and allies, and proposes to visit Iran on 30 July.[2] In that event, as I pointed out to

[1] Mohsen Hakim: probably the most prominent of the ayatollahs of the 1960s. Died June 1970. After his death several of his children and many relatives were sentenced to death by the Iraqi regime or forced to flee Iraq.

[2] He was also scheduled to visit Turkey, but became worried by the risk of anti-American demonstrations. Rather than be seen to avoid one particular country, he cancelled his trip both to Turkey and Iran.

HIM, his own trip to America would be better postponed from October to next year. There can be no sense in a Washington visit, barely a month after a meeting in Tehran; HIM thinks otherwise, arguing that a postponement might be misinterpreted.

He rang me on my return to my office with orders to tell Zahedi, the Foreign Minister, that the Shahanshah wills him to accept an appointment as ambassador in Washington. This came as a shock to me, particularly since Ardeshir Zahedi is quite capable of regarding it as some devious scheme of my own. In any event I asked him to call round this evening and passed on the Shah's proposal. Zahedi is dreadfully upset and whilst he expressed his willingness to obey whatever orders HIM may give, personally he has not an ounce of enthusiasm for the Washington job. Naturally I did my best to be tactful and tried to explain to him that Ansari was regarded as very much President Johnson's confidant. Now Johnson has been replaced by Nixon, HIM wants a man at the embassy who has been close to the new president and Zahedi fits the bill. After all, he was ambassador once before, during the Kennedy–Nixon election campaign. Like a fool he openly supported Nixon and, following Kennedy's victory, was recalled to Tehran at the President's express command. Ardeshir saw the reason behind this and, being no great admirer of Ansari, admitted it would be wrong to keep him on in Washington. But in saying this he overlooks the fact that Ansari has managed to establish close relations with Nixon ...

Wednesday, 25 June
Attended the Shahvand Palace for a dinner thrown by the Queen Mother, who became mixed up in an unfortunate argument with HIM – she forbidding him to fly to the Caspian Sea by helicopter, he adamant that there was no danger. She continued to complain, at which HIM declared that he preferred not to be bothered by those who pronounce opinions on matters they know nothing about. Both of them lost their tempers and it ended with the Queen Mother, who lives in Shahdasht and only comes to the Shahvand Palace for special occasions, storming out in a flood of tears. I intend to have a serious word with HIM. A mother's opinions are to be respected, not harshly dismissed.

Sunday, 16 July

I write these notes on board the plane taking me to Europe. Very tired. Princess Fatemeh[1] and the wife of the PM[2] are both on board this flight ... I have neglected my diary for over a fortnight for two reasons. My lover was with me and I idled away my time, or, to put it another way, realized how much time I'd wasted away from my love. Secondly, HIM was off to the Caspian Sea. I saw him there twice and told him that although it is obvious how much he loves his mother, he should show her more respect and refrain from bickering, even when she's in her most unreasonable mood. Eventually I succeeded in getting him to phone her, but she refused to accept the call. Despite it being the chief bone of contention, he flew to the north by helicopter, which was wrong of him. Not that he appreciated the fact when I pointed it out to him.

I thought he seemed a touch depressed, but he assured me that everything was fine.

Dr Eqbal finally signed the agreement for the construction of a pipeline which will allow our oil to be pumped to a port on the Turkish Mediterranean. We could have saved ourselves $15 million if only he'd given the go-ahead four months ago, before the rise in interest-rates. But that would have been to go against every tradition by which our glorious bureaucrats operate. The proposed pipeline to run Arab oil through Iran to the Soviet Union is still under consideration. It's being promoted by Peter Stirling[3] who has written to me personally on the subject. HIM wonders whether the Russians will still be interested, following their agreement with Iraq for the development of the Rumeilah[4] oil fields ...

The Shah does his utmost to promote progress and, in all truth, he's achieved a great deal for this country. But there are always the incidental matters, things like the supply of meat or electricity, the telephone system or the asphalt in the streets; things which are relatively unimportant in themselves, but which touch on the lives of everyone and tend to mar whatever progress we make elsewhere. The blame rests squarely on the incompetence of those in command ...

On HIM's orders I last night cabled Washington about the training of

---

[1] Princess Fatemeh (1930–88). Her second husband, General Khatami, was Commander of the Air Force.

[2] Leyla Emami, whose brief marriage to Amir Abbas Hoveyda ended in divorce in the mid 1970s. A very successful horticulturist, responsible for the orchids Hoveyda wore every day in his button-hole.

[3] A Scottish businessman, married to an Iranian and living in Iran.

[4] A large oilfield in southern Iraq, near Basra.

our pilots and the supply of spare parts. In the light of recent events in Iraq and the Sudan, I asked why America is so slow in heeding our most urgent requests. HIM is particularly concerned by the situation in Afghanistan and thinks that before long there may be a leftist coup, mounted under the cover of religion, as in the Sudan. The Afghans regularly send their students and even their servicemen to study in Russia. They have also allowed in the Chinese to oversee major development programmes. The Afghan regime, if not the country, becomes shakier day by day. All of which is of tremendous significance from our own point of view.

Alikhani has accepted the Presidency of Tehran University and Ansari takes over from him as Economics Minister. The Foreign Minister's future is uncertain, but I think he will be sent to the Washington embassy to replace Ansari . . .

Sunday, 3 August
Returned from Europe last night. Morning audience. The Shah pleased to see me – we both of us seem to have missed one another. He got up from his desk and came round to offer me his hand which I kissed with real sincerity. Then he complained that my return had been a week overdue. I told him, 'My doctor warned me to spend at least 10 days convalescing by the sea or the whole journey would be wasted. I only followed his advice because I thought it would help me to serve you the better; had I disobeyed him there was a risk that the concentration of white blood cells might have killed me.'[1]

I described my meeting with Shahnaz in Geneva and passed on a letter in which she informs HIM of her love for Khosrow Jahanbani. I noticed how carefully he read it through, and with what pain. I told him that I think I may have persuaded her to return to Iran. HIM replied that she would be better off staying where she is. I could feel the tears pricking my eyes but managed to control myself.

In an attempt to change the subject I mentioned the frustrations of family life at the seaside – surrounded by beautiful girls but with my wife

---

[1] A year earlier his Iranian physician, Professor Abbas Safavian, had suspected that Alam might be suffering from a chronic infection or malignant illness. For the sake of secrecy he referred Alam to his Swiss physician, Professor Eric Martin of Geneva. A form of leukaemia was diagnosed but Alam was never told the exact nature of his illness. Safavian advised Alam to place himself under the supervision of Safavian's own teachers at the Paris Medical School, Professors Jean Bernard and Paul Milliez who, a few years later, also began to deal with the Shah's cancer.

and children there what could I do? He laughed a little, asked after my family, and added: 'Isn't that wife of yours ever going to let you off the leash?' I replied that I couldn't tell, but that despite everything I love her dearly; if only she could show me just a little more understanding. 'It's a sad fact', said HIM, 'but these women have no idea how they ought to behave.' Then he told me the good news about Her Majesty's pregnancy, and I was able to offer my congratulations ...

Monday, 4 August
Found HIM depressed this morning. I asked him the reason. 'The rest of my family are at their wits' end', he said. 'My sister Ashraf[1] wrote me a letter saying that I don't love her, that she feels that I am always cold towards her and that as a result she has left the country. If I wanted her to return I should let her know in no uncertain terms, otherwise she will never come back. I'm told that last night she flew to Paris.' I asked him what lay behind all this. 'Apparently she felt that I didn't show enough enthusiasm when she came to see me on the Caspian Sea. People like my sister seem to consider me ungrateful if I fail to regard every visit from them as a personal favour.' I told him that Her Royal Highness clearly loves him very much. Perhaps his indifference has caused her real pain. He said, 'I have too many more important things going on for me to bother about this sort of nonsense'; all of which is absolutely true. He then asked me to write to her on his behalf, telling her that she has got hold of the wrong end of the stick, and that HIM looks forwards to her return ...

Ansari, newly appointed Economics Minister, was my guest for dinner. He passed on a very interesting piece of information. Apparently he has been instructed by HIM to contact the Russians and explain to them that Iran is a free agent and that he, Ansari, is personally in favour of increased co-operation with our neighbours, amongst whom he counts Russia the most important. This is a remarkable demonstration of HIM's subtlety and attention to detail. Ansari has been our ambassador in Washington and is well known for being pro-American, so now the Shahanshah wishes to send an unequivocal message to Moscow that Ansari is equally keen to be friends with the Soviet Union. Full marks for insight.

This afternoon attended a reception at the Senate, celebrating sixty-four years of the constitution. More like a wake than a birthday party. It brought

---

[1] The Shah's twin sister: an ambitious and dynamic woman who in the 1940s was involved in behind-the-scene politics in support of her brother. In later years her requests were often a source of irritation to the Shah.

home to me that I belong to a corrupt and money-grubbing élite. Iran stands little chance under the thumb of such a motley crew.

Tuesday, 5 August

HIM depressed this morning, worrying about government finances. He told me, 'Last night in the Economic Council[1] we cancelled various items of expenditure under the Fourth Development Plan,[2] but we're still in the red.'[3] I reminded him that in the past he's dismissed my criticisms of government finance. He made no comment but there was a short pause. He then said, 'The over-run on the budgets for the gas pipeline and petrochemical projects are beyond belief. Various government agencies, the Plan Organization for example, or the Steel Mill Company, pay their employees appallingly inflated salaries. The disparity between wages in this country is shocking; the better paid receive up to one hundred times the money given to those at the bottom. Things are quite different in the developed world; in Israel wages vary by a factor of three at the most. We cannot go on like this.'

I reported an important meeting held in my office to which HIM had ordered me to invite the minister responsible for Posts and Tele-communications and our US military adviser. We dealt with the Trans-Iranian telecommunications network, badly needed for the defence of the Gulf. We need it to be completed in the next two years, in time for the British withdrawal. But the minister insists that the contract should be put out to tender, which means a completion date of 1973 at the earliest. HIM was displeased. As he said, 'How can we defend this country when we lack the proper means?'

A dreadful evening which has put me in the foulest of tempers. I went personally to the airport to greet Princess Shahnaz and accompany her to the Saadabad Palace. In the car I tried to make her see reason and to avoid any meeting with Khosrow Jahanbani before her audience with the Shahanshah. This she promised to do.... When I got home, I telephoned Jahanbani's father and told him that it was in his son's best interest to prevent him making any effort to see the Princess tonight. The poor fellow then dashed all my hopes by announcing that his son left home a week ago

[1] The council's weekly meetings were chaired by the Shah and attended by the PM, various ministers, the head of the Plan Organization and the Governor of the Central Bank.
[2] The Fourth Development Plan 1968–73.
[3] The deficit was due chiefly to increased military expenditure.

and is now living with Prince Ali, the late Prince Ali Reza's son.[1] With a sinking feeling I instructed the commander of the palace guard to prevent anyone entering the Princess's residence, and sure enough he reported back a few minutes later that her boyfriend was already inside the house. What was I to do? Have him thrown out or simply turn a blind eye? Should I telephone the Shah and risk upsetting him in the middle of the night, and what if he ordered me to take strong measures and we ended up with a scandal on our hands? In the end I decided not to bother HIM, but told the guard commander to chuck Khosrow out. He rang the Princess and warned her that unless the boy left immediately he had instructions to eject him by force. As I had feared, the Princess replied that in that case she too would leave the palace. I then telephoned her myself and pleaded with her so insistently that she eventually gave way and said she would make sure he left provided they had one more hour together. This I agreed to. I waited and waited and two hours later he left. It is now 3 in the morning. I am utterly exhausted and ready to crawl into bed, but at least I did not have to disturb my master.

Wednesday, 6 August
Audience ... A report has reached us from England that at their recent meeting Nixon and Wilson reached a firm decision that Iran's interests will play no part in any future deal between the western powers and Moscow. 'In that case', said HIM, 'they can both go to hell. We will simply not allow them to strike their sordid little bargains as if we had no say in the matter. Don't they realize how easily we can come to our own agreement with Russia? Iran is not some pawn to be shunted about by Britain and America.'

We then turned to a discussion of wider regional issues ... According to HIM the Americans have delivered fifty Phantoms to Israel, a country which annually spends nearly $500 million on arms. Yet we are accused of excessive military expenditure, when without adequate protection we would be prey even to a miserable little dwarf like Iraq ...

I told HIM of his daughter's arrival and the goings on that had followed,

[1] Ali Reza (1922–54), the Shah's younger brother. He married a Polish woman when in France at the end of the Second World War. Their only child was Ali Patrick, commonly known as Prince Ali. Ali Reza, whose wife was never acknowledged by the Court, returned alone to Iran a few years later and died in a plane crash in 1954. Thereafter the Shah took personal charge of Ali Patrick, an unstable child, who disappointed his uncle. After the revolution, he changed his name from Pahlavi to Islami, which did nothing to protect him from mistreatment by the new regime. In 1982 he fled Iran and presently lives in the USA.

begging him not to upset himself, and to talk to her calmly. His meeting with the Princess passed off this afternoon, apparently better than she had expected. Over dinner HIM told me that he too was reasonably pleased with their reunion and that he will give me a more detailed account tomorrow morning. Earlier Khosrow had called round and we had a long chat. He is well educated and seems prepared to abandon his hippyfied ways and face up to reality. I only hope that things will work out for the best; Shahnaz is as dear to me as if she were my own daughter ...

Thursday, 7 August
Audience. HIM described his meeting with Princess Shahnaz. He assured her of his love and concern for her welfare; he would allow nothing to spoil things for her. But she has a responsibility to the rest of the Imperial family since her own behaviour affects the public standing of the crown. She has agreed to abandon her wayward life-style and to persuade Khosrow to do the same. Altogether HIM seemed quite pleased ...

Friday, 8 August
Attended Lunch. Afterwards a visit from the British ambassador who raised four principal issues. Firstly, Michael Stewart has badgered the Sheikhs of Ras al-Khaimah and Sharjah into agreeing to some sort of arrangement with us over the islands of Tunbs and Abu Musa. Next, negotiations for a plebiscite in Bahrain are making satisfactory headway. Thirdly, HIM has announced that he will accept the Germans as purchasers of any shares that members of the Oil Consortium may make available. Dr Eqbal now says that NIOC considers itself a potential buyer, though the whole thing is purely academic as there's no one in the Consortium prepared to market any shares. Finally, in respect to the proposed Trans-Iranian pipeline between Russia and the Arab states, there seems little point in pursuing the matter now that the Soviets have concluded their agreement with Iraq ...

Saturday, 9 August
Attended Dinner. HIM and the Queen Mother are now fully reconciled and things went off without a hitch.

... Baghdad radio broadcasts polemic against Iran and especially against the Imperial family ... Once we get the go-ahead from our allies, we shall soon find ways to deal with these bastards. I have good reason to believe that there would have been a good many more pipelines around Mosul sabotaged by the Kurds, but for the restraints imposed on us from abroad.

Sunday, 10 August

Audience. Announced that Princess Shahnaz seems genuinely determined to turn over a new leaf, which delighted HIM. Reported my discussions with the British ambassador. HIM said: 'During the Second World War, the US Secretary of State, James Byrnes, put a proposal to the Russians. Iran, he suggested, should be divided in three, with separate zones for the Turks and Kurds, the Arabs and the Persian populations. For no apparent reason the proposal did not find favour with Molotov. Stalin then opposed it and the Americans themselves began to have second thoughts.[1] But imagine, if the Russians had gone along with the idea; it would have meant the end of us, particularly since the British had armies stationed in Iraq and the Gulf and could easily have manipulated the chieftains in Southern Iran. At the time we were powerless to defend ourselves. Hence my absolute conviction that we need to strengthen the Iranian military. We are now more or less autonomous. At all costs we must avoid total dependence on either Russia or the West. Hence, when the Americans began to hint at a withdrawal of military aid, I was not unduly concerned. We have shouldered a heavy burden but it is the price we must pay for independence.' I was greatly impressed by this analysis and the deep and tragic experience that HIM can call upon. What a pity that he prevents me from publicizing such facts to the nation . . .

Tuesday, 12 August

This morning attended a memorial service for Majid Bakhtiar,[2] whose plane crashed into the Caspian Sea killing both him and his friend Palanchian,[3] a close companion of Princess Ashraf. The accident occurred several days ago but the bodies have only recently been recovered from the water. The details are far from clear, but it seems that they were both extremely drunk and decided at midnight to take their own light aircraft from Ramsar[4] to Tehran. Whatever happened, the crash was fatal and, unless I'm much

---

[1] Repeated again and again by the Shah, this story is a gross distortion of discussions amongst the Allied powers in 1945 which had been aimed at a compromise whereby Soviet forces could withdraw from Iran.

[2] A former Deputy in the Majlis and a businessman; first introduced to court via his cousin, Queen Soraya – the Shah's second wife. He was a distant relative of General Teymour Bakhtiar, then plotting against the Shah in Iraq.

[3] Leon Palanchian, an enterprising Armenian businessman and a favourite of Princess Ashraf. With her backing, he founded a private airline in which Majid Bakhtiar was a partner.

[4] A resort on the Caspian Sea.

mistaken, is a lucky break for the Shah. These two were outwardly friendly as could be, but deep down they were dangerous men who got their rightful come-uppance.[1]

Later received by HIM, enraged and rightly so by a series of minor mishaps. For one thing he's kept awake at night by the new plumbing in the palace; apparently it kicks up a dreadful racket. For another, it's well known that the Shah detests air-coolers, but his fool of a valet turned up the air-conditioning in his office and HIM felt the draught. I was more than a little ashamed since such things are ultimately my responsibility.

HIM said, 'I have issued orders for the dismissal of the Minister of the Interior and the Minister of Housing.[2] They're both idiots, swapping insults and then running to me to tell tales on one another. I simply can't stand for this sort of thing.' I agreed. He then went on, 'I have received unfavourable reports on the Naval High Command. Today I ordered that every Admiral and senior officer accept early retirement. They will be replaced by new blood from amongst the younger generation.' 'Your own homemade *coup d'état*!', I said. The decision will have a particularly rousing effect on the morale of junior officers.

. . . The British ambassador called again this afternoon. I told him of HIM's qualified approval for Britain's moves over Tunbs and Abu Musa, but that we could not accept their unjust proposals over the Bahrain plebiscite. Britain is suggesting that U Thant's representative should report the views of the Bahraini people to the United Nations on the basis of nothing more than discussions with a few pressure groups. We could never ratify such a proposal nor justify it to the Iranian public. 'That is not so', said the ambassador. 'Should U Thant's representative fail to get a clear idea of Bahraini opinion after contacting these particular groups, then U Thant is quite at liberty to seek consultation with other sections of the population. Bear in mind that we had a very sticky time getting the Sheikh of Bahrain to accept this much; he was fundamentally opposed to anything that even looked like a plebiscite.' 'To hell with the Sheikh of Bahrain', I replied; 'HIM has wisely determined to sort out our position in the Gulf, and to that end has had the courage to propose a plebiscite as the most equitable means of clearing up the problems of Bahrain. For this he has received praise from around the world and even in Iran itself, where the

---

[1] This reflects a rumour that the two crash victims had established contact with General Teymour Bakhtiar.
[2] Respectively Ata Khosrovani and Gholam Reza Nikpay. Nikpay, who was to become Mayor of Tehran, was executed in 1979. Their squabble broke out during an inter-ministerial meeting.

issue is understandably extremely sensitive. But now Bahrain intervenes with a plan that would wreck the whole operation. I speak to you as HIM's adviser, his Minister of Court and an upholder of his dynastic interest, and I tell you that your proposals are quite unacceptable.'

Wednesday, 13 August

Audience. Reported my discussions with the ambassador. HIM unreservedly approved my stand and said, 'Repeat to him that I would be committing suicide if I accepted his proposals. I should not mind so much if it were a suicide calculated to protect the Iranian nation but in my opinion the present scheme is a betrayal of national interest and as such I can never accept it . . . ' The palace pipes have been mended which has put HIM in a much better mood . . .

Tuesday, 14 August

. . . In the evening attended a private dinner in my honour at the Russian embassy. HIM had instructed me to make some sort of light-hearted remarks to the Soviet ambassador, to the effect that Moscow would clearly be behind Iran in any future confrontation with Iraq. The ambassador began by outlining the Sino-Russian border disputes and the course of recent skirmishes, adding that the Chinese are not exactly ideal neighbours. 'Strange that you should say that', I put in, 'since we too have a rather troublesome neighbour in the shape of Iraq. Just as you say in relation to China, the Baghdad government is unrepresentative of its people and has caused us plenty of headaches. It's a relief to know that the Soviet Union would never think of supporting such a regime in a show-down with Iran.' This put the ambassador in the hot seat in no uncertain way. 'We are friends of both Iran and the Arabs', he said, 'and we hope that your differences can be peacefully resolved.' 'If you really think so', I replied, 'then perhaps it would be wise to put the Iraqis in the picture.' I think he took the suggestion to heart.

. . . Turning to the Middle East he said, 'The Israelis are proud and stubborn and backed by America; hence the stumbling block in the way of a peace settlement . . . Resolve that problem and we could look forward to tackling other international disputes, China, Vietnam, the clash between India and Pakistan, and so on, in a spirit of real co-operation with the Americans . . . ' I said, 'We share your wish, but Israel is faced by those who until recently were proclaiming their intention to wipe her from the face of the globe. How can she put any faith in guarantees of peace?' 'It's the Israelis who stand to lose out', he replied. 'The Arabs are now far better supplied with military technology than they were at the time of the '67 war.' 'For which improvement', I said, 'they have only Russia to thank.' His next comment came as something of a surprise. He said that Jordan had a fine army and that King Hussein is a brave man, but that the Egyptians were a lazy bunch headed by a group of useless, fat-bellied generals.

I remarked on the valuable oil concession that his country has obtained from Iraq. But he denied that it is as significant as some people make out, saying, 'We only have access to an Iraqi oilfield of 10 million tons annual production capacity.' This is a downright lie, since I know for a fact that they have reserves of 10 billion barrels. I asked whether the oil was for the Soviet domestic market or would be exported internationally. He replied that Russia, with her domestic production of around 500 million tons a year, has no need of oil imports but that the situation was different amongst her Eastern European partners. 'In that case', I said, 'have you considered pipelining the stuff through Iran?' He said that this would need a great deal of thought and might well prove uneconomical.

His speech at dinner was full of praise for HIM, and later he commended my own administration for the new spirit we injected into Iranian–Soviet relations.[1] I said, 'I am the Shah's servant and merely carried out his orders to the letter.' He was less than flattering about the government of Amini, my predecessor as Prime Minister, claiming that it had maligned Soviet Russia without any justification . . .

Saturday, 16 August
Audience. Reported my meeting at the Soviet embassy . . . Various members of the US Senate have proposed that America help finance the creation of an international force under the auspices of the UN, rather than engage in unilateral intervention around the world. I heard this on the BBC news and it is strikingly similar to the proposals that HIM put forward three years ago, in his speech to New York University. I suggested that he remind the public of this coincidence, so that they may know what a clear-sighted leader they have. He said, 'At the same time, three years ago, remember that we also visited Russia and warned them to watch out for the Chinese, not that they seemed to pay any attention. For the past twenty-

---

[1] On 15 September 1962, the government headed by Alam pledged itself to refrain from basing foreign missiles on Iranian soil. This was the start of an improvement in relations with the USSR.

seven years I have been at the very centre of international affairs, observing, thinking and acquiring experience. It's hardly surprising that I should be blessed with foresight. Such predictions are the very least of my skills.' After a moment's thought he went on, 'I suppose that amongst the various heads of state, only Haile Selassie has ruled longer than me.' He expressed surprise that the Soviets steered clear of discussing economic problems at our dinner. I think he may be worried that they are on poor terms with Ansari, our Economics Minister ...

Thursday, 21 August

Brief audience. I pointed out that the Minister of Telecommunications and the Head of the Plan Organization are still keen to put the tele-communications network out to tender. 'I don't give a damn for their wishes', said HIM, 'I want this system to be fully functional by 1971, which will at least give us the capacity to link up with any point inside the country. You're to tell them both that I don't care how they do it but the network must be installed by 1971 ...'

The news of a fire at the Al Aqsa Mosque[1] in Jerusalem struck me as providing a good opportunity for HIM to denounce the sacrilege. He agreed and a carefully prepared statement was broadcast shortly before midnight ...

I've been up for so many hours and have quite worn myself out. Even so, it's inevitable that Princess Shams should telephone to find me just gone to bed. She wished to discuss some utterly trivial affair, but all the same I had to get up to take the call. Now it's half past one in the morning and I am at last going to get some sleep.

Friday, 22 August

Too exhausted to go riding this morning. Attended Lunch where HIM expressed great satisfaction with last night's broadcast. Later I took the opportunity to praise his speech of last Wednesday to Iranian students on leave from their studies in America. In response HIM abruptly pointed to HMQ, snapping back at me, 'But of course, nothing we say seems to satisfy this particular lady.' I was genuinely shocked. Her Majesty did her best to placate him and said: 'I only meant to suggest that you pitched your voice a little too low.' But HIM continued to sulk and I can only regret having

---

[1] One of the holiest shrines of Islam. The fire of 1969 was started by a Christian arsonist, an Australian named Michael Rohan. Apparently insane, he was none the less sentenced to jail by an Israeli tribunal. The incident caused much embarrassment to Israel's government.

unwittingly brought up a topic which quite ruined our Friday lunch ...

Saturday, 23 August
Audience. HIM again expressed his pleasure with Thursday's broadcast statement. I told him it killed several birds with one stone. It showed us to be mindful of our duties towards Islam. It pre-empted the Arabs and turned a purely Arab into a pan-Islamic issue, and finally it should please the Israelis since we made no attempt to criticize them and merely suggested that hasty actions be avoided whilst the matter is referred to the United Nations ...

Thursday, 28 and Friday, 29 August
With HIM I visited the relief work going on in the parts of Khorassan hit by the earthquake. We stayed two nights at Birjand, but Her Majesty was in too delicate a condition to accompany us and, to forestall any misunderstanding, we thought it best to issue a special statement explaining this. We had a pleasant time in spite of our gruelling schedule ... HIM was altogether most satisfied and took the opportunity to ask many questions. Nobody would have believed a year ago that so much could be done in so short a time, although there are still several villages where no reconstruction has as yet been attempted ... Even so things are moving in the right direction. HIM issued orders that the houses provided for earthquake victims be halved in price.

We were blessed with moonlit nights, and the weather in Birjand was generally superb. Yesterday after sundown we went for a stroll and chatted for some time about past, present and future. We shared our common sense of relief at the declining influence of the mullahs. HIM said that, in a recent sermon in Qom, Ayatollah Golpayegani[1] claimed the Iranian government was doing as much harm to the clergy as the regime in Iraq; 'Shame on the man and his stupid remarks. What ingratitude we meet from these people.' 'I agree with Your Majesty, shame on the fellow', I replied, 'but we have no alternative but to put up with him.' He then asked. 'Are the mullahs still influenced by foreign powers? To what extent do outsiders still look to the clergy for support?' I said that this had always been the British policy in dealing with Iran and that I thought aspects of it still lingered[2] ...

---

[1] Mohammad Reza Golpayegani, one of the Grand Ayatollahs. He held conservative views and commanded a limited following, chiefly among the merchants of the Tehran bazaar.
[2] Various outstanding clerics played a key role in the Constitutional Movement (1905–1907).

Monday, 1 September
The Romanian President, Nicolae Ceausescu, arrived on his state visit this afternoon, accompanied by an entourage that includes the Minister and Deputy Minister of Foreign Affairs and the Minister of Foreign Trade. Both the President and HIM made excellent after-dinner speeches at the Niavaran Palace, outlining the policies of their respective nations with real sincerity. The President's was framed as a deliberate rebuff to the Soviets. We too can take great pride in our policy which is perfectly straightforward and requires no special pleading.

There's been a *coup d'état* in Libya, apparently spearheaded by the leftists.[1] Poor King Idris, a man of eighty, was away in Turkey receiving medical treatment.

Tuesday, 2 September
HIM less than cheerful this morning ... I gave him my opinion that the oil companies will hardly tolerate a left-wing coup, given the importance of Libyan oil to the western nations. Perhaps they saw how feeble the King had grown and, given the ineptitude of his nephew, his heir, staged the coup themselves, presenting it as a leftist plot to cover their tracks. 'Maybe, maybe', he said, 'your reasoning is all very well, but the companies are so dim-witted that I'd have thought such deviousness to be quite beyond them. I warned them, the idiots, that they were taking a risk in permitting such massive increases in Libyan oil production, but they paid no attention.'
...

Wednesday, 3 September
Meir Ezri, the Israeli representative in Tehran, called on me this morning with a request that his Foreign Minister, Abba Eban, would like to pay HIM a visit to discuss the Middle East. I reported this proposal over dinner at HM the Queen Mother's. HIM replied: 'You're to tell him, half in jest, that there's little point in holding talks when they never listen to a word of our advice.'

... HIM spent some time at the dinner table teasing his mother. All most amusing ...

One of the movement's earliest landmarks involved a crowd taking refuge in the British embassy. In the popular imagination the two were conflated so that the entire movement, including its religious elements, was supposed to have been inspired by the British. The Shah, clearly contemptuous of anything that seemed like popular struggle for democracy, preferred the idea that foreign influence lay behind all such disturbances.

[1] The Revolutionary Council which subsequently took charge of the country was to be led by Colonel Moammar Qadhafi.

Thursday, 4 September

I asked Meir Ezri to call round early this morning. HIM's general reaction came as a disappointment to him. I then went to see HIM who was in a pretty grim mood. We mulled over the problem of the defence budget which is already a heavy burden and grows more so every day. He said that the Rapier missile, despite its excessive cost, is of little use since its electronics are unsophisticated and it has to be guided from the ground. I said that the British would hardly rely upon it for home defence if it were redundant. 'It may not exactly be redundant', said HIM, 'but it's no match for the latest anti-aircraft guns, particularly the Orlikon system which we purchased from Switzerland; three barrels firing off 15,000 rounds a minute.'

I asked whether it would be enough to ask for $200,000 from the government to cover the expense of our American trip. 'Have you gone mad?', he said. 'Even half that amount would be too lavish.' God protect him. He considers everything ...

Saturday, 6 September

... Dinner at the Queen Mother's. HIM said the Central Bank estimates our rate of economic growth at 22 per cent in the first quarter of this year. Clearly hoping for an awed response, he prompted me even further: 'Remarkable, isn't it?', he said. I replied that I found it so remarkable as to be beyond belief; the reports are clearly false. This did not go down well, particularly since we were amongst company. I realized that I had overstepped my place, but it was too late to retract. He is so desperately keen to see development that he will believe any amount of hokum. Sometimes this leads us into genuine financial problems and goodness knows what else.

After dinner he took me to one side and instructed me to tell Ezri that his Foreign Minister is free to visit us whenever he likes, a complete turn-around from his previous declaration. It would appear that he discussed the matter with the Romanian President whose country enjoys excellent relations with Israel ...

Sunday, 7 September

Audience. Reported discussions I had yesterday with the ambassador of Morocco. He has been rattled by events in Libya, which augur badly for both his country and his King, and which in general hold out a gloomy prospect for moderates everywhere. He believes that Tunisia may take the same road once her veteran President, Bourguiba, is out of the way, and that the Moroccan monarchy may find itself encircled by hostile republics. He says that they must now build up their defence capability and that they have come to appreciate HIM's wisdom in doing this long ago. As the ambassador is a friend I told him of a conversation which took place a few years back when I accompanied HIM to America. President Kennedy asked HIM why he was so keen to buy large quantities of arms, assuring him that the USA would always rush to defend Iran should the need arise. HIM replied with a smile, 'Certainly you might defend us against the Russians if only to protect your own strategic interests. But we have other fears apart from the Russians.' This was a very shrewd assessment of the regional situation; just look at Iraq, a miserable pygmy of a country which might still have dealt us a dreadful blow at Abadan but for our ability to threaten strong retaliation. The Moroccan ambassador ended with a plea that we dissuade Israel from putting so much pressure on the moderate Lebanon. HIM was pleased with my report.

Saturday, 27 September
A lengthy audience, in which HIM summarized his recent trip to the conference of Islamic Heads of State in Morocco ... We then discussed various issues, which are way outside my own department, but over which he ordered me to keep an eye: NIOC's attempt to buy out Getty's oil interests, the forthcoming oil talks in London and the purchase of military hardware. I suggested that it might be a good idea to spend money on publicity during our trip to America. He said, 'Do you expect us to buy world opinion and broadcast our prowess in the same way one buys a whore? Our great achievements are well enough known as it is.' 'Sadly', I replied, 'today's media are quite capable of overlooking any amount of triumph to gloat over some minor shortcoming. To use your own metaphor, the press is truly a whore; to keep her sweet we have no alternative but to pay her for her services.' ...

Sunday, 28 September
Audience. HIM asked whether I had read the proceedings of the Rabat conference of Islamic Heads of State. 'Yes', I replied, 'they were most encouraging, though it's clear that there would have been no progress but for Your Majesty's guidance. I notice that despite your vigorous attack on

the Egyptian representative,[1] he chose not to respond, whether out of a realization that his country was in the wrong, or whether simply out of respect for Your Majesty, I couldn't tell.' ...

He said, 'Various people in Iran are sending money to General Teymour Bakhtiar. They've been put under surveillance and once we've found out who their contacts are, we shall have them arrested.' He then gave me their names, much to my alarm since if any of them should escape I might be suspected of giving them the tip off. As Sa'adi says, 'The confidant of a Sultan has an unenviable task.' ...

Wednesday, 1 October
... Princess Shahnaz quarrelled with Jahanbani last night. She'd taken an unknown dose of sleeping tablets and complained of feeling sick. When they told me, I could feel the whole world dissolving around me. I have no recollection of the next few hours save that at noon she began to improve. Where on earth is this love affair going to lead us?

Thursday, 2 October
Audience ... Attended Lunch, where the Sheikh Rashid of Dubai was the principal guest. I've met him two or three times and he's always struck me as a relaxed and far-sighted man, so unlike the other Gulf Sheikhs who seem cursed with inferiority complexes. Important regional issues were discussed and he mentioned the trip made to Dubai by Hardan al-Takriti, Deputy Prime Minister of Iraq. 'Oh, you should have heard the promises he made to defend us', he said with bitter mockery. In respect to oil, the delimitation of the continental shelf and the overlap in territorial waters, HIM suggested that controversial areas could be exploited by a joint co-operative. The Sheikh smiled at this and said, 'I'm sure that Your Majesty would never dream of trying to coerce a weak country like my own. You must do as you see fit, I remain entirely at your disposal.' Even in the matter of defence he said that he would prefer to rely on HIM, adding, 'What need have I of an army which might end up signing my own death warrant! All I need is an efficient police force, for the rest I am interested only in domestic development.' He was critical of Sheikh Zaid of Abu Dhabi for failing to do more for the creation of a Federation of Arab Emirates. The idea of a Federation army has no appeal for him. Rather

---

[1] The Egyptian representative was Anwar Sadat who, following Nasser's sudden death, became President of the Republic in October 1970. His courteous behaviour during the Rabat conference much impressed the Shah, laying the foundations of an extraordinary friendship.

than have officers drawn from Bahrain, England, Iraq or wherever, he'd much rather go it alone. HIM was very keen to stress our goodwill, offering him all manner of assurances and citing the case of Bahrain, where we have been magnanimous in the extreme. HIM then asked after the situation in Fujeira and Sharjah. 'Oh, the people there are miserable', said the Sheikh, 'and the Sheikhs pocket every penny that's to be had.' HIM did his best to bring up the question of Tunbs and Abu Musa, but the Sheikh simply dodged the issue ...

Sunday, 5 October
It's been a dreadful day. Received by a very depressed HIM who announced without any preliminary that the Iraqis declare we have no right to interfere in the Gulf. 'I look forward to the day when I can settle the score with these people once and for all', he said. 'Obviously', I replied, 'they're talking nonsense again but remember Sa'adi's lines:

> No matter if you have the power
> of an elephant or the lion's roar,
> Peace is better than the urge to war.'

On his return from the forthcoming trip to America, HIM has asked that I arrange a meeting with the new French President. I suggested that it might be better if such a meeting took place before rather than after HIM's talks with Nixon, but he disagreed: 'I should first like to know what weapons we shall get from America', he said, 'then, to even things up, I could hold this summit with Pompidou.'

I tried to get him to agree to attend Princess Shahnaz's wedding, whenever her marriage finally takes place, but he refuses point blank to have anything to do with it. Indeed he grew increasingly angry and used very harsh words against her. This saddened me, but I thought it my duty to say to him, 'She's your daughter, you cannot simply disown her.' 'Be assured', he said, 'there's absolutely no future in this marriage. If I thought it would last for even two years, I'd happily receive them.'

The Asian Fair was officially opened this afternoon – absolutely splendid. There was only one brief hiccup when an usher got mixed up and led HIM away from the spot where his guests were waiting. I issued specific instructions that the Protocol Department and the Imperial Guard must know the route like the back of their hand, and still some idiot messes things up. I have sought HIM's permission to punish the whole lot of them, but I doubt whether he'll give me the go-ahead ...

Monday, 6 October

At ten this morning HIM presided over the state opening of both houses of Parliament. He gave a fine address, although there was one point that jarred on me. In describing the gas pipeline project and the petrochemical schemes, he again mentioned that they've drastically exceeded their spending limit, precisely the same point he made in his New Year's message to the nation. Now in my opinion, he should either keep quiet about such things or else ensure that those in charge are brought to book.

Whilst still at the Parliament, HMQ asked me why ladies have been instructed to wear evening dress for tonight's reception for Princess Margaret. Apparently this has been done without consulting her. I passed the enquiry onto the Great Court Chamberlain and relayed his reply ... She seems to have a generally low opinion of the Court's administration, and two reasons for this spring to mind. Firstly I refuse to do the bidding of her entourage who therefore plot against me, and secondly she considers me, with good reason, to be very close to HIM, which annoys her ...

Princess Margaret was HIM's guest of honour tonight. I had never met her before and she struck me as being rather coarse, indeed more than a little common. Her husband seemed likeable enough but it's said, how shall I put it, that he's not exactly a lady's man ...

Tuesday, 7 October

Audience. Looked over the agenda for HIM's discussions in America. He has decided to concentrate on oil, Iran's role in the Gulf, and various other military and financial issues.

... Attended a dinner at the British embassy in honour of our English royal guest. Princess Shams, the PM and various of his colleagues were also invited. The set-up was fairly good and there was a Scottish pipe band, but oh dear, Princess Margaret, what a vulgar little *arriviste* she seems ...

Wednesday, 8 October

This morning the new Yugoslav and Polish ambassadors presented their credentials. Both speak the most exquisite French ... Between the two audiences I snatched a brief word with HIM. He has granted permission for Moulay Abdullah,[1] the brother of King Hassan of Morocco, to join us

---

[1] Moulay Abdullah (1935–83): served on various assignments abroad; nominated Special Representative of King Hassan in 1972. Thereafter there were rumours of disagreement between him and the King. In 1974, at least according to the official version, he asked to be relieved of his duties.

in Paris on our return from the USA, and to fly on with HIM to Tehran. He also instructed me to cable his felicitations to the Aga Khan, head of the Ismailis, who has announced his engagement to a British dowager. She, need one say, is stunningly attractive ...

Princess Margaret fell ill on a visit to Isfahan ...

Friday, 10 October

... Reported that Ayatollah Milani,[1] to whom HIM sent a specialist after his recent heart-attack, has telephoned to express his thanks. He's more or less worshipped by a bunch of cretinous acolytes here and in Pakistan.

Saturday, 11 October

... Prince Juan Carlos of Spain and his wife Princess Sofia flew in last night. This evening they were HIM's guests for dinner ...

Sunday, 12 October

Threw a lunch in honour of the Spanish couple. The PM, Prince Gholam Reza and several ministers in attendance. All very pleasant. Prince Carlos was to have an audience with HIM that afternoon and I noticed that the Spanish ambassador was sticking to him like glue. Very discreetly, Princess Sofia told me that he would much rather be received in audience alone, so I telephoned HIM and we arranged for the limpet-like ambassador to be detached.

Later had a long chat with Princess Shahnaz and told her of HIM's wish that she fly to Europe and get married without any fuss. After that she and her husband should remain abroad. God bless her, she raised no objection and I have been saved a major potential headache ...

Monday, 13 October

Presentation of credentials this morning by the Papal Nuncio and by Douglas MacArthur, newly appointed US ambassador. He's the nephew of the famous general, and was lavish in his praise of Iran's development ...

This evening, a birthday party for HMQ who has just turned thirty-one. The Spanish Prince and Princess attended and the celebrations went on until 2 in the morning.

[1] Hadi Milani: one of the grand Ayatollahs, lived in Mashad. His followers were mainly Shi'a from eastern Iran, Afghanistan and Pakistan.

Wednesday, 15 October

The Portuguese and Sri Lankan ambassadors presented their credentials. The latter is a seventy-six year old Muslim whose dentures very nearly jumped down his throat during the course of his address. He had to fumble about with them, as we strained like mad to contain our laughter. Somehow he managed to keep his teeth and we our composure.

In the afternoon HIM called on his Spanish guests before attending a ceremony for the start of the new academic year. As he went on to the stage to hand out various awards, I saw out of the corner of my eye that the PM and various other ministers had begun to drink tea. I immediately sent someone to stop them as they were sitting directly opposite HIM; they were not at all pleased to be interrupted. Nowhere else in the world would this sort of behaviour be tolerated.

Tomorrow we fly to America.

Thursday, 25 October

I must now try to set down some account of our trip, with only a few scribbled notes and a couple of official programmes to aid my memory. Our visit was brief but enjoyable. We stayed in Paris for a night both on the way out and on our return ... We began with three nights in New York where HIM met an assembly of the leading American press-barons and businessmen, and also the committee formed by major US companies which hope to convene a conference on investment in Iran ... The meeting that stands out in my memory, and which made an enormous impression on everyone else, was that between HIM and the New York Council on Foreign Relations. It's a body composed of the cream of American society, the top politicians, diplomats and businessmen and the leaders of the media. The session itself was arranged by John McCloy a good and loyal friend of Iran. HIM delivered a matchless analysis of the situation in the Middle East and spelled out his expectations of the Nixon administration and the American public.

From New York we proceeded to Williamsburg and passed an uneventful night. HIM walked in the city for some time. The following morning we flew by helicopter to Washington where we were given a rousing reception and listened to a speech by the President, well phrased and highly complimentary to HIM. I was absent from the meeting between HIM and Nixon but ... was fully briefed on it afterwards.

HIM told me that he had stressed our government's need for an increase in income, via a boost in our oil production. The President appointed one of his advisers, a Mr Peter Flannigan, to talk the matter through with the American members of the Consortium. HIM then brought up the question of oil overlift in excess of the Consortium's target, to be marketed by us in return for American goods and services. Iran's need to have 120 of our pilots trained in the USA was discussed along with the training of our technicians and our request that America send a team of mechanics to service our fleet of Phantom aircraft. Finally HIM complained that at an interest rate of 8 per cent, we will find it difficult to accept US credits for the purchase of military hardware.

That evening the President once more heaped superlatives on HIM during the course of a reception thrown in his honour. I felt particularly proud when he said ' ... All Your Majesty has achieved in your country and all that you continue to achieve, truly merits the description Majestic.'

The following day we were invited to lunch by Vice-President Agnew, a plebeian looking gentleman. Not well liked, with small eyes and the face of a not particularly intelligent sheep. Appearances are against him, but he's a wise and well-informed man ...

The next day HIM had a *tête-à-tête* with Nixon lasting two hours, after which we returned by charter flight to Paris. HIM ate nothing on the plane as I had instructed our Paris embassy to prepare a special meal. We arrived to find no feast, no dinner, no anything. I was so enraged that I could have strangled the ambassador then and there, good man though I know him to be. But HIM took it all in his stride ...

The following afternoon we lunched in the Bois de Boulogne and the King of Morocco's brother was HIM's guest for dinner ... They're bosom friends, and I left them to dine without me ... With my daughter and my son-in-law who had both come specially from London ... I ate at Lasserre. Later there was dancing. The following morning we flew back to Tehran.

Sunday, 26 October

Our return yesterday evening was followed by a reception at the Niavaran Palace to celebrate HIM's birthday. The American astronauts who landed on the moon are presently in Tehran and attended as HIM's guests, not at all big headed, but reserved and amiable. Everything went off very well. If it had been us or the Russians, the Germans or even the French who'd just come back from the moon we'd be puffed up like peacocks, but they were so modest and kept such a low profile that you'd never have guessed the immensity of their achievement. They mingled politely and even joined hands with some local ladies for a Persian dance ...

Wednesday, 29 October

... Yahya Khan, President of Pakistan, flew in this afternoon and an official dinner was thrown in his honour at the Niavaran Palace. An exchange of excellent speeches, although many guests were late to arrive because of dreadful traffic jams in the city – one of the two main roads from Tehran to Shemiran[1] had been closed to allow the presidential motorcade to pass, making life pretty miserable for other drivers.

Thursday, 30 October

I had meant to absent myself from the Senate this morning, but HIM insisted I attend so as not to cause offence to Yahya Khan who was due to deliver an address. The latter went down very well.

Later to the Golestan Palace where Yahya Khan gave a dinner in honour of HIM, complete with a Pakistani band. Tayeb Hussein, the former Pakistani ambassador to Iran, accompanies his President on this trip. He was sacked by Ayub Khan for favouring Iran over the Arabs in matters relating to the Gulf. We talked for some while and he asked me to convey to HIM that the President would appreciate a private audience for frank discussions on a number of issues including Pakistan's domestic problems ...

Friday, 31 October

A pleasant ceremony on the lawns behind my office for the birthday of HRH the Crown Prince. Yahya Khan presented him with a horse. The Crown Prince wore Pakistani costume, looking very dashing, and the Pakistani band played throughout. HIM in attendance. Subsequently we all went to pay our respects at Mashad. A marvellous day. Returned in time for a birthday party at the Queen Mother's ...

Saturday, 1 November

Rose very early, since at 7.30 a.m. I was due to attend HIM at the airport. At 8 he and Yahya Khan flew to watch air force exercises at the Vahdati airbase.[2] I remained behind but apparently the show was excellent. Air Marshal Rahim Khan, newly appointed commander of the Pakistani Air force, was unstinting in his praise ...

Received a cable from the USA where a company named Planet has just

---

[1] Northern suburb of Tehran.
[2] One of the country's two principal air bases, situated near Dezful in south-western Iran.

announced a deal to market Iranian oil in America in return for armaments and other items chosen by our government. This is an outright fiction since we have told the company that no such deal can take place. Their management had approached us with a proposal that we might use our bargaining power to obtain a special oil import quota in the USA which Planet would then market. In itself this was far-fetched, since had we been in a position to obtain such a quota we'd have had no need of an American company to market it for us. Things would have been very different if Planet, as they at one time boasted, could have won us a quota through their own contacts, but Nixon rejected their advances, arguing that to accept them would be to lay himself open to charges of corruption. HIM therefore broke off all negotiations with Planet and instead sought a straightforward, government-to-government deal. Hence he was livid when I reported the details of this morning's announcement. He ordered me to find out from Dr Fallah what has been going on. He's also keen that our ambassador in Washington should consult with the White House over the need for an official denial of Planet's claims. I did as instructed and in the process noticed Dr Fallah's reaction to my enquiries – he was clearly badly rattled.

Baghdad has put a stop to its anti-Iranian broadcasts. The fools have no doubt come to appreciate the futility of their war of words.

Sunday, 2 November
Torrential rain forced the cancellation of HIM and Yahya Khan's proposed hunting trip to the Caspian ... I suggested that since a flight was out of the question they might get there by car, but the President said it would be bad for his health. And he calls himself a Field Marshal! HIM by contrast was greatly looking forward to the adventure ...

Monday, 3 November
Audience – a full hour and a half whilst the PM, poor man, had to wait his turn outside. I'd met him beforehand in my office and he was already badly dejected, complaining of the financial situation and the $800 million deficit in the Fourth Development Plan. I'm afraid he lacks the guts to do anything about it. HIM was puzzled that an interview he gave to *Newsweek* remains unpublished: 'Perhaps the US authorities have prevented its appearance, since I state my conviction that the Russians no longer pose us any threat', he said. I replied that I thought this unlikely; 'Your Majesty gave a television interview in the USA which made several far more

controversial statements. These were broadcast without hesitation and on several channels.' ...

Sunday, 9 November
... The British ambassador called on me this afternoon. We did our best to iron out the problems associated with a missiles deal worth around £50 million. I had been instructed to remind him of HIM's advice that the British cut back their oil production in Libya and so reduce the income of the Libyan government, which in any case is already said to have cancelled a £150 million arms deal with Britain. The ambassador smiled, and said that HIM's forecasts are invariably proved correct. We then turned to a discussion of Tunbs and Abu Musa. 'We are bound', said the ambassador, 'by our commitments to the Sheikhs of Sharjah and Ras al-Khaimah, but we will nevertheless encourage them to reach some sort of accommodation with Iran, provided always that you confine yourselves to an occupation based on mutual agreement or a lease, and do not insist on pressing a claim to occupy the islands by legal right.' This makes sense; go about it any other way, and we face a new confrontation with the Arabs ...

Monday, 10 November
Audience. Reported yesterday's conversation with the ambassador. When I came to his remarks about the islands, HIM nearly exploded; 'He's talking out of his arse', he exclaimed, 'the islands belong to us.' 'We must try to be pragmatic', I said, 'Your Majesty's chief interest lies in occupying the islands to facilitate our defence of the Persian Gulf. You have already declared that any oil found there could be shared between us and the Arabs. In other words we are after occupation, not total possession.' He said nothing but I could see that my remarks were less than welcome. I went on to report the ambassador's comments on the Rapier missiles; that this is not considered to be a normal commercial deal, and that the ambassador recommends a secret agreement between our respective governments, stipulating that Britain may pull out of the sale if she begins to doubt our capacity to preserve the technical secrets of the missiles. HIM rejected this suggestion.

The British ambassador called on me again this afternoon and I passed on HIM's reaction. He said, 'My government is especially cagey about the classified aspects of this weapon; since in the longer term it is unclear how close you will stand to the Soviets. Of course, you are our allies, and we are quite sure that no such development is probable, or even very likely.'

McNamara, ex-US Defense Secretary and currently President of the World Bank, was HIM's guest for lunch. He is quite astounded by the development that has taken place in Iran, and is prepared to extend us a loan of $100 million. The PM was also at lunch. The poor man struck me as being distinctly down in the dumps ...

Tuesday, 11 November
Audience. Described my latest meeting with the British ambassador. HIM said, 'We cannot permit the defence of the Persian Gulf to depend upon some whim of the British government, or their willingness to supply us with a particular missile. The clause they propose should be withdrawn.' I telephoned the ambassador immediately on leaving HIM and spelled out our position. He said: 'Bear in mind that this is a major deal for us. It is too important from our point of view for us to refuse to supply you with the weapons. This is really your most cast-iron guarantee'. This left me unconvinced and I have asked him to call on me again tomorrow.

HIM spent some time sounding off against our Foreign Minister, Ardeshir Zahedi. He knows that we are hardly on the best of terms and probably expected me to chip in with an attack of my own ... but instead I defended the man, and think that I was right to do so. I could tell from the look on HIM's face that I'd taken him by surprise ...

Wednesday, 12 November
The British Chargé d'Affaires called round at 8 this morning – much better versed than his ambassador in relation to the agreement on arms supplies. He stressed four points:

– The non–delivery clause of the agreement has been phrased in such nebulous terms that there's not one chance in a thousand of it ever being implemented.
– The performance specifications we are demanding of the missile make no sense unless we are hoping to put the British Rapier out of the running. (Here he is right, since we are really interested in the French all-weather system, Crotale.)
– Thirdly Rapier is for use against low flying aircraft which cannot operate in bad weather. Hence an all-weather missile system is unnecessary.
– And in any event additional instruments could be fitted to Rapier to enable it to fly in all weathers.

Reported these discussions at this morning's audience. HIM instructed me to brief our military authorities and to ensure that they extract a guarantee from the British to supply us with the additional all-weather instrumentation.

Arab Heads of State have sent HIM their greetings for the start of Ramadan. Al-Bakr, the bastard President of Iraq, addresses us as brothers.

Sunday, 16 November

At eleven this morning we returned from a short visit to Shiraz, Langeh and Kish Island.[1] HIM decided to make this trip on the spur of the moment and altogether it was well worth it ... I was his only companion and hardly ever left his side. We stayed in Shiraz each night, making sorties to various locations during the day.

We went one day to Langeh and from there to a picnic on Kish Island. Here we are building a new Imperial palace, and not for mere amusement. The island lies at the very heart of the Gulf and for HIM to spend a month or so here each year would have a tremendous impact.

Over our picnic we discussed HIM's policy in the Persian Gulf, and the wisdom of his remarks impressed me greatly. 'Were I a demagogue', he said, 'I should not bother with the search for peace in the Persian Gulf, but like Nasser, I should want to stir up the hornet's nest each and every day. I'd be more than justified as the Gulf is a Persian Sea and we have legitimate rights on both sides of it. But where would such a policy lead us? Psychological war against the Arabs, confrontation with Arab nationalists, vast expense, and all for nothing. The superpowers would never allow us to seize the Arabian oil fields, at least not without a terrible struggle.' 'Only regimes which have failed at home', I said, 'turn to grandiose adventures overseas, hoping to divert their people's attention from domestic shortcomings. By contrast, Your Majesty can boast real successes on the home front and, God be praised, Iran is blessed with such resources that you have both the capability and the inclination to make her into a fabulous nation. Your triumph in this respect is assured. Before even thinking of exerting influence on the other side of the Persian Gulf, we must put our own house in order. For instance, as far back as the time I was Prime Minister, we started work on a coastal road linking Bushehr[2] and Chahbahar.[3] Yet after all these years it has got no further than Langeh.'

[1] Langeh: a small fishing port on the Persian Gulf, to the east of Kish Island.
[2] A port on the Persian Gulf.
[3] A tiny and neglected port in the far south-east of Iran, in the province of Baluchistan – the

... In reply, he instructed me that on my return I am to order the government to resume operations. On the other hand he made no comment when I outlined the problems faced by local fishermen in dealing with General Ayadi and the army.[1] Anything done by the army is by definition all right by HIM.

Thursday, 20 November

HIM is truly a workaholic, complaining today about our light schedule. 'Sadly', I said, 'Anno Domini is at last catching up with me. For the past few days my eyes have been too sore for me to work.' He prescribed Vitamin A, and added, 'I seem to be in the same boat as you; for the past few days I've quite gone off women. Old age must really be setting in.'

Later I called on Princess Shahnaz. It distresses me to see her so obsessed by this boy and so neglected by her father ...

Saturday, 22 November

After my usual morning audience received a visit from the Saudi ambassador, very flustered, with a message from his King for HIM. Apparently aided by Chinese and Soviet technicians, South Yemen can now bring modern weapons to bear in an attack on Saudi Arabia. The Gizan airbase is threatened and four batteries of up to date anti-aircraft guns are badly needed for its defence. I immediately rang through to HIM, suggesting that, if he was reluctant to offer assistance, I could easily stall the ambassador, but that otherwise he should be granted an audience without delay. HIM asked to see him straight away which delighted the ambassador ...

Sunday, 23 November

Audience ... I asked whether Tehran University will be permitted to mount a joint research programme with the University of Israel at Jerusalem. HIM advised that we wait a few days, to see which way the wind was blowing between Israel and the Arabs. Did this mean, I asked, that he expected another war to break out? He replied that given Nasser's incessant provo-

---

most backward area of the country. In the 1970s development projects transformed Chahbahar into a modern naval and air base. It became a cornerstone of the Shah's ambitions to make Iran a dominant power in the Indian Ocean.

[1] The South Fisheries Company was founded in 1963 with the active assistance of the Army Co-operative and other public bodies. Their initial objective was to help the disinherited fishermen of the Gulf. But General Ayadi, special physician to the Shah, already supervisor of the Army Co-operative, ran the company as a personal fief to the detriment of local fishermen.

cations ... Israel had few options. I suspect that he is privy to very confidential information in this respect ...

Monday, 24 November

Audience ... Once again we discussed Princess Shahnaz. HIM greatly distressed by her choice of husband whom he regards as little more than a hippy, stuffed full of ludicrous notions. He said, 'As her father I may be able to forgive my daughter her mistakes, but as Shahanshah of Iran I can never accept a good-for-nothing as my son-in-law. It would imply that I am willing to condone loose morals.' This is all too true and I could say nothing against it ... Later he received the PM and various of his colleagues in charge of the budget. A stormy meeting, so I'm told; in some part my responsibility.[1]

The ambassadors of Yugoslavia and the US called to see me. The former was openly critical of the Soviets and their imperialist ambitions, which surprised me. With the latter I discussed the possibility of marketing Iranian oil in the USA and our desire to purchase new aircraft, both subjects dear to HIM's heart ... I outlined HIM's policy in regard to Afghanistan and the Gulf: that he is a pragmatist, with no interest in striking aggressive poses to impress the people, but eager that his successors inherit a developed, free and truly independent nation. The very last thing he wants is to endanger Iran by vain gestures and buccaneering abroad. The ambassador replied that these facts were well known to him and to the USA at large where HIM's policies are held in high esteem as the hallmarks of a true statesman. I added that HIM had no need for tubthumping to win over the nation. He knows his people well, just as they know him. The ambassador approved this attitude and said, to my surprise, 'You should tell the Shah that I account myself his servant.'

Wednesday, 26 November

Audience. Again discussed Princess Shahnaz. She and Jahanbani wish to go to the USA but she has no money. HIM declared that she has no permission to go anywhere except Geneva; otherwise she will be disinherited. A limited sum of money has been deposited for her in a Swiss bank, but it can only be withdrawn under HIM's signature. In effect the poor girl is left destitute ...

---

[1] The implication is that Alam had spoken out to the Shah against Hoveyda's government and its mismanagement of the budget. No one, not even Alam, dared point out that at the root of the problem lay the ever-increasing resources allocated to the military.

Met Princess Shahnaz and Jahanbani after lunch and passed on HIM's decision. She was greatly distressed. Jahanbani, who is no Einstein, began there and then to plan their elopement. Really, I told them, this sort of hippyfied nonsense is too much. He must make some sort of provision to support himself with a job. The moment they start to go hungry he will forget everything else, love included. They gave no sign of heeding my advice.

Thursday, 27 November

... Invited to dinner at the residence of the mother of HMQ. Our Albanian visitors, ex-King Leka, his mother and aunt, were also present. The poor man hopes to start up his own business and HIM has left instructions that he be assisted in this.[1]

Friday, 28 November

... The conflict between South Yemen and Saudi Arabia grows ever more serious, with the incompetent Saudis coming out the losers. I discussed the situation with HIM over dinner and he approved our offering the Saudis help. He is livid about a recent article in the *Financial Times* critical of our military build-up. 'These bastards should know', he said, 'that but for our strength we would have been prey even to puny Iraq ... Tell the British, in no uncertain terms, that if we followed such advice the first victim would be our weapons contracts with their country.' The British ambassador is away, but I shall pass on HIM's message to their Intelligence Service representative in Iran. Since the current negotiations over Rapier missiles are worth at least $120 million to them, this is bound to cause quite a stir ...

Sunday, 30 November

Audience. Reported that after two hours of intense argument Princess Shahnaz has agreed to obey HIM's command and will go to Geneva without marrying Jahanbani. 'In conveying my orders', HIM replied, 'you must never stoop to persuasion'. I didn't bother to point out that had I merely conveyed his order she would have answered with blank disobedience and we would have been faced with a scandal. My duty as a servant lies in carrying out his wishes, not in making a great fuss over the lengths to which this puts me ...

[1] King Leka (who used the title but never actually reigned) was then the representative of a European light engineering manufacturer.

The Foreign Minister, Ardeshir Zahedi, has extended a dinner invitation for tomorrow night to HIM and the ex-King of Albania. But, as I pointed out, this is all rather sinister coming on the anniversary of the death of Imam Ali. There are so many fanatic NCO's, so many fools amongst the army, that it would be to take a very great risk to go out. HIM agreed and asked me to change the date of the reception. Ardeshir was genuinely upset when I told him our decision ...

Dinner at Princess Fatemeh's. HIM still fuming over the article in the *Financial Times*, but all the while protesting his total indifference. 'If it's so unimportant', I said, 'why bang on about it?' He made no comment, but I feel that I was wrong to say such a thing with the PM there ...

Monday, 1 December

Despite my plain speaking, HIM received me with good humour. Miss Lambton[1] has written a book on Iranian land reform. She's long been familiar with the country and has already written on land tenure. However her latest book contains praise for Arsanjani and Amini. The Minister of Co-operatives and Rural Affairs asked me to tell HIM that he can, if authorized, buy up every copy at source and persuade her to revise her account, missing out the controversial passages. HIM was seething, 'What utter crap', he said, much to my delight since it demonstrates his shrewdness; the proposal is pure humbug, intended to flatter HIM, without a hope in hell of altering a text published by the Oxford University Press ...

I asked HIM whether he intends to work tomorrow, the anniversary of the martyrdom of Ali. His answer left absolutely nothing to the imagination. All my plans to go riding have been spoiled.

Tuesday, 2 December

... After all it's supposed to be a holiday so I had a brief lie in ... followed by an audience at which HIM instructed me to finalize the telecommunications contract. A meeting this afternoon at my house to discuss this business with all the interested parties. We reached agreement after lengthy debate. Then I received Dr Amini, the former Prime Minister, a shifty individual, but as the saying goes 'a single enemy can undo the

---

[1] Miss Ann K.S. Lambton: Professor of Persian at the University of London, 1953–79; an outstanding scholar whose book *Landlord and Peasant in Persia* (London, 1953 and republished in a new edition in 1991), is considered a classic. The present entry refers to *The Persian Land Reform 1962–1966* (Oxford, 1969).

good of a thousand friends', and I've done my best to butter him up, smoothing out his relations with HIM. He was present at the *Salaam* for HIM's birthday and now requests that he be granted an audience.

Dinner at the Queen Mother's. HMQ asked me the secret to my constant politeness and formality. In reply I quoted the lines:

> Although a king may show unlimited kindness
> The servant must limit himself.

It seemed to please HIM ...

Friday, 5 December

Rode out with my love. A splendid morning and even better company. Trekked for three hours in the mountains – I wish it had been for thirty ...

Attended Lunch where HIM asked me to find out from Dr Fallah how things stand with the Planet company, following his discussions with Brownell[1] – Planet's legal adviser, US Attorney-General under the Eisenhower administration. I've already described this business. In the course of breaking off negotiations with Planet and in an attempt to register our own company to obtain a US import oil quota, Dr Fallah promised to retain Brownell's services for us rather than Planet. But I doubt the company will give up so easily.

Sunday, 7 December

... Later at night I told HIM that Princess Shahnaz asks permission to see her father and kiss his hand before she leaves for Geneva. I had no alternative but to pass on her message; I'm afraid it rather marred his good humour, but he reluctantly accepted.

Monday, 8 December

This morning Houshang Ansari, the Economics Minister, came to complain to me about the desperate state of the economy, the fading away of any enthusiasm for investment amongst the private sector, the threat of inflation, the plethora of organizations capable of influencing policy and their failure to pull together. He is in a dreadful dilemma and has no idea how to alert HIM to the situation. I encouraged him to be utterly frank, to tell the truth however unpalatable ...

[1] Herbert Brownell: US Attorney-General, 1953–7.

Surprised at my audience to find HIM in a genial mood – his meeting with Princess Shahnaz appears to have gone better than he had expected . . .

. . . HIM was a guest of Parviz Bushehri[1] this evening. I attended, and on HIM's instructions arranged the deal solicited by the ex-King Leka of Albania. Found HIM still cheerful. I took the opportunity to request that the death sentences against several army officers convicted of drug trafficking be relaxed, but with no success. 'If it were a personal matter', he said, 'I should have pardoned them, but I am powerless to show leniency when the national interest is at stake.' No doubt he's right . . .

Tuesday, 9 December
. . . Audience . . . Again mentioned the convicted officers, suggesting that their cases be reviewed by the High Court. HIM said that such a course would be without precedent as the sentences passed by military tribunals are absolute and cannot be referred to a civilian hearing. 'Perhaps, then, we should set a precedent', I said. In all, I believe I may have succeeded in alleviating their sentences, at least to some extent . . .

Princess Ashraf invited me to lunch, together with various ministers and civil servants responsible for the campaign against illiteracy. Three years ago we announced that illiteracy would be eradicated within a decade, yet our estimates now suggest that, when those ten years are up, Iran will have twice the number of illiterates she has today . . .

Wednesday, 10 December
Audience . . . Discussed Iran's intellectuals . . . 'It's surprising', said HIM, 'but every one of them who has achieved prominence in the administration has not only betrayed his own friends and colleagues in the process, but shown an inclination to resort to force and to depend upon the security agencies. How are we ever going to educate this nation of ours?' I may have gone off the deep end in replying, but I said that we're not taking even the first step in this direction, which is after all a question of public duty and popular right. Under His Majesty's protection the ruling classes, far from taking a lead and serving to leaven the whole lump, are virtually immune from criticism. We both know only too well how the politicians and their parties carry on; carving up the nation into a series of opposed camps. Instead of nursing public concerns, our Members of Parliament

[1] Businessman; brother of Princess Ashraf's husband, Mehdi Bushehri.

merely grease up to the party bosses. There's not one of them of any real substance ... and as a result their meaningless squabbles are recognized as such in the country at large. We're being engulfed by a sort of creeping, collective indifference, an apathy that grows day by day. I agreed that harsh measures were needed to push the country forwards, but now that things are moving in the right direction, it is time that authoritarianism was relaxed and HIM allow the elections to become a genuine expression of public opinion. To hell with party bickering, let's allow real and meaningful elections at every level, municipal, regional, provincial. HIM's leadership has rescued this country from chaos; our foundations are secured. The time has now come to cast off the worries of the past, to permit our people the very basis of all education by persuading them to participate in the real concerns of society ... The Shah listened to all this with evident attention, but in reply he said: 'Without constant vigilance, the whole structure will still collapse.' 'True enough', I said, 'but all the more reason to strengthen our national institutions, just as Your Majesty wishes ... There's nobody today, not even the most ill-willed, who does not support you or fails to appreciate that everything, including their own private interests, depends upon Your Majesty's survival. We must seize this opportunity, allow the people a role in national affairs, give them a genuine sense of participation. Everything will run smoothly enough during your own lifetime, but without this change who knows what our nation may face in the years to come.' Never before have I seen HIM so electrified by anything I've said ...

Dinner at the Queen Mother's. My wife subsequently pointed out to me that I was unduly obsequious towards HIM; I'm impressed by her insight, though deeply disgusted at my own behaviour.

Thursday, 11 December
A religious holiday and a special *Salaam* to mark the end of Ramadan ... Overjoyed to hear HIM in audience with the parliamentary praesidium reiterate more or less exactly my remarks of yesterday, stressing that 'the people must be allowed a greater say, and be given real freedom in elections at every level, to the regional councils, the municipalities and to Parliament itself.' This was absolute music to my ears. I may not be much of a democrat, but even so I'm sure it's the right policy ... In the same address HIM briefly mentioned our precarious financial situation and the absolute necessity of maintaining defence expenditure. He fears that financial constraints may force us to cut back on the schedule for implementing social

reform, but that defence is an absolute priority. Without secure frontiers there will be no country left for us to reform.

Friday, 12 December

Went riding with my love. A beautiful morning. In the Farahabad game reserve[1] we came across a thousand and one creatures, oblivious to our presence, all beginning their courtship. What a fierce fight the male of the species has. We lunched there.

A parade on the outskirts of the city this afternoon, to mark Army Day. HIM reviewed the troops on horseback. General Ja'far Shafeqat, Commander of the First Army, an infantry man in charge of today's proceedings, was unseated by his mount. How humiliating! The loose horse stepped out in front of HIM, ahead of the royal party, and worse still, television cameras broadcast the whole thing live. Elsewhere an officer stepped out of rank when passing the royal box and tried to present some sort of petition to the Shah. He was held back by security men, and it turned out that his sole request was to be sent to study electronics in the USA. He'll receive a summary court-martial tomorrow morning and be dishonourably discharged, yet it was a peculiar incident bearing in mind the degree of discipline that's normally maintained in the army.

These mishaps apart, the parade was well turned out. We can all be proud of the army that HIM has moulded, despite its great cost ... The march past by the extension corps and the corps of health and education – the shock troops of our White Revolution – was especially remarkable for the large number of girls who took part[2] ...

Saturday, 13 December

Audience, the earlier part taken up by shared mirth at the thought of poor Shafeqat and his horse. I then congratulated HIM on the general turn-out. 'Yes', he said, 'I believe the army has real substance.' He seems really to have taken last Wednesday's conversation to heart ...

HIM appeared anxious to say something about Prince Mahmoud Reza[3] who, it appears, has once more overstepped the bounds of decent behaviour. After much hesitation he decided to let the matter drop and I was in no hurry to prompt him further ...

[1] Close by the royal stables.
[2] Conscription was compulsory for men. Following the social reforms initiated in 1962–3, one could opt to join the corps – with four months of basic military training. A subsequent law required participation by all girls with secondary or university education.
[3] Born 1926, to the fourth wife of Reza Shah.

Sunday, 14 December

... The drug traffickers, three from the military and seven civilians, were executed today ...

Monday, 15 December

... A visit from the Moroccan ambassador who brought a message from King Hassan. He's been obliged to host a conference of Arab heads of state in Rabat, but will do his best to pass it off as a mini-conference of pan-Islamic, not merely Arab, delegates. He is also gravely concerned by developments in Saudi Arabia and the provocations presented by South Yemen ...

Tuesday, 16 December

Audience. After listening to my report on the Moroccan ambassador's visit, HIM said, 'Tell him that his country must never allow herself to be hoodwinked by revolutionaries who call for an immediate resumption of war against Israel. Boasting and swaggering are all very easy, but urging war is a different matter. Morocco must take very great care.' ...

Discussing his appointment of a new Senator for Tehran, HIM said, 'Provided one is powerful, the Speaker of the Senate Sharif Emami is full of sweetness and light, but the moment there's the slightest slackening of the rein, his docility falls away and one is faced by a very different man.' 'Many of our countrymen are like that', I said. 'Thank God, we are now firmly under Your Majesty's control, and can begin to accustom the country to true democracy. As you pointed out at last week's *Salaam*, everyone should feel that their actions have an effect, however small, on the development of the nation.' He made no comment.

Mothers' day. Lunched with mine and offered up a prayer of thanks for her.

HIM has written to President Nixon, expressing his concern over the situation in Saudi Arabia and advocating a resort to joint assistance from Washington and Tehran. But our own options, he wrote, are limited by our need to increase our oil production. America should help us here, in accepting our products onto her domestic markets ...

Wednesday, 17 December

The American ambassador is ill. Instead I received his Chargé d'Affaires, passed on HIM's letter and explained its contents ...

To a private dinner at the Danish embassy – much talk of the execution of the drug traffickers which has made a favourable impression in the West. The Europeans present agreed they wished they too had a strong man to rescue the younger generation from this scourge. Yet, by the most remarkable coincidence, today has seen the abolition of the death penalty in Great Britain. I had meant to stay only a short while, but a real beauty, apparently a friend of the ambassador, engaged me in a long conversation. It suddenly struck me that it was one in the morning and that my fellow guests were respectfully waiting for me to leave before themselves retiring. Most embarrassing.

Saturday, 20 December
The Sheikh of Ras al-Khaimah is in Tehran at the invitation of our Foreign Minister who hopes to reach agreement on the hand-over of Tunbs. I don't see any chance of a settlement at the moment; the Sheikh is too apprehensive, lest he be accused by his fellow Arabs of abandoning Arab land to Iran. What insolence. The Arabs only hold the islands as a result of their usurpation from us by the British Empire, and yet they dare to speak of them as if they were some sort of family heirloom.

Monday, 22 December
Felt well enough to attend my audience this morning. HIM kindly asked after my health. I told him that the symptoms indicated gastric trouble and fever, but that in reality mental anxiety was the real problem. He agreed. 'Why else do you suppose I take a sleeping tablet every night?', he said ...

Their Majesties plan to spend time in St Moritz, a total of forty days absence from Iran. Begging HIM to excuse my impudence, I suggested that such a long time abroad was ill-advised. 'But', he said, 'nowhere could be safer than St Moritz. And in any case, there's little to worry about when the PM tells me that we have earned great respect from Harold Wilson and Kosygin, both of whom are anxious to convey their goodwill.' 'It's precisely that sort of thing that worries me', I said, 'and remember that there are other threats besides Britain and the Soviets. What, for example, do we really know of the political climate here at home?' He seemed rather put out, but made no comment ...

Tuesday, 23 December

Audience. HIM said that he is dissatisfied by negotiations with the Sheikh of Ras al-Khaimeh. He then announced that shortage of funds makes it impossible for us to purchase Rapier missiles. Only yesterday he asked me to finalize the deal and I at last persuaded the representatives of BAC to agree to all our terms. But I fully appreciate that HIM intends to tie the missile purchase into an arrangement for increased oil production. When he was in London our Prime Minister stressed our need for increased output to Harold Wilson. Wilson replied that the British government had little influence over private enterprises, the oil companies included. But as HIM says, in that case how is it that the British lend such support to enterprises like the manufacturers of the Rapier missiles? ...

The British Chargé d'Affaires called on me this afternoon and I passed on HIM's disappointment over progress with the Sheikh ... He became very agitated over the Rapier deal and protested against our decision. I soon took the wind out of his sails by pointing out that the deal is between us and a private company, and therefore no business of the British government ...

Friday, 26 December

Beautiful ride this morning. Wished I were not on my own. Two trucks had collided on the road to Farahabad, bringing traffic to a complete standstill. I waited, and meanwhile got a glimpse of the life that goes on in that squalid district of Tehran. The street running off from the highway was filthy, not an ounce of asphalt since there's no risk of an inspection by HIM. It was still early, the traffic police had not come on duty, but a single policeman strutted around, dragging on his cigarette, puffed up like the monarch of all he surveyed. A few men, women wearing the veil, on their way home from the communal bath house ... A gaggle of children, the girls all veiled. The upper classes would never be up so early in the morning, nor would the girls wear veils. They converged haggling on a merchant selling hot beetroot. Pariah dogs and a few unwashed babies pawing over a heap of rubbish at the street-corner ... shaven-headed servicemen wearing badly-cut trousers, ill-fitting boots, strolling along clearly enjoying their Friday morning off. It was both droll and desperately depressing; a scene from a top-heavy society. The Shah struggles day and night, confident that within a decade we shall have surpassed much of the developed world; change can never come quickly enough for him. Yet no manner of wishful thinking can alter life in these streets.

In Russia too, the people are poor, morose because of the system that curtails their freedoms. But at least one sees some degree of social equality, some degree of shared benefit from the nation's resources. They dress alike, public transport is cheap, and many own bicycles; people like me, affluent, seated in my sleek Chrysler Imperial, don't suddenly pop up in the middle of Russia's slums.

I rode for two and a half hours, all the time pondering the remarkable social revolution led by the Shah, and what is to come next. A long and difficult road opens before us and we shall need men of the utmost loyalty, skill and integrity to help us on the way; such people are so few and far between ...

Saturday, 27 December
Audience ... Passed on New Year's greetings from many heads of state including a cable from the Prince and Princess of Monaco ... HIM cheerfully put in, 'It must be twenty years ago, my first visit to the USA, Princess Grace[1] was introduced to me ...'

Monday, 29 December
HIM very gloomy this morning. I realized what must be amiss and asked him whether he had heard the news that Nasser had been so feted by the Libyan crowd that it took him four hours to travel from the airport to Benghazi. HIM said he had, though he must have heard it from the BBC; one of our failings is our refusal to broadcast unpalatable information, and there's been not a word of this incident on Radio Tehran ...

The US ambassador called on me this afternoon to say that the situation on the Saudi border with South Yemen has improved, but that Saudi Arabia remains a reactionary country where anything might happen ... 'We would be the last to know', he said, 'if anything was going on there, since the progressive elements shun us as supporters, as they see it, of the old regime.' 'Good for you and the CIA', said I. We eventually agreed that our Foreign Ministry should suggest that the Saudis explain their situation to the Americans and seek their assistance ...

---

[1] Grace Kelly, as she then was, American actress. Married Prince Rainier of Monaco in 1956 and thus became Princess Grace.

Tuesday, 30 December

A visit from the Israeli representative this morning. I told him that I regard Israel's action in spiriting torpedo boats out of Cherbourg as a masterstroke.[1] He said, 'Much more significant than that, we've captured sophisticated Soviet radar from the Egyptians. We now have two of these systems and have been able to discover all their technical specifications for the monitoring of low flying aircraft.' ... It appears that the Egyptians hoped to hoodwink the Israelis by installing radar in field hospitals flying the red crescent. But the ruse was discovered and Israel sent in a commando force to make off with the equipment. Full marks to the lively spirit of Israel ...

Wednesday, 31 December

... I worked at my office throughout the afternoon. Amongst other visitors, I received various mullahs, falling over themselves to lavish praise on HIM, clearly in expectation of some sort of hand-out[2] ...

---

[1] After the Arab–Israeli war of 1967 France adopted a pro-Arab stance, refusing licences for the export of several torpedo boats, already ordered and paid for by Israel. The Israelis managed to remove the boats without the prior (official) knowledge of the French.

[2] A number of the lower-ranking clergy received regular subsidies through the Court, the Prime Minister's office and various other government agencies. In some quarters the mullahs' eagerness to join in the 1979 Revolution has been attributed to the fact that Jamshid Amouzegar, Hoveyda's successor as Prime Minister after 1977, ceased the payment of many such subsidies.

1970

As in previous years, the Shah flew to Vienna to undergo a medical check-up before proceeding to St Moritz. During the flight from Tehran, he showed concern over an issue as yet undisclosed to Alam (Diaries, 20 January). Two days later, the news broke of a botched attempt at a *coup d'état* in Baghdad – backed by Iran. For the past few months Savak had supported a plot by a group of disgruntled Iraqi officers, unhappy with the new government of Hassan al-Bakr. Agents of the Iraqi Security Services – headed by Saddam Hussein – infiltrated the conspiracy and succeeded in bugging their 'secret' meetings. As a result the coup ended in a blood bath (Diaries, 23 and 26 January). One of its leaders, General Abdul Ghani Rawi, managed to escape to Iran. Relations between Iran and Iraq, already precarious, reached a new low.

Following consultations with community leaders, the UN delegate to Bahrain reported that the people favoured independence as opposed to union with Iran. His report was accepted by Iran's Parliament and the Iranian public reacted favourably, contrary to the Shah's fears. In turn, having demonstrated his goodwill over Bahrain, the Shah believed the British government was obliged to recognize his claims to Abu Musa and the islands of Tunbs. The need for a settlement here grew ever more pressing as the deadline for British withdrawal approached. Meanwhile further complications arose. An oil agreement between Occidental Petroleum and the two Emirates of Umm al-Quwain and Ajman led to offshore drilling in an area within the territorial waters of Abu Musa – recently extended from three to twelve miles. At the same time the Sheikh of Sharjah granted oil concessions over the island and its territorial waters to Crescent Petroleum, a company operated and partly owned by Butts Gas and Oil of California. In addition to these conflicting Arab claims, Iran was vehemently opposed to exploration by either Butts or Occidental which implied recognition of Arab sovereignty over the island. The British were anxious to prolong negotiations with

Iran and agreed to force a complete halt to drilling operations.

In September 1970 Libya and Occidental Petroleum reached a new profit-sharing agreement, altering the traditional 50–50 formula, into 55–45 in Libya's favour. In addition the posted price of exported oil was to be increased. This was the beginning of a chain reaction which swept through every member state of OPEC. Iran and the other producers of the Persian Gulf agreed to hold talks in Tehran, to facilitate collective bargaining with the oil companies. In turn this led to steady increases in the posted price of oil and to reductions in the profit-share allotted to the western oil companies. In 1971 Iraq was to nationalize her oil industry, and from 1972 onwards the Arab states of the Persian Gulf began an inexorable process, taking over the assets and concessions of the foreign oil companies, reaching its climax in 1973 when the oil-producing nations were able to exploit political circumstances and for the first time set their own oil prices, previously determined by the companies.

Thursday, 1 January

Audience ... HIM stressed that he will be unescorted for much of his coming trip to Europe and expects me to keep him company as often as possible. I replied that I should be honoured, although I again suggested that forty days was too long to stay abroad. The world is not without its dangers ...

Today sees the start of a new decade ... the sixties witnessed great progress for our country under the leadership of HIM. He has enjoyed more or less absolute power except for the two years 1960–1, when the late President Kennedy foisted Dr Amini on us as Prime Minister. The Twelve Principles of the Revolution of the Shah and Nation, each of them drawn up during my own time as Prime Minister, have all been implemented.[1] Perhaps our greatest success lies in having put the clergy, landlords, chieftains and communists firmly in their place. I'm confident that the country will be free of their pernicious influence for many years to come. We can be optimistic about the fate of the monarchy, provided that HIM lays the foundations of democratic rule. We have come through the last decade unscathed, but only because the great powers were engaged elsewhere, above all with the American war in Vietnam. Otherwise we would not have been left so much to our own devices. In today's world autocratic rule by one man is neither acceptable nor likely to survive, despite the fact that Mohammed Reza Shah is kind-hearted, thoughtful, well-informed and gifted with insight into the future. His power is never wielded from personal greed but always for the greater good of Iran ...

The five Israeli torpedo boats have docked at Haifa, for all Egypt's bombastic pronouncements about her so-called mighty fleet ...

Tuesday, 6 January

This morning ... I showed HIM a book published in 1956 in Egypt, at the Al Azhar theological school. It contains specific mention of the 'Persian' Gulf. 'Yes', he said, 'Nasser too always referred to the "Persian" Gulf in his early speeches. It was the London *Times* that lent respectability to the term Arabian Gulf; Nasser simply followed suit as did all the Arabs.' 'So', I said, 'the Arabs were actually taught to use the expression.' He agreed[2] ...

---

[1] In January 1963, at the height of the campaign for social reform, the Shah put six proposals to a referendum, the most important relating to land reform, the creation of a literacy corps and women's suffrage. Later, other points were added, most of them lacking in substance.

[2] In fact, the term 'Arabian Gulf' first became fashionable in Iraq in the 1950s under the monarchy. The newly independent Kuwait followed suit with the demand that all mail and

I also reported an early morning telephone call from the US ambassador who rang to pass on a cable from his Secretary of State, William Rogers, expressing his sympathy towards our position in the oil negotiations. HIM said, 'Understanding won't solve our problems; America should act. Call the ambassador and tell him so.'

Wednesday, 7 January

... HIM seemed quite washed out; though it was only 10 in the morning, he could barely contain his yawns. I pointed this out. He replied that on going to bed at 1 a.m., he regularly takes a sleeping tablet. He can then doze off for five hours, but the drowsiness persists long into the morning ...

We are coming up to the anniversary of the assassination attempt on the Shah at Tehran University: 4 February 1950.[1] Each year we hold a thanksgiving ceremony. Alikhani, newly appointed President of the university, now proposes a different set-up; a commemoration of the university's foundation by Reza Shah, without the traditional flattery and thanks for deliverance. HIM approved the change, but I couldn't tell whether or not it pleases him. Talking of the assassination attempt, he said that the would-be assassin's girl-friend was the daughter of the head-gardener at the British embassy. I told him that I'd heard this story. 'In those days the British and Americans were undoubtedly sceptical about Your Majesty. But would they really have hatched such a stupid plot against you? Isn't it more likely that General Razmara,[2] then Chief of Staff, lay behind the attempt? He was the only official to stay cloistered in his office on the day, together with Nasser Qashqai.'[3] HIM made no attempt to argue but thought for a while. He then said, 'You realize, of course, that British communists made another attempt on my life four years ago?' I replied that neither the British nor the Americans have any interest in doing away with HIM; it would fly in the face of their own best interests. Why should they want to destabilize the only sound country in the region?

commercial shipments should be addressed 'Kuwait, Arabian Gulf'. The Shah suspected, as usual, that such anti-Iranian moves were inspired by the British.

[1] Though shot at close range, the Shah miraculously escaped with only minor injuries. The would-be assassin was killed on the spot, and it was never clearly established who his backers had been. The Shah's favourite version was to attribute the conspiracy, yet again, to British Intelligence.

[2] Lt General Ali Razmara: an ambitious and highly efficient man, he was appointed Prime Minister in 1950; opposed to the nationalization of Iran's oil industry, he was assassinated in 1951.

[3] Once powerful Chieftain of the Qashqai tribe of Southern Iran; supported Dr Mosaddeq and hence exiled from Iran in 1954.

'Perhaps you are right', he said. 'The whole thing was a misunderstanding.'

I told him that Robert McNamara, the President of the World Bank, has led me to understand, prior to his audience with HIM, that he cannot extend a loan for the construction of factories manufacturing tanks or gunpowder. HIM should go along with a fiction that the loans are intended for a tractor factory and a chemical plant ...

Saturday, 10 January

... Attended Dinner. HM the Queen Mother suggested that the *Salaam* for the New Year should be cancelled as it comes only a few days after the mourning of *Ashura*. It's a ludicrous proposition, but all the same I grew concerned that it might actually be taken seriously. Normally I remain silent at these functions but tonight I intervened vigorously. 'What can you mean?', I asked. 'We mustn't jettison national tradition in deference to meaningless protocol. Even if *Now Rouz* clashed precisely with *Ashura* we should hold the *Salaam*.' A hush descended on the conversation and someone changed the subject. HIM seemed quite pleased with my intervention ...

Sunday, 11 January

... Received a letter from Nixon to HIM, thanking him for his customary New Year's gift of caviar ...

Dinner at Princess Ashraf's. Karim Aga Khan, the new leader of the Ismailis, attended accompanied by his wife, a British widow. I'd been told much about her beauty but in the event I was disappointed ...

Tuesday, 13 January

George Brown, the former British Foreign Secretary, was granted an audience this morning. He is an alcoholic and had to be sacked from Wilson's cabinet on some pretext or other. I saw HIM before the audience; 'I intend to drink tea', he said, 'but they had better lay on some whisky for Mr Brown.'

A visit from the head of Israeli arms production. Before emigrating from the USA he held down a job worth $25,000 a month; in Israel he earns a fifth of that – a staggering sacrifice. Within two years, he told me, Israel will be producing the most advanced aircraft anywhere in the world, whilst their short-range missiles already leave the rest of the world standing. Throughout this catalogue of achievements I was close to tears; look at Israel and then turn to Iran, what a depressing comparison. The man is a credit to his country. Towards the end he proposed a joint venture with us for the production of missiles which I shall pass on to HIM ...

Wednesday, 14 January
This morning I called on my father-in-law, Qavam, who is about to fly to London for medical treatment. He has two sons, two daughters, his wife is still alive, and there's my brother-in-law as well, and yet he ordered them all out of the room and made over his will to me. It shamed me, to be there amongst them, but there was nothing to be done – you cannot force a man to trust you ...

Thursday, 15 January
The President of Pahlavi University brought me dreadful news. My father's chauffeur had a daughter, a beautiful girl whom I loved as if she were my own. She was highly gifted and I therefore financed her through college in the USA ... Later I obtained a post for her as an assistant professor at Pahlavi. It seems that she and one of her students, her boyfriend so they say, have both been killed in a car crash between Shiraz and Isfahan ...

Some time ago Vice-President Spiro Agnew wrote thanking HIM for various gifts, amongst them a splendid gold watch. As he had never sent him a watch of any description, HIM asked me to make enquiries via our ambassador in Washington. The reply reached me in this morning's post, stating that the watch was actually a gift from the Ministry of Foreign Affairs but that the Vice-President had mistakenly assumed that all his various presents came from HIM. I brought the matter up at this morning's audience, pointing out that it was unbecoming of his ministers to bestow gifts on those already honoured by HIM. It makes no sense and the Americans will merely be alarmed by our extravagance. Such a thing would be unthinkable anywhere else in the world. HIM agreed, 'You're right – it's foolish, wasteful.' I then expected him to order that such goings-on cease, but he said nothing more about it ...

Saturday, 17 January
Audience. Again reported delays in the signing of the contracts for our telecommunications network and for the Rapier missile. HIM was furious ... I then reported the concerns expressed by the West German ambassador that a man named H claims to act as our middle man in negotiations over German military supplies. This might jeopardize the entire operation.

HIM was infuriated. He knows the man to be a friend of a Cabinet minister. It didn't strike me as being the first time the matter had been drawn to his attention. He instructed me to tell the Germans to have no further dealings with the fellow ...

Sunday, 18 January

Audience. Unable to fathom why HIM appeared so agitated. The Sheikh of Sharjah was invited to lunch – a knowledgeable young Arab. He surprised me by the depth of his understanding of the problems associated with economic planning.

Ex-Foreign Minister Aram called on me this afternoon. He's been deputed to handle negotiations with the Sheikh, who he tells me is a much tougher customer than his counterpart in Ras al-Khaimah ...

Monday, 19 January

... This morning my wife flew to join our children skiing at Megève, in the French Alps ... Tomorrow I accompany HIM to Europe, so this evening I went to bid farewell to the Queen and Queen Mother ... No matter how petty the request, I was forced to receive a whole stream of petitioners. It's almost as if they think they may have seen the last of me!

Tuesday, 20 January

A bizarre accident last night. HIM was driving himself and the Queen, now six months pregnant, when he was forced to brake very suddenly to avoid a collision. The car containing their bodyguards then ploughed into the back of Their Majesties' car. It could have been very nasty given the Queen's condition but, fortunately, they were both unhurt, if a little dazed. I couldn't sleep after hearing the news, but lay awake all night, terrified that I should have to take HMQ to hospital if she miscarried.

At noon today we flew via Ankara to Vienna ... en route we had a long discussion, chiefly about oil ... HIM believes we should assume an active role within the Consortium ...

Despite this being a private trip, HIM was welcomed in person by the President of Austria, who accompanied him from the airport not just to his hotel but to his suite upstairs.

During the flight HIM asked me to consult Hafez,[1] but I'd left my copy

---

[1] Traditionally an Iranian confronted with a problem consults the *Diwan* (collection of poems) of Hafez (*c.* AD 1320–*c.* 1389). A poem from the *Diwan* is chosen at random and interpreted as seems most appropriate at the time.

in my suitcase and there the matter rested. He's never asked me to do such a thing before, from which I assume there must be something very important preying on his mind[1] ...

Wednesday, 21 January
HIM went to his doctor for a check-up. Lunch we ate at the Hofburg Palace as guests of the Austrian President. Last night General Djam, the Supreme Commander's Chief of Staff, cabled to inform us that the army had been put on red alert on the western frontier; clearly this suggests another confrontation with Iraq and may well explain HIM's recent anxiety ...

Thursday, 22 January
Rose even earlier than usual. Our ambassador called to see me in a flying hurry and told me he'd been obliged to wake HIM in the middle of the night. When I asked him the reason, and why he hadn't contacted me, he said that HIM had left instructions that he was to be woken if a crisis blew up. He then explained that there has been a botched attempt at a coup in Baghdad, but the Iraqis got wind of it and so far nine people have been executed. Our ambassador in Iraq, who was in touch with the conspirators, has been ordered to leave within twenty-four hours.

Immediately went to see HIM, and found him sitting down to breakfast, terribly tired and drawn ... He was still in a dreadful state over lunch ... News of the widespread executions from Iraq has greatly upset him.

General Djam has sent another cable, recommending a pre-emptive strike against Iraqi airstrips. HIM said, 'Ask him if he's completely lost touch with reality? What makes him think the Iraqis plan an attack? If their army has been told to stand by, it's either because they're responding to our own alert, or as a move against the coup. Not a man of ours is to move without my express approval.' ... The total of those executed now stands at twenty-nine.

Friday, 23 January
Overnight news of the executions continued to come in; more than forty so far ... Lunch was held at our embassy; the Austrian President, Foreign and Trade Ministers and the Mayor of Vienna were HIM's guests. HIM had several meetings this afternoon, and received the General Secretary of

[1] A reference to the coup attempt by Iraqi officers; see introductory note, 1970.

OPEC, a Libyan, whom he urged to increase the price of Libyan oil so as to guard their resources for future generations rather than squander them for immediate profit. When this gentleman left, I pointed out that all HIM had said to him was in direct contradiction of our own avowed policy. 'Firstly', he said, 'we sell our oil at the posted price which is high, and secondly, what better means of preventing them from upping their own production?' We both laughed.

Saturday, 24 January

The Austrian President came to the hotel to escort HIM to the airport. A bitterly cold morning. En route from Vienna to Zurich HIM, for some unknown reason, launched into an attack on his personal physician, Dr Ayadi. He was only half in jest so the doctor must have made some sort of blunder. HIM never sounds off in that way without very good reason.

Prince Sadruddin Aga Khan,[1] the uncle of Karim Aga Khan, welcomed HIM at Zurich airport. I was instructed to invite him to lunch which we ate at a restaurant in the city.

Afterwards HIM went to see his optician ... He wants to change from glasses to contact lenses but he's having great trouble adapting to the latter. I told him that quite franky I can't see why he is bothering himself over something so trivial.

Sunday, 25 January

Found HIM at his breakfast in a very chirpy mood. Before I had a chance to say anything he announced that there have been excellent falls of rain and snow, right the way across Iran ... I then escorted him to his dentist. I asked permission to miss lunch, as my love is here at the moment ... My father-in-law's cancer has finally proved fatal. The poor man died in London; he possessed great integrity and knew how to call a spade a spade, but for all that he could be more than a little miserly ...

Monday, 26 January

Again accompanied HIM to his dentist. Afterwards we lunched at a restaurant outside Zurich. I told him how this morning I'd received a visit from an Iraqi named Sadr; son of a former Speaker of the Iraqi Senate under the monarchy; he has fled the country and now has truly horrific stories to tell of the ruthlessness and cruelty of the present regime. His

---

[1] At the time UN High Commissioner for Refugees.

wife is in gaol and he has had no news of their children ... HIM was moved and instructed me to offer immediate assistance ...

Wednesday, 28 January
Arrived today in Geneva, intending to stay with my wife and children before flying back to Tehran for the funeral of my father-in-law next Saturday ...

Thursday, 29 January
Arrived back in Tehran at ten this evening and immediately went to call on my mother ...

Thursday, 5 February
The Foreign Minister invited me, along with the PM and a few of his colleagues, to discuss our policy towards Afghanistan. We concluded that the new Afghan proposals for the division of the waters of the Hirmand river are unfavourable and we shall lose nothing by refusing to sign ... Even so we ought to extend transit facilities and make various other concessions, including an offer of favourable terms for the sale of oil ... if only to reduce their dependence on China and the Soviets ...

Early this evening an important discussion with General Fardoust,[1] Deputy Director of Savak, an old classmate and a long-standing personal friend of HIM. Apparently an unknown man has been able to drive into the Palace unchallenged. We know nothing about him; his name; how he entered or how he left. Fardoust has reported the matter to HIM but has yet to receive instructions. The problem is apparently considered one for the Imperial Guard. I am extremely apprehensive, and intend to raise the matter with HIM. He must either sack me or invest me with overall responsibility for palace security ...

Telephoned HMQ and HM the Queen Mother to bid farewell prior to my flight to Europe ...

[1] Hossein Fardoust, in spite of his humble origins, was selected to join the special school for the Shah while he was Crown Prince. Subsequently he became one of the Prince's best friends, accompanying him to Le Rosey in Switzerland, and later to the Tehran Military Academy. After the Prince became Shah, Fardoust's career progressed in the Army. A secretive man, he was appointed in the 1970s as Chief of the Imperial Inspectorate. After the revolution, to the surprise of many, he remained in Iran. For some years he was apparently Chief Adviser to the revolutionary regime in military and security matters. His mysterious life none the less ended in jail where he died c.1986. Not surprisingly, rumours abound concerning the true loyalties of this apparently faithful childhood friend of the Shah.

Saturday, 7 February

Arrived in Geneva on Friday and today drove to St Moritz. My wife and children are in Arosa. Went to call on HIM at his chalet and finding him out to dinner took the opportunity to snatch a few hours' rest at my hotel ...

Sunday, 8 February

Found HIM at breakfast. Indescribably delighted to see him, and he too seemed pleased to see me. Yet whatever our personal attachment to one another I shall never allow it to stand in the way of my speaking out whenever I come across shortcomings or failings. His three children, the Crown Prince, Princess Farahnaz and Prince Ali Reza, were all there, kicking up a dreadful racket. After breakfast Ali Reza began horsing about, jumping in and out of HIM's lap. 'Watch out he doesn't put an end to your manhood', I said. HIM laughed, and said the dreadful thought had already occurred to him. He added that the boy was quite the brainiest of the bunch, blessed with an astonishing memory. When I entered the room this morning and bowed to HIM, it was Ali Reza who turned to me and said, '*Bonjour, Monsieur Alam*'; the other children sat mutely by.

We talked for an hour and a half on our way to the ski slopes. The Middle Eastern situation worries HIM; particularly the Iraqis, and the fact that they seem to have reached agreement with Mostafa Barzani,[1] leader of the Kurds ... with that problem out of the way, Iraq will be able to concentrate her forces on the border with Iran ... He then asked quite candidly, 'Between ourselves, do you suppose that we are acting as traitors to our country by going ahead with this settlement over Bahrain? Or, as many voices from around the world keep telling me, are we actually on the brink of a major achievement, rescuing the region from futile confrontation and communism?' 'Merely to demand the island as a legal right', I replied, 'would get us nowhere. If we seized it by force it could only become a millstone round our necks, and a permanent provocation to the Arabs. What's more, it would be immensely expensive, since Bahraini oil resources are gradually drying up ...'

... In regard to the appointment of a tutor for the Crown Prince, I told HIM that he must decide whether to look for a civilian or a serviceman.

---

[1] Founder and leader of the Kurdish Democratic Party; a tragic figure obsessed with the idea of bringing freedom and dignity to his people; an eternal rebel who for more than forty years led revolts in Iraqi Kurdistan. After Iran and Iraq settled their border dispute in 1975, Barzani left for the US to receive cancer treatment. Terminally ill and frustrated by years of betrayal, he died in 1979.

I'm not well up on the military, but had he considered General Arfa?[1] 'I'm not at all keen on his Anglo-Saxon manners', he replied, 'and anyway he's too old-fashioned, quite frankly a bit past it.' ... I then suggested the names of two civilians ... but he said, 'No I like the idea of a serviceman very much, and shall stick to it. The army is going to play a major role in countries like ours, at least for the foreseeable future, and it would give the Crown Prince a strong sense of discipline.' Again I pointed out my lack of inside knowledge. HIM said he would look into a military appointment, 'but it won't be at all easy, picking somebody who isn't going to develop personal ambitions.' I have a slight cold and therefore returned to my hotel without risking a turn on the piste.

After lunch, I again saw HIM and briefed him on current affairs. At the end he said, 'Now for goodness sake allow yourself dinner, tête-à-tête with you know who. I know she's around. After all we've come here for a rest.' The Shah is very humane ...

Tuesday, 10 February

Saw HIM this afternoon ... and he gave me leave to dine elsewhere. I asked that tomorrow I might go to visit my wife and children in Arosa ... Discussed Princess Shahnaz – HIM less pessimistic about her, willing to admit her merits. She's spent a few days here in St Moritz.

I warned HIM about the deplorable security arrangements at his chalet. I'm genuinely concerned and have already talked it over with the Chief of Police for the Canton of Coire. Even so we need more of our own people. HIM said I was to do as I saw fit ...

Tuesday, 17 February

Returned to St Moritz and went immediately to find HIM. He was overjoyed to see me as his children have returned to Iran and he'd begun to tire of his own company. We dined out and he asked whether I too am on my own, or was my lover here? I told him she was not and explained that we had quarrelled ... 'Be kind to her', he said; 'She loves you.' In any case, I told him, I wasn't altogether a free agent as my daughter is with me ... Returning to the chalet, HIM burst into laughter. I asked him what

[1] Major General Hassan Arfa, a former Chief of Staff and ex-minister; ambassador to Turkey and to Pakistan. A colourful Anglophile with an impressive knowledge of military history, he treated his diplomatic staff as subordinates in a barracks. This brought him into conflict with his embassy counsellor in Ankara, Amir Abbas Hoveyda, who managed to obtain a job in Tehran with the National Iranian Oil Company, the fateful first step in a new career.

the joke was, and he said 'Remember your warning about security? It's been amply justified. The Swiss police are supposed to keep a constant vigil outside the chalet, yet someone managed to steal the lobby carpet from under their very noses.' 'There have been worse lapses than that', I said, 'a man has been apprehended in the gardens of the Niavaran Palace, close by the bedroom of HMQ. Having arrested him the Guards merely questioned him and, considering him to be a harmless lunatic, let him go. A deplorable piece of stupidity.' I sought permission to follow the matter up through Savak, but I still can't understand how this man got both himself and his car into the palace gardens.

Wednesday, 18 February

... Found HIM this afternoon in the midst of his massage and bath. We chatted for nearly two hours. I told him that in my view, he is overdoing it both in his sporting and his nocturnal pursuits. He pooh-poohed the suggestion, but I pointed that men of fifty-one are ill-advised to go skiing for three hours, something he'd boasted of only today ... Again I suggested that we've stayed abroad for quite long enough and should now go home. This went down like a lead balloon, but I'm under an obligation to bring home to him that the Shah of Iran cannot spend forty-five days away from his country merely for rest and amusement! Our people cannot be expected to put up with it.

I sought permission to visit my oculist in Zurich tomorrow. This annoyed HIM, and he asked me not to dash off so soon, particularly as Moulay Abdullah is about to join him ... He then said, 'Perhaps it's Mrs Alam who has got you on the run?' I admitted that this was part of the reason – my wife is indeed convinced that I am here leading a life of utter debauchery, but all the same my eyes really do need examination. I shall see a specialist and spend Thursday and Friday in Zurich. After that I must go on to Geneva. HIM reluctantly gave way, but insisted he see me tomorrow morning, before my departure.

Victor Emmanuel[1] threw a party, attended by HIM, but as my own presence in St Moritz has gone unnoticed I was not invited. Instead I strolled round town.

---

[1] Son of Umberto, the last King of Italy, he became a friend of the Iranian royal family despite an unsuccessful proposal to marry his sister, Gabriella, to the Shah. Over time Victor Emmanuel used his contacts in Iran to sell the country large numbers of Italian-made, Augusta-Bell, helicopters.

Thursday, 19 February

Arrived at HIM's chalet at about 10 this morning. He had only just got up and was still in the bathroom where I found him sitting in front of the mirror, gargling. Was it for a cold? I asked. 'No', he said, 'but to keep the colds away I gargle every morning.' I told him it was a useless remedy and could actually bring on the ills it was designed to prevent. Again he asked me whether I was really set on leaving. 'Yes', I said, 'my eyes are playing up, and I'm feeling old and decrepit.' 'But then, don't we all', he replied. Indeed his face in the mirror looked pale and lined with care. None the less I told him he seemed to be better off than the rest of us, which is true enough. I then kissed his hand and took my leave. Drove directly to Zurich where I was met by my wife, my elder daughter and her husband ... My oculist is still away on holiday, so this evening I flew to Geneva.

Friday, 20–Wednesday, 25 February

Spent the past few days in Geneva. No news of my oculist, but various other things have kept me here ...

Bad news from Tehran. Bus fares have suddenly tripled sparking off public outcry. University students refused to attend lectures and demolished several buses. They had the sympathy of the masses behind them and their demonstration was gathering momentum until HIM stepped in and cancelled the fare increase. At first he'd reacted to the disorder by following the government's advice, vowing no surrender to the mob and harsh measures against all protestors ... When I heard this, I telephoned him straight away and told him, 'Remember, I was Prime Minister the last time we used force to quell a riot, when various groups demonstrated against Your Majesty's reforms, stirred up by General Bakhtiar, the mullahs and the communists. On that occasion we had majority support for our intervention, but the present situation is very different. For goodness sake tell the government to refrain from using force.' He followed my advice.[1] In many ways it was fortunate that the fare increase went through in HIM's absence; people naturally assumed that he was against the move and had ordered its cancellation. On the other hand I'm not at all happy about the total lack of coordination in our decision-making. Foreign powers have so far left us to our own devices, but the domestic front is far from healthy.

---

[1] In the meantime Hoveyda had summoned various ministers and the presidents of the local universities to a special meeting in Tehran. Almost unanimously they advised him to scrap the fare increases. Hoveyda then telephoned the Shah, but could not bring himself to report the meeting's judgement. He was rescued by Ardeshir Zahedi, who had the courage to report what had gone on. The Shah was persuaded to accept their advice.

I'm by nature a stoic, but recent events have given even me a fit of the shivers. Each and every minister submits an independent report to HIM whose own orders are frequently issued without any consultation with our pathetic PM. Perhaps that's the secret of the PM's survival for the past six years. But all the same, HIM has no time in which to think through his decisions, and blunders are made. With twenty-eight years' experience and great natural intelligence, the Shah is wise to a degree, but in the modern world government has become a much more complex and subtle affair. I have many times argued that we need special advisers to study each problem and submit their findings to HIM, just as they do in other countries. He himself has seen that the US President's personal advisers are a quite separate entity from the US administration. But he'll have none of it, complaining that the last thing he wants is a government within a government, and that in any case we're well enough served by the study centres attached to Savak and the military. One day, I fear we may pay for this neglect.

Thursday, 26 February
Returned to Tehran by Iranair – after all they're our own people, they operate a safe service and quite a comfortable one at that. Everything that's under the Shah's personal supervision can be relied on to work efficiently. Went straightaway to kiss my mother's hand.

Friday, 27 February
Went to see HMQ this morning who asked me to stay for lunch.

Ayatollah Hakim has fallen sick. I cabled St Moritz for permission to send him a doctor. HIM replied, 'If we send an Iranian medic and Hakim dies, Iraq will accuse us of having done him in.' The PM gave me a better suggestion; the disease has already been diagnosed as kidney and prostate trouble, therefore send him a foreign specialist. I passed this idea on to HIM who gave his go ahead.

Saturday, 28 February–Tuesday, 3 March
Several visitors, the ambassadors of Russia, West Germany, Britain and the USA amongst them ... The German brought up various commercial matters, but his real purpose was to report on discussions between the Soviets and representatives of Chancellor Willy Brandt – highly confidential, but he was anxious that HIM be put in the picture. The British ambassador asked that we delay submitting the Bahrain Report to Parlia-

ment, until U Thant has completed his work, due to be finished by 28 March. Any leaks before that date would place U Thant in a difficult position.

The US ambassador ... was keen to assure me of the goodwill that HIM has aroused in the President and the Washington administration. Nevertheless, domestic difficulties make it unlikely that they can either persuade the oil companies to up Iranian output or allocate us a special import quota for the US market. As for HIM's request for the training of 120 pilots, they will ensure that it goes ahead, despite their many other commitments around the world and the strain imposed on them by the Vietnam war. The matter will be given top priority ... Finally the ambassador asked that HIM permit the annual conference of US diplomats stationed in the Middle East to take place in Tehran rather than Beirut.

Wednesday, 4 March
HIM returned after forty-five days in Europe. His absence has done much harm – above all it's seen the bus fare increases, followed only a few days later by their cancellation. This has paved the way for further riots in the universities. If it hadn't been for the government's decision to retract, we would have faced an even graver situation. Yet why make such a foolish decision in the first place? ...

Thursday, 5 March
HIM left for Pakistan this morning ...

Friday, 6–Thursday, 19 March
Terribly busy over the past week or so – no free time in which to jot down even a single word.

HIM's trip to Pakistan was a great success, marked by a highly enthusiastic reception by the Pakistani government and people ... Our respective foreign policies have been fully aligned, and we have agreed to act as Pakistan's sole supplier of oil ... magnificent advances for both Iranian diplomacy and our oil industry ...

Recently I've noted an alarming change in HIM's general bearing. The HIM I knew of old, determined, demanding and at heart a reformer, has shown unexpected signs of wavering. Elsewhere in this diary I recorded a dinner at the Queen Mother's; how she and I had a violent disagreement following her suggestion that the New Year's celebrations be cancelled out of deference to the mourning of *Ashura*, and how HIM, despite the insults thrown at me by his mother, endorsed my recommendation that we go ahead with the *Salaam* as arranged. Indeed invitations were dispatched and everything seemed set, but then he called me in one morning to say ... that the whole operation should be cancelled. I was dumbfounded ... but he would brook no objection. Finally we agreed that some sort of ceremony, but a very low-key affair, should go ahead in Mashad.

To take another example, HIM once a year makes a habit of receiving the dependants of servicemen killed on active duty. But at the end of this year's audience HIM stayed on for nearly an hour, chatting to the women and children, a quite unprecedented move on his part ... Finally, one must bear in mind his capitulation over the proposed increase in bus fares ...

Thinking about all this, I've come to the conclusion that HIM has grown cautious, reluctant to antagonize people at a time of great tension. Our confrontation with Iraq rumbles on, the universities are in turmoil and as for Bahrain, the UN's verdict seems certain to go against us. HIM is a shrewd enough man to recognize that our people are already restive on any number of grounds and that it would be rash to add to their unease.

... Bahrain has given rise to at least one comic incident. On HIM's orders I held a meeting with the Foreign Minister Zahedi and the PM to discuss ways and means of preparing public opinion in advance of the UN's decision, which we have no alternative but to accept. However rather than discuss the substantive agreement, the two men fell to squabbling over which one of them must submit the UN report to Parliament, both of them anxious that the other should be the one to accept the poisoned chalice. What a miserable couple they make. As I said to them, 'Either you believe in the settlement you've entered into, in which case you should have the guts to defend your decision, or else you should resign rather than hoping that someone else will carry the can. In any event the cabinet has collective responsibility for government decisions and it matters not one jot whether it's the Prime Minister or his Foreign Secretary who submits the issue to Parliament.'

... Did my best to intercede on behalf of Prince Abdul Reza's wife, Pari Sima,[1] who for the past eleven years has been banned from court ... but it only served to enrage HIM. 'This woman', he said, 'wore the veil

---

[1] After divorcing his second wife, the Shah considered marrying Princess Maria Gabriella of the House of Savoy. At first everything went well and, despite the difference in their religions, a satisfactory compromise was reached. But the Princess, without any warning, changed her mind. The Shah was convinced it was the fault of Pari Sima who, by gossiping about a corrupt Pahlavi Court, had frightened the Italian away.

and she used to slip off secretly to Dr Mosaddeq's, spreading stories about the day's events at court and stirring up gossip against me. At the time I was without a male heir. I can clearly remember one day walking with Pari Sima in the palace gardens. Her son ran towards us, and as he did so she turned to me and said that she could already see in him the hallmarks of a future Shah of Iran. There's a limit to my endurance, and really that woman went beyond anything that I can be expected to forgive.' I too felt that I had badly overstepped the mark.

I told the US ambassador that HIM has been notified of a comment he made to the effect that over the next five years the USA cannot advance Iran more than $500 million credit for the purchase of arms. HIM wished to remind him that America is badly mistaken if she believes that by cutting our credit she can reduce our imports of military hardware. Credit or no credit we shall find alternative means of satisfying our needs. In the next five years we intend to purchase $800 million of arms from the USA, $200 million from Britain and $200 million from the Soviets. If America is reluctant to meet our requirements, we can turn elsewhere for assistance. This had an upsetting effect on the ambassador who denied that he'd ever said the words attributed to him and asked for an urgent audience with HIM. This was duly arranged for yesterday, when he was received for at least two hours.

... King Hussein left Tehran this morning, having stayed one night as our guest, en route from a state visit to Pakistan. He spent three hours in close session with HIM. Poor man, he's caught up in an appalling balancing act, walking the tightrope between Yasser Arafat and the Palestinians on one hand, and on the other the Iraqi army stationed on Jordanian soil. What's more, he is confronted by the Israelis and has become a partner to various blunders committed by that unscrupulous so-and-so Nasser. A hopeless situation. No king can remain long on his throne if he begins by forbidding every activity amongst the armed factions in his capital city and then is ignominiously forced to back down. The Jordanian ambassador, who struck me as being blessed with precious little intelligence, told me that full understanding has been restored between the King and Yasser Arafat. Stuff and nonsense. HIM shares my pessimism over King Hussein's fate.

Saturday, 21 March

Travelled to Mashad in company with HIM, the PM, various members of his cabinet and a few miscellaneous officials. Fine weather and an enthusiastic reception from the crowds. The Shah has grown to be a true father to his people and today there's not a man who dares hope for a quiet life without HIM to lead the way ...

After we'd paid our respects at the shrine of Imam Reza, I asked HIM whether I might stay on there for a half hour or so, to pray by the tomb of my father, next to which I hope my own body may one day rest. I sensed that this request had needled HIM, although he raised no objection. This surprised me, after all it wasn't as if I was leaving him unattended. There was nothing pressing for my attention, and in all it was a perfectly reasonable request. I can only assume that he regarded it as a foolish piece of one-upmanship: my ancestors have lain in this shrine for countless centuries; perhaps he thought I had no reason to commune with dead men I'd never once met.

We all attended Lunch and vied with one another in showering compliments on HIM ...

Sunday, 22 March

Audience ... As he described it, HIM has told the American ambassador, 'For America, the sale of military equipment is a purely commercial matter, but for us the acquisition of arms is a matter of life or death. We shall find the means to finance our defence budget, even if it means our going hungry.'

Tuesday, 24 March

Audience, despite the New Year holiday. HIM has been told by the US ambassador that Washington will not now deliver the twenty-five Phantoms requested by the Israelis, but that all the same she will continue to grant Israel economic assistance. HIM asked me to inform the ambassador that whenever Washington wishes to help a country she manages to go ahead by one means or another. However when it comes to Iran, the US administration kicks up nothing but difficulties ...

Later, inspected the Golestan Palace where Soviet President Nicolai Podgorny will stay on his forthcoming visit ...

Wednesday, 25 March

Audience. 'The Russians are excelling themselves', said HIM. 'Apparently they are to offer me a sword inscribed as a memorial of the Shahanshah's valiant struggle against fascism. Some sort of vase is to be presented to the people of Tehran. Moreover Podgorny is to be accompanied by a very high-powered mission, providing the opportunity for all sorts of discussions.'

I pointed out that the American Senate's debate on military aid to Iran has elicited high praise for us from various senators. HIM seemed reasonably pleased by this news but maintained a poker face and even began to repeat his criticism of American policy, ordering me to dress up his remarks in diplomatic language and pass them on to the US ambassador. HIM is nothing if not shrewd. Behind his comments on US policy lies a desire to pre-empt American opinion should he be seen to be going too far with the Russians. I pointed out that we are constantly coming under attack from the radio broadcasts of Soviet bloc nations, if not of Moscow itself. 'They could hardly do otherwise', he replied, 'and it's not without its uses since it shows them up in their true colours. Whenever I receive an ambassador from one of these satellite countries, I bring the matter up almost as a joke, hoping that it may get back to their governments at home. But to date they've shown not the slightest reaction.' . . .

Podgorny arrived this afternoon accompanied by the President of the Soviet Republic of Turkmenistan and fifty other ministerial officials. Dinner was held at the Niavaran Palace. HIM made an excellent speech, followed by a rather unbecoming diatribe against American imperialism from Podgorny. I was surprised that our Ministry of Foreign Affairs had made no effort to vet this speech beforehand. Podgorny is a jovial fellow, but he's over-fond of the sound of his own voice . . .

Thursday, 26 March

. . . Attended dinner hosted by Podgorny at the Golestan Palace. Afterwards talked to the Soviet ambassador who is delighted by the progress of this visit . . . He expressed his government's willingness to enter into further co-operation with Iran, within the limits imposed by Moscow's current financial constraints. When I expressed surprise at this last point he replied, 'We too are heavily committed to our defence budget. An old and trusted friend has recently turned against us and we are forced to maintain a state of constant vigilance in the Far East, to counter the threat which this has posed.' This is the first time I have heard a Russian talk so bluntly about China. 'The Chinese', he went on, 'have laid claim to our far eastern territories, claiming that we acquired them by extortion.' 'They seem to have a point', I said smiling, 'since at least some of this land was taken from China back in the days of the Tsars. China is over-populated and needs space into which she may expand. Naturally she looks to the relatively deserted territories beyond her northern frontier, the only space available, which happens at the same time to form part of Russia.' The ambassador signalled his agreement ...

I returned to the Niavaran Palace with HIM at one in the morning. There found that HMQ had begun to feel contractions. Her obstetrician assured us that it was nothing to worry about and that we should go to bed. But I was woken at 3 a.m. to be told that she had gone into labour, and with HIM I accompanied her to the military hospital. HIM and I were given adjoining bedrooms and did our best to get some sleep. At 8 a.m. Her Majesty was delivered of a daughter.

Friday, 27 March
Went straightaway to HIM's bedroom to offer my congratulations. He kindly asked me to stay to breakfast and we discussed a variety of topics, including my recent discussions with the Soviet and West German ambassadors. HIM was pleased by his own talks with the Soviets whom he had found to be open and sincere ... He too had heard their complaints about the heaviness of their defence budget. He then said, 'Look how friendly the Russians are towards us. The Americans too are overflowing with friendship, yet that bastard General Bakhtiar goes around Baghdad telling everyone he meets that the Shah's regime is about to be toppled by a joint initiative from Moscow and Washington.' 'Your Majesty should pay no attention to such nonsense', I said, 'there are bonds of mutual trust uniting Your Majesty to the Iranian people; until such bonds snap, you need pay no heed to anything said by Bakhtiar, the Soviets, the British or the Americans.'

... HIM dined with HMQ at the hospital. Afterwards we attended a Russian ballet at the Rudaki Hall – an excellent performance, showing how artistically adventurous the Russian troupes have become ...

Saturday, 28 March
Worried when HIM failed to show up at his office at the usual time. I found him safe and sound in his private quarters, reading confidential reports from abroad – clearly not those sent out by our own foreign ministry ... He instructed me to ask the British and Americans what importance

they attach to the recent Jeddah conference of Islamic Foreign Ministers. The conference appointed a Secretary-General whose residence they gave as Jerusalem, with Jeddah serving as a provisional seat until the end of 'the Israeli occupation'. Apparently our own Foreign Minister has exaggerated the significance of this meeting and HIM wants an unbiased view of its impact. He also instructed me to ask the British for an explanation of the recent black-out exercises in Baghdad; is it us they fear, or another enemy? ...

Attended Dinner where HIM expressed his delight with Radio Moscow's announcement that Iran and Russia can together safeguard peace in the Middle East. We were more or less alone at the meal, save for Princess Fatemeh and her husband General Khatami, Commander of the Air Force, and Pahlbod,[1] Princess Shams' husband. I was surprised that HIM once again launched into an attack on US policy and its insensitivity to Iran's needs. I get the impression that he wishes to enter into a major deal with the Soviets and is preparing the ground by harping on America's failings. He is prepared for me to contradict him and we argued for some time ... At one stage HIM complained that the Americans and the British can have no strategic justification for buying oil from countries such as Kuwait, Abu Dhabi and Libya. I agreed, but pointed out that under capitalism material interests dwarf every other consideration ...

Sunday 29 March
Brief audience this morning. Submitted various telegrams congratulating HIM on the birth of his daughter, and also a cable from London warning us that Ayatollah Hakim is sinking fast. HIM in a rotten temper, put out by the debates in the Majlis. Following the Foreign Minister's statement on negotiations over Bahrain, the government has come under severe attack, worse than we expected, spurred on by Pezeshgpour, leader of the Pan-Iranian party. But as I said to HIM, 'What is there to worry about? Let the voice of the minority be heard, indeed I recommend that you allow Pezeshgpour to publish his speech in full.' He approved this.

I then added, 'The other evening you expressed your bewilderment that for all our achievements, Iranians lack the sense of conviction enjoyed by the Israelis. If you would allow the people to have their say, encourage them to get more involved in national affairs, gradually you will see that such conviction develops.' With this too he agreed ...

[1] Mehrdad Pahlbod (Minbashian): Minister of Arts and Culture; brother of General F. Minbashian.

Monday, 30 March

The US ambassador called on me early this morning. Among other things
... he raised the question of Iran's military procurement in his country,
which HIM has indicated will amount to $800 million over the next five
years. The ambassador says this is simply impractical since in 1968 we
reached an agreement whereby the US would guarantee credit of no more
than $100 million a year; $500 million at most over the next five years.
Reported this conversation to HIM who said, 'I refuse to accept the
ambassador's explanation. Tell him that they must offer $800 not $500
million.'

... A private dinner at the Niavaran Palace in honour of Podgorny.
He's a jolly, well-humoured man and an excellent *raconteur*. The Russians
may be helping the Arabs, Egypt in particular, but it doesn't make them
any less resentful or alter their conviction that the Arabs are a bunch of
cowards. Podgorny told one rather good joke about Nasser who, so the
story goes, came discreetly to Moscow to ask for modern weapons and a
more sophisticated sort of aircraft. The Russians replied that they could
offer him their most up-to-date MIG, a plane of quite stunning simplicity.
'How does it work?', asked Nasser. 'Well', said the Russians, 'it has three
buttons; press one for take-off, another to guide you to the target and a
third to drop the bomb, and there you are.' 'But', says Nasser, 'what about
the landing? Surely there's another button to bring the aircraft back to
ground.' 'Ah', replied the Russians, 'the landing. Yes, the landing. That
part of the flight we leave entirely to the discretion of the Israelis.'

When he was in Isfahan, Podgorny apparently spent his entire time
praising HIM and Iran. Hoveyda, who went with him, tells me that he
was so overwhelmed that he gave the Russian a smacking kiss ...

Tuesday, 31 March

Following Podgorny's departure this morning I returned with HIM by
helicopter to the Niavaran Palace. He asked after popular reactions to the
agreement on Bahrain, and I replied that abroad and amongst the diplomatic corps it's been applauded as a sign of HIM's statesmanship –
Podgorny himself had made just this point. At home the people labour
under an illusion that the plebiscite will come out in favour of Iran. Already
various ultra-nationalists have expressed dissent and have questioned the
need for a solution at this juncture. Others, the more intelligent and the
better informed, express their approval, believing that whatever the
outcome of the referendum, we had no alternative but to grasp the nettle.

I told him that the Foreign Minister's speech to the Majlis could have been much better presented. Rather than denigrate the British ... he should have stressed that the Gulf is absolutely vital to Iran. We cannot sacrifice our interests there for the sake of some antiquated claim to Bahrain ... HIM clearly appreciated these remarks but he preferred to make no comment, having himself been responsible for approving the Foreign Minister's speech.

This afternoon, the newborn princess was named Princess Leyla with due religious formality. The same name is henceforth to be given to the hospital where the ceremony took place ...

Wednesday, 1 April

In the morning I escorted HMQ home from the hospital. After lunch, an audience with HIM and among other things ... asked him, 'Will Your Majesty allow me to reprimand the Prime Minister and the Minister of Foreign Affairs? They have been so lax in observing due deference in Your Majesty's presence.' 'What else can you expect with their Anglo–American upbringing?', he said. 'But all the same you had better remind them of what's expected.' 'I only wish that I shared your confidence in blaming their upbringing', I replied, 'I'm more concerned that they behave as they do to prove to others what big shots they are.' HIM laughed and said, 'I can't agree; haven't you noticed the way that whenever I shake hands with Ardeshir he gets down on his knees in front of me?' 'That sort of deference', I said, 'is just as bad as their excesses in the opposite direction. The last time we were in Paris, Ardeshir did just what you've described and seeing him get down on his knees, a French reporter asked me, "The Shah of Iran is known as a reformer and a democrat; how can he bear to see his ministers bow and scrape in such a grovelling way?"' HIM was far from amused by this and said, 'You should have told him that Ardeshir was observing a national custom!' It's incredible the extent to which sycophancy can turn the heads of even the most intelligent men ...

Friday, 3 April

Went riding as usual this morning ... The Crown Prince came too and we rode together for an hour. He's only eleven years old, but already an excellent horseman.

Attended both Lunch and Dinner ... Told HIM of my conversation with the British ambassador. It appears that those questioned by U Thant's special envoys to Bahrain prefer to opt for independence whilst at the same time expressing a desire for close ties to Iran. In these circumstances it may well be possible to forge a special relationship with the island.

Saturday, 4 April

... Attended dinner at the Queen Mother's. Several issues were discussed, above all the question of Bahrain. HIM said that he has been asked by various people why the question has been submitted to Parliament in such a way as to place all responsibility for its solution on HIM's own shoulders. Couldn't the government have shared at least some of the burden? But, as he said, 'I am above this sort of quibbling. If the Iranian people cannot recognize my willingness to lay down my life on their behalf, then why should I make a fuss about who takes what proportion of responsibility? On the other hand, if my self-sacrifice is recognized, then I have still less cause for concern.' All this was said in complete sincerity, since he was in the presence of only the most intimate friends ...

Monday, 6 April

Brief audience. Not without a considerable struggle I got HIM to approve the marquee that will serve as the banqueting hall during the Persepolis celebrations to mark two and a half thousand years of monarchy. He was initially alarmed by the expense and in the end we agreed to reduce both the cost and the size of the tent to a quarter of their original size. It will still cost $1 million ...

At five I met the PM at the Niavaran Palace. We discussed current affairs. The PM very gloomy. As we predicted, the Soviets have protested against U Thant's initiative in Bahrain, saying that he is acting beyond his authority, having no prior approval from the Security Council; this despite the fact that Podgorny was full of praise and support for the policy during his recent visit to Tehran. The main issue seems to be one of principle. The Soviets do not wish the General Secretary of the United Nations to supervise a plebiscite without Moscow's blessing. Clearly, they wonder if they give way to the General Secretary in this instance, where will they be in future if he decides to do the same thing in Czechoslovakia?

They may have other objections; perhaps they hope to curry favour with those disaffected elements here and in Iraq, opposed to friendly relations between Iran and Bahrain; or even amongst the Arabs, some of whom hold the naïve belief that a plebiscite will result in the unification of Bahrain and Iran.

Amongst the more significant items of world news something appears to be going on behind the scenes in the Soviet Union ... though presumably General Secretary Leonid Brezhnev has the situation under control ... Four years ago HIM and I visited Moscow. I well recall that Brezhnev made a point of showing us the extent to which he ran the show. He knew me of old and in private took me aside to tell me: 'The other comrades are wrong; nothing gets done without my making the decision', which was true enough. He is still taking the same line. Unlike Stalin, he is not a violent or a vindictive man.

Friday, 10 April
Rode out prior to ... lunch at the Farahnaz Pahlavi Dam,[1] which I attended at the PM's invitation. He wished to show HIM the rest house he has had built for him. It's not at all bad and will certainly do for our outings.

One piece of domestic news comes as a major relief. Iran has beaten Israel 2–1 in the final of the Asian football cup, held in Tehran. Jubilation ensued. In the Amjadieh stadium a crowd of 30,000 rose to sing the national anthem and the celebrations went on till dawn. HIM was fortunate that no one seized the opportunity to demonstrate over Bahrain. The latter issue seems entirely forgotten. Various people used the occasion for vigorous anti-Israeli protests, which are unusual in Iran. HIM blames the communists.

Saturday, 11 April
Audience ... HIM instructed me to call in the US ambassador. I should tell him that we have agreed to a contract for the repair of military aircraft with the American company AVCO, despite our pre-existing contract with Israel. This decision should forestall any trouble with Arab countries wishing to have their planes serviced in Iran. We have insisted that the new deal be on terms no less favourable than the last one, since we shall be forced to pay compensation to the Israelis.

After I had left, HIM received Omar Saqqaf, the Saudi Arabian Foreign Minister, who arrived accompanied by our own Foreign Minister. I joined them for lunch. Omar Saqqaf was particularly harsh in his assessment of Nasser, but said that the Arab world was nevertheless grateful that the Soviets had supplied SAM anti-aircraft missiles to Egypt. Subsequently HIM asked me to tell the American ambassador that we had enjoyed a highly fruitful meeting with the Saudis, particularly in respect to co-operation in the Persian Gulf. Even so the Americans must know that both

[1] Built on the Jajroud river and named after the Shah's second daughter.

Iran and Saudi Arabia are gravely alarmed by the situation in Iraq and Syria.[1] Meanwhile the USA turns a blind eye to our problems ... Like it or not we must be ready to defend ourselves, with or without American help.

This afternoon met the US ambassador. My assertion that we must defend ourselves elicited a far more perceptive response than I'd have met with from his predecessor. 'Ah', he said, 'I see that HIM is still determined to get that loan of $800 million ... '

Monday, 13 April
... Audience. Found HIM perplexed. When I asked the reason he replied that there have been various untoward incidents in the city. A group of students has been chanting slogans of an overtly communist nature. No manner of victory at soccer can justify slogans such as 'Long live the people of Palestine', or 'Death to all Jews'. The security agencies have been unable to identify the source of the trouble, much to HIM's scorn ...

Tuesday, 14 April
... Audience. HIM has given an important interview to a reporter with the London *Times*. BBC radio carried a commentary on this at 7.30 this morning, suggesting that the Shah's insistence on a British withdrawal from east of Suez and his opposition to their return, a policy advocated by the British Conservative party, may well affect the latter's chances in the forthcoming elections. It's gratifying to know that HIM's views have such impact in Britain. In general the BBC commentary was full of praise for his remarks. I reported this to HIM, but at the same time suggested that it may have been less than dignified of him to refer to 'the downfall' of those Gulf States which resist modern reforms. 'Are you suggesting', he asked, 'that we should merely sit back and leave that devil Nasser to make every radical statement that's going?' 'But Nasser', I replied, 'is an adventurer. HIM should maintain a more statesmanlike position.' I insisted on this so forcefully that he eventually agreed to substitute the word 'evolution' for 'downfall' in the published versions of his interview ...

Saturday, 18 April
During my audience, I pointed out to HIM that a servant of his, named Aslani, holds a master's degree and therefore deserves a less menial station

---

[1] Both Iraq and Syria were developing close relations with the Soviet Union.

in life. HIM agreed to have him promoted to the rank of Chamberlain. His colleagues will doubtless be outraged by his rise from such a humble status. However, HIM takes a radical, meritocratic approach to life arguing that the more able the man, the more suited he is to promotion. He instructed me to take care of the matter, adding, in a dignified way and with complete sincerity, 'After all, where did the Pahlavis begin? My father was a simple soldier sprung from the provinces, from an undistinguished family in Savad Kuh.'[1] It delights me to hear HIM demonstrate such common sense . . .

Forced to cancel my dinner engagement at the Queen Mother's in order to carry out various tasks for HIM. For one thing he rang me up at the house of my lover and ordered me to get on to the British and American ambassadors, to let them know that he is deeply dissatisfied by the current state of oil negotiations. I telephoned them and persuaded them to meet me at my home tomorrow morning. There was one rather surreal incident this evening; for no apparent reason my lover bit me on the cheek, so hard that it bled. I returned home with a very obvious bruise but managed to improvise, saying that I'd been bitten by my dog; another creature that shows me passionate devotion. Can Mrs Alam really have believed my story? . . .

Sunday, 19 April
The British ambassador called round at 8 a.m. I made known HIM's displeasure, pointing out that the oil talks are not coming up to our expectations and that we seem unlikely to be offered an income higher than the $1,010 million already guaranteed. It appears that the Oil Consortium has agreed to increase production to 5 million barrels a day but this will take quite a while to make any impression in cash terms. The ambassador declared that immediately after speaking to me last night he'd telephoned the oil men, but they had given away nothing of their intentions. He got the impression that they would refuse to budge whatever the circumstances. I replied that all this was very well 'But I must warn you that we may be forced to take action. If we do, I'll not stand for any whining or any accusation that we've acted without prior warning to the British ambassador.' He asked me what sort of action we had in mind, to which I replied that I was in no position to say as yet, but that I was anxious he should appreciate the basic facts of the situation.

---

[1] A district of Mazandaran, a province close by the Caspian Sea.

In answer, he said that he had grown to expect a stalwart approach from Iran and it would be undignified for us to act in any other way. 'Yes', I replied, 'a stalwart approach, but for how much longer? "A stalwart approach" requires us to solve the Bahrain question before that of Tunbs and Abu Musa, whilst meanwhile the Sheikhs of Sharjah and Ras al-Khaimah mock us behind our backs. "A stalwart approach" means that we should sit by, politely requesting an increase in our oil revenue while the Libyans see their own income soar and hand the increase straight over to our enemy, Nasser. Again, it's this same "stalwart approach" that forces us to bail out King Faisal's defence budget, effectively making him our pensioner; the same King Faisal who complains about the undue concessions made to Iran the moment the oil companies begin to review quota allocations; and we must put on a dignified front and act as if nothing were amiss. Oh yes, our approach is "stalwart", but why? Why and for how much longer?'

This was meant to hit him where it hurts. I had no alternative. The ambassador is a nice man, but even he was stung into retaliation. 'You can do what you jolly well like', he said, 'but in the end you'll find that it'll be you that come out the losers.' 'Suits me', I said; 'As the saying goes, if we're going to sink we might as well all sink together.' I was so abrupt, but in my heart of hearts there is a very real fear. The treasury is empty, the government is inept and betrays the Shah at every move; what on earth can we do? Nothing, absolutely nothing! The ambassador would have to be soft in the head to be taken in by my threats.

At 9 a.m. the American ambassador and I went through the same routine, though he at least was a little alarmed by the possibility that Iran might renege on the oil agreement and rather than the present 50/50 split, go for a 75 per cent share of profits just as we've negotiated for more recent agreements. On the whole he showed far greater sympathy than his British counterpart. He said that in the forthcoming Tehran conference of American diplomats stationed in the Middle East, his chief intention was to present a full-scale defence of HIM's ideas. In conclusion, he said it would be foolhardy to wreck the one remaining haven of peace and stability in the Middle East.

I then left for my audience in which I gave a detailed account of the problems, suggesting that we should consider independent sales of our oil now that our production capacity has increased. HIM replied that he himself has been thinking along precisely these lines. 'Then we have nothing left to argue about', I replied. But HIM expressed concern that such a move would still fail to boost our income in the immediate term. He was deeply troubled, lost in thought . . .

Sunday, 26 April

HIM was in very high spirits during my audience. He declared that the Americans have abandoned their earlier claim to be unable to extend us credit for military supplies. They have now agreed to meet our Air Force's every need! I congratulated him on this news.

. . . I also suggested to HIM that there may be benefits for us in selling oil to Red China.[1] He instructed me to get Fallah to investigate . . .

Monday, 27 April

The American ambassador called before my morning audience to say that Northrop, AVCO and Douglas, three US companies, are prepared to accept contracts for the servicing of military aircraft in Iran. HIM had been misinformed on this, having been told that no such deal was possible. He asked me to look into the matter. So I must face yet another battle with General Khatami, the Air Force Commander.

I briefed HIM on our forthcoming trip to Shiraz and he instructed me to make sure that Davallou[2] accompanies us. When I objected that this might hurt the feelings of HMQ, he replied that he cannot give way to her every whim . . .

The Crown Prince of Jordan and his Foreign Minister were HIM's guests for lunch . . . Iraq loomed large in our discussions. Jordan resents the Iraqis as bitterly as we do. King Faisal of Iraq was a cousin of King Hussein. His brutal elimination[3] by the current regime has been followed by sympathetic overtures to revolutionary elements in Jordan from amongst the Iraqi army stationed there. Once again I must record grave doubts about King Hussein's future. Not even an Arab–Israeli peace can save him, since Jordan would certainly be overrun by the Palestinians, whose leader Yasser Arafat appears to favour the left . . . After lunch we flew to Shiraz with HIM.

[1] Like many US allies at the time, Iran had yet to give diplomatic recognition to the People's Republic of China.

[2] Amir Houshang Davallou: businessman, related to the Qajar dynasty. Spent his youth in France where his father had taken up residence in the 1930s. In spite of his scant formal education, he was a man of great charm and shrewdness. He was acquainted with the Court thanks to his family connection with General Zahedi and in the 1960s, much to everyone's amazement, became one of the Shah's most intimate friends. His rakish ways and covert dealings did not endear him to those who already had misgivings about the Shah's entourage.

[3] On 4 July 1958 the young King of Iraq and his much-hated uncle, Abdul Ilah, were assassinated as part of a military coup, bringing an end to Iraq's monarchy.

Thursday, 30 April

HIM toured Pahlavi University and various military installations. He was particularly impressed by one or two of the university faculties, above all the College of Agriculture. He requested that local MPs attend our lunch at the Governor's – a gesture that made a great impression. Truly he is blessed with foresight. His every venture is radical and progressive. Someone reading this might well object, 'What's so revolutionary about all that?' But remember the context: the White Revolution is only a few years old. Yet just look at the pleasure shown by these politicians at being invited to lunch with HIM. It's not so long ago that these same people were simple labourers or farmers . . .

Saturday, 2 May

Visited Bushehr. HIM's tea was served cold and he flew into a rage. Returned to Shiraz this afternoon – HIM still in a filthy mood . . . One of the older members of our party is an opium smoker[1] and this evening he offered a pipe to the Shah, saying it would improve his temper. I objected vigorously, pointing out that though far from a kill-joy, I would consider it hypocritical of the Shah of Iran, a ruler who has ordered the execution of drug-smugglers, to smoke opium himself. My remark did nothing to calm HIM's mood, but at least he followed my advice.

We flew back to Tehran . . .

Monday, 4 May

The Oil Consortium's representatives arrived yesterday evening. Should the present talks fail, HIM has ordered a special session of Parliament for the government to present new bills on overlift and the reduction of the agreement area under Consortium management. This is intended to intimidate the oil companies into surrender . . .

At dinner he was in a relaxed mood and made no mention of oil. Once again our conversation turned to that bastard Nasser. HIM admits that he is an intelligent man, though four or five years ago I'd have had my head bitten off for saying the same thing.

The Americans have announced that they are considering supplying Egypt with food aid. As HIM put it, food from the Americans, money from the Arabs and Russian guns – Nasser is a veritable magician.

---

[1] Probably Davallou, whom the Shah had invited on this trip.

[The Shah flew to Izmir, Turkey, on 6 May. The following day, Alam left for Mashad]

Saturday, 9 May

... HMQ arrived in Mashad and went straightaway to pay her respects at the shrine of Imam Reza. From there she went on to tour a leper hospital, which distressed her greatly and sent her off into floods of tears. Precisely the same thing happened a couple of years ago – in all honesty she's deeply compassionate and warm hearted. I suggested to her that tears solve no problems and that the fault lies with the Committee for the Fight Against Leprosy who have failed to discharge their responsibilities. I asked her to allow the Astaneh[1] to finance a new leper hospital in the city. She leaped at the idea. I have determined that it should be the most splendid hospital imaginable, situated at the heart of one of the loveliest spots in Khorassan.

Some years ago the Queen broke down whilst visiting an orphanage in Shiraz. Afterwards I built another orphanage, maintained under the auspices of Pahlavi University. It served as a shining example to the entire country ...

On our flight back to Tehran HMQ asked to see me in private and we spoke for nearly an hour. She is unhappy about the Shah's sisters, and the activities of the rest of his family which she regards as potentially prejudicial to the Crown Prince, her son. Yet she is too nervous to broach the matter with HIM directly and therefore asked me to talk it over with him. Much of what she says is true, but she overlooks the way in which one of her own relatives has employed the family name in pursuit of personal interests. I tried to hint at this, suggesting that nepotism of any sort was almost always to be avoided. Her Majesty echoed this sentiment with perfect sincerity. She still urged me to draw the matter to HIM's attention ... She has a knack of putting her finger on our most serious weaknesses. She was quick to point to the government's lamentable attempts at propaganda, the inadequate attention paid to public opinion and the fact that various government initiatives are no more than superficial window-dressing. As she said, this can only undermine the people's confidence in the establishment ...

She referred to a recent book on Iranian freemasonry which cites virtually every leading official bar myself: PM Hoveyda, Sharif Emami Speaker of

---

[1] Astan-e Qods-e Razavi, the religious and charitable foundation which supervised benefactions made to Reza, eighth Imam of the Muslim Shi'a. Traditionally its trustee was the monarch. Alam supervised the Astaneh's activities on behalf of the Shah.

the Senate, Dr Eqbal Head of the National Oil Company and Mr Riazi the Speaker of the Majlis amongst them. 'One alternative is merely to accept freemasonry', she said, 'but I vote we reject it as undesirable; an instrument in the hands of foreign powers. Those who have thrown in their lot with the masons should be dismissed, every last one of them.'[1]

In general I get the impression that Her Majesty fears for the future, and not without cause. One day her beloved son must ascend the throne. Anything that undermines the present regime poses a threat to his succession. I've long maintained that monarchy accords with our national tradition and will continue to dominate the agenda for centuries to come, but that all the same we must face up to reality. Elsewhere in the world monarchy of any sort, let alone by hereditary right, is in decline. In other words dynastic rule conflicts with common sense; why should the eldest child of a king govern the destiny of an entire nation merely by virtue of his birth? For ceremonial and constitutional purposes fine, but it's a different matter when the king is also chief administrator. Yet in Iran we have no alternative: a king who agreed to a purely symbolic role would be signing his own death warrant. Look what happened to the Qajar dynasty under Ahmad Shah – only one of many examples.[2] It's undeniable that our people have not yet attained maturity, having no practical experience of democracy ...

So far we've been saved by a king who combines vision with intelligence, justice with integrity. We have been truly blessed, yet God has not vouchsafed us this blessing indefinitely. Her Majesty, like the mass of the Iranian people, has good cause to be worried.

Monday, 11 May

A hurried lunch engagement ... Then to the airport to welcome HIM's return. He landed at 3 p.m., in good spirits. We flew by helicopter to the Niavaran Palace. The Queen greeted us and apologized for her failure to come to the airport.

... I mentioned that a group of Naqshbandi[3] Kurds have agreed to 'flee' to Iraq, posing as refugees. Once there they are sure to be received by General Bakhtiar who will be at their mercy. HIM disclosed that we've already managed to infiltrate Bakhtiar's household, although our agents

---

[1] Since many prominent Iranian freemasons in the nineteenth as well as in the twentieth century were Anglophiles, the society was popularly portrayed as a vehicle for British influence in Iran.
[2] The Qajars ruled Iran from 1779 to 1925. The last Qajar King, Ahmad Shah, was deposed by a Constituent Assembly which brought Reza Shah, founder of the Pahlavi dynasty, to power.
[3] Followers of Khaja Mohammad Naqshband (c. 1250), an ascetic mystic from Bukhara.

have so far failed to deliver the goods. Even so he agreed to my scheme *vis-à-vis* the Kurds. The degree of confidence he shows in me is truly flattering.

Tuesday, 12 May

... The UN Security Council endorsed the demand of the majority in Bahrain for full independence. Our own delegate to the UN immediately promised Iranian support. It was most amusing to listen to our local radio announcer reading this news – he did it with such pride that you'd have thought we had just taken Bahrain by storm ...

The unofficial Israeli mission in Tehran celebrated Israel's twenty-second anniversary. HIM forbade anyone from the court or government to attend. For myself, I should have preferred to send some sort of representation, since we do at least maintain a consulate in Israel. But HIM was emphatic. Apparently, in the aftermath of the Islamic conferences at Rabat and Jeddah, he's keen that we should adopt a pro-Arab stand and stress our solidarity with Islam.

Wednesday, 13 May

Audience ... I was able to raise some of the points made in my conversation with HMQ. HIM listened attentively before remarking: 'The Queen is highly sensitive and her words command respect. Even so it's beyond the bounds of possibility to act on every suggestion she makes. She's well-intentioned, but no one could honestly credit her with much experience or patience.'

Monday, 18–Thursday, 21 May

We are currently entertaining the Sheikh of Abu Dhabi and a group of Americans investigating opportunities for investment in Iran. I've also been rushed off my feet by a host of other concerns, the Rapier missile deal, and a proposed purchase of helicopters for the army. Though for the life of me, I can't imagine why it should be me that's made to take charge of such things.

Properly, I should devote all my energies to monitoring public opinion and the general standing of the regime. Why else do I preside over so many committees intended to gauge the people's needs? Why else am I landed with the responsibility of finding ways to satisfy those needs? And yet the only outcome is that HIM rounds on me and accuses me of empire building. According to him I'm usurping the functions of the Information Ministry and other government agencies. When I point out that, left to their own devices, these people deliver nothing but pro-government propaganda, he assures me that he can always rely on the independence of Savak and his special Military Bureau.[1] Goodness only knows to what extent his trust in them is justified, but there is one thing of which I am absolutely sure – HIM is kept in ignorance of the true state of affairs and I am at a loss to know what to do about it. For his own part, he seems quite indifferent or, rather, blithely unaware that information is being withheld. And so, rather than allow me to serve as the nerve-centre of this regime, I'm employed as little more than a clerk, burdened with every triviality that's going.

Friday, 22 May
Went riding this morning ... On HIM's instructions I then summoned the British ambassador ... to pass on a message: 'Should the Sheikhs of Sharjah and Umm al-Quwain make any attempt to drill for oil in the waters around Abu Musa', I said, 'Iran will not baulk at military intervention. Abu Musa is ours and the British must bear in mind that it is we who they will be up against in any attempt to support the Sheikhs. Not that any such Anglo-Iranian confrontation would be without its positive side. It would clear the decks in more ways than one. Iranian pride would be satisfied, and having defeated the British we would be in a position to force the Sheikhs to accept a solution over the islands.'

The ambassador pleaded with me to discourage any confrontation over Abu Musa; if needs be Iran should lodge a written protest. At the same time he would do all within his power to prevent drilling around the island, although Occidental Petroleum has already been granted a concession there by the Sheikh of Sharjah.

Much to my relief he's been as good as his word. The BBC have just announced that all drilling around Abu Musa is to be halted following a dispute between Sharjah and Umm al-Quwain over their respective claims to the continental shelf.

Saturday, 23–Friday, 29 May
Sheikh Rashid of Dubai has been in Tehran and my negotiations with him left me no time for this diary ...

Last Saturday the Queen flew out to Isfahan to inspect various ancient

---

[1] Established in the early 1960s, to examine and evaluate all intelligence and security reports directed to the Shah. It was headed by General Hossein Fardoust.

monuments which have been badly neglected. I suppose we should be thankful that she takes an interest in such matters. Having escorted her to the airport I returned for an audience with HIM. I expressed my surprise that I'd been told nothing of the Queen's trip and had only found out about it by chance. I shall be forced to reprimand her private secretary, whatever the Queen may say. Lately I'm afraid I've been very much out of favour with Her Majesty. HIM laughed. 'But of course' he said, 'it's all quite simple. You and I are very close, and the moment anyone gets close to me they're automatically in the Queen's bad books.' I replied that in her favour or out of it she commands my loyalty as the wife of HIM and mother to the Crown Prince; HIM let the matter drop . . .

Long talk with Harry Kern, the editor of *Foreign Reports* – an American gentleman who took up a great deal of my time. Why oh why are all Americans so naïve? At one point he told me he was overjoyed by the high level of Soviet military aid and their supply of Sam 3 missiles to Egypt – it was a policy sure to bring about peace talks with Israel! He may just have a point after all. At the moment Israel has distinct air superiority over Egypt, but if the Soviets become more closely involved and the Egyptians' performance improves, who knows, it may be Egypt that calls the tune in future. Even so, how much more sensible it would be if the Americans, rather than rejoicing at Soviet intervention, were to insist that Israel take part in negotiations.

Friday, 29 May

. . . Summoned the British ambassador. Told him that HIM feels that Britain hasn't budged an inch over the islands, and he has received two alarming reports: that the British have made contact with General Bakhtiar in Europe, and that Britain lay behind the Kurdish–Iraqi cease-fire.

The ambassador categorically denied the last two points, and his denial seemed quite plausible. With regard to the islands I warned him that his country would forfeit all credibility if there were no new initiative soon. Why, he asked, were we so insistent on the question of legal sovereignty over the islands? Far simpler for us just to occupy them. Solve the issue at one fell swoop. A typically British suggestion, but a suggestion with which I just happen to agree.

I had one other important commission from HIM – to ask the ambassador to intervene on our behalf in extracting a low-interest loan from Kuwait; something in the region of £100 million, to be put towards military and other purchases from the UK.

The Shah is a man of insight, and knows full well when to throw yet another card onto the bargaining table. I cautioned the ambassador that no one except HIM and myself know about these overtures to Kuwait. They will not appear in any official figures of Iranian borrowing. Finally I repeated that we fully contemplate using force to prevent drilling by any third party in the waters around Abu Musa.

Saturday, 30 May
Audience ... Told HIM of an intriguing remark made to me by the Crown Prince of Dubai before his departure; 'We are loyal servants of HIM', he had said, 'Give us guidance.' I added that we needed to prepare several alternative strategies for our policy in the Gulf. If one proves impractical, we shall have others to fall back upon. For example, with respect to the Federation of Emirates, should we adopt a role as the Federation's guardian or seek separate agreements with each of its members? Should we even join the Federation ourselves? All these alternatives must be explored and a proper report submitted to HIM. 'But for the moment', HIM replied, 'our course is set. We shall throw a spanner in their works by forcing every one of the Emirates to conclude and finance separate defence arrangements with Iran.' 'An excellent plan no doubt', I said, 'but we must still explore the alternatives. Apart from anything, can we really expect the Iranian armed forces to assume so vast a responsibility? Is it in our own best interest?' This comment outraged HIM who took it as a slur on the army, but my duty is clear and, at the risk of appearing even more insubordinate, I told him, 'It's unusual to see Your Majesty so upset; but when it comes to the crunch, war and military parades are two quite separate affairs. Your Majesty wishes Iran to become the dominant power in the Gulf. First, however, you should assess the true capacity of your army, and you must assess it with the utmost objectivity.'

Monday, 1 June
... A busy day. Started work at 7 this morning with negotiations over the purchase of Chinook helicopters. HIM has taken a personal interest in the deal. The aircraft themselves are each capable of transporting forty men. Later the British ambassador called round and showed me the text of a letter which his government has sent to the Sheikhs of Umm al-Quwain and Ajman. The Sheikhs are firmly cautioned to desist from all drilling around Abu Musa, ostensibly on the grounds of a claim to the island lodged

by Sharjah. The ambassador was in no position to give me a copy of the letter but its gist was as follows:

1. A third party be invited to settle any differences between Ajman and Umm al-Quwain;
2. No drilling in the area claimed by Sharjah;
3. Caution be exercised by all parties, bearing in mind Iranian interests in the region; Iran's position in respect to Abu Musa to be clarified as soon as possible.

According to the ambassador, 'By playing up the disagreements between the Sheikhs we intend to bring drilling to a halt without the need for armed intervention by Iran. In the meantime we have reminded them all that Britain will withdraw from the Gulf over the coming twelve months, whereafter the Emirates will be left on their own to deal with Iran, a country far stronger than theirs. They are to make no attempt to restart drilling until Iran's claims are settled. However I must advise you that Occidental Petroleum is bringing great pressure to bear, in the hope of opening up exploratory drilling.' To this I replied that Iran has no particular interest in Abu Musa's oil resources; we wish to use the island merely as a military base, a function which should not necessarily interfere with the interests of the oil men. 'Yet', I said, 'several Sheikhs who have visited the Court tell us that Britain is encouraging them to put off any settlement with Iran, in direct contravention of your promise to foster a solution.' The ambassador denied this allegation, saying 'You know what liars these Arabs are.' 'Oh yes', I said, 'the Arabs, the British; liars one and all.' He laughed ...

Tuesday, 2 June
We learned this morning of the death of Ayatollah Hakim, the great Shi'i leader resident in Iraq. The news kept me busy until mid-afternoon. In all I must have had at least ten separate interviews with HIM; to work out various points of mourning; should HIM take part, and so on ... HIM's messages of condolence on the death of the Grand Ayatollahs have always been read as containing broad hints over the favoured succession. It's a nice tradition, generally accepted, and one which excites a great deal of interest. In this instance HIM instructed me to send the telegram to Ayatollah Shariat Madari[1] in Qom. I was forced to point out that he's not

---

[1] Kazem Shariat Madari, one of the Grand Ayatollahs; a moderate with many followers, particularly in his native province of Azerbaijan. He played a key role in the first stages of the

a cleric who commands much respect amongst the public at large. 'It's Ayatollah Khonsari[1] who has the greatest popularity', I said. 'Your Majesty well knows that the leading Ayatollahs of the past ... were extremely virtuous, with not a thought for money and material gain. Integrity should be the paramount virtue of any great Shi'i leader.' I then went on to relate an incident I'd witnessed as PM. After crushing the clergy, I put out feelers to various of the Ayatollahs with a view to some limited degree of co-operation. In response, this selfsame Ayatollah Shariat Madari suggested that I give him a provisional advance of $80,000; he would contact me again in future if he found there was anything that could be done. 'Fair enough', HIM interrupted, 'but all the same he's a loyal man, perfectly harmless.' 'Perhaps', I said, 'but that's not to say that he commands the people's respect.' After I'd hammered away for some time, HIM gave way and authorized me to send two copies of the telegram of condolence: one to Shariat Madari and the other to Khonsari.

Subsequently news came through that the campus of Pahlavi University in Shiraz has erupted in turmoil. I spent the rest of the day passing on hourly bulletins to HIM.

Wednesday, 3 June

... Our Minister of Foreign Affairs Zahedi has returned from Jordan where his principal objective was to demonstrate Iranian–Arab friendship. However, being a pushy, ambitious sort of fellow, he turned the whole trip into an exercise in self-publicity. Now he's gone right over the top and announced that Jordan is to act as a mediator, helping to re-establish diplomatic relations between Iran and Egypt. What an utter genius the man must be! For the past nine years we've been saying that the only thing standing in the way of a reconciliation with Cairo is Egypt's refusal to issue us with an apology. And yet here we are on our hands and knees begging Jordan to have the goodness to act as go-between. What a magnificent achievement for our Foreign Minister!

---

revolution, advocating a democratic, constitutional government. He was outmanoeuvred by Ayatollah Khomeini who regarded him as a potential rival, managing to rob him of his title and religious authority.

[1] Although favoured at Court, Ayatollah Khonsari commanded only a limited following, chiefly amongst the business class of Tehran.

Saturday, 6 June

Audience ... HIM in authoritative mood: 'Resummon the British and American ambassadors', he said. 'Tell them what cowards they are; that if they can't be bothered to look after the interests of Iran, at least they should have a care for their own countries. Why won't they up our production of oil? Libya's output has been reduced by 200,000 barrels a day and what with sabotage and the dispute with Syria, even the Trans-Arabian pipeline is unable to meet its daily export quota of half a million barrels. Iranian production should be increased to meet the shortfall.' I did my best to explain that the companies operating in Iran are to be distinguished from those at work in Libya and Saudi Arabia but he would have none of it. 'The West still needs our oil', he said, 'and as for the companies, they can always come to some sort of arrangement among themselves.' ...

Monday, 8 June

... This evening, a dinner thrown in my honour by the American ambassador. Following HIM's instructions, I asked why the USA has granted a special oil import quota to Venezuela. Surely we'd been promised that such privileges were available to no one? The ambassador replied that Venezuela lay in the Western hemisphere, that it was a Latin American country and as such enjoyed a special relationship with the USA ... He went on to make an after dinner speech to which, though exhausted, I had no choice but to respond.

Tuesday, 9 June

Audience ... During the recent memorial service for Ayatollah Hakim I met up with an elderly merchant from the bazaar. I passed on something of our conversation to HIM. The old man was indignant about various examples of official incompetence, and lamented the fact that there was no one in the administration to whom he could take his complaints. For example, that the intercity bus station has been removed from the city centre to the outskirts of Tabriz so that the poorer passengers, peasants and the like, must now walk into town or else pay for an expensive taxi ride. His basic point was that nobody gives a damn for the people's woes. HIM replied that the bus station had been moved solely to make life easier for the inhabitants of Tabriz. 'But at the expense of the travelling public', I said. 'I should like your permission to ask that the matter be looked into by the government.' I followed this up by suggesting that HIM do more to gauge public opinion: 'From time to time, why don't you summon representatives from all walks of life, ordinary people, off the streets, and question them about their cares and concerns. I'm sure you'd obtain a fascinating response.' 'But I already know what the people think', he replied, 'I'm fed report after report from goodness knows how many sources.' I pointed out that such reports are calculated merely to set his mind at rest; to tell him only what he wants to hear. This went down very badly; his secretariat, he said, vetted every single report for its reliability. 'Fair enough', I replied, 'but even so, why shouldn't Your Majesty broaden his horizons a little; listen to some fresh voices rather than have me droning on at you day after day?' He countered this by referring to the *Salaams* where he can always ask for people's opinions. 'But just think how seldom we hold a *Salaam*', I said, 'and bear in mind that those who attend are generally too scared out of their wits to voice any sort of complaint. There are always several hundred people in attendance. Remember that poor businessman at Bushehr; he had the audacity to mention the delays in constructing the new harbour. You, Your Majesty, were so outraged by the affair that you made life miserable for the rest of the day. Even I, your poor servant, was unable to reason with you. And yet you expect people to speak out publicly in a *Salaam*; to open their hearts to you and tell you their troubles? Even if Your Majesty were able to stomach such plain-speaking, the government agencies would.be down on the plaintiff like a ton of bricks. I'm sure that Your Majesty knows the state of play far better than I do, and the likely reaction from within the government.' He greeted these remarks in silence, but all the same I got the impression that their sincerity had hit home. Within the next few days I'm confident that he'll issue instructions to get things moving along the lines I suggest.

Three hours this afternoon with the British ambassador. I did not mince my words over the Emirates but asked him straight out, 'Whose side are you really on? We can never forgive you your audacity. Why permit the Sheikhs to travel throughout the Arab world, spreading even greater misunderstanding in respect to the islands? What do you hope to achieve? When they come to Tehran nothing ever happens, beyond an exchange of diplomatic niceties. Why won't you lend a hand? Again I tell you, the islands will be ours come what may.' 'And I tell you', he said, 'that we shall answer force with force to defend the islands.' 'You can do as you please', I replied. 'Even without their strategic importance, they mean a great deal to the Iranian people, and you cannot trifle with public opinion. We have already abandoned Bahrain. Now you expect us to do the same over the islands. Later perhaps, we'll be called upon to give way to the Arab nationalists over Khuzistan.[1] You are courting disaster, and I am bound, as a friend, to give you all due warning. Your promises have proved false once too often.' Responding to this tirade, he confessed that he's been so upset over the past fortnight that he's had difficulty sleeping. 'I'm at a loss to know what I should tell you, or what I should report to London', he said, 'and for that matter London is at its wits' end knowing what to say to the Sheikhs. We're all of us in the soup.' He confided one final point before leaving: 'Following representations from Iraq, the Soviet ambassador came to tell me that I'd be ill-advised to contemplate an Iranian takeover in the islands. So much, you see, for the friendship between Iran and her so-called comrades in the North!' I felt so ill after he'd left that I was forced to take to my bed with a temperature of 104 degrees. And here I've languished for the past three days.

Tuesday, 16 June
I rather froze the atmosphere of this morning's audience by reporting that Princess Shahnaz now demands an account of her private assets. HIM forbade me to transfer any funds to her.

Audience for Sheikh Khalifa, the Prime Minister of Bahrain, who subsequently attended lunch. He's closely related to his sovereign, Sheikh Issa. In all he struck me as being intelligent and well-informed; his English is quite superb ...

Wednesday, 17 June
This morning, discussions over the telecommunications network, followed by an audience. I was forced to report that the requirements of the military have pushed up the network's projected cost from $130 million to $200 million.

The Pakistani ambassador wants an audience with HIM; he says that Israel has failed to deliver the anti-tank guns which his country purchased through our own good offices. 'But what else does he expect', said HIM, 'when Pakistan is openly provoking the Israelis?'

---

[1] Since parts of Khuzistan are the homeland of various Arab tribes, immigrants there in the eighteenth century, Arab nationalists refer to it as Arabistan and claim it as Arab territory.

Friday, 19 June

Rode with my love for two hours this morning. All very pleasant despite the heat.

A visit from the British ambassador. He admitted that he had been unable to dissuade the Sheikh of Ras al-Khaimah from travelling to Baghdad: 'But we are pressing him and the Sheikh of Sharjah to accept a solution to the problem of the islands in line with the Iranian proposal for joint occupation. We have stressed to them that this is a rare opportunity, a genuine prospect of a settlement thanks to the magnanimity of Iran.' Like HIM the ambassador is convinced that the British withdrawal from the Gulf has already gone too far to be reversed.

Reported these discussions at lunch. HIM commented, 'We must still be on our guard. The Sheikhs may seek an agreement over the islands with one of the foreign oil companies. For us to ignore such a deal would be an implicit admission that they have a valid claim.' ...

Saturday, 20 June

Audience ... HIM gave instructions for me to summon the US ambassador, to spell out our alarm over the present situation in the Middle East. 'What if the regime in Jordan were to fall and be replaced by communists?', he said. 'Where would that leave Saudi Arabia? The situation there is already chaotic. When King Faisal and his court move out to Ta'if for the summer, communications with the outside world are more or less severed. With the existence or the threat of communist regimes in Jordan, in North and South Yemen, the Saudis will find themselves encircled. How can they defend themselves, and what will happen to the Gulf? Day by day Iran must shoulder ever heavier responsibilities. Put this to the ambassador. Tell him that the USA might at the very least advise the Oil Consortium to increase our oil output by the 800,000 barrels a day that are being lost by shortfalls in Libyan and Saudi Arabian production.'

On a separate issue HIM has been delighted by a letter from President Nixon, sent in response to the joint communiqué issued on 7 May by HIM, President Sunay of Turkey and Yahya Khan of Pakistan, the three heads of state of the RCD [Regional Cooperation for Development] countries, following their meeting in Izmir. 'Tell the ambassador', HIM continued, 'that his President has the good sense to appreciate the extent of Soviet intervention in the Middle East. But tell him also that I shall think twice before publishing Nixon's letter. In the midst of US–Soviet negotiations over the region it might be more prudent to keep the thing under wraps.'[1]

Sunday, 21 June
Audience ... Reported yet another representation from the Israeli envoy in Tehran who came to me to complain over our pro-Arab stance. 'As I see it', I said, 'we should avoid too much contact with the Arabs. We may share the one faith of Mohammed, but the Arabs are Arabs first and foremost; Islam they regard as a secondary consideration, a sort of extension to Arab nationalism.' HIM remains keen to stress our common interests, but as I pointed out, common interests have always been so much moonshine to the Arabs.

Monday, 22 June
Their Majesties have left on a state visit to Finland and Romania ... My wife went with them as lady-in-waiting to the Queen. I shall miss her about the house. If only women would be more tactful, we'd never grow tired of them. Yet they're too inclined to make one's life a misery, and then all hell breaks loose ...

Saturday 27–Tuesday, 30 June
After a great deal of toing and froing, my lover, a few friends and I set out for the Lar valley[2] to fish for trout ... We'd been there only forty-eight hours when I fell sick and had to be flown back to Tehran. I'm now confined to bed.

News has reached me that HIM is outraged that so little publicity was devoted to his gift of Marmar Palace[3] to the city of Tehran. The building was worth a fortune and could only have been given away by someone of the Shah's incredible generosity. I tried to point this out to him, that the

---

[1] Presumably a reference to the following paragraph in Nixon's letter of 19 June: 'The expression of your concern is particularly welcome at this time, in view of the recently increased military involvement of the Soviet Union in the Arab–Israeli dispute. In contrast, the US has acted with restraint in the hope that it would be reciprocated. We deeply regret that this has not been the case. The implications of Soviet involvement for the entire region of the Middle East are a matter of serious concern for all of us.'

[2] North-east of Tehran, dominated by Mount Damavand, a beautiful extinct volcano, at 5,670m. the highest peak in Iran.

[3] The Marmar Palace, in the centre of Tehran, was built by Reza Shah. Covered with white marble (*marmar* in Persian), it is arguably the most beautiful palace of its age. It served as the Shah's office and for various official functions. After 1965 and an unsuccessful attempt on the Shah's life by a member of the Imperial Guard, it fell out of use.

gesture was so sincere and so immense that it was advertisement enough in itself, but this did nothing to appease him.

Their Majesties' state tour ends today and they fly on for a private visit to the Netherlands. In Romania they were received with such enthusiasm that the whole of Iran can take pride in their triumph. What with visits from the Shah, and earlier from President Nixon, Romania is showing that she has thrown off the Soviet yoke ...

Friday, 10 July

... At two this afternoon HIM arrived back in Tehran via Brussels, seemingly in excellent shape. We were alone for dinner ... stayed until midnight ...

In Brussels HIM was delighted by his meeting with the new British Foreign Secretary, Sir Alec Douglas-Home. They discussed the Persian Gulf and the problems in respect to the islands. The British ambassador had previously been recalled for consultations in London and I rather think it may have been he who arranged the meeting ...

Saturday, 11 July

... Brief audience ... At dinner I was able to inform HIM that we have reached a deal with Occidental Petroleum, allowing us to barter up to 200,000 barrels of oil a day in return for military hardware. In addition Northrop Page, the US conglomerate, has put in a bid for 3 million tons of our oil per annum to be exchanged for US goods. HIM was over the moon. 'It's always been the Iranian way', he said, 'as soon as one door is slammed in our face, God ensures that a new one opens' ... HIM is truly a man of God, yet his trust in the Almighty makes him a fatalist giving him the confidence to take too many risks. But how is one to curb the convictions of a king? Long and varied experiences have cast him in this mould.

Monday, 13 July

The British ambassador called round at 8 this morning. I told him how pleased HIM had been at his meeting with the British Foreign Secretary. Yet actions speak louder than words and the British have still to prove their good intentions. There can be no way forward until the issue of the islands has been solved. If the British refuse to act, then it is we that shall be forced to make the running by resorting to military occupation. The ambassador replied that, whilst he fully appreciates the depth of Iranian feeling over the matter, he regards a military solution as being unlikely to cause anything but harm to our standing in the Persian Gulf. Even so, I told him, the strength of public opinion is not to be denied; we cannot go on forever presenting our people with nothing but defeat.

Saturday, 15 August

... Dinner at the Queen Mother's in Shahdasht, where we ate sitting at a round table. I was placed directly opposite HIM and could tell that there was something troubling him; he was thoroughly ill at ease. I know only too well what's been going on in Baghdad. Various of our agents were infiltrated into General Teymour Bakhtiar's household. They persuaded him to go hunting with them, and one of them, a man whom the general considered utterly reliable, managed to put a bullet in him. But the blasted man refuses to die. Perhaps it's God's will; Bakhtiar must suffer excruciating pain just a little longer, but die he must in the end. In his day he was the most ruthless and ambitious of men, but even I must admit that he didn't lack for courage ... Hassan al-Bakr, the Iraqi President, is said to have visited him in hospital on three separate occasions.

Friday, 21 August

Cancelled my ride to attend an audience from 12 to 2 p.m., followed by lunch. I asked HIM whether he had granted his consent for Princess Shahnaz to marry Jahanbani. Only after she'd plagued him with requests, he said, and even then he has made it plain that Jahanbani can never be received at Court.

I passed on Dr Fallah's report on marketing strategies for Iranian oil. HIM said, 'At the moment we can exercise only limited supervision over oil negotiations when they take place abroad. Instruct the government that all such negotiations must be carried out in Iran. Also, tell Fallah that I shall withhold his leave until he's finalized the deals with Cuba, South Africa and the Northrop company.'

A visit from the British ambassador; on HIM's instructions I told him that various rumours were circulating about General Bakhtiar; that until recently he'd been living under British protection. Most people agree that he was in the pay of the British; some suggest that it was actually the British who killed him when his usefulness expired. Never before have I seen the ambassador so outraged. 'It's almost as if we were being accused of propping up the Ba'athist regime in Iraq', he exploded. As it happened this was precisely the accusation that I'd been instructed to put to him.

Turning to the question of the islands the ambassador announced that London has appointed a special representative to help find a solution, a man named Sir William Luce, formerly British Political Resident in the Persian Gulf. He has accepted the job on one condition; that he has full power to explore every road to a settlement and to ignore any decisions that may already have been made. The Conservative government has agreed to this and now admit that their pledge to halt withdrawal from the Persian Gulf was nothing more than a publicity stunt, designed to win them votes in the general election. The ambassador also told me that the Sheikhs of Sharjah and Ras al-Khaimah look to Saudi Arabia to encourage an understanding with Iran, but that the Saudis have so far washed their hands of the matter.

Finally I brought up the possibility of bartering Iranian oil for British military equipment. The ambassador declared that Britain was almost unique amongst the western nations in having no great need for oil; what they want first and foremost is hard currency. At the same time he was concerned that we are now demanding that our production be increased by 400,000 barrels a day; surely our original demand to the Consortium had been for an increase of only half that much?

... Egypt is at odds with Iraq and has announced that she wishes to resume diplomatic relations with Iran. We've got our way without any sort of grovelling or boot-licking ...

Monday, 24 August
Bakhtiar has died at last, and at this morning's audience I was able to report what a deep impression this has made on the public. Many are delighted to see the back of such a ruthless man, but they are just as impressed by the awesome power of HIM's security forces. It's even claimed that the two young men who hijacked an Iranair jet a few weeks ago were secretly working for Savak as part of the operation to kill Bakhtiar. HIM was amused by this and said, 'Despite being utter nonsense, it's worth our while to keep the rumour alive. Remember the hidden hand of the old British Empire; we too can become a byword for secret influence.' 'Fine', I said, 'but will Your Majesty please allow me to improve your personal security arrangements? At the moment you are completely at the mercy of your guards. They're good men, but we live in a world of unpleasant surprises. Four years ago, remember, it was one of your own guards that made an attempt on your life.' This sparked off an hour-long argument. HIM will never admit that an organization he himself has

created can be anything but totally reliable. Eventually he gave in to my request and agreed that I might get Savak to check up on the members of the Imperial Guard, unsupervised by military intelligence. I am greatly relieved ...

Friday, 28 August

... Lately HMQ's attitude towards me has grown perceptibly cooler. I find her a difficult woman to fathom. Of course she regards me as being far too close to HIM and she's probably caught wind of various of our escapades ... She's basically well intentioned and I'm sorry to find her so unkind; one day perhaps she will come to appreciate my sincerity.

... The PM expressed grave concern over our financial situation. 'The government budget may be enormous', I told him, 'but that can't excuse any sort of waste or luxury. I find it quite astonishing, for example, that the Minister of Foreign Affairs has purchased 900 Vacheron et Constantin watches, merely as gifts.' The PM held forth about his trials and tribulations, but I reminded him that he has only himself to blame. He's too easily swayed by his own ministers ... he can't please everybody all of the time. 'Bear in mind', I said, 'if the economy gets out of hand it will be you that will bear the blame. Just think, the Tunisians sentenced their own Minister of Planning to forced labour; a man who had been in office for a decade but failed to make progress. Ultimately there's no one above the law. Just make sure that you don't end up in a similar situation.' This rattled him; he is clearly terrified that I might make the same suggestion to HIM.

Saturday, 29 August

Audience ... HMQ has expressed doubts over our competence to organize the forthcoming celebrations of 2,500 years of monarchy. She's keen to find a role for herself in their planning, but I told HIM this was not without its risks. 'Clearly she has a right to be concerned', I said, 'but can you please ensure that whatever she tries to do she does it through me. Otherwise goodness knows what sort of mess we might end up with. I'm not claiming for one moment that I'm better than my colleagues, but too many cooks spoil the broth and Her Majesty's entourage is not exactly lacking in potential troublemakers.' HIM was in full agreement. I then showed him samples I've had made up of commemorative books and gifts to be given out to the guests, and scale models of the tents which are to be built by the French artist, Jansen ...

Today came the official announcement that diplomatic relations between Egypt and Iran have been resumed[1] ...

Sunday, 30 August

This morning HIM declared, 'The Egyptians are really crawling on their hands and knees; they're even proposing a joint initiative to decide the fate of the Gulf.' 'At the risk of seeming impertinent', I replied, 'I see things in a rather different light. For the past ten years Your Majesty has stood out on the principle of no reconciliation with the Egyptians until they issue us with an apology. But now here we are, still waiting for our apology, and dependent on Turkey and Jordan as mediators between Tehran and Cairo ... What's worse, their mediation made not the slightest bit of difference until Egypt started falling out with the Iraqis; only then did she turn towards reconciliation with Iran, for the sole reason that she hopes it will put pressure on Iraq. It's Egypt that holds the initiative, not us. Finally, Your Majesty has all along ruled out any question of interference in the Gulf except by countries bordering the coast. Can you honestly regard Egypt's proposed involvement as a gesture flattering to Iran?' HIM greeted this in stony silence. I felt more than a little ashamed of myself ...

The Hungarian ambassador has brought me a letter from Walter Ulbricht, Secretary-General of the East German Communist Party, to be delivered to HIM. It's an appeal for diplomatic recognition by Iran and amongst other justifications cites Ulbricht's recent meeting with the West German Chancellor.

Late in the evening I received a visit from the British Chargé d'Affaires; his ambassador is away at the moment. He notified me that the British reject HIM's proposal to barter £500 million of oil over ten years in return for military equipment and a plant to manufacture tanks. He regrets that his government refuses to become involved in deals over oil. I was greatly put out and dismissed him less than politely ...

Monday, 31 August

I had invited General Fardoust to breakfast, and for two hours we discussed ways to put the entire Imperial Guard under Savak surveillance. Fardoust is a loyal friend of HIM besides being deputy director of Savak.

Audience ... HIM was unimpressed by Ulbricht's letter and asked me

---

[1] Relations had been broken for a decade at Nasser's initiative, following a speech in which he castigated the Shah's public affirmation that since 1949 Iran had granted *de facto* recognition to Israel.

to call in the Hungarian ambassador: 'Tell him he should be ashamed of himself, acting as messenger-boy to a nation which openly supports Iraq and denies our claims in the Shatt al-Arab.'

I reported on my meeting with the British ... HIM said, 'When the ambassador returns, tell him I've just heard an Oxford professor, interviewed by the BBC, describe Khuzistan as an Arab homeland. Tell him how grateful I am for this fascinating piece of information.'

Tuesday, 1 September
Brief audience and was then driven to the airport to greet Sardar Shah Vali Khan, son-in-law of the King of Afghanistan, who has come here together with his wife and daughter, ostensibly as a guest of Prince Gholam Reza. In fact his visit enables us to discuss matters of common interest. He commands the troops in Kabul and is hence the most powerful single individual in Afghanistan. Protocol debars the Minister of Court from welcoming mere princes, but in this instance HIM made an exception. Not only did I greet him at the airport but tomorrow I must throw a lunch in his honour.

The US ambassador called round this afternoon. I told him how grateful HIM was that he had travelled to Washington in person to arrange matters with Exim; they have advanced us $200 million to be spent on defence procurement. As I told him, this is sufficient to pay the advance we owe for transport planes, but we still need to find the money to pay for two squadrons of F4s and a further seven Phantoms as attrition reserve. No such funds are available here and we must look to another loan from Exim, or to a foreign military sales bill laid before Congress. Even better, the Oil Consortium at its October meeting might increase Iranian production by 800,000 barrels. This would solve more or less all our problems. The ambassador laughed: 'First you talk about an increase of 200,000; then 400,000, and now you've once more doubled your demand', he said. 'Where exactly will the matter end?' I pointed out that we were merely asking that the shortfall in Libyan output be added to our own production and that in his letter to Nixon three months ago HIM had mentioned precisely this figure of 800,000 barrels.

For our telecommunications project we've hired an American consultant, formerly a government official under President Johnson. The ambassador warned me that the man is a crook and we would be well advised to have nothing more to do with him ...

Wednesday, 9 September
Audience ... We discussed a whole range of issues touching upon Soviet policy towards the Middle East; the Cuban missiles crisis, Bay of Pigs, Kennedy's assassination, the impending election in Chile which may force a military *coup d'état*. 'For all its apparent tolerance, the USA maintains a peculiar balance between the forces of capitalism and democracy', said HIM. 'To achieve this I feel sure that the country is guided by some hidden force; an organization working in secrecy, powerful enough to dispose of the Kennedys and of anyone else who gets in its way; so far I believe it has claimed upwards of thirty victims: people who had somehow come to guess of its existence.' ...

Friday, 11 September
Went riding this morning with my two companions, beautiful girls both of them, but no real substitute for my love. HIM arrived by helicopter at about eleven, ostensibly to take a look at a couple of stallions we have had brought over from England. Really though he was more interested in being introduced to the girls. For myself I preferred the horses.

Saturday, 12 September
... The Queen flew to open the annual Congress of the Medical Association in Ramsar. In her absence HIM and I arranged a rather special little outing of our own, prior to a tour of the new installations at *Ettela'at* at 6.30 this evening. But at noon I was informed that the Queen would return to Tehran two hours earlier than expected. I warned HIM that she might wish to accompany us to *Ettela'at*,[1] but he thought this most unlikely and our jaunt went ahead as planned. Meanwhile of course the Queen made up her mind to join us, but try as she might she could get no response on the telephone. Fortunately I was aware of what was going on, and one way or another managed to get HIM to *Ettela'at* a few minutes before the Queen turned up. A lucky escape, but I'm sure she must have smelled a rat even if she didn't know exactly what to make of it.

Monday, 14 September
Audience ... 'You must tell the American ambassador', said HIM, 'that the credits offered by Exim are inadequate to meet our needs as set out by the joint US–Iranian commission on military procurement. Unless an

[1] One of the two principal Tehran evening papers.

alternative is forthcoming we shall have no choice but to turn to the Soviets for the bulk of our purchases. To us it hardly matters whether our weapons are made in the USA or in Russia. It's not as if we're ever going to wage war against the Soviets; our arsenal is needed for Iraq and the Gulf. Indeed, there are positive financial advantages to a deal with Russia. We can simply offset the cost of Russia's arms against the value of her gas imports.' On a different matter altogether he pointed out that the Queen and my wife are away today at the opening of an architects' conference in Isfahan. 'They will be gone until late', he said. 'I shall come to your house for lunch and bring a few "friends".'

Everything went well; our 'lunch' was somewhat extended and HIM didn't leave until 6 this evening. I hurried off to the airport to greet the Queen ...

Wednesday, 16 September

... Princess Ashraf is to head the Iranian delegation to this year's meeting of the UN General Assembly, much to the disgust of Foreign Minister Zahedi who bears a grudge against the Princess, blaming her for his divorce from Princess Shahnaz. I warned HIM that I am finding it impossible to steer between the two factions; 'Your Majesty must either get the Princess to withdraw from the mission or tell Ardeshir to keep his mouth shut.' 'Tell Ardeshir to stop this nonsense and give her the help she needs', he replied.

... Later I summoned Ardeshir to bash some sense into his head. He was not at all pleased.

Tuesday, 22 September

Audience ... I reported my meeting with Luce who had asked me to explain a comment of HIM's. What did he mean when he said that Iran would have no objection to a British presence in the Persian Gulf provided that it came on the basis of a bilateral agreement with the Sheikhs? 'Firstly', said HIM, 'the Emirates must become independent; only then can they negotiate any sort of agreement. A pre-condition of their gaining independence is a complete withdrawal by foreign powers from the Persian Gulf. If the newly formed Federation of Emirates was subsequently to invite the British to return, that would be quite another matter' ...

Sunday, 27 September

Audience ... We discussed HIM's family. Princess Shahnaz is behaving more to his liking ... On the other hand HM the Queen Mother continues to complain that she is neglected by HIM. I sympathize with his dilemma; as he said, 'What more does she expect me to do?' She claims that her monthly allowance is inadequate, although I know for a fact that she lacks for nothing in the way of comfort.

Monday, 28 September

... Audience ... HMQ telephoned in the midst of this and HIM told me to listen in to their conversation. She was holding forth about the Key Club and the police raid there two nights ago. The club was suspected of being a centre for drug dealing and the police were perfectly justified in closing it down, especially since the proprietor was a member of Princess Ashraf's set and gossip had begun to spread. HIM went so far as to express himself delighted by the raid and personally commended the chief of police for taking a stand against a den of hippy decadence. But it's now become apparent that the police went much too far. They not only raided the club but cordoned off the surrounding streets, arresting anyone with long hair, artists, painters and even a few university professors; carting them off to have their heads shaved. HMQ had telephoned to explain the situation, but HIM replied that it was lies, all damned lies, which made her only more indignant. HIM then turned to me for support and I was forced to admit that the Queen's account was perfectly correct and that I'd been on the point of reporting the matter myself when she called. The Shah was furious and demanded that I issue a statement condemning the police's behaviour. As for the chief of police, HIM sacked him then and there; a gesture which was well received amongst the public. Several people phoned me to express their approval.

For all that she is an impulsive sentimentalist, one must admit that the Queen is a moderating influence, complicating many issues by her intervention, but calming as many as she inflames. Long may her influence be felt; a valuable safeguard against the abuse of power. She alone has the ability to open HIM's eyes to the truth. In this respect I run her a very poor second, but I do at least try my best to be truthful, which is more than can be said for anyone else at court.

Tuesday, 29 September–Saturday, 17 October

Over the past fortnight my eyes have been too sore to enable me to write
... On 29 September, early in the morning, I was listening to the BBC
World Service when Nasser's death was announced; a shot out of the blue.
I telephoned HIM who had already been told the news ... Found him
tremendously buoyed up, as he might well be given that one of his greatest
rivals has vanished once and for all ...

Subsequently I accompanied HIM on a tour of Kermanshah and
Hamedan. HIM is truly under the protection of Almighty God. As we
were coming in to land there was a tremendous thud and the jet which he
himself was piloting jolted violently. Later he explained to me that our
landing gear had hit the airfield perimeter fence, an obstacle which he had
failed to see. I replied that certain pilots had no right even to enter a
cockpit, but he simply grinned at me ...

From Hamedan we went on to Birjand; the whole royal family together
with seventy guests. There on 14 October we celebrated the birthday of
HMQ. I myself had obtained the finest chefs in the world, flown in specially
from Maxim's in Paris. The meals I served were splendid affairs, truly fit
for a king ... and over the two days' celebrations I must have spent
altogether something approaching $40,000. The reception on the second
night I laid on at my country estate, seven kilometres from the main
residence. HIM was ferried there by car, but HMQ, the royal children and
virtually all of the guests travelled on camels. It was a moonlit night and
along the route I'd stationed folk musicians to serenade us. For the
reception itself I'd had fifty tents erected. In front of them danced the local
peasants, touched by the glow of camp fires. The whole scene was so
enchanting that HMQ leaped up and linked hands with the peasant women
in their dance. One by one the royal children and I followed suit – an
evening of pure magic. And then there was the unforgettable way in which
the people of Birjand greeted the Crown Prince; I was moved to tears ...

Sunday, 18 October

Audience ... According to HIM the Egyptian Foreign Minister has made
a speech to the United Nations containing a bitter attack against the USA.
The Minister later spoke on the telephone to Nixon who hopes for an
improvement in Egyptian–US relations. HIM himself is amazed by the
President's attitude and asked me why on earth we didn't follow the
Egyptian lead, and voice our grievances against America. 'To do so', I told
him, 'would be beneath Your Majesty's dignity. The Egyptians are mere

adventurers and we would be wrong to follow their example.' HIM replied that he only wished the US ambassador were here to listen to my remarks. 'Libya', he said, 'got all she wanted by threatening the oil companies. They upped the price of her oil without doing anything to slow her production.' This I agreed with, although I reminded HIM that something might still be done to revise the present 50/50 profit-sharing formula with the companies. If this went ahead it would have repercussions throughout the Middle East. We must put even more pressure on the Oil Consortium. HIM then announced that the Consortium's representatives are due to meet in Tehran on 8 November.

Tuesday, 20 October–Saturday, 21 November
My eyes are still sore and once again I have had to take a break from writing. I must now do my best to set down a résumé of the events of the past few weeks.

... With HIM I travelled to Isfahan where he opened the new dam dedicated to Shah Abbas the Great ... There we were joined by HMQ. Over dinner that night she announced that one of the weekly magazines, in describing her birthday celebrations at Birjand, claims that the birthday cake alone cost £200. This, she said, was a dreadful thing for the papers to print, but also an appalling example of extravagance. All of this was said in the presence of the PM and myself, but HIM did not hesitate to pour scorn on her complaints. 'I won't stand for this sort of kowtowing to popular opinion', he told her. 'In Birjand you seemed more than content. Indeed you swallowed that blasted cake with what can only be described as relish. Yet the moment the papers print some such nonsense, you come over all humble and start moaning on about extravagance.' In some ways it pleased me to hear HIM say this, but at the same time I felt more than a little sheepish about it; the PM was there and, after all, it was I that arranged the celebrations in Birjand. HMQ likewise seemed thoroughly embarrassed.

At about this time we obtained a breakthrough in the Tehran oil talks and the profit-sharing formula has been altered in our favour from 50/50 to 55/45. It was also agreed to revise oil prices ... One incident during the course of these negotiations seems well worth recording. The British ambassador called on me and announced that he strongly advised us against breaking off negotiations with the companies. I passed this message on to HIM who, for all that he is generally restrained and well-tempered, could barely contain his fury. 'The British advise me' ... he said. 'If they have the fucking audacity to advise me ever again, I shall fuck them so rigid that they'll think twice before crossing my path in future.' On a similar note, a few weeks ago when we were on Kish Island, the subject of Tunbs and Abu Musa cropped up and HIM declared: 'If need be we'll take them by force, and the Arabs and British can go fuck themselves.' Such self-confidence is a source of very real pride.

... Following the death of De Gaulle, HIM decided to attend the memorial service in person. I had only fifteen hours in which to arrange things and myself accompanied HIM to Paris. It was good that we made the effort since the service was attended by about seventy heads of state including Nixon, and Podgorny from the USSR ...

Sunday, 22 November

Audience ... I reported that Zahedi, Minister of Foreign Affairs, is unhappy with his Deputy, Khalatbary.[1] The latter had been given a signed photograph of HIM as a token of esteem, but Zahedi has had it removed from Khalatbary's office. This news enraged HIM who instructed me to tell Khalatbary to regain possession of the portrait and to warn Zahedi not to be such an ass in future.

We discussed Princess Ashraf and agreed that she stands little chance of being elected President of the United Nations General Assembly.

Monday, 23 November

... HIM commutes by helicopter between the Niavaran and the Saadabad Palaces. As a security precaution I ordered an investigation into everybody living within a 1 kilometre radius around the two compounds. The results are incredible. In both cases there were literally dozens of local residents who were either ex-army officers sacked for their communist affiliations, or else related to those who were executed for the rebellion against land reform. My report came as just as much of a shock to HIM. 'I must commend your initiative', he said, 'but what the hell do Savak, the police and even my guards think they're playing at?' I told him that it was God alone that protects him, no thanks to any human agency.

Since Princess Ashraf stands no chance of being made President of the UN General Assembly she's taken it into her head to be made Iranian permanent representative to the United Nations. 'My sister gets crazier

---

[1] Abbas Ali Khalatbary, a kindly, unambitious diplomat who became Minister of Foreign Affairs in 1971 and was executed shortly after the revolution in 1979.

and crazier', said HIM. 'It's the menopause that's done it. She's satisfied her greed for money but now she's prey to these foolish delusions. Does she expect me to put an individual's fantasy above the national interest? If she had an ounce of administrative talent, I would have been more than ready to consider her request, but because she's my sister she seems to think she can ride roughshod over the Ministry of Foreign Affairs. Her ambitions are merely preposterous.' I was instructed to obtain her immediate recall from New York to Tehran. At the moment she heads our delegation to the UN ...

Tuesday, 24 November
... Brief audience ... I was instructed to summon the US ambassador and warn him that HIM will be obliged to turn elsewhere if the USA fails to meet our demands for military equipment and for the training of our pilots. We might make a deal with the British, the Canadians or even the Soviets, although we would naturally prefer that our traditional working relationship with the USA suffer no such setback ...

Wednesday, 25 November
Audience ... HIM repeated his instructions of yesterday. In particular he stressed the point about the training of Iranian pilots. At present we have only eighty-one men under instruction in the USA. This is patently inadequate, especially since our new agreement with the Consortium will increase oil production and enable us to purchase many more aircraft ... I was to ask the US ambassador whether we might not obtain a concession like that granted to West Germany, whereby we would actually take control of an airbase on US soil and run it as a training school at our own expense. If so, we would sell our present squadrons of F-5s to Saudi Arabia and replace them with F-5 21s, the most up to date of American fighters. Even then we would be looking for an even better replacement by 1975. We shall keep our existing F-4 Phantoms and augment them with a further two squadrons. Turning to the navy, HIM expressed his desire to purchase three US destroyers. All of these points I put to the ambassador who replied by enquiring the motive for HMQ's forthcoming trip to Russia. I told him it was merely for cultural purposes ...

Thursday, 26 November

Morning audience ... HIM is extremely anxious about the general outlook in the Middle East and worried by Moscow's growing influence in the Red Sea and the Indian Ocean ... which threatens the very survival of so-called 'moderate' Arab regimes such as those in Saudi Arabia, Kuwait and the Emirates. These, according to HIM, are in any case doomed to extinction. 'We can depend on no one except ourselves', said HIM, 'not even the Americans or the British can be relied upon. They're not nearly such desirable allies as the Soviets. Just look at what Moscow has done for Egypt ... But we have a common border with Russia and would therefore find it almost impossible to get rid of them. Egypt or even Iraq is in a quite different position ...'

I then raised the possibility of promoting General Nassiri, the head of Savak who did so much in the elimination of Bakhtiar. 'Yes, yes', said HIM, 'that's all very well, but it was also Nassiri who made such a mess over our plans for a coup in Iraq. For that he deserved to be stripped of his rank. Several times I warned him against placing too much trust in the Iraqi officers who had got in touch with us, but he paid no heed and as a result we ended up with something not far short of a disaster.[1] We failed and as a result hundreds within Iraq were put to death. It was the British that betrayed us. They came to hear of our plan and tipped off the President of Iraq. Hassan al-Bakr may pose as an anglophobe but in reality he's a lackey of the British.'

Monday, 30 November

Audience ... No rain in the south and east, hence HIM's depression. He mentioned the drawing up of his will and asked me to make some preliminary enquiries, but in strictest confidence. 'My wealth should go to the nation, with only a little kept back for the children. Ideally I'd abandon my wealth even now, but in return for a lifetime serving this country I like to enjoy a certain standard of living.' 'You are a paragon of virtue', I replied, 'whom God has bestowed on Iran. Your people will one day come to appreciate your greatness. Meanwhile, bear in mind that there are three things which will keep the Crown Prince safely on the throne: intelligence and the quality of his counsel; secondly, control over the army; and finally, wealth.' 'God will provide', he said. 'Indeed he will', I answered, 'but don't forget that you yourself inherited more than $20 million from your

[1] See the introductory note, 1970.

late father; equivalent to $100 million at today's prices. It was this same money that bought you great power even when the late Shah's influence and his army had all but evaporated.' 'Yes', he said, 'but the Iranian people now love me and will never forsake me.' 'True', I replied, 'and when the people believed this country to be in risk of disintegrating, they closed ranks around you. But remember it was precisely this same nation of ours that fell into line with Mosaddeq, so that you were forced to leave the country.' 'Ah, but the people called for me to return', he said. I replied that I was not for a moment questioning the nation's collective judgment but we must never underestimate the ability of our enemies to hoodwink the public. 'If only you could be around', he said, 'to see the Crown Prince through his first few years on the throne.' 'I should consider it an enormous privilege to serve him', I declared, 'but I want not a single day's continued existence when you are gone.' And here I could no longer control my tears . . .

The US ambassador dined as my guest. He agrees with HIM's analysis of the general situation in the Middle East and promised to bring pressure to bear on the oil companies in respect to our overlift. Even so, he stressed that the US army has agreed to train 200 foreign pilots; eighty-three of these places are already allocated to Iran. He undertook to pass on our request to purchase destroyers. All in all he seems mesmerized by the Shah. He left at midnight. Half an hour later he telephoned to say that he'd been attacked on his way back to the embassy. His car was overtaken by another vehicle which then braked, blocking the road ahead. Two men leaped out and proceeded to spray his car with bullets, shattering every window. Greatly shaken I telephoned the news to HIM who was outraged and ordered me to summon an immediate meeting with the Chief of Police, the Heads of Savak, Military Intelligence and the Gendarmerie to urge them to make a speedy arrest. This meeting went on until four in the morning during which time we were informed the gunmen had smashed the ambassador's windscreen with an axe, clearly believing it to be made of bullet-proof glass. The axe itself was found inside the limousine. The embassy chauffeur has identified the assailants' car as an old model Dodge. He also remembers its colour. Road blocks were set up all the way around Tehran and it appears that a car similar to the one described sped back into the city when approached by the guards at the barrier.

Tuesday, 1 December

A special *Salaam* this morning to mark the end of Ramadan ... HIM in a terrible mood because of last night's events.

HMQ accompanied by her mother flew out at noon to begin a ten days' unofficial visit to the Soviet Union ...

I was alone with HIM for dinner. I stayed only for the meal but he certainly knows how to take advantage of HMQ's absence ...

Wednesday, 9 December

[The Shah and Alam flew back from a visit to Khuzistan – south-western Iran]

On our arrival at the Niavaran Palace last night we found the Crown Prince and Princess Farahnaz waiting for us near the helipad. HIM kissed them both and then asked whether they've been praying for rain in our absence. They said 'no', at which HIM suggested they put in a word during their bedtime prayers. Last night and again this morning their prayer was answered, and there have been excellent falls of snow and rain ...

Dinner at the Queen Mother's. I reported that Princess Shahnaz is flying in from Geneva this evening. HIM was furious that she should return without first obtaining his consent ...

Friday, 25 December

Sore eyes and a heavy workload have kept me away from this diary ...

HMQ returned, very pleased with her tour of Russia. She brought back gifts for all her admirers, but not for me. Perhaps she is right to dislike me. If I were in her shoes I too would mistrust someone so close to the Shah.

HIM is upset by nationwide disturbances in the universities. He fears that our students are blind to the magnificence of the country's present situation. In reply, I pointed out that there has never been a law against the people grumbling. 'True enough', he said, 'but the present troubles represent more than grumbling. They are an act of national betrayal. Over the past few days slogans have gone up denouncing the White Revolution as a fraud and claiming that the only true revolution must be red and bathed in blood.'

Army Day, 12 December, was held in torrential rain. HIM rode out on horseback to inspect the troops. He got drenched to the skin but was still delighted by the downpour . . .

Prior to the ceremony I went along to the palace to recommend that he wear a shirt with tight cuffs so as to keep out the rain when he lifted his arm to salute. I was amazed to find him putting on a bullet-proof jacket. This shocked me to the core, partly because the Shah has always been a fatalist, seemingly oblivious to risk, and also because the army drills with unloaded rifles. It is possible that he's received a specific tip-off, but he's so secretive about such things that I'll never be told of it if he has. Whilst there, I told him about a parade inspected by his late father. It was raining so heavily, yet as the troops marched past he came out into the open to take the salute and when his sleeves had filled with water, merely poured them out like some great hose. I suggested HIM might find himself in a similar position today. 'Ah', said he, 'my father could cope with that sort of thing. He smoked a little opium and never once caught cold; but I catch cold all too easily.' Afterwards . . . he was not at all pleased with either the parade or the drill. 'If only I knew they could fight well', he said, 'I could have forgiven them their ragged drill. What worries me is that they may know neither how to fight nor how to march.' At this point he turned to General Djam, the Chief of the General Staff, saying, 'Unless their drill gets better, it may prove necessary to send you home to a less taxing sort of life.' . . . Later he mentioned the heavy burden imposed on us by defence expenditure, saying, 'I know only too well how much the army costs us, but what alternative do we have? We cannot leave ourselves prey to a country such as Iraq.' . . .

On 14 December Abba Eban, Israel's Foreign Minister, arrived in Tehran for a private meeting with HIM. Our own Ministry of Foreign Affairs was kept in the dark about this trip until the very last minute; I alone arranged the visit. Previously, Eban made repeated requests that I meet him, but I knew this would not go down well with HIM who likes to keep certain things exclusively to himself. There's nothing to be done about this particular whim of his. For myself, I pleaded a prior engagement, and made a brief excursion to Mashad. HIM seemed pleased when I asked his permission to leave Tehran. Yet on my return he showed no hesitation in giving me a blow by blow account of his negotiations with the Israelis . . . In simple terms, he has insisted that Israel reach a peaceful understanding with the Arabs, whilst at the same time agreeing to the supply of Iranian oil and the purchase of certain items of military equipment from Israel, including rocket launchers and flame throwers. Subsequently Eban was guest of honour at a private lunch arranged by our Foreign Minister.

For the first time in 200 years a Sheikh of Bahrain has made an official visit to this country. He was received at the airport by Prince Gholam Reza, the PM and myself. It's all tremendously ironic given that until recently we were busy vilifying him as the 'so-called Sheikh, the usurper of Bahrain'. Yet today he is our dear and distinguished guest. He ate lunch with HIM who later did him the honour of visiting him for tea. This is another first; never before has HIM returned a visit by a Sheikh of the Persian Gulf. I pointed this out, suggesting that we may be taking courtesy to an unnecessary extreme, but HIM replied that he is anxious that the Sheikh become a satellite of Iran. The Sheikh himself was delighted by HIM's visit ...

Over lunch today HIM announced that he intends to take HMQ along to next Tuesday's meeting of the Plan Organization. I commended this suggestion, pointing out that it will be extremely beneficial to have HMQ better informed on national issues. This comment she greeted with indignation saying that she already knew quite enough about such affairs. I replied that this was not at all the impression I'd received.

Saturday, 26 December

Audience. HIM informed me that in addition to the 300 Chieftain tanks already ordered, he wishes to purchase a further 700. He let me know that the Americans have now agreed to supply us with the full shipment of 75 Phantoms as requested. No doubt they realize we would have made up any shortfall by purchasing Mirages from the French.

HIM in excellent mood today and we enjoyed a wide-ranging discussion; touching amongst other things on the ineptitude of King Hassan of Morocco, the dire situation in Turkey, the future of Pakistan and the Persian Gulf, and an increase in oil prices which HIM considers a foregone conclusion.

HIM signed many telegrams offering congratulations for the start of 1971, the new Christian year. Amongst the greetings he himself received was a cable from the Prince of Monaco and Princess Grace. 'Twenty years ago', he said, 'Grace Kelly and I struck up an intimate acquaintance in America.' I refrained from pointing out that this wasn't the first time I'd been told ...

Sunday, 27 December

... Some time ago I suggested that HIM might like to throw the occasional dinner to which he would invite selected outsiders; a mixture of foreign diplomats, industrialists, businessmen and figures from the arts. He approved the idea, and tonight at dinner I did my best to get Their Majesties to set a definite date for the first of these gatherings and to agree a guest list. HMQ objects to the invitation of businessmen saying that they are all of them men with unsavoury reputations. HIM lost his temper at this; 'Who asked for your opinion?', he said. 'It's I that will make these arrangements, not you. Alam is always too ready to ask your views on such matters, I can't imagine why.' ... I am sorry to have been the cause of distress to HMQ, although thereafter the conversation turned to religious matters and to some extent the tension eased ...

Monday, 28 December

Audience ... 'Please forgive me if what I am about to say appears impertinent', I said, 'but I cannot help feeling that Your Majesty was excessively harsh last night. It's humiliating for Her Majesty to be spoken to in that way, especially in the hearing of others. She already bears several grudges. These things fester and one day may make life very difficult for you.' 'I insist on dealing and speaking plainly with everyone', he replied. 'It's I that must shoulder responsibility for everything, yet every Tom, Dick and Harry wants to put his oar in and tell me what I must and mustn't do.' I told him that I agreed with him in principle but that it's sometimes wise to keep an eye on certain wider considerations. This he categorically refused to accept. It seems that there's some hidden resentment which makes him act towards the Queen as he did last night. Perhaps it's simply a question of 'one country cannot be ruled by two kings', as Sa'adi puts it. With the amendment to the constitution HMQ will become Regent should HIM die before the Crown Prince reaches his majority at eighteen. This has brought the tensions between HIM and HMQ out into the open. Although, of course, the amendment itself was entirely HIM's doing. I'm inclined to think that she has been reminding HIM of her status under the constitution, prompted perhaps by naïvety, obtuseness or by certain members of her entourage. Hence his touchy mood of late. Last night she had the good sense to react with considerable dignity ...

Tuesday, 29 December

In the morning I accompanied HIM to the Plan Organization. Speeches by Khodadad Farmanfarmayan, Director of the Organization, and by the PM. HIM then spoke for close on an hour and half, defining the broad outline of the Fifth Plan.

HIM spoke to me on the telephone later that afternoon and instructed me to call in the British and US ambassadors to tell them that we originally summoned the representatives of the Consortium to meet in Tehran on 3 January, at which time OPEC will announce the revised oil prices. The representatives now plead prior engagements, but if they fail to attend on the 3rd, they should be in no doubt that we will go ahead regardless and reach a decision in their absence. I passed this on to the ambassadors who seemed pretty much in the dark over the whole affair.

Wednesday, 30 December

Attended Lunch. Dr Joseph Luns, the Dutch Foreign Minister, was our guest . . . I know him well, a jolly, well-humoured man. Serious topics had been got out of the way in an hour and a half of discussions beforehand, so the meal itself was chiefly given over to badinage and stories. HIM told one rather amusing anecdote. 'At the Tehran Conference',[1] he said, 'during the last war, Churchill and Roosevelt made no attempt to come to see me, but Stalin did pay me a call. I was then a young man, bursting with enthusiasm, and I complained bitterly to him about the state of our army which was completely bereft of armour or aircraft. In response Stalin promised that the equipment of a whole tank regiment and a Russian air squadron already in Iran would be put at my disposal. I was over the moon until a month later I heard from the Russian ambassador. Of course, he told me, the Soviets would be happy to give me these weapons but only when the war itself was over; in the meantime the Red Army would look after them.'

Thursday, 31 December

Audience . . . HIM repeated his conviction that we've earned greater respect from the British. Luns has told him that there is strong support for Iran within NATO; no other Middle Eastern country is regarded as being reliable. Apparently the British are doing their utmost to secure the islands of Tunbs and Abu Musa on our behalf . . .

[1] The first tripartite meeting of the Second World War. Held in Tehran, 28 November–2 December 1942 between Stalin, Roosevelt and Churchill, the leaders of the Allied Powers.

1971

The oil producers of the Persian Gulf held negotiations in Tehran with representatives of the oil companies, paving the way for an increase in oil prices and a reduction in the companies' profit-share. The Shah played a crucial role here, emerging as one of the principal spokesmen for the oil producers in their bid for a fairer percentage of profits. Alam was jubilant: 'All of this has been a triumph for the Shahanshah who is rapidly assuming leadership not only over the Persian Gulf, but over the Middle East and the entire oil-producing world.' (Diaries, 12 February)

Alam's diary ceases abruptly, resuming only in April 1972. He was preoccupied during the intervening months with celebrations to mark the foundation of Iranian monarchy by Cyrus the Great, traditionally dated to 558 BC. The main festivities took place in October in Persepolis, attended by the heads of state (or their representatives) of sixty-nine countries. Hundreds of millions of dollars were spent in providing hotels and other facilities besides a luxurious encampment of tents close to the ruins of Persepolis. Though the celebrations were intended to commemorate the glories of Iran, ironically it was French firms which laid on most of the catering and supplies. Despite this, President Pompidou of France, in company with several heads of state, among them Queen Elizabeth of England, preferred to steer clear of the entire event. The celebrations themselves were spectacular, but lacked meaning or popular support, earning scorn within Iran and abroad, well summed up by the caption to a cartoon in the French newspaper *Le Figaro*: '*Persepolis oui, mais Perse et police non!*'

On 30 November Iran occupied the islands of Tunbs, followed the next day by the abrogation of Britain's treaties with the Trucial States and the foundation of a federation of United Arab Emirates. Ras al-Khaimah objected to Iran's actions and delayed a year before joining the new federation. With respect to Abu Musa, Iran and Sharjah agreed to divide the area into two equal parts, the inhabited territory remaining with Sharjah. As a conciliatory gesture Iran agreed that her own part of the island and its territorial waters should continue subject to the oil agreement with Crescent Petroleum. To facilitate this, Iran offered various confidential financial incentives to the Sheikh of Sharjah.

Ardeshir Zahedi, one of the Shah's closest confidants, was replaced as Foreign Minister by his deputy, Abbas Ali Khalatbary.

Saturday, 2 January

Brief audience ... I was not at dinner at the Queen Mother's, but I know that Pari Sima, wife of Prince Abdul Reza, intended to take the opportunity to throw herself on HIM's mercy and beg his forgiveness for past wrongs. For the past thirteen years she's been banished from Court. Several times I've tried to intercede on her behalf but with no success ... Yet, as I told HIM, although she may have been instrumental in disrupting his plans to marry Princess Gabriella of Italy, it was actually a great service that she rendered to Iran. I know only too well the sort of life that Princess Gabriella was leading in Europe. When I described it to HIM even he was shocked ... Thanks God, the marriage never came off and instead we now have Queen Farah, an absolute angel. Fair enough she may not care for me, but she's hardly to be blamed for that. She doesn't know me well enough and it's virtually impossible for a wife – just think of my own – to be on good terms with her husband's best friends. HMQ believes that her husband and I go philandering together, and in that she's not far wide of the truth.

Sunday, 3 January

... Two new ambassadors, from Nationalist China and Egypt, presented their credentials ... For the past ten years we've had no diplomatic relations with Cairo. In the meantime I should have expected a young, dynamic group to come to the fore, replacing the old ruling class. The new ambassador and his staff are undoubtedly young, but I found them utterly devoid of life or enthusiasm. I wouldn't be surprised if they still need their mothers to tie their shoe laces ...

HIM has ordered me to send a request to the British Foreign Secretary to extend the tour of duty by Sir Denis Wright, the ambassador, due to be recalled in April. I am to say that we wish him to stay for the celebrations of 2,500 years of monarchy next October. Wright is a worthy man, but I doubt we stand much chance of keeping him, since the London Foreign Office rarely gives way to this sort of request, being very keen to create openings for a younger generation of diplomats. HIM's real motive is fairly transparent. He wishes to settle the problem of the Gulf islands and would prefer to do so with Sir Denis, whom he knows and who is undoubtedly a friend of Iran. Of course he could say nothing of this in his message to the Foreign Office ...

Monday, 4 January

HIM decided to go skiing and so I had to cancel all his appointments. There were various urgent matters to be reported so he received me at breakfast ... I then insisted, in the interests of security, that he fly to the slopes in a different helicopter from HMQ and the Crown Prince. He agreed to go first. HMQ's flight was timed for half an hour later and meanwhile I stayed at her side, playing football with the Crown Prince. The boy is left-handed and also shoots at goal with his left foot. I pointed this out to HMQ, telling her that the same was true of his grandfather, Reza Shah ... It was quite clear to me that she was being deliberately icy in her replies, and I had to keep reminding myself, '*Je m'en fous ... Je m'en fous ...*'

Yesterday, without telling me anything of its contents, HMQ delivered a speech to the Committee on Social Reform. With fifteen minutes to spare before this afternoon's main news broadcast, the speech itself was passed on to me. Much of it struck me as wrong headed, running contrary to the policies espoused by HIM. He himself was away, and so on my own initiative I gave instructions that the speech could be broadcast on the radio, but that the press should delay publishing its text. An hour later I was informed that HMQ's private secretary had already distributed printed copies and that nothing could be done to prevent their appearing in tomorrow's editions. This is bound to put the cat amongst the pigeons.

Tuesday, 5 January

Sure enough at this morning's audience HIM kicked off with a sarcastic enquiry. 'Please tell me what precisely it is you do', he said. 'I would be fascinated to know.' 'I am your obedient servant', I replied. At this he exploded. 'Then pray explain why it is that HMQ's speech has appeared in the newspapers unauthorized.' I told him what had happened; that I had no alternative but to allow the thing through. To have ordered a full-scale confiscation at the presses would have caused even more of a stir. HIM immediately rang through to the Queen and told her in no uncertain terms that her private secretariat is in the hands of subversives. I could not hear her reply, and their conversation was in any case very brief and to the point, but I could tell that she was wounded to the quick.

She rang me herself later on and asked me to look into the matter. 'I'm afraid that I hardly need to investigate any further', I told her. 'There can be no doubt that it's all the fault of your own secretariat; they themselves already admitted as much.' It is much to be regretted that the stupidity of her entourage is driving a wedge between HMQ and HIM ...

Thursday, 7 January

On HIM's instructions I invited the ambassadors of France, Holland, Denmark and Great Britain to dinner at my home. I remarked to the French ambassador how surprised I am by President Pompidou's reluctance to attend the monarchy celebrations here, given the close relations between Iran and France and the fact that HIM made the effort to attend similar commemorative ceremonies for De Gaulle. 'For goodness sake', replied the ambassador, 'don't make the mistake of comparing the present lot with De Gaulle; they're in quite another league – a bunch of cringing politicians without an ounce of international standing. Even so I shall go to France and see if there's anything to be done.' This from a man who is supposed to act as Pompidou's representative! I found his words utterly astounding.

In a similar vein I told the Dutch ambassador that I was surprised that the Queen of the Netherlands had turned down our invitation; HIM has shown nothing but kindness to the Queen and Prince Bernhardt. The ambassador replied that the royal couple had already agreed to visit Indonesia. This, I told him, struck me as odd, since the President of Indonesia has himself agreed to attend our celebrations; presumably he will be away from home when the Dutch royals call on him. The ambassador was understandably embarrassed and promised to see what he could do.

Discussed the islands and our purchase of tanks with the British ambassador ...

Friday, 8 January

Rode out early this morning. With my heavy workload, riding is about all I have to keep body and soul together ... Audience from 12 until 2. We managed to clear a large backlog of work, besides discussing various political and personal matters.

HIM complained that his workload increases day by day and that he can no longer hope to cover it all. Every day for an hour and a half he reads reports from the Foreign Ministry. Three to four hours a week he spends on economic affairs; two full days he devotes to the army, gendarmerie, police and Savak. Then there are the confidential foreign policy decisions which he deals with through me; on top of which comes the weekly Economic Council, a lot of personal and family matters, and meetings with his other ministers, most of whom endeavour to see him at least once a fortnight.

In reply I pointed out that by no means all of this work is essential. 'The burden could easily be reduced', I said, 'but whenever I make any suggestion you merely accuse me of empire-building. What can I do if you won't trust me? Let me throw up my present job and work for your private secretariat in an unofficial capacity.' He replied that he is already delegating far more to his secretariat. 'I'm well aware of it', I said, 'but I had far more sweeping reforms in mind. The modern world demands deep thought and penetrating analysis; every problem requires examination by first-rate experts before its submission to you. Remember, it was I myself that put forward the name of the man who now heads your secretariat.[1] I like him very much. But honest and loyal as he is, you must also be aware that he has next to no academic qualifications. He never attended university, speaks no language other than Persian and has no grasp of the problems of the modern world.' I sensed that some of this may have got through to him, but even so he replied: 'What if I could reduce my workload, what then? I'd merely find my time taken up by family problems. No, I prefer to stay at my desk.' 'Unfortunately', I said, 'you are only human and no human being could cope with your present workload without facing mental and physical collapse. The country needs you to be fit. Relaxation comes in more than one form. You could find more time for sport, for riding and skiing and indulge yourself in the companionship of people you like.' He remained silent and I tactfully changed the subject, even though I have a clear duty to make him reform his life-style. More and more I get the impression that national affairs are uncoordinated with no firm hand on the tiller, all because the captain himself is overworked. Every minister and high official receives a separate set of instructions direct from HIM and the result is that individual details often fail to mesh with any overall framework. Thank God, the Shah is a strong man, but he's no computer; he cannot be expected to remember every one of the thousands of instructions he issues each week. Occasionally one set of instructions contradicts another ...

Tuesday, 12 January
Audience ... Reported that General Hashemi Nejad, Commander of the Imperial Guard, is seeking permission to make the pilgrimage to Mecca together with his wife. I told HIM my own response to this request; that the general might just as well send his wife to Mecca and stay at home

---

[1] Nosratollah Mo'inian, ex-Minister of Information.

himself; a far easier way to find heaven on earth. HIM laughed. 'Yet isn't it exactly these sort of people that accuse us of being morally bankrupt?', he asked. 'No', I said; 'People of that rank are well aware that from the very bottom of your heart you are a man of God ... but the ordinary soldiers are too easily influenced by religious fanatics and must be carefully watched. Hence one must be particularly on one's guard during nights of religious mourning. On one such occasion my lover and I were in Shiraz. We behaved with absolute discretion but even so my servants refused to serve us dinner.' ...

HIM is outraged by a recent comment by his sister, Princess Ashraf. She told him he was permanently surrounded by flatterers and sycophants. No doubt I am to be counted amongst their number, but nevertheless I suggested he should be less critical of his sister, particularly since she's his twin – 'Sometimes she really does tell you the truth.' The Shah is a reasonable man and I'm sure he took my hint, although he made no attempt to reply ...

Wednesday, 13 January
Audience ... The oil negotiations are clearly worrying HIM. The Consortium's representatives arrived here to discuss oil pricing with the Gulf members of OPEC but they've since cancelled all further negotiations without setting any date for them to be resumed. HIM has ordered the Minister of Finance to explain our aims to the press. I too have been delegated to set out our position at my dinner this evening with the British and US ambassadors. The uncertainty has forced HIM to delay his trip to Switzerland ...

Thursday, 14 January
Morning audience ... reported my conversations at the US embassy reception. The US and British ambassadors were both due to be received by HIM on my departure. In addition I mentioned the trip made by ex-Queen Soraya to Bangkok. HIM was enraged by the press photographs I showed him of this visit.[1]

A mixed group of diplomats and Iranians dined at the Niavaran Palace. The British ambassador, presently doyen of the diplomatic corps, told me in confidence that Sir Peter Ramsbotham has been chosen to succeed him.

[1] The photograph published in the *Bangkok Post*, 5 January 1971, showed the ex-Queen in a bathing suit, accompanied by the Italian film director Franco Indovina who had rented a private beach bungalow in the Penang resort.

He also informed me that the oil companies will submit counter-proposals within forty-eight hours. I reported both these matters to HIM who afterwards called the ambassador and spoke to him for some while ...

Friday, 15 January
Despite the heavy snow, rode out for two hours. HIM has postponed his planned trip to Vienna until early February in order to cope with the oil negotiations.

Saturday, 16 January
Lengthy audience this morning ... The oil companies' counter-proposals include a suggestion that we agree a settlement to last for the next five years. But they make no mention of what sort of price increase the companies themselves are contemplating. HIM and I went through every detail of these proposals and HIM several times telephoned through to Jamshid Amouzegar, the Minister of Finance. In the end we decided that, provided the companies offer us a fair share of the price increases they have already introduced on western markets, we are prepared to reach some sort of agreement. Libya's reaction to any such deal remains an unknown quantity ...

Reported a telephone call from the US ambassador. He rang me this morning to announce that John Irwin, President Nixon's special envoy, and Under-Secretary at the State Department, is on his way to Iran and asks that he be granted an audience by HIM, to submit his views on the oil negotiations. HIM told me that two days ago when he received the US ambassador and his colleague, the US ambassador to London, he dealt with them harshly. For example when they advised him to moderate his stand against the oil companies, he replied: 'Am I hearing the big voice of a superpower?' The two Americans were dreadfully embarrassed. HIM is sure he put the wind up them – hence their decision to send Irwin here.

I also passed on the terms and conditions for our purchase of Chieftain tanks from the British. HIM was impressed and said: 'Tell the Americans and the British that, as they can see, an increase in our income merely leads us to purchase more goods and services, chiefly to the benefit of their own two countries.'

Princess Ashraf lunched with me at my office. She now wants to be chosen UN Secretary-General, an appointment due to be made in 1973. Neither HIM nor I reckon she stands much chance of success. Apart from anything else she's on rotten terms with our own Foreign Minister who will do his best to undermine her position.

The British ambassador telephoned me this evening to ask for an urgent meeting. He is keen that our negotiations with the oil companies be held in an atmosphere of calm and moderation. Their eventual outcome perplexes him. I assured him that we will proceed with all the tact in the world, providing only that we are offered a reasonable share of the latest price increase. I also told him that oil prices should be raised on an annual basis in future to keep pace with inflation in the industrialized world. Before he left I personally telephoned HIM who said, 'You must tell the ambassador that his government appears to identify itself with the interests of the oil companies. At the same time, he may rest assured that we shall proceed with calm and dignity. Iran has no need to resort to cheap rhetoric. That calm would be broken only if the companies were to prevaricate. It would be best if their representatives arrived here to open discussions with Iran, Saudi Arabia and Iraq, before the Tehran OPEC meeting next Saturday.' ...

Sunday, 17–Friday, 22 January
Tremendously busy with the oil negotiations, and not enough time even now to set down more than a general outline of what's been going on. OPEC's negotiations with the oil companies were based on a resolution passed at the organization's last meeting, in Venezuela, where it was agreed that there should be a revision to the taxes paid by the companies to their host countries, and that the old profit-sharing formula of 50/50 be altered to 55/45. The posted price of oil should be increased, and pressure brought to bear to ensure that the companies invest more heavily within the oil-producing nations. Libya and Algeria later went further than this and demanded profit-sharing on a 60/40 basis in their favour. They also envisage increases to the posted price way beyond anything we in the Persian Gulf have contemplated ... In the light of all this, we are now attempting to make the companies see sense. If only they will comply with the spirit of the original OPEC resolution and reach some sort of agreement with the oil producers of the Gulf, we shall moderate our demands and withdraw all support from the radical measures proposed by Libya and Algeria. In the meantime we insist on certain conditions. Above all we wish to obtain an increased share of future profits, but repudiate any attempt by the companies to anticipate this by imposing massive price increases which

will only serve to drive consumers away from the market and so deplete our share.

The basic justice of our cause has already been accepted by various of the company representatives including Lord Strathalmond of BP and George T. Piercy representing US oil companies, both of whom are in Tehran at the moment for negotiations with our Minister of Finance and the oil ministers of Iraq and Saudi Arabia. However they argue that the US law dispensing American companies from anti-trust regulations stipulates that they function together as a single cartel in negotiations with all the oil producers. HIM, on the other hand, insists upon a separate agreement with the Gulf states.

On his instructions I summoned a lunch meeting between the US and British ambassadors to which I also invited our own Finance Minister, Jamshid Amouzegar, a shrewd individual. Together he and I prevailed upon the ambassadors to see sense. We warned them that unless the company representatives come here before next Thursday and make a separate agreement for the Gulf, we of the Gulf states will throw in our lot with those countries which have made the most radical claims, namely Libya and Algeria. In the Gulf alone this would cost the companies $1,500 million. Of course we'd much rather stand apart from Libya and Algeria, whom we regard as mere adventurers. Even so there is little to stop us following their lead: our own market lies chiefly in the Far East whereas theirs is around the Mediterranean. Libya itself is in a very strong position; she can afford to live without any oil income for at least two years. If she and Algeria closed down their exports to Western Europe, bearing in mind the shortage of tankers and notwithstanding the oil piped to the Mediterranean from the Gulf, it would result in a shortfall of 3 million barrels a day; a quite staggering loss ...

Sunday, 24 January
HIM's press conference on the oil situation lasted three hours and he carried it off so superbly that I found myself reciting a verse from the Koran that God might continue to guide him. Despite threatening the oil companies with dire consequences if they fail to heed our demands, he managed to leave the way open for some sort of compromise. To the journalists' various questions he replied in fluent English, Persian or French. It was a literally dazzling performance, made all the more impressive by his complete mastery of the subject in hand ...

Monday, 25 January

Audience. Reported the reaction to HIM's speech which has sent shock waves across the international media. Later we escorted HMQ and the royal children to the airport; they are off to ski in Switzerland. HIM prefers to stay here for a few more days, to deal with the oil negotiations, and to enjoy a little peace and quiet to tackle the rest of his work.

I and another dined alone with HIM; a very pleasant evening.

Tuesday, 26–Thursday, 28 January

Too busy over the past few days to jot down a single word. The ménage for lunches and dinners has continued; HIM eating alone with me and his other guest ...

The companies gave way in the end, and agreed to negotiate two separate deals, one with the Gulf states, the other with Venezuela and the oil-producing countries of the Mediterranean. They've sent out two negotiating teams, one to Tehran and another to Libya. However the Libyans refuse to begin their own talks whilst the Tehran leg of the negotiations is still in progress. The Algerians are more conciliatory and seem to have reached some sort of understanding with France; perhaps not surprisingly, since their whole economy depends on the French ... From our own point of view things could hardly be better. The only dark cloud on the horizon has been the in-fighting amongst various members of the Iranian negotiating team[1] ...

Saturday, 30 January

Audience. Discussed the oil negotiations and the position of Libya.

I then asked straight out whether he would grant his consent to a marriage between Princess Shahnaz and Khosrow Jahanbani. He nodded agreement, saying he had little alternative ... It saddens me to see the Shah so helpless, but I said nothing beyond asking where he wished the ceremony to take place. He suggested our embassy in Paris. There I let the matter rest. Since I am anxious to spare him further anxiety, I shall try to make sure the wedding takes place as quickly as possible ...

---

[1] This refers to Jamshid Amouzegar – a man of hawkishly nationalistic views – and Dr Reza Fallah, well-known for his friendly relations with the major oil companies. The Shah was far from unhappy that these two prominent personalities failed to see eye to eye with one another (see the main introduction).

Tuesday, 2 February

The OPEC ministers have arrived: should the negotiations break down we are now in a position to resort to collective action. The Queen of England has informed us that her husband will attend the monarchy celebrations in place of Prince Charles, the British Crown Prince. Unofficially, she is prepared to allow Princess Anne to attend as well, provided we agree. All of this infuriates me but HIM seemed content with the arrangement and instructed me to invite both Prince Philip and Princess Anne.

... The oil negotiations have more or less collapsed ... Dined with HIM ... and then went to see my lover. Returned home at 2 a.m. to be told that the British and US ambassadors had both tried to reach me several times to arrange a meeting. I immediately rang them back and it was agreed that the British ambassador will call on me early tomorrow morning to act as joint spokesman for them both.

Wednesday, 3 February

The British ambassador brought round an urgent message from Prime Minister Heath to HIM. He also asked to be received personally, if possible before the lunch which HIM is throwing for OPEC ministers. He told me that the oil companies would like to see a halt in proceedings for at least forty-eight hours. He complained that we are seeking to raise our demands: in his press interview HIM gave the impression that the oil producers were after a price increase of 30 cents per barrel with no mention of any regular escalation for the future, but now the talk is of an immediate rise of 46 cents, linked to annual increases to keep pace with inflation. In the ambassador's presence I telephoned through to HIM, who instructed me to reply that he was too busy to grant an audience today; if the ambassador had any particular message he should convey it through me. Likewise HIM refused to contemplate any delay in negotiations. The companies, he said, have already been warned. They must now sit back and await a resolution from the OPEC oil ministers. HIM will himself address a special session of Parliament, in order to spell out OPEC's position; a session attended by the foreign oil ministers. Finally he said, 'You might be good enough to thank the ambassador for his efforts, but tell him he's missed the boat.' The ambassador eventually left in a dreadful state.

Audience later on. HIM couldn't even be bothered to read the message from Heath and instead asked me to fill him in on what it's all about. 'More time', I said; 'They're anxious to play for more time, and are terrified meanwhile that we shall bring forward confiscatory legislation, even before the talks are officially ended.' HIM chuckled knowingly, 'They're much too late', he said, 'the game is already afoot.'

He instructed me to call in the British and US ambassadors. I am to tell them that they cannot be received by HIM in person since he has a prior engagement with the OPEC ministers whose conference will go ahead this evening as planned. Nevertheless, they can rest assured that we shall not resort to any cheap gestures and will do our best to persuade the conference to resolve upon moderate proposals. In any event, it will take a considerable time for all of the member states to force through any sort of legislation; the companies will have ample breathing space in which to submit new counter-proposals. We are merely seeking what is ours by right and demanding our just share of the last set of price increases imposed by the companies themselves. In these circumstances it would be quite wrong of the USA and Britain to turn against Iran and the other moderate Gulf regimes, Saudi Arabia, Kuwait and the Emirates. To do so would be merely to play into the hands of the extremists. The West can surely learn from its past mistakes. Yet still we and the other friends of Britain and the USA find ourselves pressured beyond endurance to the advantage of no one save our mutual enemies. I am to tell the ambassadors from HIM that he has ruled this country for the past thirty years and has seen more than enough mistakes made by the West in virtually every corner of this region; in Iraq and Syria, Egypt, Aden and Lebanon, and in Iran itself. His only desire now is to act in the best interests of his people. 'Spell all of this out to them', he said, 'and tell them there can be no going back on whatever I say in my address to Parliament this evening. We have total support from Kuwait, Saudi Arabia, even from Iraq, despite what the Iraqis may lead outsiders to believe. How can we be wrong? The posted price of oil is today even lower than it was ten years ago, yet over the same period the cost of industrial goods has soared ahead. Of course they may harbour some delusion that by spending a few million dollars they can topple me and my regime. But they should realize that the days when that sort of thing was possible have vanished forever. As for organizing a coup amongst the army, my generals distrust – and lack professional respect for – one another.' At this stage I butted in with a couple of comments which I'm not sure were to his liking. 'Don't let confidence run away with you', I said. 'If these foreigners had it in mind to bring down our regime, they would simply remove the half dozen people at the top, and leave the rest of the country to sort itself out at some later date. God help Iran if that should be the case. I only wish I shared your confidence in the army. If it really were immune to foreign influence we could all sleep much more soundly in our beds.' 'But that's the point', he replied, 'I don't think there's a single member of the army prepared to betray us, and in any event, they're too much at one another's throats to constitute a threat. There's no point in empty speculation. We've taken the plunge and you must now hurry to brief the ambassadors and be back in time for lunch.'

I carried out his instructions to the letter. The ambassadors winced visibly, alarmed especially when I repeated HIM's declaration that there's no going back on anything he may announce to Parliament later today. They again pleaded for a minimum forty-eight hours, delay in proceedings, but I told them it is already too late to call a halt. Naturally they were anxious to know the details of HIM's speech but despite having a good idea of its outline, I gave nothing away ... They both of them left in a pitiful state ... their only ray of hope was my assurance that whatever HIM may say, he will say it with dignity and without any of the tricks and flourishes that a Nasser or a Mosaddeq would have used. Our cause is just and we deserve to triumph.

Rushed back to the Niavaran Palace, arriving only five minutes before our guests. HIM was amused to hear of the ambassadors' reaction. Lunch was attended by the PM, our Finance Minister Jamshid Amouzegar, the mastermind behind these negotiations, and by Dr Eqbal who was invited at my insistence. I also recommended that HIM invite our Foreign Minister, chiefly to show that I bear no grudge against the man, but HIM insists that oil is a commercial rather than a political matter and Zahedi was left out in the cold.

Whilst aperitifs were being served, HIM addressed the OPEC ministers and with great subtlety sketched a veiled outline of his speech. This won him a general promise of support. Our lunch only broke up at 3 and for the whole meal I sat stunned by HIM's shrewdness; his *savoir-faire* in knowing precisely how to address the Iraqi representative or how to suggest an idea to the Saudi Minister, without the latter even knowing that he was being led to adopt the Shah's own point of view. In short he knew exactly how to get everybody to agree with him.

Once the guests had departed, HIM sat down with the PM, the Finance Minister and myself and we ran through his speech one last time. HIM is generally reluctant to have his speeches committed to writing but I was glad that in this case he made an exception. I am also indebted to the PM who urged him to cut a whole series of statistics. I myself had made this point to HIM several times over lunch but he paid me no attention. I'd even mentioned it to the Finance Minister who apologized but said that it was HIM who insisted the figures be included. Luckily, with the PM's backing we persuaded HIM to revise his decision.

The joint session of Parliament was convened for 6 this evening; HIM was expected to start on the dot – he's usually incredibly punctual. However the Finance Minister, poor man, was still busy editing in the revisions we'd agreed upon after lunch and arrived with the revised text half an hour late. Meanwhile people sat at home glued to their televisions and radios and no one could understand the delay. The city buzzed with some pretty far-fetched rumours and my mother even telephoned me at the Senate to ask what was going on.

The meeting itself is quite unprecedented in Iranian history. It was brought to order by the Finance Minister who as Chairman of the OPEC summit called upon HIM to deliver his address. Our Protocol Department originally suggested that HIM should leave as soon as he had finished speaking. 'Rubbish', said HIM, 'this is an OPEC meeting held before a joint session of Parliament and I intend to sit through the whole thing, alongside my Prime Minister, Finance Minister and various members of the cabinet.' Never before can anyone have witnessed a Shah of Iran defer to his Finance Minister and call him 'Mr Chairman', before turning to his audience, addressing them as 'gentlemen' . . .

The whole thing was a triumph and confirmed us in unrivalled leadership of the entire Gulf. Not even the Iraqis dare challenge us now. HIM gave the oil companies seven days in which to resume negotiations, and yet he steered clear of forcing any sort of deadlock by the masterly way in which he analysed the position of the oil-producing countries. To cap it all, the Gulf members of OPEC have now given powers to our own Finance Minister to negotiate on their behalf with the company representatives.

Thursday, 4 February
The US and British ambassadors both rang me early this morning, full of praise for HIM's statesman-like speech . . .

Audience . . . Passed on the news that his speech has been universally well received. 'For myself I desire nothing', said HIM, 'but our cause is undeniably just. You must once again summon the US and British ambassadors and spell out our demands.'

This I did. I told them that they can rely on HIM to act wisely. 'For example', I pointed out, 'he was wise to reject your suggestion that proceedings be delayed. Had he followed your advice, nothing could have been achieved in the interim and he might have sacrificed the confidence of the other OPEC states. As it is, the oil companies now have a whole week's breathing space rather than a mere forty-eight hours, and they have been granted it with unanimous approval from OPEC.' Last Wednesday the British ambassador did his best to lower my spirits by claiming we stood no chance of keeping the Iraqis in line; 'Iraq is a tiger; you may think you can ride a tiger, but the tiger will end up riding you.' Today I was able to pay him back in kind. 'Now you see', I told him, 'HIM can not only ride tigers but donkeys as well.' Oh, what a donkey the British ambassador was to underestimate the Shah.

I told both men that they should press the oil companies to see sense. In reply they repeated that it is essential that we avoid any sort of pattern of leap-frogging – one country increasing the price of oil, encouraging the others to follow suit, and so on without end. They also suggested that Iraq and Saudi Arabia should set a lower posted price on the oil at their pipeline terminals in the Eastern Mediterranean than that set by Libya and Algeria. I pointed out this was pure nonsense; neither the Iraqi nor the Saudi governments would ever dare do such a thing. The American nodded his agreement but the British ambassador refused to be drawn. I was anxious that the latter harbour no hard feelings about my little joke and so at the end of our interview I invited him to come out riding with me tomorrow.

... The Soviet ambassador called round, praising HIM's speech and congratulating me on our success ...

Friday, 12 February
Too busy over the past week to keep up with this diary ... and what a week it's been. The oil negotiations ended in what I can only describe as a blaze of glory for HIM. Our own income for the current year is set to rise by 30 per cent ... The posted price of Gulf crude increases 33 cents a barrel rather than the 20 cents proposed by the companies. Company expense allowances have been abolished, giving us a further 6 cents a barrel, and for the next five years the posted price is due to rise 5 cents per annum to compensate for the devaluation of the US dollar. On top of all this, the posted price is to be inflation-indexed against a range of western industrial products. This is the very point which HIM was so keen to have recognized, and now everybody refers to it as 'the Shah's provision'. All of this has been a triumph for the Shahanshah who is rapidly assuming leadership not only over the Persian Gulf, but the Middle East and the entire oil-producing world.

Saturday, 13 February

Audience ... HIM seemed anxious, and explained that the Iraqis threaten to refuse to sign the new oil agreement, demanding that a special export tax be imposed on oil leaving Southern Iraq to help finance the port of Basra. They said nothing of this at the OPEC meetings, either in Caracas or Tehran. Even so, with or without Iraqi participation, we and the other Gulf producers – Kuwait, Saudi Arabia, Abu Dhabi and Qatar – will press ahead with the negotiated terms. 'And fuck Iraq', said HIM, 'After all, what right have they to demand an additional $200 million a year?'

The telephone rang shortly afterwards – it was Amouzegar reporting that Iraq has agreed to abandon her demands and will now sign as agreed. HIM was over the moon ...

Sunday, 14 February

Audience ... HIM still buoyed up as the final details of the agreement slot into place ...

At 4 p.m. a communiqué was issued to announce the successful conclusion of negotiations. What a triumph. On HIM's instructions I sent straightaway for the Finance Minister and invested him with the order of Taj, first class, on the Shahanshah's behalf. He was taken completely by surprise since there can be no more than ten men holding this decoration at any one time and it's generally reserved for the present and former Prime Ministers. Amouzegar was quite overwhelmed and could not hold back his tears. HIM rang meanwhile, to remind me that the honour was to be bestowed at once. I was able to tell him that his wishes had already been carried out and that Amouzegar was at that very moment sitting beside me at the telephone, weeping for joy. HIM laughed good humouredly ...

Monday, 15 February

Special *Salaam* for *Eyd-e Ghadir*. Truly a day for celebrations. The oil negotiations have ended triumphantly, rain is falling across the whole of Iran and HIM has emerged as the undisputed leader of the Middle East ...

A less than celebratory evening for me I'm afraid. My wife went alone to dinner at HM the Queen Mother's and returned home in an even filthier temper than when she set out. The blame lies with our dear Queen Mother who has nothing to do with her time except recount tittle-tattle; whispering sympathy to one or other of her lady friends and then spreading scandal about her the moment her back is turned ...

Tuesday, 16 February
Flew Iranair charter to Zurich with HIM. Chatted about the international
situation, various new weapons systems ... my domestic difficulties ...
HIM in a euphoric state; 'Look how things have sorted themselves out',
he declared; 'The oil problem solved, rain for our crops, and Iran's
leadership of the Middle East acknowledged throughout the world' ... He
then showed the extent of his faith in divine providence by a most peculiar
remark: 'I have learned by experience that a tragic end awaits anyone who
dares cross swords with me; Nasser is no more, John and Robert Kennedy
died at the hands of assassins, their brother Edward has been disgraced,
Khrushchev was toppled, the list is endless. And the same thing goes for
my enemies at home; just think of Mosaddeq, or even Qavam.' ... He is
convinced that the American oil companies showed more understanding
than the British during last week's negotiations, and has instructed the
Finance Minister to point this out to the US ambassador ...

[Alam's diaries end abruptly at the end of February to resume only in
March 1972]

1972

Alam and the Shah's family spent the Iranian New Year on Kish Island, where Alam was supervising the development of a major winter resort. This project, financed entirely from government funds, was to drag on until the revolution, six years later. The ostensible purpose was to attract rich Arab holiday-makers from around the Gulf, but in practice Kish remained a private playground for the Shah and his court.

In December India and Pakistan went to war, leading to the secession of East Pakistan as the newly formed state of Bangladesh. More than ever, Iranian foreign policy became focused on the problems and territorial integrity of what was formerly West Pakistan.

The Arab oil producers demanded participant status in the oil companies operating within their borders, beginning at a 25 per cent share and set to rise to 51 per cent. Iran had nationalized her oil resources as long ago as 1951, a move tacitly acknowledged by the oil companies in 1954 in the agreement between Iran and the Oil Consortium. An act of nationalization was passed and compensation paid to British Petroleum – the former owner. Even so, with a view to dissuading others from following Iran's example, the Consortium agreement had imposed conditions limiting Iran's oil income per barrel to much the same level as that enjoyed by countries where oil production remained under foreign control, Saudi Arabia for example. Consequently, as these other countries steadily increased their share in their own oil industries, formulae had to be devised to award equivalent financial advantages to Iran.

Following the success of his interventions the year before in the politics of the Persian Gulf, the Shah turned his attention increasingly to events in the Indian Ocean. Already he had begun to contemplate yet further expansion in Iran's military potential, the cost of which could be met only by increases in oil revenue.

During a visit to Iran by President Nixon, various acts of terrorism and sabotage were carried out (Diaries 30–31 May). Even after the presidential motorcade had set out for the airport, students threw stones at the passing cars. Nevertheless, given the turbulence and violence prevailing elsewhere in the world, Iran's situation appeared comparatively tranquil.

Wednesday, 22 March–Sunday, 2 April

Since 22 March I've been in Kish Island with the royal family. Every day I've been out riding with HIM; I had ten horses flown here specially. HIM is keen that I get the hotels, casinos and other developments we have planned for the island finished as soon as possible. 'Before my death', he told me, 'I want to see the place looking as I should wish.'

A new round of negotiations has opened with the oil companies. The Arab oil producers now demand 20 per cent shares in the companies operating on their soil, but as Iranian production has long been nationalized, we are looking for different but none the less significant concessions. Representatives of the Consortium have twice flown to Kish and on each occasion spent upwards of five hours with HIM. Before coming here HIM held discussions on the same subject in Tehran with the British Foreign Secretary, Sir Alec Douglas-Home ...

I myself have been heavily involved in extricating Amir Houshang Davallou from his brush with the Swiss police. Davallou, a Qajar Prince, is a man of great shrewdness who by intelligence and sycophancy has risen high in HIM's favour. At Court we know him by the accurate enough nickname 'Prince Pimp'. Every year he accompanies HIM to St Moritz, to carry out his rather sordid functions and to indulge his taste for opium. However, during their latest trip, the Swiss police raided the house of a Mr Q ..., a friend of Davallou's, and found 25 grams of opium on the premises. Q ... claimed under interrogation that the drugs were given to him by Davallou who wanted them sent on to Germany to a mutual friend, Khosrow Qashqai.[1] The police were unable to interview Davallou since he enjoys diplomatic immunity as a member of HIM's household. Thus a scandal arose, widely reported in the European press, only further exacerbated by the fact that Davallou, despite the attempts to bring him to justice, was allowed to return to Tehran in HIM's private aircraft.

I myself have volunteered to tackle the problem since it threatened to blacken the name of my own dear Shah and of the whole Iranian people. I shall begin by having the case against Davallou and Q ... dismissed. Then I shall kick-up a fuss against the iniquitous manner in which the Swiss and other foreign journalists have handled the affair. The western press is full of attacks on our mass execution of terrorists and is currently reporting an accusation that Princess Ashraf is guilty of smuggling heroin.

[1] Brother of Nasser Qashqai; both left Iran in 1954 after the fall of Dr Mosaddeq's government. After the revolution of 1979, Khosrow returned to Iran, only to fall out with the new regime and to be executed a few years later

It's all a lot of hot air and I have been assigned to scotch these rumours. They're spread about by our enemies who have been quite active of late ...

Friday, 7 April

Returning from my ride this morning I encountered HIM also out on horseback. Rode with him for half an hour but my mount was restive and I felt too tired to continue. With HIM's permission I made my way home, but only after he'd made me promise to lunch with him.

... On his return ... we once again discussed the Davallou case. I reported that our legal adviser and our mutual friend in Switzerland both recommend that Davallou return to Europe to face the music as swiftly as possible. HIM objected that the man has only recently recovered from a heart attack; the trip abroad might kill him. Whilst congratulating HIM on his generosity in this respect, I pointed out that if we are to stand any chance of silencing the anti-Iranian propaganda, we have no alternative but to persuade Davallou to go. I sensed that HIM was pleasantly surprised by the firmness of my stand ...

Saturday, 8 April

Audience ... Discussed the practical side of Davallou's proposed return to Switzerland. Again HIM stressed that the man should travel only if he feels up to it. I myself am caught in a dilemma: should I allow the whims of some crooked old opium addict to tarnish the reputation of my beloved Shah?

HIM outlined his intention to address the annual conference of the International Labour Organization in Geneva next June, but I warned him that the Swiss authorities disapprove of the trip since it is bound to cause them major embarrassment.

The Queen of England has invited HIM to continue on from Switzerland to the UK ...

Dinner at the Queen Mother's. HIM was opposed to our plan to send Davallou to Switzerland the day after tomorrow. I pointed out that our arrangements have already been made and that he will be met on his arrival by his lawyer, one of the most outstanding in Europe, who intends to open his attack on the Swiss authorities with a press conference, there at the airport. If Davallou fails to arrive we shall forfeit a major public relations coup. HIM is still concerned that Davallou will collapse under the strain, but I assured him that the man is in good shape and perfectly capable of making the journey. Once again I insisted that we proceed as arranged. 'You're being influenced by the lawyer', said HIM, 'and will swallow whatever nonsense he tries to sell you.' 'In which case', I replied angrily, and without pausing for thought, 'You, Your Majesty, are under the spell of Amir Houshang Davallou.' Only then did the rashness of my words come home to me, but HIM was unperturbed and made no comment. He can be tolerant to a fault.

I have been instructed to investigate the real reasons for the Swiss government's reluctance about HIM's trip to Geneva – does it mask some sinister intrigue by one of the superpowers, or by Britain or France? Again I told him there was no such plot, and that the Swiss are merely keen to forestall demonstrations by our own nationals. He remains unconvinced by this ...

Sunday, 9 April

HIM told me that even if he must cancel his visit to Switzerland he still insists on accepting his invitation to the UK. I should arrange things ...

Dinner at Princess Ashraf's. The PM was amongst the guests, so I was unable to raise anything of significance with HIM ... He has been told that vandals have been stealing the bathroom taps from the great Tehran Stadium, and he asked our opinion as to why people sink so low. The PM blamed the general lack of education. I agreed that this might be so. 'But at the same time', I said, 'it strikes me that most people are unable to grasp the fact that places like the Stadium are public property and that therefore they are merely robbing themselves when they resort to vandalism.' 'I find that even harder to believe', said HIM. 'But why?', I replied; 'One only need look around this country to realize that we, the ruling class, behave as if we were conquerors in a vanquished land. The people not surprisingly resent this attitude.' Princess Ashraf agreed with this. HIM heard us out in silence. He only changed the subject when the PM made some attempt to interrupt us.

Wednesday, 12 April

Throughout my audience poor Dr Eqbal, the Chairman and Managing Director of NIOC, was kept waiting outside. Most of HIM's conversation was devoted to oil negotiations and he gave me various opinions to pass on to the head of the Consortium. Why, I kept thinking to myself, why does he leave this all to me when that poor man Eqbal is left to twiddle his thumbs next door? ...

Tuesday, 18 April
Audience. HIM in excellent spirits. I showed him cuttings from the French and Swiss press. Not long ago they treated us like mud but now we can do nothing wrong. Davallou is made out to be nothing short of an angel. HIM had already received similar cuttings via the foreign ministry ...

Wednesday, 19 April
Audience. HIM unaccountably bad tempered. Even on unimportant matters he made me unhappy with his constant grumbling. It being morning, and I being stone cold sober, I was able to restrain myself from making any remark.

Amongst other international affairs, we discussed Morocco where the king has been forced to grant elections and a limited degree of political freedom to his people. Likewise in Pakistan, Bhutto has been obliged to relax martial law, five months before time, in order to implement a provisional constitution ... HIM believes that Bhutto had no alternative since he cannot rely on his defeated army[1] and must instead resort to political sleight of hand. Even so, I pointed out, the sort of chicanery going on in many of our neighbouring countries is bound to present us with problems in the end ... Whether we like it or not, we must adapt if we are to survive in this changing world. 'Your Majesty is always saying that he wishes to be ahead of events', I said, 'why not then implement change before change is forced upon us?' 'But what more do you expect me to do?', he replied; 'No one could have accomplished more than us.' He then went on to say that he has discovered the root cause of discontent amongst the younger generation; the disparity between their wages and those of men already in established positions. I suggested that this is only one of several factors at work. If people could be persuaded that they are working to achieve some basic goal, a goal respected by the ruling class, they would be prepared to put up with any amount of deprivation, even real hunger. 'But what principles do you suggest we put to the nation?', asked HIM. I replied that the public must feel that they are more than mere spectators of the political game. We must prepare the ground for their greater integration into this game; only then will they be satisfied and learn to play by the rules. HIM totally lost track of what I was saying, since he objected: 'But we lack the equipment; our department of physical education hasn't enough sports fields, trainers or even simple cash.' I explained that this wasn't

[1] The Indo–Pakistan war of December 1971 achieved independence for Bangladesh – previously East Pakistan.

exactly what I had in mind; that I was talking about popular participation in the game of politics. For example, why does the government continue to meddle in local elections? Leave the public to fight their own political contests and to choose whatever local representatives they prefer. Parliamentary elections may still require a degree of management, but surely this is untrue of elections in the municipalities. Why not allow the people free discussion of their local cares and concerns? What harm could it possibly do? 'What are you talking about; of course it would be harmful', he declared, 'they'd begin moaning about inflation, or some such rot.' 'Sadly', I replied, 'what they say about inflation is all too true. But even assuming it to be nonsense, why not open the safety valve and allow them to talk nonsense, freely, amongst themselves?' 'Precisely the reason I've allowed the opposition party to continue in existence', he replied. 'Yes', I said, 'but an opposition deprived of free discussion is surely no opposition at all?' At this point he asked my why the people pay so little attention to the progress we have made. 'Because' I told him, 'our propaganda is applied in quite the wrong directions. So much of our self-advertisement is patently untrue, and for the rest it's so mixed up with adulation of Your Majesty's own person that the public grows tired of it. Even I found it difficult to swallow the exaggerated propaganda over oil negotiations and the islands, though both of them were in reality very great triumphs.' ...

Dinner at the Queen Mother's. HIM spent much time arguing with HMQ that it's pointless to show greater sensitivity to the way in which events at Court are reported abroad. In reality, I'm sure his words were meant for me; my comments of this morning were not appreciated. Amongst other things I pointed out to him that, like it or not, we are exposed to scrutiny and criticism by the foreign press. Not that we should give way whenever they print unfavourable comment, but we cannot afford to ignore their opinions ...

Wednesday, 26 April
Audience. HIM approved an outline itinerary for Nixon's forthcoming visit to Iran. Some time ago, when Willy Brandt was our guest, HIM warned him that one effect of East-West *détente* in Europe would be to allow the Soviets to increase pressure on the Middle East. Today I reported a telephone call from the German ambassador, who told me that on his recent visit to London, Brandt raised precisely this point with the British, recommending that the British and Germans make private representations to the Soviets, warning them against further intervention in the Middle

East and threatening vigorous western reaction. HIM remarked that Brandt appears to be more reliable and responsible than he'd supposed.

... Later I received the new Chinese ambassador who wishes to invite HMQ to Peking. So much has changed over the past few years. How can any of these fools purporting to follow left-wing ideologies not realize that they are merely the puppets of the superpowers?

... In the evening escorted HMQ to a reception, to mark the end of the Tehran film festival. She distributed various awards. The PM was there, drunk as a lord and making an utter fool of himself.

Friday, 28 April

Audience. Reported the Chinese invitation to HMQ which has now been communicated to her by their ambassador. HIM was flabbergasted, firstly that HMQ had told him nothing about it, and secondly that the ambassador should have asked her directly without addressing his invitation to HIM as head of state. He urged me to reprimand the ambassador, but then he had second thoughts and said, 'Better still, do nothing. If we simply refuse to approve her visit, it will come to the same thing in the end.'

I also passed on a request from the Israeli envoy here, that HIM accept a visit from Prime Minister Golda Meir or from Abba Eban, the Israeli Foreign Minister, prior to the arrival of President Nixon. 'We have nothing of importance to discuss with Israel', said HIM, 'but if they're really determined to see me, they must bear full responsibility for keeping our meeting a secret.' He then went on to say that he would like to meet Nixon in private on the first day of his stay. Only Kissinger should be allowed to attend a second meeting. HIM requires only a secretary to take notes, though even that might be dispensed with if Kissinger can be persuaded to write the minutes. What faith HIM puts in our PM and Minister of Foreign Affairs!

... Over dinner the PM told me that he was up until 3 a.m., dancing the night away with actresses attending the festival reception. 'Good for you', I replied ...

Friday, 28 April

... Lunch at home with various French actors and actresses attending the film festival. They most of them struck me as plain and decidedly ignorant, but the young people, my daughters and sons-in-law amongst them, seemed to appreciate their company ...

Sunday, 30 April

Audience ... HIM said that he's thinking of appointing special advisers to counsel him in various issues. 'This is a suggestion that I have put to Your Majesty on at least ten separate occasions since my appointment as Minister of Court', I replied. 'Given that Your Majesty's present great authority means that your orders are immediately carried out, I have long considered it advisable, especially in social and economic affairs, that each case be examined by an expert before you issue any irrevocable order.' 'But surely that's the purpose of my government and my Plan Organization', he said. I reminded him that at present each minister receives his orders direct from HIM. Once such orders have been issued the minister in question quite naturally tends to ignore the wider aspects of government policy. On occasion this has led to something little short of chaos and has severely disrupted the co-ordination of any overall policy. There is a pressing need for a regulatory authority, which would best be located in HIM's personal secretariat. But HIM would have none of this and asked straight out, 'Did anyone ever "advise" me to achieve the many great things I have done for this country?' 'Of course not, Your Majesty', I told him, 'but the issues which face you today are of much greater technical complexity. No one could cope with all of them single-handed. Why else does a man like Nixon surround himself with specialist advisers?' He made no reply ...

Monday, 1 May

Despite it being the anniversary of the Prophet's birth and a national holiday, HIM remained at his desk. During my audience he seemed depressed. *Towfiq*, a satirical paper, excellent in its heyday but suppressed recently, has now re-opened, much to HIM's disgust. He has severely reprimanded those he holds responsible.

... 'Ask the Queen if she wants to accompany me to London', HIM said; 'She claims to have no interest in the visit, but I want you to make sure. If she really is determined against coming, then we can arrange a few amusing private excursions.' I telephoned HMQ who confirmed that she was uninterested in the trip. I reported this to HIM, but much to my surprise, she rang me back a few hours later and announced with a laugh that she had decided to change her mind. I again telephoned HIM who had already been put in the picture ...

Tuesday, 2 May

Audience. Submitted the itinerary for HIM's visit to the UK and asked him who he wished to accompany him. 'A few knowledgeable naval officers, Dr Ayadi and one or two personal servants', he said. Before leaving, I pointed out that I myself accompany him to Geneva, as someone must be on hand to keep an eye on developments.[1] There I shall take leave of him. 'As you say', he remarked, 'it is imperative that you keep an eye on things in Geneva.' Of course, I should have loved to go on with him to London. I love the city, British pomp and circumstance and their devotion to horses, but I long ago decided never to ask HIM for any personal favour, not even to accompany him on a trip ...

He instructed me to remind X that whenever he contacts some woman, he should report back to Davallou and never directly to HIM. I didn't understand this message, and in explanation he said, 'You know, people like X are always trying to wheedle their way into my affections. They compete with one another for the privilege of rendering their rather squalid services.' ...

Wednesday, 3 May

Audience. Amongst my many reports submitted a letter from Dr Amini who pledges his complete devotion to HIM. HIM laughed after reading it. I quite understood why. Even so I remarked that Amini might be sincere in what he says. 'Yes, but it depends entirely on the political situation from one moment to the next', said HIM. 'Men like yourself or Dr Eqbal never change, but the same cannot be said for the Aminis or the Sharif Emamis of this world. Their reactions at moments of crisis are always open to doubt.' I took the opportunity to ask if he holds such a low opinion of Sharif Emami, a freemason, why has he entrusted him with the supervision of our students overseas? 'For the moment', he replied, 'Sharif Emami is behaving himself and doesn't dare step out of line. Even so, you may instruct your deputy, Dr Mohammad Baheri, to offer his assistance and keep an eye on things.' I didn't bother to point out that to team up Sharif Emami and Baheri is to construct one of the strangest partnerships imaginable.

... The Saudi ambassador threw a dinner party in my honour, attended by the ambassadors of Pakistan and Jordan. They notified me that Bhutto

---

[1] The Shah was expected to deliver a speech at the annual conference of the International Labour Organization, before proceeding to the UK. Alam was concerned over the possibility of demonstrations against the Shah in Geneva.

and King Hussein would both like to visit Tehran during Nixon's forth-coming stay.

Tuesday, 9 May
The US Chargé d'Affaires rang me early this morning to arrange an urgent meeting. He arrived in person at 8 a.m., bringing a message from Nixon to HIM, announcing the US decision to mine the waters of North Vietnam, to resume bombing operations there, and to break off the Paris peace talks. According to the Chargé d'Affaires this news has only been divulged to America's closest allies, in London, Paris, Brussels, Rome, Bonn, Tokyo and Tehran. I passed the message on to HIM at my audience and suggested he reply to it in favourable terms. 'But how can we?', he said. 'For goodness knows how many years we've been insisting that both sides honour the 1954 Geneva accord.' 'But all the same', I replied, 'we and the Americans stand together. A defeat in Vietnam would spell disaster for the whole free world.' 'True enough', he said, 'but what are we to do with the Soviet bear breathing down our necks?' Subsequently I drafted a reply to Nixon but HIM insisted on expunging from it anything that might be read as an endorsement of America's actions.

Wednesday, 10 May
Audience. Reported that Golda Meir is due to arrive here on Thursday 18 May. I am doing my utmost to keep this visit a secret and can only hope that the Israelis won't let the cat out of the bag. Informed HIM that our press intends to condemn recent American actions in Vietnam. He ordered me to prevent publication in any way I can.

Our ambassador in Morocco writes that he has been contacted by Palestinians seeking financial support. 'We may have helped them once or twice in the past', said HIM, 'but they ended up backing our enemies, and actually training Iranian terrorists. Tell him that they can go fly a kite' – an attitude which I strongly support . . .

Saturday, 13 May
Audience . . . Reported that Ayatollah Milani of Mashad wishes to com-municate with HIM via the Ministry of Court. 'Why?' said HIM; 'Have you made him a courtier like the others? In the past he's always struck me as loathing the Court, or at least as being a very tricky customer.' I explained that the man wishes to emulate the success of Ayatollah Khonsari who presently basks in royal favour. Similar yearnings by Ayatollahs

Shariat Madari, Golpayegani and Marashi[1] of Qom have already been rebuffed by HIM, 'But we'll bend the rules for Milani', he said.

Sunday, 14 May

Audience ... Discussed the independence movement in Baluchistan. HIM agrees that this is the work of Russia and India. 'For the moment the Russians are unable to impose a communist regime in Afghanistan', he said. 'By seeking a weak and independent Baluchi state, they hope to get access to the Indian Ocean more easily than by going through Bangladesh, or through Iraq which has only a short coast-line at the far end of the Persian Gulf. Either one behaves like me, self-reliant, trusting in God Almighty for the good of my nation, or else one ends up like the King of Afghanistan. He goes around telling everybody that he will be the last king to rule over his people.' ...

Dinner at Princess Ashraf's marred by a fierce argument between her and myself. So swollen-headed has she become, and so vast does she believe her international experience, that she's taken to treating us like a bunch of cretins. What's even more ridiculous, she claims that whatever credit she's won for us abroad, we squander as we steer this country towards disaster. Tonight I had more than I could bear of all this, and although I love her dearly, I told her precisely what she can do with her opinions, even to the point of saying that it's she and people like her who are really responsible for discrediting the Shah. HIM seemed most amused by my outburst. The Princess, realizing that she was dealing with a madman who just so happened to be speaking the truth, made a complete about-turn and announced in joking tones that I must be drunk. The fact was I hadn't taken more than a glass of red wine. How bloody astute these women think themselves to be ...

Monday, 15 May

Audience. HIM was evidently pleased by last night's war of words. He laughed loudly and said, 'You gave her precisely what she deserved. Really, these people ought to be ashamed of themselves. They do untold damage to my reputation, yet have the audacity to pose as the defenders of national honour.'

... After lunch we held the inaugural session of the Council on Social Affairs. HIM declared that a third of shares in industry should be sold to

---

[1] All three played important roles in legitimizing the 1979 revolution.

the workers. This is a significant breakthrough as until now workers have been entitled to no more than 20 per cent of the net profits of their labours. Ironically, his speech made no mention of the word 'workers', referring to them throughout as 'third parties'. Only at the end did he realize that the point was unclear, so the session was resumed and he repeated his declaration clarifying it for the benefit of radio and television.

Audience later. Reported that the Davallou case has ended satisfactorily. HIM was delighted but asked me to say nothing to HMQ who will be less pleased by the news. 'She dislikes my entourage', he said, 'and with good reason. I'm sure you know why.' I told him that he's more than welcome to sack me if I'm the cause of tension with HMQ – it's obvious that my presence infuriates her. 'Of course you're a cause of her displeasure', he said, 'but I never allow other people to meddle in my affairs, not HMQ, not anybody.' ... He then asked me whether industrialists will comply with his request and sell shares to their workers. 'There's no doubt about it', I said; 'People are convinced that your policies are in their own best interest.' ... In all we spoke for close on an hour. At one point, apropos of nothing in particular, he remarked, 'It's extraordinary, but all my ministers assure me that whatever I say to them they know to be true from the very bottom of their hearts.' I refrained from pointing out that his ministers are all adept at the most preposterous flattery ...

Thursday, 18 May

Audience. Golda Meir flew in at 7 this morning and I reported that she was taking a short rest. 'That old woman has such stamina', HIM said. He then asked after the time of their meeting which was scheduled for 3 p.m. She was received for around two and half hours, before returning to the airport for her flight back to Israel.[1]

Friday, 19 May

Rode out with my wife early this morning ... Audience later. HIM had just returned from the hospital. He had a swelling behind his ears, probably due to his smallpox vaccination, but the dim-witted surgeons have insisted

---

[1] Iran, careful not to offend Arab friends, avoided any publicity about her high-level contacts with Israel. Relations with the latter, although outwardly limited to an exchange of consular missions, were in practice very close and encompassed an array of economic, security and political issues. During the above-mentioned meeting, the Shah, who had developed friendly relations with President Anwar Sadat, tried his best to persuade Golda Meir to show more understanding towards Egypt. The Shah guessed correctly that there was a good chance of freeing Egypt from the Soviet stranglehold.

on giving him massive doses of antibiotics and they now want to take X-rays. I opposed the suggestion, but HIM paid me no attention and followed the advice of his witch-doctors. On his return today he told me that he has agreed to a few days of diathermic treatment. Again I grumbled at this, but he only laughed saying, 'You've got it in for the doctors, and for any sort of medical advice.' I replied that his doctors seek any pretext to wheedle their way into his favour.

Reported that Davallou has delivered an excellent statement to the press in Geneva, but then spoilt everything by announcing that he is to return to Switzerland with HIM on 14 June. What a stupid blunder. I could sense how much it had upset HIM. From then on he turned a deaf ear to all my proposals.

Saturday, 20 May
Audience. HIM in a good mood. His new policy on industrial participation has gone down well at home and abroad. The British press have been particularly enthusiastic, especially *The Economist*. 'Just as you told me', he said, 'it appears the British are greatly impressed. Hence the change of tone at *The Economist* – a magazine which previously opposed virtually everything we did. It only goes to show that the British government still pulls all the strings; one word from their ambassador and their newspapers are falling over one another to praise us.' I suggested this might be going a bit too far: the British praise us or damn us according to the merits of our actions. I referred to a broadcast speech I made a few days ago, setting out HIM's new policies. Without mentioning the British ambassador by name, I remarked how a highly qualified foreign observer had told me that previously he had always believed that the Iranian government lay behind our stability, the rule of law, the absence of strikes and social disorder, but that since listening to my speech he had come to realize that all of these qualities spring from the foresight and common sense of the Shah. HIM denies having heard my broadcast, though I'm absolutely sure he has, both on radio and television, as well as reading it in the newspapers. This is always his way: he likes to give the impression that anything we say is far too insignificant to merit his attention. Though God help you if you ever make the slightest error. One false word and before the broadcast has even finished, he is bawling you out on the telephone, dictating what you should and should not have said . . .

Sunday, 21 May

The new US ambassador Joseph Farland presented his credentials this morning. God help us, but he shows few outward signs of intelligence. He is due to call on me tomorrow.

Monday, 22 May

Audience. Submitted the final proposals for Nixon's stay in Iran ... HIM asked me to arrange audiences this afternoon for representatives of the oil companies and for Onassis who is keen to lease us some of his tankers ...

Received the new US ambassador at my office. He still strikes me as being far from ideal, although he appears well-intentioned. We must simply wait and see ...

Tuesday, 23 May

As usual, many petitioners visited me at home before my departure for the office. Amongst them was a sheep farmer from Firouzkuh who claims to have been swindled by an individual close to the Shah. The man leased the farmer a pasture, banked the money and then rented out the selfsame land to another man without allowing the farmer to take possession. I examined his case and found that he's telling the truth. Accordingly I mentioned it at this morning's audience. HIM has instructed the gendarmerie to ensure that the poor man is able to graze his sheep as originally agreed ...

Audience later at which I submitted a draft of the speech to be delivered by HIM during Nixon's stay here. HIM is livid with the Soviets for having contracted a friendship agreement with Baghdad despite all our efforts to warn them against the Iraqis. Even so he agreed to tone down various bitterly anti-Soviet remarks which he yesterday ordered to be included in his speech. We discussed the addresses made to a reception at the Kremlin last night by Nixon and Podgorny, both of whom expressed a desire for mutual co-operation to achieve world peace.

HIM is delighted by the attitude shown recently by the British. 'They have become more European', he said, 'and as a result they seem to have altered their approach towards us; it's much more sincere.' I replied that the same sort of thing could be said of the Americans. He agreed, remarking that it's all due to the fact that Iran is their only reliable ally in the region. Discussed Saudi Arabia and the increasingly reactionary line being adopted by King Faisal, poor man. He's had every cinema in the country closed down. I remarked that I would have expected him to adopt a more enlightened attitude, but HIM told me I should bear in mind some of the

King's more absurd pronouncements last year, when we held a lunch in his honour at the airport. For example he declared that every Jew has a sworn duty to dunk his bread in the blood of a Moslem at least once a year. We considered the various possibilities for the succession; HIM believes Prince Fahd[1] is most likely to become king, though he added that an Englishman – probably the British Foreign Secretary – has told him Fahd is too much of a lecher. 'Not of course that that ought to be a hindrance to him', he said, 'after all I myself have never been averse to a bit of good old-fashioned lust.' I retorted that he should distinguish between a man like himself, who enjoys a few hours' relaxation each week, and an out-and-out lecher obsessed with carnal pleasure ...

Wednesday, 24 May

Audience ... showed HIM a pro-Iranian article in *Süddeutsche Zeitung* which pleased him very much ...

Submitted the guest list for Nixon's dinner; all the Shah's relations have accepted their invitations. 'We have Nixon to thank for that', said HIM; 'Normally they avoid my receptions like the plague.' Yet he continues to invite them; what a tolerant man he is ...

Saturday, 27 May

Audience. Mentioned that *Ettela'at* has printed a picture of the policeman tragically killed by terrorists, side by side with a report that a royal pardon has been granted to various of the terrorists condemned to death by military tribunal; the remainder have already been executed. 'I'm personally unfamiliar with those I pardoned', he said, 'but our investigations proved that they were relatively minor offenders.' 'God grant you long life', I replied. 'You have no desire to mete out death to those whose hands are unstained by innocent blood. The death sentence is almost certainly too harsh a punishment for those who merely assist the terrorists.' 'Even so', he remarked, 'the military penal code classes such people as conspirators against national security, deserving nothing short of execution.' I pointed out that this was morally unjustified, however much it might be correct in law. Most of the culprits can be persuaded to mend their ways in less drastic fashion. 'I hope you're not turning soft', said HIM. 'Perhaps I am', I replied, 'but quite frankly I have no confidence in the people who head

[1] Younger brother of King Faisal. In fact Prince Khalid succeeded King Faisal in 1975. Prince Fahd became King only after Khalid's death in 1982.

our security services. By excessive zeal they threaten to involve Your Majesty in the shedding of innocent blood.' He assured me that I was mistaken, adding, 'What do you suppose the terrorists would do with the likes of you and me, given half a chance?' I replied that I could imagine our fate only too well, but that this was no excuse for harshness. We must not sink to their level. He smiled at this but none the less I sensed he was impressed. 'Why need Your Majesty drive these people to the point of no return?', I said. 'After all, they're our own fellow countrymen, whatever their crimes.' ... 'And it's our own innocent fellow countrymen that they slaughter', he declared. 'I cannot ignore the rights of their victims.' I replied that two wrongs can never make a right.

... Turning to Nixon's forthcoming visit, HIM instructed me to ensure that Nixon and his entourage, especially Kissinger, are presented with gifts truly worthy of the occasion ...

Monday, 29 May

Audience ... HIM carefully read through the draft programme for his trip to the UK, but was surprised to find so little of interest in such a heavy schedule. It includes an expedition on horseback, so he asked me to buy him some impressive riding kit.

I reported that the mayor of Tehran has assembled the architectural plans for the Pahlavi museum; should he submit them to HIM or HMQ? 'To me, of course', he replied.

Our Foreign Minister was my guest for lunch. He told me that the Chinese ambassador is keen to know whether HMQ will accept her invitation to China ... I immediately telephoned HIM who was lunching with HMQ. They discussed the matter for some time. I know that he was displeased that she alone had been invited, but in the end he approved the trip.

HIM most impressed by the biography of Mrs Nixon which I passed on this morning; 'What an extraordinary woman', he remarked ... I hope that everything is now set for Nixon's visit. My own office has been primed to work round the clock. We've armed ourselves with every sort of telecommunications device, besides limousines, helicopters and motorcycle escorts ...

Tuesday, 30–Wednesday, 31 May

The presidential visit is over and at last I have time to jot down a few words ...

On Tuesday morning I inspected the White Palace at Saadabad,[1] the residence we've put at the disposal of Mr and Mrs Nixon. I then went on to look over the court guest house we've set aside for part of his entourage; the rest have been assigned to four separate hotels. From there I dashed off to the airport, noticing on the way that the streets were not nearly so well-lined with people as we'd planned. I'd apportioned school children to one part of the route but my orders had not been implemented; likewise the political and corporate representatives had been placed too far out of the city, along the road to the airport. I cannot describe my fury at all this. I was cursing everyone around me, and above all myself, for having trusted the assurances of the Chief of Police. As it was, I did what I could to ensure that 5,000 children and the corporate representatives be relocated inside the city limits ...

Nixon flew in at 4 p.m. and the ceremony of welcome went off very well. Even so, whilst the President was inspecting the guard of honour a gust of wind blew the cap straight off the head of the guardsman carrying the flag. We all laughed, but I took it as an ill omen. The weather cleared as the procession moved off towards the city, and many more onlookers turned out to catch a glimpse of the President. HIM and Nixon travelled the whole route in an open car and Nixon was greatly impressed by the enthusiasm of the crowds. At Saadabad he was welcomed by HIM's children – a charming sight.

There followed an hour and a half's private talks between HIM and Nixon, and then a well-managed reception. Dinner, I found less impressive, largely because we can no longer depend upon our excellent French chef who gave in his notice sometime ago. Another annoying incident: instead of the broth described on the menu, we were served cream of asparagus soup. I was in an agony of embarrassment but no one appeared to notice the mistake. Both after-dinner speeches were excellent ... I then went to my office, the nerve-centre of this entire operation. Terrorists have set off a few explosions. Nothing very serious, though we could have prevented them altogether if we'd been a little more vigilant.

Meanwhile the PM escorted Assistant Secretary of State Sisco and Kissinger, Nixon's national security adviser – some would say his intel-

---

[1] The Shah used the White Palace as his summer residence.

lectual mentor. He was supposed to show them the sites of Tehran, but, as I see it, he was really out to prove that he's still a lick-spittle of the Americans; after all, he was one of the traitors around Mansour who only achieved power with American support. He still knows on which side his bread is buttered. HIM would not allow him to attend the private discussions with Nixon and Kissinger, so I presume he was keen to get some sort of inside line to Kissinger. At 3 in the morning whilst I was still at work I caught sight of Kissinger returning to the guest house. Apparently the PM took his guests first to a nightclub and from there to a reception, thrown by the Ministry of Information for the presidential press corps.

Rested for a bare three hours before returning to my post. At half past six I heard a bomb go off at no great distance. It turned out to have been planted in the car of a US general acting as adviser to the Iranian army; he himself was wounded ... Later came news of yet another explosion, this one demolishing part of a wall at the mausoleum of Reza Shah. I was amazed so little had been done to guard the site, despite my categorical orders. Fortunately I can depend on the minutes of our discussions to bear me out. I wonder whether the security authorities will be for the high jump. These particular gentlemen enjoy every advantage, yet they couldn't so much as guard a sack of potatoes let alone a national monument.

According to his schedule, Nixon was due to leave his residence at 8.30 a.m. to lay a wreath at the Reza Shah mausoleum. I was not required to accompany him and so waited in my office for the cortège to set off. By 9 a.m. there was still no sign of movement, and a few minutes later the head of the American security team rang to tell me that he had advised that the wreath laying ceremony be cancelled in view of the earlier explosion. This infuriated me, but when I telephoned HIM he merely told me to leave it to the Americans to do as they wish; we shouldn't insist they comply with the pre-arranged schedule. He added that he had issued similar instructions to the commander of the Imperial Guard. 'But, Your Majesty', I said, 'if we accept the situation we'll be discredited right across the world. I myself shall escort the President to lay his wreath.' 'What if something should happen?', said HIM. 'Nothing will happen', I replied ... Hurried to the presidential residence where I came across Nixon sitting in his car; he had been there an hour, prevented from setting out by his security men. I opened the car door, wished him a good morning and asked why he had not yet set out. I've known him for some time and can afford to be rather familiar with him. When he explained that his security men had advised him to cancel the visit, I said: 'Nonsense; you're in absolutely no danger.

I myself shall escort you. Let's get going.' Clearly he was infected by my own self-confidence, for he replied, 'You're quite right. These people are being far too cautious. Let's be off.' He offered me a seat beside him, but I pointed out that the schedule assumed he would work with his advisers. Instead I took up a place in the next car back. We went. We returned, and not a thing went wrong. The crowds were much thicker than they had been the day before. When we got back, I pointed out what a shame it would have been to disappoint so many people. He thanked me warmly.

According to the schedule, at 10.30 a.m. Mrs Nixon was to be received by HMQ. Together they would then visit the children's library in the Niavaran park ending up at a day creche nearby. Yet, somehow, her escort got confused and drove first to the creche. One day these idiots will get their just deserts. But we managed to correct the mistake and the morning passed off satisfactorily.

Meanwhile HIM had another set of talks lasting an hour and a half, with only Nixon and Kissinger present. For lunch Nixon invited us to his residence; twenty-four of us sat down to an excellent meal. Discussions ranged widely. Various American students are ignoring national interests and causing turmoil in the universities. Nixon remarked that he'd like to see the culprits executed. We then touched on the tragedy at Tel Aviv; a few Japanese terrorists, Palestinian sympathizers, have machine-gunned the airport; thirty-three innocent men, women and children were slaughtered, eighty wounded. Mrs Nixon sitting next to me remarked that one never reads of this sort of atrocity happening in a communist country, but, as I pointed out to her, such atrocities are the price we must pay for living in a free society; only under communism, as her husband so rightly suggests, would saboteurs be executed before trial. I also remarked how strongly we support the President's stand over Vietnam; an action vital to the survival of the free world. She was delighted. I was speaking from sincere conviction, not plying her with flattery.

Nixon gave a very friendly informal address, announcing that the Kremlin may be a palace but an eight-day stay there was absolute purgatory. Only now, in the Shah's own private residence, could he learn to breathe freely again. Indeed he considered it to be very much a home from home. There were relatively few people present, but even so I was surprised to hear a head of state speak so bluntly at what was, after all, a semi-official luncheon. HIM replied in equally warm terms. This too came as a surprise; normally he is far more guarded.

At 1.30 p.m. the motorcade set out for the airport. En route the highway passes close by the halls of residence of Tehran University and a few students took the opportunity to throw stones at the passing cars. Luckily they had not got into their stride by the time Their Majesties and our guests passed by, though my own car was hit. Once again the police failed to predict the problem. Our guests flew out at 2, and I was able to breathe an enormous sigh of relief ...

Thursday, 1 June

Audience. HIM gave me a brief sketch of his discussions with Nixon who seems to have agreed to every request that was put to him ... According to Nixon himself, his decision to resume bombing in North Vietnam was opposed not only by Congress, but by the State Department and the Pentagon. Yet he refused to give way, even if it meant cancelling his visit to Moscow, or forfeiting his chances of re-election. Apparently he is now gaining ground against his critics. HIM is convinced that he greatly appreciates the stability of Iran and the responsibilities we've assumed in the Persian Gulf. Kissinger told HIM that the Russians have gone too far in their relations with Iraq, adding that something would have to be done to stop the rot ...

The Soviet ambassador dined as my guest this evening. HIM had asked me to raise the subject of Iraq. The ambassador himself began by praising HIM's speech at dinner two nights ago; at the same time describing Nixon's as inappropriate. When I disagreed with this, he went on to say that Nixon should have stuck to the agreed text, and not spoken about the enemies of America as if he meant to include every socialist country. 'Surely he was only speaking the truth', I said. The ambassador laughed. I seized the opportunity to point out that, much as we should like to see world-wide peace, we must continue to strengthen our defences so long as we are up against countries like Iraq, in thrall to foreign imperialism. 'What's more Mr Ambassador', I said, 'it's a peculiar fact, but Iraq could not hope to make so much trouble for us without support from your own country.' At this, he categorically denied that Moscow is backing Iraq against us ... He added that the whole Iranian–Iraqi conflict can be too easily exaggerated, and that there are some countries which have no wish to see the conflict resolved. Even so, as I put it to him, 'How can you, our friends, conclude an agreement with our enemies in Iraq?' 'The two friendships need not be mutually exclusive', he replied; 'Iran herself already has a friendship agreement with America.' At this I reminded him that he had begun by insisting that there was no longer any enmity between Washington and

Moscow. He was lost for a reply and was forced to fall back on whisky and Russian jokes ... On the whole, he's an agreeable sort of man ... Later we discussed the importance of Soviet–Iranian friendship for the preservation of peace ...

Monday, 5 June

Brief audience. Reported the complaints of Dr Kani, leader of the Mardom party, who claims that the government secures the dismissal of anyone in an official post who joins his party, citing the example of the headmaster of a government-run secondary school. HIM took the whole thing very seriously and straightaway telephoned the PM to express his concern. He then instructed his principal private secretary to launch an enquiry; a few hours later the man reported back to say that Kani's complaints were justified. In the past HIM would have brushed this sort of thing aside, so his change of attitude came as a great surprise to me. It may not do much to improve the outlook for Mardom, but at least they'll be free to attempt a come-back. According to one British newspaper, we have two political parties in Iran; the 'yes' party and the 'of course sir' party. Would it be right for me to express the hope that Mardom may now be less of a rubber-stamp when it comes to debating government policies? ...

Tuesday, 6 June

Audience. I told HIM that I'd now read the *Economist* article, and that it's a fairly light-weight piece. What it says about our military tribunals being hole-in-corner affairs, closed to outside observers, is no more than the truth. I cannot describe the rage with which HIM snapped back at me, 'Why don't you go away and write them a letter, thanking them for their well-timed remarks?' ...

Wednesday, 7 June

Attended Dinner. HIM in a genial mood. 'Tell the British', he said, 'that our press is about to make life hell for them. They can protest as much as they like that this will have no impact in Britain, but it will be enough for us merely to discredit them here in Iran.' Of course, he'd be quite right, if only our press commanded an ounce of credibility even here.

[There follows about a month's interlude in which no diary appears to have been kept. The Shah was away in Switzerland and the UK. Alam too went abroad. The diary resumes after Alam had returned to Tehran, the Shah to Nowshahr on the Caspian Sea.]

Monday, 10 July

For some time the British ambassador has been insisting that I take up an invitation to lunch. In the end I accepted, although I'm by no means in perfect health. He complains that I was much closer to his predecessor than I am to him.[1] Well, it's true that the previous ambassador was a likeable man, and I had far more in common with him; a shared love of sport and horses. Even though he was no longer ambassador, last February he spent five days as my guest at Arosa. I don't give a damn who the British appoint as their ambassador, but my friends are mine for life. I can't pretend I think much of his successor; too much of an old woman for my liking, but I had no choice but to accept his invitation. He's hinted on nearly a dozen occasions that I've never been to his residence, though he has been my guest both privately and at Court. It might discredit him with his superiors, and now that HIM has returned from his visit to London trailing clouds of glory, I thought it best to put the poor man out of his misery. As HIM remarked when I told him about it, 'If he's that keen for you to go, you had better accept.'

In the event I spent a full three hours at the residence and he gave me a run down on HIM's trip to England. At the airport before setting out for Switzerland and thence to London, HIM apparently remarked to the ambassador, 'There can be little point in my visiting your country given the way Iran is presented by the BBC and Fleet Street.' As a result, the ambassador sent off an anxious memo to the Foreign Office, but it turned out that HIM had received false reports about press coverage in the UK. The ambassador is indignant about this, and with just cause.

He declared that Iran is the only country in the Middle East that the British can rely on; the most stable and the strongest power in the region, governed by a leader of unparalleled standing. 'So you see', he said, 'we've put all our eggs in one basket, and if I criticize from time to time it's only because I'm so anxious to avoid future problems for Iran, and by inference for my own country as well.' He added that whilst on a tour of duty in Paris, he'd been instructed by the Foreign Office to make a character study of De Gaulle. De Gaulle, he believes, resembles HIM in many ways. The General declared that he was France, and the Shah thinks in much the

---

[1] The previous ambassador, Sir Denis Wright, had left Iran in 1971.

227

same way about Iran. I could only agree with this and, as illustration, I cited the case of the palace on Kish. When I submitted the title deeds for this palace to HIM and registered it in his personal name, he threw them back at me, saying, 'Why make me the owner of some trifling plot of land? The whole nation is mine without my having to stake some petty private claim. Everything is at the disposal of a ruler of strength. But for my strength, title deeds and all such trifles will avail me not one jot.' The ambassador went on to say that HIM may share De Gaulle's failings as well; obstinacy and wilfulness. 'Perhaps', I replied, 'but I've yet to see any sign of it. For the moment HIM tempers his strength with clear logic, prudence and calm.' ...

We turned to a discussion of the House of Commons. The British Prime Minister and the Leader of the Opposition have both praised HIM and Iran, but one catches no echo of this in the Iranian press. On the other hand, the moment a British newspaper, and the British government has no control over such things, prints the merest whisper of criticism against us, our own press erupts in fury. I must admit that here again the ambassador has just cause for complaint.

He then remarked that HIM's orders tend to get mixed up once they are transmitted to the lower levels of the executive, a fault he puts down to a shortage of men with the requisite administrative skills. He also suggested that it might be better for the country if HIM were to remain more aloof from details. All this was expressed with the utmost courtesy, and profuse apologies for interfering. As the ambassador put it, his only justification was that Britain now feels duty bound to assist her great ally to the best of her abilities ...

Tuesday, 11 July
Flew to Nowshahr with the Minister of War, arriving there at 10 a.m. The Minister was granted a brief audience and then HIM emerged from his shack bare-chested. Straddling the parapet of the jetty he asked that I deliver my report. It was 39 degrees in the shade with 80 per cent humidity, so I suggested that there might be more suitable places for us to work. 'But I like it here', he replied.

We talked for two hours and in the meantime HMQ arrived accompanied by the King and Queen of Greece. They eventually became so impatient with the delay that HIM was forced to tell them that he and his Court Minister always have a great deal to discuss.

I began by reporting my conversation with the British ambassador. HIM listened attentively throughout, and although it's my duty to keep nothing hidden from him, I endeavoured to present the ambassador's words in the best possible light. For example, I said that he had drawn a major distinction between HIM and De Gaulle, saying that HIM had acquired far more experience in his early youth and was still a young man. 'As such, according to the ambassador, you will never grow so stubborn or wilful as old De Gaulle.' HIM agreed with this, saying, 'I shall do my best to live up to that particular forecast, even in my dotage.'

I also reported my latest meeting with the US ambassador. I had told the ambassador that Nixon is said to have great confidence in him, at least according to the Shah. 'You did well', said HIM. 'When you next see him let him know that I shall rely on him in future if ever I need to relay a confidential message to his President without the knowledge of the State Department.' HIM is keen to obtain American credit for the development of Chahbahar, crucial for the control of the Indian Ocean and for economic progress in Baluchistan. As a result he authorized me to invite the ambassador on a tour of Birjand and Baluchistan. On 23 July I must be in Tehran, when HIM arrives to begin oil negotiations.

Again the question of the opposition party cropped up, and I described how Kani, poor man, had enthusiastically shown me the newspaper pictures of popular jubilation at the Mardom meeting in Rasht.[1] HIM smiled: 'We'll know the truth of the matter soon enough, after the next local elections', he said. I replied that Kani is equally keen for the issue to come to a vote, providing only that HIM appoints an unbiased Minister of the Interior to handle the elections. HIM made no comment. His attitude is altogether a puzzle to me; what can be wrong with suggesting he make such an appointment? Why on earth should he feel obliged to support our present PM, creepy old Quasimodo? . . .

Friday, 14 July
Flew once again to Nowshahr and went directly to see HIM who I found taking his bath. He signalled to me that we could be overheard from the next room, remarking as he did so, 'I'm sure it's much too hot for you in here. Go and pour yourself a whisky and then we'll be off to the King of Greece's reception.' As I was sipping my drink, the Queen came in. 'Presumably you're waiting for His Majesty', she remarked coldly. I replied that this was indeed the case, and she breezed out again. HIM then joined

[1] Provincial capital of Gilan, on the Caspian Sea.

me and we discussed various items of news, besides drawing up his schedule for next week, when he's to spend a couple of nights in Tehran – hence his anxiety that HMQ should not eavesdrop on our plans ...

Saturday, 15 July
Returned to Tehran where I lunched at my mother's with my daughter Naz. Then went home for a siesta, but before I had put my head down the telephone rang. It was Naz to say that she'd narrowly avoided being kidnapped on her way home. At 3 p.m. in summertime the streets of Tehran are more or less deserted. Naz found her way blocked by a group of terrorists who made a grab for her. Fortunately she was nearly home, separated from her house only by a plot of waste land running alongside the road. Keeping her cool she slammed on the accelerator, swerved across the road and, after pulling herself out of a deep ditch, not without difficulty, reached the safety of her house. For this I gave heartfelt thanks to the Almighty. I immediately telephoned General Ja'farqoli Sadri, Chief of the National Police, who in his customary Isfahani drawl told me I was worrying myself over nothing. 'It's nothing very serious; she's a pretty girl, a few men take a fancy to her, so what?' On the day when Nixon was here and the American general's car was bombed, it was this self-same General Sadri that I phoned to ask about the explosion. 'Oh, it's nothing very serious', he said; 'a car's brakes failed descending the hill. It hit a lamp-post and the petrol tank went up in flames, so what?'

Monday, 17 July
Discussions with a certain Englishman, an expert on Iraq and Kurdistan. Together we have come up with a well-thought-out plan to topple the present regime in Baghdad by bringing together the Kurds and the Iraqi opposition in exile. We are working closely with the British and Americans on this, but must wait and see whether anything comes of it.

The American ambassador called round. He gave his assent to every request I put to him, promising that we will be supplied with DC-10s, Lockheed 10–12s, F-15s and F-111s, the last two types of aircraft still on the drawing board. He agreed that whatever fuss BOAC and the other airlines kick up, Iranair may operate a scheduled service to Los Angeles, a longstanding ambition of HIM. He also remarked that, following the resumption of diplomatic relations with North Yemen, his government intends to shower the Yemenis with all manner of aid. His intelligence services report that Sheikh Zaid, the head of the UAE, is adopting a far more sensible line, being anxious to see closer ties to Iran and Saudi Arabia. I replied that my own sources tell me that the Sheikh has abandoned his idea of opening diplomatic channels with the Soviets, at least for the moment. The ambassador was surprised I should have heard of this.

I then raised the subject of our secret manoeuvres with respect to Baghdad, expressing the hope that our plans will not be exposed as they have been in the past . . . The ambassador suggested that he establish direct links with our own military commanders and security officials, on the quite preposterous grounds that he is interested in keeping an eye on the US military advisers within Iran. I told him that his suggestion came as something of a shock; that it hardly struck me as being very appropriate but that I would refer it to HIM. In reply he made the utterly irrelevant remark that he would like every member of his embassy to know who's boss . . .

Tuesday, 18 July
Flew to Nowshahr. Unbearably sticky heat. Audience . . . In response to the US ambassador's request, HIM said, 'Make him understand that in no circumstances can he approach our military and security commanders without prior approval from the Court. If he has information to pass on, he may in certain circumstances be allowed to meet them in person, but he must report every meeting either to me or you.' . . .

Wednesday, 19–Thursday, 20 July
. . . Sadat has without warning sacked every one of the 20,000 Russian military advisers stationed in Egypt. Quite an army! Moscow has taken it all very calmly . . . For several months US and particularly British intelligence sources have warned us to expect such a development . . .

Saturday, 22 July
Met the Russian ambassador before lunch and discussed HIM's forthcoming trip to Moscow. I asked his opinion on the oil negotiations and Middle Eastern politics in general. He ducked my questions but I sensed he is put out by events in Egypt.

. . . Then left for the airport to greet HIM and escort him to Saadabad. Walking together in the garden there, I got the distinct impression that he was angry with me. Suddenly he turned to me and said, 'Why has Kani started spouting all this rubbish? At a party rally in Isfahan he accused the government of being reactionary, saying that Mardom would be elected if only the elections were not rigged. How dare he accuse my government of reaction, and how dare he so much as suggest that elections held under my rule are anything but completely free?' I assured him that this was the first I'd heard of the matter, and pointed out that as leader of the opposition Kani feels obliged to say something, nonsense though it may be. If HIM is determined to read it in a sinister light, the man's speech will naturally seem shocking. It all depends on how broad-minded HIM is prepared to be, and how such speeches are reported to him. Naturally an opposition leader will regard the government as reactionary, and as for the elections, we know jolly well that he's speaking the truth. The real issue is whether it's right to air such views in public. 'But what on earth is the bloody man on about?', said HIM. 'He's got about as much hope of winning the election as of teaching a pig to fly.' Kani would say, I replied, that the government is just as unpopular as his own party, and that Mardom stand a real chance of winning, if only by default. 'What bullshit', HIM retorted angrily and I thought it best to let the matter drop ...

Monday, 24 July

... Received for about three hours after lunch. I reported that Kani is so upset by HIM's reaction that he has resigned as party leader and now begs to be appointed to some sort of position at Court. Handed over his letter explaining all this to HIM who answered that he had sacrificed his chances at Court along with everything else; 'There can be no place for him here.' Clearly HIM's anger is more deep-rooted than I at first suspected, and it will take much longer to cool.

HIM said, 'On your trip together to Birjand, remind the US ambassador of Nixon's promises. I asked that they supply fully qualified blue-suiters[1] for our airforce, but they now propose to hire retired military mechanics and even civilians, who will be of little use to us. And what about Kissinger? He told our PM that Nixon would have given me every weapon in America if only I'd asked for it.'

Tuesday, 25 July

King Hussein and his sister stopped off here before flying to the Caspian with HIM. Muna al Hussein, his Queen, is elsewhere and instead he's brought along a stunningly attractive British girl who we're supposed to think is merely a friend of his sister. He's also accompanied by his close

---

[1] On active service with the US air force.

confidant, General Amash, head of Jordanian military intelligence. The latter has spent the past week flying to and fro between Tehran, Amman, Jeddah and Abu Dhabi in an effort to improve our relations with the Arab states.

Wednesday, 26–Friday, 28 July
... Flew with the US ambassador to Birjand where we stayed for two nights. Early on Thursday we set out on a six-hour tour of inspection, flying high over Baluchistan and Chahbahar. I had ample opportunity to chat with him and to raise the various topics suggested by HIM ... Having talked over Egypt and the Middle East we moved on to discuss the imminent US presidential election and the fact that a defeat for Nixon would strike a blow at the entire free world. Turning to the practicalities of the election, the ambassador put a request to me that even fifty years from now I could never divulge for fear that it would irreparably damage relations between our two countries. Whilst I dare not set down his request in black and white, I can say that it demonstrates the extent to which Nixon is willing to rely on HIM. I promised to convey the President's suggestion to HIM and assured the ambassador that we shall be only too happy to do all we can to help.

Saturday, 29 July
Flew to Nowshahr to report Nixon's message. HIM was delighted and immediately gave his approval in principle. We must now wait for Nixon to make the next move ...

Saturday, 5 August
Around noon HIM and King Hussein arrived back from the Caspian, the King flying straight on to Amman. Accompanied HIM to Saadabad and lunched there with him and the Queen Mother. He was in high good spirits, talking about the British dock strike ... 'What does their government think it's up to?', he said, 'allowing a small minority to hold the country to ransom. Likewise in the USA, the former Attorney General flies off to North Vietnam, makes some flattering remarks about the regime there, and actually ends up being applauded by various of his fellow Americans. Thank God we in Iran have neither the desire nor the need to suffer from democracy.' 'But sooner or later we shall have no alternative', I replied. 'For the moment we are blessed with a wise and great monarch, a truly benevolent dictator; but without him we shall be forced to choose between

totalitarianism or democracy. There will be no middle way.' HIM nodded his agreement ...

Monday, 7 August

... The British ambassador lunched as my guest. The British are so forlorn that nothing interests them these days save commerce and arms deals ... Discussed the success of the army of Oman which with British assistance has crushed the Dhofari rebels. However the weapons we ourselves sent to Sultan Qabus along with C-130 transport planes were simply turned away by British military advisers. The ambassador apologized for this incident and said it was due entirely to the absence of the air-base's commanding officer on that particular day. 'Nevertheless', I said, 'our countrymen sometimes suspect that you would like to hold on to what remains of your vanishing influence at all cost.' 'I swear that the incident was the result of nothing more than human error', he replied, 'but we have broad shoulders and take criticism without flinching.' He then asked about HIM's discussions with King Hussein. 'I am afraid I know no more than you', I replied. He clearly didn't believe this so I remarked how peculiar it was that he too should have suspicions about what people like me tell him. 'I'm sure the feeling's mutual', he replied ...

Tuesday, 8 August

Flew to Nowshahr to lunch with HIM. Commenting on my discussion with the British ambassador, he said, 'Tell him it's not the broadness of their shoulders that marks out the British, but the size of their arse.'[1] ... Passed on a letter from Bhutto. I was instructed to write back that we shall not recognize Bangladesh until Pakistan herself has done so. It may seem surprising that HIM should give the Pakistanis such a firm commitment, but then he's never fully appreciated the extent to which Mujib ur-Rahman has thrown himself into cahoots with India, whilst from any point of view, good relations with Pakistan are of the utmost importance to us ...

Thursday, 10 August

... Commenting on HIM's Constitution Day message (4 August), both *Ettela'at* and *Kayhan*[2] write that we shall gradually develop Western style democracy, as the people become accustomed to political participation at

---

[1] In Persian 'broad arsed' is an epithet applied to the lazy; hence the play on words
[2] Tehran's two principal evening newspapers.

village, county and provincial levels. On HIM's orders I summoned the editors of the two papers and instructed them to print a second set of articles stressing that we have no desire to have western democracy established here so long as in practice it merely encourages treachery and leads to tyranny by a minority. These are far from being my own sentiments, a point I made plain to HIM ...

Sunday, 13 August

Audience ... Showed HIM the first two parts of a series of articles on Iran by Hirst, a well-known journalist with the *Manchester Guardian*. On the whole, the articles were in our favour and HIM, being in a good mood, gave his permission for them to be reprinted by the local press.

At about 2 p.m. my special telephone rang and I found myself being addressed by HIM in such gloomy tones that I became seriously concerned. He wanted to know whether I had read the third of Hirst's articles. I replied that I hadn't but had been warned by our press office that it was not so good as the first two. 'What on earth do you mean, not so good?', he snapped. 'The mischief of the thing defies belief. His allegations must be refuted by the British government at the very highest level. The consultant for the gas pipeline where there's such an overrun is a British company; but our arms deals with the Americans, the Soviets and the British themselves are entirely government to government, so how on earth can he accuse us of corruption? The man is an utter shit.' All of this upset me greatly, not only because I hate to see HIM so annoyed, but because, at the British ambassador's insistence, I personally arranged for that scoundrel Hirst to be granted an interview with HIM.

This morning terrorists gunned down General Taheri, Governor of the Tehran prison, outside his own front door. This has only added to HIM's burden of woes. I reminded him that we must all learn to take the rough with the smooth ...

Monday, 14 August

Audience. HIM's first question was again about the *Guardian* articles – his sensitivity and suspicion are quite extraordinary. 'I still can't understand what induced him to write the final part', he said. Since it is I that was so vociferous about the opposition party and the need for greater political freedom and participation, I get the distinct impression that he suspects me of spurring on the journalist. When, I wonder, will he realize the true extent of my devotion to him? Not until doomsday perhaps. Of course I'm only going by instinct and I may exaggerate the depth of his suspicion.

I should set down here that the US ambassador came to see me last Saturday. He brought me messages from Nixon ... relating to the matter we discussed in Birjand ...

Wednesday, 16 August
Audience. Reported that the British ambassador has rung me several times to request a meeting. 'Go ahead and receive him', said HIM. 'After all it's not as if we intended leaving him out in the cold.'

The ambassador duly called round after lunch and we talked for a couple of hours. I told him that HIM has used private channels to convey the following message to the British Foreign Secretary: 'We were wrong to believe the British are our friends. You are obsessed solely with your own selfish interests and treat us as a people beyond the pale. But your attitude is a matter of profound disinterest. Your democratic system has already erupted in chaos. We shall soon overtake you and in a decade you will be struggling in our wake. Perhaps then you will remember how once you treated us.' ...

The ambassador protested vigorously at this, although I had by no means finished and had yet to raise the issue of Hirst's *Guardian* articles. When I'd had my say, he replied with admirable calm, 'We are attacked in your own newspapers every day of every week, indeed HIM's interview with Hirst itself contained yet another attack upon us. If anyone is entitled to complain it is us. How can HIM, who returned from London fully satisfied, vowing the warmest friendship to Her Majesty's government, how can he throw everything away for the sake of some load of nonsense concocted by a journalist. Let's face it, the *Guardian*'s articles were actually a boost to Iranian pride. Your country is now a power to be reckoned with and HIM is a very great man. The choice must be yours; either you behave like a totalitarian regime and refuse access to western journalists; or else you let them in and accept the consequences without boiling over at the first hint of criticism.' ...

Prior to dinner at the Queen Mother's attended a reception at the Israeli delegation in honour of General David Elazar, the Israeli Chief of Staff. HIM had ordered me to go, as he believes the general to have been favourably impressed by the progress we have achieved for Iran. It was whilst I was at the reception that I heard the news from Morocco. King Hassan was returning to his country after an absence of three weeks when his plane was fired upon by the fighters supposedly sent to escort him home. Two of the engines on board his 727 were put out of action, but somehow the pilot managed to land safely. I immediately sent a cable of congratulations on HIM's behalf and am now waiting to hear the latest developments ...

Thursday, 17 August
Audience. Naturally Morocco dominated our discussions. I remarked that the King must be at his wit's end. 'It would certainly appear so', said HIM. 'He spends half his time asleep and the rest of it buried between the legs of the fairer sex. It's no way to run a country.' I reported that the Moroccan Defence Minister, General Oufkir,[1] is said to be implicated in the plot ... 'It wouldn't surprise me', said HIM, 'But he would have acted only out of patriotism. For too long he's been a witness to the sheer indolence of his King.'

I then said that much as it pained me to introduce an element of comedy into the conversation I felt obliged to report an incident at last night's reception. I was talking to the Israeli Chief of Staff about the progress we are making when his Iranian counterpart, General Azhari, butted in with an appalling howler, remarking that we owe any progress we have made to one fact; that everyone here is scared rigid by HIM. If someone fails to carry out an order on time he knows only too well that there will be hell to pay. 'What's so wrong with that?', said HIM, and I was forced to explain that fear is no substitute for patriotism as a spur to duty. 'I still can't see what he said wrong', HIM replied, clearly hinting that I'd be well advised to keep my mouth shut in future ...

Sunday, 27 August
Audience. Talked first of Morocco and then of the Hirst article which alleges corruption in the Iranian army. HIM wonders whether Hirst was in receipt of information from a source within the regime.

... The trial of a terrorist, Rezai, has begun in open session following pressure from Amnesty International. I've several times suggested that these sorts of trials be open to the public but HIM was swayed by the military judges who claimed that the accused would seize the opportunity to shout obscenities at the court. Having been roundly abused by Amnesty

---

[1] General Mohammad Oufkir, former Minister of the Interior, was a member of the Regency Council as well as Minister of Defence and Head of the Armed Forces. As one of King Hassan's closest confidants, his unsuccessful attempt on the King's life was particularly shocking to Hassan and led to his immediate execution.

International we must now sit back and suffer the abuse of our own home-grown offenders.

The ambassadors of Jordan, Qatar and Saudi Arabia dined as my guests so that I might thank them for refusing to sign a letter to the UN Security Council circulated by various Arab governments, claiming Tunbs and Abu Musa as Arab land ...

Monday, 28 August–Tuesday, 19 September

... Negotiations are still going on between the oil companies and the Arabs of the Persian Gulf. We have warned the companies that we ourselves shall reach no firm agreement until these other negotiations are settled; largely to ensure that the Arabs are not offered more favourable terms than us.

For the past few days HMQ has been in China accompanied by her mother, Mrs Farideh Diba, and the PM. She's received a tumultuous welcome; a good indication of the respect which this country and our sovereign now command. HMQ should not make the mistake of thinking she alone has inspired such enthusiasm.

We've now gone overboard on the publicity attending the terrorism trial. So far have we exceeded the bounds in inviting along journalists, photographers and TV crews that we're rapidly becoming an international laughing stock. A BBC correspondent has already dubbed it a 'show trial', much to the fury of HIM. The other day he asked me whether I'd read the transcript of the BBC news, and not having done so I promised to look it over ...

Again, over dinner at the Queen Mother's, HIM asked me what I made of the BBC report. 'Trivial stuff', I said, 'it merely sticks to the facts.' At this he produced a copy of the text and began to read excerpts out loud. They concerned the public prosecutor who was described as having delivered a swingeing attack on terrorism in general, without once descending to the specific charges against the accused. 'Well, well', said HIM, 'and yet you still maintain this is trivial stuff?' 'Yes', I said, 'the report is factually quite accurate.' 'Well now we know then', he said, 'now we know what some people consider to be factually accurate', and he launched into such an outburst of ranting and shouting that his mother, HMQ and the whole royal family gasped in alarm. I too was shocked, not only because the report was perfectly true, but because the whole business is of such stunning inconsequence. Never before has HIM abused me like this, but all the same I managed to maintain my composure, nor did I once feel anger myself. On the morrow I accompanied HMQ on a twenty-four hour tour of the Shiraz festival and all the time I was turning HIM's words over in my mind. I concluded that this trivial business about the BBC was merely the straw that broke the camel's back – he'd never have exploded in that way unless there had been something far more important that had already upset him.

He was much calmer on my return from Shiraz and spoke to me of his disappointment with Sheikh Zaid of Abu Dhabi, head of the UAE, who continues to sound off against Iran. He's still inclined to believe that for all their lip-service and growing dependence on Moscow, the Iraqis are secretly manipulated by the British. All in all his suspicions of the British are quite incredible; he tends to see their secret hand behind virtually every international incident. For myself I'm convinced that they're more or less incapable of achieving anything on the international stage, to such an extent has their power declined. The Americans by contrast are stupid and naïve enough to use their power in a manipulative and interfering way.

On three or four occasions I met the British ambassador and discussed the articles in the *Guardian* and the BBC. I pointed out that if they sincerely desire to maintain their relations with us on a cordial, let alone special, basis they should make some effort to discipline their media. To begin with he merely pleaded the impossibility of intervention. I then threatened the cancellation of every commercial deal we have with his country. This put the wind up him soon enough and at my insistence he requested an audience with HIM.

Also met the Egyptian ambassador who was full of complaints against our close relations with Israel, citing several specific examples in support of his case. When I reported this to HIM he said: 'Tell the ambassador that his own regime in Cairo does precisely what it likes; signs petitions and circulars vilifying us yet praising Iraq and Kuwait. Now he complains that we've grown too friendly with the Israelis; small wonder, is all I can say.'

The Moroccan Minister of Court came to Tehran to deliver a message from King Hassan. Much to my surprise HIM forbade me to welcome him in person. Apparently he's convinced that the King's days are numbered, an opinion he's had confirmed by the US ambassador ... The Minister stayed here for thirty-six hours during which I met him twice and gave a special lunch in his honour. He asked me how many hours I worked, and I explained that as HIM works about twelve hours each day I need to spend at least fourteen hours putting his orders into operation. 'Yours is a fortunate country indeed', he replied. 'Our own King leaves his private apartment for no more than two hours each day; and then it's only to go and play golf.' He spent most of his audience with HIM pleading for military assistance. HIM agreed to send military instructors and equipment, but pointed out that in the modern world a country's army cannot be kept apart from its people; if the people are dissatisfied with a particular regime then a well-trained army becomes more a threat than a safeguard.

... Following his audience with HIM the British ambassador came to see me. Apparently HIM remarked to him at one stage: 'I intend to live well in my old age, so I shall deposit all the kick-backs I have received from my nation's commercial transactions in one of the British banks for safe-keeping.' The ambassador was non-plussed by this and asked me what it meant. HIM had already briefed me on their conversation, so I explained that it was intended as heavy irony; ridiculing the press allegations of corruption in arms deals ... The ambassador blushed scarlet and asked me whether he could report the conversation to London. I told him to go ahead.

Wednesday, 20 September
Audience. Found HIM in a good mood which only improved when I reported last night's discussions with the ambassador. He suggested that next time I should add that HIM will likewise deposit in the UK all the kick-backs he receives from America; they might do something to save the British banking system, fast disappearing down the drain. What a pity that the general public has no idea how hard he fights to preserve our nation's dignity; and what a pity that our present government's behaviour merely drives another wedge between the people and their Shah ...

A second audience lasting two and a half hours this afternoon, to get through some of the backlog that has built up. Discussed the recent visit to Moscow by the President of Iraq and the joint Soviet–Iraqi communiqué stressing Soviet military aid. 'Its main purpose', said HIM, 'is to enhance their mutual prestige, but even so we must be vigilant. In my own forthcoming trip to Moscow I shall be freer than I've been in the past to speak my mind. I intend to make it plain that, as we can never put any real trust in the Soviets, we have no choice but to throw in our lot with the Western bloc.' And then, once again, he returned to his old obsession that the Iraqi President, al-Bakr, is an agent of the British.

Dinner at the Queen Mother's. HIM in excellent spirits. Among the guests was the head of the Imperial Inspectorate, General Yazdanpanah, who remarked that he's received far fewer complaints of late, suggesting growing public satisfaction with the government. 'Or maybe they've simply given up complaining because they know that it gets them nowhere', I replied. Neither HIM nor Yazdanpanah appreciated the joke, but I was pleased none the less to have had my say; it will have opened HIM's eyes when otherwise he might have been misled ...

Monday, 25 September

Audience ... I suggested that now we've moved to Saadabad for the summer and the Crown Prince must commute to school at the Niavaran, it might be best if he did so in the bullet-proof Mercedes I purchased last year for HIM. HIM replied that he was reluctant to do anything that might unsettle the boy, but, as I pointed out, we have no real alternative. He then went on to praise the boy's intelligence and his skill at driving, which I have always believed puts him unnecessarily at risk. 'Better that he take risks', said HIM, 'than that he ends up a shrinking violet like Ahmad Shah Qajar.'[1] He then added that Prince Ali Reza has asked whether he will take him to school in person as he did the Crown Prince; 'But I had to explain to him that I can't, as the school he's going to is French. Boys of his age are uncommonly sensitive about such things.' I replied that it might be advisable if Prince Ali Reza were taught that he should always look to the Crown Prince as a protector deserving his allegiance, however highly he may rate his own intelligence. Things are bound to turn out that way given the great difference in their ages ...

Saturday, 30 September

... The police chiefs of Bern and Geneva lunched as my guests, as part of their complimentary visit to Iran. Hardly the briefest nor the most sparkling of receptions I have thrown.

Then met Miss Lambton, an Oxford don and an outstanding expert on Iranian land reform. She has just returned from inspecting our latest achievements, which for the most part she praised.

Attended Dinner. HIM told me, 'Ask the British ambassador in a light-hearted way whether his country still regards Syria as a moderate, despite her accepting goodness knows how many Russian arms and agreeing to the establishment of Russian military bases. You might also remind him that the Chieftain tanks produce 50 to 60 horsepower less than their stated engine capacity.'

[1] The last Qajar King (1897–1930); acceded 1909; deposed in 1925. In colloquial Persian, his name is a byword for ineptitude.

Monday, 2 October

... Reported a conversation with the Chinese ambassador, who has been deeply impressed by HMQ's sincerity and her simple good nature on being introduced to strangers. 'People get quite the wrong idea about us', said HIM: 'They expect us to be aloof and superior, totally lacking the common touch. The ambassador should know better, but even he is pleasantly surprised to find his preconceptions confounded.'

... The US ambassador is away at the moment, and so it was through a special channel that HIM instructed me to send a message to President Nixon, urgently warning him of a report from King Hussein that the Syrians have taken delivery of T-62 tanks from the Soviets. Meanwhile the Red Army's General Babajanian is in Iraq. Should the Iraqis receive similar tanks and MIG-23 aircraft, the whole balance of power will be altered. Jordan asks that we help refit her own tanks with new engines, but we are in no position to supply the parts, and unless the USA goes to her rescue, the situation will be grave indeed. HIM instructed me to issue an identical briefing to the British ambassador.

Discussing the contrast between youth and old age, he said, 'In no time at all we shall both of us be sixty. How time marches on!'

'Quite right too', I replied. 'It's not the march of time that worries me, but as the poet[1] says:

> For judgment day my one and only fear
> Is that from out the grave the same old faces reappear

Tuesday, 3 October

This morning I was surprised to find the PM at the White Palace, requesting an unscheduled audience with HIM. Apparently Hormoz Qarib the Great Court Chamberlain, a freemason like the PM, had promised to arrange things. He's always the first person to be received each morning if only to discuss HIM's forthcoming appointments. This morning he emerged very down in the mouth, announcing that HIM was ready to receive the Minister of Court, an awful put-down for the PM. Once inside I told HIM what had gone on and suggested that unless we kept my report as brief as possible the poor PM was likely to have a nervous breakdown. HIM laughed in agreement.

Again he stressed that Nixon must be made aware through our private

[1] Saeb Tabrizi (AD 1607–75): a prominent poet of the Safavid period.

channels of the urgency of Jordan's need for tanks. If the Americans give the go-ahead and supply us with the necessary parts we can refit the existing Jordanian vehicles in our tank maintenance plant; our mechanics are working round the clock.

'Everyone in Morocco', he went on, 'agrees that the only hope for King Hassan is if the Shah of Iran comes to his aid. The Moroccan Minister of Court made exactly this point during his recent visit, but I have yet to receive a written request from the King himself. I'm in a quandary. You should make this point plain in our message to Nixon.' . . .

As I left I had to walk past the PM who was literally speechless with rage. Why oh why does he get so wound up?

. . . The British ambassador called round after lunch. I told him how pleased we were that Sheikh Zaid of Abu Dhabi has issued a communiqué on the establishment of diplomatic relations with Iran. According to our ambassador it is an exact carbon-copy of the text we ourselves approved; a real sign of Britain's sincerity and influence. As instructed, I then pointed out the problems with the Chieftain tank engines.

My comments on Abu Dhabi made him almost jump with joy; he declared that my message was so significant that he would immediately transmit it to the British PM and Foreign Secretary . . . As for the tanks, he said that a Ministry of Defence representative will shortly arrive in Tehran to offer us a written guarantee that the necessary engine modifications will be made at no extra cost to Iran . . .

Later I received Nixon's go-between and passed on HIM's messages which he promised would be dispatched to Washington within a matter of a few minutes. We discussed Morocco and HIM's problems in offering effective aid directly to King Hassan. He expressed an opinion that the Moroccans lack any firm policy and are at a loss to know what to do. I replied that as a descendent of the prophet, Hassan may have considerable influence amongst the Moroccan Bedouins, 'But unlike us, he is powerless to control the farmers, the workers or the middle classes. As the patron and protector of various corrupt elements, he lacks the support of both the army and the politicians. How on earth can anybody hope to save him?' My visitor agreed, and promised to keep me informed of Washington's views on the matter . . .

Wednesday, 4 October

Audience. Reported a meeting I've had with Henry Kern, the editor of *Foreign Report*, recently returned from Saudi Arabia where he was entrusted with a message from King Faisal. The King suggests that as a step towards solving our differences, we should agree a comprehensive package of defence measures for the Persian Gulf, which would cover amongst other things the islands of Tunbs and Abu Musa. In this way the King would find things much easier in future, when it comes to negotiations with his fellow Arabs. 'Nonsense', said HIM. 'Neither King Faisal nor Henry Kern have the faintest idea what they're asking. The islands are ours, and now that they're actually under Iranian control no outsider will be permitted to meddle with their future.' Bravo, I say, for such a hard-headed attitude ...

Friday, 6 October

Despite the holiday, HIM fulfilled his constitutional duty and opened the new session of Parliament. He made a long, perfectly excellent speech, cataloguing the remarkable advances we've witnessed in Iran ... Their Majesties then retired to a special ante-chamber set aside for royal visitors and HMQ remarked that the speech had done nothing but praise our achievements without mentioning a single shortcoming. HIM smiled as he replied: 'Today we harp on about our successes yet there are still subversive elements around, prepared to answer us in bombs and bullets. Just imagine how much worse it would be if we gave vent to self-criticism.' Turning towards HMQ he added: 'You're becoming quite a revolutionary yourself. I'd like to see you try and run this country at the same time as making revolutionary pronouncements and heaping your own administration with abuse. But do tell me, now that you've joined the revolutionaries, how is it that you continue to dress yourself in jewels and finery?' All this was said in a bantering sort of way, since HIM was acutely conscious that he was talking in front of the PM, the Speakers of Parliament and myself, but even so it didn't prevent HMQ from getting decidedly hot under the collar.

Prince Gholam Reza, presently a brigadier in the army, has allowed his hair to grow too long. HIM remarked to him, 'I've told you before that it's against regulations. For goodness sake get it cut.' Again, this was put as light-heartedly as possible, but the Prince refused to pass up the opportunity to show off his customary wit. 'Of course I shall do as you suggest', he replied; 'If only it does something to improve the quality of our army.' The smile vanished from HIM's lips, and turning to me he said: 'Ensure that this gentleman has his hair cut tomorrow.' Alas, I shall have no choice but to obey this command ...

Returned to the palace by helicopter, taking Prince Behzad, the son of Prince Hamid Reza,[1] with me to pay his respects to the Shah. Until recently he's been leading a dissipated life in Britain, but I had him brought home and enrolled him in the military school. He's now a completely reformed character; a well behaved, highly articulate boy. HIM was pleased to see him so changed ...

Suggested that it might be a good idea if the British and Americans co-ordinated their actions in Iraqi Kurdistan.[2] 'I disagree', HIM replied, 'I much prefer it that they keep us informed of what they're up to separately.' I could make no sense of this ...

Saturday, 7 October

... At dinner we were joined by Prince Gholam Reza who has still not had his hair cut. I was worried that HIM might berate me for failing to implement his orders, but luckily he seems to have forgotten the instructions to me. This did not prevent him from being enraged with the disobedience of the Prince. He showered him with insult after insult; never before have I seen HIM so furious. The poor man and his wife were humiliated before their fellow guests; perhaps to pay him back for his impertinence the other day. HIM never forgets.

Tuesday, 10 October

Their Majesties flew out at 11 this morning to begin their ten-day visit to the Soviet Union. The international media is buzzing with speculation about the trip, but as far as I'm aware the chief topics on the agenda will be Iraq, relations between India and Pakistan, and our own trade with Russia; we hope to sell them more gas, to dissuade them from getting too close to the Iraqis.

Asked HMQ at the airport whether I might take the Crown Prince to the première of the film documentary about last year's monarchy celebrations, telling her that HIM had already approved the suggestion. 'For goodness sake, leave me alone', she said, 'I want our names to be utterly disassociated

---

[1] Prince Hamid Reza: the last child of Reza Shah (1932–). A problem child and a drug addict. His scandalous life-style and brawls forced the Shah to ban him from the Court and remove his title Prince. After the revolution he stayed in Iran and (like his nephew Ali Patrick) changed his name to Islami. The regime in Iran currently subsidizes his living expenses.

[2] Both countries – as well as Israel – backed the Barzani rebels in their fight against Baghdad.

from those ghastly celebrations.' There was no time to argue about this; to remind her that, like it or not, the celebrations are now past history and were too well publicized for us to shrug them off as if they never happened. But to my utter amazement she then said, 'HIM and I see eye to eye on nothing; almost invariably I disagree with him.' Never before have I heard her dare to speak so bluntly, for all that she knows I would never repeat her comments to my beloved sovereign. I wonder what old Quasimodo, the PM, has been whispering in her ear? God preserve us! ...

Saturday, 14 October

HMQ's birthday – the Soviet Chargé d'Affaires called round to offer his congratulations and to ask that I pass a similar message on to the Crown Prince. I thanked him for the warm reception granted in Moscow. We then discussed Iraq. He claims that the Soviets are keen that we settle our differences with Baghdad, and that they'll do what they can to help us achieve this; 'It's now entirely up to Iran', he said.

My friend Denis Wright, previously British ambassador, lunched as my guest. He believes that Edward Heath could win the next British election if only he manages to conquer inflation. I replied that Heath had proved far less dynamic that we'd expected, a sentiment with which he agreed ...

Saturday, 21 October

HIM flew in at 1.30 p.m., direct from Souchi in Georgia. I was surprised to find him in a far from happy mood. He chatted for a while with the PM, and then asked that I make my report after lunch ...

Audience, lasting two and a half hours. Commenting on his trip, HIM said, 'It went very well. We got exactly what we wanted and gave away nothing in return ... Fortunately I'd cleared the ground beforehand by my speech to the Defence College. It certainly made the Soviets sit up and take notice. I stressed that problems concerning the Persian Gulf must be handled by the Gulf states alone, without any intervention from outsiders. The Soviets remarked that this meant I was bound to oppose American bases in the Persian Gulf, but I pointed out that by the same token I should have to demand their own withdrawal from Umm al-Qasr.[1] At that they rapidly changed the subject.' He then went on to relate that on his last day, waiting at the airport, Kosygin came up to him and whispered in his ear, 'You can rest absolutely secure in regard to us. We have no intention

[1] Iraqi port on the Persian Gulf.

nor any advantage to be gained from provoking hostility.' I remarked that despite this, His Majesty appeared upset. 'It's the British and their disgraceful impertinence', he said. I asked whether he was referring to the article in *The Times*, describing our local council elections. 'Of course', he replied. 'Why can't they mind their own damned business. Some bastard on *The Times* claims I have abandoned any idea of instituting a two-party system. They're deliberately blind to the progress we've made. It's the pro-Arab lobby within the British Foreign Office that lies behind all this mischief.' For myself, I can't for the life of me believe that the two things are related.

HIM then fell silent for a couple of minutes, apparently debating with himself whether to bring something into the open. I waited in considerable trepidation, worried that he may suspect me and my friend Kani, the former leader of Mardom, of having egged on the man from *The Times*; the article makes quite a lot of Kani . . .

Monday, 23 October

Audience. *The Economist* has unfortunately followed up *The Times* article with a few blunt comments of its own. Again they relate to the council elections and have only inflamed HIM's rage. I reported that a man named Housego is responsible for both sets of articles; we investigated his contacts and found that they're mostly with the British embassy staff. 'Didn't I tell you that those bastards are behind it all?', said HIM . . . I thought it best to change the subject, passing on a message from Nixon delivered this morning via the US ambassador; he no longer needs our F-5 aircraft for Vietnam, but all the same he's extremely, repeat extremely, grateful to HIM for agreeing to put them at his disposal.

Imam Jom'eh[1] claims that the bazaaris and clergy are grumbling against HIM's birthday celebrations, which will take place on the eve of the anniversary of Imam Ali's sword injury. 'Fair enough', said HIM when I reported the matter. 'The birthday celebrations are such a bore, we'll simply cancel them.' 'Your Majesty should not kow-tow to the clergy', I said, 'the eve of a holiday is no concern of theirs. Our own celebrations are a national event and cannot be cancelled. I recommend an announcement

---

[1] The Prayer Leader of Tehran appointed by royal decree; chosen for more than a century from amongst the qualified members of the Emami family. The then holder of the title, Dr Hassan Emami, professor of law at Tehran University, was educated in France as well as at Shia madrassehs. An elegant man of the world, much liked by the Shah. The traditional clerics, who saw him as a courtier in mullah's garb, had little time for him.

stating that the *Salaam* will go ahead, but without any illuminations or public festivities.' He agreed to this.

... At her personal request I paid a visit to Princess Shahnaz. She asked why I've been avoiding her and I had to tell her quite bluntly that I could have nothing to do with her when her behaviour is so utterly at odds with the interests of HIM. 'Not only shall I continue to avoid you, but I shall force you to mend your ways. Don't think that being the daughter of HIM will protect you in any way. Your husband is a disgrace.... You're a hopeless case, and if HIM takes any care of you it's only because he'd do the same for a sick animal.' She was badly shaken by this.

This morning I asked HIM's permission to attend dinner with Van Reven, head of the Oil Consortium. Normally I avoid such invitations but the man assured me that his only other guest would be Denis Wright. 'You should go', said HIM, 'and point out that our oil production has remained stationary at 4.2 million barrels a day; we must have 4.4 million if we're to finance our defence budget. Why haven't they increased our output when they've allowed a sharp increase to Saudi Arabia?' At dinner, Van Reven promised that one way or another the Consortium will up our production to the level demanded by HIM.

Tuesday, 24 October
Audience. Reported yesterday's meetings, and the advice I'd given the PM not to suggest to HMQ that she might like to attend the meeting in Shiraz to review the Fifth Plan; since the PM had originally intended to do just this, he did not take kindly to my advice. 'It's extraordinary', said HIM. 'What right does he think he has to stick his nose into such affairs?' I replied that I couldn't imagine, but in fact I know full well that the PM harbours ambitions of surrounding HMQ with his own adherents. Hence the appointment of Karim Pasha Bahadori as HMQ's principal private secretary. The PM's people strive hard to do me down as they regard me as the only man at Court who still dares to speak the truth to HIM ...

The British ambassador called on me after lunch. Again I mentioned that our whole deal over Chieftain tanks is jeopardized by the below-par performance of their engines.[1] 'I'm afraid that there must have been an error in the specifications supplied to your government', he replied, in a very offhand sort of way; 'But the tanks themselves are more or less identical

---

[1] They were ordered by the Shah himself on the grounds of their specified performance, without any prior technical tests or any comparison with rival American or German tanks. As it turned out they were unsuitable for use in Iran.

to those in service with our own army, and there's really no call for the extra engine capacity.' I then put to him our suspicion that British officials have sponsored the hostile articles in *The Times* and *Economist*. He expressed his surprise that I should even entertain such an idea; newspaper correspondents are paid to report the truth and cannot be expected to file a lot of lies. He repeated that Iran is now a great and powerful nation and should be less sensitive to pin-pricks. 'We're not so broad-shouldered as you', I replied, and we laughed, though this did little to relieve what was really quite a tense discussion.

Birthday dinner for HIM at Prince Abdur Reza's. HIM asked after my meeting with the British ambassador; had he kept his composure? When I replied that he had, HIM declared, 'Then it looks as if I must do something to shake him up.'

Friday, 27 October

Returning from my ride this morning I caught sight of HIM a long way off, just setting out. I was too tired to gallop over to join him, and in any case it's unfair that he should see nothing but the same tired old faces. The US ambassador telephoned just as I got home, announcing that he's received a message from Nixon asking that our F-5 aircraft be dispatched to Vietnam. Immediately I rang through to HIM who gave his approval, provided that the Americans undertake to make good any losses within a year. I passed this on to the ambassador, who was delighted by our decision, and most surprised by the speed with which I can contact HIM ...

Saturday, 28 October

Audience. Reported yet another visit from Mahdi al-Tajer, presently ambassador of the UAE in London, who was received yesterday by HIM. He wanted to tell me that during his audience he had forgotten to mention that he can persuade Ahmad al-Suwaidi, the UAE's Foreign Minister, to adopt a less hostile attitude towards Iran. 'Tell him to go ahead', said HIM. 'All these people are under the influence of the British; he's merely doing his master's bidding.' HIM's suspicions of the British are quite incredible; but on this occasion he's got even me wondering whether he may not be correct ...

The Afghan Parliament is about to debate our new agreement on the Hirmand river. The proposals are much in their favour, but even so it appears that we shall have to distribute quite a few favours before their MPs will approve the plan. 'Their Parliament is a complete bear garden', said HIM, 'and I've recommended that the King scrap it in favour of a less chaotic system. But quite how and when he will be able to do anything remains open to question. Send someone reliable to assist our ambassador, and authorize him to make the pay-offs if you really think they're necessary.'

Fallah called round at noon, reporting that the oil companies have conceded more than we expected to the Arab producers ... It was a wise decision of HIM's to wait for the outcome of these negotiations before starting on our own ...

Sunday, 29 October

This morning HIM received representatives of the Oil Consortium and so my own audience was postponed until after lunch. I showed him samples of the fruit, rice and saffron he is sending to Podgorny, Brezhnev and Kosygin in Moscow ... HIM complained of insomnia; he sleeps even worse than before, despite taking sleeping pills. 'Today', he added, 'is the anniversary of the assassination of Imam Ali, and as you've no doubt noticed I'm wearing a black tie. Not out of mere respect for tradition; I have a deep belief in God and his saints. It's a great consolation, though I couldn't attempt to explain to you why.' I replied that whilst his deep religious convictions will be apparent to all who know him, he's nevertheless wise to observe the formalities when it comes to religious mourning; this is a Shi'a country, and he heads a population, 90 per cent of which is made up of convinced believers ...

In a religious broadcast on the radio, I was surprised to hear the preacher, a magnificent orator named Hejazi, wind up with a prayer in which he asked God's blessing on many things, the seminary at Qom included, but never so much as mentioned the name of HIM. 'What a farce', said HIM. 'Anyone courting popularity does his damnedest to steer clear of the court. That bastard Falsafi did precisely the same and ended up being sacked as a result. Now this other gentleman follows suit, though it's entirely thanks to our own approval that he's permitted to enter the pulpit or even a radio studio.' He then became pensive, ordering that the matter should be investigated more closely.

He seems satisfied with this morning's talks with the Consortium, and suggested that we might propose a new formula under which Iran becomes the seller of oil and the Consortium the purchasers. In that way responsibility for output levels, overlift, etc., would no longer be in their hands ... The telephone rang as he was speaking, but he made no attempt to lift the receiver. Only when it had stopped did he phone through to the operator to trace the call. Learning that it had been from Fallah, he asked to be reconnected. He subsequently explained that he's resolved not to answer the telephone after lunch; in that way he can prevent HMQ from checking up on whether or not he's at his office.

Mrs Diba has drawn my attention to the fact that the invitation card for the state opening of parliament neglected to mention that it was to be held 'in the presence of Their Imperial Majesties' in the plural. Also, that the customary reply from the Senate was addressed to HIM alone with no mention of HMQ. I passed her complaints on to HIM, remarking that I'd told her she could hardly expect anything else when it's HIM and not HMQ who actually delivers the speech to Parliament. As for the invitation cards, I told her that the omission could be rectified with HIM's approval. 'The matter will be considered in due course', said HIM. I sense that for the past few months, things have been far from all right between HIM and HMQ. Let's hope that with God's grace the situation improves.

It's surely rather droll that Fallah should be our only representative in the oil negotiations; Dr Eqbal, the managing director of NIOC, like our Finance Minister, has effectively been left out in the cold.

Tuesday, 31 October
... Attended the PM's farewell dinner for Asadollah Saraj, the retiring ambassador of Afghanistan ... Saraj's time as ambassador to Turkey coincided with Hoveyda's appointment as counsellor under General Arfa at our own embassy in Ankara. Hence at the end of dinner Hoveyda made a speech recalling the old days, going on to make a totally inopportune series of jokes at the expense of Arfa who is now President of the Iran–Pakistan Friendship Society. The Pakistani ambassador, needless to say, was amongst this evening's guests. The whole thing made me cringe ...

Wednesday, 1 November
... A second audience after lunch. Reported that Kani is to sue the journalist Housego over various allegations in his article. HIM was delighted. 'That bastard Housego is full of shit,' he said. He then remarked that we have devised a new formula for inclusion in the coming oil agreement which marks an advance on every other oil-producing country and will be the envy even of the radicals such as Libya and Iraq. We shall all of us become sellers of oil in our own right, although some provision needs to be made to reduce the tax pressures on the oil companies within their home countries.

Saturday, 4 November
At 10 a.m. this morning HIM and I landed on Kharg Island for the opening of the new oil terminal. Tankers up to 500,000 tons will be able to use these facilities. The whole visit could not have passed off better. What is at present the largest tanker in the world lay at anchor offshore, all 300,000 tons capacity of her, an incredible floating city, walled and turreted ... Lunch was held in the presence of the PM, various of his Ministers, both Speakers of Parliament and the ambassadors of four countries with companies belonging to the Oil Consortium: France, the USA, Britain and the Netherlands. HIM was beaming with goodwill.

Later we toured the Kharg naval base. The navy helicopters gave a magnificent aerial display, firing off their missiles with deadly accuracy ...

Dined at the Naval Officers' Club where the Admiral of the Fleet made an excellent speech to mark the fortieth anniversary of the navy's creation. In his reply, HIM set out our continuing ambitions in the Gulf, and even in the Indian Ocean beyond. It was superbly put, swelling my heart with pride. I'm sure that these contacts with the military are tremendously beneficial; what a pity there aren't more of them ...

Sunday, 5 November
Storms during the night. After rising we toured various public institutions arriving in time for the navy parade at 10. Because of the unsettled weather, it was impractical for us to observe manoeuvres from the royal yacht moored off Kish, and instead we climbed a naval observation tower. Amongst our guests was the grandson of the Emperor of Ethiopia, commander of his country's fleet. Twenty-nine ships and a whole flotilla of torpedo boats swept by, firing off a salute as they passed our position. They were followed by a dozen helicopters and sixteen hovercraft. On the spur of the moment HIM requested that a couple of the ships armed with missiles take a shot at the targets, hit so accurately by the helicopters yesterday. Two vessels were selected for the display. The first missed the target altogether; the second could not even get its missiles off the launch pad. A total shambles, made still more embarrassing by the presence of our Ethiopian guest. The strain gave me a headache and I subsequently fortified myself with more than one glass of vodka. HIM was absolutely seething, although maintaining a poker-face. Lunch, not surprisingly, was held in an atmosphere of tension and barely suppressed gloom. As I remarked to the Minister of Finance sitting next to me, if the target practice had gone according to plan, we'd have heard an endless panegyric of the

navy, and much talk of how we shall dominate not only the Gulf but the entire Indian Ocean. As it was, the only safe topic of conversation consisted of amateur analysis of the various species of fish inhabiting our offshore waters. Even so, since the Ethiopian admiral cannot have been entirely unimpressed by this morning's display, HIM ended lunch with a description of our fifth Five Year Plan, under which per capita income will increase from $500 to something between $1,000 and $1,200. We then climbed into a helicopter to make an over-flight of the oil terminal; twenty-seven tankers lay at anchor alongside our fleet. On landing we boarded another plane which took us on to Shiraz.

There I accompanied HIM to the Eram Palace[1] before taking my leave of him to join my lover who was waiting nearby at the house of a friend of mine. An excellent dinner and an equally memorable night. I paid a brief visit to the palace to make sure that HIM was enjoying himself as much as I was.

Monday, 6 November

At 10 a.m. we held a meeting in the great royal tent[2] at Persepolis to finalize the Fifth Development Plan. An interesting debate ... The heads of various departments of the Plan Organization reported those aspects of the plan to which they had been assigned, followed by a questions and answers session between HIM and his ministers.

All the government representatives lunched with HIM before resuming the discussions which lasted until 5 p.m. We then returned to Shiraz, the PM and his ministers staying in Persepolis at the Hotel Darius. Things thereafter went much as the night before ...

Tuesday, 7 November

In the morning, once again accompanied HIM to Persepolis ... At lunch he asked after domestic and international news and I was able to report the excellent commentary on his Kharg speech, broadcast this morning by the BBC ... To the right of the Shah sat the PM, keeping a beady eye on us as we talked, and doing his best to attract HIM's attention by presenting him with the morning papers. After glancing through them, HIM let out a cry of rage at a misquotation from his speech of yesterday. He demanded to know why the correspondents have made such a mistake and the PM

---

[1] A magnificent nineteenth-century palace, renowned for its gardens.
[2] The tent had been erected for the celebrations of 2,500 years of monarchy in 1971. A few years later it was completely destroyed by a fire rumoured to be an act of sabotage.

could do nothing but squirm on his seat and promise over and over again that the matter would be investigated; forgetting, of course, that no journalists were allowed into yesterday's meeting and that they relied entirely on a bulletin provided by the government's own Ministry of Information. I'm not sure whether or not HIM was aware of this, but I restrained myself from dropping any hint. The Shah continued to sulk throughout the remainder of the meal, whilst the PM sat there, clearly cursing himself for making such a foolish blunder ...

Whilst the debate in Persepolis continued, HIM instructed the Foreign Minister, the Minister without Portfolio and myself to attend a reception at the Russian embassy to mark the anniversary of the October revolution. The three of us flew back to Tehran where our attendance was warmly welcomed by the Soviets as a sign of HIM's goodwill.

Wednesday, 8 November

Returned to Shiraz at dawn, arriving at the Eram Palace by half past eight. Surprised HIM taking a stroll in the garden. 'Doubtless you'll have heard the results of the US presidential election', he said. 'I must send my warmest congratulations to Nixon; instruct the Court to prepare a draft.' 'It's already been done, Your Majesty', I replied. He was delighted and after adding a few words of his own authorized the cable's dispatch.

... Lunched at Persepolis sitting next to HIM. 'The development plan for the next five years has been finalized', I said, 'and Nixon's re-election now means that the political agenda for four of those five years lies clear before us.' He nodded his approval, saying, 'Quite so; the world is moving towards a new peaceful equilibrium. Nixon is a strong leader with a good grasp of the world's problems. He knows that the only way to argue with the communists is from a position of strength. This is precisely what he's done and no doubt will continue to do.'

Saturday, 11 November

... Flew back to Tehran yesterday ... The US ambassador called round this afternoon and we talked first about the presidential elections. He admitted that he would have resigned immediately if Nixon had been defeated. We then discussed the trip which HMQ made to Rasht whilst HIM and I were in the south. HMQ had forbidden any obtrusive security presence in the streets. As a result she found herself mobbed by a crowd which practically lifted her car into the air in its jubilation – basically a good sign despite the obvious risk. The ambassador suggested that she behave less recklessly in future. 'Both Their Majesties are fatalists', I replied. 'They have not an ounce of fear between them ...'

The ambassador also expressed anxiety over the attitude of the clergy. 'You needn't worry', I said, 'their time has passed; they're powerless in the face of HIM.' I then related how we crushed them during my own time as Prime Minister. Following their opposition to land reform we came down on them so hard that never again can they be considered a significant contender for power. The grumbling of a couple of Mullahs should not conceal the fact that such wretches are a complete irrelevance so long as the Shah is at the helm. 'The only possible way they could make a come-back would be if HIM were rendered powerless and you and the British promoted the clergy as a bulwark against communism', I said. God forbid that this should happen, but even if it did it's still an open question whether the clergy would actually be capable of seizing their chance. Their present grumbling is a direct result of their deep inner divisions. The ambassador replied that it is no more than his duty to pass on to me whatever rumours he hears, but that as I was so confident his fears are groundless, he had nothing more to add.

At dinner the talk centred on our trip to the south, the Fifth Plan and HMQ's experience in Rasht. Since her promotion as prospective Regent, there's been a perceptible upsurge of rivalry between her and HIM.

Sunday, 12 November
Audience. Having listened to my account of yesterday's meeting with the ambassador, HIM said: 'You had better tell him that, even assuming the clergy assumed power, they'd be of absolutely no use in the fight against communism. Indeed they'll merely turn communist themselves, or at least "Islamic socialists" – some new monstrosity dreamed up by the radicals amongst them. You should also remind him about Nixon's promise to replace our aircraft; when will it be honoured?'

A meeting with the British ambassador, whose first priority, as always, was commerce ... Before leaving he touched briefly on the subject of the journalist Housego who has been summoned by our own public prosecutor on the basis of Kani's complaints. I assured him that the case is entirely a private one, between Kani and Housego; if the latter is proved innocent, that will be the end of the matter as far as we are concerned. The ambassador showed me a recent series of articles in *The Times* which I'd already seen; they're by Housego and are really rather good ...

A dinner presided over by HMQ to mark the seventh Tehran International Film Festival. The Soviet ambassador caught my eye across the room and rushed to greet me, full of flattering remarks about HIM's speech in Persepolis. I'm sure that what really pleased him were HIM's favourable remarks on the newly approved fifteen year economic agreement with Russia. I was worried that the ambassador would go on to ask me about HIM's references to the importance of establishing a two-party system. I'd have been at a loss to know what to say, but fortunately he steered clear of the topic.

Monday, 13 November
Audience. Reported my conversations with the British and Soviet ambassadors ... Referring to the Housego case, HIM said: 'You gave precisely the right answer. We should now pretend complete indifference to the affair, though don't hesitate to intervene if you think you can make trouble for the man without being detected. We shall refrain from putting undue pressure on the judge.' ...

Wednesday, 15 November
Audience. The *Financial Times* intends to bring out a special supplement on the Fifth Plan; I've already spoken with their correspondent and sent him on to the PM and the head of the Plan Organization. 'The bastards will in any case write whatever they like', said HIM. We then discussed the prevalence of corruption in both the western and the Soviet blocs. I pointed out that the West had a much worse record in this respect. 'I know', said HIM, 'it's difficult to believe that things can be as bad as that in the East.'

General Ali Hojjat, National Head of Physical Education, complains that the new sports facilities are behind schedule if they're to be ready for the Asian games, due to be held here in just under two years time. 'Tell my private secretariat', said HIM, 'to write to the Minister of Housing and Development; they should warn him that any delay to the construction work for the games will be interpreted as deliberate disobedience to my orders and will be punished accordingly.' ... He then went on, 'Inform those idiots in the protocol department that they make even bigger fools of themselves, instructing foreign journalists how to enter my room, how to bow and so on.'

At dinner HIM announced that he will grant no more interviews to foreign journalists except at his own express invitation. A former British cabinet minister, speaking on BBC television, has come out with a statement to the effect that the Shah of Iran is the only living statesman of the calibre of De Gaulle or Churchill. HIM made no mention of this, although I'm sure he knew all about it. Fortunately, I too had been told the news and was able to introduce it into the conversation.

Friday, 17 November

... Army Day, so this evening attended a reception at the Officers' Club. All the guests were whispering about yesterday's sacking of General M. There were plenty of theories floating around and everyone seemed to assume that I knew the real reason. I couldn't for the life of me persuade them that I was just as much in the dark as everyone else.

Attended Dinner. Reported that Baghdad has sent what amounts to an ultimatum to the Kurds. HIM instructed me to get the Kurds to prepare a response which we shall make public via the Beirut newspapers.

Saturday, 18 November

Audience ... I passed on General M's request that I see him today; we met briefly at the Officers' Club reception. HIM told me to go ahead and receive him. I then asked the reason for M's dismissal. HIM explained: 'The bloody fool suggested at a meeting with the Minister of Finance that we increase the medical allowance for army personnel sent abroad for special treatment. As he put it, the expense would be a drop in the ocean compared to the profligacy of Princess Ashraf. I had to remind him that I myself paid out $30,000 to settle his private gambling debts.' He then asked what other people had made of the incident. I told him that there were any number of rumours going the rounds last night; that M had shot his mouth off once too often; that he'd got too friendly with the Americans; his gambling, his laziness, his unreasonable demands for an increase in officers' pay. 'What shall I say to him when he calls?', I asked. 'Tell him he's a bloody fool who would have done better to learn a little wisdom and to keep his mouth shut', said HIM, adding; 'Which doesn't alter the fact that he was an able officer, well-suited to his job.'

M called at my home this afternoon. The man is a complete buffoon and we wasted an hour together in idle chatter. He told me that he'd been summoned by HIM who announced, 'I always knew you were a clown but had no idea quite how stupid a clown you were.' HIM must have been dreadfully angry to have passed such an uncharacteristically harsh judgment, merely on the basis of a report from the Finance Minister. When we were at Kharg Island M showed a complete lack of tact by sounding off about the disparity between civilian and military salaries. I noticed then how much this irritated HIM, although he managed to put a brave face on things ...

Sunday, 19 November
... Passed on a report from our ambassador in Rabat on his discussions with King Hassan.

[Excerpts from the report of the Iranian ambassador A. Nayyeri, dated 16th November 1972]

... I reported to His Majesty that HIM was anxious to know whether any foreign power was implicated in the recent attempt on His Majesty's life. In an earlier report I cited unofficial rumours of American involvement. His Majesty confirmed that certain American elements had taken a hand in events, commenting: 'Our investigations have brought to light various new aspects of the case. We are aware *"cela dépasse largement le cadre du Maroc"* ' ...

His Majesty continued: 'The Americans wish to gain hegemony over every state bordering the Mediterranean ... Qadhafi is undoubtedly a product and an agent of American policy, however strongly he denies it. Italy ... is economically dependent on the Americans ... who enjoy complete control over Greece and Turkey. The rightist regime in Spain complies with Washington's opinions and policies. The only countries not to enjoy total confidence amongst the Americans are Algeria and the Maghreb, hence America's connivance in the plot of 16 August, which was designed to bring about a reshuffle ... Boumédienne telephoned me later that night to tell me ... that if a military regime had seized power in the Maghreb, the Algerian army were set to move from Oujda into Moroccan territory, making a push towards Rabat ...'

... His Majesty then remarked: ' ... When the plot was revealed, every officer in the air force was placed under arrest and we concluded that we must train an entirely new lot of pilots for our F5s. From the start I was convinced that I could depend upon my brother (HIM) in this respect. From that day onwards all our 20 F5s have been grounded for lack of pilots, but even so I shall never send men to be trained in America, and would suggest that His Imperial Majesty think very carefully before doing likewise. Such trainee officers are not segregated in any way from American personnel. The Americans are there to learn how to kill; how to go off to Vietnam and bomb the innocent; how to become murderers ... Foreign pilots trained in America are rendered useless to the service of their own home countries. America wants only lackeys and foreign agents; she wants only to stamp out all independent voices abroad ... '

HIM read it through, remarking, 'What poor Hassan doesn't appreciate is that it's only because he himself has become such a lost cause that the Americans act against him ... Why else does he suppose we in Iran are spared similar interference? Tell the ambassador that he needn't be so keen to stand up for the King, particularly for a King who has proved himself so unreliable.' I was instructed to transmit this message verbally, not to put it in writing.

Reported my meeting with General M who claims that if he mentioned the name of Princess Ashraf it was merely to suggest that she might be a bit less lavish in her expenditure, not out of any ill-will towards her. 'Rubbish', said HIM. 'The man is lying out of his teeth; he lost his head and must now bear the consequences. Princess Ashraf's travelling expenses have nothing whatsoever to do with the military or, for that matter, with civilian affairs. General M should never have mentioned them; he did so merely to show off in front of his colleagues. I know his stupid clowning better than you.' I could do nothing to soften HIM's heart; indeed he's even angrier than before, since General M has approached the Queen Mother to intercede on his behalf ...

HIM asked me what popular reaction there's been to General M's sacking. I replied that the general opinion was unchanged, including the view that the General got too friendly with the Americans. 'What nonsense', HIM replied; 'Who would dare even contemplate collusion with a foreign power? ... Last year when we sacked General Djam a similar false rumour got about, that it was because of his too close relations with the British. It was nothing of the sort; the man was simply a blabbermouth.' He then asked why there's been no reply from Nixon to our cable of congratulations. 'The whole thing is rather off-putting', he said; 'You had better send a reminder to the Americans.' I'm surprised to find HIM attaching such importance to the affair. I say, to hell with Nixon; why should we pay any attention to his lack of manners? ...

Saturday, 25 November

Audience. HIM most gracious . . . He remarked: 'A couple of nights ago I caught sight of your lover in one of the boxes at the Rudaki Hall.' 'Yes, Your Majesty', I replied. 'Imagine, her being there and me in my deplorable condition'[1] . . . He laughed.

Reported last night's conversation with the US ambassador who promises that once Nixon has been sworn in he will do everything that we require, although he must tread carefully if he's to avoid trouble with Senator Fulbright, Chairman of the Senate Foreign Relations Committee. 'And yet', said HIM, 'Fulbright raises no objection to US aid to India, despite the fact that India has a defence agreement with the Soviets and has defeated Pakistan with Soviet support.' . . .

I then went on to outline the ambassador's anxieties over the clergy; how he's read intelligence reports claiming that the mullahs now demand that the slogan 'For God, King and Country' be replaced with 'For God, Country and King'. At the time I replied that this accords precisely with HIM's own view, that the country must come first, since without it there would be no need for a king. We've only refrained from altering things out of respect to HIM's late father, whose regime coined the phrase. 'Is he so idle that he can find nothing more important to discuss?', said HIM. 'The man's an ass, but all the same he's tough and a close friend of Nixon's. We must continue to humour him.'

Le Monde claims that a student named Shamekhi has been killed whilst in police custody. 'An outright lie', said HIM. 'He was a terrorist and when they arrested him he took his own life by swallowing cyanide.' In that case, I suggested, we should deny the report. 'There's no need', HIM replied, 'but you should issue instructions so that henceforth the local newspapers cease to quote stories out of *Le Monde*.' 'To what end?', I asked. 'So that *Le Monde* comes to realize that it cannot influence opinion here', he said. I pointed out that on the contrary, people will only become all the more curious to read *Le Monde*, but he refused to alter his instructions . . .

Sunday, 26 November

Audience. The famine around Kabul now threatens the lives of nearly 200,000 Afghans, but as I told HIM, nobody seems willing so much as to lift a finger to help. 'Their country is completely bereft of government',

---

[1] Alam's leukaemia meant that he fell increasingly ill.

said HIM. I asked about the King. 'He doesn't give a damn', he replied, 'it's as if he were just hanging around waiting for death to claim him. He's told me himself that so long as he lives nothing will change and the Russians will keep their distance; once he's gone, however, he says God alone knows what might happen. It's quite beyond me how the man can hope to rule a country when he adopts that sort of attitude ...'

Tuesday, 28 November
The Consul-General of South Africa called on me at noon – seemingly well-informed and well-pleased by his recent audience. He was especially impressed by HIM's proposal for a tripartite defence agreement between Iran, South Africa and Australia. He felt it showed the Shah's great breadth of vision, whilst admitting that Australia will need to be pressed if she's to overcome her initial scruples. HIM had already raised the matter with me; it will be practicable only in the longer term. As regards intelligence gathering, we're currently benefiting enormously from the South Africans' willingness to pass on information about every Soviet ship that rounds the Cape of Good Hope en route to Iraq. In this way we can build up a picture of the sort of equipment the Soviets are supplying ...

Wednesday, 29 November
Audience. At last night's reception at the Yugoslav embassy, the US ambassador discreetly passed me a note which I assumed was to do with recent events in Jordan. In fact when I got home I found that it was yet another commercial proposal; an American company seeking a factory here to manufacture copper and aluminum wire. What a farce! As HIM remarked, 'They can no longer sell arms to Vietnam, so they must look for new markets to conquer.' He then instructed me to pump the ambassador for information on Richardson, the new US Defense Secretary, previously Secretary of Health, with no previous experience of military affairs. How on earth is he expected to master such a vast new assignment? 'Likewise', said HIM, 'ask the same thing of Aslan Afshar, our ambassador in Washington. Tell him to make enquiries of Kissinger, or even of the President. How will this appointment affect our plans? All that high-flown rhetoric about their love of peace is so much window dressing. I can't believe that the Americans really intend to disregard their own fundamental interests or those of their allies.' I replied that a man of Nixon's great experience would never be so foolish. 'Quite so', said HIM; 'He's grasped the point that strengthening Israel is a key factor in securing a Middle Eastern peace.'

I replied that Nixon faces up to harsh reality. He, at least, avoids the temptation to retire to a world of make-believe.

Much to my alarm Dr Hossein Nasr, the new President of the Aryamehr Institute of Technology, has reported that many of his students are poor, and a great number of them fanatical Moslems. 'They're merely communists masquerading as religious fanatics', said HIM, 'and they're manipulated by men of high intelligence, the same group that has begun proclaiming the cause of Islamic Marxism. Warn Nasr to tread carefully but to make a thorough investigation.'

Reported that the public prosecutor of Geneva is to issue a communiqué exonerating Davallou from any suspicion of wrong-doing. 'I should be pleased if you could have the thing put out as soon as possible', said HIM, 'so that it's published in the Swiss papers to coincide with HMQ's trip to Zurich. When Davallou was indicted last year she was down on me like a ton of bricks. Perhaps now she'll realize that there was more to the case than met the eye.'

The Prime Minister of Yugoslavia lunched as HIM's guest and discussion became focused on the relations between the superpowers and smaller nations. HIM declared: 'The great powers claim that whatever they possess is theirs by right, but that whatever we, the smaller countries, possess is negotiable.' Turning to subversion he remarked: 'We shall oppose it with every fibre of our being; *et Le Monde pourra dire ce qu'il voudra.*' ['The world, (*Le Monde*), can say what it pleases']; a pun which was well received by the Yugoslavs who are themselves under attack from that infamous newspaper ...

Thursday, 30 November
Audience ... HIM signed a congratulatory telegram to Prince Sadruddin Agha Khan on the occasion of his marriage. The lady in question is a forty-four year old Lebanese of Greek extraction, widowed with three children by her previous husband. 'Is the man off his head?', HIM asked. 'Your Majesty surely realizes', I replied, 'that it's all the rage to marry ladies of a certain age.' ...

Saturday, 2 December
Audience ... HIM is furious at a letter from Lord Louis Mountbatten which ends 'Your friend' rather than the customary 'Your obedient servant'. I pointed out that Mountbatten holds no official position and is therefore dispensed from some of the rigours of protocol. What's more he

was himself once Viceroy of India. 'Your Majesty accepted an invitation to tea at his private residence', I continued. 'Since he holds no official position, you can only have done so because he is your friend.' I'm not at all sure that he found this explanation acceptable.

... Lunched with Lord Victor Rothschild, senior adviser to Edward Heath, following his audience with HIM. He is uneasy about recent events in Britain, remarking that there can be no improvement until a government emerges prepared to confront the unions. He merely laughed when I suggested that his own government should face up to the task ... The British ambassador was present and enquired whether HIM might take the opportunity of Prince Philip's stay here in March to invite the Queen on a private visit next year. I replied that HIM would not consider issuing such an invitation unless he knew in advance that it would be accepted ...

Sunday, 3 December
... Khodadad Farmanfarmayan, Head of the Plan Organization, lunched as my guest. He sought my help in submitting his resignation as he finds it quite impossible to work with the present government ...

After lunch HIM and I went to inspect the house I have rented via my friend M ...; a veritable palace. I suggested we buy it outright. 'No need', said HIM, 'the present arrangement will suffice.'

Monday, 4 December
Audience. Expressed my surprise that both the BBC and *The Economist* have devoted attention to our Fifth Plan and referred to Iran's importance in the world at large ... The BBC suggests that it's in the oil companies' own interest to reach a settlement with what they describe as a powerful and stable nation. HIM remarked that the British have become much more reasonable over the past month or so.

... A cable from our ambassador in Washington describes Richardson as a friend of Iran and a close confidant of President Nixon. Hence our plans for the military seem secure, a point confirmed by the US ambassador.

Tuesday, 5 December
Audience. Reported a request from the Romanian ambassador. On 20 January, President Ceausescu would like to stop off here for twenty-four hours en route from India, to pay his respects to HIM. I told the ambassador that HIM would be pleased to accede to his request but that the

proposed visit should be prolonged. 'Well done', HIM said, 'repeat the point to him.' ...

Saturday, 9 December

... Audience ... HIM informed me that Joseph Farland, the US ambassador, has been replaced by Richard Helms, previously head of the CIA. I am surprised that Farland should be recalled; he's been here less than a year and is very close to Nixon. And what a peculiar choice of replacement ... Later I rang Farland who was literally in tears of grief ...

Monday, 11 December

Brief audience. HIM instructed me to remind the Americans that it was agreed they should supply tank engines to Jordan whilst we would merely service and repair the chassis. Now the Jordanians seem to expect us to take on both the supply and servicing. We then returned to the recall of the US ambassador. 'There's no reason why they should have any sinister intentions towards us', HIM said. Telephoned the CIA representative in Tehran to discuss the business of the tanks. He declared that the Jordanians are mistaken and that the USA has no intention of reneging on its promise to supply engines; however the cost will be met by a deduction from the overall budget for military aid to Jordan ...

Professor Paul Milliez, my French physician, dined as my guest.

Tuesday, 12 December

... Army Day parade after lunch. Went off well although the bitter cold and the driving rain set me shivering. After three hours in the open air I went home to take a brandy. HIM then telephoned to say he had forgotten the address of the house we have rented. I hurried round to act as his escort; the house was in a shambles, only the library having been made ready in time, and even that was cold and without light. I retired to a lavatory and there went through my papers, amongst other things signing a reply to Mountbatten's letter. As we left to return to the palace, we were caught by Mrs Diba just emerging from a house directly opposite. I knew that she would be dining at my sister's that evening. I was feeling far from well but even so I dropped in to find out whether her suspicions had been aroused. Indeed they had, since she said to me in a very pointed way, 'You're always hard at work, aren't you? Only this afternoon I caught sight of you with HIM.'

Wednesday, 13 December

Audience ... repeated Mrs Diba's remark about how hard we work. HIM laughed: 'She's got enough sense to say nothing to HMQ', he said, 'especially as her present life-style is too comfortable for her to want to throw it away.' I agreed, reminding him that although she was a guest on her recent trip to Turkey, the woman had still spent $20,000 of our money. 'Never mind', he replied, 'we must put up with these extravagances. The only problem is that HMQ allows her own people a degree of licence which she'd be scandalized to see in us.'

The British ambassador called after lunch to discuss Sharjah and the oil drilling around Abu Musa ... He asked the purpose of the Saudi Foreign Minister, Omar Saqqaf's recent visit. I replied that I hadn't a clue. He laughed, adding that according to rumour Saqqaf talked himself hoarse and all to no avail. Again I had to confess myself completely in the dark. He then asked why Farland had been recalled and who would succeed him. 'I'm afraid I seem to be just as much in the dark on that matter as well', I replied.

Thursday, 14 December

Brief audience ... The representatives of the oil companies have had three hours of talks with HIM, who intends to scrap agreements and concessions altogether. We shall become the suppliers and they the buyers of oil, as simple as that. This is a quite extraordinary step which will have repercussions on oil production right across the world ...

Friday, 15 December

Two and a half hours' audience ... Referring to current oil negotiations I remarked that HIM is once more causing the world to tremble. 'There's no alternative', he said. 'We must secure our interests as opportunity arises. A few days ago the United Nations declared that every state has autonomy over its own natural resources. What better opportunity for us to act ...'

Saturday, 16 December

Audience. Submitted the reports of Davallou's acquittal printed in the Swiss newspapers and related how the PM had telephoned to congratulate me on the outcome and to suggest we capitalize on the situation by proclaiming that the entire business was a put-up job intended to discredit us. HIM was sure at the time that Davallou's indictment was well received by the PM, and so he smiled knowingly when I told him this latest development. 'Thank him very much for his most helpful suggestion', he said, 'but we feel that the matter is too unimportant for us to bother with. Remind him that, to begin with, various people jumped off the deep end or lost their heads; whatever you do don't suggest that they were pleased by Davallou's misfortunes – but we have always been confident that truth would triumph in the end.' . . .

Later HIM rang me to ask that I invite the British ambassador and the US Chargé d'Affaires to my home to brief them on his views about oil. I should also express our appreciation of the support we have received from Van Reven.

Monday, 18 December
Audience . . . HIM instructed me to help out the ex-King of Bulgaria[1] who is in dire financial straits. He has a plan to export gourmet sea-food to Germany in association with various German business partners, but needs bank credits to get the thing started . . . He then asked whether I had passed on his comments to the PM and seemed quite amused when I told him how embarrassed the PM had been. 'The man is by no means lacking in intelligence', he said – a comment which I could tell meant in effect 'The man's a bastard but no fool.' The Shah has quite incredible patience. Sometimes his tolerance of a particular person or situation is so great that one could almost mistake it for positive approval . . .

Tuesday, 19 December
I have given an interview to *Kayhan*, propounding my views on the White Revolution. The thing is now the talk of Tehran and I'm pretty sure that HIM approves. He has undoubtedly read it, although as I know from long experience, he's never in a hurry to sing one's praises. On the other hand, a single word not to Imperial taste, and one faces stern reproach . . .

Audience. I described an encounter I had with the PM at a wedding yesterday. Normally he's so tense and keen to remind me of his importance, but on this occasion he rushed out to greet me: 'I wish to congratulate you on three counts', he gushed; 'Firstly on HIM's negotiations with the oil men; I should gladly kiss his feet in gratitude; secondly for your triumph in the Davallou case . . . and finally for your quite superb interview in *Kayhan*.' The latter was a bare-faced lie, as I'm sure the interview will

[1] Simeon of Saxe-Coburg; with German and Iranian partners he tried unsuccessfully to export delicacies from Iran (goose liver, smoked sturgeon, cat fish, etc.).

have upset him. HIM laughed and said: 'Clearly my remarks about Davallou have got him worried.' ...

Wednesday, 20 December
Early this morning Mehdi Samii[1] called round to say that HIM has asked
him to form an official opposition party; what should he do? I replied that
he should obey HIM's instructions but that he had a difficult task ahead.
To survive, an opposition party must be able to speak out freely and have
some prospect of coming to power. Here, by contrast, the opposition's
chief function is to remain silent, since whatever it says is likely to meet
with HIM's displeasure ...

Dinner at the Queen Mother's to mark Their Majesties' thirteenth
wedding anniversary. The royal children attended and were allowed a few
sips of champagne. They were a delight to behold, especially the Crown
Prince who combines great good humour with sagacity. The PM had taken
several too many drinks, and was really quite amusing. HIM was keen that
this year's celebrations should be much less elaborate than the parties we've
thrown in the past. HMQ, of course, is keeping an eagle eye out for
extravagance. She's right to avoid provoking people's envy, but she's still
too young and inexperienced to appreciate that modesty and simplicity are
themselves a sort of luxury, purchased only through HIM's firm command
of power.

Thursday, 21 December
Audience. Passed on dozens of Christmas greetings from around the world.
HIM was especially struck by the card from the Prince and Princess of
Monaco showing a picture of their children. 'What a beautiful daughter
they have', he said, 'I wish we could have invited her here.'

Sunday, 24 December
Audience ... Related a conversation I had with Mrs Diba following dinner
last night at the Queen Mother's. She dropped a series of hints to suggest
that all men are depraved, I more than most. She said too, that HMQ is
by no means happy with her situation. As I remarked to HIM, 'Your
Majesty must take care lest the same gossips who are ruining my marriage
take an interest in your own.' 'What precisely did you say to her?', he

---

[1] Former Governor of the Central Bank of Iran and Managing Director of the Plan Organization,
Samii was a competent technocrat who enjoyed wide respect in Iran and abroad. He was to
abandon any idea of launching a new party after only a few weeks.

asked. 'I left no holds barred', I replied, 'and told her I am what I am and that Mrs Alam must either take it or leave it. As for Your Majesty, I warned her against listening to rumour, and even if she did, to say nothing herself, out of love for her daughter.' HIM fully agreed with this.

Submitted a profile of Helms, the new US ambassador. He's recently divorced his first wife of twenty-eight years standing, and remarried a divorcée with four children.

Monday, 25 December

Audience ... Submitted a draft of the cable to be sent to Nixon on his sixtieth birthday. HIM considered it too formal. 'Rewrite it in more friendly tones', he said, 'and send him a present or two. Do the same for Podgorny's seventieth birthday next February.'

Reported HMQ's instructions to cancel the furs bought for her in Russia. According to HIM, she can buy a fur coat for the same amount of money far more quickly from Paris.

A greetings telegram to King Hussein, congratulating him on his wedding, his third, to a twenty-four year old Palestinian girl, needed to be signed by both HIM and HMQ. HIM remarked that HMQ is reluctant to celebrate a marriage she disapproves of, but I replied that there is no alternative, as the girl has been proclaimed Queen of Jordan. 'The thing could hardly have come at a better moment', said HIM, 'bearing in mind your recent conversation with Mrs Diba.'

Tuesday, 26 December

Audience. HIM at last agreed the text of the cable to Nixon, redrafted several times over the past two days. 'All the same', he said, 'the cable marking the fiftieth anniversary of the formation of the Soviet Union is far too dry.' I pointed out that it was I who had drawn his attention to this fact. 'Well, now I've decided to agree with you. Prepare a better text', he said. Alas, poor me.

Passed on various comments made by the BBC about changes around the world ... amongst them the fact that Iran now has an economic growth rate of 10 per cent and possesses unrivalled military power in the Middle East; in short that we're becoming the region's most important nation. HIM was delighted, saying, 'If we continue to depend upon ourselves, the world will be obliged to sit up and take notice.'

I then put my foot in it by suggesting there are shortcomings none the less, for example the inefficiency of government agencies and the public's dissatisfaction at being excluded from a role in national affairs; HIM should find a way round these problems. He was not pleased by this and it effectively cancelled out the effect of the first part of my report. However, I am duty bound to tell him the truth.

Wednesday, 27 December

HIM went skiing this morning ... audience after lunch. Submitted a long report from our ambassador to Rabat, describing Prince Abdul Reza's visit to Morocco. 'Poor King Hassan seems to be going off his head', remarked HIM. 'Yes', I said, 'I'm afraid the game is up for him.' He replied, 'But if it's the Americans who are to blame, why is it that they have refrained from curbing my own independence?'

Thursday, 28 December

Brief audience. Our Paris press attaché states that a correspondent of the French magazine *L'Express* has been making enquiries about the new oil deal. 'Tell them to release no information as yet, absolutely nothing', HIM said angrily, adding: 'I'm sure that the leak can be traced back to the PM.'

Later I went to sign the book at the US embassy following the death of former President Harry Truman. The US Chargé d'Affaires let me know that Farland will return to America sooner than was expected – a hint, no doubt, that I'd better hurry if I want to throw a farewell party ...

Towards evening I attended a meeting chaired by HMQ, intended to coordinate the works of various organizations for the handicapped. She devotes a great deal of energy to this cause and to my delight the meeting produced a sound set of resolutions ...

Friday, 29 December

It's freezing cold, 15 degrees below zero. Worked at home all day. Phoned HMQ to bid farewell – my wife and I are flying to London tomorrow to join our daughter who is expecting a child.

1973

Western governments had grown increasingly concerned by the pace with which the oil producers of the Persian Gulf were assuming a share in the operations of the oil companies. As recorded in the diary (20 January) President Nixon was moved to write to the Shah, reminding him of the potential consequences for US–Iranian relations. Yet circumstances were radically different from those of 1954 when Iran had been forced to sign the Consortium agreement, sacrificing many of the advantages of nationalization. By contrast, in 1973 Iran obtained an agreement placing her national oil agency, NIOC, in charge of operations throughout the area previously assigned to the Consortium. In return, member companies of the Consortium were to be treated as privileged buyers under a sales-purchase agreement valid for twenty years.

The Arab–Israeli war of October caused a sharp increase in oil prices on the international market. A revised posted price was set by OPEC ministers meeting in Tehran on 23 December. The price of Arabian light crude, regarded as a marker, was to rise to $11.65 per barrel, $9.27 of this being allocated as the government take, compared to the $2.18 established only two years earlier by the Tehran agreement of 1971. Iran's oil income, which had risen from $90 million in 1955, to $1.1 billion by 1970, now soared to a staggering $21.4 billion.

The Shah revelled in the attention he attracted as leader of the oil-producing nations, pressing their claim to higher income. Many more countries opened embassies in Tehran. Foreign governments and private businessmen flocked to share in Iran's new found wealth.

In July the King of Afghanistan was toppled by a *coup d'état*, and a republic declared. Iran observed these developments with anxiety, perceiving a new threat in the east when her western border with Iraq had long caused misgiving. Alam suggested that help be given to the deposed King, exiled to Italy, to retrieve his throne. The Shah replied that 'The King lacks the guts for anything like that.' (Diaries,

17 July) Subsequently he decided that it was in Iran's best interest to cultivate friendly relations with the new regime and to help it against communist infiltration.

Iranian military support for Oman increased, troops being sent to assist the Sultan against the Dhofari rebels led by the Popular Front for the Liberation of Oman and the Arab Gulf (PFLOAG).

As inflation soared, the Shah threatened to put the military in charge of his campaign against profiteering. Meanwhile the government issued warnings that businesses convicted of over-charging would be liable to expropriation by the state. Alam believed that much of the blame for price increases lay with the government. He warned the Shah 'People are dissatisfied, and ... this could pose a serious threat.' (Diaries, 26 September)

Friday, 12 January
President Ceausescu of Romania flew in at 1 p.m. together with his wife. Later he spent two and a half hours talking with HIM. For dinner I laid on a small reception – about 60 guests ... The President left at midnight but HIM stayed on to watch a movie. I bid my farewells and returned home. Meanwhile a cable arrived from A.Kh. Afshar, our ambassador in London, announcing that the oil representatives intend to propose Iranian participation in the Consortium on far better terms than those offered to the Arabs. The representatives themselves arrived tonight. At 1 a.m. my telephone rang and I was ordered to cancel my attendance at the airport tomorrow morning, and proceed directly to the palace.

Saturday, 13 January
Audience. HIM in a grim mood despite the excellent snows. 'Have you seen Afshar's telegram?', he asked. 'You must immediately summon the British ambassador and ask him the meaning of all this skulduggery. There can be no comparison between us and the Arabs; our oil production was nationalized long ago and we shall insist on the purchase/sale formula which we proposed, as the only possible basis for settlement.' ... I was also instructed to telephone through and brief the US ambassador.

In the afternoon following Ceausescu's departure, the British ambassador called round. To the best of his knowledge, he said, he thought the Consortium's proposals were reasonable, although he is unaware of their exact details. The US ambassador said much the same.

Reported these conversations at dinner. According to the British ambassador, HIM himself hinted at the possibility of a partnership during his stay in London last June. 'Tell him', said HIM, 'that we were expecting the Arabs to be offered a maximum 25 per cent share, but it has since been agreed that this should rise to 51 per cent in 1981. I can hardly maintain my former standpoint now that the whole situation has altered in this way. Nevertheless, tell him that, whilst refusing to abandon our basic principles, we shall judge each proposal on its merits.' The ambassador had also suggested that the companies have certain contractual rights, despite the fact that our oil has been nationalized. 'That's a matter of opinion', said HIM. As to the purchase/sale formula he dismissed the ambassador's objection that it implied a complete take-over, saying that since 1954 Iran has already owned 100 per cent of her oil.

Sunday, 14 January

... This afternoon the oil representatives were received by HIM and put forward proposals similar to those already offered to the Arabs, saving the one difference that we would receive our 51 per cent immediately on signing. HIM rejected the suggestion out of hand ...

Monday, 15 January

... A second audience for the representatives, discussions going on for several hours. HIM emerged in an excellent mood, saying that he'd put his case quite bluntly: 'Either accept my proposal to sell you oil at a reasonable discount over the next twenty-five years, or I shall terminate the present agreement in 1979. Then I shall be free to do exactly as I choose. I was surprised that they took my ultimatum so calmly.' ...

Tuesday, 16 January

HIM flew to Pakistan, ostensibly to go hunting, but in reality for talks with Bhutto ...

Thursday, 18 January

... He returned shortly after noon, and immediately asked whether there had been any news on the oil negotiations. I replied that I'd met with the Tehran representatives of British Intelligence and the CIA, both of whom, especially the British, believe that HIM will get his way, whatever gloomy forecast the British ambassador may make. Apparently the ambassador met with both the British and American oil representatives following their audience with HIM ...

Saturday, 20 January

Audience. Reported that the US Minister-Counsellor called round this morning and handed me an urgent letter for HIM from Nixon. He also expressed his government's concern that HIM may take the opportunity of the forthcoming National Congress, marking a decade of the White Revolution, to outline his views on the oil negotiations and so jeopardize the whole continuation of the present talks. 'Frankly', I told HIM, 'I'm shocked by the President's letter. For all its outward politeness, it's nothing short of an order.'

[Text of the letter of President Nixon to the Shah,
dated 19 January 1973]

Your Imperial Majesty,

As Your Majesty knows, I have followed with great interest the negotiations between Your Majesty's Government and the Oil Consortium.
Recent reports on the present state of the negotiations have deeply
concerned me, and I am writing now in the light of our long friendship
and our mutual concern for stability in your area of the world.

My concern is that the most recent proposals of Your Majesty's
Government could seriously affect the entire area and the whole course
of our mutual relationship. As you are aware, I'm at the moment deeply
involved in the activities related to the negotiations for peace in Southeast
Asia, the reorganization of my own Administration and my Inauguration,
and am not in a position to address the substance of the present situation.
However, since a unilateral step which doesn't meet the legitimate
interests of both sides could have serious consequences for the objectives
which we are pursuing together, I do want to express the hope that you
might defer any unilateral action until I can study the issue and put my
consideration before you.

HIM pondered a while before dictating a reply which I noted down. At
the end I remarked that his own letter gives me as much joy as Nixon's
had angered me ...

[The Shah's letter, dated 20 January 1973, is warmly phrased but stands
firm on his basic policy towards the oil companies. The most important
clauses are as follows]

We ... think that the oil companies had ample time to reach an agreement
with us but they spent time doing otherwise.

I am convinced that after the announcement of our policies which are
the best guarantees of the secure flow of oil supplies ... there will still
be time for the parties concerned to meet our legitimate. rights and
reasonable demands ...

... At dinner HIM said: 'Summon the US ambassador and ask him what
makes ours such a "special" relationship, when it can be jeopardized
merely by the complaint of an oil company. Up until now his country has
maintained that it is unable to offer advice to the companies, which are
independent of government control. You should tell him on your own

behalf how surprised and dismayed you were by the tone of Nixon's letter.'
I suggested that this was perhaps a little too harsh but, try as I might, I
could do nothing to make him soften his attitude. 'Nixon', he said, 'has
the audacity to tell me to do nothing in the interest of my country until he
dictates where that interest lies. At the same time he threatens me that
failure to follow his so-called advice will be to jeopardize the special
relations between our two countries. I say to hell with such special relations
...' He added, 'We shall accept no further advice from friend or foe.' The
spirit he has shown is tremendous. I regret that there were so many others
present, otherwise I might have been tempted to kiss his feet ...

Sunday, 21 January
Brief audience. Yesterday HIM saw the British ambassador to reply to the
message he delivered from his Foreign Secretary. Subsequently I received
a text of this message and, having discussed it with me, HIM today dictated
a written reply. Home's message and HIM's answer were both extremely
polite, totally different from the response we sent to Nixon's letter. 'Tell
the British ambassador', he said, 'that I must outline the principles of my
oil policy in a speech to my people. I shall not enter into details and I shall
leave the companies some room to manoeuvre.'

He then asked whether I had read Nixon's inaugural speech. I had heard
it on the radio but not read it. 'Do you recall', he said, 'that at one point
he specifically advocates non-interference in the internal affairs of other
countries? And yet the blasted man has the audacity to write me such a
letter.' ...

Received the British ambassador who asked about HIM's answer to
Foreign Secretary Home. With HIM's prior consent I showed him a copy.
He then wanted to know about HIM's letter to Nixon but I stonewalled
him. He said that the US ambassador had shown him the text of Nixon's
letter. 'In that case', I said, 'you can guess the sort of response it merited
and received.' He replied that he himself had helped to draft Home's letter
and had suggested the appropriate tone. I told him that, like it or not,
HIM's proposals will be accepted in the end; they represent the best
solution to the problems of every oil-producing country. He agreed, con-
fessing that at yesterday's audience he had been completely flattened by
the force of HIM's logic. 'For instance', he said, 'I reminded him that Iraq
has lost nearly $300 million as a result of nationalizing her oil. He replied
that Iran underwent this trauma years ago, and that Iraq will make good
her losses in the long term. Next I suggested that the policies he is pursuing

may have an adverse effect on foreign investment within Iran, but he pointed out that the country has quite sufficient capital of its own, and that foreign investors will have no misgivings once his policies have been properly explained to them. I then suggested that Iran lacks sufficient qualified personnel to manage its industries, but HIM replied that most of the expatriates presently working in the oil industry will stay on regardless, and that even if they leave, replacements can always be found.' ... He ended by remarking that the Americans might accept HIM's less radical formula, by which the present agreement would be terminated in 1979. I assured him that this would more than meet our requirements ...

Monday, 22 January
The PM telephoned me before my audience saying that he had been instructed by HIM to read through the replies we are sending to Home and Nixon. Audience. HIM's first question was whether I had sent the PM the letters he requested. I replied that I had sent HIM's replies, but he berated me for not having sent copies of the letters we received. I explained that the PM had not asked me for these, nor would it be appropriate for Nixon's peremptory message to become common knowledge. After thinking for a while, HIM replied that both sets of letters had to be read together in order to appreciate the harshness of his reply. 'Your Deputy Bahadori can take the thing round to the PM and then return it.'

For some time we discussed the extent of foreign interference in our affairs, and how the Americans – Kennedy that is – helped Amini to achieve power[1] ...

I remarked that any manner of foreign backed conspiracy could always be thwarted if a few determined people were in the right places, reminding him how we crushed the Mullahs and our other enemies during my own time as Prime Minister. 'Who else except Your Majesty had the courage to support me?' 'Nobody', he confessed. Once again, I ran through the events of 1963, how violent disorders broke out on 5 June following Khomeini's arrest; how HIM had rung me to ask what action I intended to take. 'Remember', I said, 'how I told Your Majesty that I would hit them where it hurt, and how you laughed when I said I would give them the screwing they'd been asking for. There was no alternative. Had we backed down, the rioting would have spread to every corner of Iran and

---

[1] As Iranian ambassador in Washington, Ali Amini had already got to know the then Senator John Kennedy. It was not only Kennedy, but the entire American administration which felt the urgent need for a change of government in Iran. See introduction.

our regime would have collapsed in abject surrender. I even told Your Majesty that, should I myself be brought down, you could always rescue yourself by having me indicted and executed as a scapegoat. On the other hand, if I won through, we'd be rid of clerical skulduggery and foreign manipulation for ever.' 'Oh yes', he said, 'I remember it well enough. I shall never forget the service you rendered.' ...

Tuesday, 23 January

The *Salaam* of *Eyd- e Ghadir*. In a steady snowfall, a host of children was assembled in the gardens of the Golestan Palace to demonstrate popular enthusiasm for ten years of the White Revolution. HIM became annoyed that the children should be kept outdoors in such weather and ordered that they be invited inside and given tea. How on earth was I expected to arrange tea for 2,000 school children? Instead we laid on a whole mountain of pastries and the kids were hurried into the newly decorated hall, passing from room to room with their pockets crammed full of cakes. A pair of little girls refused to leave until they'd had their picture taken alongside HIM ...

In the afternoon he attended a special national congress to mark the anniversary, delivering a magnificent speech in which he stressed his determination to implement the oil policy which he then proceeded to outline ... Later I heard on the BBC news that there's been a fall in oil company shares on the London stock market. AFP, the French news agency, quoted a spokesman for the Oil Consortium, announcing that their representatives will continue to seek a mutually acceptable solution via negotiations with Iran. Bravo for the Shah. I've just this minute rung him to pass on the latest developments ...

Ex-President Lyndon Johnson has died – a good personal friend but by no means a first-rate president. He was too slow to take decisive action. One evening at a White House reception I asked him what he hoped to gain by an escalation of the war in Vietnam, and why instead of sending off a few thousand more soldiers each week he didn't simply finish the job and send in a hundred thousand overnight. He replied that he had to keep an eye on the opinion polls. 'In which case', I said, 'if I were you I should be a very worried man indeed.' Mrs Mariam Ansari, the wife of our then ambassador in Washington, kicked me vigorously under the table warning me to curb my tongue.

The British ambassador rang to inform me of the furore that's broken out over a young Englishman, an assistant in the English department of

Tehran University, and temporary tutor last summer to the Crown Prince, who was actively involved in anti-government demonstrations at the university. It was decided to expel him, the government using him as an example of British intrigue in the midst of the oil negotiations. I passed on the news to HIM, reminding him that he is sufficiently powerful not to have to resort to such cheap propaganda from his government; this kind of exercise, spreading false rumours and so on, was all too common when Mosaddeq was Prime Minister. I had tremendous difficulty persuading him to change his mind. He gave way in the end, thank goodness, otherwise we'd have had the world media round about our necks again, alleging that we're an autocratic police-state.

Saturday, 27 January
Audience ... Discussing the developments over oil HIM said, 'Nixon would like to consign us to the level of the most backward countries in the whole Middle East. Why lower us to the standard of the Saudis rather than raising the Saudis to meet us? Iran has a population and development needs out of all comparison to those of our Arab neighbours.' ...

The British ambassador telephoned me at home late this afternoon to lodge a vehement protest against the arrest of that blasted Englishman, mixed up in university demonstrations. I did not take kindly to the ambassador's hectoring, and told him so, quite bluntly. I reminded him that it is entirely due to HIM's desire for closer relations with the West that I allow him to ring me up like this; by rights he should approach our Foreign Ministry, and even then, he's not supposed to deal with anyone higher up than the head of the British desk. 'In future', I told him, 'you'll no longer be permitted to visit me at Court.' Sure enough, this put a whole new complexion on our conversation, and he ended up pleading for forgiveness ...

Reported this at dinner. 'Well done', said HIM, 'but you should have gone even further.' ...

Monday, 29 January
... In spite of my acrimonious remarks, the British ambassador called at my office to offer a personal apology. I kept him waiting outside for nearly an hour – something I hate doing, but in this instance I felt I had no alternative. The ambassador was brimful with remorse, but even so I made my point, forcing him to admit that the English student at the centre of the row must leave Iran for good. When he objected that the boy has no

money, I promised that we will bear the cost of repatriation.

A visit from the deputy manager of the Oil Consortium, bringing a letter to HIM from J.K. Jamieson, Chairman of the Exxon Corporation.

[The letter, dated 26 January 1973, runs as follows]

The Consortium member companies have read with concern the remarks concerning the consortium made by Your Majesty in your speech to the National Congress on 23rd January 1973.

As discussed during the last audience, it is in our mutual interest that discussions continue looking towards achieving a satisfactory solution. This continues to be our wish. Accordingly, we are desirous of seeking a further audience with Your Majesty in the near future.

The companies have asked me to mention that, as Your Majesty will appreciate, your speech raised certain questions reflecting on the provisions applicable to the companies and the Government of Iran under the Agreement of 29th October 1954. The companies reluctantly feel that they must write formally to the Minister of Finance of Iran, being the designated person under the 1954 agreement, to protect their legal position under the Agreement. Such a letter is being sent.

May I emphasize that the necessity to send a formal letter to the Minister of Finance will in no way inhibit the companies' efforts to reach an appropriate understanding ...

HIM rang me as soon as he'd read it. 'Tell them', he said, 'that they are a bunch of thieves; they tried to pay what was due to us in sterling at a time when sterling was devalued. It was only our alertness and our power to persuade that saved us from a loss of several million pounds. What's more, it was only under pressure that they began paying tax at our ports; for years they'd been getting away scot-free. Even now they refuse to pay compensation for the quantities of associated gas that they burn off in oil production. It's only recently, with no help from the companies and in the face of a host of obstacles, that we've been able to pipeline a small proportion of this gas to the Soviet Union. Remind them that the UN Charter states quite clearly that every individual country has sovereignty over its own natural resources, and can dispose of them as it sees fit. You should also remind them that the proposals I made in last week's speech to the joint session of Parliament were two days later incorporated into unalterable law. The companies should be grateful that I refrained from exposing their shortcomings in public.' ...

Tuesday, 30 January

... Series of lengthy meetings this afternoon; secret sessions with our own heads of security and with representatives of British Intelligence and the CIA, amongst other things, going through the precautions for HIM's forthcoming stay in St Moritz.[1] I'm having nightmares about this trip, which has so far been kept out of the foreign media. The state of play in the oil negotiations only heightens my anxiety, although HIM's wisdom and good fortune will probably see him through ...

Wednesday, 31 January

Audience ... 'The US ambassador is outside waiting to be received', said HIM. 'Greet him as you leave and tell him casually that my proposals to the joint session of Parliament have since become law and are no longer open to debate.' ...

I myself went to the airport and waited there for HIM ... He was accompanied onto the plane by the PM and the Minister of Finance, busily briefing him on their discussions with the companies. Meanwhile the rest of us were made to wait outside in the cold ...

Towards evening I attended the wedding of my secretary, the daughter of General Oveissi. She already has a son by a previous husband; she's thirty years old, but goodness what a fuss she's made about this marriage. Nevertheless she's a good girl, and a considerable beauty; beauty licenses behaviour we might otherwise resent ...

Saturday, 17 February

A meeting with the President of Pahlavi University and with Abdol-Majid Majidi, newly appointed head of the Plan Organization. The government originally assigned $25 million of next year's budget towards building at the university, but it now appears that only $9 million will be available. By contrast, according to Majidi, military investment is set to rise by 300 per cent and current expenditure is to be doubled; a total of $500 million from the budget. He begged me to report the situation to HIM. I was forced to reply that this is the PM's duty, not mine. 'But the PM is terrified to spell out the facts', said Majidi. 'His idea is to fob the responsibility off on me, by insisting that I go to St Moritz to report in person. I'm at my wits' end to know what to do.' Once again I disclaimed any responsibility,

[1] Whenever the Shah travelled abroad this was an aspect of the standard co-operation between Iranian Security Agencies and their western counterparts, particularly those of the United States and Great Britain

pointing out that HIM resents my interfering in such matters. He left my office a very disappointed man.

After lunch I received a visit from Dr Hammer of Occidental Petroleum. He described his recent discussions in Tehran and St Moritz and proposed that we sign a tripartite deal; Iran to deliver gas from Sarakhs to Russia; the Soviets to supply an equivalent quantity of gas from Siberia to Alaska; the Americans to finance the operation by paying us in US dollars.

Sunday, 18 February

... The US ambassador called round to bid me farewell. I gave him a signed photograph of HIM. Overall he is optimistic about the outcome of the oil negotiations ...

My secretary came to see me. Having got married a fortnight ago she now seeks my advice on obtaining a divorce. How droll!

Saturday, 3 March

... HMQ flew in at ten tonight, later than expected as she had made her pilot stop off in Rome so that she might lunch with her guests, the King and Queen of Greece. At the airport she was most effusive towards the PM – who has bought up virtually every member of her entourage – inviting him to dinner. I myself am not nearly so well favoured, for the usual, obvious reasons ...

Monday, 12 March

Today is Princess Farahnaz's birthday. While in St Moritz I overheard a telephone conversation in which she made her father promise to be back in Tehran in time for the occasion. Sure enough, he flew in at 5 this evening ...

Sunday, 15 April

Audience. Submitted various cables for HIM's signature. One of them was addressed to the Syrian President, Hafiz Assad, who sent HIM no telegram on the latter's birthday. I pointed this out but HIM signed the cable none the less, remarking: 'You shouldn't be so surprised. We're in the midst of negotiations with a view to establishing diplomatic relations with Syria; in the meantime we must turn a blind eye to such minor irritations; after all, unlike them, we're not burdened with an inferiority complex.' ...

Monday, 16 April
Audience ... HIM reminded me that the cable to President Assad should be read out on national radio ... He also instructed me to summon the US ambassador Helms, to complain about the shortage of spare parts for our Phantoms ...

Met the ambassador at my home. He asked me to advise him on those people he is free to meet in Iran without risking disapproval from HIM. I replied that this is not a dictatorship; foreigners are free to consort with whomever they choose. In answer to a question I asked some time ago, he told me that President Nixon is indeed a candidate for the Nobel Peace Prize ...

Tuesday, 17 April
Audience. Related an amusing exchange I had at last night's reception at the Pakistani embassy. The Egyptian ambassador approached me, expressing a hope that we shall not invite the Israelis to take part in the forthcoming Asian Games; otherwise the Arab countries will be forced to stay away. To avoid giving a direct answer, I replied that long before the games take place we expect that the Arabs will have wiped Israel from the map. The ambassador was well aware of the ludicrous nature of this proposition and burst into one of his notorious guffaws. HIM was amused at this, but remarked, 'You should have told him even so, that we have absolutely no say in these invitations. They are issued by the international sports federations.' I pointed out that I'd been anxious to steer clear of any sort of argument over details ...

Wednesday, 18 April
HIM was too busy to receive me this morning, following the presentation of credentials by our first accredited ambassador from East Germany. Instead I sent round those reports I considered most urgent, together with a note that the Consortium's representatives have arrived in Tehran and are requesting an audience. He phoned back to say that he would receive them after lunch, adding: 'As they're being good boys, you are free to organize a reception for them.' ...

At dinner Their Majesties discussed the future of the environment. HMQ maintained that Iran's natural beauty must be protected at all costs. HIM said, on the contrary, that the country requires rapid development; in the process, some degree of damage is bound to be inflicted. We must set against this the fact that many thousands of hectares have been planted as forest. 'But what of the natural splendour of the deserts?', said HMQ. 'Are you blind to their beauty?' 'I shall make sure that you are created Viceroy of every desert in Iran', joked HIM. But HMQ refused to be side-tracked, remarking: 'You see these gentlemen around us? They all agree with what I say, but not one of them dares express his opinion.' At this stage I quoted the lines:

> If once a King declares that day has turned to night
> Make sure to marvel at the moon's bright light.

HMQ was amused by this, but I'm not at all sure that HIM shares her sense of humour . . .

Thursday, 19 April

Audience . . . We talked about the new US ambassador Helms. 'He seems a good appointment', said HIM. 'I've come across him in the past; he's chiefly interested in getting close to us, rendering us whatever service he can.'

Back in my office I received a phone call from Princess Ashraf, asking after the *Légion d'honneur* that was promised her by Pompidou. 'It's a shame to put yourself in Pompidou's debt', I said. 'What advantage can you hope to gain from a French decoration? Why aim so low?' As soon as she'd rung off I phoned through to HIM to report the matter. 'You did well', he said, 'very well indeed.'

Saturday, 21 April

Audience. Despite this being a religious holiday, the anniversary of the Prophet's birth, we worked on regardless. I was expecting to find HIM buoyed up with the success of the oil negotiations, but on the contrary he was red with rage. Some time ago he ordered the government to allow farmers to increase the price of sugar-beet, and in compensation to the sugar refineries allowed a reduction of 2 rials per kilo in the tax paid on refinery products. The price of beet has already been raised; the deduction in tax is to follow next year. 'But now', said HIM, 'I've heard that S . . . has contacted the management of the sugar companies, demanding $4 million to speed up the introduction of tax concessions. You must issue instructions to the government, ordering them to prosecute any company which has agreed to pay this commission; they must be severely punished. Likewise, notify S . . . that unless he curbs his greed I shall have him thrown out of the country altogether.' Only then did he express his satisfaction with the oil talks ...

Sunday, 22 April
Audience. Reported that I had implemented his instructions of yesterday but I have found that S ... was not alone in the deal. 'What did I tell you?', said HIM; 'He's had the whole bloody pack of vultures crawling around him.' I refrained from mentioning the names of S ...'s two associates, Amir Houshang Davallou and a government minister, nor did he press me for details. Hence I can be sure that he's already in the know. We must simply wait and see how he reacts ...

Tuesday, 24 April
Audience. Abba Eban, the Israeli Foreign Minister, is due here for a secret audience next Friday. I reported that he has asked to see me, but HIM brushed off the suggestion as 'totally unnecessary'. As I've remarked in the past, such is *l'ingratitude des grands* ...

After lunch attended the Association of Scholars and Intellectuals,[1] established on HIM's own orders to assess the progress of the White Revolution. Goodness knows what role it will find for itself. If only its members could learn to work together, or dared speak their minds. Then perhaps it might become remotely useful ...

Wednesday, 25 April
Audience. Reported that the Spanish Foreign Minister has invited me to an embassy dinner during his forthcoming visit; should I accept? 'Act according to form', HIM replied. I had no idea whether this was a yes or a no, but thought it best to probe no further. I'm not sure that HIM likes me to be openly involved in political affairs. In general I do my best to conform to his wishes and only risk causing offence when I believe it to be in his own or the country's best interests.

A two-hour meeting this afternoon with the editor of *Newsweek*. Discussing Sadat he made a startling remark to the effect that the Egyptians intend to provoke Israel into hostilities which will mobilize world opinion against her. Kissinger has apparently confided in him that the US administration can do nothing for the Arabs given the pro-Israeli bias in Congress.

---

[1] At the Shah's suggestion on the tenth anniversary of the White Revolution various Iranian academics formed this group with a view of studying and debating aspects of the country's social reforms. They were not taken seriously either by the Shah or Hoveyda

The only thing to change this would be if Israel were to overstep the mark, causing the Arabs to sever oil supplies to the West; even a brief period without oil, and the Americans would be free to pressure Israel into more moderate policies. In other words Kissinger and Sadat appear to think alike. According to the Chinese, Egypt is set to attack Israel within a matter of two to three months. My reply to all this was to say that a regime defeated in war loses all room for manoeuvre. I cannot believe that Sadat is stupid enough to take such a risk ...

Thursday, 26 April
Audience ... Reported my meeting with the editor of *Newsweek*. 'So Saudi Oil Minister Zaki Yamani's grumbling is directly inspired by the Americans', HIM remarked ...

Saturday, 28 April
... Attended HIM's lunch for Moulay Abdullah. We spoke of nothing except last year's failed coup in Morocco. Afterwards, Moulay Abdullah informed me that HIM has recommended him to hold discussions with General Nassiri and myself ...

Declined several official engagements in order to dine at the British residence with my old friend Denis Wright. I'd made it plain beforehand that the British ambassador should invite no one else ...

Sunday, 29 April
Audience. I asked what tone HIM wished to adopt in replying to a letter from King Hassan of Morocco. 'Limit the thing to generalities', he said. 'One daren't do more, as who knows what such people may be up to.' ...

Attended Lunch in honour of the Crown Prince of Bahrain. We discussed HIM's address to the Association of Scholars and Intellectuals ... HIM remarked to the PM that the Association was useful, in that it distracted the attention of the younger generation. Apparently this is the limit of its usefulness as far as HIM is concerned ...

Subsequently I met with Moulay Abdullah and General Nassiri. Moulay Abdullah's chief concerns were as follows:

- The situation in Morocco is explosive. King Hassan expects HIM to bolster up the present regime.
- There is need for direct liaison between the King and HIM. No such

go-between can be found amongst the Moroccan army or intelligence agencies, whose officers are completely unreliable.
- King Hassan is a well-intentioned man who too easily puts his trust in those around him; a case in point being General Oufkir, against whom Moulay Abdullah says he warned the King on several occasions.
- The axis of co-operation between Rabat, Riyadh and Tehran should be reactivated.

What surprised me most in all this was the extent to which Moulay Abdullah seems to fancy himself as ruler of Morocco.

Sheikh Hamad, the Crown Prince of Bahrain, called on me at six this evening; Sandhurst educated, capable, well-informed, and only twenty-three years old. Subsequently I dined as his guest. The PM was disgracefully drunk; at least five or six times he toasted the health of the American ambassador, an appalling piece of flattery, all the worse for having taken place in front of so many foreign dignitaries.

Monday, 30 April
Audience. Reported my discussions with Moulay Abdullah. 'A gentleman who has a reputation even more crimson than that of King Hassan', remarked HIM. 'None the less you should tell him to come to dinner with me tonight.'

... He then asked about the Crown Prince's dinner party. I described the PM's drunkenness and his impropriety without entering into details. I also passed on remarks made to me by the US ambassador, who had lavished flattery on HIM, even suggesting that he should act as a tutor in good government to the Crown Prince of Bahrain and the Sultan of Oman, indeed to every ruler in the Emirates. 'But where's the flattery in that?', asked HIM, a remark that rather threw me off balance. 'Yesterday', he continued, 'the members of the US staff college told me precisely the same thing; the ambassador was there and heard every word of it.' ...

Wednesday, 2 May
Audience. We discussed Watergate. HIM declared that the entire system of American presidential elections is founded on deceit. 'Big business always has the final say in which candidates are nominated, both by the Democrat and the Republican conventions', he said; 'But it appears that they're now treating what would normally be considered a straightforward piece of gamesmanship, as if it were some sort of scandal.' ...

... HIM informed me that Davallou will accompany him on his forthcoming visit to southern Iran, although three days ago he told me quite the contrary. It's beyond me, how someone as intelligent as HIM can tolerate such people when they do so much damage to his reputation. But then Persian history is full of scoundrels like Davallou, men of no apparent talent who nevertheless bask in their sovereign's favour ...

Thursday, 3 May
Brief morning audience. HIM signed various letters and telegrams including one congratulating the Israelis on the twenty-fifth anniversary of their country's foundation ...

Flew to Shiraz after lunch ...

Saturday, 5 May
Flew on to Bandar Abbas, where we spent a couple of hours under a scorching sun, touring the naval installations. Over lunch HIM asked that his tour of the hospital of the Red Lion and Sun be cancelled. He subsequently explained that the hospital is named after his second wife, ex-Queen Soraya, and he's worried that HMQ may get the wrong impression if he shows any interest in the place. Pauper or prince, no one can ignore the complexities of marriage.

In the afternoon we flew to Kish ...

Sunday, 6 May
After rising we sailed to the island of Abu Musa in order to observe naval operations; a series of rapid manoeuvres by the fleet, firing cannon and missile launchers. None of the cannon hit their targets, much to the rage of HIM who roundly cursed the navy's commander. I did my best to calm him down, reminding him that the fleet is still inexperienced and needs time to improve, but he would have none of it. I pointed out that the Sea-killer missiles with a range of only 24 kilometres are merely practice weapons, very different from those that would be taken into a real engagement. 'Forget about the missiles', he said; 'it's the cannon that disappoint me; they're fired at fixed targets, in peace time with no real pressure on the gunners ... These are the people that I rely on in planning my foreign policy, in risking confrontation with foreign powers; and yet you can see for yourself what a bunch of cretins they've turned out to be. What's to be done with them?' Any pleasure I've had over the past few days has been utterly erased by this incident. HIM was so upset that he dined alone;

tense and on edge. Even so he's a fair man; he instructed me to cancel tomorrow's visit to the Bushehr naval base. 'Firstly', he said, 'I do it to punish them. But at the same time it would be unreasonable for me to go there now. I'd start off prejudiced against their likely performance.' ... Instead, we returned to Shiraz.

Monday, 7 May

Dr Fallah was received this morning to report on negotiations with the oil companies ... My own audience followed. 'Notify the fleet', HIM said, 'that we could hardly have been less pleased by their performance. I specifically promoted younger officers to command, expecting them to put their backs into the task; but just look at the result!' I remarked that Admiral Ramzi Atai, the Commander of the Navy, had been utterly prostrated when I told him of the decision to cancel today's visit to Bushehr; he had pointed out that he's only been at his post for the past six months and will require at least as long again to get things into any sort of order. HIM fears that rapid promotion from amongst officers of the same rank has wrought havoc with discipline[1] ...

Thursday, 10 May

Brief audience. Submitted a draft of HIM's speech for the forthcoming dinner in honour of Bhutto – due to arrive this afternoon. HIM had asked for a text that lavished praise on our guest ... He showed me a letter from Paris, from his brother, Prince Abdul Reza. The Prince and his wife had been invited to dinner by the Queen of the Netherlands, but the spread was so frugal that they returned home nearly fainting from hunger. The Dutch royal family is as miserly as it is rich ...

Friday, 11 May

... A dinner at the Golestan Palace, thrown by Bhutto in honour of HIM ... Afterwards the Soviet ambassador approached me to complain that Princess Shams has turned down an invitation to Russia from the Soviet Red Cross.[2] I pointed out that the invitation should have come from the Soviet President, since the Princess is HIM's own sister. The ambassador promised to see what could be done ... He then referred to an article in

---

[1] A few months earlier on the Shah's orders all the leading naval officers had been put into retirement and replaced by younger men.

[2] Princess Shams was President of the Red Lion and Sun, the Iranian equivalent of the Red Cross.

the *New York Times* by Cyrus Sulzberger, according to which HIM intends to intervene should any sort of crisis develop in Baluchistan. In fact this is misleading; HIM's real object is merely to prevent disorder spreading to Iranian Baluchistan. I told the ambassador that, as HIM made plain to Kosygin, we shall do everything in our power to prevent the disintegration of Pakistan ... 'Don't paint yourselves in the same light as Pakistan', replied the ambassador; 'Iran is a powerful, self-reliant nation; the Pakistanis are a very different bunch.' ...

Saturday, 12 May
Audience ... Bhutto has declared himself willing to open direct talks with Bangladesh, although the latter has yet to be accorded official recognition by Pakistan. Accordingly, HIM has suggested that Pakistan convene a round table conference with India and Bangladesh, to examine their mutual differences, and who knows, perhaps even to settle them. 'Bhutto accepted the proposal', he said; 'You must get in touch with the British ambassador. Tell him the time has come for his government to act as a go-between; they have a role to play in getting this conference off the ground.' ... He then expressed surprise that the morning papers make no mention of the speech he gave at dinner. I explained that the copy reached them only after they'd gone to press; it's been held over for the evening editions.

Transmitted HIM's message to the British ambassador, who claimed that it would be inappropriate for his government to interfere when Pakistan and India are already in direct contact with one another. He further remarked that the Bangladeshis have ruled out any negotiations with Pakistan until the latter grants them diplomatic recognition and amongst other things agrees to the resettlement of Bihari refugees ...

Reported this conversation at dinner. 'Call him again immediately', said HIM. 'Tell him that if his own government is unwilling to get involved, they can nevertheless persuade a third party to set about organizing this conference.' ...

Bhutto has left for Shiraz but will return tomorrow. Hoveyda is now back after three weeks in Holland and Tunisia. What a lucky man he is, to go swanning off with not a care in the world.

Sunday, 13 May
Audience. Passed on a letter from Kenneth Rush, the US Deputy Secretary of State, thanking HIM for the audience he was granted whilst attending the US regional ambassadors' conference in Tehran. 'From the tone he

adopts', said HIM, 'it's almost as if the arrogant bastard assumes that he and I are equals.' ...

Thursday, 17 May

Audience ... Reported that the local French and English language newspapers have published HIM's interview with *Newsweek*. A Persian translation was due to appear this evening but apparently HIM has vetoed its publication. Now the papers are anxiously asking for instructions. 'Quite so', said HIM; 'I wish to go through the Persian translation.' Clearly he wants the thing suppressed – he takes such interviews very seriously. Three months ago he declared that he would refuse to grant them as they're more trouble than they're worth. It was only after Hoveyda travelled to London and made such a splash in the papers there, that HIM changed his mind and agreed to speak to *Newsweek*, basically as a means of snubbing his PM. Not, of course, that he's admitted this to me, but I'm well aware of what's been going on ...

After lunch I attended HMQ's acceptance of a decoration from the Italian Women's Association. She paid me a great deal of attention and personally straightened my tie for the group photograph. Most gracious, it took me quite by surprise ...

Subsequently I held a small 'at home' for the US ambassador's wife and various American friends. These people have spent so long complaining about Iranian corruption that they're now horrified to find their own dirty washing aired in public.

Friday, 18 May

... Submitted a letter from Indira Gandhi, the Indian Prime Minister. She writes about her meeting with Asadollah Rashidiyan[1] and their discussions on the state of relations with Pakistan. As I remarked to HIM, I am surprised to find Rashidiyan sticking his nose into affairs which are none of his business. 'Not at all', said HIM; 'He's acting on my own direct orders. You must prepare a reply to be handed to him direct. There's a great deal to be said in favour of these sorts of unofficial channels, not least that they're maintained unbeknown to our Ministry of Foreign Affairs.' I am amazed to find HIM putting any trust in unreliable characters such as Rashidiyan, but I thought it best not to voice my anxiety.

---

[1] Asadollah Rashidiyan and his elder brother Seyfollah were known to be in close contact with British Intelligence. Instrumental in the mob uprisings which toppled Mosaddeq's government in 1953, they were ostensibly nothing more than successful businessmen.

Wednesday, 23 May

Flew to Mashad with HIM and a wide range of government officials. As always, we went directly to the Holy Shrine ...

Over lunch we discussed national development and HIM's ambitious plans. Our annual steel production is supposed to reach 15 million tons over the coming decade; railroads are planned right the way along the coast of the Gulf; HIM wants to build nuclear power stations; to harness our resources in natural gas, and so on *ad infinitum* ...

Fallah telephoned this evening to report his successful negotiations with various members of the Consortium. The agreement signed in 1954 is to be scrapped, to be replaced by a twenty-year contract for the supply of oil to the Consortium from NIOC.

Thursday, 24 May

Flew to Sarakhs, HIM touring the new gas deposit and the vast agricultural development scheme ...

At lunch he received a cable, announcing that the oil agreement has now been signed, though unofficially. He passed it on to Dr Eqbal; the first Eqbal has been told of recent developments, despite the fact that he's theoretically Chairman and Managing Director of NIOC. HIM remarked that our agreement will force every other oil producer to follow suit ... but he expressed his consternation that the new agreement has so far excited little enthusiasm. 'Perhaps it's only to be expected', he continued. 'We've done little to keep the public informed or to give them any sense of participation in the contest with the companies.' I'm at a loss to know why our great Shah has neglected such a crucial point until this late stage ...

[The Shah and Alam returned to Tehran on Friday 25 May]

Saturday, 26 May

Audience. Amongst the backlog of work, I had to report a request from the English royal family. Prince Philip wishes to be elected to the governing committee of the Iranian Imperial Equestrian Society. HIM was amused by this, commenting, 'In days gone by, an Iranian politician would have considered it a catastrophe if he'd been missed off the guest list to a British embassy cocktail party. Now it appears the boot is on the other foot; a request from the British royal family is filed away amongst insignificant trivia.'

He instructed me to summon the British ambassador to express our surprise that the Foreign Minister of India apparently discussed the security of the Persian Gulf and the Indian Ocean with the Iraqis on a recent trip to Baghdad. Do the Indians want to threaten Iran by the formation of a Delhi–Baghdad axis? Or are they merely reacting to our own joint communiqué with Pakistan, issued during Bhutto's visit? We have repeatedly expressed a willingness to act as intermediaries between India and Pakistan, indeed to settle all regional conflicts. Have the Indians been spurred on by Moscow? HIM wishes to discuss all these matters with the British Foreign Secretary, Sir Alec Douglas-Home, on his forthcoming visit to Tehran, and also to explore the wider prospects for the Gulf Emirates, Saudi Arabia and Iraq. I was to assure the ambassador that none of this implies a hitch in Anglo-Iranian dialogue; we are delighted by the current state of our relations and interested solely in strengthening them ...

Sunday, 27 May
Audience ... On returning to my office, received reports of a mutiny in the Greek navy, supporting the exiled monarchy against the colonels. Apparently a group of retired admirals attempted to seize control of a couple of naval destroyers, intending to occupy one of the islands in the Aegean and thereafter to force the colonels to relinquish power. HIM was made aware of the situation. This afternoon ... I received a phone call from our ambassador in Rome, who claims that the King of Greece – living in exile in Rome, but not officially deposed – has made an unsuccessful attempt to contact HIM and is now pestering the ambassador beyond endurance. I immediately rang through to report this to HIM. He replied that he was already aware of the situation but preferred not to speak to the King. 'The poor fool doesn't realize his telephone is tapped', he said.

... We met later at Princess Ashraf's and HIM ordered me to call in the US ambassador. 'Tell him that the King of Greece is worried that the present rumpus is a put-up job, intended to force his deposition ... Are the Americans aware quite what they would be up against if the Greek monarchy were abolished? Do they want to end up with another Italy or a second Iraq? The US ambassador must make an urgent approach to Nixon, to spell out my anxieties.'

... The ambassador duly came to my office. He is just back from a trip to Tabriz and had no fresh news on the Greek situation. He promised none the less to pass on HIM's message to Nixon. At 11 p.m. I rejoined HIM, reporting the ambassador's words and mentioning how intrigued he had been to know the source of our information. 'But I've already told you', HIM snapped back; 'The King of Greece has spoken to me in person.' Yet earlier this evening, HIM was busy stressing his unwillingness to speak to the King. 'Your Majesty has not told me of this before', I said. 'Yes, I have', he replied. 'The point is not worth labouring', I said. 'I must contact the US ambassador straight away and let him know.'

Monday, 28 May

Audience. For some while we discussed events in Greece. I suggested that they spelt disaster for the King, predicting that a similar fate awaits King Hassan. The latter had insisted that we send General Nassiri to Morocco, yet the general has now been there three days without any attempt on the King's part to receive him.

A second audience after lunch ... Earlier HIM had received Camille Chamoun, former President of Lebanon, who brought a message from his successor, Sulaiman Frangieh, requesting military aid. 'Summon the US ambassador', he told me, 'and ask him whether his country will supply us with a battalion of 155 millimetre long-range artillery, to pass on to the Lebanon; and may we send them 3 F-5 planes?' I remarked that the Lebanese ambassador has already asked for supplies of ammunition, but we are in no position to help as they rely on French as opposed to our own American weapons systems ...

The US ambassador called at my house to receive our request. 'If HIM commands it', he said, 'I shall do my best to get Washington to approve.' ...

Tuesday, 29 May

... Went to the airport to bid farewell to Their Majesties who are off on a trip to Yugoslavia, Romania and Bulgaria ... Passed on a report on the Greek situation prepared by the US ambassador. An impressive document, implying that nothing can be done to alter the course of events. HIM read it through carefully, remarking: 'Tell the ambassador that I'm displeased to find his government so indifferent to the fate of the Greek monarchy.' ...

Friday, 1 June

Colonel Papadopoulos, head of the Greek military junta, has declared Greece a republic. The announcement was not unexpected but none the less I am grieved both by the demise of the monarchy and by the almost superhuman stupidity shown by the Americans ...

Saturday, 2 June

... Attended the British embassy reception, on the occasion of Queen Elizabeth's birthday. I have steered clear of this event for more than a decade, but this year HIM instructed me to put in an appearance, since his own birthday reception in our London embassy was attended by both Lord Mountbatten and the Duke of Gloucester ...

Met the US ambassador who tells me that the Lebanese have made a request for military aid to Washington, similar to that submitted to HIM. They are asking specifically for Sky Hawk aircraft, type A 4-B. The ambassador requested my permission to check that the Beirut government is coordinating its requests with those made by Chamoun. He then filled me in on the latest terrorist outrage: the murder of Colonel Hawkins, one of the US military advisers in Tehran ...

Thursday, 7 June

Early morning meeting with the British ambassador. He outlined the topics which Sir Alec Douglas-Home wishes to explore during his forthcoming visit; Indo-Pakistani and Indo-Iraqi relations, the situation in the UAE, our relations with Saudi Arabia, Gulf security and the concept of collective defence ... which the ambassador believes will be difficult to implement given the hypocrisy of the Arabs. The British have no official diplomatic relations with Iraq, but even so they've received reports via the French embassy in Baghdad, indicating that Iran has opened secret negotiations with the Iraqis. Sir Alec would like to know whether there is any truth to this rumour. I strenuously denied it ...

He closed our conversation with a confidence. 'My government and my Prime Minister', he said, 'are anxious to conclude the deal on Chieftain tanks which promises Britain employment and considerable revenue. However, I cannot help thinking that 800 tanks may be too many for Iran to cope with, given the cost of maintenance and your shortage of skilled technicians. Moreover the tanks themselves are ill-suited to mountainous or marshy terrain such as you have in the west and south-west of Iran. I should hate the deal to go ahead at the risk of jeopardizing the excellent relations which prevail between our two countries.' His frankness made a great impression on me and I suggested that he might like to repeat these remarks to HIM in person. This he agreed to do ...

Then to the airport, to welcome Their Majesties on their return from Eastern Europe ...

Audience lasting two hours. Reported various developments, and pointed out that HIM's forthcoming state visit to the USA should be accompanied by full pomp and ceremony. 'I have suggested to the US ambassador', I went on, 'that it might be appropriate if their President attended a reception at our embassy on the last night of Your Majesty's stay.' 'What's all this nonsense about "might be appropriate"?', retorted HIM. 'Why dress it up like that? Nixon is obliged to attend, and that's the end of the matter.' He's quite right of course. Several times he returned to the subject, rebuking me for my feebleness. Fortunately I was able to pass on a letter from a delightful young lady which went some way towards appeasing him ...

Saturday, 9 June

... HIM received the British Foreign Secretary at eleven thirty this morning, their talks lasting two hours. I then joined them in the palace gardens to escort them to lunch where we were to be met by HMQ and Lady Home. HIM greeted me in English, saying: 'The Minister of Economics, Ansari, is in Italy, but you must contact him immediately and ask why he has cancelled his trip to London. I'm told that he refuses to go because the British Prime Minister has not arranged a lunch in his honour. Ansari must answer this allegation, and whatever his excuse, his visit to London must go ahead.' Over cocktails before lunch, Home confided that it was he who had reported the Minister's behaviour to HIM, fearing that it threatened Anglo-Iranian relations. During the meal I was able to contact Ansari and got him to change his mind. He claimed that his reluctance had sprung from the insufficient time allocated to discussions on the economy; it had nothing whatsoever to do with pique at the reception he was promised. When I reported the matter at the lunch table, HIM was pleased and the British clearly impressed at the efficiency of our Court. I was placed on the left-hand side of HMQ who had Sir Alec to her right as guest of honour. 'The poor man's growing old', she whispered to me discreetly; 'He dribbles so much, especially when he's drinking.' ...

Sunday, 10 June

The Moroccan ambassador called round early this morning; King Hassan wishes to send his Court Minister to Tehran to be received by HIM. HIM subsequently approved the proposal. 'How lucky you are', said the ambassador when I rang to let him know. 'You are blessed with a king to whom you have immediate access, who allows you to pass on his orders unhindered.'

At home that evening I fielded a telephone call from HIM complaining about the media coverage of Home's visit. 'Look in the evening papers. The bastards have printed a picture which makes it look as if I'm bowing to the blasted man. The parties responsible should be taught a lesson they won't forget.' My subsequent enquiries revealed that some time ago HIM forbade the press to publish shots of foreign ambassadors bowing during the presentation of their credentials. Consequently, when it came to Home, the picture they printed was one of only two that they considered remotely suitable. Even so I had no alternative but to order the arrest of everyone involved, up to and including the editor of *Ettela'at* and the head of the Association of Press Photographers. We shall see whether this leads anywhere, but in the meantime I'm disgusted with myself for having to take such drastic action . . .

Monday, 11 June

. . . Dined as the Soviet ambassador's guest . . . at his summer residence . . . I expressed disappointment that there were no nightingales to serenade us. He explained that it was too late in the year for the real thing, but that even so he could remedy the situation. At which point he put on a cassette of nightingale song that he himself had recorded. Strangely touching to find a man like this, outwardly so hard-headed, willing to devote hours to capturing a simple bird song. How the world around us is changing. The Soviets have thrown off their past brutality and stand revealed as human beings like the rest of us. We can meet like this without even an interpreter, or to put it more accurately, without a KGB man posing as an interpreter.

Tuesday, 12 June

Audience. A girl named G . . . is spreading rumours all around Tehran that HIM is head over heels in love with her. I reported this, remarking that I was surprised to find HIM so smitten. 'Bloody woman', said HIM, 'I met her a few times, admittedly, but I too have heard what she's saying and the rumours are getting perilously close to HMQ. Warn her that unless she puts a stop to her tittle-tattle she will end up behind bars.' ...

'Incidentally', he continued, 'as to my trip to the USA, I've told Rogers that I'm completely indifferent whether it's presented as a state or merely as an official visit.' This I found especially galling, given the fuss he made on just the same point only a few days ago. I pointed out that the trip coincided with Nixon's new term of office, and that in my opinion this justifies its being upgraded, and Nixon being obliged to visit our embassy...

Wednesday, 13 June

Ellingworth, the British Chargé d'Affaires, called round this morning with a letter which his ambassador addressed to HIM before setting off on his holidays:

> When Sir Alec Douglas-Home called on His Imperial Majesty on 9 June, His Majesty referred to a possible declaration by Iran and the other Persian Gulf States, asking the Great Powers not to interfere in the region. After Sir Alec had asked how this would affect British operations, for example in Oman, His Imperial Majesty said that these would not at all be affected if the personnel were hired by Oman.
>
> Sir Alec has asked me to write to you to ask if you could possibly lay the following before His Imperial Majesty. Many of the British personnel serving in Oman and in the United Arab Emirates are, of course, officers seconded to the local forces or on contract to the States concerned. There are, however, both in the United Arab Emirates and in Oman, certain elements of the British Forces which are directly responsible to Her Majesty's government in the United Kingdom. There is, for instance, a military advisory team at Sharjah concerned with training and the organization of visits by the British Armed Forces to the United Arab Emirates. There are also serving Royal Air Force officers at Masirah manning the staging post there in addition to the Royal Air Force and British Army personnel serving at Salalah in connection with the operation and protection of the airport.
>
> I'm sure that His Imperial Majesty is aware of the presence of these personnel and shares our view that they are playing a vital and effective role in the protection of Oman and the Lower Gulf. Sir Alec was, however, anxious that I should write to you about this in case there should be any misunderstanding about the status of these personnel.

Passed this on to HIM at my audience. He remarked that there is no problem with British forces stationed in Oman to the east of the Straits of Hormuz. However, as for those within the Gulf, the British might follow the lead of the ARMISH-MAAG,[1] and make it appear that their troops are merely advisers, without any established bases of their own. This would be in keeping with HIM's declared policy to have the great powers evacuate the Gulf ...

Submitted various newspapers which have now printed photographs showing Home bowing to HIM. I pointed out that the photographers in custody are completely blameless and should be released immediately. Delighted that HIM agreed to this ...

At dinner HIM was fulminating against the *Washington Post* and their report on terrorism which claims it is inspired solely by the Shah's autocratic style of government, stating that the terrorists' demands are by no means unreasonable. 'What else can you expect from the *Washington Post?*', I said; 'The paper that's trying to make a mountain out of a molehill over Watergate. We should simply ignore them.' He nodded his approval.

Wednesday, 20 June
Audience ... The German ambassador has asked that HIM receive the Chairman of Mannesman, a company which hopes to be awarded a contract to build a plant here, manufacturing industrial pipes. 'There's no call for an audience', said HIM. 'Tell the ambassador in a light-hearted sort of way that I'm no longer interested in any project or proposal that costs under $500 million.' ...

Thursday, 21 June
Audience ... The PM is suggesting that we shelve the building of a hospital in Lebanon for Shi'a muslims, until our new ambassador there, Mansour Qadar, has had time to study the proposals. 'Bullshit', HIM exclaimed. 'No ambassador has a right to interfere in plans I myself have approved. Tell them to go ahead with the thing without any further delay.' ...

Friday, 22 June
... Our PM has appointed a politician, Nasser Ameri, to take over as leader of the Mardom party. This is the way the opposition is organized in Iran, its leadership is selected in consultation with the government party,

[1] Acronym for the US Armed Forces Mission Military Assistance Advisory Group.

its *soi-disant* rival. Of course the appointment is dressed up in a different way for public consumption ...

Saturday, 23 June

... At dinner the discussion turned on the sentimentality of the late Reza Shah, the way in which he wept even on behalf of his children. Princess Shams described how, as a small girl, she had gone to her father, full of rage, declaring that she wished she were dead. The old man had tears in his eyes. 'Why should you want to die?', he asked her. 'I would much rather die myself than see you so upset.' HIM, who has inherited none of his father's emotionalism, was clearly put out by this story, but I came to his rescue by declaring that no modern leader can afford to be so easily moved.

Monday, 25 June

... Granted interviews to reporters with the *Daily Telegraph* and the *Guardian*. The thing went on for three whole hours and left me completely exhausted ... The *Telegraph* correspondent asked why we are so keen to suppress freedom of speech and expression. I replied that the public have little left to say or express now that the White Revolution has enabled them to achieve their every goal. This was a shameful reply, all too reminiscent of the line that communist regimes adopt; but then what else could I have said?

Wednesday, 27 June

Brief audience. Submitted the final schedule for HIM's trip to the USA, mentioning that Nixon has agreed to dine at our embassy. Sensed that HIM was pleased by this ...

This afternoon King Hussein of Jordan arrived in Tehran, accompanied by his wife Queen Alya and his children by his two former wives. Here they were joined by HIM and HMQ before flying on together to the Caspian Sea.

Sunday, 1 July

Meeting with the Managing Director of the Ashland oil company who proposes a joint venture with NIOC to market oil on world markets. Over the next ten years our profits from this operation would enable us to buy up Ashland's oil installations in the US mainland. A radical new departure, but as it was Dr Fallah who initiated the proposal, Dr Eqbal is against it.

Received the British Chargé d'Affaires after lunch. He stated that his Foreign Office is studying the position of US military advisers in Iran to see whether a similar status might be awarded to British forces stationed in the Gulf ... He then expressed satisfaction at our government's decision to purchase Scorpion tanks ... Turning to the new leadership of the Mardom party he asked me whether I had any opinion on the matter. I replied that he was here to discuss Anglo-Iranian relations, not to meddle in our internal affairs, a remark which made him blush red with embarrassment. I regretted my harshness, but it was too late to retract. Merely to change the subject he asked whether I knew of Bhutto's forthcoming visit to India, and I chatted on aimlessly for some time, in an effort to appease his wounded pride.

Monday, 2 July
Flew to Nowshahr where HIM received me from noon until two. Amongst other things, we discussed the King of Greece's imminent visit to Iran. 'In his place', I remarked, 'I should have called the whole thing off.' HIM asked me to explain myself, so I reminded him that it is the colonels who actually rule Greece and with whom we have diplomatic relations; King Constantine has been branded their enemy. 'I couldn't give a damn', said HIM.

We arrived an hour late for lunch. HMQ chided us for the delay, but HIM would have none of it, telling her that there was much work that had to be seen to. King Hussein had also been kept waiting, but seemed not at all put out, merely nodding in agreement when HIM referred to his heavy workload.

Over the meal we discussed the latest developments in Iraq where only yesterday the head of the government security agency invited the Ministers of Defence and the Interior to his home and there attempted to place them both under close custody. A struggle broke out, in which the Defence Minister was killed and the security chief was forced to flee his own home. He was subsequently rounded up and arrested. HIM and King Hussein both seemed more than a little pleased with the course of events.

Whilst lunch was being cleared away, HIM asked me to inform the British Chargé d'Affaires that he would like to discuss our military relations with the British Defence Secretary, Lord Carrington, during the latter's forthcoming visit to Iran. Above all he wishes to talk about new weapons systems, such as the application of laser technology to tank guns, the construction of a new arms factory outside Isfahan and the purchase of a through-deck cruiser.

'Tell the Chargé d'Affaires and also the American ambassador that King Hussein's army has nothing left to fight with except good morale', he said. 'Syria has 2,000 tanks, besides the latest Soviet MIG fighters. Jordan by contrast has nothing. Why don't the Americans or the Saudis do something to save her? If the Saudis had the sense to give Hussein $200 million rather than squandering ten times that amount on their own defence, it would benefit their own security infinitely more than anything King Faisal may do on his own behalf.'

Flew back to Tehran with the Queen of Jordan who subsequently dined as my guest ...

Tuesday, 10 July

Their Majesties flew with their Jordanian guests to Tehran airport and there bid them farewell. King Hussein flew on to London and his wife in another Jordanian plane to Amman. The Jordanian Prime Minister, the Chief of Staff and the head of their intelligence agency arrived on the King's flight, ready to accompany him to London ... King Hussein welcomed them and embraced them all, although not one of them bothered to kiss his hand.[1]

HIM passed on a letter from Mrs Gandhi which I assume to have been forwarded via Rashidiyan. In it she turns down an invitation to visit Iran, and suggests instead that HIM go to India. I was surprised by the calmness with which he ordered me to prepare an appropriate response and asked that I examine the possibility of the Indian Foreign Minister visiting Iran. We then turned to discussing the current visit by the French head of protocol, here to make arrangements for President Pompidou who is to stop over in Tehran en route from Peking. HIM indirectly revealed something of his feelings about the French, remarking: 'There's no need to flatter the Frenchman. I shall not go to the airport. Instead you should escort him to the palace. We shall dine together and then you can take him back to his plane. If he objects to this arrangement he's quite free to go straight on from Peking to Paris.'

Ezri, the Israeli representative in Tehran, has been awarded the order of Taj, second class. HIM instructed me to alter the date of the Firman certifying this award to before the Arab–Israeli war of June '67.

---

[1] Iranian officials were expected to kiss the Shah's hand.

... Princess Ashraf and a few others lunched as my guests. She intends to bequeath her entire fortune to a charitable foundation. The lunch went well and we had an opportunity to sort out the various details of this proposal ...

Tuesday, 17 July
Audience. A black day: there has been a *coup d'état* in Afghanistan. Sardar Davoud Khan, ex-Prime Minister, cousin of the King and husband of the King's own sister, has masterminded a plot against his royal brother-in-law. What a filthy world we live in. Apparently the rising has already claimed the life of Abdul Vali Khan, the King's son-in-law, Commander of the Kabul garrison; a good friend of mine.

The news has come as a dreadful shock to HIM, especially since Davoud, though a wealthy landowner, is markedly pro-Soviet ... He was Afghanistan's PM and absolute ruler for nearly fifteen years, and yet he claims that the present coup is intended to bring freedom to the people ... Nevertheless we could cope with all this, were it not for the position of the Afghan military. Every officer in her army has undergone training in the Soviet Union and no doubt been brain-washed into Marxism – given the extent of material deprivation and backwardness in Afghanistan this is hardly surprising. It will not be long before Davoud himself falls victim to a military coup, and we shall be faced with a situation no less calamitous than that which plagues us in Iraq.

Meanwhile Davoud has declared Afghanistan a republic. I suggested to HIM that if only the deposed King, presently in Italy, were to seize the initiative and fly to Western Afghanistan, we would be in a position to offer him all the help he could possibly need. If only he can get the tribes behind him we could topple Davoud without needing to send in a single military unit. 'Unfortunately', replied HIM, 'the King lacks the guts for anything like that. We must simply have patience and await developments.' From my own point of view, I fear that such patience may be the death of us.

... I've been contacted by Sir Alec Douglas-Home, asking whether anything's expected of him during HIM's coming stop-over in London, en route to America. I replied that the stay in London is unofficial but that it would be a nice gesture if Sir Alec went to the airport and extended a personal welcome. This the dear man has agreed to do. HIM, on the other hand, was upset when I told him what had been decided, complaining that I should never have asked such a favour of the British. However, I'm not at all sure that his indignation was sincere, and in any event I have merely done what I considered proper. HIM deserves to be treated with the utmost respect, particularly after the shock of recent events in Afghanistan.

Wednesday, 18 July

Audience. Davoud appears to have established some sort of order in Afghanistan. Meanwhile we have been in contact with the King who claims that for the moment he prefers to await developments – what utter nonsense! It is still unclear whether Abdul Vali Khan has really been killed. We have little to go on save the reports from Savak ...

Friday, 20 July

Audience followed by lunch with HIM. Afshar, our ambassador in London, reports that following Home's decision, the British PM would also like to meet HIM on his brief stop-over. 'Next', said HIM, 'you'll be telling me that Pompidou and the French cabinet have put in a similar request. For goodness sake do nothing to encourage these proposals.' But in fact, I have already taken the initiative in this respect and must weather the storm if things turn out not to HIM's liking. In this respect, he's a difficult man to work for. Try as one may to please him, you can never be sure that his pleasure is sincere, or that his anger is not mere play-acting. In these circumstances it can be something of a nightmare attempting to predict the unpredictable.

Saturday, 21 July

... The ambassadors of Venezuela and North Yemen presented their credentials. As the Yemeni was ushered in, HIM turned to me and whispered: 'Just look at the brute. How many throats do you suppose he's slit?' ...

Our own Foreign Minister, Khalatbari, was not invited to an hour-long audience between HIM and the Foreign Minister of India. Afterwards over lunch, discussion centred on economic matters ... Dinner at the Queen Mother's. Again Mrs Diba did nothing but spout nonsense about HIM's marriage ... It all got too much for me and I'm afraid I laid into her in no uncertain way ...

Sunday, 22 July

Audience. Little to do as HIM was due to depart for London within a couple of hours ... Referring to Afghanistan I remarked that, but for the King's lack of initiative, we might have done something to resolve the situation; as things stand I'm convinced that we granted recognition to Davoud's regime with undue haste. 'We could not have gone it alone', said HIM ... Apparently he's unconvinced that we could count on British and American assistance against the Soviets ...

Reported Mrs Diba's goings-on last night. Although she never once mentioned the word divorce, she made one very significant statement to the effect that her daughter was unaccustomed to luxury – implying that a separation from HIM would cause HMQ little material hardship. 'Crap', said HIM. After much debate we agreed that the bloody girl G ... who began all these rumours must be found a husband post-haste.

As there was nothing more of any weight to be reported I passed on a letter addressed to HIM by a charming young creature. He was greatly flattered, allowing me to read her message, and chatting to me about it for some while. He then suggested that we continue our conversation over tea. At this point HMQ rang, anxious to leave for the airport and asking why we were taking so long. 'We have been discussing affairs of state', replied HIM ...

Their Majesties flew out at one thirty this afternoon ...

Friday, 27 July

... Much to my relief, Abdul Vali Khan turns out to have survived the coup ...

I was due to fly to Paris at noon. Tried to tune in to the news on my way to the airport but they were broadcasting nothing but unctuous telegrams, expressing popular jubilation over the victory on oil,[1] so I switched it off. It's incredible how easy it is to undermine even the greatest of achievements by this sort of propagandist sham. My chauffeur is an intelligent chap and quickly spotted how infuriated I was. 'Yes, Sir', he said, 'the oil thing is a great success, I don't doubt, but how are people supposed to appreciate the fact when there's no meat nor anything much worth eating in the shops? Thanks to you Sir, and though I say it myself, to a great deal of pushing on my own part, I've at last persuaded the city council to grant me planning permission for a house. After all that, though,

---

[1] Sales-purchase agreement; see introductory note 1973.

it turns out that I can't buy cement for love nor money.' His remarks cut me to the quick. But what on earth does Hoveyda think he's up to? Is he deliberately trying to wreck this country?

Sunday, 29 July

Their Majesties arrived in Paris at nine this morning, on their way back from the USA, to be greeted by Pierre Messmer, the Prime Minister, and a guard of honour. I had spoken with the French Prime Minister beforehand for over an hour. He's a staunch Gaullist, and a man of great integrity ...

Once the royal flight had touched down I went on board to extend my own greetings. HIM asked me in a rather arch way what all the fuss outside was about. There was no hint of reproach in his voice, and I replied that he could guess the answer well enough. 'Your Majesty is an important statesman, and these people feel duty bound to pay you their respects', I said. Messmer then escorted HIM to our embassy. The entire route into the city was lined with policemen; an extraordinary act of courtesy given that this was an unofficial visit. Of course, much of the credit must go to Amir Mottaqi, my assistant, who made all the arrangements, although I hardly dare spoil HIM's illusion that the whole thing is a spontaneous act of homage from the French ...

This afternoon with HIM and his children, I walked for three hours in the Bois de Boulogne ... I asked him how he had got on in the USA. 'Superbly', he replied. 'The Americans gave me whatever I asked for and promised support for whoever I recommended.' ...

Dined at La Closerie des Lilas. An excellent evening, given over to anecdotes from Their Majesties and myself ...

Monday, 30 July

The French Prime Minister and Foreign Minister called at the embassy this morning and, with the same ceremonial as yesterday, escorted Their Majesties back to the airport. HIM gave a brief interview to French television before his departure. Asked whether the military played an excessive role in Iran, he replied that ours is a great and dynamic nation which has no need to justify itself to the outside world; we shall do whatever is best calculated to enhance our grandeur. It was a superb response, and was broadcast verbatim by the French. Once HIM had taken off, I set about putting his children on board their flight to the USA.

HIM arrived in Tehran today to be greeted by a crowd which some have estimated at one and a half million. Every single member of Parliament turned out to meet him at the airport. What a total waste of time. Who do they think they're kidding? Certainly not the Iranian public who know well enough how such crowds are, as they say, spontaneously co-opted; nor the foreign media which is completely indifferent to such events. If the idea was to welcome HIM on his return from the USA, then I can only say that he has been there before without needing to return to this sort of hullabaloo. If, on the other hand, it was intended to celebrate our victory in the talks on oil, then Parliament has already uttered every flattery imaginable on that particular subject. The Minister of Finance remarked to me the other day that not a single member of Parliament had debated the substantive provisions of the oil agreement; they merely shouted themselves hoarse in praise, and crept, and crawled and went down on bended knee. What a miserable nation we are. And as for the present public relations exercise, its only effect will be to stir up even further hostility against us, at the height of the summer heat ... It pains me to see one of the Shah's greatest achievements belittled so ... The whole thing, needless to say, has been stage-managed by Hoveyda, who's as anxious as ever to pull the wool over HIM's eyes. I am mystified as to how such a miserable creature can have gained such a hold over a man of HIM's great wisdom ...

[For the next three weeks Alam stayed with his family in France, returning to Tehran on 16 August. The Shah meanwhile was holidaying on the Caspian]

Saturday, 18 August
Went to the airport. HMQ flew in first, followed shortly afterwards by HIM. As usual HMQ was offhand with me, but HIM was most gracious, inviting me to join him in his helicopter to the Palace. He's extremely anxious about developments in Baluchistan. The Afghans are growing increasingly aggressive and have used our embassy in Kabul to send a message to the Pakistanis warning them that Afghanistan can no longer turn a blind eye to the sufferings of Baluchis living on the Pakistan side of the border. 'I can detect the hand of the Soviets and maybe that of India behind this ultimatum', said HIM. I replied that he was undoubtedly correct, 'But why don't we place ourselves in a position of strength before negotiating with them; meet force with force? Why doesn't Your Majesty allow me to raise Western Afghanistan against the regime in Kabul? It

could be done quite easily, and at the moment we hold every trump in the pack; the King of Afghanistan will be behind us and need only rally support from Pakistan, Britain and the USA. Right from the start I have warned where appeasement will lead us.' 'There seems to be much to be gained from the action you propose', he replied. 'Have a plan of action prepared for submission as soon as possible.' ...

Sunday, 19 August

Saw HIM off on his return to the Caspian. 'I'm afraid I have some bad news for you', he declared. 'Several Iraqi-trained guerrilla units have infiltrated Iranian Baluchistan. I want these men caught, tried and executed.' I replied that everything was under control, although we need to act swiftly. As for my proposals on Afghanistan, I promised to pay him a visit in Nowshahr to report on these ...

Colonel Papadopoulos has been sworn in as the new President of the Republic of Greece ... He has promised to end press censorship and to hold free civilian elections within the next twelve months. Meanwhile King Constantine is our regular guest, using HIM's private flight as if it were his own. HIM rejects any suggestion I make that the King's presence here is undesirable ... but the King, although he may be a fool, should know better than to embarrass us. Sadly he's mean as well as stupid, and takes advantage of our generosity. Last year, for example, even before he was dethroned, he and his family stayed with HIM in St Moritz; they ran up bills at the hairdressers all of which they had charged to us.

Monday, 20 August

A meeting at my house with the head of Savak and various tribal leaders from Baluchistan. Issued instructions for the capture of the guerrillas, but I doubt this will be sufficient and am therefore determined to take charge of operations from a base to be located in Chahbahar ...

The British Chargé d'Affaires called round to express his thanks on behalf of Queen Elizabeth who is due to stop off in Tehran en route from Australia. HIM has invited her to lunch with him at the airport. I am annoyed at this proposal which was made whilst I was abroad. Far from HIM going to her, the Queen should be driven to the Palace there to have the privilege of lunching with the Shah. But it's now too late to alter the arrangements.

Wednesday, 22 August

Flew to Nowshahr. My audience over-ran, lasting nearly two hours. Around noon I saw fit to remind HIM that Dr Eqbal was being kept waiting outside; the poor man would die of wounded pride if we went on much longer ... 'Too true', laughed HIM. 'Tell him to come in, but you must have lunch with me and afterwards we can resume our discussion.'

We devoted a great deal of attention to Baluchistan, Afghanistan and the various measures we have undertaken. I remarked that we'll face little trouble from a few Iraqi-trained guerrillas but that I'm concerned by Afghan infiltration of the Baluchi population in Pakistan. Once we've mopped up our own problem with the guerrillas we need to teach the Afghans a lesson they won't forget. 'But', said HIM, 'they can count on support from Moscow.' 'So what', I replied; 'The Soviets cannot send in troops. However difficult a task we're faced with, we can no longer stand by and leave our enemies to their own devices.' I reminded him that in Kurdistan our support for Mustafa Barzani has gained tacit approval from the British and Americans. 'Quite so', he said, 'but what precisely do you propose we do in Afghanistan?' I explained that it would be relatively simple to foment a rising in the country's western provinces. We should then reintroduce the King to his people. HIM interrupted at this point, saying that the King is utterly spineless; 'He's incapable of decisive action. He's not even interested in speaking with our ambassador in Rome, despite several attempts to make contact.' I pointed out that the King is now little more than a prisoner of his former Prime Minister, the present Afghan ambassador in Italy, Nour Ahmad E'temadi, who is not to be trusted an inch. In these circumstances it's hardly surprising that he rejects all contact with our Rome embassy. We must try a different approach. For example, Dr Khanlari,[1] the writer, is highly respected by the King and by the Afghans in general. We might send him to Europe to act as a go-between. To begin with he might simply offer the King financial assistance. But once the King feels indebted towards us, he might well change his mind about returning to Afghanistan, particularly if we can persuade the British and Americans to bring further pressure to bear ... HIM approved this scheme.

Likewise he accepted my proposals for wiping out the guerrillas. 'Above all act quickly', he said. 'The present situation is totally unacceptable.' I

---

[1] Parviz N. Khanlari: an outstanding scholar and ex-Minister of Education; Professor of Literature at Tehran University.

told him the more haste the less speed, but that God willing we shall resolve the problem before too long.

I then asked why we have sent no congratulatory telegram to the new President of Greece. HIM replied that he could hardly send such a message when King Constantine is staying here as his guest. 'It's precisely for this sort of reason that I advised you to limit your hospitality', I said. 'He's nothing more than a free-loader.' HIM merely laughed at this. 'Admit it', he said, 'you just happen to have taken a dislike to him.' ...

'As Pompidou sent his PM to welcome Your Majesty to Paris', I said, 'you will no doubt see fit to send me and the PM to greet Pompidou when, returning from China, he stops over here.' 'Ah but the two situations are quite different', he replied. 'Pompidou was not in Paris when I arrived. Hence I see no need for our PM to greet him at the airport.' I was surprised by this and asked whether he was suggesting that he himself should go to greet the Frenchman. 'Of course not', he replied ... At that stage I thought it best to let the matter drop. HIM bears Pompidou a grudge for not having attended our monarchy celebrations. I'm convinced that we should at least provide the poor man with a guard of honour, but this was not the occasion to raise the matter.

I pointed out that it was a shame that he'd agreed to lunch at the airport with the Queen of England, rather than have her brought to the Palace. He became distinctly uneasy at this, agreeing that more thought should have been given to the arrangements, but affirming that it was now too late to alter anything. 'Even so', he said, 'there's no need to provide her with a guard of honour.'

Saturday, 25 August

Their Majesties returned from Nowshahr this afternoon. HIM's first words to me were to ask whether I'd heard about the King of Afghanistan's abdication: he's sworn allegiance to Davoud Khan and declared the monarchy abolished in favour of the new republic. The news was already known to me; as I told HIM, it's largely our own fault. We should have agreed to finance the King rather than leaving him stranded in Europe with a host of dependents to support ... Our conversation was interrupted by the arrival of the Foreign Minister, reporting that Prince Mohammad Na'im, Davoud's brother, wishes to visit Iran to discuss the situation in Baluchistan and Pashtunistan. 'Tell him he can go to hell', said HIM. 'He can't ride roughshod over me, in the way he did with Pakistan.' ...

Thursday, 30 August
Flew to Shiraz with Their Majesties to attend the annual Arts Festival. I sat beside HIM for the entire flight. Reported on various issues and showed him the newspaper reports categorically denying the rumours that he has married a second wife. He asked me to show this to HMQ who sat apart from us during the flight.

The King of Nepal is to make a brief stop-over in Tehran. I suggested that rather than inviting him to the Saadabad Palace, it would be better merely to offer him lunch at the airport – we must be careful not to discriminate between visiting monarchs. 'Quite right', said HIM. 'Our protocol department is staffed by idiots who have no grasp of this sort of nicety.' He also agreed that we should provide a guard of honour for Pompidou ...

Attended the ballet at Persepolis – an intriguing piece by Maurice Béjart,[1] based on a poem of Sa'adi.

Saturday, 1 September
Brief audience ... According to HIM, HMQ is now convinced that the girl he is supposed to have married is actually having an affair with General Khatami, the Commander of the Air Force. She suggests it's unfair that she and HIM should bear the brunt of all these rumours, merely to protect the general's reputation. In fact, it's true that HIM did meet the girl in question on a number of occasions. Later she was seen gadding about in official cars and helicopters, although by that stage she was Khatami's lover, not HIM's. Even so people jumped to the conclusion that she and HIM were engaged. She's a beauty, but vain and ruthlessly ambitious. The rumours flattered her, so she did nothing to discourage them.

Monday, 3 September
... Went to the airport to greet the King of Nepal, en route to the conference of non-aligned countries in Algeria. Their Majesties joined us a little later. Over lunch, which as agreed was laid on at the airport, I asked the King for his definition of non-alignment. The poor young man was quite bewildered by my question. HMQ then said how much she would like to visit Nepal to take a look at all the hippies. The King was not at all amused by this, but otherwise things went well ...

[1] French dancer and choreographer; Director of the *Ballet du XXe siècle*.

Tuesday, 4 September

... Audience. *Le Monde* has published an article suggesting that if the worst comes to the worst in Afghanistan, Herat[1] and the country's western provinces could always seek unification with Iran. 'We must simply wait and see', HIM remarked. 'Patience is undoubtedly a virtue', I replied, 'but all the same it might land us in very hot water.' HIM then complained how little information we have on the intentions of the great powers, adding, 'The British are much weaker now than in the past, but they are by no means without influence. I know how closely they control Iraq ... and the same appears to be true of their relations with India ... At the moment we have no complaint against them; they seem sincere in their desire to co-operate with us, almost to rely upon us. Even so, you can never trust an Englishman to tell you all his secrets.' ...

Turning to the behaviour of the King of Afghanistan, HIM repeated that the man is of no possible use to us. After some time lost in thought, he added, 'See whether you can arrange for Abdul Vali Khan to escape from Kabul.' I replied that I would think it over, but that he is imprisoned more or less next door to Davoud's residence. He is not, like Mussolini,[2] to be spirited away from some remote mountain top. Even so, if we can't risk sending in a rescue squad, it may still be possible to bribe his jailers.

Wednesday, 5 September

The new Polish ambassador presented his credentials at the White Palace. He turned out to be of rather over-ample dimensions and with a great deal of huffing and puffing he only just managed to climb the stairs from the Saadabad gate to the reception hall. HIM happened to arrive a few minutes early and immediately issued instructions for the ambassador to be shown in. I suggested that the poor man might well have a stroke unless we gave him time to catch his breath, but HIM would brook no delay. Fortunately the ambassador survived his ordeal.

Went to the airport this afternoon to welcome the royal children, returning from their trip to Europe and the USA. The PM and the two Speakers of Parliament were also in attendance, and even Their Majesties put in a surprise appearance. A touching reunion.

---

[1] The principal city of Western Afghanistan.
[2] After Benito Mussolini's overthrow in 1943 he was jailed on a mountain-top, but rescued by German paratroopers.

Saturday, 8 September

Presently I'm in Ramsar for the annual conference on education ... My wife has accompanied HMQ to Shiraz for the closing stages of the Arts Festival ... The conference opened this morning in the presence of HIM, the PM, various ministers and academics. My deputy, Dr M. Baheri, began proceedings with an hour-long report. Each year, on HIM's orders, he draws up a survey of higher education and the universities, and his performance on this occasion was particularly impressive ... Referring to the general attitude of our students, he stressed that despite their access to a wide range of scholarships and other privileges, they are completely disinterested in the progress this country is making. A significant point, which I'm sure can be explained by the fact that they are denied any role, either in university or in national political affairs. Fair enough, a few may be manipulated by our enemies abroad, but this would hardly explain the indifference towards us shown by the entire student body: it's inconceivable that the Iranian people have become subversives, every man, woman and child of them. If only we could root out this problem, then we might truly count ourselves the most outstanding power in the Near and Middle East ... It is a tragedy that our government should be so negligent ... Its indifference and, on occasion, its brute aggression towards the people remind me of the way an army of occupation might treat a nation defeated in war. At every level, from Parliament down to local and municipal elections, the government denies freedom to the people, imposing its own will and returning its own candidates as if the electorate had absolutely no say in the matter. Having for so long been deaf and blind to the nation's wishes, we should not be surprised that the nation itself regards us with a similar degree of bland disinterest.

I have gradually persuaded HIM that material progress on its own can never be enough. He's recently hinted that future elections will be conducted freely, although, as I see it, for this to go ahead we must first get rid of the present government and appoint a caretaker cabinet to oversee a general election.

Sunday, 9 September

... Lunched with the PM, leaving HIM to his own devices. He's entitled to his privacy, though he soon gets bored of being on his own. Likewise, even when he finds a companion, however attractive she may be, he sooner or later tires of her; work alone commands his absolute devotion ...

Half-hour audience this evening ... We discussed the arrest of a pair of Baluchi guerrillas, caught red-handed with their machine guns and ammunition ... I suggested that HIM pardon them and he agreed, provided they're not convicted of murder ... I left soon afterwards, being reluctant to trespass any further on his time ...

Monday, 10 September
The education conference came to an end this morning ... Returned to Tehran ... where HIM opened the autumn international tradefair ...

Tuesday, 11 September
Audience ... Until recently HIM was accustomed to receive fortnightly reports from representatives of the CIA and British Intelligence. But it's now been several weeks since he granted them an audience and they're wondering what to do. 'I simply can't afford to waste my time listening to the rubbish they give me', he declared. 'They expect me to accept as intelligence reports what are no more than transcripts of broadcast news items.' I suggested that this might be something of an exaggeration, but he was adamant. 'If and when they have something worthwhile to report, then I shall receive them; meanwhile they should present you with whatever material they come up with. Of the two of them, I'm much more inclined to receive the American, even though the British have at last realized that it's no longer in their interest to pull the wool over our eyes.'

Wednesday, 12 September
Audience ... Reported that we shall need to mobilize another force of Baluchis if we're to wear down the guerrillas. Confronting them along a single front will get us nowhere. 'But what about the gendarmerie?', HIM asked. I replied that they are a bunch of ninnies, unfit to wage a real war. He gave me the go-ahead to send in more Baluchis.

Turning to family matters, he said, 'Tell my sister Ashraf that she can either indulge her taste for philanthropy and drop these ridiculous acts of self-advertisement, in which case I'm willing to support her, or she can carry on as she is, and count me out of her performance. I simply don't understand her ... My sister Shams sold some of her land and set herself up in style; she has the most exquisite palaces and a luxurious life-style, yet nobody bears her a grudge because she's been completely open and frank about what she was after.' I promised to speak personally to Princess Ashraf.

A meeting with Princess Shahnaz after lunch. She and her husband are beginning to regret their past follies ...

Dined in Mehrdasht,[1] at Princess Shams'. A vast party to celebrate the twenty-first birthday of her daughter Shahrazad. The Princess' newly built house struck me as looking more like a casino than a family home. Her daughter, on the other hand, is blessed with every grace including beauty.

Thursday, 13 September
This morning received various Baluchis who have been set to track the guerrillas. I awarded a couple of them cars as a prize for their successful man-hunting.

Audience ... Attended the Court celebrations marking the birthday of the twelfth Imam.[2] Usually I avoid such religious occasions ... but I went today with the deliberate intention of distinguishing myself from the Baha'is, who it's said can count half the present government amongst their followers. Such cliques and cabals only put people at one another's throats. It's unfortunate, for example, that HIM's special physician, Dr Ayadi, should be a well-known member of the sect; it does much to detract from HIM's standing with the religious ...

The Chinese ambassador has passed on to me an invitation for HIM to visit China, signed by the Prime Minister, Chou En-lai. Peking is well aware that HIM expects Chou En-lai to visit Iran before reciprocating with a visit of his own, but they pretend that Chou is too busy to travel abroad, being preoccupied with the China People's Congress – a Congress different from that of the communist party ...

Saturday, 15 September
... Over dinner our talk centred on the scarcity of certain basic commodities, HIM suggesting that people must simply learn to go without. HMQ interrupted at this point, saying that she and HIM are the only two people in the court or the administration to practise this maxim, since they have deliberately given up sugar. I fully agreed with what she said but held my peace. HIM likewise said nothing ...

---

[1] An estate 45km west of Tehran, owned by Princess Shams.
[2] The Shi'a believe that the five-year-old son and successor of the eleventh Imam (c. AD 850) was spirited away into hiding. His return will herald the rule of supreme justice in the world.

Sunday, 16 September

Audience. Offered my congratulations on the thirty-third anniversary of HIM's accession. 'Just think what calamities we've been through since then', he said. I agreed, remarking how hard things had been during the last world war, but he brushed this aside. 'The war years weren't really that difficult', he said, 'since we had no alternative but passive resignation.[1] No, the worst years of my reign, indeed of my entire life, came when Mosaddeq was Prime Minister. The bastard was out for blood and every morning I awoke with the sensation that today might be my last on the throne. Every night I went to bed having been subjected to unspeakable insults in the press.' ...

Pompidou is presently in Peking, due to stop off here on his way back to France. He has sent us a copy of the speech he intends making during his stay. It's full of the most flattering remarks about HIM who ordered me to prepare a reply in kind, stressing the similarities between Pompidou, HIM and De Gaulle ...

Called on Princess Ashraf this evening. She was anxious to know what she's done to incur HIM's displeasure. I told her she had no one to blame but herself ...

Monday, 17 September

Audience ... 'Our national radio and television agency has been infiltrated by subversives', declared HIM. 'You and the Savak Chief, General Nassiri, must purge the organization from top to bottom.' ...

Since it forms part of my will, I asked his permission to establish an Alam Foundation in Birjand. He approved the idea, but only after considerable hesitation. His reluctance surprised me, and I am led to assume that enlightened and warm-hearted though he is, he cannot abide being upstaged by anyone.

Pompidou arrived this afternoon ... and I ferried him by helicopter to Saadabad. After dinner, once the speeches were over, he spent an hour and a half alone with HIM. On the journey back to the airport he did little else but hold forth on HIM's breadth of vision ...

---

[1] In 1941 the British and Soviet forces occupied Iran, being joined later by the Americans. They remained in control of the country for the duration of the Second World War.

Tuesday, 18 September

Audience ... Reported an argument I had with Princess Shams last night. With only a few hours to go before her planned departure for Moscow, she rang me to say that the trip would have to be cancelled as she was suffering from an upset stomach. I told her in no uncertain terms that her trip must go ahead regardless; if she was really ill, then the Russian hospitals could take care of her. I was quite shameless in my insistence. 'Well done', was HIM's only comment.

I went on to say what a pity it was that Pompidou was granted a personal welcome by HMQ. 'A rather unnecessary gesture if Your Majesty doesn't mind my saying so.' HIM replied that the French have always gone overboard whenever HMQ visits France, but all the same I repeated that she need not have gone so far herself ...

Wednesday, 19 September

Meeting with the British ambassador early this morning, recently returned after ten weeks leave in England. Discussed the forthcoming visit by Lord Carrington, the British Defence Secretary. It was suggested that HIM might agree to lunch with him, but I pointed out that even with visiting Ministers of Foreign Affairs this is an honour which HIM only rarely extends ... Briefly touched on the situation in Afghanistan. The British believe that the coup can be blamed principally on the ineptitude of the King. Apparently a similar move had already been contemplated by some Afghan leaders, but they had been unable to agree on the King's successor ...

Audience ... According to HIM, his discussion with Pompidou centred on relations with China and the Soviets. Pompidou was told in Peking that the Soviets contemplate making a push towards the Gulf of Oman, via Afghanistan and Baluchistan ... He intends to stand for re-election to the French presidency, if only to avert the catastrophe for France of Mitterrand becoming President ...

Saturday, 22 September

Early this morning I received the British ambassador accompanied by their Chargé d'Affaires in Kabul, here to brief us on Afghanistan ... Apparently the Afghans believe our fears of Soviet influence within their country to be groundless. They are as keen as ever to maintain friendly links with Iran; hence their appointment of Mohammad Ghazi, Davoud's son-in-law, as ambassador in Tehran. He's a reliable individual, previously loyal to the Afghan monarchy and instrumental in persuading the King into closer relations with the West. His wife, Davoud's daughter, has made a point of attending official engagements in Kabul, alongside her father, to demonstrate their desire for a rapprochement with Iran ...

The British ambassador asked whether our aid to Pakistan is to be of a military nature, or merely to help the victims of the recent flood. I replied that it was both; that we had no alternative but to do what we can to prevent the disintegration of Pakistan. We have made no attempt to conceal this from India, which in any case is well aware that our military supplies would be of little consequence if Indo-Pakistani hostilities were to flare up again ...

Audience. Reported my meeting with the British ambassador ... 'Tell him that in the case of Pakistan, our helicopters are flying under Iranian insignia, and the pilots have been ordered to wear Iranian uniforms', HIM said. 'We have nothing to hide. Our intervention is at the request of Pakistan and aimed solely at defending her integrity. We have ensured that the rest of the world has been notified of this, especially the Indians.' ...

Sunday, 23 September

Audience. HIM in a foul mood ... 'It's that bloody girl again', he declared. 'Her relations have been interviewed by some Turkish woman journalist. They claim that, although the rumours of a marriage were unfounded, their daughter was undoubtedly my mistress. For God's sake look into the matter as soon as possible. The people involved must be taught a lesson.'

Bozorg Alavi,[1] notorious as a leader of the Tudeh communist party, has asked permission to return to Iran to live out his last few years. 'He may come', said HIM. 'Though goodness knows whether he deserves it; yet another of those men the British indoctrinated with communism.' ...

Monday, 24 September

... Audience ... Passed on a letter from our ambassador in Morocco:

[The ambassador reports a secret audience with King Hassan who was surprised to have received no reply to a letter he sent the Shah three months earlier, via General Nassiri. Both General Moulay Hafid, the Court Minister, and King Hassan suspect that the Shah's recent coolness may have been inspired by Moulay Abdullah, the King's brother.]

[1] Bozorg Alavi (1905-): writer; jailed in Iran as a member of the illegal Communist Party, 1936–41; a specialist in German language and literature, he lived in East Germany after the war, teaching at a University in East Berlin.

HIM could not recall what he'd done with King Hassan's letter, and instructed me to hunt it out ...

Reported that Ayatollah Khonsari is very worked up over a recent decree from the Minister of Education, forbidding girls in the so-called 'Islamic high schools' to wear the veil. I pointed out that, as a leading figure within the Shi'a community, he has every right to be upset. 'Fair enough', replied HIM, 'but without such measures, left-wing propagandists would have a field-day. We shall go ahead with the decree even if it leads to school closures. This is not exactly the first time the mullahs have criticized our social reforms.'

Thursday, 27 September
... Audience ... Reported sharp increases in the price of foodstuffs; meat is now selling at 40 per cent more than it did only a matter of days ago. HIM was furious about this. 'What on earth do you expect?', he said. 'Meat is in short supply so the price goes up.' 'But why is it in such short supply?', I replied. 'As Your Majesty's servant I am duty bound to inform you how dissatisfied the people are becoming. No doubt international factors account for at least part of the price increase, but much of the blame must rest with our government, especially the Council of Corporations which does nothing but abuse the functions entrusted to it.' 'Absolute nonsense', he snapped back. 'You're an outsider; you know nothing of what's really going on.' 'Doubtless Your Majesty is correct', I replied. 'But the fact remains that the people are dissatisfied, and as I see it, this could pose a serious threat. However, Your Majesty is free to act as you see fit.' He made no attempt to reply ...

Over dinner the talk was about the eradication of illiteracy. According to Princess Ashraf, despite all the new schools and the introduction of special literacy corps, the rapid growth in the population means that we're still burdened with 8 million citizens unable even to sign their names. Bearing in mind the atmosphere of this morning's audience, I thought it best to remain silent. In any case there was really no need for me to intervene; the Shah's sister knows how to put her points across.

Monday, 1 October
Audience. Passed on a report from our ambassador in Morocco.

[The ambassador writes that Moulay Abdullah is passing snide remarks about his brother, King Hassan, and that relations between the two men are extremely tense.]

HIM remarked again that he could see absolutely no reason why the Americans should have tried to bring down King Hassan ... 'Yet even in Iran', he continued, 'they seemed to regard Amini as their only hope, giving him every support and encouragement. Likewise, there seems no rhyme or reason to their overthrow of Ngo Dinh Diem in Vietnam ... At least King Hassan can breathe a sigh of relief that the Americans have ditched that bastard Rockwell.'[1] ...

Tuesday, 2 October
Audience ... HIM announced: 'I have told the PM that girls attending the so-called Islamic high schools must not wear the veil in school; outside they can do as they please.' ...

Wednesday, 3 October
Audience. 'They still haven't arrested all the guerrillas', HIM said. 'Why doesn't your Baluchi chieftain get his act together?' I assured him that if only we can exercise a little patience, the thing will soon be successfully completed. 'I'll allow you forty-eight hours to finish the job', he replied. Once again I assured him that it was all over bar the shouting, begging him to be a little less hasty. 'Forty-eight hours', he repeated, 'my final word.' HIM is always issuing this sort of ultimatum. You are expected to accept them with a due display of deference. You and he then get on with the job in hand exactly as before.

Saturday, 6 October
... Open hostilities have broken out between Egypt, Syria and the Israelis. Phoned through as soon as I heard this and was the first to break the news to HIM. He ordered me to summon the Chief of Staff and the commanders of the army to meet him in Saadabad ...

Sunday, 7 October
Audience. Discussion dominated by the Arab–Israeli war ...

[1] Stewart Rockwell, US ambassador to Morocco and, during the early 1960s, Minister Plenipotentiary at the US embassy in Tehran. A staunch supporter of Prime Minister H.A. Mansour, he was popular neither with Iranians nor the staff of the American embassy.

Submitted a report from our ambassador in Rome describing his meeting with the King of Afghanistan.

[The ambassador writes that on 3 October he called at the King's modest residence, an hour or so's drive from the centre of Rome ... There he found the King, his daughter Princess Belqis and altogether twenty-two members of the royal family living in only five rooms. Despite being completely without servants, they had only just enough money to support themselves for a further two months. The King hoped that thereafter his expenses might be met by Iran, Saudi Arabia and Kuwait.]

I suggested that HIM might contribute $10,000 a month, since neither Kuwait nor the Saudis are likely to respond to the King's entreaties ... We might have to persuade them to chip in, if the King needs to buy a new house, but even then it would be preferable for HIM to meet the entire expense unaided. HIM agreed, and instructed me to communicate this decision to the King ...

Referring to a recent broadcast on the BBC, he declared, 'The bastards have the audacity to state that the chances of a revolution in Iran have receded, since our army will be able to crush any rising, now that we've purchased so many new weapons. What the hell do they mean "the chances of a revolution"? Our farmers and workers are far too happy ever to contemplate becoming revolutionaries.' In the same way, he's outraged by an article in the *Financial Times*, describing the problems we face with inflation ...

With respect to the Arab–Israeli war, Kissinger has notified HIM by word of mouth that regardless of the actual military situation the USA are doing all they can to bring about a cease-fire on the basis of the *status quo ante bellum*. However if this fails, they intend to rescue their own international standing by lending outright support to the Israelis.

Monday, 8 October
Audience. Reported that the Israelis seem to be making less progress than was anticipated. 'There's been no official confirmation of that', said HIM, 'and whatever happens, you can be absolutely certain that Israel won't emerge the loser. The Americans will move heaven and earth to prevent it. They're determined to preserve Israel as a stick with which to beat the Arabs.' ...

The BBC broadcast continues to prey on his mind to an alarming extent. I'm surprised by this, since we can surely afford to ignore their criticisms, however impertinent. I put this to him directly, saying he should be more sanguine about the affair. 'Who says I'm not being sanguine', he replied. 'I couldn't give a damn for their criticisms. But, all the same, the bastards seemed at long last to be showing us more understanding; why this sudden about face? In future you should be very cool in your dealings with them.' ...

This afternoon I was shown a recording of the BBC Panorama programme which has caused all the rumpus. I jotted down a few notes, and intend to discuss it again with HIM tomorrow ...

Tuesday, 9 October

Audience. Remarked that on balance I considered the programme to have been well made and could see nothing in it calculated to arouse HIM's indignation ... 'But the commentary was disgraceful', he replied ... 'I shall get my own back on them in my own way; in the business world, there I can put the squeeze on them. Do you suppose Pompidou would have been so keen to visit us if it hadn't been for the commercial pressure we exerted? We began cutting back on trade-links with France, cancelling their feasibility study for the Tehran metro. They were in a desperate state.'

Referring to the Arab–Israeli war, HIM declared that it would be wrong to underestimate the Arabs. 'They have an enormous stock of weapons, including the Soviet Sam missiles which have proved so effective against Israel's planes.' Even so, I suggested that victory is bound to go to whichever side has the stronger convictions, not the most weapons.

Wednesday, 10 October

Audience ... 'The Israelis may be courageous', said HIM, 'but they stand no chance of breaking through the Egyptian defences; a steel wall of tanks. What's more, the Sam missiles have denied their air force freedom of action.' ...

Dr Gholam Hussein Mosaddeq – son of the legendary Dr Mosaddeq – has asked permission to import a car via the Court, thus saving himself customs duties. HIM agreed to this, showing his customary generosity. Mosaddeq, on the other hand, showed nothing but impertinence in asking such a favour.

... Over dinner ... I remarked that the King of Greece should never have accepted the $4 million he was offered in compensation for his property seized by the new Republic. 'Why ever not?', said HIM. 'The land was his and they took it.' I explained that by accepting compensation he showed that he has no real expectation of returning to Greece.

Thursday, 11 October
Audience. 'The Americans and the British now admit that they were wrong to believe the Arabs incapable of waging war', declared HIM. 'I knew this all along, and on many occasions did my best to warn them. Nobody listened.' ...

Reported a meeting I had last night with the British ambassador. Apparently he's been reluctant to contact me for the past few days as he sensed that I was cross about something. He says that whenever I'm angry it's a sign that HIM is in a dreadful mood; on such occasions I am best avoided. Yesterday however he escorted Selwyn Lloyd[1] to an audience with HIM who received them with a radiant smile. He knew straightaway that my mood would have lifted. HIM was greatly amused by all this, asking me what the ambassador was after. I replied that he was anxious to pass on news of the Arab–Israeli war. Secondly he invited me to dinner to meet Selwyn Lloyd, an invitation which I declined. Finally he asked that we meet for an extended discussion, but I replied that I was too busy to receive him until next week. 'You are prone to exaggerate', said HIM. 'Let him call on you if he wants to.' ...

The Israelis claim to have broken through on the Syrian front and to be making a push towards Damascus. It may well be true, as the Soviet ambassador rang up this afternoon, asking for an immediate audience with HIM. He was duly received this evening at half past six ...

Friday, 12 October
... Audience ... For a while we discussed the latest rise in oil prices which have doubled our income more or less overnight to a quite staggering level ...

... We read through a series of confidential British and US reports on the course of the war. Apparently the Syrian front is holding and the Israelis have turned to settling their account with Egypt ...

Saturday, 13 October
Audience. 'Last Thursday', HIM said, 'their ambassador asked that Soviet planes be allowed to cross Iranian air space on their way to Baghdad and

[1] British Foreign Secretary 1955–7, subsequently Speaker of the House of Commons.

Damascus. When I refused this, he asked that Aeroflot at least be permitted to transport spare parts to Baghdad. Aeroflot is a civilian airline, and so I agreed to the request. Now I am wondering whether I should inform the Americans.' I replied that if he considers the Americans as friends then they should certainly be told; if not, then it would suggest a fundamental change in our foreign policy. He gave me the go-ahead to alert the American ambassador, adding, 'Tell him he's under an obligation to find some sort of solution to this blasted war. It's America's inaction, or possibly America's impotence, that has landed us all in this mess. Meanwhile I've agreed to supply Saudi Arabia with transport aircraft, flown by our own pilots. They're strictly for local use. It's the very least I could do, given that the Saudis are our fellow Muslims, and I've long been keen to cement our friendship. If they ask for anything else I shall be only too pleased to oblige them ... '

Sunday, 14 October

Met the British ambassador this morning. Discussed oil and the war. In his opinion the Arabs must be made to appreciate that threatening oil supplies is a double-edged weapon; it will do little to hurt the USA, but will have a serious effect on the countries of Europe, many, perhaps most, of which are basically pro-Arab. He asked that I raise this point with HIM.

... Audience. Reported my meetings with the British and US ambassadors. Referring to the former's comments about Arab oil, HIM remarked that he himself had made precisely this point in a recent interview with the *Egyptian Gazette*. He instructed me to send copies of this to both ambassadors ...

Monday, 15 October

Went to the airport to bid farewell to HMQ, on her way to France where she is to be awarded the *Couronne Civique*.

Audience. Bhutto arrives here tomorrow and I submitted the schedule for his visit.

Passed on a letter from our ambassador in Rome, describing another meeting he's had with the King of Afghanistan. The ambassador reports that the King has written to Davoud. Should the Afghans agree to pay him a salary, he will no longer be in need of assistance from Iran. Whilst the King is waiting for a reply from Kabul, HIM ordered that he be given a provisional advance of $20,000 and an assurance that we are handling the matter with the utmost discretion ...

Later the US ambassador handed me a letter, setting out his government's basic approach to the war. He also asked me to convey Washington's deep appreciation of HIM's courage in refusing military access to Iranian air space. I asked him what route the Soviets are using to transport military supplies. He was not altogether sure, but has a hunch that they're flying directly along our border with Turkey ...

Brief audience. Via the Americans, the Israelis have asked whether an attack might be launched within Iraq by Kurdish guerrillas. The US ambassador believes this to be a reckless undertaking, as the Kurds are totally unequipped for operations beyond their own mountains. 'Tell him I'm entirely in agreement', said HIM, 'and in any case I've no desire to have the Kurds branded as mere henchmen of Israel and the USA.' HIM is convinced by air force reports that not a single Soviet plane has violated our air space in flying to Syria or Iraq. They must have found some alternative route for supplies ...

The Pakistani ambassador has suggested that, as HIM and Bhutto are personal friends, HIM might greet him personally at the airport. 'Crap', said HIM. I went on to explain that I had already rejected the proposal. 'Naturally', he remarked; 'I'd have been amazed if you'd reacted differently.'

Then took a helicopter to the airport, arriving at exactly the same time as Bhutto. Escorted him to the guest house at Saadabad ...

Returned to the palace. Bhutto is fasting,[1] which came as a considerable shock to HIM. As a mark of respect I was instructed personally to escort Bhutto from his residence to the palace. There he stayed talking to HIM until 1.30 in the afternoon. Meanwhile I had a chance to speak with Aziz Ahmad, the Pakistani Foreign Minister, and various others of the President's retinue ...

Bhutto dined as my guest and at his request I also invited the US ambassador. To my surprise Bhutto soaked up a substantial quantity of wine and whisky. On my asking how this accorded with his fast, he replied, 'Today I fasted, and tomorrow I shall fast again. But as for night time, now that's a different matter altogether.'

---

[1] The visit coincided with the month of Ramadan, when Muslims are expected to spend the daylight hours fasting

Wednesday, 17 October

... Early this evening I met Israel's new representative in Tehran. He remarked on the damage that's been done to his country's air force by the Soviet Sam 6 missiles – a new system, light enough to be carried on a man's shoulders. All in all, this is the first time I have heard an Israeli bemoaning his country's situation. Over dinner last night the US ambassador told me that Israel has lost 105 aircraft. They started the war with only 400, though the Arabs, of course, claim to have destroyed 600 or some such preposterous figure ...

The Arabs have just announced a 5 per cent reduction in their oil supplies to the USA and to every other country which has lent support to Israel ...

Thursday, 18 October

Met the British ambassador who informed me that he is shortly to be posted to Washington. He said how much he would regret leaving Tehran, although I doubt the sincerity of these remarks. I told him, on HIM's orders, that we are shortly to increase our oil prices to the levels set by Nigeria and Venezuela. 'But why is it', I asked him, 'that your government has accepted Nigerian and Venezuelan pricing, yet the moment we decide to keep pace with them, you turn up here with a begging letter from your Prime Minister?' ... The ambassador believes that he owes his Washington appointment to a long-standing acquaintance with Kissinger – they were at the Defence College together in Britain and know the way each other thinks ...

The US ambassador called at my home early this evening to confess that his information on Soviet planes being routed along our border with Turkey has since been proved false. He also passed on the figures for Arab and Israeli casualties ...

OPEC has doubled the price of oil ... Further to the monthly 5 per cent reduction in oil supplies to the USA, Saudi Arabia has decided on a cut of 10 per cent, whilst Abu Dhabi is to cease supplies altogether.

The Israelis have now broken through on their front with Egypt.

Sunday, 21 October

... Meeting this afternoon with a group of Islamic diplomats; the ambassadors of Morocco, Egypt, Kuwait, Saudi Arabia and the Lebanon come to complain of our failure to support the Arab cause. I denied this, reminding them how helpful we have been in the past, and adding that it's we, if anyone, that should be complaining. The Arabs are consistently unfriendly, always sounding off about the islands, or talking about the so-called 'Arabian Gulf', whilst the President of Algeria used the latest conference of non-aligned countries to launch a bitter verbal attack on Iran ... Together with the ambassadors I then went on to Mrs Diba's residence for a reception to celebrate the end of Ramadan ...

Monday, 22 October

... Audience. Passed on a message from Kissinger, notifying HIM of a joint US–Soviet resolution to the UN Security Council, calling for a prompt end to the present war and for negotiations towards a lasting Arab–Israeli settlement ...

Submitted the menu for tomorrow's lunch in honour of the Queen of England. HIM changed virtually everything, insisting for example that the Queen dislikes caviar and that *pâté de foie gras* should be served in its place ...

Went to the airport this evening to welcome HMQ on her return from Europe ... She was accompanied by the PM who had been with her in Paris. Despite the present crisis, he seems to have had no qualms in escorting HMQ on what was basically no more than a week-long sight-seeing trip. Though he has used the Arab–Israeli war as a pretext for cancelling his official visit to Hungary ...

Tuesday, 23 October

Audience ... Queen Elizabeth of England flew in shortly before noon and spent an hour or so before lunch discussing the international situation with HIM; the war, security in the Gulf and the Indian Ocean, HIM's forthcoming trip to Australia and so on. In general she seems to be kept well-informed of events ... She's just returned from Australia and was delighted by her visit, though critical of the £60 million being spent on the Sydney Opera House ... In confidence she mentioned to me her sense of shame that the British government has refused Israel's request for spare parts and other supplies ...

Thursday, 25 October

... Went to a performance of *Carmen* at the Rudaki Hall. The whole world is reeling from the news that the Soviets have agreed to Sadat's request to send troops to supervise a cease-fire. The Americans have reacted by placing various of their troops on red alert ... though Kissinger has put

out a plea for the avoidance of confrontation between the superpowers ...
HIM was dreadfully anxious when he arrived and ordered me to give the
opera a miss in order to keep an eye on developments ... In due course
Moscow announced that it had lost interest in sending troops. We all
heaved a sigh of relief, including HIM who declared that the Soviets would
never have backed down had it not been for the speed of America's reaction
... As it happens, the British have been warning us for nearly a week that
the Soviets were contemplating just such military intervention.

Sunday, 28 October
Special *Salaam* to mark the end of Ramadan ... The Speaker of the
Majlis delivered an address, expressing Iranian solidarity with our Muslim
brothers presently engaged in war. HIM was outraged by this, whispering
to the hapless Speaker, 'Muslim brothers be damned; they're our greatest
enemy.' Later he confided in me how mystified he is by the current fashion
for Islamic solidarity. 'You know yourself that I'm a Muslim, even a
fanatical Muslim', he said; 'But that does nothing to alter my opinion of
the Arabs.' ...

Sunday, 4 November
Audience ... I asked why Mir Fendereski has been sacked as Deputy
Foreign Minister.[1] 'He told the Russians they could fly their planes through
Iran', said HIM. 'He then came to me and justified his actions on the
grounds that Iran has always been "the Bridge of Victory".[2] How the hell
can he have been so stupid? He must have known that it contradicted
everything I've said on the subject ...'

The US ambassador has written to inform me that a naval task force
consisting of the US ship *Hancock* and accompanying destroyers is due to
move to a holding area some 180 miles south-east of Muscat on 6 November.
He was anxious to know how the Shah would react to this; would he, for
example, allow the USA to make use of the air base at Bandar Abbas, to
fly long-range surveillance missions by America's P2s, as well as to enable
short-range flights to and from the *Hancock*. The latter will be in the
immediate vicinity of Bandar Abbas for roughly twenty days. Finally he
was interested in the possibility of our selling fuel oil to the task force.

[1] Iranian ambassador to the USSR and later Foreign Minister in Bakhtiar's short-lived government during the revolutionary turmoil, 30 December 1978–February 1979.
[2] A nickname applied to Iran during the Second World War when US forces made extensive
use of Iranian roads and railways in transporting supplies to the Soviet Union.

Immediately passed this message on to HIM who sent for me and asked me to find out from the ambassador how much fuel the ships will require. He also suggested that it would look better if any such fuel were supplied to them indirectly, via our own navy. They may use Bandar Abbas, but only if they do so on the pretext of training Iranian pilots to fly the P2 aircraft we ourselves have bought ...

Monday, 5 November

... My friend Rasoul Parvizi telephoned late last night, to say that my family has been lavished with praise by the BBC's Persian Service. I can't imagine why, and all in all I'm in a quandary as to how to break the news to HIM, given the extraordinary depth of his suspicions. At the moment I have the good fortune that HIM trusts and favours me more than anyone else, hence my annoyance at Parvizi's news ... In the end, I reported the matter straight out during my audience, adding that Parvizi suggests we seek out whatever idiot is responsible for the broadcast. I'm by no means sure this allayed HIM's suspicions ...

Later I received the Saudi ambassador who had what he termed a minor request to put to me; that we ban El Al, the Israeli airline, from using Iranian air space, and that we cease to pipeline oil through Israel. I was shocked by his audacity, replying that it's the companies rather than we that use the pipeline to supply the Israelis with oil, and that we can hardly ban El Al short of declaring open war on Israel. The ambassador did not press the point, merely remarking that he and his Arab colleagues had spent the afternoon discussing matters with our Minister of Foreign Affairs ...

Wednesday, 7 November

Audience ... The Saudi ambassador told me yesterday that his Crown Prince[1] wishes to go bustard-shooting in Southern Iran. 'He's most welcome to pay us a visit', said HIM, 'but as for the bustards, they're a protected species. Our hunting restrictions have rescued them from near extinction. I'm not about to undo the good work.' Discussed the general situation in the Middle East, touching on Kissinger's tour of North Africa and Asia. He's expected here next Friday en route for the Far East ...

[1] This refers to the present King Fahd Ibn Abdul Aziz who in fact did not become Crown Prince until 1975.

Friday, 9 November

... Called at the Niavaran Palace this morning. HIM kept our Foreign Minister Khalatbari outside whilst he received Kissinger and the US ambassador. I couldn't help feeling sorry for the poor man and invited him to join the US Assistant Secretary of State Joseph Sisco in my office where we discussed the Middle East before going in to lunch. Sisco says that Egypt and Israel have agreed on a six-point disengagement formula, due to be announced this evening ... He also remarked how reluctant the Israelis had been to consent to Kissinger's efforts at shuttle diplomacy. Apparently he and Kissinger have slept for less than three hours in the past three days.

We then joined HIM and the others for lunch ... Kissinger is quite transformed from the man he used to be; much more dignified and, at least in my opinion, much more arrogant. He gave us his impression of the Soviets, who he considers both shrewd and flexible. For example in their negotiations over Vietnam, they didn't hesitate to slam their fists on the table, but the moment discussions broke up for lunch or dinner, they returned to being friendly as could be. Later it was discovered that they'd had the whole performance taped, in order to demonstrate how strenuously they'd defended Vietnamese interests. It was only away from the nego-tiating table that they were able to reveal the sort of deal they were really after ... We also discussed the high level of Israeli casualties, especially amongst the air force ... Kissinger believes that on this occasion neither side will emerge as absolute victor, all of which increases the chances of a lasting peace maintained under UN supervision.

He and the US ambassador complimented me on the efficient and cheerful way I always respond to their approaches. HIM countered this by saying that my efficiency was the direct result of my being able to reach him at any hour of day or night. 'As for his cheerfulness, it's only to be expected when he lets slip no opportunity to savour a fine wine or a specimen of female beauty.'

Afterwards I made moves to escort Kissinger to his helicopter, but HIM dissuaded me with a shake of his head ...

Saturday, 10 November

Flew with HIM and the PM to Shiraz. At HIM's request I had instructed Amouzegar, the Finance Minister, to come to see us off at the airport. HIM wanted to give him a letter and a personal message for King Faisal. The PM however had been kept entirely in the dark about all this, and naturally asked Amouzegar what he was doing there. He in turn replied that he had no more idea than the PM; he had merely obeyed HIM's orders as passed on by me. This left the poor PM terribly embarrassed; faced with such a situation, who wouldn't be? But what can one do? Just as there is only one God, there can only be one Shah. The more his subordinates are humbled, the more it pleases him ...

After lunch he opened an impressive new refinery outside Shiraz ...

Saturday, 17 November
Audience ... Bhutto has written to HIM, endorsing the proposal for a conference of Islamic heads of state to discuss the Middle East, first suggested by Tunku Abdur Rahman, ex-Premier of Malaysia and currently Secretary-General of the Islamic Council. HIM has pointed out in his reply that, in present circumstances, such a meeting might only inflame the situation. As I see it, Bhutto cannot possibly share HIM's knowledge of recent Soviet–American accords, or he would never have supported the idea of a conference.

Tuesday, 20 November
Audience. HIM is furious with a recent speech by Nasser Ameri, leader of the Mardom party, calling for health care and university education to be entirely state-funded ... Why, asked HIM, should the children of the wealthy be exempt from university fees ... On the other hand, as he made plain in his address to the education conference at Ramsar, he's fully in favour of scholarships for the most gifted, regardless of a student's family background. 'Why won't these damned politicians ever read my speeches?', he complained. 'And why on earth don't they make an effort to grasp the basic principles behind the policies we've adopted?' This is all very well, but what on earth is the role of an opposition leader if it's not to criticize the government and promise better ways of doing things? Current thinking is that Ameri should restrict himself to 'constructive opposition', which means, I suppose, that he's not to tread on anybody's toes ... If the opposition is merely an exercise in window dressing, I can see no point in carrying on with it ...

Attended a dinner in honour of Prince Hendrick, the Prince Consort of Denmark ... I've heard various rumours about this particular gentleman which, having met him, I can well believe.

Wednesday, 21 November

Audience ... Reported that I've told the Saudi ambassador that his Crown Prince will be allowed the same privileges with respect to hunting in Iran as are enjoyed by members of our own royal family. The ambassador got my point – that the bustard is a protected species and not to be hunted for at least another three years. Even so he confessed that he's got himself into a tight corner since he led the Crown Prince to expect that permission would be granted without any problem. To help him out, I suggested to HIM that I'd had no idea when I was first approached that there would be an absolute ban on the sport. It would save face all round if HIM were to allow the Prince to hawk for a few of the birds. 'Absolutely not', he replied. 'You got yourself into this mess, now you must admit to the ambassador that you misled him.' ...

Thursday, 22 November

A memorable turning point in our history: the day when HIM delivered what was little short of a political will and testament. Over dinner last night he informed me that he would not be coming to the Jahan Nama Palace this morning for his weekly meeting with the army high command. Instead he would remain at the Niavaran Palace; the meeting was to take place there, and would be followed by a second session which the PM, the Speakers of the two Houses of Parliament, HIM's Chief private secretary and I would also be expected to attend ...

We were duly received at half past eleven this morning. Much to my surprise, we were joined by HMQ.

[The following is Alam's resumé of the speech delivered by the Shah]

I have summoned this meeting in the presence of the Commanders of my army, my Prime Minister, the Speakers of Parliament, the high officials of the Court, and Her Majesty the Queen, so that I may lay before you certain grave and important matters. God alone determines the hour of our deaths, but we live in an age in which the instruments of death are wielded by terrorists and subversives. At any moment my life may be snatched from me. In the event of this and until the Crown Prince attains legal age, authority is to lie with Her Majesty the Queen and the members of the Regency Council. My armed forces will be as obedient to Her Majesty the Queen and later, once he has ascended the throne, to the Crown Prince, the future Shah, as ever they were to me. Their orders may come from a woman or a man of tender years, but they are to be obeyed with no less respect. The safety of all your lives depends on this ...

Today I intend to apprise each one of you with your future duties. In doing so I trust to demonstrate to our enemies both at home and abroad, that we have made provision for every eventuality and that it will be in vain that they contrive to shift us from the steady course of policy by accident or act of violence.

First I shall speak of the armed forces whose foremost duty lies in preserving the integrity of this nation. They are the defenders of our constitution, the constitution as I have enforced it. Their role lies not in the political arena but in absolute loyalty to the Shah or to whoever performs the duties of Shah according to the constitution ...

They must respect the established order. The Commander in Chief will issue his commands through the Chief of the General Staff. Should the head of state be familiar with military affairs, such affairs are to be at his personal disposal; if not, he must first consult the council of army commanders or an equivalent body of military advisers. None the less, the head of state is to retain the ultimate right of decision and is not to be gainsaid by any man. The men of the armed services owe nothing but blind obedience to his commands.

However, should the head of state neglect to exercise his constitutional prerogative, the armed forces may be obliged to remind him that national interest and legal duty require him to exercise that authority as I do and have always done. The armed services must permit no change to the established order through which this country has progressed so far ...

No commander would be so foolish as to connive with politicians in pursuit of selfish ambition. So long as each officer puts obedience to the Shah above loyalty to fellow members of his class, this country will be secure against military dictatorship ...

The achievements of the past decade stand testimony that whatever goal has been set and whatever triumph won, it has been for this nation's good. As God is my witness, if a better course had been available to me I should have seized it. The constitution awards executive power to the monarchy ... At every level, through the councils of villages, counties and provinces, our people must learn to share in their political duty and to participate in the construction of their own destinies and future. The political parties must act as the people's guide in this enterprise, not squander their energies in faction and cabal ... The executive and the legislature must act as the twin pillars of the White Revolution, divided yet inseparable ...

I pray God that he may yet vouchsafe me time to witness and to celebrate the dawning of our Great Civilization. For this to be achieved, the orders I have given you today must be obeyed in every detail, not only in my own lifetime, but thereafter ... The man who issues them and who stands before you now has delivered you and your country from the despair of 1941 to the dawn of a great new era; nor has he ceased to dream of what that era may one day bring.

The room was in absolute silence as HIM finished; everybody too electrified to utter a sound. I myself was so overwhelmed that I could think of nothing, save that I no longer wish to live a single moment once the Shah has gone. Pray God that I die before my beloved Shah.

Afterwards HIM spared a few minutes to chat with the PM, the parliamentary Speakers and myself. He wanted to know how his statement might be made known to the country at large. I stood out strongly against this; it might spread chaos and give rise to goodness knows what sort of misinterpretations. HIM agreed with me, suggesting that the general tenor alone need be publicized and then only indirectly, just to make it clear that the succession and related questions are no longer in any doubt ...

Saturday, 24 November

Presentation of credentials by the new ambassadors of Mongolia, Bulgaria and Afghanistan. The latter is Davoud's son-in-law, a very shrewd diplomat. He delivered an excellent address and altogether behaved with considerable dignity. It was he as much as anyone else that persuaded the King to abdicate ...

Sunday, 25 November

Audience. Discussed the arrangements for the King of Afghanistan's pension, $10,000 a month out of secret government funds. 'Apart from yourself and our ambassador in Rome, no one in the government is to know anything about this', HIM declared.

The Prime Minister of Mongolia and his Russian-born wife lunched as HIM's guests. A very humdrum conversation ensued, turning mostly on the qualities of mare's milk and other such fascinating issues ...

Monday, 26 November

Audience. HIM is infuriated with an article in the *Financial Times* which flatters the Arabs whilst subjecting us to quite unjustified criticism ...

He has been told that the PM has forbidden any public announcement of the forthcoming visit here by the mayor of Johannesburg. 'Tell the PM to keep his nose out of matters which don't concern him', he said.

Submitted a transcript of the speech which the leader of the Mardom Party made in Tabriz, retracting everything that he'd said earlier about free health care and higher education. HIM expressed himself well satisfied ...

Tuesday, 27 November

Audience ... I reported that demonstrations have broken out in the School of Agriculture at Tehran University. HIM was dismayed by this, and furious that the students should care so little for the great progress that this country is making ...

Wednesday, 28 November

Audience ... Israel's representative here asked me to congratulate HIM on the interview he gave to the Lebanese magazine, *Al Havadess*.[1] He was also keen to be granted an audience. 'Some other time', HIM said.

Discussed how a copy of HIM's statement on the succession can be passed on to senior officers in the military. I remarked that in effect he has appointed the armed services as tutors to HMQ and the Crown Prince. 'Precisely as I intended', he replied. He left instructions that every officer, from brigade commanders upwards, is to be shown a copy of his speech, and must sign to record their having done so. Likewise, their successors must do the same ... Once again he voiced grave concern for the future.

The demonstrations at the School of Agriculture were referred to at dinner and HIM became quite heated about the students' ingratitude. 'Calm yourself', said HMQ; 'Just look at our own children. They've decided to answer only half the questions in their exams as a protest against the amount of work they're given. What do you suppose we should do?

---

[1] The Shah declared that the use of oil as a weapon during the war was understandable. 'But since you [Arabs] have accepted the cease-fire for the sake of a peaceful settlement, why do you continue to cut oil supplies and reduce production?' ... He went on to say that his government had always called for the fulfilment of the legitimate rights of the Palestinian people, but criticized the Arab states for pressuring Iran to close down the Israeli trade mission in Tehran. He remarked that the Arabs were not making a similar demand of Turkey, despite its being an Islamic country.

Send in the army?' A point well made. Once again I must record the moderating influence exercised by HMQ. What a pity that she's so often led astray by her entourage ...

Friday, 30 November

Audience ... Submitted a report on Sir Maurice Oldfield, head of British Intelligence, who is due shortly in Tehran for an audience. I pointed to the fact that he is unmarried. 'How lucky he is', said HIM, which led us on to that proverbial topic, woman ... 'I'm convinced that bachelors outlive married men', he declared; 'They live longer and more successful lives because they're spared at least half the worries that afflict those of us with wives.' 'Surely Your Majesty means three quarters rather than half', I replied. 'Quite so', he agreed. 'But just think of the lack of freedom we men must put up with.'

Monday, 3 December

Audience. Reported meeting the US ambassador at a reception last night. The US Indian Ocean Task Force requires a substantial quantity of fuel – about half a million barrels a month – and I had to tell the ambassador that we can no longer supply it at local prices as we did to begin with, but must charge the full international rate. He took this in good part ... I also warned him that if US aircraft from Europe are to join the fleet they should do so only in small numbers and on the pretext of joint military exercises with Iran. If not, we'll face justifiable protests from the Soviets, who may even ask the Indians to provide them with a base of their own.

In response to our enquiries about reports reaching Washington on local corruption, the ambassador categorically denied that any such reports have been sent. 'In that case', HIM interrupted, 'why did Kissinger raise the subject with Ardeshir Zahedi [by now Iran's ambassador in the USA]?' I made no effort to reply ... 'What hypocrisy', he went on. 'The US President and Vice-President stand accused of corruption, precisely the same charges they level against us. But in what way are we supposed to be corrupt? Every defence contract takes place on a government-to-government basis, within the guide-lines laid down for FMS (Foreign Military Sales). As for ordinary commercial transactions, no one would bother with a deal unless it was set to make a profit.' I replied that he need not pay so much attention to idle rumour ... although I made it clear that our administration does indeed harbour corruption, however limited that corruption may be ...

Reported another conversation I had last night, this time with George

Ball, former US Deputy State Secretary. He is convinced that Nixon should stand down and that the Republican Party as a whole is keen to see the back of him; they regard him as a millstone around their necks, in the run up to next year's elections[1] ... He also suggested that the USA is in a position to force an Israeli withdrawal from the occupied territories ... Nixon cannot afford to run such a risk. Instead we must wait until Gerald Ford takes over at the White House, when he and Kissinger might tackle it together.

There's been further unrest in various of Tehran's universities ... 'I'm all but certain that the Soviets are behind this', said HIM. 'Tell the authorities that they must take firm action.'

Tuesday, 4 December

Audience ... Ayatollah Milani's son has been arrested on pilgrimage to Mecca; the Iraqi police caught him in possession of opium. 'Make sure that he's released', HIM said, 'but at the same time collect enough evidence so that we can jog his memory in future; these religious types can be so frightfully forgetful.'

A meeting with the new ambassador of Afghanistan, a graduate of Harvard and Columbia who speaks the most exquisite Persian besides fluent French and English. He's a talkative fellow and required little prompting to open up about recent events in his country. He claims to have paid money to the former King – a fact borne out by reports from our ambassador in Rome to whom the King admitted that he has sorted out the problem of school fees for his youngest child. The ambassador then went on to describe how he bamboozled the King into abdicating and declaring allegiance to the new republic ... The younger Afghan officers, he complained, are ignorant and wet behind the ears, and he was equally scornful of Abdul Vali Khan. Apparently when the latter was in London last summer, he totally ignored a telegram from Kabul, forewarning him about the coup. It was even found after his subsequent arrest that he'd got a full list of the conspirators locked away in a drawer, but had been simply too lazy to do anything about it ... For my own part I told the ambassador how keen HIM is to support Davoud; should Davoud fall the whole of Afghanistan might be plunged into chaos. I asked to what extent the army

---

[1] Since July 1973 Senate hearings had resulted in confessions by John Dean and various other members of the White House staff. In October of the same year, Elliot Richardson, Attorney General, and several of his assistants resigned in protest against the decision of President Richard Nixon to dismiss the special prosecutor in these proceedings, Archibald Cox.

is under control, but received no clear answer. Presumably the ambassador believes I'm spellbound by Davoud, since he left me looking thoroughly pleased with himself ...

Wednesday, 5 December
Audience ... HIM explained that Abdul Vali Khan took no action against the conspirators on direct orders from the King.

... Later chaired a meeting to look into the security arrangements for HIM's forthcoming trips; he's to visit Austria, Switzerland, Senegal, Kenya and the Sudan ... I called in the Senegalese ambassador and asked him whether his government can guarantee HIM's safety. 'No', was the simple answer. Even so the poor man promised that we'll be given every assistance we ask for ...

Thursday, 6 December
Audience ... Last night the BBC Persian Service broadcast a report claiming that the Baluchi rebels in Pakistan are being crushed through the use of HIM's money, helicopters and troops, and that this has inspired a wave of resentment amongst the Baluchi and Pathan populations ... HIM express-ed his surprise at this. 'You don't suppose it might possibly have anything to do with the British Foreign Secretary's recent visit to Moscow?', he asked. I replied that this was out of the question. Even supposing that there had been an Anglo-Soviet understanding on the matter, which I very much doubt, it would never have been publicized so swiftly by the BBC. In any event the British, especially the present Conservative government, are utterly opposed to the Soviets gaining access to Baluchistan and the Gulf ... 'Fair enough', said HIM. 'Hence Mrs Gandhi's refusal, when Brezhnev visited India, to agree to his request for a naval base.' I agreed, pointing to the high regard in which Mrs Gandhi is held by the British; they would be bound to consult one another on such a matter.

We then turned to HIM's trip abroad and my worries over the security arrangements. I suggested that for the various legs of his tour we might call upon the assistance of French Intelligence in Senegal, the British in Kenya, and the CIA for the Sudan ... Reported that General M has been admitted to hospital in Paris. HIM instructed me to ensure that we pay his medical expenses. 'The man had to be punished', he said, 'but that's no reason to hound him to his grave.' After pausing a while, he continued, 'I don't suppose he'd have been any good in a fight. He got by on bombast, bombast and showmanship. Come to think of it, there's not a single one of our generals has real backbone. They're all of them mere exhibitionists, except perhaps Azhari. He keeps a low profile but he might well show real valour if he were put to the test.' He then reeled off the names of several generals, dismissing them each in turn as gutless wonders. Referring to Khatami, the head of the air force, he said that though he may have proved his organizational abilities that's no guarantee he will stand up under the pressures of war.

Sunday, 9 December

Audience. Passed on a cable from the ambassador in Tokyo. Apparently the Japanese are willing to accept almost any conditions so long as they can secure regular oil supplies. A mission headed by their Deputy Prime Minister hopes to visit Tehran at the end of this month. 'Tell the ambassador that I shall be abroad by then', HIM said.

He is extremely anxious about student unrest which has now infected every campus save the Pahlavi University at Shiraz. 'Mark my words, Moscow is behind it all', he said. I replied that this might be so, but that we should bear in mind that they would have to be sowing fertile ground if their success is to be explained. For my own part, I'm convinced that the university authorities have made the mistake of refusing any sort of dialogue with the students. The same goes for the country at large; our government behaves like the conqueror of a vanquished land. As I said to HIM, for all his achievements and his tireless endeavour, there's a growing sense of alienation between regime and people. 'I'm afraid you're right', he replied. 'I've sensed the same thing myself. Something must be done.'

Yet another telegram has arrived from Prince Fahd of Saudi Arabia requesting permission to go bustard shooting. 'You must prepare a reply over my own signature', HIM said. 'Spell it out to the man; like it or not, we have laws in this country which even I am powerless to ignore.' ... On a different tack he continued, 'Look around you. America, Japan, Europe, their leaders are running scared, every one of them.' ... Referring to the Saudi oil boycott, he said, 'You never know, perhaps it's the Americans that put them up to it. Their oil is owned entirely by US companies who stand to lose very little from any sort of boycott. By contrast, America's competitors in Japan and Western Europe are bound to be severely hit; their costs will soar, leaving America to sweep the market.' ... I replied that whilst such a plan is all very well in theory, I doubt the Americans have that degree of intelligence. 'Don't be so sure', he remarked ...

Monday, 10 December

Audience ... 'What on earth's going on in the universities?', he asked. 'It's the Soviets that are to blame. We must act now, and with force. Tell the presidents of every university that leniency will not be tolerated. Just as in the army, I've ordered that academics should be graded according to the effort they put in to winning loyalty from their pupils.' ... 'But even so', I replied, 'there's no one that can be bothered really to discuss matters with the students. It's the same old story all over again.' As an example of the sort of thing I meant, I cited the recent by-election in Tabriz. Last year the senator there obtained over 200,000 votes thanks to ballot-rigging by Iran Novin. But HIM has since insisted on free elections and ordered a careful check of voter identity, and this time the party polled no more than 34,000 ... With the government's deceit shown up in this way, it's hardly surprising that the people should be disaffected ...

HMQ has asked Mrs Diba to attend a conference in Paris on vocational training. I asked HIM what sort of expenses she should be allowed. 'As much as she asks for', he said. 'Hopefully that will encourage her to keep her mouth shut.'

... Invited the British ambassador to dinner to discuss the security for HIM's trip to Kenya and the Sudan. He could offer no guarantees as far as the Sudanese are concerned, but assured me that things were likely to run more smoothly in Kenya ...

Tuesday, 11 December

Audience. Referring to his African trip, I suggested that there was no particular urgency for him to visit the Sudan. Wouldn't it be better if the thing were cancelled, particularly since the country is wide open to organizations such as the Palestinian Black September, and to mad Qadhafi and his Libyan millions? HIM eventually agreed, authorizing me to cancel the Sudanese visit on grounds of security ...

The situation in the universities is still causing him grave anxiety. Perhaps he knows more than he lets on to me, otherwise I find it difficult to understand why he should attach such importance to the matter ...

Wednesday, 12 December

Army Day. There was a fly-past by 150 Phantoms, and a magnificent parade of tanks and missile carriers. We spent the entire time discussing oil prices. Our latest auction has raised the level to $17.4 a barrel ... which means we've already exceeded the target for next year's budget by a factor of 30 per cent. We discussed how the surplus can be spent. Released into the domestic economy it might only fuel inflation, so it may be wiser to invest it abroad ...

Met the US ambassador. Referring to HIM's African trip, he said that there's very little the USA can do, even in the Sudan. I told him that we've cancelled the Sudanese leg of the visit.

HIM has sent a message to Washington stating that the King of Greece still commands great popularity and wishes to return to his country within the next ten days, before the drafting of a new constitution which will settle the fate of the monarchy. The US ambassador asked me to tell HIM that there is no way the King will be allowed to return. General Ioannides, the Chief of Military Intelligence who masterminded the coup, and all his colleagues are utterly against it. In any event, according to the ambassador, the King is not nearly so popular as he likes to pretend, nor will the constitution be drafted so quickly as he claims. I suggested that Washington may have reached some sort of understanding with Athens against the King, but that a stable monarchy would be preferable to rule by a bunch of conspiratorial army officers. The ambassador made no comment. Personally I have no faith in Greece's playboy King, but I did my best to stand up for him on orders from the Shah.

Thursday, 13 December
Audience. Reported the US ambassador's remarks. 'Tell him', said HIM, 'that we must warn his government that monarchy is far preferable to martial law. Washington may live to regret its present attitude.' I asked why the USA is so set against King Constantine. HIM replied that they fear, with his restoration, Greece would once again be plunged into turmoil, weak government by discredited veterans clinging to power. 'Given the current state of play in the Middle East and the Eastern Mediterranean, the USA cannot allow yet another trouble-spot to develop', he said ... 'The trouble is, I myself am unconvinced that the King can provide the sort of strong leadership that's required.' ...

Reported the press statements made by Senator Barry Goldwater on his return from Iran. 'The man has shot his mouth off about matters that are none of his concern', said HIM. 'His remarks are not to be reported in the local press.'[1]

[1] Senator Goldwater stated that the Shah and his military advisers were concerned about Soviet attempts to establish a foothold in the Indian Ocean through Afghanistan and Pakistan, and that Iran's armed forces were determined to resist a Soviet break-through via neighbouring countries.

... Bhutto is doing the rounds of various Arab states, presumably to drum up financial support and to demonstrate his lack of dependence on Iran ...

Friday, 14 December

Prior to my audience HIM received Mrs Marcos, wife of the Philippine President, making a brief stop-over in Tehran. 'She's desperate to get her hands on our oil', said HIM. 'In exchange she's offering us a fifty-year lease on land where we might grow rice or breed cattle. In addition, despite the international shortage of cement, they can provide us with 2 million tons of the stuff straight away.' I remarked that Mrs Marcos is quite a beauty and therefore her request merits our attention, even without the added attractions of land and cement. 'Ah, but she's growing old', he replied.

Saturday, 15 December

Audience ... Discussed the broadcast by Radio Moscow, objecting to our stand over oil. Our refusal to reduce production and our criticism of those Arab states which have agreed to cut-backs have been interpreted as signs of an anti-Arab bias. The Soviet ambassador made exactly the same point at his audience a couple of days ago, to which HIM replied that at heart the Arabs agree with our stand, whatever they may say in public.

Once again he complained that the university authorities have made no effort to establish a dialogue with the students to ease the present unrest. 'People get away with the bare minimum', he said. 'There's no sense of national or moral obligation. It's exactly the same with the military. The whole thing makes me fear for the future.' I replied that since it's HIM who has achieved so much for this country, it is he too that must reform popular attitudes. But by subtlety; it cannot be achieved merely by issuing commands. 'Something must be done', he replied; 'We must talk about it soon.'

Sunday, 16 December

As HIM went skiing this morning, I had the opportunity to call on an old flame of mine who'd been nagging me for neglecting her: 'Noblesse oblige'. She gave me coffee.

Met the Lebanese ambassador. Our Foreign Ministry complains that he showed unnecessary zeal, supporting a joint Arab plea that we close the Israeli mission in Tehran. He's a member of a highly respected Lebanese

Shi'a family.[1] His recent behaviour has been both unexpected and hurtful to HIM, who had previously treated him with particular favour. To make the point quite clear, a couple of days ago I declined a courtesy invitation to the Lebanese residence and made him call at my office to explain himself ...

Afternoon audience ... Suggested that the painting HIM bought in England might be paid for with government funds. 'Out of the question', he replied. 'It's to hang in my private apartments at Saadabad.' I pointed out that several of the pictures at Saadabad already belong to the government. He insisted that they be included in future inventories of government property ...

Monday, 17 December
Audience ... Bhutto has invited Princess Ashraf to visit Pakistan. He's chiefly interested in obtaining cut-price Iranian oil and the Princess wanted to know whether HIM was likely to accede to this request. If not, there would be no point in her making the trip. 'Never', said HIM. 'Mr Bhutto is so anxious to please the Arabs that he's even started talking about 'the Gulf', without a hint of the all-important adjective 'Persian'. If he wants cheap oil, then he can damn well sort something out with his Arab friends.'

... Late this evening the Romanian ambassador called round with a message for HIM from President Ceausescu, asking for oil. In the past we've supplied him with 2 million tons a year to support his stand against the Soviets. But now, the oil price increases make it impractical for us to maintain this level of support. The Romanians have no illusions about our selling oil to them below the international rate; they're merely keen to secure the same quantity as in the past. I assured the ambassador of HIM's continuing respect for President Ceausescu, and told him that we shall do our best to meet their needs[2] ...

Tuesday, 18 December
Audience. Reported that the British are fairly confident over the security arrangements for HIM's visit to Kenya, but that I myself am far from happy about his safety in Switzerland. 'Nonsense', he retorted.

[1] Khalil al-Khalil; Lebanese ambassador to Iran, 1971–8. His father, Kazem al-Khalil, was a prominent politician and Secretary-General of the Liberal National Party.
[2] It was not the supply of oil which worried the Romanians, but rather the fact that they wished to keep their transactions within the framework of the barter agreement which regulated their trade with Iran; this stipulated that payments be made in Romanian goods and not in hard currency.

Discussed ... the general outlook for Morocco. 'The King is doomed', HIM declared. 'One minute he's announcing his absolute allegiance to the Arab cause; he's willing to sacrifice anything, even his life, for the common good. The next moment he's busy squandering money, chartering a yacht, to sail the seas to indulge himself.'

Thursday, 20 December
Audience. HIM was poring over a bulging file which turned out to contain details of students awarded scholarships by the Pahlavi Foundation. I suggested that a world leader of HIM's calibre need not waste his time on such trivia ... 'But I enjoy it', he said. 'Just think of it as my hobby.' Reported a meeting I had last night with the Pakistani ambassador, to discuss the conference of Islamic states. Bhutto has telephoned in person and has twice sent ministers to brief HIM on this conference. We now want the thing postponed from January until late February. However the ambassador claimed this will cause grave embarrassment to Pakistan. HIM was infuriated. 'Why the hell should I let King Faisal dictate the date?', he said. I reminded him that he'd already discussed timing with Bhutto, who needs the publicity and is anxious to obtain oil at a favourable rate. 'In that case', he said, 'we'll follow the example set by Indonesia, Turkey and the Lebanon and merely send our PM.' I replied that this would be a slap in the face for Bhutto, given the extent of HIM's past support ... This seemed to make little impression, so as a last resort I suggested that, if only he would agree to divide up his trip to Europe, he might take a few days' rest in Tehran, reduce the length of his absence abroad, and still be in a position to attend Bhutto's conference. Having pondered for a while, he replied: 'Don't reject the ambassador's request. Merely tell him I consider the conference to be a waste of time. Let's see what they make of that.'

... Reported a meeting with the French ambassador to discuss the security for HIM's trip to Senegal. According to the ambassador, President Senghor of Senegal was at school with Pompidou which has led to excellent Franco-Senegalese relations. The French will be allowed to send in their own men to assist our security operation.

... Just as I was about to take my leave, HIM asked who owned the magnificent Range Rover he'd seen parked in front of the palace. I replied that it belongs to Princess Shahnaz who was there to go skiing with HMQ. 'Astounding', he said in an angry tone. 'That husband of hers doesn't stint on the luxuries, for all his hippy pretensions. A Rolls and a Lamborghini to swan about town in, and now a Range Rover to go skiing.' ...

Over dinner at Princess Ashraf's HIM informed me that for this Saturday's Tehran OPEC conference, he will receive the visiting ministers at 11 a.m. after which they will lunch as his guests. There will be no meeting beforehand. Amouzegar, the Finance Minister, is to attend on our behalf, but I remarked that Fallah and Eqbal hadn't received invitations. 'Fair enough', said HIM; 'Invite them, although Eqbal has no say in these affairs.'

Saturday, 22 December

Audience ... Two days ago HIM instructed Princess Ashraf to accept an invitation to Pakistan, but she's since complained to me that she cannot go there empty-handed. Bhutto is bound to talk about oil and financial aid, in which case what is she to say to him? 'Tell my sister that her trip is no longer necessary', HIM replied with evident satisfaction. 'Now that Bhutto has agreed to postpone the Islamic conference to February, I shall be able to attend in person.' Apparently Bhutto telephoned last night and agreed to the change of date. HIM is clearly delighted, which may mean that Bhutto's other problems will be easily solved ...

HIM subsequently chaired the OPEC meeting, lasting two and a half hours. I took no part, but was afterwards allowed to join them for lunch ... Before the delegates left, HIM delivered a brief address: 'Remember', he said, 'we have decided that there are three possible courses of action, two of which are your suggestions, the third of which is mine. Should I agree to either of your proposals, the responsibility for success or failure will rest with you. If you adopt my formula I am quite prepared to bear the consequences. I shall defend our action before the entire world, confident that my nation will support me.' ... I've no idea what three formulas he was referring to, but doubtless he will let me know ...

The Pakistani ambassador called round and again requested the purchase of 700,000 tons of oil at a favourable price. He strenuously denied that Bhutto has ever spoken of 'the Gulf' rather than 'the Persian Gulf' ...

At dinner, HIM declared his intention to meet the local and foreign media at half past ten tomorrow morning. I asked whether the OPEC meeting had resulted in a joint resolution. He replied that it had not, but that he was keen to spell out his own approach. I did not press him for details; clearly things haven't gone as he expected, and now '*il n'était pas dans son assiette*'.

Sunday, 23 December

Met Dr Fallah early this morning to receive an account of yesterday's negotiations. He spent the afternoon session analysing HIM's position and now wants to distribute a copy of his findings to each of the delegates. The posted price is to rise to $12 a barrel, $7 of which constitutes our income.

Arrived at the Palace to find HIM at breakfast. Passed on Fallah's text. Much as I expected, when I turned up for my audience at ten, HIM waved the document at me, saying, 'Tell Fallah that I want my own statement distributed, not this thing of his.' Nobody is ever allowed to steal HIM's thunder.

... The press conference went superbly. Beforehand, I received a letter from the British ambassador, Peter Ramsbotham, expressing concern over the outcome of the OPEC meeting. Apparently he was moved to write by reports in this morning's newspapers, claiming that OPEC is greatly to increase the posted price of Gulf crude.

I showed the letter to HIM after his meeting with the journalists. He was livid. 'Remind the idiot that his Prime Minister and his cabinet received Fallah in London and agreed my proposals were perfectly fair. I myself told the ambassador a couple of days ago that we expected to receive $8 income for every barrel sold. Yet now we've reduced it to $7 pending a decision on the price of energy sources other than oil. What on earth is all the fuss about? Summon him and give him a dressing down.' I duly gave the poor ambassador a very rough ride. He was dreadfully embarrassed, apologizing over and over again, saying that he had misunderstood HIM's position. Never before have I seen him in such a pitiful state ...

Thursday, 27 December

Confined to bed for the past few days ... HIM flew out this morning. I was too weak to escort him to the airport and had to bid my goodbyes on the telephone ...

His going makes me miserable, not just because I'll miss him, but because he's to be absent at such a critical time. We have reached a political zenith. HIM's leadership is acknowledged throughout this part of the world. Our western allies support us to the hilt and are unlikely to abandon us in future. But the situation on our borders, or within Pakistan and Afghanistan, might easily turn sour. Pakistan is so poor and so much at the mercy of India and the Soviets. Earlier this week, although he knew I was sick in bed, the Pakistani ambassador insisted on coming to see me to lament our asking $12 a barrel. I reminded him that this is still $5 less than the price we're asking elsewhere. He admitted this, but it did nothing to staunch his complaints ...

We're at a critical moment of history, yet HIM goes abroad for two months. Why does he take such risks? Anything might happen. It's not as if the domestic scene were exactly calm. Our people are deeply dissatisfied ... despite every effort of the Shah, and his many achievements ... This was precisely how the Iraqi government collapsed under Nouri Said.[1] He too created an economic miracle and expected it to suffice. But people want more than material progress; they demand justice, social harmony and a voice in political affairs. Why don't we make any effort to meet these demands? I'm apprehensive, gravely apprehensive ...

Sunday, 30 December

Returned to my office after four days' lost work ... The US ambassador handed over an important message from Nixon to HIM.

[The most significant passages in this letter are as follows]

The US government is greatly concerned over the destabilizing impact that the price increases agreed to at Tehran for Persian Gulf crudes will have on the world's economy and the catastrophic problems it could pose for the international monetary system. Not only will it result in raising the prices of manufactured products but it will have severe repressive effect on the economies of oil consumers which could cause a world-wide recession and which eventually would benefit no-one, including oil exporters ...

The US endorses the idea of greater consultation and mutual understanding between oil producers and consumers which was most recently reaffirmed in Secretary Kissinger's initiative to establish an energy action group. We strongly urge that:

(1) the recent decisions made in Tehran be reconsidered;
(2) steps be initiated to hold the kind of consultations that we believe most consumer and producer countries endorse ...

Immediately cabled HIM in Vienna. Drew up a report of my meeting with the ambassador and had it sent by courier. I had told the ambassador how

---

[1] Nouri Said (1888–1958); dominated Iraqi politics in the aftermath of the Second World War. Openly pro-British, he was loathed by Iraqi nationalists. During the military *coup d'état* of July 1958, he was brutally put to death together with Iraq's royal family.

surprised I was that knowing HIM's views he had made no attempt to explain them to Kissinger prior to the OPEC meeting. 'As I recall, HIM granted you an audience', I said, 'in which he would certainly have explained that oil prices can only be set in accordance with the price of alternative energy sources. I know for a fact that HIM made this point to the British ambassador.' He duly admitted that he'd been briefed by HIM. 'In that case', I asked, 'what's your objection? Our approach seems perfectly rational.' He replied that he had no objection and that he had sent a detailed report to Washington. Even so he'd been ordered to submit Nixon's message unaltered.

He then asked whether he might raise a rather impertinent question. I replied that we know one another well enough not to be bashful. 'Well', he said, 'most of the Arab delegates at the conference tell us, Zaki Yamani in particular, that they wanted to fix a lower price and only agreed to the present rise out of respect for HIM. It is I that have the responsibility of preserving good relations between Tehran and Washington. I'm anxious to know the truth of the matter.' I replied that I had been absent from negotiations ... but that one thing was quite certain: after lunch the delegates left HIM. He did not attend the meeting where they resolved on $12 a barrel ... Even so, if the Arabs turn out to be telling the truth, there is nothing for us to be ashamed of. The price resolution was simple common sense ...

1974

In reaction to the steep increase in oil prices, the industrialized nations adopted a common front, establishing the International Energy Agency, and promoting both the conservation of energy and the development of alternative energy sources. Iran, Algeria and Venezuela were identified as the most hawkish oil producers and pressured towards a reduction or at least a stabilization in oil prices. The Shah's response was to advocate parity between increases in the prices of oil and of manufactured goods imported from the western world.

In February the Iranian government announced an ambitious Foreign Aid Programme. But over-production of oil and a slackening demand on the international market forced the programme's reduction before the end of the year.

State education to the age of fourteen, school meals and complete health care were declared free to the consumer. Private schools were to be abolished.

Faced with housing and food shortages caused chiefly by inflation and its own mishandling of the economy, the government attempted to offload the blame on private business, which became the scapegoat for the nation's every ill. Besides the campaign against profiteering and hoarding, new price regulations were introduced and the army employed to enforce them.

With a view to staking a larger claim to the bonanza in oil prices, the US government proposed 'ways to deepen and broaden the already strong ties' existing with Iran (Memorandum from the US ambassador addressed to Alam but intended for the Shah, 13 April 1974). These included the establishment of a Joint Economic Commission at cabinet level to 'address general areas of concern or specific projects'; a most improbably centralized and bureaucratic venture for a nation supposedly pledged to free enterprise. The memorandum also referred to 'cooperation' in the development of Iran's potential for nuclear energy, her petrochemical industry and communications.

In practice this amounted to a suggestion that Iran buy goods and services from US companies without access to competitive offers from America's trading rivals. Alam warned that 'The sort of fixed agreements the Americans propose do not accord with the policy of independence we've pursued to date.' As the Shah put it, 'You're warning me that we mustn't end up an American colony like Saudi Arabia.' (Diaries, 14 April) The Joint Economic Commission was duly established and an impressive list of projects worth tens of billions of dollars submitted for its consideration. But in coming years, with the gradual deterioration of Iran's finances and the relative slump in the oil market, the entire venture was discreetly put aside.

The first signs that things were far from well with the Shah's own health emerged during a trip to Kish Island. Alam records how he was met by Dr Ayadi, the Shah's special physician, who advised that Professor Jean Bernard, the French haematologist, be invited to examine the Shah (Diaries, 9 April). The diagnosis of Waldenstrom's disease − a form of leukaemia − pronounced by a team of French specialists was made known only to Professor Safavian and later to Dr Ayadi, not to the Shah himself. Experienced in treating prominent personalities elsewhere in the world, the French believed that absolute secrecy was essential to prevent others exploiting the Shah's situation. The French medical reports sent to Professor Safavian referred to the Shah merely as 'number two' − 'number one' being Alam, treated by the same doctors for some time past. The Queen was shielded from the truth for the next two years. Alam was never told. The Shah himself was unaware of the exact nature of his illness, though its full seriousness gradually began to dawn on him even before the revolution.

Tuesday, 1 January
The British ambassador called round, despite the New Year holiday. On his government's orders he asked whether they might approach HIM to suggest the oil price increase be implemented in several stages. According to the ambassador there is now genuine concern that doubling the price so soon after the October increase may bring about world-wide recession. What would HIM make of this, he wanted to know? I assured him that HIM has no desire to undermine the industrialized economies, but that we consider the price increases to be natural and unavoidable ... By suggesting we stagger this increase, I told him, he was basically asking us to make sacrifices on behalf of advanced countries such as his own ... I doubt whether HIM would agree to this and in any event it would have to be agreed by every member of OPEC ... The ambassador replied that to his certain knowledge, some producers, Saudi Arabia for example, are already willing to stagger the increase ...

Later met the US ambassador for lunch. I asked whether the British ambassador had approached him to suggest measures to stave off recession. He replied that he had indeed been approached, but was in no position to comment until he'd been advised of Washington's reaction ...

Wednesday, 2 January
Handed HIM's reply to Nixon's message of 30 December 1973 to the US ambassador.

[The Shah's handwritten comments are set down in the margin of Nixon's message:]

First, persuade Venezuela, Nigeria, Indonesia, Libya and Algeria to lower their prices; then we shall sit up and take notice.

[In the margin of Alam's letter of 30 December 1973, reporting his meeting with the US ambassador, the Shah wrote:]

Tell the ambassador, write to him if need be, that the Iraqi delegate said $12 a barrel was too low. Zaki Yamani felt it was too high. Everyone else was in broad agreement with us, although on arriving home the next day the Kuwaiti Oil Minister declared that $12 was too low. We'd have stood out for $12 even if all the Arab delegates had said it was too high.

I asked the US ambassador whether he thought it reasonable to expect half the oil producers to lower their prices. 'Quite honestly, and in confidence, I would have to say that it isn't reasonable', he replied. 'But what else can

Nixon do? Put yourself in his shoes. He's got a serious problem and is doing his best to resolve it.' ...

Shapour Reporter telephoned to report Zaki Yamani's announcement that he originally suggested $6 income a barrel, but gave way to the Shah's demand for $7. He claims that King Faisal reprimanded him for agreeing to the higher price.

Yamani's claims about King Faisal are either exaggerated or a complete pack of lies. No king would act against his interests in that way, to the extent of reprimanding a minister for what is actually a considerable triumph.

Friday, 4 January

... Had an urgent meeting with the Finance Minister whom HIM had sent to brief me on his discussions with the US ambassador ... He told the latter that Zaki Yamani did indeed come out on the side of moderation ... at first suggesting $5.45 a barrel to the producer and only agreeing to $6 under pressure from Kuwait, Abu Dhabi and Iraq. We ended up suggesting $7, and it was accepted as a compromise between radicals and moderates. In effect we limited the posted price to $12 a barrel, when Iraq, Abu Dhabi and Kuwait were all pressing for $14. He also told the ambassador that Saudi Arabia's demand to up her participation from 25 per cent to 51 per cent immediately rather than waiting until 1980, combined with the Kuwaiti demand for 60 per cent participation, means that the oil put at these countries' disposal can be sold on the free market at up to $17 a barrel. On the other hand, Kuwait's proposal to purchase company shares at book price rather than market value will mean a $1 billion loss by the companies to Kuwait. In turn it would automatically be adopted by Iran, Saudi Arabia and Qatar for their new agreements, which would spell a further $3 billion transfer of assets.

Apparently the US ambassador has begun to realize the true implications of the Arab proposals, which has really put the wind up him ...

Monday, 7 January

... Flew to London this morning ...

I haven't seen my daughter Naz for nearly five months. I love her dearly but even so, it was with the greatest reluctance I agreed to fly all the way to London to see her. I'd much prefer to have stayed in Tehran, shuffling through the snow. Normally when I go abroad I notify Tehran of my safe arrival. My wife wanted to know why this time I sent no cable. But the person I used to reassure with these telegrams, the one with whose heart my own beat in unison, lies buried under the snows of Mashad.[1] Those who remain look to me not with love but merely because I occupy a certain rank. For my own part, I can summon up nothing more than courtesy in return ...

London, Tuesday, 8 January

... Arab propagandists in Europe are doing their best to blame price increases on the Shah. They hope to divert criticism from their oil embargo which HIM was so forthright in opposing ...

[No diary survives for the following two months. In March Alam returned to Tehran.]

Tuesday, 5 March

Audience ... HIM in a rotten mood over last night's border clashes with the Iraqis. We were constantly interrupted by phone calls from the Chief of the General Staff, passing on the latest news. HIM issued his orders with admirable sang-froid ... a true professional at work ...

Wednesday, 6 March

Audience. Yesterday our soldiers gave the Iraqis a thrashing and it's greatly improved HIM's temper. I told him that I'd heard on the radio that the Western Europeans have agreed to bilateral agreements with the oil producers. This spells the undoing of the recent Washington conference, despite all the publicity hype that accompanied it. 'Quite so', HIM said; 'I'm not exactly mourning their failure. These blasted Americans, especially our dear friend Mr Kissinger, must give up pretending that whatever they say has the authority of holy writ.'

He then referred to various articles in the *New York Times*, the *Washington Post* and the *Daily Star* which congratulate HIM on his proposals to assist the Third World. 'McNamara had a hand in this', he said; 'He's a left-wing Democrat through and through.'

He instructed me to inform the Foreign Ministry that they must allow no one to intervene in their activities save HIM. 'I've even forbidden

[1] Alam refers here to his mother who had died the previous year.

Hoveyda's brother, our representative at the UN, to report directly to the PM.' ...

Later I received a large number of Kurdish tribal chiefs. Their morale seems excellent.

... At dinner the chief topic was our defeat of the Iraqis. They've lost fifty men killed in action and a wide variety of weapons including two armoured trucks ...

Thursday, 7 March
Accompanied HIM to the airport where we bid farewell to Sultan Qabus of Oman ... HIM still over the moon, since the Iraqis this morning sued for an end to border skirmishes, so badly have they been beaten. The Soviet ambassador was also at the airport and spent a short while alone with HIM, apparently offering to act as go-between with Iraq. Likewise Davoud Khan of Afghanistan has cabled us, soliciting a role as mediator ...

HIM received the Soviet ambassador again at 7 this evening. Meanwhile I had a meeting with the ambassador of Pakistan. He did his best to smooth things over in respect to Bhutto who realizes he can count on no one except HIM. He also knows our loathing for Qadhafi, and that by inviting him to the Islamic Conference in Lahore, he ruled out any possibility of HIM being able to attend. Worse than that, he has actually gone ahead and signed military, political and economic agreements and a full-blooded friendship treaty with Libya. Of course he's come to regret this folly, but much too late in the day as far as we're concerned. At one stage it was Bhutto who was so insistent that HIM visit Pakistan. Now he begs to be received by us here. HIM quite rightly has turned him down ...

Friday, 8 March
Audience ... Discussed the unrest in the universities. 'It puzzles me', HIM declared. 'Most of our problems are behind us and our soldiers have shown they can fight like lions. Yet still we're plagued by the fuss generated by a tiny minority of students.' 'Some of them are keen to become martyrs', I said, 'and others draw unfavourable comparisons between our political system and that of the European democracies.' 'But what has democracy ever done for Europe?', he retorted ... adding, 'Many of these subversives are in the pay of foreign powers.' I pointed out that they were bound to appear so if we maintain that with so much material progress people are not entitled to express any sort of complaint. On the other hand, if we

honestly admitted that our regime has its shortcomings, then we'd learn to regard these so-called subversives in a very different light. 'Tell the President of Tehran University that I expect his students to display their dedication to this country. The same goes for our students everywhere', he replied.

A few Iranian students have occupied our embassies in Stockholm, Brussels and The Hague and are demanding greater political freedom here in Iran. Thanks to the BBC, the incident has been blown up out of all proportion. Ridiculous! ...

Saturday, 9 March

A further meeting with the Pakistani ambassador. He's utterly distraught about recent events and pleaded for Bhutto to be received by HIM. Reported this at my audience. 'I suppose I can't put it off forever', HIM said. 'Find a suitable date for his visit.' I suggested that he might be invited to Kish Island – he'd doubtless be flattered to be offered admission to HIM's inner circle. HIM thought for a while before replying that in that case Bhutto should come here to Tehran before we set out for Kish.

... HIM instructed me to pay $10,000 a month as a subsidy to the King of .... At the same time the monthly subsidy we're paying the King of Afghanistan is to be increased from $10,000 to $11,000 to cover his children's school fees; we are also to buy him a house in Rome. All these expenses are to be met from the government's secret funds, but even so HIM insists that the government be provided with detailed accounts of how the money is spent ...

Monday, 11 March

... Attended Lunch. Sheikh Mohammad bin Mubarak, the Foreign Minister of Bahrain, was there. An intelligent young man blessed with fluent English ... We discussed America's insistence that oil prices remain as low as possible. 'Washington relies on Zaki Yamani', said HIM. 'But not even a hundred Yamanis could interrupt the flow of events.' Towards the end of the meal someone mentioned the special relations which exist between us and Bahrain, remarking how smoothly the whole issue had been settled. Normally I keep silent on such occasions, but today I had to make our guest appreciate the great sacrifices we suffered in order to achieve the Bahrain settlement. 'No mere politician, certainly no demagogue', I said, 'would have dared to take the path we chose. Such audacity is reserved for men of the calibre of De Gaulle or HIM.' HIM's reply to this was characteristically impressive: 'I am free to take such decisions solely because of the bonds of mutual trust binding me to my nation.'

Tuesday, 12 March
Audience ... Passed on the text of HIM's interview with the *Sunday Times*. He approved it for publication in the local press. He also read through his transcript interviews with the US networks, NBC and CBS. The first was excellent, but the CBS interview left him in a very poor temper.[1]

... Ardeshir Zahedi has cabled to say that Kissinger may have to postpone his visit here, from the Iranian New Year to some time around 28 April. He also says that, following Simon's published remarks, Nixon has issued an apology via Kissinger. I phoned the news through to HIM who agreed to the change in schedule ...

Friday, 22 March–Wednesday, 3 April
For the past fortnight we have been on our traditional jaunt to Kish. HIM rode or swam every day. Perfect weather ...

I remarked to him that every one of his dreams seems to have come true. It's almost unbelievable, but our oil income has rocketed from $2 billion to $16 billion; heavy rainfall suggests a bumper harvest, and HIM is now unrivalled amongst Middle Eastern statesmen. 'But I have so many more aspirations', he replied. 'To be first in the Middle East is not enough. We must raise ourselves to the level of a great world power. Such a goal is by no means unattainable.' ...

At long last he agreed that Bhutto might come to pay his respects to him on Kish ... Things went well, HIM seeming quite happy with their discussions.

[During this period the Shah received an important letter from President Nixon]

Your Imperial Majesty,
I'm writing in relation to the public statement made recently by the administrator of our Federal Energy Office, Mr Simon, following the

---

[1] In his CBS interview the Shah had pointed out that the USA was presently receiving more oil than it had done prior to the date of the so-called embargo set by Arab producers. Asked for his reaction, the administrator of the Federal Energy Office, William Simon, dismissed the Shah's remarks as irresponsible nonsense.

televising here of your own comments regarding the effect of the Arab embargo on US oil imports.

I want to say to you quite directly that there were no excuses for Mr Simon's rhetoric, and you have our apology. As I indicated in my press conference, I dissociate myself and my government from his remarks.

. . .

I want to emphasize once again that, as I believe you know, I continue to attach the highest priority to the warm and cooperative relations that exist between our two countries, and to the strong bond of friendship that has characterized our personal relations . . .

Thursday, 4 April
Audience. Discussed the death of President Pompidou. The man knew he was stricken with cancer, yet he carried on with his official duties right up to the end . . . His courage has awed the world. I asked HIM whether he would attend the funeral. Nixon, Brezhnev and most European heads of state are to be there. 'I've thought long and hard about it', he said. 'The fact is that we were never very close. It would be a nuisance if it set a precedent and I had to attend the funeral of every head of state. It was a different matter with De Gaulle and Eisenhower. They were of a far higher calibre; men I knew well.' I pointed out that HIM is now a statesman of international reputation and as such he must not let his actions be guided by personal likes and dislikes. 'Quite so', he replied. 'HMQ offered to represent me but I'm sure it will be quite acceptable if Prince Gholam Reza goes in my stead.' I questioned whether the Prince enjoys sufficient standing; at the very least HIM should be represented by Prince Abdul Reza or the PM. He disagreed: 'Gholam Reza will do well enough. It's not as if he were expected to make a speech or take part in discussions.' . . .

Sunday, 7 April
Audience. Passed on a letter from Sultan Qabus of Oman who is anxious that we send him military instructors as soon as possible. Reported that Savak have impounded the libraries of several student unions within Tehran University. They claim that all the books are subversive. 'No book can be deemed subversive at a university', I said. 'In any event, Your Majesty left specific instructions that students should be free to read whatever they like, to study a problem from every possible angle.' 'Make sure that the books are returned', he replied, 'and tell the parties responsible that such stupidity will not go unpunished in future'.

... Flew with HIM to Kish this afternoon. For once I have brought no companion with me ...

Monday, 8 April

Flew to Bandar Abbas. There we boarded a US Navy helicopter and were taken to the US aircraft carrier *Kitty Hawk*, currently stationed in the Sea of Oman. A fascinating excursion. I'm particularly impressed by the discipline of the American sailors; quite a contrast to the hippyfied lifestyle of other young Americans ...

The task force mounted a magnificent series of exercises; incredible fire-power.

Lunched with the US Navy Chief of Staff, their ambassador and the task force commander. HIM displayed his knowledge of every subject, military affairs, politics, economics. Someone mentioned the naval base on Diego Garcia, which the British have recently handed over to the USA. The Americans are pleased that Congress has approved funds to develop the site. I remarked that we must still wait and see what approach the new Labour government in Britain will adopt, but according to the US Chief of Staff there seems little likelihood that they'll raise any objection. HIM joined in at this point to say that traditionally Labour governments in Britain have been closer to the USA than the Conservatives; a remark which won full agreement from the US ambassador, for many years head of the CIA. 'Even so', said the ambassador, 'I'm at a loss to know why this should be so.' 'But it's obvious', said HIM. 'They rely on the Americans to shoulder the burden of defence so that they can divert their own resources to education and social development!' – an analysis which earned general admiration.

Flying over Qeshm Island on our way back, I joined HIM in the cockpit – he was piloting his own Jet Star. 'I can read your mind', I said. 'Your Majesty is imagining what it will be like when we've harnessed the island's gas deposits and established a vast local steel industry ... You're thinking too, what we might do with the finished steel, and where we might build a desalination plant to supply fresh water.' He agreed that this was exactly what was on his mind. 'But I was also wondering', he said, 'whether we should acquire aircraft carriers. It might be a waste of money. At the moment we aren't involved in ocean warfare, and even without the planes, the cost would be something approaching $1.5 billion. As things stand we can build as many air bases as we like along the coast of the Persian Gulf ...

I wonder what I should make of today's visit. On the one hand HIM is emphatic that the great powers should withdraw from the Gulf and the Sea of Oman. At the same time, it's no bad thing that our allies can still put on a show like today's, given that the Iraqis are receiving so much assistance from Moscow, regularly opening their harbours to Soviet shipping ...

Tuesday, 9 April
Left my official residence on Kish this morning and drove to meet HIM, expecting to find him in high good spirits; he enjoyed the time of his life yesterday afternoon and last night. Instead I was met by his special physician emerging from HIM's apartment. The man took me aside to advise me that we must send for Professor Jean Bernard, the French haematologist, to come and examine HIM. I asked him why, but he would give me no details, merely repeating that Bernard must be sent for urgently. It was as if my whole world had crumbled about me; so upset was I that I even forgot to leave a tip for the servants on the island. When HIM eventually came down he seemed to be perfectly fit and I could not bring myself to ask him what was the matter. Yet in the car to the airport he only heightened my anxiety, asking what was being done about the other two hotels to be built on Kish. 'They must hurry up. I want them finished in my own lifetime.'

I was in a dreadful state, wondering what sort of disease can show up so suddenly. On the plane I could think of nothing but what will happen to this country shorn of its leader ... Had the Shah not been on board I truly believe I'd have preferred the plane to crash; at least in that way I'd have been spared such agonizing thoughts ...

Wednesday, 10 April
Audience. I immediately asked after HIM's health, explaining that yesterday I telephoned Paris only to find that Jean Bernard is to be away for the whole of this week. HIM replied that there was some doubt over his spleen; it was swollen and he's keen to establish that there's been no change to his circulation. At this I heaved a sigh of relief. I suggested that since it's merely a question of a check-up, he might consent to an examination by Professor Milliez – a specialist in internal problems, who treats me and is currently in Tehran. HIM rejected the idea since he already has an annual check-up with Professor Fellinger of Vienna and believes it wrong to solicit too many different opinions. None the less he agreed that we

can afford to wait another week until Professor Jean Bernard is free to see him ...

Met the new British ambassador Sir Anthony Parsons after lunch ... He's actually a very wise man and has seen service in every country of the Middle East save Saudi Arabia ... It was a pleasure to talk to him ...

Saturday, 13 April

... Received a letter from the US ambassador. On behalf of his administration and Kissinger, he proposes to broaden US–Iranian co-operation along similar lines to those agreed between the Americans and Saudi Arabia[1] ...

At dinner HIM reminisced about his childhood. Apparently Dr Nafici, his tutor, never allowed him to go skiing or swimming when they were in Switzerland. He thinks as a result he may have grown up with some sort of complex. In my opinion the Shah has no complexes whatsoever, save perhaps an occasional liking for flattery. We Iranians are so accustomed to sycophants that we've a tendency to be pleased whatever lies they may tell us.

Sunday, 14 April

Audience. The US ambassador's letter formed the chief topic for discussion. HIM instructed me to prepare a reply and to summon the ambassador to an audience next Tuesday. I felt duty bound to warn him that the sort of fixed agreement the Americans propose does not accord with the policy of independence we've pursued to date. The USA relies on us, and HIM has quite understandably co-operated with them; what need have we of formal agreements? We must maintain a balance in our foreign policy. 'In other words', HIM retorted, 'you're warning me that we mustn't end up an American colony like Saudi Arabia. I've thought through every aspect of the problem and shall do no more than reinforce our present level of co-operation with Washington.' ...

Monday, 15 April

... Once again I drew his attention to the scarcity of basic commodities, the high price of sugar for example. I'm surprised he still has nothing to say on the matter ...

Chaired a board meeting of the governors of the Rural Cultural Centres.

[1] See introductory note 1974.

To my chagrin, it was announced that so far only 1 per cent of our villages have been supplied with clean, piped drinking water. Though the problem is not as serious as it might appear, since most of the others can draw clean water from their wells or *qanats*.[1] Far more shameful is the fact that only one in twenty-five villages has electricity, a ludicrous figure given the rate of national development. I must alert HIM.

Audience. Following the buy-out of company shares by Qatar and Kuwait, both of whom now control over 50 per cent of their own oil production, Iran's income is bound to rise by some $4 billion.[2] In other words we are looking to a net income of $22 billion for the present financial year. HIM agreed with this analysis. 'We have the money', he said. 'Now we must use it to fashion "The Great Civilization".'

I suggested that we increase the allowance of Princess Esmat, the last wife of Reza Shah.[3] 'Very well', said HIM. '..., but I can't ignore the fact that the cost of living has risen by 12 per cent in the past year'. Rather audaciously I butted in to say that he had been misinformed: the real figure is something in excess of 20 per cent. 'Nonsense', he replied. 'It's you, not me, that's been misled.' ...

Tuesday, 23 April

... Audience. Passed on a letter from our ambassador in Rabat.

[In his report, dated 18 April, 1974, the ambassador describes an interview with Prince Moulay Abdullah. The latter confided that his brother, King Hassan, suspected him of being in cahoots with the Shah and King Faisal in a plot against the throne. The Prince confessed that there might well be a coup in the making, led by Colonel Delimi, Morocco's Chief of Intelligence.]

Met the Lebanese ambassador and discussed the position of Lebanon's Shi'as. I told him that our mutual friend, Mousa Sadr,[4] has put up a most

---

[1] An ancient system for raising water, relying upon the power of gravity and a system of underground canals.

[2] See introductory note 1974.

[3] Reza Shah's first wife died when he was still a young army officer. His second wife, who became Queen, was the mother of the Shah. Later Reza Shah married, successively, two Qajar princesses; one was the mother of Prince Gholam Reza and the other – Esmat – the mother of the Shah's half-brothers Abdul Reza, Mahmoud Reza, Ahmad Reza, Hamid Reza and his half-sister Fatemeh.

[4] An Iranian clergyman who became the most influential Shi'a leader in Lebanon and in the 1970s was appointed as President of the Lebanese Shi'a Council. He disappeared in mysterious circumstances, during a trip to Libya in August 1978.

disappointing performance; he takes money from whoever will give it to him, Iraq, Egypt, Morocco or even Libya. The ambassador warned us against abandoning the Lebanese Shi'as merely because of Sadr's misdeeds. Valid argument though this may be, I doubt it will persuade HIM to maintain support.

Later met the Israeli representative. He feels there's recently been a cooling of relations between our two countries ...

Wednesday, 24 April

Audience. HIM is adamant that we cannot support the Lebanese Shi'as so long as Mousa Sadr remains in place. He has instructed our ambassador in Beirut to offer Sadr one last chance to prove his reliability.[1]

HIM denied any hitch in relations with Israel. 'If we're backing the Arabs it is only because their claims are valid', he said. 'We could hardly act otherwise. Indeed we did precisely the same thing after the war of 1967.'

The US ambassador informed me that, contrary to expectation, Kissinger has no intention of visiting Iran. I suggested this implies he is in a sulk about something. 'To hell with Kissinger', HIM said. 'Pay him no attention, and tell Ardeshir Zahedi that he's to avoid offering any sort of invitation or giving any hint that we're expecting a visit.'

Discussed the Crown Prince who is due to visit England this summer. Once again I suggested it is wrong to allow him to be constantly surrounded by women. There are so many of them: HMQ, Mrs Diba his grandmother, the governess Mademoiselle Joelle, and a whole host of schoolmistresses. 'As I have several times hinted to Your Majesty', I said, 'the boy needs a tough tutor, a military man.' HIM replied that he was still considering the matter and that meanwhile we might find the Prince a girl friend or two. I pointed out that he's probably too young to take any interest in such matters. 'Not at all', HIM retorted. 'At his age I had a thorough understanding; I was head over heels in love with Iran Teymourtash.'[2]

... The British ambassador called round and we discussed our economic relations, the military, and the present state of Middle Eastern politics. Referring to the Crown Prince, he said that should we require the services of an English teacher, his own daughter, a girl of eighteen, would be willing

---

[1] Sadr was asked to refrain from further contacts with countries unfriendly towards Iran.
[2] Daughter of A. Teymourtash (1882–1933), who as Court Minister was the second most powerful man in Iran after Reza Shah. He was subsequently arrested and put to death. His daughter, Iran, became a journalist, serving as press attaché at the Iranian embassy in Paris during the 1950s.

to take on the task. He assured me that she's neither a hippy nor a communist. I didn't dare ask whether she's good looking, but promised to give the matter due consideration ...

Friday, 26 April

... Audience. For a while we talked about modern youth and the university disturbances. I remarked that the unrest has many causes; natural youthful rebelliousness, lack of dialogue with the students, the ineptitude of the university authorities, and last but by no means least, the pitiful performance of our propaganda agencies. It's almost as if by heaping ridiculous flattery on HIM they were setting out to obscure his real achievements ...

Wednesday, 8 May

... In the evening HIM entertained President Amin of Uganda who has made a sudden decision to fly from Jeddah to Tehran to offer his services as mediator between Iran and Iraq.[1] He's quite a character, a former sergeant in the British army and an avid boxer. He's had himself promoted Field Marshal and issues endless preposterous statements and communiqués. Recently he cabled Nixon suggesting that he be invited to the USA, to explain to the American nation that the President is innocent of any involvement in Watergate ...

Tuesday, 14 May

Houshang Ansari, the new Finance Minister,[2] rang at midnight to tell me that the Arab oil producers have accepted HIM's proposal to deposit part of their income with the International Monetary Fund ... although they've accepted an interest rate of 7 per cent on the money, as opposed to the 8 per cent we recommended. Unless we too agree to the lower rate, HIM's whole initiative will have been in vain. Ansari had been asked by the Arabs to reply within the hour. Reluctantly, I roused HIM who has been feeling rather under the weather. He agreed to the altered rate.

[1] Although totally unexpected, Amin's intervention was received with courtesy. Overwhelmed by the gracious manners of the Shah, who described to him the origins of the dispute, he apparently forgot the purpose of his self-appointed mission, advising the Shah to finish with the Iraqis once and for all!

[2] He succeeded Jamshid Amouzegar who was appointed Minister of the Interior whilst remaining Iranian representative to OPEC ministerial meetings (see the introduction on the Shah).

Wednesday, 15 May
Audience. Discussing the French presidential elections, I expressed my conviction that Valéry Giscard d'Estaing will come out on top, but HIM disagreed, saying that it's too early to tell and that this morning's edition of *Le Monde* was firmly in favour of François Mitterrand ... He remarked how uneasy he is about the present state of Western Europe; only Germany and Britain inspire any confidence, since they alone have maintained some sort of respect for tradition. Meanwhile the USA remains the only fulcrum for the free world ...

Thursday, 16 May
Audience. HIM has been troubled by a skin rash for the past two days and is not in the best of health ...

Reported that Mrs Diba intends to visit Shiraz. I have left instructions that she is to be accommodated in the governor's guest house, not at the Eram Palace. 'Quite right', HIM said. 'Royal palaces are not to be treated like hotels, though I doubt my mother-in-law will appreciate your arrangements.' ...

Ardeshir Zahedi recently cabled us to recommend we organize a very warm welcome for a visiting US congressman, a Democrat whose party Ardeshir claims is bound to win the next presidential elections. HIM's reply was to question whether a member of our own Majlis could ever expect such a welcome from the White House. In other words, are we expected to behave like yet another American colony? Ardeshir was clearly embarrassed by this, since much to HIM's amusement he's now cabled seeking to justify his actions ...

After lunch I called round on Princess Belqis and Prince Mahmoud, children of the King of Afghanistan, staying in Shahdasht as our guests ... I passed on HIM's reply to the letter sent by their father and asked Prince Mahmoud to convey to the King how anxious we are that he should maintain contact with his former kingdom and not abandon hope of a restoration; who knows what the future might have in store for him?

We dined at Majid A'alam's. I told HIM of a telephone call I'd received from Ayatollah Milani of Mashad, who informed me that Ayatollah Khoyi,[1] presently living in Iraq, is suffering harassment from the Ba'athist regime

---

[1] The most prominent Shi'ite cleric in Iraq. Born and raised in Iran, but for many years lived and taught in the holy city of Najaf, in Iraq. At the start of the revolution he showed a relative degree of sympathy towards the monarchy, by receiving Queen Farah and her children – most probably because of his opposition to Khomeini's political ideas.

and has made discreet enquiries whether he might seek refuge in Iran. 'By all means, let him come', said HIM. 'We'll let bygones be bygones and make no demands of him.' ... Subsequently he told me that Bhutto is due to pay us a brief visit tomorrow, for which I should make all the necessary arrangements.

Friday, 17 May

Bhutto's arrival put paid to the Friday day of rest. He was accompanied by his Ministers of Defence and Foreign Affairs. I lunched with them whilst Bhutto ate alone with HIM. I'm sure they've come here to rattle their begging bowl again.

After his meal I escorted Bhutto to the airport, where he confided an account of his audience and asked that I do my best to follow up his requests with HIM. Apparently, he stressed the special relationship his country enjoys with Iran, declaring that he quite understands our need for closer links to India. In the long run these would be to everybody's advantage, but we cannot expect the Pakistani public to understand; they require some demonstration of Iran's continuing support (an obvious bid for more money) ... 'I may have accepted a military agreement with Libya', he added, 'but I did so only because the military told me that we need to procure arms from whoever will supply them, the devil himself if needs be. Even so, I've warned them to accept economic aid from no one save Iran. During my time in Kish I was promised $1.2 billion over the next three years, but HIM has since agreed to only $450 million. I'm now asking him to loan at least $300 million in the first year, followed by loans of $200 million for the second and third years.' ... As he boarded the plane, he remarked that HIM has promised to send a reply within the next two days and asked that I try to ensure this promise is kept.

Later this evening the Pakistani Minister of Foreign Affairs called on me to suggest that the credit terms we've offered are remarkably tough – a loan over seven years, with a two-year grace period before repayment, interest set at 2.5 per cent. He claims that virtually everyone else, Britain, the USA and even the Australians, have offered more favourable arrangements, and he asked me that I draw the fact to HIM's attention without making it seem like yet another Pakistani request.

... This morning, chatting with HIM before Bhutto's arrival, I was confirmed in my impression that Hoveyda enjoys a far stronger position ... I'm afraid we shall have to put up with him for many years to come, though goodness knows what the secret of his survival may be. Pray God that if Hoveyda remains Prime Minister he damages neither HIM nor the foundations of our regime. I can hold out little hope in this respect. If only I knew how to voice my misgivings to the Shah ...

Saturday, 18 May

The PM was granted an audience of about ten minutes before I myself was received. HIM opened our conversation by demanding that I tell Ameri that his statement in the opposition party paper calling for a premium to be paid to teachers is nothing short of scandalous. 'It's downright sabotage', HIM said. 'Is he deliberately trying to stir them up? ... Tell him if he carries on spouting this sort of seditious nonsense he can expect to be punished.' Clearly the PM had worked HIM up to a pitch of indignation.

The Government is drafting legislation which will make businessmen convicted of overcharging liable to every punishment up to and including the death sentence. I suggested it's unseemly for HIM to make virtually every crime a capital offence. 'We're doing no more than the Soviets', he replied. But I pointed out this was irrelevant. He then attempted to justify the move on the grounds that it's intended merely as a deterrent. I was unconvinced, and repeated that it's too draconian and will dent our reputation abroad. I also suggested we devise some sort of protection for the relations of executed drug smugglers; innocent families must not be punished. He gave his approval and instructed me to discuss the matter with HMQ ...

Later this evening I had a meeting with former US Vice-President Agnew. He was extremely bitter about Nixon who he believes made him a scapegoat, leaving him to bear the blame for Watergate. He also criticized the Jewish lobby in the USA who he says engineered the entire Watergate affair as a means of weakening Nixon and preventing him switching support to the Arabs. All in all, he had a great deal to say about the secret Jewish influence within the Washington administration. He strikes me as rather forlorn; he's been in Tehran for the past two days and has made every effort to contact me, but this was the first free time I had to see him ...

Monday, 20 May

Audience ... About six months ago the President of Finland wrote, recommending somebody to HIM who was subsequently granted an audience. However the President's letter has since gone unanswered, lying unnoticed on HIM's desk. 'What do you suggest I do?', HIM asked. I replied that it was too late to send a reply. To tease him I added that I'd sack any member of my own staff found guilty of such negligence. He took the joke in good part.

... Today the Crown Prince took his first solo flight, though we issued a statement that in the national interest he will always be accompanied in future. Once again I remarked to HIM that the boy should be more cautious. 'Never fear', he replied; 'He's calm and self confident. He knows what he's up to.' ...

Wednesday, 22 May
Audience ... Asked HIM whether it was true that he's forbidden any publicity about yesterday's flight by the Crown Prince. If so, what should I do with the letter of congratulations which I'd prepared? 'Send it', he replied. 'Send it. It's the Prince himself who wants to avoid the limelight. Ask those bastards in the media whether they really believe my son's achievements merit less attention than a knife fight between a pair of hooligans. I'm reluctant to try to influence the press, but really they should be ashamed of their priorities.' ...

Fereidoun Hoveyda, our ambassador to the UN, has told us in confidence that Kurt Waldheim, the UN Secretary-General, intends to offer HMQ the post of patron to an international relief campaign for Africa. She summoned me after lunch and told me how upset she is that Princess Ashraf has already made a pronouncement on Africa's needs. I explained that the Princess's remarks bear no relation to the UN scheme; they were made off the cuff, to a gathering of advertising executives. We then agreed to issue a statement on the UN proposal. However when I reported this to HIM he quite rightly pointed out we are in no position to issue a public statement until Waldheim has actually made his approach. In other words I'd entirely wasted the past two hours ...

Friday, 24 May
... Asked the West German ambassador what sort of send-off he'd like organized to mark the end of his assignment to Tehran. He suggested a few hours on horseback, so this afternoon I took him and his four children out riding ...

Tomorrow HIM and I are to fly to Mashad for the day. On such occasions I'm expected to pass the flight reporting on all manner of current affairs. I must spend tonight arranging this as best I can. From past experience I know that I stand a better chance of obtaining HIM's approval for whatever proposals I raise if they're put to him in a particular order. If I leave in too many details, he tends to get side-tracked and decisions are postponed. He's only human, and it's natural that he grows tired of problems. One must sugar the pill and feed him more enticing morsels in between the serious items. Two things relax him; reports of successful national achievements, and the intimate letters which I alone am given to pass on to him. Hence such matters form the twin poles around which I organize my file.

Monday, 27 May
Audience ... Reported that Ameri, head of the Mardom party, has requested an audience. 'He's an idiot', said HIM; 'Sounding off about what he calls the government's anti-revolutionary tendency. Tell him to go to hell.' ... Speaking of governments and oppositions, I described how Edward Heath had been received in China. He's no longer Prime Minister, merely leader of the opposition ... but according to the BBC, the Chinese lack any understanding of official opposition and can only refer to him as ex-Prime Minister. HIM smiled dutifully at this, although I could tell he was far from amused ...

Tuesday, 28 May
Audience, later than usual as HIM had gone to observe test firings by our new Maverick missiles. He returned in a filthy temper, presumably disappointed with the target practice ... Nothing I said could cheer him up, until I passed on one of the *billets doux* that's arrived for him ...

Remarked that the Crown Prince would be unwise to fly to Kermanshah this Friday in a Bonanza light aircraft. HIM replied that there would be an experienced pilot on board, but I questioned what use experience would be in face of the high mountains that block their path. 'I know what I'm talking about', he replied; 'You don't. What's more it's my son, not yours that we're discussing. I've given him permission and I cannot go back on my word.' ...

The soaring cost of newsprint has forced *Ettela'at* and *Kayhan*, the principal evening papers, to double their cover price. Yesterday I met the papers' two chairmen who complained that circulation is falling and that HIM should adopt a practice, common abroad, whereby the government subsidizes their production. This would permit them to re-establish their former price, and at the same time HIM could take credit for the reduction. 'Well, well', HIM remarked. 'So these gentlemen are out to bribe me. Why on earth should we imitate what's done abroad? ... They must cope as best they can with the price increases. Sooner or later people will accept them.' ...

Mr Robert Mellish lunched as my guest. He's the British government's chief whip in the House of Commons; a pleasant man with an unmistakable Cockney accent. He'd just been granted an audience, and was greatly impressed by HIM, saying how much he wished Western Europe possessed a leader of comparable stature ...

Saturday, 1 June

Audience ... Passed on a cable from Ardeshir Zahedi, reporting an article in the *Washington Post* and setting out a range of opinions on Iran canvassed from prominent American personalities. 'Ask him why he pays so much attention to what's written in the press', said HIM. 'Whether they're for or against us, it makes not a blind bit of difference to our conduct of policy. Who do you suppose brought Iran to its current state of grandeur: foreign journalists or myself?'

Nixon intends to make a tour of the Middle East and has asked whether HIM wishes him to include Iran in his itinerary. 'By no means', HIM replied. 'His present trip has nothing to do with us, though of course I'll be happy to receive him if he particularly wishes it. All in all the Americans have been behaving with admirable tact towards us and there really is very little for us to discuss.' For myself, I assume that HIM's reluctance to issue an invitation stems from Nixon's deteriorating position at home ...

Sunday, 2 June

Audience ... Submitted an outline of Their Majesties' forthcoming trip to France. HIM crossed out various of the names of those I'd suggested for his retinue, including that of my assistant Amir Mottaqi. Presumably Mottaqi is out of favour with HMQ, or else he's been the victim of some sort of plot by somebody at Court ... I pointed out what an asset he would be, given that he knows virtually everyone of note within the French government and media. 'Redundant skills, I'm afraid', HIM replied. 'I'm now sufficiently important in the world to be assured excellent coverage in France just as everywhere else.' I made no attempt to respond to this ...

Monday, 3 June

Audience. The Crown Prince has left instructions that his training aircraft be kept on permanent stand-by at the hangar so that he may fly it whenever he wishes. 'He can do as he likes with it', said HIM. 'There's no reason why the army or whoever shouldn't make use of it when he's not there.'

Reported the bread shortages in the city; all the more scandalous because there are at least a million tons of wheat left stored in silos across the country . . . Precisely the same thing happened last month with sugar. What an example of administrative incompetence . . . Last night I was telephoned by a couple of palace guardsmen who'd been unable to buy bread to feed their families. As I said to HIM, 'How can we expect people to go without bread when we're busy telling them that we're in the midst of a golden age?' HIM seemed thoroughly taken aback and ordered me to set up a committee to look into the matter . . .

Tuesday, 4 June

Audience. Asked after HIM's health as he seemed rather under the weather. 'I'm as well as can be expected', he said. 'But tell me this; why do the people I allow access to me grow so puffed up and self-important? Despite all he's got up to in the past, Amir Houshang Davallou has asked to accompany me to France. Doesn't he realize the harm it might do me? Apart from anything else, HMQ would be down on me like a shot. Yet nobody gives a damn for my feelings, merely for what they can get out of me. Tell Davallou that his request has been refused. To justify himself, he told me he sent a bouquet to Giscard d'Estaing to congratulate him after the election. Who the hell does he think he is to send flowers to the President of France?'

King Hussein has written to HIM asking for some of our F-5s as a free gift – the US ambassador warned me about it yesterday. 'Give him what he asks for', said HIM. 'We can't expect the poor man to pay for his planes; and anyway, who else would want to buy them?'

Wednesday, 5 June

. . . This afternoon met the Afghan ambassador who showed me a letter from Davoud Khan . . . Davoud expressed his satisfaction with the way I denied rumours that Princess Belqis had been seen in Tehran . . . But I never made such a denial, indeed as I said to the ambassador, she came here asking news of her husband. Following assurances from the ambassador, HIM told her she had nothing to fear about his safety. The ambassador was disconcerted by my bluntness, explaining that he'd made his false report to Kabul for the sake of good relations between us and Davoud. I then asked whether his government was in contact with the exiled King. He replied that they pay him a monthly pension of $7,000, $2,000 to the Queen and $1,000 to each of their children. On the other hand they've rejected a demand to pay compensation for the monarchy's confiscated property.

He then turned to Davoud's forthcoming trip to Moscow. Apparently the Soviets will be assured of Afghanistan's friendship but at the same time warned to steer clear of intervention in her internal affairs. He believes that Davoud will get his way, stressing what an important development this would be. As for the Afghan communists, he was full of scorn, claiming that Davoud will purge every one of them as soon as he returns from Moscow ... I told him I wished Davoud every success, and asked how things stood with the army. He remarked that control of the army is of critical significance but avoided any clear reply ...

Sunday, 9 June

Presentation of credentials by the new West German ambassador. As usual I was passed a copy of his speech a couple of days ago. It concentrated on Germany's willingness to exchange technological know-how for Iranian goods and services, making great play of the continuity in such relations between past, present and future. I did my best to warn him that HIM likes a major distinction to be drawn between Iran in the past and the country as it stands today. I was sure the man had heeded my advice, but in fact he delivered his speech more or less unaltered. HIM took him to task in no uncertain terms, replying that German technology is no longer of much interest to us; if Germany wishes to carry on good relations with Iran her best bet would be to learn to keep her place. It's unprecedented for a ceremonial speech to provoke such a reaction, but I was genuinely proud of the Shah. The ambassador can't say I didn't warn him, but all the same he may be fool enough to blame me for what transpired.

... Attended a reception for foreign diplomats at the Niavaran Palace ... At table I was sat next to HMQ, opposite HIM. I remarked that Dr Fereidoun Mahdavi, the Minister of Commerce, has returned from Italy. He found the whole country in deep economic and political crisis, everybody praying that God will grant them a leader of HIM's stature. 'I suppose I might rent them my services for a while', HIM commented. HMQ joined in at this point, saying that for all the progress we've made, people remain dissatisfied; above all by commodity shortages and bureaucratic mismanagement. I was forced to agree with her, but could tell how displeased this made HIM ...

Monday, 10 June

Early this morning I met Houshang Ansari, Minister of Finance. We discussed the various economic and administrative problems that confront us. For example, is it right that Amouzegar should continue to be in charge of oil and relations with OPEC now that he's been made Minister of the Interior? He's talented, but no one can discharge so many responsibilities unaided. I can't understand why HIM knocks affairs off course by making such deliberately perverse appointments ...

Audience. Discussed Nixon's Middle Eastern tour. HIM was surprised that he should choose to spend a full three days in Saudi Arabia. I suggested that this might be one way of diverting attention from Watergate, and that he may also have some idea of pressuring the Saudis into reducing oil prices. Kissinger has made his own intentions in this respect quite plain. HIM doubts whether Nixon can get his way and once again remarked how peculiar it was for an American President to devote so much time to Saudi Arabia ...

I got the impression that he was anxious. To lighten the mood I passed on some of the letters he so enjoys reading and we chatted about his favourite private subject ...

Subsequently I escorted HMQ to the airport to welcome the Queen of Jordan, invited here as HMQ's personal guest to observe the measures we're undertaking in social welfare ...

Wednesday, 12 June

Audience ... Once again Princess Ashraf is making representations on behalf of various private businesses with which she is involved. 'How can she play at being a businesswoman', HIM remarked, 'and yet at the same time give away her entire personal fortune, or at least claim that she wants to give it all away? ... I'll not listen to her demands.'

Saturday, 15 June

Audience ... HIM complained that Davallou is still pestering him to be allowed to join in his trip to France. 'People are all too ready to abuse Your Majesty's kindness', I said. 'Allow me to tell him that he stands no hope of success.' HIM asked me to do what I could.

Later this afternoon he rang me. 'Warn all those scum we see at palace dinner parties', he said, 'that they're not to discuss their private business interests with me; if they have requests to make they should do so via you, likewise if they want to make complaints.' Apparently he's exhausted his patience with those members of his entourage who have long abused his kind nature.

In the evening I received a visit from the Tehran representative of British Intelligence who warned me that the palace housekeeper, an Englishwoman known as Florence, is having an affair with the chief KGB man at the Soviet embassy. I was both shocked and alarmed . . .

Reported this at dinner . . . HIM ordered the woman sacked without notice . . .

Sunday, 16 June–Friday, 21 June
I've just returned from a brief visit to Paris. For the past year my white blood cells have been multiplying at an abnormal rate, apparently due to some sort of virus. I'm under the care of Professors Milliez and Jean Bernard, and must go to Paris for check-ups . . .

In my absence, those fools in the protocol department made a hash of things. Giscard d'Estaing is no longer to accompany HIM on his tour of the French provinces. HIM can surely expect more courtesy from the President of a country asking us for $5 billion. De Gaulle certainly accompanied the Queen of England when she made a similar tour, even though it meant rising from his sickbed . . .

Sunday, 23 June
Brief audience . . . after which HIM received the PM, the Minister of Finance and several members of the cabinet for talks on inflation. The Chief of the General Staff attended, accompanied by his advisers, since HIM has appointed the army to enforce price controls around the country . . .

HIM then left to fly to Zurich from where tomorrow he will go on to France.

Saturday, 29 June
HIM returned by Concorde, taking a mere two and a half hours to fly from Paris to Tehran . . . He expressed great satisfaction with the entire trip and told me that the French had dealt with him as with an equal . . .

Attended Dinner . . . Afterwards he instructed me to sort out the mess that Davallou has got himself into. The fellow is officially recognized as a drug addict and is entitled to receive opium from a special government agency. None the less he decided to send his driver to Isfahan to pick up 30kg. of the stuff. On his way back his car was involved in an accident and the driver's wife was killed. The other car was to blame, but as soon as the gendarmerie and the coroner's office began to investigate the possibility of a manslaughter charge they naturally lighted on Davallou's opium ...

Back home I summoned the Commander of the gendarmerie who announced that in addition to opium, they've found traces of heroin in the car. This was a crushing blow. In this country a man can be executed and his family left to starve for possessing as little as a gramme of heroin. What on earth am I to do? ... In the end I decided that should HIM demand a cover-up, I shall ask to be relieved of my appointment at Court.

Meanwhile I told the Commander to carry on with his investigations. I then telephoned Davallou who categorically denied that there could have been anything other than opium in the car. A little later the Commander rang back to confirm that this was true; their earlier report had been misinformed. A real weight off my mind.

Sunday, 30 June
Confined to bed ... but was able to telephone through to HIM and tell him amongst other things that the Davallou case has been successfully wound up ... Even so, I remarked how shocked I was that the man's first question to me had been to ask what had become of his opium, with never a thought for the driver's injuries or the tragic fate of his wife. 'People like Davallou merely wallow in corruption', said HIM. 'They can see no further than their own selfish squalor.' ...

Tuesday, 2 July
Audience. HIM's face was slightly swollen. Apparently his allergy has once again brought on a rash ...

A few months ago the Israelis agreed to buy 400,000 tons of oil from us; part of the deal being that 130,000 tons would be sold to them at the old rate of $4 a barrel, the rest at $17. They're now complaining that the bargain has not been honoured. HIM reluctantly agreed to my suggestion that we allow them a discount on future sales ...

Thursday, 4 July

Audience ... HIM announced that he's been converted to the view that capital punishment is too severe for opium traffickers. Apparently it's led to us being branded butchers by various people in France. I welcomed his change of heart, but pointed out that if drug smuggling is no longer to remain a capital offence, it's even more scandalous that overcharging by businessmen is shortly to merit the death sentence, according to the government's new bill ...

Saturday, 6 July

Audience ... The door burst open in the midst of our conversation and in walked the Crown Prince. HIM reacted calmly and replied to the various questions that the boy wanted answered. By contrast, I managed to put my foot in it, by asking him whether he knew that Queen Elizabeth has invited him to lunch during his forthcoming visit to England. HIM made frantic signs at me and hastily changed the subject. As soon as the Prince had left, he told me, 'We must be careful not to pressure Reza. If we tell him about the lunch in advance he'll refuse to attend. On the other hand, if he learns about it after reaching London he'll assume it's a fixed part of his itinerary; he'll appreciate how important it might be for Anglo-Iranian relations. There will be no arguments and he'll put on an excellent show.' Then, as if it were an afterthought, he added, 'From now on the Prince and his brother and sisters are not to enter my office during working hours, without first asking my permission.' ...

Monday, 8 July

Audience ... Reported the demolition of Princess Fatemeh's house in Nowshahr to make way for a new extension to the royal palace. The government have agreed to pay her $600,000 compensation. 'Nonsense', said HIM; 'What business is it of the government's? It's I that took the land and so I must pay whatever damages she's claiming.'

He also agreed to give Princess Shahnaz $400,000 to meet the cost of her residence and other household expenses. I'm delighted to see him acquiring a better opinion of his daughter. She and her husband can take some of the credit for adopting their new lifestyle, but above all she has HMQ to thank for intervening bravely on her behalf.

... HMQ has announced she'd like to build a guest house in Aqdasiyeh, not far from the Niavaran Palace. But the idea was angrily rejected by HIM. 'Tell HMQ', he said, 'that the Niavaran can be left to our guests, whilst we shall have a new palace built just for ourselves.' I didn't dare ask him where and how he wants this new palace built. Whenever he's raised the idea in the past he's been piqued to find HMQ reject it. She may be sincere, but I suspect her of a misguided anxiety to appease public opinion.

Wednesday, 10 July
HIM is away at the Caspian Sea ... The US ambassador called round with a memo concerning their naval base on Bahrain. I forwarded it to HIM together with an account of our conversation. According to the ambassador, the government of Bahrain some time ago announced it wished to terminate its agreement to act as home port for the flagship of the Commander Middle East Force; all of this as a result of tensions generated by the October 1973 Arab–Israeli war. Under the terms of the existing agreement Bahrain must give at least one year's notice to the Americans. In other words, unless they change their minds, they'll be rid of the US fleet by this coming October. Given current instability in the Gulf and the extent of Soviet assistance in beefing up the Iraqi navy, it would be extremely detrimental to the USA, ourselves, Saudi Arabia and others were Bahrain's deadline enforced. Hence the ambassador is keen to drum up support from our government and the Saudis. Prince Fahd promised to talk to the Bahrainis but so far without result. 'As you know', said the ambassador, 'the Arabs say one thing but do quite another.' I assured him that this could never be said of HIM. He was astonished I could believe him so naïve as to doubt HIM's word. As far as he can tell, the Sheikh of Bahrain and the Crown Prince both favour a continued US presence; the problem lies with their Foreign Minister who waxes hot and cold and dissuades them from cancelling their ultimatum ...

Sunday, 14 July
Audience followed by lunch with HIM in Nowshahr ... Discussed Nixon's deteriorating position. 'There's more than meets the eye to his present predicament', HIM remarked. I asked whether he was referring to the Jewish lobby. 'Not the Jews', he replied. 'No, the whole thing is a conspiracy put together by the CIA, big business and a handful of influential men whose identities remain a closely guarded secret. It was they that arranged Kennedy's assassination. Now they have a score to settle with Nixon, though I don't know why.' After a few moments thought he went on, 'Maybe I'm just imagining things. But I sincerely hope I'm right about

the conspirators. If all this is the result of mere chance it doesn't bode well for the future of the free world.'

HMQ insists that we send a private plane to bring the King of Greece to Iran but I expressed doubts about the wisdom of this. 'Do as she asks', HIM replied, 'though the King is likely to remain an ex-King for good and all. The Americans fear they will lose control if Greece reverts from military dictatorship to constitutional monarchy, in which case the country might fall into the hands of who knows what sort of leftist fanatics.' ...

Returned to Tehran this afternoon in time for a meeting with the US Chargé d'Affaires. It appears that *American Banker* magazine has once again printed disrespectful remarks about HIM made by the US Deputy Treasury Secretary, William Simon. The Chargé d'Affaires delivered a cable from Simon repudiating the comments made, but I could not control my temper and roundly abused both men. I told the Chargé d'Affaires that I was no longer prepared to listen to the sort of rubbish he brings me. He was thoroughly ashamed of himself, but assured me that *American Banker* have agreed to print Simon's denial.[1]

Monday, 15–Wednesday, 24 July
The five days up to Friday 19th, I spent trekking on horse-back across the high mountains of Alborz ... It was at this time that the Greek military launched an assassination attempt on Archbishop Makarios as a first step towards *enosis*, the reunification of Greece and Cyprus. Turkey reacted swiftly and in force, sending an army of occupation to the island which toppled the short-lived regime established by the Greek coup. Thereafter the Greek military command resigned 'en masse', humiliated by their defeat ... Hence, whatever the Americans may say about it, there's a real possibility that King Constantine will be invited to return ...

Travelled to Nowshahr on Monday for an audience. Pointed out how vexed the Americans have been by recent events in Greece ... 'It's always the same', HIM said; 'They ignore my advice at their peril.'

Yesterday King Hussein and his family flew in to join HIM in Nowshahr.

---

[1] As reported in *American Banker*, 15 July, 1974, Simon said that 'The Shah is a nut.' His subsequent telegram addressed to the US embassy in Tehran reads as follows: 'In talking with the reporter from the *American Banker* I made no statement intended to characterize the Shah in an offensive manner. The article prepared by the reporter was the result of a gross misunderstanding of my views, since in fact I have the greatest respect and admiration for the Shah's leadership in his country's far reaching economic and social development programmes.'

Saturday, 27 July

Audience ... King Hussein interrupted us for a few minutes to chat with HIM. Earlier that morning he'd met with Mustafa Barzani. I was ushered back in at the end of their conversation. In King Hussein's presence HIM said to me in English, 'Tell the US ambassador that Egyptian sources warn us that Iraq intends to reverse her policies and fall into line with her fellow Arab nations. King Hussein and I doubt her sincerity in this ... We wish the Americans to investigate and, when our doubts are confirmed, to advise Egypt against falling into an Iraqi trap. If we ourselves issued such a warning the Egyptians would probably dismiss it as mere prejudice.' ...

Tuesday, 30 July

... This afternoon HIM and King Hussein flew together from Nowshahr to Tehran airport where they bid one another farewell ...

Reported that the British ambassador believes King Constantine stands a good chance of being restored. HIM declared he's done all he could to put pressure on the Americans ...

Thursday, 1–Saturday, 3 August

For the past three days I've been at the Ramsar conference intended to increase the scope of the fifth development plan ... My head is spinning with a whole series of incredible statistics. Two years ago the target outlay was $24 billion. Today it's more or less trebled to $68 billion ... Truly the reign of Mohammad Reza Shah will go down in history as the most glorious in all the two and a half millennia of Iranian monarchy ...

HIM declared during the conference that the terrorist outrages of two years ago were linked to our negotiations over oil. I subsequently asked him what evidence he had for this claim. 'None at all', he said, 'but that's no reason why it shouldn't be true.' ...

Monday, 5 August

... Audience at Nowshahr ... HIM asked whether there'd been any popular reaction to the Ramsar conference and the improvements to the plan. I replied that it had been well received but that the figures we'd bandied about were beyond most people's comprehension, even mine. These things need to be set out in straightforward layman's language, and even then the best way of bringing it home to people is for them to experience a real improvement in living conditions. At the moment all they can understand is that inflation is a crippling problem and that the standard of public services is deplorable ...

He then asked whether he'd caused offence by lashing out at the national propensity for sloth. I replied that people knew only too well what he'd said was accurate. 'A man who is not dependent on people's votes', he said, 'is free to act directly in the national interest.' I admitted that there might be some truth to this, remarking that a member of the British House of Lords has recently called for an autocrat to rescue his country from its plight. However *The Times* poured scorn on his proposal. Autocracy is no longer acceptable to a country that has once experienced democracy. 'In other words they prefer chaos to reform', HIM replied. 'Quite so', I said. 'For them even the most intense misery or chaos is worth enduring so long as their freedom remains intact. We in Iran rejoice that Your Majesty is a benevolent dictator, utterly devoted to the good of all. However we may not always be so fortunate in our rulers.' ...

Friday, 9 August

... Nixon resigned last night. Gerald Ford stepped in to succeed him ... We had to cable the new President and I read several drafts of the message down the telephone to HIM. Much argument whether we should apply the adjectives 'illustrious' or 'eminent' to his predecessor, 'who made such efforts to preserve world peace'. In the end we agreed to dispense with an adjective altogether. The vast majority of Americans have grown to despise Nixon's administration, but there can be no doubt that he possessed strength and great experience in foreign affairs. His achievements in regard to China, the Soviets and the Middle East cannot be brushed aside.

Ford had been sworn in for a bare three hours when the US ambassador telephoned me, at 10.20 this evening, to ask whether he might bring round a personal message from his new President to HIM ... He seemed in good spirits and laid great stress on the speed with which Ford has sought to establish contact. For my own part I suggested the whole thing reeked of one of Kissinger's famous ploys. He laughed, saying that in any case there could be no doubting the importance Washington attaches to HIM and Iran ... I cracked a bottle of champagne and we toasted the health of HIM and President Ford. Sat chatting until midnight.

Nixon was brought down not as HIM believes by some great conspiracy but through the re-assertion of fundamental principles, the very stuff of which democracy is made ...

[Alam spent the next three weeks abroad in Europe]

Saturday, 31 August

Flew in at dawn ... called briefly on HIM who was most kind ...

This afternoon the Soviet Chargé d'Affaires brought round an important message. Before going away on holiday, his ambassador apparently invited HIM to make an unofficial visit to Moscow. They're now suggesting 18 November as the date ...

Sunday, 1 September

HIM received me over breakfast ... and agreed to the Soviets' date ... Submitted a report addressed to me by our ambassador in Rabat.

[The ambassador mentions discussions with General Moulay Hafid. The latter had invited Alam to visit Morocco at the bidding of King Hassan but as yet had received no reply. The King had several times made enquiries on the subject. Much to his embarrassment the General had exhausted excuse after excuse. The ambassador wondered whether Tehran was deliberately cold-shouldering Morocco. He had come to feel that the Shah bore a grudge against King Hassan. None the less he would appreciate it if he could have these suspicions either confirmed or denied so that he might act in accordance with whatever policy the Shah had adopted.]

'I'm glad the Moroccans are beginning to feel uneasy', HIM remarked. 'King Hassan put his name to a joint communiqué with the Sheikh of Abu Dhabi in which they refer to the 'Arabian Gulf'. No wonder we're displeased.'

Attended the Tehran Olympic stadium for the opening of the seventh International Asian Games. Later flew with HIM to Ramsar ...

Monday, 2 September

Joined HIM at his villa and drove together to the Ramsar Palace for the annual education conference. As we sped past, many people were cheering by the roadside; an honest and touching scene. 'Look how the people react when they see you face to face', I said. He replied that their sentiments were bound to show themselves in this way. He then referred to American naïvety. 'That idiot Kennedy', he said, 'once told me that Dr Amini was the only hope for Iran just as Karamanlis was for Greece ... Yet just think what Amini actually did. Had I allowed him to carry on, he would have brought this country to its knees. Likewise in Greece, the Americans were stupid enough to give open support to the military. As a result Karamanlis had no choice but to adopt an anti-American stand. Again and again I warned them that the Greek military were doomed to failure. Yet they paid me no attention. They went ahead and backed an obvious loser.' ...

HIM received several visitors after lunch; Kamal Adham,[1] the head of Saudi Intelligence; Prince Saud al-Faisal,[2] in all likelihood King Faisal's chosen successor to Zaki Yamani; and an Egyptian special envoy, Moham-mad Ashraf Marwan, bearing a letter from President Sadat. They were all three adamant that Iraq is striving to free herself from Soviet domination – a diagnosis confirmed by the Americans.

Wednesday, 4 September
HIM was present for the closing session of the education conference ... One of the peculiarities of this gathering is that it's open to university and high school teachers holding no official position. They're even allowed to express their opinion on various of the topics under discussion. Today, for example, they dared to challenge HIM's views on the relation between teachers' salaries and their sense of duty. It was all done most politely, and was a joy for me to observe ...

Last night the PM and the Ministers of Education and the Universities submitted what they described as a conference resolution to HIM and obtained his approval. He was naturally taken aback today when he asked the conference if it had any comments and discovered that no one had seen the document in question. He got himself off the hook by suggesting that, perhaps, they'd been too busy to hold discussions. But he surely can't suppose that between eight o'clock last night and ten this morning they couldn't have spared the matter so much as half an hour? Even in its dealings with the élite, our government shows nothing but contempt. Yet they expect people to take an interest in national affairs and to fool themselves that they have some sort of share in decision-making ...

Returned to Tehran after lunch. Met the US ambassador ... who spoke of HIM as the chief 'coordinator' in Middle Eastern affairs. Someone once asked what he meant by this phrase and he explained that by coordinator he was implying a political juggler; a man who keeps his own and other

---

[1] King Faisal's brother-in-law and close ally; the King's trouble-shooter in foreign policy.
[2] Son of King Faisal, the then Deputy Minister of Petroleum and Mineral Resources; later Minister of Foreign Affairs.

peoples' interests constantly in play; in other words, as the ambassador put it, 'a man with a lot of balls'.

Thursday, 5 September

Audience ... On 23 September HIM will be unable to attend the start of the academic year at Tehran University as he will be away on a state visit to Australia. I asked who he would like to act as his proxy. 'The Crown Prince is still too young', he remarked. I replied that I'd not been thinking of the Prince, but of one of HIM's brothers or sisters. 'No, not them', he said. 'Let Shahnaz do it.' I am both surprised and delighted to see how much their relations have improved.

Later this evening I learned that Ayatollah Shahroudi had died in Najaf. Recently he'd been at odds with the Ba'athist regime in Iraq. I straightaway informed HIM, and dispatched telegrams offering condolences to the old man's son and to Ayatollah Khonsari. All in all I was kept at my desk until the small hours, drafting the cables and preparing copies for the media ... But it was a task that deserved to be done well. This country rests on three basic foundations: Shi'ism, the Persian language, and the monarchy. Each one of them must be treated with appropriate respect ...

Sunday, 8 September

Audience ... Reported that Princess Shahnaz is unable to stand in for HIM at the University as she has a dental appointment in Europe. 'She's already told me', HIM replied ... Reluctantly he suggested I ask Princess Shams to represent him.

Monday, 9 September

Audience, longer than usual, the discussion centred chiefly on HIM's health. He complained about his spleen which is still distended, and about his recurring skin rash, suggesting that Jean Bernard should fly to Tehran for yet another consultation. I simply can't understand what's going on ... I did my best to hide my anxiety, assuring him that there can't be anything seriously the matter. 'But I must emphasize one point to Your Majesty', I said. 'Last June when I went for my own check-up in Paris, Jean Bernard confided that Your Majesty's health is being badly messed about. ... Your private physician, Dr Ayadi, wouldn't know a scalpel from a garden spade.' ... I told him that I'd long been waiting for an opportunity to speak out on this, and suggested we summon Professors Jean Bernard and Milliez, telling them it's I rather than HIM that am in need of treatment. He agreed ...

Tuesday, 10 September
Audience ... Asked HIM how he was feeling. He merely pointed to the continued inflammation of his face. To cheer him up I told him that, sitting with his back to the window and his face in shadow, I'd be hard put to see that anything was amiss.

Ardeshir Zahedi has suggested to President Ford that he make a stopover here on his way to Tokyo. 'I told Ardeshir he was wasting his time', said HIM. 'Ford can do as he likes; it's a matter of complete indifference to me whether he comes or not.' ...

This afternoon met the British ambassador and, amongst other things, discussed Queen Elizabeth the Queen Mother's forthcoming visit to Iran ... He remarked that the Iraqi army has gained ground in Kurdistan. I'd already been given a full report on this, but preferred to feign ignorance ...

Thursday, 12 September
Audience. Discussed the British general election from which it seems no party is likely to emerge with an overall majority ... 'They're in serious trouble', HIM remarked, 'whereas despite the grumbling that goes on, in this country I alone have the final say, a fact which I believe most people are happy to accept ... If my ministers carry out their orders promptly and without hesitation, it's only because they are convinced that whatever I say is correct.' I replied that this was true in most respects, but that he should never underestimate the extent to which he puts the fear of God into people. He seemed to find this most amusing ...

Friday, 13 September
Before lunch HIM and I made an inspection of the superb furniture that's been ordered for the Shahvand Palace. To begin with he tried to give orders how each and every piece is to be displayed, but after a fruitless forty-five minutes it dawned on him that this really wasn't his cup of tea and that we need an interior decorator to decide which items to retain and which to send on to the other palaces. HIM may be a great king but soft furnishings are certainly not his forte. Luckily he had the intelligence to appreciate this fact and beat a hasty retreat.

... Told him that Mrs Diba still longs to be awarded the Order of

Khorshid ('The Sun') reserved for members of the royal family. She never refers to it by name, but goes on and on about 'the other decoration' ... 'How peculiar', HIM remarked. 'Tell her that it doesn't befit her status as a self-confessed dervish to covet such baubles.'[1] 'None the less', I said, 'you had better let her have her way.' 'You must be joking!', he replied.

The Emperor of Ethiopia has been deposed by a military coup ... Poor Haile Selassie; over the past few years he'd lost control of his country and the inevitable was bound to happen. I remember his attendance at the monarchy celebrations, how he snatched his hand away when I tried to help him from his car, telling me he could manage well enough on his own, thank you very much. Likewise during the recent drought when thousands of his people were dying he refused all HIM's offers of help, denying that anyone was suffering or even that there was a drought. He saw himself as a mighty ruler but now the truth has caught up with him. At the Shahvand Palace today I could think of nothing but Haile Selassie's fate. Inevitably one is inclined to draw parallels ... They are not reassuring ...

Sunday, 15 September

Presentation of credentials by the ambassadors of Ghana and Saudi Arabia, the latter speaking English superbly. He seems to represent the younger generation of his countrymen ...

British customs officials have caught Prince Behzad, the son of Hamid Reza, trying to get through Heathrow airport with a small quantity of hashish in his pockets. The boy was fined £50 but our ambassador managed to prevent the story being leaked to the press. HIM was extremely annoyed; how much he suffers from the stupidity of his relatives. In my opinion it's best for a king to have as few relations as possible ...

Monday, 16 September

Today marks the thirty-third year since the start of HIM's illustrious reign but instead of bringing him my congratulations, at 8 this morning I ushered the French physicians Milliez and Jean Bernard into his bedroom. He seemed in more or less perfect health save for this infuriating allergic rash ... He took it all very calmly, even whilst the doctors were aspirating samples from his bone marrow, a very painful exercise but necessary if they're to make a proper laboratory analysis. He chatted with them whilst

[1] In Persian the term 'dervish' implies a person inclined towards mysticism, who leads a simple life and is therefore disinterested in worldly riches.

they went about their business, recommending that they take a look round our new heart hospital. However I reminded him that it's better that they keep a low profile in Tehran; for them to be seen in a hospital would be especially likely to start rumours. He agreed I had a point ... At the end I showed them out of the Palace by a discreet back entrance ...

The Asian Games have come to an end leaving us in second place, next to the Japanese. HIM was pleased by this coincidence since he holds that of the continent's more advanced nations, Japan should lead in the East and we in the West.

Tuesday, 17 September
Audience ... HIM seemed fretful and preoccupied, paying little attention to my report ... Somehow the conversation got round to his doctors, who lunched with me yesterday and spent a full three hours discussing his symptoms. It dawned on me suddenly that it was precisely this that made him anxious, since he knows his spleen was once again found to be enlarged. I assured him that I'd have told him straightaway if something were amiss. As it is the doctors made all the tests they could, and found nothing particularly the matter. I spoke with so much conviction that it seemed to put his mind at rest. Nor was I being insincere; the doctors would have warned me if anything were wrong ...

Friday, 4 October
Following more than a fortnight in the Far East, Their Majesties returned to Tehran ... I got the impression that HIM achieved far less on the economic front than he'd hoped for. The Australians were unable to agree terms for the exploitation of uranium and bauxite, a failure for which I suspect the British are responsible. None the less the Shah worked hard. He even came up with new proposals for an Indian Ocean pact, encouraging greater co-operation amongst the region's states and an end to great power intervention. As the saying goes, this is bound to pay off in the long run.

Saturday, 5 October
The State opening of Parliament, after which I flew with HIM to the Palace. He talked about his trip and the interview he's given the press; a sharp rejoinder to President Ford's declaration that OPEC risks retaliation from the world's oil consumers. 'Ford is an utter booby', he remarked. 'He does nothing but repeat whatever cretinous nonsense he's fed by Simon.'

I suggested that Kissinger was the real power behind the throne. He agreed this might well be so . . .

He then asked whether there'd been any news from his doctors. I did my best to feign indifference, replying that there was no real urgency and that they're bound to send word sooner or later. Unfortunately he's been anxious ever since his spleen began to harden. No cause for concern, but he's naturally apprehensive . . .

Sunday, 6 October

Audience . . . Again we discussed the problems with his spleen . . . I assured him the doctors told me there was nothing to worry about. 'You're not a child for me to try to hide the truth from you', I said. 'Honestly, if there were anything seriously the matter I would tell you.' The doctors' report, and whatever medicines they prescribe, are to be sent here as if intended for me. I then went on to describe an incident that's supposed to have occurred under Karim Khan Zand.[1] One day the palace doctor told him he needed an enema. Karim was outraged, saying how disgraceful it was, how dare they make their ruler suffer such humiliation. 'Think carefully before you answer', he said to the doctor, 'and then tell me again, who is it that needs the enema?' – The poor doctor had only one way out; 'I of course', he replied. 'I shall take the enema. Your Majesty will reap the benefit.' HIM was greatly amused by this. He also got the message; if I were seriously concerned for his safety I should never have been so flippant . . .

Monday, 7–Tuesday, 8 October

Early morning meeting with the US ambassador, followed by my audience. Submitted draft proposals for Kissinger's visit. I'd allocated an hour and a half for his discussions with HIM, but HIM ordered this extended by a further hour . . .

Some time ago General Khatami, the Commander of the Air Force, confided in me that we're ordering far more planes than we can possibly use. We simply haven't enough pilots, or the facilities to train more. This has obvious implications for the effectiveness of the air force. Yet, despite being his brother-in-law, the Commander dares not draw the matter to HIM's attention. Instead he asked me to bring it up when an opportunity arose, being careful not to reveal who had supplied me with my information.

[1] Ruler of Iran, 1750–79.

This put me in a dilemma; on the one hand HIM is bound to resent any remark I might make, particularly as the subject lies quite beyond my own competence. But at the same time, duty bade me enlighten him, regardless of the cost to myself. A way out presented itself a couple of days ago during a meeting with the US ambassador. The US Aviation Minister was due to have an audience with HIM. I advised the ambassador that it would be foolish to object, should HIM take the opportunity to call for further supplies of aircraft, regardless of the fact the planes may be left to rot in their hangars. The poor man fell straight into my trap, remarking that the Aviation Minister would tread carefully; 'Although the truth is, your air force simply hasn't the capacity to cope with so many new planes.' This morning I was able to quote these words verbatim to HIM. 'Tell him he should credit me with more intelligence', HIM replied. 'I fully appreciate the problem, but he must still supply the aircraft. At least that way we'll have no worries about basic machinery. As for manpower, I'm determined our air force college should train more pilots, even if it means their working round the clock ... '

Thursday, 10 October
Audience. Discussed the guerrillas' defeat in Iraqi Kurdistan. HIM hopes the Kurds' situation may improve once they've received our supplies of long-range artillery and anti-tank missiles.

Kissinger's reputation seems to be in decline – he's begun to receive unfavourable notices in the US press. 'Quite so', said HIM. 'Pride comes before a fall – although in his case it's more conceit than pride.' ...

Surprisingly he still seems worried about his health ... I suggested he allow me to tell HMQ that his weekends need to be spent in complete rest, away from everybody. She may boil over, in which case I shall be for the chop. On the other hand, it might actually do the trick. Even so, HIM rejected the proposal ... saying he must resign himself to his present mode of existence ...

Sunday, 13 October
Audience ... Reported information from a highly reliable source. It appears that the US President recently held a meeting at Camp David attended by Kissinger, an observer from the French government and the Foreign Ministers of Great Britain, Germany and Japan. We've obtained what are virtually the minutes of this meeting. They deal with the international position in regard to oil and show that various possibilities were discussed,

including an armed occupation of Libya and Algeria, although some of those present felt that a bargain may still be struck with the Algerians. The Japanese Foreign Minister demanded that pressure be brought to bear on every oil producer including Iran. His British counterpart disagreed, saying that the Shah will find a compromise acceptable to everybody if only he's left to his own devices. At this point the French observer intervened to offer his government's services as mediator between oil consumers and producers, should a major confrontation arise. The Foreign Minister of Germany remarked that strong measures will solve nothing and that the only hope lies in reduced oil consumption. All of this was most useful in briefing HIM for his forthcoming meeting with Kissinger[1] ...

Monday, 14 October

Audience. The doctors' report has come through, giving HIM a clean bill of health; although, as arranged, it was worded as if I were the patient. HIM seemed pleased, though determined to avoid any outward show of emotion.

We've bought anti-aircraft missiles of British manufacture. At dinner I reported that the British have agreed they may be operated on the Iraqi border by retired officers from Britain's own armed services. HIM was delighted, presumably because of the political implications ...

Sunday, 20 October

Audience ... Submitted the schedule for Kissinger's visit. We're to hold a reception in his honour and the Great Court Chamberlain has prepared a guest list including a whole host of prominent people such as the PM and various members of his Cabinet. 'Tell the Chamberlain not to be so bloody subservient', said HIM. When he saw I hadn't grasped his meaning, he went on, 'Why treat Kissinger any differently from the way we treat every other Foreign Minister that comes to stay? The standard procedure is to hold a reception, to which only you and our Minister of Foreign Affairs are invited.'

Monday, 21 October

Audience. I've received further information from a British source independent of their embassy, suggesting the British are inclined to leave any

---

[1] In light of the entry for 21 October 1974, it appears that it was the British who had reported the Camp David meeting to the Iranian authorities.

compromise between oil producers and consumers to the discretion of HIM. I suppose they have little alternative.

Prince Saud al-Faisal was received this afternoon. It turns out that the Saudis are proposing a minuscule price reduction, for which they will obtain compensation by massive increases in company taxes and royalties. In effect, the market price will actually go up rather than down. Their show of sympathy towards consumers is nothing more than a publicity stunt ...

Wednesday, 23 October
Audience. Discussed HIM's proposals for price stability. Apparently he told the Saudis we can only support a price freeze on oil provided the cost of manufactured goods remains stable ...

One of our ministers was assigned to negotiate a co-operation agreement with Kissinger. The man has come to me to object that a senior cabinet colleague should not be invited to our reception. He fears that it will mean his losing face with Kissinger, since protocol insists he be placed below his colleague at the dining table. HIM and I were heartily amused by this, HIM remarking, 'These people have about as much intelligence as a herd of sheep.'

Monday, 28 October
HMQ has set out on a tour of north-eastern Iran, visiting the cities on the edge of the desert ...

I then went to see the guest HIM was due to meet this afternoon. She struck me as being either half-witted or a positive menace, possibly both. I warned HIM to watch his step. At dinner he took me aside and assured me that he'd been extremely cautious ...

Tuesday, 29 October
Audience ... Briefed HIM on my meeting yesterday with the British ambassador. Apparently the British government intends to announce that Harold Lever, a Cabinet Minister, will make a visit to Iran at HIM's invitation. I made it quite plain how much I disapproved of such an announcement, cautioning the ambassador that the invitation must be said to have been issued by the Iranian government, not by HIM personally. In reply he attempted to dispel any resentment we may feel that Denis Healey, the British Chancellor of the Exchequer, is to visit Saudi Arabia at the same time as Lever is in Tehran; we should appreciate that Healey

and Lever enjoy equal status, and not suppose that the Saudis are being singled out for special treatment. He seemed quite taken aback when I replied that we regard every member of his government with an equally profound degree of disinterest.

To add a little diversity to my report, I told HIM that the girl he saw yesterday, the one I thought half-witted, clearly mistook me for the Shah since she gave me a solemn bow and then launched herself into my arms. The whole thing was dreadfully embarrassing; I was lost for words to correct her mistake. Even so, according to a mutual acquaintance who met her later, she's simply naïve and there can be no harm if HIM consents to have dinner with her. HIM replied that he'd come to much the same conclusion ...

Wednesday, 30 October

Audience ... HIM's spirits dampened by an article in *Time* magazine. They've printed his picture on the cover – generally considered a mark of great favour – but he's dissatisfied by what their article says about Iran ... For example they claim that 40 per cent of the country's wealth belongs to only 10 per cent of the population ... and yet they overlook the extent to which workers have been granted a participation in industry. In the past these bastards in the international press made up lurid stories about what they dubbed 'Iran's one thousand families'. They've now invented yet another myth, talking about Iran's 'new bourgeoisie' ...

The Prime Minister of Sri Lanka lunched as our guest but HIM was in a far from hospitable mood, troubled by a head-cold and by the article in *Time*. HMQ did her best to persuade him to join in the conversation, but it became apparent that this was getting her nowhere. She then switched from English to Persian, saying, 'All this work is wearing you out. I'm seriously worried. Why else do you suppose I insist you relax at the weekends?' – 'There's only one way you can get me to relax', he snapped back at her. 'Stop inviting all these pretty faces who are always traipsing after you. Surrounded by people like this, how on earth do you expect me to relax?' HMQ was too shocked to reply and the meal petered out in an atmosphere of sullen gloom ...

Friday, 1 November

... Met the British ambassador on HIM's instructions and complained about the unfavourable coverage afforded the Iraqi Kurds, poor fellows, by Britain's Independent Television network ...

Kissinger flew in this afternoon accompanied by his wife. He was received by HIM between six and eight thirty. At dinner he was placed to the right of HMQ with me on her left. He was full of praise for HIM, saying how much he wished President Ford could emulate his example ... Afterwards he and HIM resumed their private discussion, breaking off at midnight. Meanwhile HMQ and the ladies watched a film, after which they retired, Mrs Kissinger being very worn out after her flight. She's no beauty but is reputed to be worth a fortune. Kissinger I found far more polite than last time ... His discussions with HIM were attended only by the American ambassador. I felt quite sorry for our own Foreign Minister, poor man ...

Saturday, 2 November
... This afternoon flew with HIM to Kish. Superb weather, blissful peace and quiet. Later we sat reminiscing by the sea shore ... Quite out of the blue he remarked that drug smuggling is to be reduced from a capital offence to one meriting life imprisonment. 'The foreign press, bloody fools, accuse us of executing 200 such smugglers', he said. 'It's not that influenced my decision one iota. Our harsh measures were entirely justified. However there's no point in going on with them when they don't appear to deter people.' ...

Sunday, 3 November
Spent the morning relaxing. After lunch we joined the PM and Admiral James Holloway, Commander of the US fleet, on board the Iranian destroyer *Palang*, a vessel equipped with all the latest technology from missiles to computers and communications systems ... Holloway took part in both the Second World War and the war in Vietnam; a man of great wisdom and experience ...

Monday, 4 November
Twenty-one ships, besides countless planes, helicopters and hovercraft, took part in today's naval manoeuvres. The thing went on until nine this evening, all in all an excellent performance. The Crown Prince got his first taste of a military exercise, attending as an official observer on board the destroyer *Babr*. The cruiser *Artemis* was set aside for Prince Gholam Reza and the uncle of the Sultan of Oman.

HIM was overjoyed, remarking that the targeting was so good that people were surprised when the odd dud shot failed to hit home. Perhaps the most interesting aspect was the display of laser-guided bombing put on by our Phantoms. They hit their targets at the very first attempt, much to everyone's delight.

The naval officer who two years ago was severely rebuked for the mismanagement of just such an exercise, found himself promoted Rear Admiral, so well did the whole thing go. HIM commended the entire naval staff.

Tuesday, 5 November
... HIM reviewed the fleet to mark the end of their manoeuvres ...

This afternoon we returned to Kish ... My lover joined me here and I've passed a very pleasant few hours. Sadly the same cannot be said of HIM whose groin and genitalia are inflamed with a nasty rash ... As a result he's been forced to cancel tomorrow's visit to Bushehr.

[The Shah and Alam returned to Tehran on the 9th]

Sunday, 10 November
Audience. His health and the oil policy of Saudi Arabia are both causing him anxiety. I told him he has nothing to fear. The rash on his groin will soon clear up, though he should seriously consider dismissing the local quacks who attend him, as well as that fellow in Europe ... HIM's health is not to be tampered with; it deserves the attention of the world's leading specialists. I suggested that Professor Abbas Safavian, a reliable man, be sent to Paris to liaise with Professors Milliez and Jean Bernard. Together they should try to devise an overall strategy to monitor and speed his recovery. He approved the idea.

He is surprised to find the Saudis proposing a reduction in oil prices. 'What are they up to?', he remarked. 'Either they're being incredibly naïve or else they've embarked on a devious scheme of their own which we've yet to latch on to.' ...

Submitted a schedule for his forthcoming trip to the Soviet Union. I asked who he wished to accompany him. 'No one but the Minister of Finance', he replied. 'It's an unofficial trip so I shall require no assistance from the Minister of Foreign Affairs.' ...

Wednesday, 13 November
Audience ... *Newsweek* intends to circulate heads of state, soliciting opinions on the problems most likely to occupy them in 1975. 'I shall

refuse to grant them an interview', HIM announced. 'Tell them they're a bunch of rascals who do nothing but twist my words.' ...

The British ambassador called round this afternoon ... His Foreign Office is anxious about the British technicians who are to install Rapier missiles on our western frontier. On no account are they to cross the border into Iraq or it might spark off an international incident ...

Monday, 18 November
HIM set out for Moscow this morning ... As he boarded the plane he turned to me and said: 'I may have accepted their invitation, but goodness knows what the Soviets are hoping to get out of me.' ...

Wednesday, 20 November
... HIM returned this afternoon in excellent spirits.

I then went to meet the US ambassador who ... was keen to know whether HIM had brought back any message for the US President who is shortly to meet Brezhnev in Vladivostok.

Reported this over dinner. 'Tell him I stood firm on political issues affecting the Soviets but agreed to extend economic co-operation across a far broader front', HIM said. There were too many people around the table for him to risk giving me further details.

Thursday, 21 November
Audience ... Asked after HIM's talks in Moscow. 'Things went very well', he replied. 'To begin with they did their best to brow-beat me, complaining about our military build-up. Why do we feel it necessary to purchase so many new weapons? Against whom do we intend to use them? What purpose is served by our reviving CENTO? They said they were justifiably concerned. I told them that they could make of it what they liked, but that I'll tolerate no criticism of legitimate improvements to national defence and that I'm under no obligation to justify myself to outsiders. I reminded them that twice in Arab–Israeli confrontations and again in Cyprus, we've seen the international peace-keeping organizations proved worse than useless. No one lifted a finger to oppose the aggressors in these situations nor was anything done to aid their victims. For my own part I refuse to let myself or any of this country's resources fall prey to foreign bullies, however powerful – a clear warning to the Soviets themselves. By standing up for myself like that I altered the whole tone of the debate. The Soviets did their best to laugh off their earlier remarks as if they'd been intended

as a joke. On the economic front they even proposed some degree of Iranian investment within Soviet industry. As for Iraq they suggested, very politely of course, that we need to reach a permanent understanding.' ...

Friday, 22 November
Unable to go riding. HIM demanded I go to the Palace, ready to be received as soon as he'd finished his audience with the Bulgarian President. This was expected to last no more than an hour but in the event I was kept waiting a full three and a half.

HIM seemed tired and I suggested that instead of working in his office we take a stroll around the palace gardens. I steered clear of topics likely to cause him anxiety, although he insisted on briefing me on this morning's negotiations. 'We agreed on many issues', he said. 'And I even undertook to loan them money to build roads at 11 per cent, 1 per cent below current interest rates. I can't see any harm in it. By all means, let's encourage what support we can within the eastern bloc.' ...

Saturday, 23 November
Audience ... Again HIM referred back to his talks in Moscow. 'On the first day', he said, 'Brezhnev warned me that existing problems in the Gulf could all too easily escalate into world war. Goodness knows what he was implying.' I suggested it might be a reference to Moscow's recent agreement with Baghdad which risks involving the Soviets in an armed confrontation between Iran and Iraq. 'Maybe that's it', said HIM. 'In any event, Brezhnev was slamming his fist on the table as he said it, ranting on about the revival of CENTO, declaring that the present disputes in the Middle East were a threat to world peace.'

Sunday, 24 November
Audience ... HIM was still dwelling on his Moscow trip. 'They complained about our support for the Kurdish guerrillas', he said; 'So I asked them how one was supposed to distinguish between Iranian assistance to the Kurds and their own aid to North Vietnam. In Kurdistan the people are being wiped out by the most devastating weapons of modern warfare: aircraft, missiles. But in Indo-China, the Soviets are effectively supporting the chief aggressor, North Vietnam. They then tried to object to the way we approve US intervention in the Indian Ocean. I told them that we'd much prefer a complete superpower withdrawal, but that the Americans are bound to take a hand, given that the Soviets have already staked a claim

in the region. As for the new naval base at Diego Garcia which clearly has them worried, I pointed out that the latest developments in warships mean that such bases are not nearly so significant as some people think. In any event, if they wished to raise a complaint they should do so directly with Washington.' ...

Hardly had I set foot outside his office when my telephone rang and he informed me that in Ethiopia a group of young officers has executed the chairman of the so-called Revolutionary Council together with a whole host of others; at least two former prime ministers and the Emperor's grandson, previously Commander of the Navy. HIM insisted I tell the US ambassador that communists are responsible for this outrage. The ambassador should appreciate that the Soviet Defence Minister is presently in Iraq, and Brezhnev himself is due there shortly. In these circumstances the optimism of America, Egypt and Saudi Arabia is utterly misguided. They all forecast an improvement in respect to Iraq and the Middle East, but this is arrant nonsense, particularly given Brezhnev's attitude to the Gulf. 'Tell the ambassador', he said, 'that I wish to know whether his government intends standing up to these threats. At the same time, tell him, I have no desire to see my prophecies splashed across the front pages of the American newspapers. I trust his discretion, but wouldn't put it past the State Department to leak whatever I say in confidence directly to the press.' He finished by asking for news of the Vladivostock summit meeting ...

Saturday, 30 November
Audience ... Discussed Iraq and the extent to which she's being propped up by the Russians. 'Moscow is doing no more than defend her own interests', said HIM. 'But we too must stand up for ourselves. We've given the Iraqis a real thrashing with our long-range artillery and I doubt they'll be in a hurry to relaunch their offensive against the Kurds. For all their missiles and what have you, the Iraqis were quite incapable of silencing these so-called "Kurdish" guns. Their training and discipline are a complete shambles.' ...

Attended lunch held in honour of President Kaunda of Zambia. In the midst of a wide-ranging conversation HIM expressed satisfaction with China's conduct of diplomacy ... 'Even so', he said, 'I made my acceptance of an invitation to Peking conditional upon their first sending us a figure of recognized stature, in return for the visit HMQ made to China. But now I'm faced with a dilemma. I am keen to enforce the rules of protocol, but they seem to be quite out of fashion. American Presidents, Nixon, Ford, travel to China one after another with never a thought for the diplomatic niceties.' . . .

Sunday, 1 December

I brought Professor Safavian with me to this morning's audience in order that he might spell out the health care programme devised by Professors Milliez and Jean Bernard. HIM approved the scheme, which seems highly satisfactory . . .

Later I received word from a reliable source at the Vladivostock summit that the Soviets have complained about our military build-up, describing it in front of the US delegates as a threat to world peace. They announced that during the Shah's visit to Moscow they failed to dissuade him from his crazy re-armament and that they would therefore like the USA to try to make him change his mind. The USA replied by defending HIM's policy, stressing that Iran is free to act as she sees fit. Immediately reported this to HIM . . .

Monday, 2 December

Audience . . . HIM instructed me to write to Princess Ashraf asking her what on earth made her commit $2 million of Iranian money to the UN Commission on Women's Rights. 'Does she imagine she's running this country?', he asked. 'Just for this once we'll honour the commitment she's foisted on us, but she'd better not make the same mistake in future.'

Showed him an article in *New Yorker* magazine; a fictitious sketch of HIM, quite amusing, but bearing no relation to fact. He read it with a wry smile . . .

Wednesday, 4 December

Audience . . . He's outraged by student unrest, declaring he has two reasons for his anger: 'Firstly, the kids seem to lack any sense of patriotism, and secondly, why are the university authorities so lax in identifying the chief trouble-makers?' He instructed me to liaise with Savak and the other security agencies and to notify the Chief of the General staff that if the Kurdish guerrillas prove incapable of resisting an Iraqi counter-offensive, we must remove our long-range guns from the front line to prevent them falling into enemy hands . . .

Friday, 6 December

... HIM was due to receive Yitzhak Rabin, the Prime Minister of Israel, this morning. I made all the necessary arrangements, sending General Nassiri to greet him at the airport, instructing the guard how to transfer him to the Palace without arousing suspicion, and even selecting a servant to attend HIM; I picked a man of quite outstanding stupidity in the knowledge that he would be incapable of recognizing Rabin. Even fools can sometimes have their uses! ...

Despite Rabin's express desire to see me, I avoided putting in an appearance. HIM would have told me if he wanted me there ...

Saturday, 7 December

Audience ... according to HIM, Rabin promised to do all he can to reach an understanding with Egypt, and asked HIM to support any initiative that arises ...

Having read through a report from Dr Eqbal, HIM began to set down his comments in the margin. All of a sudden he hesitated, asking me the spelling of an incredibly simple word ... I was quite taken aback and can only assume he must be exhausted ...

Ardeshir Zahedi telephoned later, to say President Ford had only just that moment left our Washington embassy – at three in the morning – and that his daughter and various relations were still there gorging themselves on salmon and caviar. What status this country of ours has achieved! I prayed God to protect HIM, who has brought us to such greatness. Passed on Ardeshir's news.

Tuesday, 10 December

Audience. Submitted a letter from Princess Ashraf. HIM was clearly furious with it, since he began tearing it to shreds. But then he broke into a laugh, saying, 'Write to my sister. Up to now she's made such a fuss about donating her money to charity. Ask her why in that case she's so keen to be involved in private business deals ...'. Needless to say he turned down all the business requests she's made ...

Discussed the King of Greece and his defeat in yesterday's referendum. Less than 40 per cent of the electorate voted for the monarchy to be restored ... 'To cheer him up a little', said HIM, 'you'd better send him an extra something.'

... Met the ambassador of Afghanistan after lunch ... He described the chaos that's erupted at home. For example, there's a governor in the north of the country who simply auctions off positions in local government to the highest bidder. They have no domestic television service, although those living near the Soviet border listen in to the Soviet networks. I asked him about Davoud's future plans. How does he intend to deal with his army, the majority of whose officers are Russian trained? How can he forestall a coup? And what about the clergy and the tribesmen in the provinces; has Davoud any sort of popular power-base? The ambassador's replies to all these questions made very depressing listening. He blamed virtually everything on shortage of finance. In that case, I asked him, why doesn't Davoud turn to HIM for help? Apparently he's biding his time until his forthcoming visit to Tehran. I told him that there's no love lost between us and Davoud, particularly when one recalls what he did to the rest of the royal family. We will support him only because there is no other alternative. God knows what will happen to Afghanistan once he's gone. I then made discreet enquiries as to the ambassador's own financial situation; was his father-in-law, Davoud, keeping him well-supplied? He replied that he had been granted a modest allowance ... He seemed positively delighted by my interest.

Wednesday, 11 December
Audience ... Apropos my meeting with the Afghan ambassador, HIM expressed himself well pleased with the arrangement we've come to. 'Just as I'd hoped', he said. 'These people must learn that it's we that call the tunes.'

Sunday, 15 December
... President Giovanni Leone of Italy flew in this afternoon at the start of his official visit ... Dreadfully embarrassed over dinner at the Niavaran Palace to discover that my idiotic subordinates had failed to provide any sort of white wine. Somehow HIM failed to notice the blunder ... Leone is a handsome and personable individual ... his wife turned out to be a real beauty ...

HIM instructed me to use his private account to buy gold. He anticipates a sharp rise in its price.

Wednesday, 18 December
The ambassadors of Algeria and Pakistan presented their credentials this morning. For several years our relations with Algeria have been suspended, but now that we've adopted a common policy on oil, the time has come

for us once again to exchange ambassadors. The Pakistani ambassador made a speech reminding us that Persian was his mother tongue but that it had grown rusty through lack of use and so he was forced to address us in English. He apologized for this lapse; a charming gesture.

Audience this afternoon ... HIM expressed grave suspicion about various leaders of the domestic opposition. He believes they're in the pay of foreign powers. A shocking fact if true.

Reported a meeting I had yesterday with the British ambassador. The man was quite over the moon about the successes scored by British-made Rapier missiles. They've brought down two Iraqi planes in as many days ... He was anxious to sound us out on our reaction, should Britain sell helicopters to Baghdad. 'Let them go ahead and supply them', remarked HIM. 'They can't afford to throw up such a lucrative deal, and anyway Iraq is bound to buy helicopters from someone. Better they obtain them from our ally than from the Soviets.' ...

Sunday, 22 December
Audience ... HIM then received Jacques Chirac, the French Premier, who had asked to meet him in private, unattended by our own PM. HIM was more than happy to agree to this ... We've fallen out with the French over the price of gold. Giscard d'Estaing and President Ford agreed at their Martinique meeting to joint control of bullion prices, which are rocketing ever higher on the international markets. Apparently these rises assist the western powers in reducing their balance of payments deficits. From our point of view, however, the situation is wholly undesirable. Originally we agreed to a freeze on oil prices for the next nine months, but we may be forced to jettison that resolution ...

Chirac passed on a letter from Giscard d'Estaing to HIM, asking for a meeting sometime in the near future ...

Monday, 23 December
Audience. HIM instructed me to reply to the French President's letter, suggesting that they meet either in Zurich on 18–19 January, or sometime in February at St Moritz. Failing that, HIM could stop-over in Paris on his way to America this coming May. I suggested that this last proposal was unduly submissive, given that Giscard really ought to come to pay his respects to HIM rather than the other way round. 'Nonsense', replied HIM, 'I refuse to listen to such petty considerations.'

... I myself received Chirac after lunch. It was billed as a fifteen minutes courtesy call but in fact went on for nearly an hour ... Discussed Iran's relations with her neighbours; a subject of which the Frenchman seemed more or less wholly ignorant. He didn't even know the reason for our dispute with Iraq. I gave him a brief run-down on the situation, before reminding him how close Franco-Iranian relations have been, leaving aside such temporary disappointments as Napoleon.[1] Here again it was apparent that he hadn't a clue what I was talking about. I would at the very least expect a Prime Minister visiting a foreign country to have been briefed on something of past relations with his host, and to have at least a basic idea of that host country's present situation. Chirac struck me as being far too inexperienced to hold down such an important office. He's barely out of short trousers. A cabinet minister by all means, but not a man to head a government. Trade and economic affairs seemed the one subject that interested him ...

Tuesday, 24 December

Audience ... Dr Eqbal had called round to offer HIM a helicopter as a birthday present from NIOC; an offer which HIM refused, pointing out that there were bound to be problems over spare parts and maintenance as all our helicopters are US-made. Even so Eqbal insisted I tell HIM that the manufacturers have guaranteed to service the aircraft. 'What he doesn't realize', HIM said, 'is that he's being manipulated by the British or some agent of theirs. First they hope to see me using their blasted helicopter. Then they'll gradually persuade the military to follow suit.' ...

Over dinner HMQ described an amusing French cartoon she's seen. Various French politicians are asked if they believe in Father Christmas. Giscard answers no; Mitterrand likewise. But when the same question is put to Chirac, just back from his trip to Iran, the cartoonist shows him hesitating whilst above him hovers an image of HIM disguised as Santa Claus. The fact is that Chirac managed to obtain trade agreements here worth $6 billion. Giscard has rewarded him with the Order of Merit, First Class.

Saturday, 28 December

... At dinner ... we discussed the careers of various Iranian politicians. 'In all fairness', I said, 'whenever I meet Amini he's full of praise for Your

---

[1] In May 1807 Napoleon concluded a military agreement with Iran which, like France, was at war with Russia. Barely two months later, he made peace at Tilsitt with Tsar Alexander I, totally ignoring his promises to Iran.

Majesty. He says he prays for you.' 'Such men are merely reeds blown in a wind from Washington', HIM replied. 'When the time is ripe, Amini and many like him will come oozing like worms from the mud.' ...

Sunday, 29 December

... Instead of planting nothing but pine trees, HIM suggested recently that whenever possible plane trees and other more attractive species be substituted. As a result the authorities in various parts of Khorassan now contemplate grubbing up their ancient pines; the effect will be to leave a total desert. Reported this at my morning's audience. HIM was greatly upset, saying I should ask the Minister of Agriculture whether the men in his ministry have completely lost touch with reality.

Princess Ashraf has requested an audience. Amongst other things she wants to ask HIM to set aside $40 million for the UN family planning scheme. She believes a gesture like this might improve our standing abroad; at the moment we're regarded as a militaristic and authoritarian regime. 'Are you sure that's all she wants?', said HIM, laughing. 'After all, she's already forced us to pay $2 million to the UN Commission on Women's Rights.' I remarked that the Princess is keen to prepare the ground for what she hopes will be her election as Secretary-General of the UN. In addition, when HIM opens next month's conference on women's rights, she intends taking the opportunity to call for equal rights of inheritance. This may be a desirable goal, but it's simply impracticable in Iran, as it runs quite contrary to Islamic law ... HIM pondered for a while before replying. 'Tell her', he said, 'That I shall punish anyone who calls for such a change in the law, even if it means prosecuting my own sister.' I heaved a sigh of relief ...

1975

Arguing that his own personality and social reforms commanded universal support, the Shah determined to dispose with what had previously passed for multi-party politics, declaring the old system redundant and a hindrance to minority interests. Henceforth there was to be a single party, the *Rastakhiz* (Resurgence). To stimulate debate inside this monolith, two factions were formed, each headed by a cabinet minister nominated by the Shah. Any hope that the new party would offer real opportunity for debate evaporated after only a few months. As Alam reported to the Shah, *Rastakhiz'* only concrete achievement was 'to get everyone's photograph in the newspapers and to provide a forum for the ridiculous antics of Hoveyda' (Diaries, 29 November).

Inflationary pressures intensified. A new statute empowered military tribunals to hear cases of hoarding or profiteering; evils against which the new party was invited to crusade. In his September address to Parliament the Shah boasted that prices had actually fallen by 2 per cent since the start of the year, although even the official index registered a rise of nearly 13 per cent.

At the Algiers conference of OPEC heads of state, Iraq agreed an end to its border dispute with Iran, conceding critical Iranian demands over the Shatt al-Arab waterway. This represented a diplomatic triumph for the Shah, boosting Iran's status as the paramount power in the Gulf. Deteriorating relations with the new revolutionary regime in Iran were to lead in 1980 to Iraq's unilateral abrogation of this agreement. More recently still, in August 1990, following her invasion of Kuwait and wishing to transfer Iraqi troops southwards from the frontier with Iran, Iraq declared her willingness to resume talks on the Shatt al-Arab based on the Algiers settlement. In 1975 this had led to devastating consequences for the Kurdish forces seeking independence from Baghdad. Deprived of Iranian military support, the Kurdish force proved to be no match for the much larger Iraqi army. Some 60,000 Kurdish guerrillas or their relations accepted the Shah's offer of haven within Iran, obtaining Iranian nationality. They were generously treated, many being recruited by government agencies. Their commanders received salaries equivalent to those of the Iranian army. Four hundred houses close to Tehran were put at the disposal of the Kurdish leader Mustafa Barzani and his immediate family. Despite this, the Kurds felt bitter disappointment. Alam writes of a plot by Kurdish nationalists against the Shah's life (Diaries, 21 March–3 April).

Thursday, 2 January

Audience. Various clergymen mixed up in anti-government politics have been awarded heavy prison sentences. But Ayatollah Khonsari has put in a request that they be granted royal pardons in return for undertaking to refrain from any future misconduct. 'Not a bad idea', said HIM. 'Fair enough, we'll let them go, provided they were jailed for simple subversion. Anything more serious, like murder, and they remain in gaol.'

Brezhnev has cancelled a trip to Egypt on the grounds of ill health. I pointed out that he may be faking. 'No', said HIM, 'I'm pretty sure he's telling the truth. He seemed far from well when I met him in Moscow. Part of the time he was totally incoherent. He couldn't even get to the end of his sentences.'

Friday, 3 January

... Audience. HIM had received Princess Ashraf beforehand. Normally on these occasions I expect to find him in a very touchy mood. Today on the contrary he beamed at me when I was shown in ... 'The Iraqis have taken a dreadful beating', he said. 'Our troops are fighting like lions. Barzani's guerrillas were preparing to turn tail and run, but they've rallied and put on a brave show of resistance.'[1] ...

Reported that I met the Soviet ambassador yesterday. He was complaining that our government intends to put the building contracts for several major power stations up for international tender, despite the fact that HIM agreed in Moscow that they should go exclusively to Soviet contractors. 'Totally irrelevant', said HIM. 'We can't be expected to give them the contracts regardless of whether or not they can come up with a competitive bid.'

The Egyptian ambassador has asked that his government be granted a discount on 600,000 tons of oil to mark HIM's forthcoming visit to Egypt. I was instructed to look into the matter with NIOC ...

Saturday, 4 January

Audience ... Showed HIM drafts of the speeches he's to deliver in Amman and Cairo. 'The Cairo speech puts too much emphasis on Islamic solidarity', he said. 'What have we ever gained from this so-called "solidarity"? I don't like to get so closely mixed up with the Arabs.' I pointed out that the tone of the speech was designed to mirror that of the welcoming

[1] See introductory note 1975.

411

address to be delivered by Sadat. 'Bully for him', said HIM. 'But what may be to his advantage is to our net loss. Delete, or at least tone down, the references in question.'

... Reported that NIOC has agreed to supply 400,000 tons of oil to the Egyptians at discount. As for the Soviets, our government has agreed to purchase Soviet generators for several towns and cities provided the price, and above all the delivery terms, are competitive. 'Fair enough', HIM remarked. 'But remind the ambassador that they're no longer supplying us with arms and spare parts as promised. Worse, they've failed to offer us any explanation. Tell him this flies in the face of every accepted tradition of etiquette.' ...

Sunday, 5 January

Audience. Again raised the subject of security for HIM's visits abroad. He hates discussing such matters but I am obliged to draw them to his attention, especially as I have peculiar misgivings about this particular trip. 'If Your Majesty disapproves of my suggestions', I said, 'you can at the very least try to reduce the length of time you're to be away. For example, there'd be no harm in leaving HMQ in Europe whilst you yourself fly home.' He made no comment, merely changed the subject; his way of telling me to mind my own business ...

[On 6 January, the Shah and the Queen flew out on a state visit to Jordan and Egypt, proceeding thence to Switzerland where they were joined by their children. Alam also joined the Shah in Europe but for a few days only, returning to Tehran on 8 February.]

Friday, 21 February

... HIM and Giscard d'Estaing have held a meeting in St Moritz. This is the first time in the past seventy-six years that a French President has visited Switzerland, and even then it was not the Swiss he went to see but the Shah of Iran.

Kissinger stopped off in Zurich on his way from the Middle East, specifically to call on HIM. The CIA representative in Tehran told me in confidence that HIM's recent discussions with Sadat of Egypt laid the foundations for a whole new initiative by Kissinger ...

President Boumédienne of Algeria has sent a special envoy with an invitation for HIM to attend the OPEC summit in Algiers ...

Lunched with William Rogers, former US Secretary of State, now legal adviser to the Pahlavi Foundation in America. He told me an extraordinary story relating to our negotiations with the British over the islands of Tunbs and Abu Musa. Sir Alec Douglas-Home, the Conservative Foreign Secretary, whom we took to be a friend of Iran, several times asked the Americans to pressure us into abandoning our claims to the islands. By the same token, the Americans, although friends of King Faisal of Saudi Arabia and therefore supposedly hostile to our claim, refused to get mixed up in the affair ... This is how friends behave towards one another, when it comes to diplomacy ...

Saturday, 22 February

... HIM returned from Europe today, apparently in excellent shape ...

We have cancelled the trip Their Majesties were due to make to Pakistan on 25 February. The chaos there made it impossible to guarantee security. Bhutto is naturally upset; he'd planned to take his guests on a whistle-stop tour of the country. But the risks were simply too great. HIM is annoyed at having let down Bhutto at the very last moment. 'Why don't I visit him at home?', he asked. I agreed that this involved less risk. He decided to telephone him tonight. In due course he rang me back to say that he will travel to Larcana, Bhutto's home town, next Tuesday ...

Over dinner he remarked that it's no longer acceptable for our opposition party to have so little freedom of speech. He's thought about it long and hard, and shortly intends making an announcement to the nation. He gave nothing more away, although I could tell how anxious his remarks had made the PM ...

Sunday, 23 February

Audience. Found HIM twiddling his thumbs – always a sign that he's lost in thought – his feet up on the desk. In the past he used to play with his hair when thinking, but just as his power has increased so he has altered his outward signs of concentration. It was quite some time before he noticed my presence.

... I suggested that he be accompanied on his trip to Algeria by a high-level team, comprising the Minister of Finance, the Minister of the Interior who doubles as our chief intermediary with OPEC, the governor of the Central Bank and various assorted experts, including Dr Fallah. 'But what would all these donkeys find to do?', he asked. I replied that call them whatever names he likes, they are none the less essential. He admitted I might be right ...

He is also furious with the Great Court Chamberlain for suggesting that Prince Charles, the heir to the British throne, be welcomed on arrival at Tehran airport by our own Crown Prince. 'Did Prince Charles go to Heathrow when the Crown Prince visited London?', he asked – a very reasonable question ...

Monday, 24 February

Audience. Just as yesterday, I found HIM sunk in thought, drumming his fingers on the desk-top. I was pretty sure that whatever I said would go unnoticed but all the same did what I could to attract his attention, reporting that *Paris Match* want to feature him on their cover and have asked that he grant an interview to their correspondent. 'I'm not interested', was all he said.

Reported the findings of our enquiry into student unrest ... He showed complete disinterest. Next, I described the discussions I've held with Senator Charles Percy, a supporter of Kissinger. Still not a spark of interest ...

He telephoned me after I'd left and instructed me to arrange a meeting next Sunday to be attended by the PM, the Speakers of Parliament, the head of his private secretariat, press representatives and myself. He said merely that he wishes to elaborate upon a few issues that have occurred to him. None the less, I now know why he's been lost in thought for the past couple of days ...

Wednesday, 26 February

... Received Lord Mountbatten at my office ... Once a dashing and witty man, the years are beginning to tell on him. He is here with Prince Charles, both of them having attended the coronation of the King of Nepal. They are our unofficial guests so I did not go in person to the airport to greet them but sent Amir Khosrow Afshar, previously our ambassador in London. Mountbatten explained that he's grown tired of destruction and war and is anxious to foster harmony by establishing international colleges in various parts of the world. Three have already been set up, in Wales, Canada and Singapore, and it's hoped that HIM will consent to Iran playing host to a fourth. Together with the British ambassador, our Education Minister and my deputy Homayoun Bahadori, we spent about an hour and a half discussing the proposal and drawing up a report to be submitted to HIM.

This evening HMQ entertained Mountbatten, Prince Charles and their retinue. Our own Crown Prince and I joined them for dinner. An enjoyable occasion ...

Thursday, 27 February

... Houshang Nahavandi, the President of Tehran University, called round full of anxiety about his position. I couldn't help feeling sorry for him. He's worked with dedication, but faces endless stratagems from the PM and his accomplices within Savak. They fear that Nahavandi's Association of Scholars and Intellectuals will one day come to rival the PM. The PM is convinced that Nahavandi must go, but as usual, he's far too devious to voice this opinion openly. Only last Tuesday when I met him at the airport he declared that whatever HIM may have decided about Nahavandi, he'll be sorry to see him go. Meanwhile HIM has instructed me to liaise with Savak to investigate the poor man's position. I didn't dare point out that before turning our attention to Nahavandi we should first find out who is pulling the strings at Savak.

HIM returned from Pakistan this afternoon ...

Sunday, 2 March

Audience. After lunch HIM was due to address the meeting he'd convened but he seemed already to have decided what he would say. Certainly the pensive look of the past few days has vanished. Discussed those aspects of his forthcoming visit to Algeria that are under my control ... Reported that Libya is not to be represented by Qadhafi in person but by his deputy who in effect holds the rank of Prime Minister. Rumour has it that the Algerians weren't looking forward to receiving Qadhafi. 'Even so', said HIM, 'I wouldn't have pulled out, even if Qadhafi had been there. I'm not about to stake this country's future on the whim of a Libyan lunatic.'[1]

... This afternoon HIM addressed the special meeting, announcing his views on the political system. He declared the old idea of an opposition party is moribund; in future there will be only one party including both government and opposition across a spectrum from left to right. Political debate will take place within the confines of this one party, which should make it easier to challenge and if necessary to replace the party leader ...

---

[1] The Shah had already been informed by Boumédienne – who was acting as go-between – that Saddam Hussein would take advantage of the Algiers Conference to reach agreement with Iran.

Malcontents within the ruling party will have greater freedom to speak out, without risking a charge of heresy[1] ...

Monday, 3 March

Audience. HIM was in high spirits, asking my views on yesterday's statement. I replied that it had been greeted enthusiastically ... with everybody scrambling to jump aboard the Shah's new party ...

He confessed that he'd pondered the issue for the past four or five months and in the end could think of no better alternative ...

Reported that Spiro Agnew, ex-Vice President of the USA, is presently in Iran looking up business contacts. I was unable to receive him but arranged for him to meet my deputy Homayoun Bahadori. I passed on Agnew's various requests. HIM said they should be forwarded to the appropriate government departments. All in all he seemed amused to learn what a low ebb the man has sunk to.

... 'By the way', he added, 'HMQ has told your wife to cease nagging you all the time; either she learns to cope with the situation or she should pack her bags and leave.' I replied how surprised I was to find HMQ taking sides with me; normally women are only too ready to gang up against us men ...

At two this afternoon HIM left for Algeria ...

Tuesday, 4 March

... I have discovered a growth in my armpit similar to the cancerous tumour that killed my late sister. If this means my life is coming to an end, I confess I feel more relief than regret. I shall put an end to myself if the growth proves malignant; I couldn't bear the lingering agony that awaits me otherwise. I find that life has little meaning, even without this latest threat ...

The OPEC summit has begun. The Algerian President made a speech of welcome, announcing his willingness to see oil prices stabilized for the coming decade, provided only that the West agrees to control the price of industrial goods and puts an end to inflation ... He has HIM's full support in this. Indeed he asked that HIM's arrival be arranged in such a way as to allow a personal display of greetings at the airport followed by two hours

---

[1] This meeting proved to be the birthplace of the Rastakhiz party, for which see the main introduction on the Shah.

of private discussion. Saddam Hussein,[1] Vice-President of Iraq, is also at the summit. He's been received by HIM ...

Wednesday, 5 March

... The doctor examined my tumour and pronounced it benign. Is this good news or bad? A sense of duty alone bade me thank God for my deliverance[2] ...

HIM has twice received Saddam Hussein ...

Thursday, 6 March

... President Boumédienne of Algeria has declared that the Iran–Iraq conflict is dead and done with. HIM and Saddam Hussein publicly embraced one another, and expressed their thanks to the Algerian ...

Friday, 7 March

HIM flew in at two this morning, apparently fit and full of optimism. He deserves to be, given the triumphs he has won ... Audience at noon ... Told HIM that in my opinion this is the most successful trip he has ever made. 'Just so', he replied. 'Although it's quite worn me out. I slept no more than two hours a night. On the bathroom scales this morning I found I'd lost a full three kilograms. The OPEC side of things went well, nearly as well as our settlement with Iraq. I had to cope with two infuriating problems inherited from my father: his extension of the oil agreement and the treaty he signed over the Shatt al-Arab.[3] I can't really blame him, he probably had no alternative. Even so thank God I reached a radical new solution to the oil problem, and now at long last I've been able to tear up the Shatt al-Arab treaty.' ...

I asked what the fate of the Kurdish guerrillas will be. Apparently he has already ordered General Nassiri to offer them shelter in Iran. But what about the idea of an autonomous Kurdistan? 'Moonshine from the word go', said HIM. 'They've suffered defeat after defeat. Without our support they wouldn't last ten days against the Iraqis. I spent four and a half hours

---

[1] Because of President Hassan al-Bakr's long illness, Saddam Hussein was already effective ruler of Iraq.

[2] Alam's physicians had agreed not to reveal to him the exact nature of his illness.

[3] In 1933 Iran concluded a new agreement with the Anglo-Iranian Oil Company, extending its concession by an additional sixty years – to 1993. The terms of the agreement were considered most unfavourable to Iran. A new agreement on the Shatt al-Arab was signed in 1937, to a large extent merely updating the Constantinople treaty of 1913 which, in Iranian eyes, had granted excessive privileges to Iraq – then a part of the Ottoman Empire – over what was supposed to be an international waterway.

with Saddam Hussein, and he admitted that several times the presence of our troops and artillery had been the only factor to stand between the Iraqis and total victory ... ' Even so, I suggested that Kurdish claims might one day prove useful. 'Perhaps so', he said. 'But I wouldn't be surprised if our agreement with Hussein proves permanent. Baghdad may well opt for a closer relationship with us and shake off foreign, particularly Soviet, influence.' 'But last year, Your Majesty', I replied, 'the Iraqis were on the brink of accepting Kurdish demands. Indeed it was only at Your Majesty's prompting that the Kurds rejected the offer.' 'Both sides knew that Iraq had no serious intention of honouring her promise', he retorted. 'It was more a cheap gimmick than a promise.' ...

Wednesday, 12 March
Audience. Found HIM in a far better mood than yesterday. The reason is simple. Yesterday afternoon he was apprehensive about receiving Mustafa Barzani, the Kurdish leader. Naturally he was a little embarrassed to meet the man face to face, though the Kurds would have been wiped out long ago if it hadn't been for our support. Something approaching 100 pieces of field artillery, besides countless anti-tank and SAM missiles, are under Iranian command in Kurdistan. The whole lot must be destroyed as soon as possible since there's no chance of our retrieving them in the time available ... The international community is accusing us of betrayal. They don't spare a thought for where the Kurds would be today, but for Iranian support. In any case an independent Kurdistan was never likely to do us much good ...

HIM received the Deputy President of North Korea who subsequently lunched as his guest ... The man is anxious to lay his hands on a loan; what he describes as 'only' $1 billion, repayment to be discussed later. HIM shot me a surreptitious smile ...

Thursday, 13 March
... Attended Lunch given in honour of the Turkish Foreign Minister, following his audience at noon. Discussing various regional issues HIM remarked that he's warned the Pakistanis against any further clash with India; they'd be bound to come out the losers which would be to no one's advantage, least of all ours. Meanwhile he has notified the Indians that we would be unable to remain neutral should they launch an attack on Pakistan ... 'The position of Afghanistan is even more ridiculous', he continued. 'On top of their long-stated ambitions in Pashtunistan, they've now laid

claim to Pakistani Baluchistan. It's India and the Soviet Union that have egged them on. The idiots can't appreciate that even if they manage to snatch Baluchistan and so get access to the sea, the Soviets would march straight in and claim the spoils.' ... Concerning our own arms build-up and our purchase of 80 F-14s – the Americans themselves have only 300 – HIM declared, 'We must be strong if we're to discharge our responsibilities in the Gulf and the Indian Ocean.' Our Turkish guest was quite taken aback by the boldness of this remark. I too was more than a little surprised ...

Thursday, 20 March
... Audience ... Reported that the Iraqi Kurds are asking for more time to get their families across the border into Iran. Barzani fears for his friends and relations left behind. None the less HIM insists that the guerrillas alone are to be offered sanctuary, saying that Iraq will do no harm to women and children. I replied that whilst this may be true, we can hardly expect the Kurds to believe it or to abandon their families. HIM suggested that the latter be put under the protection of the International Red Cross, indeed he promised to arrange this ... He can see no other alternative if we're to honour our agreement with Iraq ...

Friday 21 March–Thursday, 3 April
New Year fell on 22 March. The following morning I flew with Their Majesties and most of the royal family to Kish. We spent the next few days motor-boating or swimming, riding out most afternoons ... The ex-King and Queen of Greece were there as HIM's guests ... As a result HMQ put me to a lot of trouble, making arrangements for Greek singers to be laid on as part of the entertainment. HIM and I took a day off to fly to Abu Musa and another to visit Chahbahar where we've invested hundreds of millions of dollars developing the port, Iran's gateway to the Indian Ocean ...

The Soviet ambassador and his wife stayed as my guests for a couple of days. It gave me an excellent opportunity to get to know them. I get the distinct impression that the ambassador's far from being a committed communist. He made one particularly ludicrous remark to the effect that Iran can never be friends with China, though he soon withdrew when he saw how much fun I was able to poke at him.

... Our ambassador in Amman arrived with a letter from King Hussein, supplying the names of several Kurdish nationalists plotting against HIM's life. I duly forwarded it to Savak ...

On 21 March King Faisal was cruelly murdered by one of his own nephews – the young man is said to have been deranged ... I can't claim we were ever on good terms with Faisal, particularly towards the end when he grew into a dreadful old wind-bag, obsessed with the liberation of Jerusalem. None the less, there's no guarantee his successor won't be a damned sight worse ...

Returned to Tehran on Thursday, 3 April.

Saturday, 12 April
Audience ... Submitted the schedule for HIM's trip to Venezuela, Mexico and the USA ... remarking that over the next ten days we've somehow got to cram in receptions for the British Queen Mother, Prince Bernhardt of the Netherlands, Saddam Hussein of Iraq and the Afghan President, besides goodness knows how many visiting Foreign Ministers. And that's regardless of the fact that HIM is to spend forty-eight hours in Saudi Arabia. Really he's making life terribly difficult for everyone, himself included ...

Monday, 14 April
Audience ... *Ettela'at* has published a letter from one of its readers asking why the constitution of the new party lays so little stress on the appointment and conduct of the government. HIM was outraged, ordering me to tell the paper's editor he's a fool to print such nonsense. 'Spell it out to him', he said. 'The appointment and dismissal of ministers are prerogatives of the Crown. I and my successors remain the supreme authority over and above the executive. Tell him his paper would better serve its readers not by pandering to their ignorance but by explaining just such constitutional realities.'[1] ...

Thursday, 17 April
Audience ... Once he's returned from America HIM wants to visit Azerbaijan. I was surprised to have this sprung on me but then I realized that he's anxious to cap HMQ's recent success in Kermanshah ...

---

[1] The Shah clearly had in mind his own idiosyncratic interpretation of the Constitution.

Friday, 18 April

... A private dinner party given by HIM in honour of the British Queen Mother – the first time I have met her. Greatly impressed by her unostentatious good manners and her lack of conceit. Likewise her retinue was made up of delightful, highly cultured individuals. She's to be our guest for the next three days ...

Saturday, 26 April

... Met the British ambassador. He declared that despite the outward lack of success of the Paris talks on energy and commodity prices between producers and consumers, they must nevertheless be regarded as an achievement just in themselves; the first sign of dialogue between opposing camps. He assured me on behalf of his government that Britain is against any manner of confrontation between oil producers and the industrialized nations. 'We shall adopt a flexible approach', he said. 'Whether it be at the Paris talks or within the context of direct negotiations with Iran, HIM can rest assured that his opinions will receive full consideration.' I remarked that this was a wise move, but could he vouch for his cousins in Washington? He replied that he could speak only for the British government ...

Again he apologized for recent events, saying that he'd lost a whole night's sleep worrying about it.[1] I told him I had already passed on the facts to HIM and had been empowered to accept whatever apology might be offered. HIM considers the project we're engaged in as being of the utmost importance and has declared that however badly one particular individual may have behaved, it shouldn't be allowed to interrupt the legitimate activities of other British companies ...

President Davoud Khan of Afghanistan flew in this afternoon. He seems greatly aged and has lost all his former vigour. The speech he made at dinner rambled on and on ...

Tuesday, 29 April

Yesterday morning HIM travelled to Riyadh to spend twenty-four hours with King Khalid, Saudi Arabia's new King.

[1] The events referred to involved negotiations by a British company to secure a major contract for the construction and equipment of hospitals in Iran. Their principal agent was a well-known British peer whose political career had been blighted by involvement in a sex scandal. He was misled into believing that his local Iranian partner had passed on bribes to Alam. Alam was outraged when these allegations surfaced, professing ignorance of the entire affair. He duly received a letter of profound apology from Sir Anthony Parsons, acting 'as British ambassador [and] guardian of the honour of England'.

Saddam Hussein was granted a two-hour audience this afternoon and later attended a dinner in his honour. His pictures in the newspapers fail to do him justice. He turns out to be tall, slim, handsome, a young man of considerable intelligence. Over dinner the talk centred on our joint communiqué about security in the Gulf; the need to exclude all foreign influence ... Hussein's response to all this was most impressive ...

Wednesday, 30 April

On HIM's orders I attended the first Congress of the new party, the Rastakhiz movement. There were some 4,400 delegates from across the country, ready to debate the provisional party constitution. The whole thing was excellently stage-managed, but hollow; utterly hollow and false ...

Davoud Khan was due to lunch privately with HIM before returning to Kabul. I sent a note reminding HIM to press Davoud for the release of Abdul Vali Khan. Now that we're giving Davoud so much assistance, it's the very least we can expect in return ...

Thursday, 1 May

Audience. HIM remarked that he'd found King Khalid good-natured and more than the mere puppet he's made out to be. 'None the less', he said, 'all the serious business was left to me and Fahd.'

The Crown Prince has been invited to the ceremonial re-opening of the Suez Canal. HIM insisted that I ask him, man to man, whether he wishes to attend. The stress on 'man to man' was intended to rule out any approach via the women who surround him, HMQ or Mrs Diba.

The Foreign Minister of the UAE attended lunch. Again we discussed Gulf security. He had little alternative but to endorse the resolution arrived at by HIM and the Iraqis.

Saturday, 3 May

Audience prior to HIM's departure for Venezuela, Mexico and the USA ... Reported a meeting between Afshar and the British ambassador and their discussions on political developments in Oman. The British are highly critical of the Sultan's entourage and the spread of corruption. In reality, their irritation springs from the fact that the Sultan's most trusted adviser is a man called London, a Canadian who was his fellow classmate at Sandhurst. 'How ridiculous', HIM remarked. 'The British can't even rid themselves of such a minor nuisance.' ...

Wednesday, 21 May

Their Majesties have returned from America ... Attended Dinner, over-joyed to see HIM once more ... The PM was there, heaping praise on HMQ for the speech she made at Georgetown University. Indeed it was an excellent speech, but the PM was really out to remind her it had been prepared by his brother, Fereidoun Hoveyda ...

Saturday, 24 May

... The Crown Prince received me after lunch. He approved the schedule for his visit to Egypt and insisted I accompany him. He's such a charm-ing boy, and stands so high in my affections that I had no choice but to accept ...

Sunday, 25 May

Audience ... Remarked how impressed I am by the Crown Prince's shrewdness and intelligence. For example, discussing his retinue, he made a point of saying how essential it is that I should be on hand to deal with any problems beyond his competence or that of his aides. 'Quite so', said HIM. 'He's a very bright boy, with a well developed talent for avoiding responsibility.' ...

Monday, 26 May

Audience. Discussed Senator Edward Kennedy's stay. He is due to lunch as my guest and so I asked HIM what topics I should raise in conversation. He told me to stress the importance of the Persian Gulf, the free flow of oil, developments in the Indian Ocean, Soviet–Indian plans for the dismemberment of Pakistan, and the possibility of a Soviet invasion of Afghanistan ... Our own policy in all these fields is to stand firm, and resolutely to oppose such changes ...

I pointed out that Kennedy's Middle Eastern tour is being justified on the grounds that he's a member of the Senate Energy Committee, yet that really he's edging towards a bid for the US presidency and hopes the trip will bring him good publicity. HIM agreed, saying he'd heard rumours to this effect during his stay in the USA. I remarked that in Iraq Kennedy was welcomed by the Minister of the Interior – a peculiar mark of honour. HIM was so surprised by this that I had to show him the Reuters report to convince him it was true. He then asked what sort of welcome we ourselves had arranged and I explained that at Abadan he was received by the city's mayor but that at Tehran there was to be no official ceremony;

he would merely be driven from the airport to my private residence. I suggested it was not too late to send a junior member of the Foreign Ministry's protocol department to the airport, but HIM said this was unnecessary ...

Kennedy duly flew in at half past one this afternoon, accompanied by various relatives, friends and photographers. We had little time to discuss politics since he was expected to attend a meeting with the Foreign Minister at half past three followed by visits to the PM and the Finance Minister. At lunch his wife was placed next to me and we had a most enjoyable chat ... She's still quite a beauty ... She agreed to remain in Tehran for a short while longer than the Senator ...

Tuesday, 3 June
This afternoon, flew to Cairo with the Crown Prince. He was received by the Egyptian Vice-President with full military honours. The boy behaved magnificently, with a dignity well beyond his years. I was so proud of him.

Thursday, 5 June
... Accompanied President Sadat on board an Egyptian destroyer from Port Said to Ismailia ... With a break of only half an hour for lunch Sadat spent the entire journey talking to various Egyptian and foreign journalists. He carried the thing off shrewdly and with great patience. I presume that some of the foreign correspondents had been prepared beforehand since one or two of their questions, and even Sadat's simulated rage at various points, seemed pre-arranged. For example when the ABC man asked why Israeli shipping has been permitted to use the Suez Canal, Sadat affected a fit of temper, snapping back at him, 'Why make a mountain out of a molehill? I am bound by the Suez treaty of 1883. It stipulates the canal must only be closed to countries at war with Egypt.' ... He went on to say that he believes Israel's decision to reduce her ground forces in exchange for free passage of the canal is a sign of goodwill towards Egypt. Moreover he declared his readiness to fight to keep the canal open, as a signal to the rest of the world that he intends to maintain the peace ...

Over lunch we talked about the late Reza Shah, and of how HIM and Sadat had both been of the same rank, lieutenant, when HIM first came to Egypt. Sadat said how much he admired Reza Shah who was banished by the British at the same time that Sadat was languishing in a local British prison.[1] He also expressed a strong desire that his children might visit Iran. I promised to arrange this at the earliest possible opportunity. Throughout he referred to our own Crown Prince as 'my son' ...

From Ismailia we returned to Cairo having meanwhile bid farewell to Sadat. He spent a good two minutes shaking my hand, saying how much he appreciated HIM's decision to allow the Crown Prince's exams to be postponed in order that we might make this trip ... 'Tell HIM', he said, 'that I badly need his wisdom and assistance.' He struck me as being entirely sincere, a quality I would credit to all the Egyptians we met. Last night for example, my servants went shopping in Port Said, and having no local currency offered to pay for their purchases in Iranian rials. As soon as the shopkeeper realized they were from Tehran he offered to give them whatever they wanted, entirely free of charge ...

We dined this evening as the guests of Mrs Sadat. The Crown Prince carried on a conversation in fluent English, a language he knows not nearly so well as French. I assumed he'd be feeling worn out, but in the event he stayed until past midnight. Doubtless he found Sadat's beautiful daughters an incentive for remaining behind ... The President has four children: a son aged nineteen, two married daughters and a third aged thirteen, very pretty but apparently rather spoilt ... We'd brought carpets and Iranian gold for the family. In return we were given various antique Egyptian guns and a superb Arab stallion. Mrs Sadat neither drinks nor smokes, altogether a very attractive and distinguished host. She's studying Arab literature at the university and is so worried about her coming exams that she finds it difficult to sleep ...

Friday, 6 June
Toured the Pyramids this morning and the museum of Egyptian antiquities. Flew home at 2 p.m., our departure marked by the same ceremonial that greeted our arrival.

Saturday, 14 June
Audience. Discussed the forthcoming elections[2] I consider HIM's moves towards relatively free elections a most important step, although in the short term it's causing us any number of headaches ...

---

[1] Following the occupation of Iran by British and Soviet armies in 1941, Reza Shah was forced to abdicate. He contemplated going into exile in a neutral country, but the British thought differently and moved him first to Mauritius and subsequently to Johannesburg, where he died in 1944.
[2] Parliamentary elections, held every four years.

HIM complained about the greed of his entourage. 'How much more do they expect to get out of me? They're already jeopardizing my reputation.' I was saddened by this, reflecting that I myself might have done far more to protect him. But then there's very little I can do, given the way things work in this country ...

Monday, 16 June

Audience. Again discussed the elections and the way the changing political climate has encouraged people to volunteer their names for the electoral register ... We then turned to the question of female suffrage and from there got round to the subject of women in general. HIM remarked that every woman is flawed in some way, however trivial. I reminded him that no one, either man or woman, is perfect and that if he'd forgive my impertinence, criticizing the fairer sex is invariably a sign of approaching old age ... He laughed at this, saying that old age has its advantages. At least it would stop him growing too attached to some harpy, and so save us all a lot of trouble ...

Wednesday, 18 June

Audience. So far 11 million people have registered to vote and been issued with polling cards ... There seems to be a great deal of enthusiasm for the change, with long queues forming outside many of the registration offices ... 'And yet no one has a clue how they're going to vote', said HIM. I agreed. It's true that there's been no reliable forecast of the outcome, although I'm told that students, university teachers, the working class and small businessmen have been particularly keen to register. This news seemed to worry him, but after a brief pause for thought his expression cleared and he remarked that it matters not one iota who gets elected, at least as far as we're concerned ...

Saturday, 21 June

Audience. HIM very pleased both with the conduct of the elections and the popular reaction to them ...

At dinner he ... instructed me to go immediately and telephone the Minister of the Interior. 'Ask him why he's been spouting such nonsense; saying that we've no idea how the newly elected MPs will behave. Doesn't he realize that they're all of them members of the one political party, and as such will follow the party line? Tell him to issue a correction immediately.' ... I did as I was told and rang poor Jamshid Amouzegar. He was already quite worn out by the elections and what I had to say to him got him badly shaken. I did my best to calm him down . . .

Tuesday, 24 June

Audience. Reported a meeting with the Israeli representative in Tehran . . . His government is keen to propose various joint ventures with us but is apprehensive we may reject them . . . 'Too damned right we will', said HIM. 'They know as well as anyone that the Jewish press in the USA is solely responsible for our poor publicity.' . . .

Thursday, 26 June

Audience . . . Passed on a letter from Kissinger reaffirming his government's eagerness to seek a long-term contract for additional supplies of oil, offset against Iranian purchases of US goods. He asks that HIM receive Robinson, his Deputy, in order to discuss the matter at length. In reply HIM told me to point out that Robinson is already in touch with our Finance Minister, and that he can be granted an audience should this prove strictly necessary. I remarked on how cold this sounded but HIM replied this was precisely what he intended. 'These aren't exactly the most sincere of people we're dealing with', he said.

He then asked about the speech made last night by President Ford, setting out America's attitude to any further price rise by OPEC. Ford raised the possibility of the USA seeking alternative sources of energy. HIM chuckled at this, saying, 'But that's precisely what we've been telling them for ages. What asses these people are. They set out someone else's policy as if they themselves had invented it.'

I then passed on a very friendly thank-you letter from Senator Kennedy. 'If the man is so keen on us', HIM said, 'why on earth did he give a television interview criticizing our military build-up?'

Later met the local Israeli representative . . . I informed him that HIM disapproves his suggestion for joint Israeli–Iranian ventures. I explained that the hostile attitude of the US press was to blame for this, though he denied that their attitude was anything like so negative as we claim, offering to invite the President of the American Union of Jewish journalists to Tehran so that we can tell him exactly what we require . . . Before he left I presented him with a few books of HIM's political philosophy and a carpet. They're to be delivered to Yitzhak Rabin, the Israeli Prime Minister, to thank him for the little statue I was given on his last visit to Tehran.

The ambassador was delighted, knowing I must have got the go-ahead for this from HIM ...

Saturday, 28 June

Audience ... Reported my conversation with the Israeli representative ... HIM very much doubts whether the Jewish union referred to can include leading journalists such as those on the *New York Times* and *Washington Post* ...

At dinner Princess Shahnaz and HIM argued over recent outrages by Muslim fanatics (outright lunatics I would call them), who on their own authority have taken to murdering, or, as they put it, 'executing', innocent victims; for example Professor Adl's daughter[1] and her husband who murdered a few poor farmers and gendarmes before being gunned down. I gave it as my opinion that the sanctity of human life lies at the root of every religion. Those who deny this principle do so on no authority save their own. They either deserve to be confined to a psychiatric ward, or else to be given 100 strokes of the lash each day in a military prison until they regain their sanity; it's not something that's open to argument. This put the Princess in her place and much to HIM's relief she preferred to change the subject ...

Thursday, 3 July

... Audience ... The air force has asked that the Crown Prince's training aircraft be painted in the same colours as every other military trainer. HIM retorted that on the contrary, all the others must be altered to match the prince's colours. Apparently the boy refuses to accept any other solution ...

Monday, 7 July

Audience. I pointed out that, in seeking approval for the colour change, the Air Force Commander was merely reporting something that has already been done. The Prince's plane has been repainted. Should it now be restored to its previous colours? 'No', said HIM. 'Let's just forget about it, shall we?' ...

---

[1] Catherine Adl; a well-known figure at Court and very close to Princess Ashraf's children. She and her husband, both drug addicts, became devout Muslims, under the influence of Khosrow Jahanbani – husband of Princess Shahnaz. Their zeal turned gradually into a death wish. Although they had no connection with any opposition group, quixotically they twice provoked armed clashes with security forces and were both killed. Catherine's father, a leading surgeon, was a personal friend of the Shah.

Mr Carlos Lacerda, a Brazilian politician and HIM's host some time ago in Rio de Janeiro, is in Tehran and has called round with a gift for HIM and a request for an audience. 'Neither you nor I need receive him', HIM remarked. 'He's an opponent of the current regime in Brazil. Send him some sort of token, to thank him for his gift.' As I've said so often, the ingratitude of great men knows no bounds.

Asked if I might go to Paris for a check-up to establish whether I really do have cancer ... 'You talk about it as if it were a mild head-cold', HIM said with a smile. I sensed that he was embarrassed and so changed the subject. We chatted about various lady friends. He said how surprised he is to find the women he meets growing less and less attractive as the years go by, but as I pointed out, it's only because his own tastes grow more difficult to satisfy the older he gets. I immediately regretted my impertinence but HIM laughed it off, saying I might well have a point ... 'And yet', he said, 'if it weren't for this one little indulgence of mine I'd be an utter wreck.' I agreed, remarking that every man in a position of responsibility needs some sort of distraction, female company being in my opinion the one cure that really works. Without such diversions men grow callous – yet another impertinent remark, and one that I compounded by saying it explained why a eunuch like Hoveyda can be so dangerous. 'Oh, I don't know about that', said HIM. 'Hoveyda keeps himself occupied with his work.' I pointed out that this is an even greater danger; scheming is his only substitute for sex, and scheming in turn is bound to have practical consequences. HIM made no comment ...

Thursday, 10 July

Audience. The new parliamentary party – Rastakhiz – has resolved itself into two factions, one headed by the Finance Minister Ansari, and the other by Amouzegar, Minister of the Interior. As a result the Association of Scholars and Intellectuals is attempting to form an alternative group, to be called 'The Rationalists', objecting that the present two factions are merely the outcome of ministerial cabal imposed from above, rather than developing to meet real political needs at grass-roots level. HIM declared he has no intention of allowing the Association its way. 'They must fall into line with the existing groups, or even assume leadership of one of them if they can muster sufficient support. But they must on no account challenge the basic structure.' I reported that the same Association has criticized both Ansari and Amouzegar for being too close to the Americans.

'It's none of their business', HIM remarked. 'I'm the best judge in such matters.' ...

Friday, 11–Wednesday, 16 July
Flew to Paris for a thorough examination by four French specialists: Milliez, Jean Bernard, a gastro-enterologist from the Cochin hospital, and a leading dermatologist ... They found no serious disorder; merely strain from overwork ... Apparently the tumours on my chest aren't malignant. Thank God, but even so I feel a strange sense of anti-climax, unsure whether I might not have preferred death to a few more years of dull survival ...

Saturday, 19 July
Audience ... Discussed the plight of Western Europe, soaring inflation combined with economic stagnation ... HIM remarked that we, by contrast, have achieved a 30 per cent growth rate, unparalleled elsewhere. I replied I had my doubts about the exact figure, but even if it's only 15 per cent it's none the less extraordinary. HIM went on to claim that our price controls ensure that inflation stands at under 5 per cent. Again I expressed doubts about his figures ... remarking that, do what he may, HIM cannot deny the fundamental laws of economics. If need be, I shall pluck up the courage and tell him quite what misleading figures he's been given ...

Sensing that HIM was growing tired, I switched to discussing the fairer sex, reporting an incident which has at long last been resolved. HIM was annoyed by this but calmed down when I showed him the file I'd prepared on the affair.[1]

Tuesday, 22 July
Audience ... A unanimous resolution by the Jeddah conference of Islamic Foreign Ministers agreed by our own Minister demands the exclusion of Israel from the United Nations. I pointed out that this runs contrary to our traditional policy, but HIM denied this, saying that we simultaneously repudiated any conference resolution at odds with Iran's present com-

---

[1] Various British and German newspapers had published photographs of girls invited to Geneva by a Mr Q ... and from there dispatched to Tehran with promises of extremely generous remuneration. Interviewed by the Geneva police, Q ... denied acting on behalf of the Shah of Iran or anyone at his Court, claiming that the girls were employed solely for his own entertainment; an explanation the police were content to accept.

mitment to the UN; a neat way of ducking the issue over Israel.

Submitted the programme for Mrs Sadat's visit here on 25 August. HIM has always been most kind to the Sadats. He instructed me to tell her she should stay longer than the five days arranged ...

Wednesday, 23 July

Audience. Passed on a copy of *Bunte*, a German magazine which claims the relationship between HIM and HMQ has entered stormy waters. HIM declared such sensationalist nonsense must be treated with the contempt it deserves. I warned him that although we've banned its circulation in Tehran, one or other of HMQ's well-wishers is bound to send her a copy. 'Even so', he said, 'the thing's so utterly vulgar, HMQ will merely laugh at it.' ...

King Hussein flew in this afternoon, accompanied by his Queen ... HIM and HMQ flew on with them to the Caspian ...

Saturday, 26 July

... After lunch bade farewell to King Hussein and his retinue at Tehran airport. Their Majesties and I then paid a call on HM the Queen Mother. HIM complained to me how irrational his mother's requests have become, but I reminded him it's the duty of all of us to do what we can for her. 'A mother', I said, 'is the most absolute ruler of all. She must be obeyed however illogical her orders.' 'Quite so', HIM replied, 'I wouldn't dream of disagreeing.' ...

Tuesday, 29 July

Flew to Nowshahr, arriving at half past nine this morning to find HIM seated alone at the breakfast table ... Told him that I'd watched his broadcast interview with Lord Chalfont,[1] representing the BBC, and suggested it was so good that we should have it shown on the local networks. HIM agreed to this, although he said that watching the film he'd realized how many grammatical slips he made in his English. I confessed I'd noticed nothing of the sort ...

Before taking my leave, I accompanied him to the jetty next to his hut and there we stood chatting about this and that. I pointed out that Soviet ships anchored across the harbour were perfectly capable of photographing us, or even of eavesdropping on our conversation. Surely this was a serious

[1] Former journalist and Foreign Office Minister under the 1964–70 Labour government.

security risk? But he shrugged it off, saying that if he needs to hold important discussions or to meet foreign dignitaries he does so at Ramsar not at the beach. Even so, I remarked, the PM and myself are always received at Nowshahr. 'Neither of you ever has anything very important to say to me', he replied, putting an abrupt end to the conversation . . .

Saturday, 2 August
Flew to Nowshahr. Again found HIM at the breakfast table. I brought no important news. Four years ago during the monarchy celebrations we promised every visiting head of state a beautiful carpet woven with his or her portrait. In the event five of our guests accepted their invitations so late in the day that their carpets couldn't be got ready in time. They have only now been completed. I asked HIM's permission to have them delivered. 'You'd better check beforehand', he said with a smile; 'Find out how many of them have died or been chucked out of office.' Excellent advice. It turned out at least three of the five have vanished into thin air . . .

The most significant local news focuses on price control and a government campaign against businessmen accused of over-charging. Some cases have actually led to arrests; actions quite outside the law, since no managing director should be accounted responsible for the actions of his employees. Yet this is the way we carry on in Iran, much to the public's satisfaction I have to admit. For myself I see no good coming from this campaign. The only solution to over-charging is to increase supply to meet demand; the present price controls only make matters worse . . .

Sunday, 3–Thursday, 21 August
Holiday, and three weeks rest in Europe, beginning in Cap d'Antibes where I'd rented a large villa and an even bigger garden. Stayed there with my whole family, wife, children and grandchildren. God knows I must be growing old since I find young people and their ways quite impossible to cope with . . . a constant round of throwing, attending or recovering from parties. Once or twice I met up with Princess Ashraf and various of my friends. All most pleasant. Swimming or water-skiing from dawn to dusk has done a little to improve my health.

The villa was a veritable paradise, the property of a lady member of the French parliament, a leading radical.[1] As for myself, a man of the bluest

[1] The Villa Eleric, the property of Mrs Jacqueline Thôme Patenôtre.

of blue blood, such a house is quite beyond the dreams of avarice. But then that's the way things are in this world of ours ...

Sneaked off to Switzerland for a few glad days alone with my lover. Later joined my wife in Zurich where she had a dental appointment. From there we returned together to Tehran ...

Saturday, 23 August

Audience. HIM was the very soul of kindness, asking after my health and suggesting he be sent a copy of my doctors' report, that he may know what's really the matter. 'Have you ever wondered whether they're telling you the full truth?', he asked. 'You must take greater care of yourself. I need to know what's the matter, if I'm to find out whether there's anything I can do to help.' I was so touched by this that for several moments I stood there, quite speechless with gratitude ...

I asked whether it is true that HMQ is to attend this year's education conference in Ramsar. 'Quite true', said HIM. 'She likes to be numbered amongst the intellectuals.' ...

Reported that St Moritz is becoming a very risky place. Two days ago in Zurich the head of Swiss police showed me a bulging file, full of reports on people suspected of plotting to assassinate HIM. A copy of this file is to be made available to us in Tehran. HIM was quite taken aback and said that if that's really how things stand he will cancel this year's visit ...

Over dinner I told HIM how delighted I was that he'd sent such a forthright reply to the King of Saudi Arabia, in other words to the Americans by proxy, defending our stand on oil prices.

[King Khalid in a letter to the Shah dated 2 August 1975 stated that Saudi Arabia was opposed to any further rise in the price of oil at the forthcoming OPEC meeting in Vienna on 24 September. He referred to the international recession and the declining demand for oil to justify his caution. By resuming their talks in Paris, he claimed, the industrialized nations had shown their willingness to reach some sort of understanding with OPEC. In these circumstances a price increase would be politically untimely and likely to provoke an unfavourable reaction.

The Shah's reply stated that oil prices must accord with the price of alternative sources of energy; indeed that they should be designed to encourage consumers to explore and develop such alternatives in order to reduce the rapid depletion of natural oil resources. He reminded the

King that the industrialized nations had increased the price of their exports by 25 per cent during the course of 1974.]

'These bloody Americans', said HIM. 'They imagine they can get their own way, by manipulating the Saudis, and relying on their vast oil supplies.'

Sunday, 24 August
Audience ... Submitted a draft of HIM's reply to Kissinger's message of 22 August [reporting his efforts for an interim settlement between Egypt and Israel].

[The Shah in his reply adds]

... Regarding our own bilateral relations, I am very much disappointed that our talks on oil have not been successful and might even be inconclusive. Although, I appreciate your personal efforts that we first discussed when we met in Zurich. I am also disappointed that your authorities have not placed an order for our 'Spruance' class destroyers as this will postpone for at least two years our presence in the Indian Ocean ...

Expressed my doubts as to how much we can rely on Kissinger's goodwill in fixing oil prices. HIM admitted he too was unsure. 'But still', he said, 'we've got to go through the diplomatic niceties.'

Passed on a report by the Court Ministry's Social Department, dealing with education and the campaign against illiteracy ... Most significantly they suggest that seven years into the project and despite a declaration that illiteracy would take no more than a decade to eradicate, the number of illiterates has actually risen from 12 to 14 million. No doubt this results from the general population explosion, but even so it's a matter of great regret ...

Monday, 25 August
Prince Abdul Reza, HIM's brother, telephoned me last night to say that as Chairman of the Trustees of the National University he intends to sack Professor Safavian, the University's President. He reminded me that he'd accepted the honorary position of Chairman on the condition that he be given complete freedom of action and that he'd never put himself forward for the job. Now after a month studying the possible options, he is determined to make a clean sweep. He's convinced that Safavian must go.

HIM was dead set against this move when I reported my conversation, and declared that nobody is to be sacked without a thorough investigation and cast-iron justification. Moreover, he remarked that the Chairman of Trustees should have absolutely no say in hiring or firing the University President. 'Tell that to the Prince', he said. I naturally agreed, although I warned him how upset the Prince was likely to be. 'I couldn't give a damn', HIM replied.

... Immediately did as I'd been told. The Prince was badly rattled and declared that if this was how HIM intended to handle the matter, he preferred to be relieved of his appointment as Chairman. Reluctantly I telephoned HIM and explained how things stood. He was outraged that the Prince should take such a selfish attitude, saying, 'Tell him he can go to hell for all I care, and make sure you use exactly those words.' Even so in breaking the news to HIM's brother I had to think of a less brutal way of putting things. The Prince is no fool, though he's got a very sharp tongue. He'd already told me he considers Safavian to be my own placeman. As it turned out my scruples were entirely unjustified since the moment I told him HIM still refused to sack Safavian, he started banging on and on in exactly the way he had before. I'd had enough of this nonsense and told him straight out I didn't give a damn for his opinions but that he had better do as HIM ordered and look sharp about it, at which point I slammed down the receiver.

An hour later I rang through to report yet another urgent matter to HIM. He naturally asked how things had gone with the Prince. I explained that I'd carried out my orders to the letter and that as a result it was highly unlikely that the Prince would ever speak to me again, not that this bothered me unduly. 'Well done', said HIM. 'He's been asking for this for a long time.' ...

Saturday, 30 August

Their Majesties attended the opening of the annual education conference in Ramsar ... As expected the PM ensured that the party's report on the universities was highly critical – there's no love lost between the PM and Houshang Nahavandi, the President of Tehran University.[1] HIM made some excellent forthright remarks but in general came down on the side of the universities. HMQ also had her say ... She really is a moderating influence, besides being able to raise topics that no one else dare refer to.

---

[1] Hoveyda regarded Nahavandi's activities as President of the Association of Scholars and Intellectuals as a threat.

For example, she announced that the lack of free dialogue between students and academics is due to the fact that the students are afraid they'll be accused of political trouble-making. This is absolutely true, but who else would have the courage to say it? ...

Tuesday, 2 September
Audience in Nowshahr ... Submitted a message from Kissinger informing HIM that negotiations between Israel and Egypt have been successfully concluded ... HIM instructed me to get the Israeli ambassador to convey our congratulations to Yitzhak Rabin ...

Without any warning he then asked me when he could expect to receive my medical report. I assured him I'd asked my doctors to forward it direct ...

Wednesday, 3 September
The Ramsar education conference is still in session ... Apparently Majidi, Head of the Plan Organization, has persuaded the PM to bury his dispute with Nahavandi, provided that the Association of Scholars and Intellectuals, a body controlled by Nahavandi, refrains in future from submitting reports direct to HIM. Since Nahavandi himself has put these rumours about, I can't vouch for their reliability. If what he's saying is true, then both he and the PM have taken a very bold step ...

Thursday, 4 September
The conference came to an end, Their Majesties attending the closing ceremony.

Flew back to Tehran for the wedding, held at my own house, between the daughter of my chauffeur and a fellow Birjandi. Everyone was in excellent spirits save me, and even I had to pretend to be happy. The poor girl has cancer. I sent her to France for treatment last year but the doctors warned me she has only a few years left to live. I couldn't bring myself to tell her or her family, and allowed the wedding to go ahead. Oh, they had a marvellous celebration in my house, but for myself I've never felt less like rejoicing.

Sunday, 7 September
Brief audience ... Showed HIM a pamphlet by one of the underground opposition groups. It was found under his chair at the Ramsar conference. He was extremely indignant and ordered an immediate investigation ...

Monday, 8 September

State opening of Parliament ... Subsequently HIM and I returned to Saadabad by helicopter. I always enjoy watching HIM at the controls, dressed in full military regalia ...

He remarked that so many books have been written about him that it's about time someone wrote a book on HMQ. I told him I'd already mentioned this possibility to her, but that she thinks it's still too soon. 'But that's what she always says when she wants something but won't admit it', he replied. 'Pay no attention; just get on with whatever you're doing and you can bet she'll be pleased in the end.' ...

Tuesday, 9 September

Audience ... HIM rejected a proposal that we arrange a lunch with Saud al-Faisal, the Saudi Foreign Minister and second son of the late King Faisal. 'The thing will have to be rearranged', he said. 'How can I invite the man to lunch right in the middle of Ramadan?'

Wednesday, 10 September

Confined to bed with a fever. Wrote to explain this to HIM. He rang as soon as he received my note and asked whether I felt any better. Took the opportunity to discuss various items of business. Later I was handed letters for HIM from Kissinger and President Ford which made me apprehensive. I'm afraid I guessed correctly. The Americans are furious about the latest oil price increase. They're even ready to scrap the bilateral agreement which we signed in the mistaken belief that it might placate them. Tension between us and Washington is particularly unfortunate at a time when excessive co-operation with the Arabs has blackened our reputation with the US media.

... Last night met the Finance Minister who was moaning on about the chaotic state of our affairs ... As he is a friend and I can talk to him frankly, I told him he was behaving like an outside observer, like the Finance Minister of Mars might behave. Instead of wringing his hands he should take action or at least have the courage to report the situation to HIM. He replied that he and his colleagues have been expressly forbidden to report such matters; the PM has told them it only gets HIM worked up, which put another way means that HIM gets angry with the PM. The government's role is to gloss over harsh realities ...

Thursday, 11 September

Twice read through HIM's reply to President Ford. Thank God for the Shah. At last he's achieved a standing from which he can address the President of the United States, courageously, on equal terms. What a pity that etiquette forbids us to publish this exchange that our people might read it ... Even so HIM has insisted the letters be read by the PM, our Foreign Minister and our ambassador in Washington.

[In his letter dated 9 September 1975 President Ford had written:]

... We have undertaken a fundamental review of our overall policy towards the developing countries. This review has resulted in a new approach to the producers/consumers dialogue that responds more fully to these nations' concerns, particularly those raised by your government's representatives and other delegations during the Paris meeting ...

As you can appreciate, the support of the American public for the new United States position must be based on an awareness of the concerns of the oil producers and other developing countries and the need to seek cooperative solutions to our common economic problems. I am concerned, however, that this necessary support will be jeopardized should the member countries of OPEC increase the price of oil this fall.

I am also concerned that such action could raise serious questions among the American public regarding the close cooperation we seek and are actively developing with your country in several fields of our bilateral relationship. I value this relationship greatly and sincerely wish to continue to broaden and deepen it ...

[In his reply dated 10 September 1975 the Shah wrote:]

... At my suggestion OPEC agreed to freeze the price of oil until the end of September 1975, although we were subject to the continued inflation exported to our country.

However I feel constrained to say that it does not appear justifiable to us to continue the freeze and to tolerate a decrease of about 35 per cent in our purchasing power before such a dialogue takes place. In this context it is worthy to note that we have no influence on the prices of commodities and manufactured goods which are imposed upon us. There are many items of goods that we buy this year 300 to 400 per cent more from the United States of America than we did 18 months ago ...

With regard to the adverse effect of any increase in oil prices on the recovery of the industrialized countries, I would like to draw your attention to the fact that firstly, the tax imposed by the consuming industrialized nations on oil products, which on average nearly equals the government take of the oil producing nations, can very well be adjusted to take care of any increase in oil prices. In the case of the United States of America, considering lifting the 2 dollar tariff imposed on imported crude which has been under discussion could very well serve the same purpose.

Secondly ... an increase in oil prices is imperative to create sufficient incentive for the development of alternative sources of energy which in the case of the United States in particular would render 'project independence' a reality ...

I also appreciate very much and greatly value the special relationship that exists between our two countries which as you fully realize, Mr President, is not only in favour of Iran but is mutually and equally beneficial to both sides. If in defending our legitimate interests, we might raise serious questions among the American people, we would be very sorry to ascertain that the real facts have not been set before your public ...

Friday, 12 September

... A dreadful tragedy; General Khatami, the Air Force Commander has been killed in a hang-gliding accident over the reservoir of the Dez dam.[1] He was a stubborn man, but likeable; highly efficient and utterly devoted to HIM. Throughout the long years of confrontation with Baghdad, it was the strength of our Air Force that deterred the Iraqis from overt aggression ... Khatami was generous, disciplined, with a will of iron. Needless to say there have been rumours about the vast personal fortune he managed to accumulate, and for all I know these rumours may be true. But as I see it, an able servant deserves every penny he earns ... He was fanatically devoted to sport, and in the end this cost him his life; an irreparable loss to the country. Several times I've discussed the matter on the telephone with HIM who expressed sincere regret for what's happened ...

---

[1] In spite of various rumours, every serious investigation concluded that his death was purely accidental.

Sunday, 14 September

Audience ... 'Have you seen the letter I received from that idiot, Ford?', asked HIM.[1] I replied I had, but that HIM's reply[2] to it was sure to put the President firmly in his place. 'Yes', he said, 'but what on earth made him send such a letter in the first place? I'm convinced it was Simon or that devil Kissinger that put him up to it.' ... I pointed out how often I've warned him that the Americans are behind Saudi Arabia's recent series of letters and official visits here. When it became obvious to Ford that the Saudis were getting nowhere, he had no choice but to come out into the open. 'He'll achieve nothing by his latest move', HIM said. 'We reacted even more firmly against Nixon, although at that time oil prices were increased by a full 500 per cent. Now we're asking for a rise of no more than 15 to 20 per cent.' 'None the less', I said, 'we must remain on our guard. The Americans feel strongly enough about it to resort to who knows what sort of tricks.' HIM replied that they actually stand to benefit from a price increase since it may make it economical for them to develop alternative sources of energy, and so reduce their dependance on oil. But I pointed out that they still prefer cheap oil as a route to prosperity. 'Maybe so', he said, 'but they're powerless to get what they want. The merest hint of their moving against us and the Russians wouldn't hesitate to intervene.' I suggested that there are plenty of precedents for the superpowers reaching agreements on matters of mutual interests, behind our back. 'Ah, but not in this instance, I believe', said HIM ...

Monday, 15 September

Audience ... Submitted the doctors' report on my progress. HIM read it with considerable interest. He then suggested that although there appears to be nothing seriously the matter, I should none the less go to the USA for a thorough examination. I assured him my French doctors are more than satisfactory, as witnessed by their diagnosis of his own case, a highly complicated one, and the excellent treatment they've so far given him. 'Quite so', he replied. 'They're looking after me splendidly. But still you must go to America ... Take a complete rest. And mind you go alone. Your wife is not to go with you. Understand what I'm saying?' I gave in to this, thanking him sincerely for his kindness ...

---

[1] See the entry for 11 September 1975.
[2] Idem.

Wednesday, 17 September

HIM was due to grant an audience to a team from ABC television, but the Court Chamberlain who was present telephoned me to say that HIM had been so outraged by various of their questions that he'd stormed out of the room. Normally he keeps a tight rein on his temper. Indeed so surprised was I by this outburst that I immediately telephoned to find out what had gone wrong. 'The bastards questioned me about Savak', he said, 'asking whether it's true that suspects are induced to confess by being made to sit naked on red hot iron bars. Who on earth can have persuaded them to ask such a preposterous, such an insulting question? I want every one of them chucked out of the country, and make sure to be quick about it.' Despite this, I've delayed issuing a deportation order. I hope I can persuade them to offer some sort of apology for me to pass on to HIM . . .

At dinner . . . HMQ quite rightly reminded HIM how reckless he is to pilot so many different planes and helicopters. The talk then turned to the fate of General Khatami. HIM surprised me by once again declaring that Khatami had been depressed before his death . . . He also referred to his interview with ABC, suggesting that the whole thing may have been a deliberate provocation stage-managed to coincide with the forthcoming OPEC conference . . .

Saturday, 20 September

Audience . . . The ABC journalists have presented an official apology to the relevant officers of the Court, besides writing to me in person. HIM read their letter and seemed not at all displeased. He almost never expresses satisfaction in such cases, indeed his only comment on this occasion was that the journalists might remain on assignment in Iran . . .

Sunday, 21 September

Audience . . . HIM has been annoyed by a television interview given by Ardeshir Zahedi who announced that oil prices are set to increase by 5 to 10 per cent. To allow himself greater room for manoeuvre, HIM has always maintained that the increase will be nearer 20 to 30 per cent . . .

He then received the Speakers of both Houses of Parliament, taking the opportunity to announce that the newly elected parliament is now ready to hold its first session. As is customary, the PM has tendered his resignation and was duly reappointed by HIM to head the new government . . .

Monday, 22 September

Audience ... The US ambassador had been my guest for breakfast, and I reported our conversation to HIM. US Defense Secretary James Schlesinger has appointed a civilian to be his special representative in Tehran, in charge of all military transactions and reporting direct to his employer so as to cut down on red tape.[1] The ambassador asked that HIM grant the man an audience, also for the US general appointed to head their military mission, as well as for their latest CIA representative. HIM agreed.

I had asked the ambassador about the sale of Pershing missiles to Israel, a deal which has caused uproar amongst the Arabs. Apparently even the US Defence Secretary is against it, and has told the Israelis that Washington may be unable to honour its promises on the grounds that the missiles are no longer in production. The ambassador remarked how embarrassing and incomprehensible he finds this latest move, though he promised to look into it on my behalf. 'What a mess', HIM said. 'And to think that we are forced to depend on these people. Talking of which, Kissinger really is an old twister.' ... I had also asked the ambassador what sort of increase in oil prices he's anticipating. He replied he was unwilling to commit himself, saying he'd heard what a blunder Ardeshir Zahedi has already made in this respect. 'At least the rascal is kept well informed', HIM said.

Hoveyda, always ready to bend with whatever wind is blowing, proposes to install in his cabinet several people recommended by HMQ, Princess Fatemeh and others of his cronies. HIM was far from pleased and has forbidden any new ministerial appointments ... Having already discussed his plans with various people, Hoveyda was thoroughly taken aback to have them rejected. He was in a very forlorn state when I saw him this afternoon ...

Tuesday, 23 September

Audience. HIM has signed a cable, congratulating President Ford on yet another narrow escape from assassination. 'But why on earth do people want to dispose of such a hopeless old donkey?', he asked with a smile.

... I remarked that HIM's decision over the cabinet has badly disappointed those who thought they'd been promoted to office. 'But what else could I do?', he said. 'These idiots think they can get away with what the hell they like.' ...

Submitted the programme for Princess Shams's visit to Rome and the

[1] The man appointed was Erich Fritz von Marbod, previously principal Deputy Assistant Secretary at the US Defense Department.

Vatican. HIM gave his approval, provided she doesn't make a great song and dance about her meeting with the Pope.[1]

Finally I reminded him of our promise to supply the Israelis with oil. 'Quite so', he said. 'I've already told Kissinger that I fully intend to honour our commitment.' ...

Wednesday, 24 September
Audience. HIM declared that some day soon he would like to invite HMQ and the Crown Prince to his office so that I may brief them on the functions of the Court Ministry and its relation to other branches of the administration. He intends organizing similar meetings where the various government ministers and military commanders can explain their roles ... I suggested that above all else we need to make the Crown Prince familiar with Iranian history and traditions; also to turn him into a master of the Persian language and literature, aspects of his education which have been sadly overlooked ... Three institutions, the language, Shi'ism and the monarchy lie at the very foundation of this country ... 'Your Majesty might bear in mind', I said, 'that you are not only Shahanshah of Iran, but of the Shi'a community throughout the world.' He replied that the Shi'as living abroad lead miserable lives and that he's come to expect nothing but hostility from their clergy. Even so, I suggested, the possibilities opened up by appealing to the entire Shi'a community have been somewhat neglected in the past ...

Zaki Yamani has declared that the forthcoming increase in oil prices will be purely nominal. 'His usual rubbish', was HIM's only comment ...

Later met Uri Lubrani, the Israeli representative, who is extremely grateful for the congratulatory telegram sent by HIM to Yitzhak Rabin ... None the less he expressed regret that political considerations have led us to limit our co-operation with Israel ... He announced that his Prime Minister has commissioned him to prepare a plan whereby Iran will receive more favourable coverage in the US press, currently dominated by the Jewish lobby ...

Spent an hour and a half with Professor Peter Avery of Cambridge University. He hopes to write a book about the White Revolution ...

---

[1] Princess Shams and her husband, Minister of Culture Mehrdad Pahlbod, had quietly converted to catholicism in the late 1940s – an extremely sensitive issue in an Islamic country.

Thursday, 25 September

Audience ... 'Find out exactly what the Israeli representative has in mind', said HIM. 'Obviously if they can persuade the US press to adopt a more friendly attitude towards Iran, we shall be prepared to resume closer co-operation with Israel.' ...

He then discussed the army and the late General Khatami, disclosing various highly confidential matters that I shall never be in a position to disclose. HIM relies on the army, and he knows its every in and out, every detail, every rumour relating to its commanders. Where on earth would we be were it not for his insight and knowledge of what's really going on? The suspicions he confided in me are a sign of great trust, but none the less a heavy burden which I must carry with me to the grave[1] ...

Sunday, 28 September

Took advantage of the religious holidays last Thursday to fly to Kish together with my wife, General Nassiri, my friend Azimi and my grand-daughter. It may be hot and sultry but somehow my sweet memories of this place enable me to ignore its less than perfect climate ...

Whilst away I received a cable from our ambassador in Caracas, con-veying an urgent message for HIM from the President of Venezuela. Apparently in the event of other OPEC members agreeing on price increases, Saudi Arabia has threatened to withdraw from the organization. The President also complains that he is coming under strong pressure from the Americans to reach an understanding with Zaki Yamani. I immediately telephoned HIM, holidaying in Nowshahr. He admitted to having already endorsed a move by the Kuwaitis, a compromise solution whereby oil prices will rise by 10 per cent but remain frozen thereafter for at least nine months. Our representative in Vienna, Jamshid Amouzegar, has been instructed to go along with this plan, and although it will give us an

---

[1] At various critical moments Khatami had shown unwavering loyalty to the Shah and until his final few months continued to enjoy favour at Court. At the end, not only to the Shah but to other observers as well, he seemed depressed. One can only speculate on the reasons for this or the accuracy of the Shah's opinion confided in Alam. It appears that in the late 1960s the US administration devised a contingency plan in case of the Shah's sudden death. A key role was to be played during the interim period by the Iranian military and in particular by General Khatami. Khatami himself may have known nothing of all this, but the Shah probably found out about it and it may have turned his suspicious mind against Khatami. Hence perhaps the general's depression towards the end and his cold-shouldering at Court. Ironically, the Americans made no attempt to revise their contingency plan, despite the death of its key actor, leading to their utter confusion during the 1979 revolution. For my knowledge of the contingency plan I am indebted to my friend, Cyrus Ghani, and his perceptive interpretation of discussions held with various high-ranking US officials between 1976 and 1980 – Ed.

additional $2 billion in income, it can only be regarded by the Saudis, and for that matter by the USA, as a relative climb-down by us and our supporters ...

Wednesday, 1 October

Audience ... HIM asked me to ensure that Bhutto, during an upcoming visit to Tehran, is accommodated at the Shahvand Palace. When I pointed out that this is an honour reserved for heads of states, he replied that Bhutto is far more than a mere Prime Minister. 'For us he's more important even than a head of state.' In other words I was left in no doubt as to the sort of reception that's required. Despite this being a private visit I asked whether we should arrange for a guard of honour. 'But of course', he said.

Submitted a letter from the British ambassador, dealing with the proposed arsenal in Isfahan. The ambassador undertakes to ensure that the British companies presently acting as consultants will do their utmost to supply the best equipment at competitive prices, provided they're awarded the contract. It's worth £500 million. 'I'm told that their terms are far from satisfactory', HIM remarked. 'More like daylight robbery than an honest deal.' ...

Reported a meeting I held yesterday with Lubrani, the Israeli representative, to discuss the projected press campaign. I was shown a detailed schedule based on up-to-date market research – quite a contrast to our own amateur approach. Furthermore, Israel is willing to put all manner of information at our disposal and to introduce us to various leading experts on public relations. Needless to say this is to be kept entirely confidential.

Lubrani stressed that we cannot expect them to work miracles, but that they will do whatever is humanly possible. He then referred to the late President Johnson, saying that he once asked the Israelis to persuade the US press and its leading Jews to improve popular perceptions of the Vietnam war, particularly amongst the younger generation. The President refused to believe them when they replied that the issue was quite beyond redemption, until a categorical statement to that effect was delivered to him by a joint committee of American and Israeli experts. In the present instance HIM is extremely keen to keep the matter secret and has therefore ordered that it be handled under my supervision via the Ministry of Court. Should need arise, we can advise the government of the best way to handle public relations but without revealing full details of the scheme ...

This afternoon went to welcome Bhutto at the airport and escorted him to the Shahvand Palace ... Subsequently he was received by HIM ...

Thursday, 2 October

Audience. Reported that recent surveys suggest our international image is deteriorating. The reasons for this are unclear and in any case I doubt it's a matter we need worry about unduly. It's far more important that we retain a solid foundation of support within Iran ... 'I tend to agree with you', HIM said, 'and I blame US reaction to OPEC and oil negotiations for our declining popularity abroad; this too relates to Jewish opinion.' In that case, I replied, I had done all I could to square things with the Jews. We now need to find someone to handle public relations from our end; someone reliable, well informed on international politics yet at the same time free of influence from the CIA and other such mischievous organizations ...

Discussing OPEC, I remarked how strongly Amouzegar has attacked the Saudis. He claims they're being propped up by another Arab country. I assumed he was referring to Abu Dhabi and was therefore surprised when HIM told me the country concerned is Algeria. I pointed out that up to now the Algerians have always been considered amongst the most radical of the oil-producers. HIM admitted he finds it hard to understand what they're up to ... 'Abu Dhabi joined in the movement against price increases', he added, 'but in general it's difficult to know whether she's for or against us, or playing some moderate line of her own.'

Met the British ambassador after lunch. Discussed various commercial matters, which seem to be the one and only subject in which the British show any interest; arranging a deal in one place and a new business in the next, out for whatever profit they can lay their hands on ...

Monday, 6 October

Audience ... Proposed that MG be appointed head of our joint project with Israel to influence American public opinion. HIM approved ...

Discussed a recent article in the *New York Times* which in my opinion does HIM less than justice. 'The bloody fool dubs me Louis XIV', HIM declared. 'Yet I'm the leader of a revolution; the Bourbon was the very soul of reaction.' ...

Wednesday, 8 October

Audience ... Talking about the development project for Kish I told HIM that he could expect to see the whole thing completed within four years. 'But by then I'll be sixty', he said. I assured him that men of sixty are not exactly in their dotage. 'It'll be many years before Your Majesty resorts to a walking stick', I said.

Attended Dinner, a select gathering consisting only of HIM, Her Majesty the Queen Mother, Princess Shams, her husband and myself. HMQ has flown out to the Caspian ... The Queen Mother told us stories of her married life with Reza Shah. On her wedding night, her husband, then a mere brigadier, was forced to ply her with brandy to calm her nerves. Even as Queen, she said, she did her best to keep out of his way. HIM was amused by this, gently teasing her for having avoided his father ...

He then declared how impressed he is with Denis Healey, the British Chancellor of the Exchequer, currently attending the Tehran conference on Anglo-Iranian investment. He was granted an audience this morning. 'He's always been a friend to this country', HIM said.

Saturday, 11 October

... Introduced MG to the Israeli representative so that they may make a start on their joint assignment ...

A meeting with the Conservative MP, Anthony Royle, formerly an assistant secretary in the British Foreign Office, currently a member of Healey's delegation to Tehran. He asked whether it might be possible for Mrs Thatcher, his party leader, to be received by HIM. I could see no grounds for objection, but he pointed out that it might not go down well with the present Labour government. This rather took me aback. As I told him, I'm surprised to hear such partisan nonsense from an Englishman, and in any case we don't give a damn for the feelings of the British government, whether it be Conservative or Labour. He blushed with embarrassment ...

Monday, 13 October

... An informal reception at the Saadabad Palace to mark HMQ's birthday. Ex-King Constantine ... deigned to honour us with his presence ...

This afternoon HMQ opened the Farah Sports Stadium in the eastern suburbs of Tehran. Prior to Their Majesties' arrival I noticed that the seats reserved for the ex-King and Queen of Greece were set slightly behind those for our own royal family. However the Great Court Chamberlain assured me that HIM approved the arrangement. In the event, of course, HMQ kicked up a dreadful fuss and insisted that the chairs be brought forward ... I then heard her turn to HIM and say, 'Look how we've become slaves to protocol. We should take a lesson from King Hussein. He manages to behave with such natural informality.' ...

Wednesday, 22 October
Audience ... Passed on a clipping from the *New York Times* which claims that intellectuals in this country are demanding radical social reform. HIM was not at all amused. 'The bloody fools', he said; 'They're doing no more than repeat exactly the points our own advisers made at the Aspen conference in Shiraz, a meeting under the direct patronage of HMQ. And in any event, who the hell do these intellectuals think they are? A lot of paranoid nobodies whose criticisms have been made solely at our invitation.' ...

The PM has called in a friend of mine and badgered him for information on the fortune left by the late General Khatami ...

Tuesday, 28 October
HIM set out for Turkey at nine thirty this morning ... Later I granted an interview to a Mrs Laing who is preparing a biography of HIM.[1] She asked me a series of very tricky questions; for example, what did I consider to be HIM's greatest failings? I replied that in my opinion he has made only one real error; to assume that those around him are just as honest and well-intentioned towards Iran as he is himself ...

Flew to Kish after lunch, accompanied only by my wife. Kish is a true paradise. Superb weather, far away from the horrors of city life.

Sunday, 2 November
... HIM flew in from Turkey at two this afternoon, cheerful despite a toothache. At the airport he presided over a special meeting of the Economic Council. We then flew by helicopter to the Niavaran Palace ... He's been greatly impressed by the popular enthusiasm that greeted him in Turkey ...

Gave a dinner at home in honour of Senator Fulbright, former Chairman of the Senate Foreign Relations Committee. It was an all-male gathering and we spent the entire time talking politics. I took issue with Fulbright when he began denouncing the Vietnam war as a senseless waste. If it hadn't been for the war, Indonesia, Thailand and Burma would have been over-run by communism ... I could tell the US ambassador agreed with

[1] Margaret Laing, *The Shah* (London 1977).

me, although he was in no position to admit it openly. Fulbright was lavish in his praise for HIM, comparing our policies with those of Finland; both we and the Finns remain staunchly anti-Soviet whilst admitting a wide range of co-operative ventures. Throughout the vicissitudes of Senate politics, Fulbright never wavered in his support for Iran. I gladly raised my champagne glass in his honour.

Tuesday, 4 November

Audience. Ardeshir Zahedi persists in asking that HIM receive representatives of the US media. 'Does he take me for a film star that I need to appear on every available front page and chat show?', HIM said. 'I'm simply too busy to see these blasted people. Make it known that visitors of this sort are unwelcome, regardless of where they come from, be it the USA or anywhere else for that matter.'

HIM is displeased with an interview given by Fulbright who took the opportunity to express reservations about our military build-up. I pointed out that off the record the man expressed an opinion totally at odds with his press statement. Indeed he told me straight out that he appreciates our motives in defence matters. 'These people are ham-strung by their need to play to the masses', HIM remarked.

Wednesday, 5 November

Brief audience, HIM postponing various matters until Friday when we shall travel to Kish for a weekend's rest. What a prospect for a holiday! Three hours talking shop and a further three hours spent transmitting his orders! ...

Passed on a letter I've received from Senator Edward Kennedy:

[The Senator, writing on 24 October 1975, asked Alam to receive a prominent constituent from Massachusetts, and his associate, who were due to arrive in Tehran on 10 November. Their purpose was to discuss the sale and transportation of materials for the Iranian Air Force.]

I remarked that these are precisely the same people who are always so ready to accuse us. 'I agree', said HIM. 'The whole thing is incredible. I recently suggested a UN resolution, blacklisting any company resorting to sharp practice in its international dealings. The Americans are doing their best to bury the scheme ...'

Friday, 7 November

Magnificent weather, but I spent the whole morning working with HIM at his residence on Kish ... Reported that according to the US ambassador, Defense Secretary Schlesinger never had much time for our demands – a few days ago he was removed from office. HIM disagreed, saying that the man always leant a sympathetic ear. 'Tell the ambassador', he said, 'that the price of the US destroyers we ordered has jumped from $180 million to $260 and now to $338 million, way above the rate of inflation over the past three years. In these circumstances we have no alternative but to cancel the contract, which in turn will mean that America remains totally reliant on her base at Diego Garcia for Indian Ocean defence. The Indian navy is unreliable and Pakistan will never find the money to pay for ships at that sort of price. We ourselves are at present incapable of operating outside the Gulf. Nothing stands between the Soviets and dominance in the Indian Ocean save God and the Americans.' ...

Turning to the problems of the Lebanon, HIM pronounced the country doomed. In his opinion the likeliest scenario will be partition; rival zones for Christians and Muslims, with the south falling under Israeli occupation ...

Poor Franco has cabled his thanks for a sympathetic enquiry from HIM ...

The afternoon we spent resting or swimming. Oh the pleasures of swimming in paradise whilst Tehran shivers in temperatures well below zero! ...

Saturday, 8 November

Returned from Kish on board HIM's most elegant jet, the Shahbaz. He himself took the controls for take-off and landing, spending the rest of the journey with me going through our backlog of work. He approved the purchase of a house for Prince Davoud, son of the King of Afghanistan, currently working as a pilot with Iranair.

Sunday, 9 November

Early this morning met the US ambassador who expressed his embarrassment at the exorbitant price asked for our six destroyers. He suggests we postpone any decision until we've heard from the new Defense Secretary. Meanwhile he will launch an enquiry into the 300 per cent increase. Personally I detect Kissinger's hand behind all this; his way of paying us back for our policy on oil ...

Tuesday, 11 November 75

Audience ... The Arab–Israeli conflict is being debated in the UN, and charges of racism have been levelled at Israel. HIM agrees with me that it would be irresponsible of the USA to support any Palestinian resolution against the Jews, and he immediately telephoned our Foreign Minister to tell him so. The latter replied that it was already too late and that the Palestinian motion was passed last night with Iranian support. He was berated on this but pointed out that it was HIM who had personally instructed our representative how to vote. 'In that case', HIM replied, 'it must be explained to the press that we were merely showing solidarity with the Arabs, and that the vote bears no relation to our real feelings on the matter.' I refrained from reminding him how often I've advised the appointment of men at Court to study such issues in advance and so avert precisely this sort of mess ...

Wednesday, 12 November

... Met the two Americans recommended to me in Senator Kennedy's letter. We've recently introduced regulations requiring all foreign companies dealing with our government to submit an affidavit that no middle man has been involved in such transactions. Now, however, these two gentlemen would like me to procure them an official letter exempting American companies from this restriction. I laughed when they told me, making them squirm with embarrassment. They then sought to justify themselves, saying that every company needs agents and that agents in turn incur expenses if they're to maintain an efficient staff ... undertook merely to draw the matter to HIM's attention ...

Thursday, 13 November

Brief audience ... HIM was much amused by my account of Kennedy's friends and their attempt to protect their commissions ...

Reported a meeting with the ambassador of North Yemen who came to complain about Al Hamadi, Chairman of his country's revolutionary council. Despite being a Shi'a he's busy supporting the Yemeni Sunnis in return for $400,000 a month, paid into his account by Saudi Arabia. As a result many prominent Shi'as have fled the capital to rejoin their tribes, presaging the outbreak of a new civil war. The ambassador's testimony may be biased since he's under threat of dismissal, but all the same I'm inclined to take it seriously ...

HIM personally welcomed the Sheikh Khalifa of Qatar this afternoon at the start of an official visit. The Speaker of the Senate asked him at the airport why he'd bothered to give the Sheikh such a generous reception. HIM replied that he's been supporting us in OPEC, having been a staunch friend of Iran since his days as Qatar's Prime Minister. Qatar is a small country with an inferiority complex. It's our duty to treat her as if she were our equal. Full dress reception at the Niavaran Palace in honour of the Sheikh; the full works, white tie, decorations and all.

Monday, 24 November

Their Majesties welcomed the Turkish President Fahri Korutürk and his wife, making a stop-off on their return from an official visit to Pakistan. Their entourage included various Turkish MPs and a luncheon table seating thirty-four people had to be laid on at the airport.

I was placed next to HMQ who was asked by Ihsan Çaglayangil, the Turkish Foreign Minister, to jot down a few verses in Persian as a souvenir of the occasion. She turned to ask my advice and I suggested that since both she and the Foreign Minister had been casting aspersions against a bearded fundamentalist MP, a Turk seated at the far end of the table, the following lines from Hafez might be appropriate:

> Come, come, the glamour of this day's success will never fade
> No matter what my sins, or how sincere your pious masquerade.[1]

HMQ remarked that despite being a close friend of Çaglayangil, she dared not resort to such a double-edged compliment, particularly about a Turkish MP. Instead I suggested:

> The ascetic spends his life desiring paradise,
> But paradise lies in the renunciation of desire.

She liked this and, having copied and signed it, passed it across the table to Çaglayangil.

The President and his entourage left shortly afterwards ...

Tuesday, 25 November

Audience. At lunch yesterday HMQ confided that she would like to attend Juan Carlos' coronation as King of Spain.[2] She suggested that it was a timely gesture given that the monarchy has at long last been restored. I

---

[1] Translated at the request of the Editor, by Mr Ebrahim Golestan.
[2] Franco had died on 20 November.

also pointed out to HIM how keen she had been that he approve what I myself regard as a thoroughly sensible suggestion. He replied that as far as symbolic gestures go, Iran will be represented by his brother and that in any case the forthcoming ceremony is to be merely a solemn mass, not a real coronation; a Christian mass moreover. If HMQ wants to follow the example of Giscard d'Estaing or Prince Philip then she should think again. Nor should we adopt the undignified approach of King Hussein who plans to attend accompanied by his Queen and half the Jordanian government. 'Moreover', he said, 'I told her last night that she is not to go, and that's my final word on the subject. Good day to you.' . . .

Wednesday, 26 November
. . . Brief audience. Reported various plans for the jubilee to mark fifty years of Pahlavi monarchy . . . A special film was to have been made by David Frost but the government has scrapped this important project to save costs. HIM ordered it be reinstated . . .

Saturday, 29 November
Audience. HIM in low spirits, complaining of dizziness. His special physician, Dr Ayadi, suggests it may be due to excess cholesterol. What a joke! I couldn't restrain my laughter, and pointed out that Ayadi is a good comedian but a hopeless doctor. I suggested we contact the French specialists via Professor Safavian who by a stroke of good luck is presently in Paris . . .

Passed on the reports prepared by Dr Etemad, head of the Nuclear Energy Agency, detailing his recent agreements with France and Germany. HIM has a great vision for the future of this country which, though he denies it, probably includes our manufacturing a nuclear deterrent.

Reported that the new Rastakhiz party's activities have ground to a halt, with no real opportunity for discussion or debate. Despite the great song and dance, their only concrete achievements have been to get everyone's photograph in the newspapers and to provide a forum for the ridiculous antics of Hoveyda. Something must be done if people are not to lose all faith in the venture . . . HIM listened carefully to what I had to say, before announcing that he himself had various ideas on how to get things moving again.

. . . Described my meeting with the ambassador of North Korea, come to complain that we've yet to sort out the $200 million loan promised to his government. I'm aware that the delay springs directly from HIM's own orders, but even so I feigned ignorance of the whole affair and in the end the ambassador took pity on me. HIM laughed, remarking that we simply don't have the money to make such a loan. 'Added to which', I said, 'the Americans have asked us to postpone the thing for as long as possible.' HIM replied that much as he takes note of American opinion, we should go ahead with the loan regardless were it in our interest to do so.

... Subsequently contacted the doctors in Paris who assured me that HIM's problems have nothing to do with cholesterol and strongly advised against administering any drugs in this respect. Professor Jean Bernard will make his own diagnosis when he arrives here on 11 December.

Reported this conversation at dinner. 'You're turning into quite a medical expert yourself', said HIM with a smile.

Monday, 1 December
Flew to Paris to see my doctors.

[From Paris Alam proceeded to the USA and thence to Morocco, returning to Tehran early in January 1976.]

1976

High oil prices led to a reduction in fuel consumption, forcing OPEC members to reduce their output. Iranian oil production fell by 1.6 million barrels a day, representing a loss of $6 billion in revenue over the year. Shortage of funds brought many development programmes to a halt. Priority was given to military projects upon which vast resources were squandered. Elsewhere the Shah concentrated on the more grandiose of civilian schemes; the building of large steel mills, or of nuclear power-stations. The basic infrastructure, transport, education, power supply, was almost entirely ignored. This misallocation of resources in turn exacerbated the high rate of inflation. Across the country the inadequacy of housing, food supplies and basic services led to havoc and outcry. Alam writes sarcastically that 'We claim to have brought Iran to the verge of a Great Civilization, yet the country is constantly hit by power-cuts and we can't even guarantee water and power supplies in the capital.' (Diaries, 2–11 July)

Once again the government attempted to offload the blame upon private businessmen. A national campaign against profiteering and hoarding was intensified and coupled to a movement against administrative corruption and inefficiency. The Shah nominated his own Principal Private Secretary as head of an Imperial Commission established to monitor the performance of various government agencies.

Protests against the regime grew more shrill, particularly in the universities and amongst Iranian dissidents living abroad. Many students turned to religion to give vent to their dissatisfaction. During a visit to the Pahlavi University at Shiraz Alam was surprised to see many girls wearing the veil, a practice he believed had been more or less done away with. He was also informed that some of them refused to shake hands with the University's president, on the grounds that Islam forbade any sort of physical contact between the sexes outside marriage (Diaries, 27 April). Various of Iran's embassies and consulates were occupied by demonstrators. Meanwhile the Senate in Washington engaged in a debate designed to discourage the US administration from granting military aid to countries guilty of political imprisonment.

The Shah became convinced that the Jews were capable of moulding western, especially US, opinion. Israel offered its services and a prominent American public relations firm was retained with a view to improving Iran's image abroad. However, the Shah's expectations were too unrealistic. By the end of the year, when no miracle had been effected, he abandoned all interest in the project.

Beginning at the Iranian New Year, 21 March 1976, celebrations were held to mark the fiftieth anniversary of the foundation of the Pahlavi dynasty

Monday, 5 January

HIM's personal valet called round to tell me his master intended going skiing this morning and would therefore not be at his office. Instead I got through to him by telephone, and told him that at yesterday's meeting with HMQ I managed to persuade her that she should take her holidays not in St Moritz but somewhere in France. HIM approved the arrangement and said he would grant me an audience at 3 this afternoon.

Audience. Reported that Princess Ashraf has taken no security precautions for her forthcoming trips to Africa and Switzerland. 'For God's sake do something', HIM said.

The American ambassador met me for breakfast bringing a message from Kissinger to HIM:

> Please thank His Imperial Majesty for any help he can give in Angola. Please inform him that the United States government has received a report via British MI6 that the Saudis have agreed to provide £13 million to the FNLA, at Egyptian urging. Secretary Kissinger emphasizes that the United States government cannot confirm this report but he thought that His Imperial Majesty would be interested.

'Tell the ambassador straight out, that we are in no position to offer financial assistance', HIM remarked.

... Passed on a rumour I've heard through British channels that their Energy Secretary Anthony Benn is prepared to pressure the oil companies into increasing their purchases from Iran in return for certain concessions. 'Quite impossible, I'm afraid', HIM replied. 'Our output has dropped by 1.7 million barrels a day.' I was astonished, a shortfall of $6 billion over the coming year means that we've lost the battle against Kissinger and the Saudis ... Yet HIM seems as confident as ever ...

Remarked that Mrs Gandhi is apparently contemplating imposing limitations on the Indian parliament. 'Good for her', HIM said. 'It's about time she freed herself from some of the more ridiculous trappings of democracy.'

Tuesday, 6 January

Audience. Referring to the oil companies HIM said, 'The bastards have thrown down a serious challenge to us. So much for their protestations of goodwill.' ...

Following his long audience with HIM this morning I invited Alain

Peyrefitte to lunch. Formerly Education Minister of France, he's a highly intelligent man who has agreed to write a book about Iran.

Wednesday, 7 January
... Attended the official opening of the Farah Pahlavi University – a women's college. HMQ was late in arriving and apologized for this in her address – a touching gesture ...

Sunday, 11 January
HIM received me at breakfast since he was due to accompany HMQ to the airport prior to her departure for Paris. Passed on a letter from King Hussein who is in the process of buying a property in St Moritz. 'But how on earth did he get hold of the money?', HIM asked, clearly surprised. I remarked that it's only a few years since he was given £12 million by the Saudis. 'But that was all to do with the inheritance from his great grand-father, Sharif Hussein', HIM replied, 'And by now it will have been divided up amongst goodness knows how many heirs.'

... The contract we've agreed for some military housing constructions amounts to straightforward theft by the British company. I pointed out that they're effectively demanding $600 million over the odds. I was expecting HIM to order a stop to this, but though he listened carefully to what I had to say, he made no comment ... Perhaps he intends acting via the government. Alternatively he may regard it as a premium that must be paid to the British if they're to persuade the oil companies to buy more from us ...

... We then turned to discussing Admiral A, the former commander of the Navy who has been sacked amidst accusations ... HIM asked me to enquire amongst my business acquaintances whether there are any rumours about naval procurement contracts. He also referred briefly to the wealth of the late General Khatami, estimated as $100 million. The figure strikes me as being way over the top, but HIM would never have cited it without knowing his facts. He's determined that the money be confiscated should any evidence of sharp practice emerge ...

Monday, 12 January
Audience ... Reported that my enquiries indicate that whilst A, poor bastard, was not himself involved in any wrong-doing, his ineptitude allowed free rein to various of his subordinates ...

Ex-Queen Soraya has written asking that we buy her a flat in Paris. HIM agreed, ordering me to make the necessary arrangements.

... Passed on a cable from one of the Baluchi chieftains informing me that he's accepted the surrender of a band of dissidents formerly supported by Iraq. 'Following my decision to call off the local chieftains in order to leave things in the hands of the gendarmerie', HIM remarked, 'we've achieved excellent results.' However I pointed out that, on the contrary, my cable shows it's precisely the chieftains who have been obtaining surrenders. He made no comment, although it's clear the gendarmerie have been trying to steal all the credit ...

Tuesday, 13 January
Audience ... Discussed the various guerrilla networks unearthed in the north of the country. 'The determination with which they fight is quite unbelievable', HIM said. 'Even the women keep battling on to their very last gasp. The men carry cyanide tablets in their mouths and commit suicide rather than face capture. And yet the people of this country lack for nothing. There are jobs for everyone and endless opportunities for people to enrich themselves. There's even a serious shortage of technicians and skilled labour. How can such things be?' I explained that the terrorists have been brainwashed ... into seeing only our shortcomings and nothing of our achievements. The younger generation is naturally idealistic and all too easily led astray. Even the Crown Prince was outraged after witnessing the squalor of south Tehran. We lack any sort of coordinating body to ensure that young people are shown the picture in its entirety, not just our more deplorable shortcomings. Our ratio of success to failure must be at least 100 to 1, and I'm confident that young people would realize this if only we could present it more clearly. And yet, take the example of the daughter of one of my servants. I spent $15,000 on sending her to Germany for a whole year's medical treatment, yet she returned a committed communist, loathing me and all I stand for ... demanding to know where I'd got the money to pay for her treatment ... I added that we need to be particularly vigilant when it comes to the army ... HIM agreed, admitting that a few subversive elements have already been uncovered within the military and will be dealt with. 'But prevention is better than cure', I reminded him, 'and we can only forestall such developments if we enable the younger generation to take pride in their country.' Again HIM was in agreement, instructing me to do whatever I can to help ...

Saturday, 17 January

Travelled with HIM to the hills south of Isfahan to attend the closing stages of a military exercise mounted over the past four days. A magnificent spectacle; thirty thousand fully equipped men, supported by tanks, planes and helicopters. The US military adviser told HIM that, with a force as well trained as this, he'd be prepared to go to war against all comers. We ourselves fared worse than the soldiers, having to stand in the open for close on three hours, buffeted by a cold head wind. At one point I whispered to HIM that there wasn't enough tea to go round, but that he should take the one cup available. 'How can I drink tea and leave you and guests, those Egyptian officers for example, to go thirsty?', he retorted. A generous sentiment, but I reminded him that he'd come to watch manoeuvres, not to catch his death of cold. 'Oh go on then', he said, 'And be quick about it as I'm very nearly frozen already.' An hour later he asked for a second cup, insisting it be just as hot as the first ...

At dinner Dr Eqbal had been asked to provide HIM with a detailed briefing on the way the oil companies have violated the agreement on sales and purchases. Unfortunately he became totally confused and put on a pitiful performance, getting his notes mixed up and losing his place every second sentence. HIM kept sneaking glances in my direction, clearly on the verge of bursting into laughter. Later he told me to come armed with Fallah's more coherent notes to tomorrow's audience.

Sunday, 18 January

Audience ... 'Unbelievable', announced HIM. 'Eqbal has not invited Fallah to today's meeting with the oil companies. I expressly ordered that he attend. This sort of petty backbiting over matters of national importance makes my blood boil.' ...

Again discussed embezzlement in the Navy and Air Force. 'Why on earth do people do these things when they're already perfectly well paid?', HIM asked. 'After a point money becomes more of a burden than a pleasure, and yet still they're greedy to grab more.' ...

Reported that we're expecting the arrival of an Israeli delegation to discuss our public relations campaign for the USA and the foreign media. They intend to pose various fundamental questions about the image we hope to present, and how we want it done, through the press, the television or the academic community ... It's a good indication of how far we lag behind their systematic approach. 'But I've told you over and over again', HIM said, 'that we lack a propaganda machine. As for our so-called image, it's set out perfectly clearly in the seventeen points of the revolution.' With a knowing smile he went on, 'If it's an inquest into past failings you're after, you had better approach the Minister of Information.' They're also keen to know whether we want to be regarded as a democracy or as something else ... 'Our system is unique', he replied. 'It has nothing to do with "isms", "ocracies", or anything else churned out by the westerners.' I pointed out that, rather than sound off against the West, we'd be better advised to deliver a positive statement of what we ourselves have achieved. We should emphasize that true democracy lies in popular participation in every aspect of social and economic policy, not in handing over power to a self-elected minority of trade-unions. 'Excellent', said HIM. 'You should work that up into a full-scale declaration.'

Monday, 19 January
The Israeli representative and their Deputy Minister of Information called at my house early this morning accompanied by an American Jew named Daniel Yankelovich.[1] We spent an hour and a half discussing our propaganda campaign and have agreed to meet again tomorrow. They had already been briefed by the Israeli Prime Minister.

Audience ... HIM was ashen faced and I guessed, correctly, that things must be going badly with the oil companies. 'The bastards won't accept the level of off-take they originally agreed to handle', he announced. 'They've got some cock and bull story about there being a glut on the international markets. If that's the way they want to play it, I shall go straight ahead and cancel most of the import arrangements I've made with the West.' I agreed with this. Now that they've called our bluff the last thing we should do is meekly to give in to them ...

Tuesday, 20 January
Audience. Reported that the British are asking permission to fly spy planes, five hours a day for three days, between Astara and Ourmiah.[1] They hope to monitor troop movements by the Red Army in Transcaucasia. HIM gave his approval ...

MG was then ushered in, to deliver a detailed report on his discussions with Yankelovich and the Israelis. HIM agreed that the exercise cannot be

---

[1] Public opinion analyst; Chairman of Yankelovich, Skelly and White Inc., N.Y.C.
[2] Astara, a border town between Iran and the Soviet Union on the west of the Caspian Sea; Ourmiah, the old name of Rezaiyeh, lies in the north-western corner of Iran, close to the Turkish and Soviet borders.

kept secret, and that our best bet is to operate in the USA under cover of a new body to be called 'The Centre for Media Research'. At least that way we shall avoid disclosing Israel's involvement ... 'We must present ourselves exactly as we are', he went on, 'warts and all. The world will come to realize that over the next decade we are set to achieve a comparable standing to France or West Germany; a nation of 50 million, provided with all that is best in the way of education and an advanced standard of living.'

Before I left, HIM asked me to remind the British that we shall cut back on our imports from them in direct proportion to any fall in our oil sales ...

Friday, 23 January

... Rode for a full two hours, a whole series of thoughts buzzing around my head. Above all I was worrying about the discussions I had last night with Majidi, head of the Plan Organization. Going through the various projects of particular interest to HIM, he recited a depressing catalogue of financial shortages and the squandering of what resources we have left. I genuinely fear that this may be the first vague rumbling of impending revolution.[1]

He told me that we're in deficit on this year's budget by as much as $4 billion and that the government is conniving at the most senseless extravagance; for example, they've purchased 4,000 lorries without having a single man qualified to drive them. The losses we've incurred in buying wheat, sugar and other basic foodstuffs are beyond belief. And then again, a further $2 billion has gone on loans to foreign countries. According to Majidi the government agencies didn't even see fit to inform him of their expenses until after the event.

These people are outright traitors; they have betrayed the Shah and they have betrayed the country. Nor have they the courage to tell HIM what's really been going on. The net effect is that we have no alternative but to surrender rather than risk confrontation with the oil companies ...

A day of perfect blue skies and yet my mind is clouded by the darkest imaginings. The Shah has sacrificed everything to make this country great, and yet he is now in the power of traitors, or at the very least of mealy-mouthed incompetents. When I think of his own blind confidence in the public's goodwill ... He is betrayed, and not one defence remains intact in our battle with the oil companies ...

[1] See the main introduction on the Shah.

Saturday, 24 January

The US ambassador met me for breakfast and we had a lengthy conversation about the situation with regard to oil ... He is fully aware of recent developments and promised to do what he can on our behalf ... I warned him that the fall in our production will hit first at our imports from the USA; for example, we've already been forced to cancel our order for ocean-going destroyers ... He then asked the purpose of the current visit to Tehran by an emissary from Mauritania. I feigned ignorance, assuring him that I would raise the matter with HIM.

Audience ... HIM instructed me to put the ambassador fully in the picture concerning our Mauritanian guest, here to ask our assistance against Algeria. The Algerians have been supplying the Polisario Front with heavy artillery, but we could offer nothing definite to relieve this situation. 'Even so', HIM said, 'one might ask the Americans what, in their view, the Algerians are up to with so many Russian weapons? Also what's General Giap[1] doing in their country? In the south of the continent, in Angola, pro-western forces have been wiped out by a joint Soviet-Cuban campaign. France has announced her intention of granting independence to Djibouti, at which stage the Somalis will be bound to stir up trouble. Africa is being encircled in a red ring of fire. Yet the Americans remain utterly indifferent to our attempts to relieve the pressure they're under in the Indian Ocean. We alone are capable of achieving parity with the Indian navy, and so lending the USA a helping hand.'

Wednesday, 28 January

Audience ... Reported that the Moroccan Minister of Court wishes to pay us a visit at the earliest possible opportunity. He's almost certainly determined to obtain military assistance in the Sahara against the Algerians ...

There is a debate going on in the US Senate, intended to deter the administration from granting military aid to any country with a record of imprisoning political dissidents. 'What a joke', HIM remarked. 'It would serve the Americans right if we emptied the prisons and let the subversives take power. They'd soon show Washington just how much they appreciate good old American values.' ...

[1] General V. N. Giap, the Defence Minister of Vietnam was the most outstanding Vietnamese military commander during the wars against France and the USA.

Monday, 2 February

... Received the PM at my office and talked with him for close on an hour. He is concerned by the harmful side-effects of HIM's campaign against corruption and believes it may eventually undermine our entire regime. He asked me to help by persuading HIM to tone things down. 'But if you were opposed to the scheme', I said, 'why on earth did you ever support it? Indeed, why did you go to such extravagant lengths to give it publicity?' He replied that nothing could have deterred HIM, and that whenever he tried to reason with him he met with very short shrift. I admitted I shared his anxieties about the campaign and undertook to raise the subject at tomorrow's audience.

Earlier on I'd shown HIM a leader in *Le Monde*, criticizing us for recent executions of terrorists. When he described the piece as irrelevant, I pointed out that our image is deteriorating throughout the western world. 'So what?', he replied. 'We mustn't become slaves to western opinion. These bastards in the press spout nothing but rubbish. A murderer, particularly a terrorist, deserves nothing short of death.'

Tuesday, 3 February

... Audience. Submitted an outline of HIM's schedule up to next October, a particularly gruelling programme, including visits by the Presidents of Egypt, Tunisia, Austria, France, and the Crown Princes of Jordan and Bahrain. HIM must also fit in trips to Pakistan and Italy, and an extensive tour of the provinces to mark the fiftieth year of the Pahlavi dynasty ...

Ayatollah Khonsari has backed out of his commitment to deliver a public condemnation of terrorist activities by the so-called Islamic Marxists.[1] He claims that the time is not yet right ... 'One thing I don't understand in all this', said HIM. 'Is the Ayatollah anxious to withdraw because the terrorists are too powerful?' I replied that this was not at all the case; it's merely that Khonsari, like all the mullahs, is conservative, stupid and deceitful. There's no changing human nature ...

The PM telephoned to say that he'd already raised the matters we discussed last night and that the Shah had been suitably impressed. Would I therefore refrain from saying anything at my own audience? Little does he realize that I report everything I hear to HIM, within twenty-four hours at the latest ...

---

[1] The name given by the Shah to the People's Mojaheddin, later to play a prominent role in the revolution.

Wednesday, 4 February

Audience ... Forwarded a letter from Prince Bernhardt of the Nether-lands – yet another damned wheeler-dealer. 'I see that the Prince is as anxious as ever to stamp out corruption', HIM remarked sarcastically ...

Thursday, 5 February

... As today's audience was drawing to a close, I sensed there was still something HIM was keen to tell me, and so I waited in silence for him to take the plunge. 'Remember that so-and-so, NH?', he said; 'That military engineering man we had arrested? The bastard has confessed to an unsuc-cessful attempt to embezzle a contract to the tune of close on $120 million.' I pointed out that I'd several times passed on rumours that would fit in with this story; indeed I'd given fair warning that the contract we were about to sign with a British consortium was set at four times the proper asking price. 'But I simply couldn't believe it', he said. 'I thought it was just scare-mongering.'

Friday, 6 February

... Welcomed the Moroccan Minister of Court, Moulay Hafid, and chatted with him for a couple of hours. He asked us to supply all manner of military technology to assist the fight against the Algerian-backed Polisario ... He's accompanied on this visit by a Moroccan air force colonel,[1] a well-informed gentleman, who was able to quote the exact number of our F-5s, a few of which they're hoping to obtain. When I asked him what he intended doing about pilots, he assured me they already have fifty men trained to fly these particular aircraft; a reply that caught me off guard ...

Despite Algeria's failure to support us at the latest OPEC meeting, we've been getting on better with her recently. I wonder how HIM will manage to duck the Moroccan request.

Saturday, 7 February

Audience. In response to Morocco's enquiry, HIM claims we have no F-5s to spare ...

Tomorrow he is due to set out for Gajereh on a four-day skiing expedition. 'You are to fly over every day to make your report', he said. I replied I was loath to waste so much of His Majesty's time. 'In other words', he said, 'you're too lazy to make the effort.' 'Not at all', I said;

---

[1] Colonel Mohammad Kabbaj; Inspector and Commander of the Moroccan Air Force.

'Gajereh is only ten minutes by helicopter and I always consider it a privilege to be received by Your Majesty. But aren't you just a little fed up, having to see me every day?' He laughed.

Passed on a letter from Princess Ashraf, who wants to buy a house in New York. HIM was not at all pleased. 'She wants to set up home amidst the chaos of America. In so doing she risks causing even more uproar against us in that country. She must be going off her head.'

At dinner we once again discussed Morocco ... Afterwards I called on our guests and told them that in the immediate term we are prepared to supply them with seven F-5s via the Jordanian government. They were delighted.

Monday, 9 February
Arranged for HIM's French doctors to visit him in Gajereh to take further blood samples ...

The campaign against corruption is reaching new heights of sensationalism. Strange how this government consistently transforms HIM's high ideals into the most vulgar of clichés ...

Wednesday, 11 February
... At dinner HMQ remarked that Giscard d'Estaing was most kind during her recent skiing trip to Val d'Isère, telephoning her several times. Likewise, I said, I'd received an extremely courteous reception during my trip to Morocco, but not out of simple kindness; it's because our sovereign commands such awe and respect. This last remark was received in chilly silence. Someone tactfully changed the subject ...

Friday, 13 February
Audience. Following discussions with Fereidoun Movassaqi, our ambassador in Jordan, I reported that the Moroccans are now asking Jordan to pass on the weapons we've agreed, pending replacements from Iran. King Hussein is apparently far from happy with this arrangement but is prepared to go along with it if HIM so wishes. I pointed out that it was never part of the plan to have King Hussein supply the weapons, and that there must surely be a more sensible solution. 'Summon the US ambassador', HIM replied, 'and tell him the Moroccans are putting both King Hussein and myself in an embarrassing position. Politically it's worse for Hussein since he's so keen to improve his relations with Syria, one of Algeria's staunchest allies. Morocco is a neighbour of the USA, albeit they are separated by the

Atlantic Ocean. She is not our neighbour, nor King Hussein's. Why should we be the ones to supply her with arms?' ...

Princess Ashraf has asked permission to set 22 March as the date for announcing the establishment of her charitable foundation. HIM burst into laughter at this ... 'Tell her she can make her blasted announcement, but she should be under no illusion that she can hoodwink the public.' ...

Saturday, 14 February

Met the US ambassador, who told me King Hussein is prepared to supply Morocco with F-5As ... on condition that Morocco guarantees to replenish his stocks within eighteen months, repaying him with F-5Es which are more advanced than the 5s ... I was surprised by this since it is directly contrary to what I was told by Movassaqi ... The ambassador then asked whether Morocco has enough money to honour such a guarantee. I replied that they enjoy a lucrative export trade in phosphate. I didn't reveal that HIM has already indicated his willingness to help out financially.

On HIM's instructions, I enquired after the forthcoming visit here by ex-US Treasury Secretary John Connally,[1] stressing that the man has used an intermediary of the worst possible reputation to request an audience. Surely Connally himself was accused of accepting bribes from the US dairy farmers? How on earth could I allow him to meet HIM in these circumstances? The ambassador replied that the intermediary I mentioned is not a friend of Connally's; he is merely acting on behalf of a company for which Connally works as legal adviser. Connally himself was acquitted of any wrong-doing and might even run as a Republican candidate in the next presidential election. What a bizarre country America is!

Audience. Suggested that HIM agree to receive Chesnoff, the editor of *Newsweek*, who's been briefed by the Israelis to give us an excellent write-up. HIM gave his consent ...

Monday, 16 February

The US ambassador telephoned last night to say that Washington has given us the go-ahead to supply US-made weapons to Morocco. Unfortunately, they're imposing one quite impossible proviso; that the arrangement be disclosed to Congress, which means the press are bound to get wind of it ... Reported this to HIM ...

---

[1] In July 1974 the Watergate grand jury had indicted Connally for bribery and perjury, accusations that stemmed from an increase in federal subsidies for milk production authorized during his time as Treasury Secretary. He was acquitted the following year.

Tuesday, 17 February

Met the ambassador of Afghanistan who seems concerned by his country's situation. Davoud Khan is suffering severe back pains which may well be diagnosed as tubercular osteomyelitis. The ambassador asked if I could find a job for his sister, who's in the process of divorcing King Zaher's son. He also told me that the ex-Queen is making life hell for her husband, exiled in Rome. She's constantly quarrelling and has several times threatened to leave him altogether. Apparently she was up to these antics even whilst they were living in Kabul, hence the King's inability to concentrate on affairs of state.

Received the Israeli representative. His chief purpose was to remind me of the obligation I'm under, now that our propaganda campaign has started to show results. The Jewish-owned German magazine *Quick* has published an interview with HIM which was also transmitted by Radio-Television Europe I in its hourly news bulletins for a full twenty-four hours ...

Saturday, 21 February

... Audience. Asked if HIM had reached a decision on Moroccan arms supplies. He replied that the weapons are to be shipped to Jordan which will assume responsibility for their final delivery. In these circumstances it will make little difference whether or not Congress is told of the deal. Even so, I remarked, King Hussein stands to lose out badly from such a revelation, bearing in mind his rapprochement with Syria. 'That's his problem', said HIM. 'Though we'll make sure nothing is done without his approval.'

Sunday, 22 February

Audience. HIM in low spirits. Refrained from asking after his health, although I sensed that the problem was psychological rather than physical. He paid not a moment's attention to my report, which worried me more than ever ... Perhaps he's worrying about the Lockheed scandal; they recently supplied us with a number of C-130 transport planes, and it may be that this will turn sour on us. The US Senate committee has already unearthed cases of corruption in Japan, Holland and Italy, and they've announced that an as yet unspecified Middle Eastern country is implicated in the affair ...

Submitted an unintentionally amusing letter from Princess Ashraf, proposing that we get Cuba involved in the World Campaign Against Illiteracy.

'What nonsense', HIM remarked. 'How on earth can we work with a bunch of mad Cuban revolutionaries?' ...

Monday, 23 February

... Met the Israeli representative ... We're shortly due to receive a delegation from the US Congress, touring countries in receipt of American arms. The ambassador supplied me with details on every member of the mission, assuring me that they're all of them staunch supporters of Israel. He suggested we prepare a thorough briefing for them; they're such donkeys that they might otherwise vote a complete arms embargo against Iran ...

Tuesday, 24 February

HMQ has set out on a state visit to Senegal ... HIM confined to bed with a heavy cold ...

He was too ill to receive Colonel Kabbaj of Morocco who met me instead. He told me that, following his last visit to Iran, he and Moulay Hafid proceeded to Jordan where they persuaded King Hussein to act as intermediary in our supplies to Morocco. In turn, Hussein sent them on to brief Hafiz Assad of Syria, and to explain the nature of their dispute with Algeria. They found Assad most sympathetic. Apparently he told them he could never forget the brave Moroccans who died fighting alongside their Syrian allies in the war against Israel. They said nothing to Assad of their trip to Iran, nor did they tell him that it is we who are actually forwarding the arms to Jordan. Subsequently King Hassan sent Kabbaj and Moulay Hafid to Washington where they spoke with General Vernon Walters. It was the general, an important figure in the CIA, who persuaded the US administration to accept our proposals ...

Later received Lord Chalfont of the BBC. We spent an hour together, discussing the negative image this country receives in Britain where we're branded a nation of bankrupts. I pointed out that a $2 billion shortfall in a budget of $45 billion can hardly be considered bankruptcy; it's a mere hiccup when compared to the dire plight of the British economy. He promised to write this up as an article for *The Times* ...

Saturday, 6 March

Audience. Reported that HMQ has instructed the Omran Bank[1] to lend

---

[1] The Omran Bank was set up in 1952 when the Shah began his land reforms, being primarily intended to help tenant-farmers on Crown estates to purchase their own land. Its activities gradually diversified and by the end of the 1970s it was the fifth largest bank in Iran. It was owned entirely by the Pahlavi Foundation.

$100,000 to the ex-King of Albania, on top of his earlier advance of $400,000. 'There's nothing to be done', HIM said. 'Get them to pay the money.'

At dinner HMQ made a determined effort to stop HIM's dog, an enormous Great Dane, from poking his nose into people's plates. HIM asked what she thought she was up to. 'Flatterers everywhere!', she said. 'I refuse to follow their example. Even this dog is fawned upon just because he's yours. I alone refuse to stoop to such nonsense.' I doubt HIM was particularly pleased by this remark.

Thursday, 11 March

... Met F, a prominent American, who visits Iran from time to time to see to a small business he has here. He told me that, if we like, he can ensure that Washington keeps the names of those found to have received major bribes from US companies entirely under wraps. I replied that we have no particular worries on that score and that, having been so long attacked for corruption, it's reassuring to find our American accusers, especially those in Congress, found guilty of even worse dishonesty. He said he was reluctantly inclined to agree with me. I told him we are actually keen to have the names of the guilty parties disclosed. Should Washington be unwilling to do this, we shall endeavour to obtain a list and publish it on our own initiative. He was dreadfully disappointed ...

Sunday, 14 March

Audience ... Reminded HIM that New Year is approaching and that Mrs Diba expects to be granted either the honorary title Princess, or the Khorshid decoration. It would be unwise to disappoint her. 'I've talked the matter over with HMQ', HIM replied, 'and she too is astonished by the vanity of this dervish mother of hers.' I remarked how surprised I was that the two ladies hadn't already discussed the matter; I had assumed HMQ would be the first person to whom Mrs Diba put her request. 'Well, you assumed wrongly', said HIM. 'Let's just suppose I agreed to give her the Khorshid thing. How on earth could I explain it to my mother? My sister Shams would be certain to stir things up with her. Yet another row!' I quite took his point and promised never again to raise the subject, though I added that Mrs Diba's brother, Mohammad Ali Qotbi, wants to be awarded the title 'roving ambassador'. 'Incredible', said HIM ...

Monday, 15 March

... Audience ... For the fiftieth anniversary celebrations of the Pahlavi dynasty, it's been arranged for 3,000 representatives from each and every province to attend a special gathering at the Olympic village. It would be appropriate for members of the royal family to be there, and I suggested we invite the Crown Prince. HIM approved, but left it up to me to persuade the Prince to attend ...

By long tradition all the members of the royal family join Their Majesties at the moment the clocks chime in Now Rouz – the New Year. Now, however, Princess Ashraf has asked to be received either shortly before or shortly after the others. I have never seen HIM explode with such rage. 'Who the hell do they think I am?', he bellowed. 'They are a lot of good for nothings who'd be totally lost without me. I refuse to be treated this way. My sister need no longer attend the ceremony. As for you, why on earth do you bother me with such nonsense? You'd serve me better by reminding my relations of their obligations towards me.' I regretted ever having opened my mouth, but by then it was too late ...

Wednesday, 17 March

A very busy day. Audience ... HIM has turned down a request for an audience from the President of Lockheed. King Hussein and his wife are due in Tehran, on their way back from a tour of the Far East. HIM expressed a hope that they stay no more than twenty-four hours here, since we have so much work to get through ...

Met the British ambassador and amongst other things discussed HMQ's forthcoming trip to London, for the opening of the Exhibition of Islamic Art by Queen Elizabeth. HMQ is to stay with the British Queen Mother as a semi-official guest. I warned the ambassador that although I have not yet had time to raise the issue with Their Majesties, I shall insist on cancelling the arrangement if HMQ has to walk behind Queen Elizabeth at the opening ceremony. She must either precede her fellow sovereign or walk alongside her. The ambassador was very reasonable and promised to refer the matter to London ...

Next I went to the airport to bid farewell to the President of Gambia, our guest over the past few days. I stayed on there to await King Hussein's arrival and was joined by HIM. He asked whether like last year the Soviet ambassador had expressed a desire that I invite him to Kish. I replied that he had not, despite my pointedly telling him at the recent reception for the Gambian President that we intend spending the entire New Year holiday on the island. 'They must be in a sulk with us', HIM remarked. 'They disapprove of our army's intervention in Oman. In Africa or wherever else, they believe they have an absolute right to interfere, and yet they're scandalized the moment we volunteer help to a friend in need.' ...

Thursday, 18 March
... King Hussein was due to leave at 10 this morning but his discussions with HIM meant he didn't arrive at the airport until nearly midday. Meanwhile I spent an hour there talking to Zaid al-Rifa'i, the Jordanian Prime Minister, and another hour with him playing backgammon. He plays like a real professional.

Subsequently escorted HIM back to the Niavaran Palace. He handed back the US ambassador's notes I'd passed on to him before our Jordanian guests arrived.

[The memorandum referred to described plans to supply 14 battalions of improved Hawk missiles and 100 Vulcan anti-aircraft guns, to provide Jordan with a credible air defence ... Since Jordan lacked the requisite funds ... King Hussein had persuaded Saudi Arabia to pay for the entire affair. The Saudi government had been under the impression that the cost would be approximately $300 million ... However this figure covered only the basic hardware. The package as a whole, including delivery and servicing, amounted to something nearer $800 million. The Saudis withdrew their offer when this became known, notifying King Hussein that they would nevertheless stand by their commitment to spend $300 million. In turn Jordan attempted to divert this sum to purchase a comparable air defence package from the Soviet Union, confident that the Saudis would agree. The US ambassador wrote that Jordan might well be taking too much for granted. On behalf of Washington, he asked HIM to tell King Hussein he would be well advised to persevere with Saudi Arabia and the USA, without involving Moscow.]

He told me that he and King Hussein had talked things over in detail. 'Tell the US ambassador', he said, 'that if Washington persists in disappointing Hussein, they will live to regret it. Who on earth do the Americans suppose their allies are amongst the Arab world? Even Saudi Arabia they seem to regard as nothing more than a reservoir of oil and money. They must give assistance to Hussein, and they must do so as a matter of great urgency. I intend raising the matter personally with President Ford.' ...

Friday, 19 March

HIM was too busy to receive me this morning and asked me to call round later whilst he was taking his bath. HMQ came in unannounced in the middle of our conversation. She had come to tell him that people were growing impatient for their lunch, and was quite taken aback when she realized he was not alone. HIM briefed her on my meeting with the British ambassador, and my reservations about her trip to London. She was shocked by the blunt language I'd used, but HIM assured her that what I said had been quite in order.

He remarked today how much more enthusiastically the dynasty's jubilee has been greeted by the Soviet rather than the western bloc; apparently the warmest messages of congratulations have all come from communist regimes ...

Saturday, 20 March

Audience ... Earlier on I'd met the Israeli ambassador, who claimed that the Senate mission sent to report on Middle East arms sales has filed a highly favourable report on Iran. Their only caveat lay in whether we or the Saudis should be given first priority. HIM laughed when he heard this. On occasions he finds American stupidity almost beyond belief ...

Submitted a report by Dr Fallah, relating to the BP shares previously owned by Burmah Oil, currently held by the Bank of England.

[The report indicates that Anthony Benn, the British Energy Secretary, has succeeded in buying up 3 per cent of these shares, on behalf of the British government, subject to goverment approval, the balance – less than 18 per cent of the shares – to be offered in equal proportions to the governments of Iran and West Germany.]

Sunday, 21 March

Despite the rain, the dynastic celebrations went ahead this morning with a ceremony at the tomb of Reza Shah, first of the Pahlavis to rule Iran. Beforehand people had warned what bad luck the celebrations would bring; the Qajar Shah, Nasser ed Din,[1] was assassinated on the eve of celebrating

[1] Born in 1831, he ruled Iran from 1848 to 1896. Calculated according to the lunar calendar, his reign lasted nearly fifty years.

his own golden jubilee. By comparison we escaped with only a minor hitch; the Crown Prince had to dash off into a corner to be sick ...

After lunch flew to Kish with my wife and family ...

Monday, 22 March

HIM and HMQ arrived on separate flights ... The Crown Prince is already here, arriving two hours before me ... He took his parents off to see the residence that's been provided for him, the first he's had of his own. HIM went riding but I was too exhausted to accompany him.

Tuesday, 23 March

Walked with HIM along the sea shore. Dr Ayadi and I dissuaded him from going swimming; the water was far too cold ... HMQ then joined us as we were sitting on the beach. She and HIM have had a blazing row, all because of some sycophantic woman who has been caught embezzling funds set aside for interior decoration. Many times I'd warned HIM against her but he always told me to turn a blind eye to her goings-on. He said it was the only way to avoid offending HMQ, she being a close friend of the lady concerned. Needless to say, he's now changed his tune entirely, declaring: 'She's a downright thief and deserves to be sacked.' I was startled by the harsh way he said this, not least because HMQ's embarrassment began to make even me feel uneasy. HIM confessed later on that the woman has being saying harsh things about him and HMQ, something that HMQ has no idea about.

This evening we welcomed Nelson Rockefeller, the US Vice-President, who dined as our guest. There was a brief exchange of speeches ... Rockefeller praised HIM, comparing him to Alexander the Great ...

Wednesday, 24 March

Attended HIM whilst he received Rockefeller and Helms, the US ambassador.

[The minutes of this meeting relate to a wide range of issues:]

HIM expressed concern over Russian and Cuban intervention in Africa, coinciding with US support for the regime in Pretoria and the consequent waning of US influence in Black Africa.

Despite Iran's firm links to South Africa, HIM recommended that

Washington adopt a more flexible approach, proclaiming its support for human rights and denouncing apartheid ...

With regard to Afghanistan and Pakistan, HIM stressed that Soviet imperialism is a greater threat than communist ideology. Since the time of the Tsars, Russia has sought access to the Indian Ocean and its warm waters. As HIM has made plain in his public statements, Iran will tolerate no challenge to the territorial integrity of Pakistan; a warning issued to India, with whom Iran's relations have greatly improved. At the same time he has advised Pakistan against deliberately provoking India. 'This', he said, 'is our policy towards our eastern neighbours, even if it involves us in confrontation with the Soviets. Needless to say, Mr Vice-President, you would come to our aid should Moscow threaten to use nuclear weapons against us'. Rockefeller: 'Of course we would.' HIM: 'My policy is honest and straightforward and I have no hidden agenda. I say quite openly that I wish Iran to play a role in the Indian Ocean. I have no objection to America being present, indeed I shall actively defend your interests' ... HIM expressed concern over the situation in Afghanistan. He believes that Davoud Khan's position is under threat and that a group of communist army officers are in the ascendant ...

... Later a private reception at the Yacht Club in Rockefeller's honour. People were greatly impressed by the native singers who'd been laid on, and perhaps most of all by the belly-dancers ...

Friday, 26 March
Rockefeller left for the Far East and Australia early this morning. On the way to the airport I chatted with him about this and that, and he admitted how much he resents the slowness of decision-making in the USA, a great contrast to the way things are done here. 'You should lend us HIM for a couple of years', he said; 'He'd soon teach us how to govern America.' ...

[The royal family and Alam returned to Tehran on 3 April 1976]

Sunday, 4 April
Audience ... Princess Ashraf is asking permission to make a public broadcast on radio and television, announcing the establishment of the Ashraf Pahlavi Foundation for Charitable Causes. 'No', HIM said. 'Categorically

no. If it's a worthwhile venture, and I very much doubt it deserves such a description, it will need no such publicity.' ...

Wednesday, 7 April
Audience ... Discussed the Crown Prince. Pointed out that HIM might spare the boy more time and attention. In Kish, for example, they spent less than half an hour alone together during the entire twelve days. 'I don't want to put him under any obligation', he said. 'At his age too much responsibility might put him off administrative work for life.' I replied that this was not at all what I had in mind; merely that they might occasionally lunch or dine alone, so that the boy can benefit from his father's wisdom and experience ... I added that I fear HMQ's unwarranted liberalism may so influence the child that he grows up incapable of taking hard decisions. His French governess has an equally unfortunate effect ...

Thursday, 8 April
Audience ... Reported meeting the ambassador of Gabon who expects us to give his country full financial support. 'Why on earth should we?', HIM replied. 'They promised to sell us uranium but it now appears the French control their entire supply. They also asked us to train their pilots, yet we have no facilities and I refuse to give up any of the 300 places we have each year for training in the USA; the largest quota of any single country.' I remarked that, according to the poor old ambassador, they've already arranged to supply 120 tons of unrefined uranium below the market price. HIM denied any knowledge of this, instructing me to contact Etemad, head of our Nuclear Energy Agency. If what the ambassador says is correct, then we shall respond favourably to all his requests.

Met the British ambassador ... Willingly agreed to arrange a visit to Kish for him. He presumes that either Roy Jenkins or Denis Healey will be appointed Foreign Secretary in the new Callaghan government. He was proved wrong late this evening when the job was awarded to Anthony Crosland, Environment Secretary under Wilson and a man with no previous diplomatic experience.

Friday, 9 April
Went riding, despite a pain in my arm. Beautiful weather. My wife was ill in bed for a fortnight over New Year. She and my grandchildren went for a walk whilst I went to say hello to my dearest friend, my horse. Being an

obliging beast he took pity on his poor one-armed master and somehow or another we managed to get by ...

Audience ... The North Korean ambassador has suggested that HIM cable President Kim Il Sung, congratulating him on his sixty-fourth birthday. HIM was bemused by this. 'Fair enough if it were his sixtieth or his seventieth birthday', he said. 'But sixty-four makes no sense. This ambassador of yours must be a dreadful old toady.' ...

Earlier on he'd undergone a medical examination and seemed pleased that his spleen is now back to normal. No thanks to Beglou, his valet, who made a stupid mistake the other day. HIM's tablets are deliberately kept in a bottle whose label bears no relation to the contents. Not realizing this, Beglou used the label to order fresh supplies from Paris. Needless to say as soon as HIM began using these, his spleen blew up like a balloon. Goodness knows what might have happened if Beglou hadn't boasted about his thoughtfulness to Professor Safavian. Safavian got the fright of his life when he realized what had happened. He rushed round to see me, apart from anything else to complain that that idiot Ayadi, HIM's special physician, had totally failed to notice anything was amiss. HIM took it all in good part, even forbidding us to tell Beglou, so as to spare the poor man's feelings.[1]

Camille Chamoun, ex-President of the Lebanon, is peeved that HIM made no attempt to sympathize with him when his house was bombed. HIM replied that the news had not reached him in time ... and that in any case he has little sympathy for the Lebanese Christians and their nonsensical views ...

Monday, 12 April

Audience ... Princess Shahnaz's husband is still trying to build a motor-cycle factory, but they're having problems finding a suitable site west of Tehran. On behalf of my friend Kani and myself I offered to give her land from our own estate there ... HIM reluctantly approved this, though I had to use all my powers of persuasion.

Reported that men convicted by military tribunals are being held in gaol long after their sentences have expired. This is terribly unjust. HIM replied that 90 per cent of terrorists are men recently released from prison. I

---

[1] Ayadi had warned the French physicians that the Shah – a rather fussy patient – was keen to read the label of any medicines administered to him. To prevent him from discovering the true nature of his illness, it was decided to put his tablets in a different bottle. Hence the bungling by the Shah's overzealous valet.

replied that this was no excuse and that the present policy is a dreadful blot on the nation's reputation. If particular men are suspected of terrorist sympathies following their release they can always be banished to some remote provincial town and placed under police surveillance, but at least that way they'll be relatively free. HIM agreed with this, instructing me to explore the matter with General Nassiri, head of Savak.

Ayatollah Khoyi of Najaf has contacted HIM to request help for Najaf's religious schools which are threatened with closure by the Iraqi authorities. 'I have already spoken out on their behalf', HIM said, 'and shall do so again, though I doubt the Iraqis will pay any attention. Right across Islam, the mullahs are doomed.' . . .

He then expressed his intention of flying to Kish on Wednesday. I assured him that everything will be prepared . . .

Tuesday, 13 April
Audience . . . Tomorrow HIM flies to Kish, so I cancelled an invitation to the British ambassador, due to visit the island on Thursday. HIM asked me why and I explained that although the ambassador was to have stayed somewhere away from our own quarters, it might be best if we avoided him altogether. HIM replied this was surely rather embarrassing given that I'd already invited the poor fellow. But my first objective is to provide for HIM's comfort, even if it means causing offence to others . . .

The King of Afghanistan wants $10,000 to buy another limousine. 'But of course, we'll grant his request', HIM replied. 'God has granted us the means to help those less fortunate than ourselves.' He also instructed me to discover whether Abdul Vali Khan needs any financial support. 'We've made an allowance to Princess Belqis, but it would be wrong for her husband to be entirely reliant on her. Remember what I told Nelson Rockefeller', HIM continued. 'One day we may install Abdul Vali Khan as the new ruler of Afghanistan.' I pointed out that the Americans are unlikely to support such a scheme during an election year, especially given the hostility it would arouse from India and the Soviets. In the longer term our best bet would be to have it implemented via the British and their own Afghan contacts, provided we can trust them and they can count on financial support from Washington. 'The British have grown too lazy', HIM retorted. 'They've turned their backs on Afghanistan and her problems.' . . .

Wednesday, 14 April

Audience ... Told HIM an amusing tale relating to one of his lady-friends, a Swedish girl. She was taken ill last night as a result of eating too many green almonds. As soon as I heard I sent my driver round to collect Professor Safavian. However the poor fool paid no attention when I gave him the girl's address, and instead drove Safavian off to see my own French girl-friend. She, of course, denied any sort of stomach pains and was even more bemused when the professor began reassuring her that she had nothing to fear, that she could confide in him, that Iranian doctors are discreet and entirely reliable, and so on and so forth. Thank goodness, after they'd both got thoroughly bewildered, she rang me and I was able to put matters straight ... HIM nearly wept with laughter when I told him. Goodness only knows what the servants would have made of it, coming in to find us both rolling around in hysterics ...

Friday, 16 April

Spent the past two days in Kish with HIM. A welcome rest ... Reported various matters to him during the flight back to Tehran, including my recent meeting with the West German ambassador. The ambassador expressed amazement at his country's failure to sell us Leopard tanks. Apparently the deal proposed went far beyond the simple commercial procedures employed by Britain and the USA, and included an offer to build a tank factory here in Iran. Even if the price per tank were slightly more, surely it is far more important for us to concentrate on the opportunities for future industrial development? ... HIM remarked that the Leopard costs precisely twice as much as the Chieftain and that if we opted for local manufacture we'd be forced to wait a full ten years ...

This evening Princess Shams invited us to meet Karl Münchinger, the German orchestral conductor. Accompanied HIM there in his new fast-flying helicopter[1] ... Complained that he was flying it at its maximum 140 knots an hour. 'Who is the better pilot?', he said. 'You or I?'

Over dinner ... we discussed various notorious examples of embezzlement by American big business ... Concluded that the highly industrialized nations are the very byword for corruption, yet it's always they that accuse everyone else of dishonesty ...

A wonderful concert after dinner. It was past midnight when we returned to Tehran, but HIM still insisted that he and I take a stroll around the

[1] Princess Shams's palace was situated in the countryside, west of Tehran.

palace gardens. I remarked that news of tonight's reception was bound to leak out, and that Princess Shams's extravagance would be contrasted with Princess Ashraf's announcements about her charitable foundation. None the less, put their reputations in the balance and Princess Shams would still emerge the popular favourite. 'Alas', HIM said with a laugh, 'I'm afraid you're only too right'.

Saturday, 17 April
Audience. Reported that Princess Belqis's allowance is set at $2,500 a month. HIM instructed me to arrange further monthly payments of $1,000 to Abdul Vali Khan. I pointed out that they're keen to obtain title deeds to the residence we bought on their behalf. HIM agreed to this, provided they intend to stay put in Rome ...

HIM was teasing his mother over dinner, asking how much she'd really loved his father. 'How could I have been in love with him?', she said. 'Most of the time I was far too cross'. 'But, mother', he replied, 'that in itself is a proof of love. You don't lose your temper with those to whom you're entirely indifferent.' He went on in this vein, embarrassing her by asking how many nights a week they spent together and what precisely they got up to on such occasions ...

Monday, 19 April
Ex-King Leka of Albania called on me early this morning. He's desperate for money and like the ex-King of Greece is eager to snatch at any sort of business deal. They're both of them envious of the enterprise shown by Prince Victor Emmanuel, the son of ex-King Umberto of Italy, whom HIM has helped become a very rich man indeed ...

Audience ... HIM authorized me to recommend that ex-King Leka approach our Finance Minister ...

Wednesday, 21 April
HIM flew to Izmir at 8.45 this morning to take part in the RCD conference. Although it was a rather early hour for the ladies, HMQ accompanied him to the airport. I was a little surprised by this. Then I remembered that HIM's failure to see off or welcome back HMQ on her own trips has led to rumours in the city that the couple's relations are increasingly strained. I had further proof of these rumours two hours later when HMQ's uncle, Qotbi, paid me a visit. He wanted to know whether there's any truth to

the stories he's heard. I assured him in all sincerity that they are entirely unfounded, at least as far as I can judge ...

Met the Israeli representative who passed on a summary of the US Senate Defense Committee's report, following their fact-finding mission to Iran. Apparently they were favourably impressed by the degree of training in our armed forces. They had expected much worse ...

Friday, 23 April
Lunch with the US ambassador ... I asked what Rockefeller had made of his meeting in Kish. Apparently HIM's suggestion that the USA side with Black Africa had never occurred to them before. Rockefeller immediately put a call through to Kissinger, before embarking on his African tour ...

Saturday, 24 April
HIM returned from Turkey ...

Special dinner at the Foreign Ministry to commemorate a joint anniversary: the coronation of Reza Shah and the abolition of Capitulations,[1] part of the festivities to mark fifty years of the dynasty ... The diplomatic corps turned out en masse, and the whole thing was a great success. However, HIM made no attempt to reply to the speech delivered by our own Foreign Minister.

Tuesday, 27 April
Audience. HIM complimented me on my speech yesterday to the Pahlavi University in Shiraz; a rare sign of approval ... I told him how enthusiastically I'd been received; 3,000 students packed into the university's gymnasium ... Though I was rather alarmed to see so many of the girls wearing the veil. During my time as the university's President the veil was more or less done away with. We'd have scorned any girl inclined to wear it. Yet there were several dozen of them at yesterday's conference. I considered it inappropriate to make any comment at the time. I was also informed that some of these girls refuse to shake hands with Farhang Mehr, the university's new President, claiming that Islam forbids any sort of physical contact with the opposite sex outside marriage. HIM was extremely indignant ...

---

[1] Capitulations were the legal and economic privileges extended to foreign nationals, exempting them from the jurisdiction of Iranian law. Imposed by a series of nineteenth-century treaties. Abolished in 1928.

Saturday, 1 May
Labour Day. HIM delivered an address to a crowd of 3,000 trades union delegates.

On the way back to the Niavaran Palace he asked me to ride with him in his car. I remarked that even five years ago no one except HIM would have dreamed of the rise in working-class living standards. 'Your Majesty perseveres in turning your dreams into reality', I said. He replied that the idea of land reform occurred to him when he was still only heir to the throne. 'As to worker profit-sharing in industry, and part ownership, it was in 1954 that I first began to realize what might be done. Ironically, the same year I made a trip to West Germany and raised the idea with the president of their trades union congress. He considered the scheme totally impractical. I couldn't understand his attitude, but I suppose he realized the struggle between workers and the capitalist ruling class evaporates once workers become shareholders in their own endeavours.' . . .

Monday, 3 May
Audience . . . Passed on a long report prepared by the South African Consul-General, detailing his country's investment opportunities in gold, uranium and other minerals . . .

'Ask the US ambassador for information about this man Jimmy Carter', said HIM. 'He seems to be making a clean sweep of the Democrat primaries.' I replied that according to my one and only source, a brief biography in *Time* magazine, he's a political lightweight. He's managed to duck out of any clear statement on the more important policy issues, but then again, 'The White House makes the man', as the saying goes. HIM is anxious to open up some sort of channel of communications with him . . .

He is puzzled by the fact that both *The Times* and the *New York Times* have simultaneously published criticisms of Iran. 'They're particularly opposed to our treatment of the communists', he said. 'James Callaghan claimed at our latest meeting that communism can be defeated merely by the existence of a democratic regime. It's strange and not insignificant that his views should be so exactly mirrored in the newspapers.' . . .

Tuesday, 4 May
Audience. I've now read the offending newspaper articles but could find no trace of a deliberate ganging up against Iran. The *New York Times* merely quotes an Iranian source to the effect that torture is practised in

our gaols. This is simply to repeat what the communists have been claiming for years. We must resign ourselves to the fact that such allegations will crop up elsewhere. *The Times* contains absolutely no criticism, though the weekly magazine *Time Out* prints some sort of anti-Iranian diatribe which can safely be ignored. Presumably whoever reported the matter to HIM got the magazine and the newspaper confused. 'Perhaps you're right', said HIM, 'in which case we should let the thing drop.'

I should have liked to raise the whole question of anti-Iranian propaganda, and its roots in the unjust acts perpetrated by Savak and other government agencies. But as HIM was rather preoccupied, I decided to wait for a better opportunity . . .

Wednesday, 5 May

Audience. On HIM's instructions the Protocol Department has prepared a schedule for a week long visit to Shiraz. I pointed out that this is an unnecessarily long time, particularly since the Crown Prince of Jordan is expected here next Monday and HIM's absence from Tehran might be misinterpreted as a deliberate insult. He agreed, requesting that I shorten his trip in Shiraz . . .

Princess Ashraf has appointed a certain young man named Golesorkhi to manage her household. He has no administrative or Court experience and yet she wants him ranked at the same level of protocol as a deputy minister of Court. I told HIM that her request was quite out of order and that I have turned it down. 'Well done', he replied. 'These people are a selfish bunch. They don't give a damn for me. They forget that without me they'd be utter nobodies.'

Later HMQ telephoned, asking for the dates of HIM's visit to Shiraz. When I gave her them, she began complaining she'd been kept entirely in the dark about his plans. 'This is just as a King ought to behave', I replied. Had I not been so forthright, she'd no doubt have got other ideas about this trip; ideas which would not have been far wide of the mark. As it was, she completely changed tack, saying she'd phoned merely to ask that I ensure HIM isn't overtired. I'm concerned by the present state of relations between Their Majesties. I trust their family life won't be wrecked. HMQ commands my fondest affection and for various reasons my sympathy . . .

Thursday, 13 May

Audience ... Reported a conversation I had with the US ambassador about the presidential elections. As yet no one can say what the outcome will be, nor whether Carter will maintain a lead over his rivals. According to the ambassador, as an ex-naval officer who worked under a conservative commander, Carter is unlikely to adopt an unreasonable approach to foreign policy ...

Passed on an American newspaper cartoon. Convinced that Carter's success in the primaries is due to his buck-toothed grin, President Ford is shown doing his best to adopt the same sort of expression. I remarked that the artist had grasped Ford's native stupidity. HIM was much amused, recounting President Johnson's comment that Ford was so thick he couldn't chew gum and walk straight at one and the same time. None the less, I remarked, Carter may turn out to be an even greater ass than Ford ...

Submitted a memorandum from the US ambassador.

[The note reads as follows:]

We are aware that Iran has recently discussed with Northrop and associated US firms a possible barter of oil for the land-based F-18L aircraft. According to information from the Department of Defense, there are several factors that Iran should be aware of as it considers the Northrop proposal.

First, the current estimate in the Department of Defense is that the full scale development of the F-18L aircraft will cost 250–300 million dollars. The present indications are that the Department of Defense will not fund the full development of this aircraft and that the development cost will be the responsibility of non-US buyers of the aircraft. To our knowledge, Iran is presently the only active customer.

Secondly, if an F-18L aircraft is developed, it would have an estimated 40 to 60 per cent commonality of spares and support with the F-18L. According to information now available to us, the US Navy is not now in a position to make a commitment to support the F-18L aircraft. There might, therefore, be problems with arrangements for support by non-US buyers of the airplane.

Both of these questions are now under review in the Department of Defense. A DOD position on these questions is being developed. When the DOD position is received, it will be immediately communicated to the Imperial Government of Iran.

I was instructed to inform Northrop that HIM will buy the aircraft only if the US government places its own order first.

... This afternoon HIM received the British ambassador, come to discuss an urgent matter relating to Jordan. I was subsequently instructed to contact King Hussein via our ambassador in Amman, to let him know that the British are prepared to devise a package deal for Jordan's air defence, involving the supply of Thunderbird and Rapier missiles ... HIM is keen that the Jordanians refrain from purchasing sophisticated weapons systems from the Soviets ...

Saturday, 15 May

Audience. Submitted cables from our ambassador in Jordan who has since returned to Tehran. Apparently King Hussein is determined to buy weapons systems from Russia, claiming that the British offer is mere wishful thinking. They made just the same proposal on missiles when he was in London but absolutely nothing came of it. The King fears the Syrians will devour him unless he demonstrates a firm will to resist. None the less he will follow the advice of HIM, whom he describes as his elder brother, trusting that HIM appreciates his tricky situation. 'He's quite correct', HIM remarked. 'Hence in my message to him I spoke of the overall interests of the region, not merely of his own position. The Saudis have let him down, whilst the British talk and talk but take no action ...'

The ambassador also reports that our supply of military equipment to Morocco is now public knowledge, with the Jordanians recognized as being no more than intermediaries in the deal. He suggests that Jordan take various steps, a token supply of their own weapons for example, to keep up appearances. 'There's no need', HIM replied. 'What can it matter if our role in the affair becomes known by Algeria and the Palestinians?' ...

Sunday, 16 May

Audience. Good news to report; the security forces last night shot dead eleven terrorists. HIM asked me to look into the details of this engagement which he'd been expecting for some time. 'There are others of them', he said, 'who will either be arrested or killed before long ... Their hide-outs have all been identified. We should be able to annihilate them.'

... We then turned to discussing recent developments in Jordan. 'There is one point that I simply don't know how to put to King Hussein', HIM said. 'Jordan will continue to exist just so long as she poses no threat to Israel. At the moment she acts as a buffer between Iraq, Syria and Israel.

But were she to be regarded as the slightest threat by the Israelis, they would wipe her out in a couple of hours ... I have asked our ambassador in Amman to raise this issue with the King, using whatever tact and caution he can muster.' ...

Sunday, 23 May
This morning I met the President of Tehran University. He delivered a detailed account of the student unrest that's broken out in the past few days. He claims that reports of students mourning for the dead terrorists have been grossly exaggerated. HIM at first ordered that the Polytechnic as well as the University engineering school be closed down, but apparently this would have caused only worse uproar, playing directly into the hands of the terrorists. The President blames the unrest on Hoveyda whom he believes is manipulating it to distract people's attention from the government's shortcomings. I find this hard to accept, since it is unlikely that Hoveyda would encourage precisely those actions most likely to threaten his own position. He has far more subtle ways of distracting the public, just as he knows how to distract HIM.

Reported this conversation at my audience. Suggested that we refrain from putting undue pressure on the university presidents. They have troubles enough as it is and are literally battling for survival. HIM questioned what grounds they have for fear, and I explained that they are genuinely afraid of assassination by the terrorists. 'Yet what's the point of their surviving?', he retorted, 'when they forget their country and think only of themselves?' ...

Monday, 24 May
... King Khalid of Saudi Arabia has arrived on a state visit ... Dinner in his honour. No speeches as the poor man is totally at sea when it comes to public speaking.

Wednesday, 26 May
Audience ... HIM remarked that he's sent a message to King Hussein, notifying him that the Saudis are prepared to finance his programme of air defence. They are keen to know whether this will incline the King more towards buying a western system ...

The BBC announced this morning that we and the Saudis have agreed a 5 per cent increase in oil prices for the forthcoming OPEC summit in Bali. 'What bastards these people are', HIM said. 'How on earth can they claim to know that?' I replied that the report was not even in their main news broadcast but relegated to their account of the London Stock Exchange. Apparently share prices in the oil companies have risen steeply as a result. HIM smiled at this in a self-satisfied sort of way.

Monday, 31, May

Early morning meeting with the US ambassador ... Discussed the hand-over of the US army's radio TV system to our own national network ... We then turned to the issue of terrorism. In reply to his enquiring its origins I remarked that the entire movement is obviously inspired from abroad. To this he replied that we cannot rule out public dissatisfaction here in Iran. I suggested that the majority of our population is made up of farmers, workers and the professional middle class. None of these groups has much to complain of ... The ambassador replied that none the less various hot-headed idealists are determined to protest against virtually everything we've done. I could only agree with him ...

Tuesday, 1 June

Audience. HIM far from happy. He explained that besides stomach pains, he's suffering from a skin rash and headaches. I asked whether he'd consulted a doctor. He replied that Ayadi had seen him and prescribed various medicines. I remarked that most doctors are idiots but that Ayadi is the biggest idiot of them all ... To calm his anxiety I told him that he'd soon put his own problems into perspective if he could see me without my clothes on. I'm literally a mass of sores and boils. 'Then why on earth don't you get something done about it?', he asked. I explained that since all doctors are idiots there's little hope of their arriving at a diagnosis let alone a cure. 'As simple as that?', he asked. 'As simple as that', I said.

Princess Shams is considering making a trip to Johannesburg, to visit the Reza Shah museum.[1] Her private secretary has approached the South African Consul-General in the hope of obtaining an official invitation. The Consul in turn sought my advice which was that such an invitation would be a grave mistake. The trip had much better remain unofficial, thus saving us the headaches involved in taking sides over apartheid. 'Quite so', said HIM. 'These people have no sense of reality.'

HIM interrupted suddenly as I was talking about the universities. 'Did

---

[1] Reza Shah's residence while in exile in Johannesburg was bought by the Iranian government in the 1970s and turned into a museum.

you know', he said, 'that according to an NCO serving with a regiment outside Tehran, the terrorists are actually courageous heroes? He's announced that without them the government would have bled this nation dry. I don't suppose anyone bothered pointing out to this fine young gentleman that the provision of countless social services can hardly be considered "blood-sucking" ...' I remarked that in this particular instance the man falls under military jurisdiction and deserves whatever he has coming to him ... but that in general we must just learn to put up with such grumbling ...

'Even more remarkable', HIM continued, '*The Times* and the *Guardian* accuse us of operating a police-state. The BBC Persian programme has made similar allegations, saying that countries such as Iran and Saudi Arabia should be denied access to western military technology. What are the bloody fools on about? Do they seriously regard Iraq, or Algeria, or Libya as liberal regimes? Tell the British ambassador that if his media and political bosses really feel this way, we shall be forced to reconsider our purchase of weapons from the UK. Remind him that *The Times* and the *Guardian* are widely regarded as the voice of the British government.' I confessed myself surprised by all this, not having seen or heard anything like the criticisms he was alluding to. The most the papers have done is to quote from a report by the International Commission of Jurists ... I added that we ourselves are to blame for whatever false allegations arise, since we do so little to make a good impression. Why is it that our terrorist trials proceed in secret? Why do we forbid the accused to see their families? Surely what we're aiming at is to prosecute the enemies of the regime who are without a doubt the enemies of the people. With such just motives spurring us on, it can benefit us not one iota to hold these trials away from public view. HIM pondered for a while but made no attempt to respond ...

Wednesday, 2 June
Met the British ambassador and warned him that if his government and ruling party adhere to the anti-Iranian views of the British media then we shall cease to purchase weapons from the UK. He was greatly annoyed by this. He told me he'd just returned from a trip to London, to get to know the new Foreign Secretary. He denied the British government has any bias against Iran and expressed bafflement about the BBC programme we found so offensive, suggesting that subversive elements may once again have penetrated the foreign language service. For example it was recently dis-

covered that Palestinian agents had infiltrated the BBC's Arab department and had come close to disrupting relations with Kuwait and Saudi Arabia ... He remarked that he's several times advised the BBC to discontinue their Persian service as a waste of time and money; there are quite enough people in Iran capable of understanding the standard English language broadcasts. Referring to Jordan he said that the British have not abandoned hope of supplying missiles. King Hussein may well prefer this option to supplies from Russia. I warned him that this is not at all the impression we have received ...

Audience. HIM in much better spirits than yesterday ... He claims to have received information suggesting that the International Commission of Jurists is a tool of the CIA, and has ordered the Foreign Ministry to publicize these allegations in the *Guardian*, *The Times* and the *New York Times*, if needs be by buying up advertising space.

... Met the Soviet ambassador. He has issued an official invitation to the Crown Prince for the first week of July ...

Monday, 7 June
Audience ... Our consulate in Geneva has been occupied briefly by a group of Iranian dissidents who carried off various classified documents. Originally HIM instructed the Foreign Ministry to ensure the guilty parties were tried before a local Swiss tribunal. However I spent ninety minutes on the telephone last night discussing the matter with Maître Nicolet, an outstanding Genevan lawyer and a valued friend of Iran. In his opinion it would be unwise to proceed in this way since it will give each of the thirteen accused the opportunity to appoint a communist defence counsel. For weeks on end they'll have the attention of the international media. Moreover the most we could hope for by way of punishment would be fines of 100 Swiss francs or five days imprisonment. Nicolet suggests as an alternative that we register our protest by refusing to re-open the consulate. This might embarrass the Swiss into expelling the dissidents. Sooner or later we'll be presented with a better opportunity to bring a prosecution in some other country ... It took a great deal to persuade HIM to follow this advice ... When I passed on the news to the Foreign Ministry, the officials there were overjoyed. They had seen all too clearly where we were heading but lacked the courage to say a word to HIM ...

Tuesday, 8 June

Audience ... Some time ago HIM sent a message via the US ambassador, claiming we had connived at the recent OPEC meeting in Bali, staving off an agreement in order to save President Ford embarrassment in the midst of his re-election campaign ... Ford has now replied thanking us for maintaining oil prices at their present level but making no allusion to HIM's comment about the election. On HIM's instructions I established that the ambassador passed on the full text of Ford's message, without omitting anything.

Submitted a copy of HIM's interview with *Al-Ahram*, Egypt's principal newspaper, which is shortly due to be published. 'They've made at least one mistake', he said. 'Last year our rate of inflation was precisely nil.' I replied that this could be corrected, but was it really true that there had been no inflation whatsoever? 'Of course it's true', he snapped back. I didn't press the issue but he could see from my expression that I had not been taken in ...

Wednesday, 9 June

Audience. Passed on significant cables from Movassaqi, our ambassador in Syria ... King Hussein claims he has yet to receive a firm undertaking from the Saudis to finance his missile purchases ... On HIM's instructions, Movassaqi is to be sent to Saudi Arabia to discuss the matter.

... Submitted a provisional schedule for the Crown Prince's visit to Russia, pointing out that he's decided against touring the Moscow Military Academy on the grounds that he's not yet a soldier. 'In that case why has he agreed to visit the Naval Academy in Leningrad?', HIM asked with a frown. 'Tell him he can do what the hell he likes.' Although this annoyed me I refrained from enquiring the reason for this outburst ...

Later passed on a copy of the same schedule to the Soviet ambassador, adding that HIM insists I accompany the boy on his trip. The ambassador seemed delighted, inviting me to stay on after the Crown Prince has left and suggesting that I meet Kosygin and take a well-earned rest including a thorough medical examination.

I replied that this was quite out of the question. It's against every rule of protocol to leave the Crown Prince on his own half way through a visit abroad ...

Thursday, 10 June

The US ambassador telephoned early this morning to ask for an urgent audience with HIM. I passed on this request. Subsequently, during my own audience, HIM asked why the ambassador was in such a hurry. I explained that he has some sort of message to deliver from King Hussein. 'Presumably it's to do with Syrian action in the Lebanon', he remarked. 'The Syrians have got bogged down outside Sidon and Beirut.' ...

Met the US ambassador who showed me the cables from Jordan. The Jordanians and the Syrians are seriously worried that Iraq may launch an attack on Syria. King Hussein would have no choice but to intervene on Syria's behalf, although he's learned that the Soviets have assured Iraq they will pressure the Syrians into breaking off operations in the Lebanon. This might spell the end for Hafiz Assad, in which case the leftists would come to dominate the entire region from Damascus to Baghdad; a grave threat to the Saudis and a destabilizing factor throughout the Middle East. King Hussein has warned HIM via the US ambassador that he will cancel his trip to Moscow if it's confirmed that the Soviets are pressing for Syrian withdrawal from the Lebanon. He is anxious to know what our attitude would be towards Iraq if she attacks Syria, forcing Jordanian intervention.

Friday, 11 June

Totally exhausted. Spent the entire day at home ... I miss my poor old horse, but I'm no longer well enough even to think of riding[1] ...

Saturday, 12 June

... Audience ... Discussed Syria and the Lebanon ... HIM announced that he's sent a message to King Hussein, supporting his resolve to stand behind the Syrians and declaring that there can be no going back. He's also notified King Khalid that he should dissuade the Iraqis from any hostile action against Syria.

Expressed my unease about King Hussein's involvement in this mess. 'He's complicated his position for no valid reason', HIM said. 'He doesn't appreciate that Jordan's greatest strength lies in the very fact that she's always been so weak. He's got ambitions way beyond his proper station, yet the more powerful he seeks to become, the more he risks annihilation. He's sincere, he's young and he doesn't lack for courage. But why does he overplay his hand? Why go swanning off to Australia or, as he's doing now,

---

[1] For much of his last year in office, Alam was confined to bed.

plan a daft trip to Austria? These people have nothing to offer him, nor he to them.' ...

Met Movassaqi after he'd been received by HIM. His talks with King Khalid went well and the Saudis have agreed to purchase up to $500 million worth of missiles for Jordan, provided they are not supplied by the Soviets ...

Wednesday, 16 June

Audience. Ayatollah Khoyi of Najaf is once again asking for HIM's support. In particular he complains of harassment by Khomeini who is making trouble for him with the backing of the Iraqi authorities. HIM instructed me to notify Ayatollah Khonsari. 'Incidentally', he continued, 'whatever happened to Khonsari's promise to publish a pamphlet condemning Islamic Marxism? I see that he's not a man to be trusted.' I replied that the clergy think only of how to attract more followers. They don't give a damn for anything else ...

President Sadat of Egypt arrived here yesterday on a state visit. HIM received him following my own audience ...

Saturday, 19–Sunday, 20 June

Accompanied Their Majesties and the Sadat family to Ramsar [on the Caspian Sea]. A welcome rest for all concerned ...

Monday, 21 June

Returned to Tehran around noon. Sadat flew on to Saudi Arabia ...

In the Marble Palace at Ramsar, whilst we were waiting for the scheduled time to fetch our guests, HMQ remarked quite out of the blue that she worries the public is growing fed up with her and HIM. 'They don't seem to show anything like the enthusiasm for us that they once had.' Like me HIM was rather taken aback but he disagreed with her strongly. 'Even so', she said, 'if I were made to wait in a crowd for hours to see my King with an officious policeman blocking my way, I too would be fed up.' I butted in at this point since I could see that HIM was on the verge of losing his temper. I reminded her that she is hardly likely to see eye to eye on all this with the Iranian public. The public see Their Majesties only too seldom, but they are always delighted, even if it's only to catch a brief glimpse of them and their guests ... Incidentally, popular enthusiasm this morning seemed to me to be as great as ever it was ...

Subsequently Sultan Qabus of Oman arrived in Tehran and was escorted to his residence by HIM ... There was a private reception in his honour this evening and HMQ has begun arranging a similar dinner-party for tomorrow. As discreetly as possible I warned HIM that the Sultan normally shuns such occasions. He's come here, unaccompanied by his wife, with the sole intention of finding a little extra-marital entertainment. HIM duly informed HMQ that tomorrow's dinner will be a very brief affair. She was not at all pleased.

Tuesday, 22 June
Audience ... Submitted the draft of a cable, sending congratulations for the bi-centenary of American independence, and praising the achievements of the USA over her short but glorious existence. HIM insisted that I delete the word 'short', declaring that Americans feel a sense of inferiority about such things ...

Over dinner at the Sultan's residence, the PM informed HIM that the British film crew presently working in Iran today visited Tehran University and incited the students against the government. HMQ was particularly upset by this since it was she who helped arrange the film crew's stay here ...

Thursday, 24 June
Having bid farewell to Sultan Qabus at the airport HIM and I flew back to Saadabad. 'He's a good sort', HIM said of the Sultan. 'He doesn't do a thing without asking our permission.' I replied that this was a wise approach, given that HIM's advice springs from no motive save a desire to protect the security of the Gulf. 'Quite so', HIM replied. 'I don't think he has any wish to see our troops withdraw from Oman.' ... He then asked what the Sultan had got up to over the past two nights. I replied that both evenings he'd met a bevy of four or five women outside the residence. I can't vouch for what happened later on, though the Sultan seemed more than content.

He asked whether I'd read a particular article in the *Financial Times*. I said I had, at which he continued, 'What a coincidence that the BBC Persian service have also got hold of it and quoted large chunks. Tell the British ambassador that we can no longer turn a blind eye to this deliberate anti-Iranian campaign.' I pointed out that the article was by no means wholly critical. 'Yet the bastards still moan on about there being misery in Iran', he said. 'On the contrary we have a positive shortage of labour, a minimum wage of $7 a day, free health and education. Industrial workers are given shares in their companies and the farmers own their own land. What the hell is miserable in all that?' ...

Reported that Grumman Aerospace have offered to entertain Prince Gholam Reza during his trip to the USA. The company stands accused of bribing several of our countrymen in order to increase sales and it would be most inadvisable for the Prince to accept their hospitality. HIM said: 'Tell him not to go. He'd bring discredit on us for the sake of a few lousy dollars.' ...

Saturday, 26 June
Audience. Talked about the Crown Prince's forthcoming visit to Russia. HIM gave me instructions in case I find myself in discussions with Soviet officials. 'If they raise any objection to our military build-up', he said, 'you're to remind them that we're more than willing to be friends with them but that we are under no obligation to justify our own national defence. Why should they be allowed to set themselves up as some sort of grand inquisition against us?' I pointed out that I would have difficulty conveying this message without sounding unduly harsh. 'Then so be it', he replied. 'If they raise the subject, then you're to reply exactly as I've told you. If not, then you're free to keep your mouth shut.' I suggested that he give a similar briefing to the Crown Prince when he returns on Thursday. He needs to be told how to handle himself and which topics are best left for me to deal with.

Reported that Prince Gholam Reza has abandoned his plans for a trip to the USA. 'Good', said HIM, 'notify every member of my family that they're to accept no foreign invitations, either from companies or governments, without the prior approval of the Court.'

The Great Chamberlain is in a dreadful state. HIM instructed him to reduce drastically the length of the route taken by the Indian President when he arrives here later today. The poor man had barely an hour to make the necessary changes and he's worried that HIM will dislike certain aspects of the revised plan. 'Rubbish', said HIM. 'The whole thing's childishly simple. Why take the President on a great long ride in a sealed car when he's known to suffer from a heart condition? Fair enough if it weren't so hot. Then we could have used a convertible.'

Escorted Their Majesties to the airport to greet our Indian guests. Whilst there I heard news which convinces me more than ever that HIM is under the protection of the Almighty. Apparently a girl had been waiting besides the original route to the palace, ready to assassinate HIM. When she realized the route had been changed she lost her head and lobbed a grenade at two policemen standing nearby. They, thank God, escaped with only minor injuries, whilst she was killed in the ensuing scuffle. Meanwhile HIM, HMQ and their guests returned safely to the Saadabad Palace.

A group of Cambridge academics who have already published several volumes of a history of Iran arrived with presentation copies for HIM. They lunched as my guests together with various local scholars and the British and US ambassadors. I warned the British ambassador of HIM's reaction to remarks made by the *Financial Times* and the Persian service of the BBC ... The ambassador was most upset. He declared that if HIM refers to the matter at his next audience he will personally undertake either to shut down the Persian language broadcasts, or at least to ensure they're brought under stricter control. I was impressed by his eagerness to help ...

Sunday, 27 June

Audience. HIM in an excellent mood ... Referring to yesterday's assassination attempt, I remarked that had the girl's plans worked out, they would have had grave consequences for international politics, even if HIM had escaped with his life. No other head of state would dream of escorting a guest on a 13 or 14km car journey. In future I suggested the route be limited to a brief procession between the airport and the city limits, at which point our visitors should proceed directly to the palace either by car or helicopter. HIM agreed to this.

I added that it was only his change of plan, a stroke of pure inspiration, that had saved him. Had the Protocol Department got their way the route would have been left unaltered. 'Not inspiration', he said, 'merely common sense ... Though perhaps the Almighty does have some sort of desire to protect me. No doubt so I may fulfil my mission to the people of Iran.'

A message then arrived that the Indian President was on his way to meet HIM. His heart condition makes it impossible for him to climb stairs so HIM went out to receive him in the palace gardens. I accompanied him from the office and en route suggested that, as it's summer, he might like to work in the garden if we could arrange some sort of tent. 'It's not practical, I'm afraid', he said. 'You can't expect people to work outside with a mountain of files and confidential papers.' Fair enough as excuses go, but the fact is he himself prefers working indoors ...

Wednesday, 30 June

Returned to Tehran following a brief trip to see my dentist in Zurich ...

A further ten terrorists have been killed. They were found in possession of papers linking them to Libya and the Palestinians.

Friday, 2–Sunday, 11 July

For more than a week I've been in Russia with the Crown Prince. Imposs-ible to keep a diary there as however sophisticated the combination lock on my briefcase, Soviet agents would have had no trouble breaking into it.

As usual the Soviet public is obsessed with food and housing shortages. They're proud of their country and its Slavonic heritage, but in spite of all the propaganda, they seem to have precious little faith in communism. The gang of party bosses uses the secret police to keep people on the straight and narrow. In all fairness I suppose they've at least provided basic services such as schools, public transport and some sort of improvement in housing, water and power.

None the less thinking about all this spoiled my trip. At home we claim to have brought Iran to the verge of a Great Civilization, yet the country is constantly hit by power cuts and we can't even guarantee water and power supplies in the capital. Damn the incompetence of our government. I'm determined to get them replaced within the next twelve months, not out of selfish ambition but because my loyalty to HIM demands it ...

In some respects Soviet industry has made great progress. One advantage of this trip was that it opened the Crown Prince's eyes and taught him not to underestimate our northern neighbours. Up until last week he'd assumed that an American F-14 could out-manoeuvre any number of MiG 23's. He now knows differently. It was wrong he should have been misled about this great Russian bear which could swallow us whole in one gulp.

In general the Prince was on his best behaviour and asked intelligent questions. Visiting the Hall of the Supreme Soviet, for example, he enquired the meaning of the emblem plastered across one wall; a hammer and sickle dwarfing the globe. Our hosts were at a loss how to reply.

Only once did he put his foot in it. There was a reception at the embassy at which our host, Mr Niazbegof, expressed his hope that Iranian–Soviet relations will never be spoilt by the appearance of a black cat – an old Russian expression derived from the superstition that a black cat walking on the wall between two houses spells discord between neighbours. The Crown Prince had spent the evening proclaiming the merits of Iranian wine and had drunk two glasses rather than his customary one. At the mention of the black cat he butted in, saying, 'Yes, just like the American black Cadillac.' I was extremely embarrassed but remained silent rather than spoil the boy's evening. The following day we toured the Soviet Space Centre. The Prince made a delightful impromptu speech praising all the world's astronauts, American and Soviet alike. Outside as we were getting into the car I told him his remarks had more than made up for last night's gaffe. He turned to me perplexed and asked what gaffe I meant, but there was no time to explain. I'd quite forgotten this exchange by the time we arrived back at the residence. But the boy came straight into my room where I was resting and asked me to explain myself. To avoid the hidden microphones I took him out into the corridor and whispered that his comparison between black Cadillacs and the unlucky black cat might be regarded as an indirect criticism of the Americans, our natural allies and the only power capable of protecting us against the Soviets. The boy was awestruck but I told him he needn't reproach himself; he'd not been at an official meeting and had said nothing particularly horrendous ...

Tuesday, 13 July
Flew to Nowshahr. Overjoyed to see HIM after all this time ... He immediately asked how the Crown Prince had behaved. I replied that his bearing had been impeccable but that he needs HIM to teach him political wisdom. He's an intelligent boy, handsome and sensitive with a sound general knowledge ... I avoided giving him orders, trying merely to offer advice and let him make up his own mind. Indeed I'm sure that if I'd been more forthright he'd have done precisely the opposite of what I told him; something I regard as a sign of strong character. HIM was pleased ...

He asked whether the Soviets had pulled out all the stops for us. I replied that they had shown as much warmth as they considered necessary which wasn't perhaps as much as we'd wished. For example, they could have ranked the Crown Prince above the Deputy Chairman of the Praesidium. HIM agreed. I explained further that, on our arrival in Moscow, I was told by Podgorny's head of protocol, our guide throughout the trip, that Podgorny would invite the Prince to tea as soon as we returned from the Crimea. In the event no such invitation materialized, which I consider surprising and more than a little rude. Perhaps the fault lay with us. We should have ironed out all such details in advance ...

I then showed HIM a copy of his interview with the German magazine *Blitz*. There was an editorial comment on the final page describing Iran as a camp follower of America. I suggested that we delete this section before having the piece republished in the local press, but HIM disagreed and insisted it be left in. I'm pretty sure he'd have reacted differently if the Crown Prince and I had received a warmer reception in Russia . . .

Wednesday, 14 July
. . . Met the Israeli representative. He told me that Prime Minister Rabin is due in Tehran this Friday for an audience with HIM.

Saturday, 17 July
I'm writing these lines on board the plane to Geneva. Jimmy Carter has obtained nomination as Democrat candidate by an overwhelming majority. He will probably win the presidency in which case who knows what sort of calamity he may unleash on the world. He's no more than an ignorant peasant boy. There again, if his only achievement were to rescue America from its all-consuming permissiveness, he would render a great service to humanity.

Tuesday, 3 August
. . . Congress has debated the sale of US arms to Iran. Various senators claim these weapons are so powerful that not even the US could use them effectively; that they'll only result in further problems all round. Kissinger hit back, reminding them that a strong Iran guarantees US security and that the managerial problems we suffer can be attributed in part to mistakes made by our US military advisers. A special force of these men has been sent out to put things back on course . . .

Thursday, 5 August
Returned alone from Europe. Kissinger is here.

Saturday, 7 August
Attended the reception in Kissinger's honour given by the US ambassador. I told him how much I appreciated his standing up for us in the Senate Foreign Relations Committee. Kissinger replied he'd acted as he had from a conviction that we are a staunch US ally. As for the senators, he declared they were only out to grab the limelight, given that this is an election year.

He questioned me on what role the Court plays and how HIM's timetable is arranged. I explained it all, remarking that HIM spends on average twelve to thirteen hours a day hard at work. 'Which must surely make him the most diligent statesman in the entire world. An honour I'd previously reserved to myself', Kissinger replied. He was full of praise for HIM, saying, 'There's not a greater man around. I say this not to please you but because it happens to be true.'

The ambassador then commented on the great speed with which HIM and the Court spring into action. Kissinger admitted he'd often been amazed to receive answers to his messages, sometimes within as little as sixteen hours. He then asked after the Crown Prince. I assured him that he has inherited all his father's strengths. No one need fear in that respect ...

Dined with Kissinger at Ansari's. On HIM's instructions I brought up the dire financial situation of Jordan ... He promised to give the matter serious attention. 'Tell HIM', he said, 'that Hafiz Assad is a little shaky and needs propping up. HIM must let Assad know that we Americans will back him all the way.' So much for the Soviets, who seem to regard Assad as a creature of their own; a belief I myself used to share ...

Kissinger expressed gratitude for the financial help HIM has given Egypt ... I warned him that, now our oil income is in decline, it's time the Saudis came forward to help Sadat. He replied with a scathing attack on the Saudi ruling class, saying that they're a stupid, narrow-minded bunch interested in nothing save money. I told him that Jordan, Egypt and even Syria are Saudi Arabia's buffer of defence. 'Provided they're willing to accept the responsibility', he said. 'As things stand they seem to live in a world of make-believe. Jordan spent so long sitting on the fence, she was very nearly picked off by the Soviets. Only HIM's intervention saved the day.' ...

He then asked whether his talks with HIM had proved satisfactory. I replied I had not seen HIM since their meeting but that, if things had gone amiss, he could rest assured I should never have been allowed to attend the embassy lunch, let alone this evening's reception.

Monday, 16 August

Audience ... Bearing in mind HMQ's recent order that the Court avoid unnecessary expense, I reported my intention of offering the Crown Prince a Rolls Royce as a birthday present. 'I hope', I said, 'that Her Majesty will not regard this as a bad example to the Prince. I should be publicly humiliated. Hence my desire to clear it with you first.' HIM replied that the choice of gift was my own affair. I thanked him. Thanks to HIM I am now a very rich man; last year alone I sold over $5 million worth of land to the government. In these circumstances I can see no point in my behaving like some miserable old pauper ... I detest such dissimulation ... I went on to say that part of my fortune will be left to found an Institute of Higher Education in Birjand, to be named in honour of my late father. HIM asked whether the promotion of carpet-weaving would be amongst the Institute's functions, but I pointed out that the trade is already so flourishing that it can't keep up with demand. 'Under Your Majesty's guidance', I told him, 'there's not a person in this country need lack for money or employment. In the old days in Birjand my father was the only man to own a car. Now there are more than a thousand of them and they've even had to introduce one-way streets to cope with the congestion.' HIM was delighted, saying we should tell this to some of those idiots in the media; tell them to go and see for themselves and then report what they've seen fairly and accurately ...

Wednesday, 18 August

Audience. Discussed the celebrations of fifty years of Pahlavi rule. So far everything has gone smoothly and it's especially encouraging that so many books have been published or reprinted to mark the occasion ... About seventy are due to appear in Iran this year and several more will be printed abroad by the world's leading academic presses.

I remarked that my old friend Sir Denis Wright, former British ambassador, has sent us a copy of the dedicatory address to his latest book.[1] 'With that sort of preface', HIM said, 'he can hardly have written anything particularly offensive.' I replied that, from what Sir Denis himself has told me, the book deals mostly with the Qajar period, with only a brief epilogue on the rise of the Pahlavis ... describing Reza Shah as a great patriot whose seizure of power coincided more or less with what were then British interests ...

On a different note, I pointed out that Kim Roosevelt,[2] a CIA official who helped bring down the Mosaddeq regime, is trying to get his memoirs published – a complete load of nonsense ... HIM was amused, instructing me to do as I see fit ...

---

[1] 'To my Iranian friends with the sincere wish that the progress and prosperity which have marked the first half century of Pahlavi rule will long continue' – *The English Amongst the Persians* (London 1977).

[2] Kermit (Kim) Roosevelt; grandson of President Theodore Roosevelt. In 1952 as a CIA official he coordinated a joint Anglo-American plot, code-named Operation Ajax, to bring down Dr Mosaddeq, the Iranian Prime Minister. Subsequently he acted as a consultant to US firms trading with Iran. His book, *Countercoup: The Struggle for the Control of Iran*, was eventually published in New York in 1979. For a critical review, see Cyrus Ghani, *Iran and the West* (London 1987).

Saturday, 21–Thursday, 26 August

For the past few days I've been touring Azerbaijan with Their Majesties and the Crown Prince. A heavy schedule, but all went well ... Great enthusiasm amongst the local people ...

Spent the flight back to Tehran with HIM catching up on our work ... We then sat chatting, since HIM had no desire to mingle with the other passengers. Reminisced about our younger days and the girls we knew. I told him the first woman I ever had was my mother's forty-year-old maid. How keenly I recall that evening; she'd eaten a more than generous helping of garlic, which seemed to me then like the very breath of paradise. HIM burst into such prolonged laughter that HMQ and the others became seriously alarmed ...

Saturday, 28 August

Audience. HIM was very downcast. Before I'd had a chance to open my mouth he told me terrorists have this morning assassinated three of the US military advisers with our army. 'Telephone the ambassador as soon as possible', he said. 'Offer our condolences to him and the victims' families. They should also receive personal letters. Tell the military to provide the highest pensions that can be paid in such cases, as we do with our own men killed in action. You should also make sure the Court social department arranges a personal deputation to each of the families at their own homes. Above all, let the ambassador know that in our opinion the blame for this atrocity rests with the communists. They're taking advantage of the US Senate and the idiotic questions raised in its committees. Various senators suggested US advisers might one day be taken hostage. The terrorists are now trying to impress this fear on the minds of the American public. They hope that violence will excite a popular backlash, forcing Congress to ban arms sales to Iran. I'm also convinced, tell him, that various US journalists and newspapers are controlled by communists. Why hasn't the ambassador kept us informed of subversive activities by Iranian students living in the US? ...' When an opportunity arises I shall remind HIM that, following the Senate debate on arms sales, we were warned by Israeli Intelligence against just such attacks on US advisers here. The accuracy of their forecasts is quite phenomenal ...

At dinner ... HMQ said how much she would like to spend her birthday in Birjand. I told her there was no wish I felt more keenly myself.

Tuesday, 31 August

Audience ... That lunatic Qadhafi of Libya has cabled his best wishes for the start of Ramadan. HIM was quietly amused by this since the man not only cut his diplomatic relations with us but finances all manner of Iranian terrorists and left-wing radicals. I was instructed to liaise with the Foreign Ministry to determine whether or not we should send a reply.

Talked about the Swiss and their decision to declare our Savak representative in Geneva as *persona non grata*. 'They must explain themselves', HIM said. 'They knew perfectly well that our man kept in close touch with the Swiss security authorities.' I replied that there is no end to the depths a government will sink in grovelling for votes, and I reminded him of the case of Princess Beatrix, heir to the Dutch throne. She avoided attending our monarchy celebrations so as not to offend the leftists in Holland, but then came here personally to apologize to HIM. Meanwhile her father, the great Prince Bernhardt, was busy taking bribes from Lockheed, the American aircraft manufacturer. 'Indeed', said HIM, 'corruption has reached an unbelievable level abroad.' I pointed out that, at the same time our man is being ostracized in Geneva, a top Swiss official has written me a confidential letter, assuring me that he is at our disposal and that we should contact him indirectly via Maître X. Quite extraordinary!

Reported that *The Economist* has printed a lengthy piece about Iran. I only received it this morning and so must suspend my judgment until I've had a chance to go through it. 'No matter', HIM replied. 'I can guess what you'll have to say; that it's a load of utter balls.'

Wednesday, 1 September

Audience ... As expected *The Economist* article was extremely hostile; about 70 per cent criticism and 30 per cent praise. 'Quite so', said HIM. 'That bastard Housego either has a grudge against us or he's working on someone else's orders. The same goes for Eric Pace of the *New York Times* – every time he refers to our government he feels obliged to describe it as a "dictatorship".' ...

Thursday, 2 September

... Audience. HIM in high spirits as his French doctors gave him a checkup this morning and found no further inflammation of the spleen ...

Passed on a note from the US ambassador, concerning Kissinger and his reaction to questions about arms sales, put to him at his meeting with the Philadelphia World Affairs Council on 31 August.

[Kissinger's response was reported by the ambassador as follows:]

... Iran is a country whose independence has been considered important to the United States ...

It's threatened by the Soviet Union to the North. It has as its neighbour Iraq, which is one of the most radical Arab States and which, in relation to per capita, is armed much more effectively by the Soviet Union than we are arming Iran.

...

So nobody is pursuing a policy of selling arms for their own sake. But especially in the case of Iran, I think that it is on the whole in the American interest to enable it to defend itself; all the more so as it is done entirely with its own resources.

'That bit about "on the whole" rather weakens the argument', HIM remarked, after he'd read it. 'You had better say as much to the US ambassador.'

Reported that the British ambassador appears upset by the article in *The Economist*. He's since met my deputy, Homayoun Bahadori, and expressed his intention to give that bastard Housego a piece of his mind. 'Nonsense', said HIM. 'He could never do it. Yesterday evening, by the way, I was interviewed by Claire Hollingworth of the *Daily Telegraph*. Half way through, it dawned on me these people are not only ignorant but completely indifferent to the fact. I told her the British media tend to twist things. If the Americans refuse to sell us arms, we shall assume that they and the Soviets are in league with one another in a scheme to carve up the world.' I replied such a plot would not be such a bad idea, since at least we'd be saved the worry and expense of defending ourselves. 'Yes', he said, 'but what if we were part of the portion given to the Soviets?' As best I could, I expressed my unwillingness to believe that the USA will ever abandon the chain of security provided by Turkey and Iran ...

Later I met the US ambassador ... and discussed Kissinger's statement to the US Senate Foreign Relations Committee. The latter gave an estimate for the price of the 160 aircraft we're to buy, far above the FMS[2] unit price which has previously formed the basis for such calculations. The

---

[1] One of the best known and most respected of British foreign correspondents, whose active career spanned several decades of reporting.

[2] Foreign Military Sales: the standard price-list approved by the US Defense Department, put at the disposal of friendly foreign powers as a guideline for the purchase of US military hardware.

ambassador replied he had already noticed this discrepancy and had cabled Kissinger for an explanation ...

Saturday, 4 September
Accompanied Their Majesties to Ramsar for the annual education conference. At the airport HIM showed me a cable from Ardeshir Zahedi, our ambassador in Washington. Apparently Senator Goldwater has supported military sales to Iran before the Senate Foreign Relations Committee. HIM seemed pleased.

Monday, 6 September
Audience ... I began by reporting the acute shortages in basic foodstuffs but HIM blamed the problem entirely on hoarding by businessmen. I pointed out that, if only we could guarantee regular supplies, then there'd be no incentive for hoarding of any kind ... I believe the government has once again been caught off guard. HIM made no attempt to reply.

Discussed the case of an army officer who seems to expect particularly favourable treatment from HIM. 'But if I show partiality towards one individual', he said, 'how can I justify it to all the others? ... I suppose that it's a common problem, not only in Iran but throughout the Middle East. Hence the criticism we have to put up with from those bloody westerners, accusing us of flouting democracy. If I were to stand down tomorrow and ask the people, all 35 million of them, to nominate a president, there would be 35 million candidates polling one vote each. What's happened recently in Pakistan, India and Kuwait only goes to show that it's futile to imitate western democracy. They've ended up back exactly where they started.' ...

I've received highly confidential information from a British source indicating that the Pentagon is pressing General Dynamic, the company which manufactures the F-16, to double the price it is asking from Iran. They are to use inflation and past miscalculations as a pretext for this increase. Washington seems to think we will pay anything just to have the aircraft. HIM took some time to think about this before remarking that he had already begun to have doubts, hence his insistence that I ask the US ambassador whether the figures bandied about by Congress covered 160 or 300 planes. 'Even so', he said, 'the manufacturers have sent written confirmation that the price is to be $6.5 million per aircraft. How then can they raise it to $18 million; almost a three-fold increase?' I replied that this is precisely what they did over the Spruance destroyer; half a dozen of the ships were estimated at $280 million, but we still ended up paying nearer $600 million. 'It would appear', I said, 'that the Pentagon is wasting no time, appropriating what little remains of our oil revenue.' ...

Discussed a report our security services had prepared on the safety of American military advisers living in Tehran. I suggested the report's proposals don't go nearly far enough and that the only practical way to protect these people is to arm them and advise that they stick to one another's company. HIM instructed me to liaise with the US ambassador ...

... Met the American Jews who are assisting our push for better publicity in the US media. HIM had instructed me to tell them that we are well aware that the Jewish lobby has been opposed to our arms purchases. In the event I remarked to them that, on their own admission, they originated a campaign against US arms sales to Saudi Arabia and in the process unwittingly gave rise to restrictions subsequently applied to Iran. They promised to redress the situation.

Wednesday, 8 September
Audience. Gave a detailed account of my meeting with the Israeli representative who tells me that Yankelovich, our consultant for the propaganda or 'Information Plan' in America, has recently been appointed public relations officer to Jimmy Carter. Kalman Druck,[1] who is to serve as overall head of the plan, occupies a similar position under President Ford. HIM was amused by all this ... I told him that the Israelis are past masters at this sort of operation and that according to their own account their most fervent lobbyists in the US Congress are men who outwardly feign support for the Arabs. Our Jewish friends suggest that HIM receive three specially selected journalists and two prominent TV interviewers on the understanding that their questions and HIM's answers will be carefully vetted beforehand. HIM was hostile to this suggestion, but I pointed out that we must do as they recommend since they know more than anyone what is likely to prove popular with the American public ...

The Israeli representative recommended that in improving our image we should try to take a more active stance, not only in terms of the media, but within US political circles by more effective lobbying in Washington where we are at present badly under-represented. He says that it will do us no good merely having close relations with Kissinger and the State

---

[1] Public relations consultant; President of Harshe-Rotman & Druck, Inc., N.Y.C.

Department or handing out free caviar and party invitations to particular senators. Now that Congress and the presidency are at odds with one another we need to establish direct links to Capitol Hill. HIM suggested that I send someone to consult with Ardeshir Zahedi in Washington, but then changed his mind, saying: 'No. Better still, write to him and tell him that he's been working too hard and that we've decided to lighten his burden by sending out a few high-ranking people to assist with our public relations in respect to Congress. You should dress it up as if we're paying him some sort of compliment.' ...

Reported my discussions with US Democratic Senator Birch Bayh, who is fascinated by HIM and claims that there's not another leader in the world that can stand comparison to him ...

Friday, 10 September

... Met the Israeli representative this evening. Discussed joint action to persuade the US Senate to accept arms sales to Iran. He suggested that HIM raise the issue with Shimon Perez, the Israeli Defence minister, who is due to be received tomorrow. He also told me that Senator Hubert Humphrey is considering making a tour of the Middle East; Iran, Israel and Saudi Arabia in particular ... It would be a good idea if our Washington ambassador could extend an invitation along these lines, since it would help our position in regard to arms. He stressed that we must act quickly if we're to forestall Saudi Arabia and so be the first to attract the senator's attention ...

Tuesday, 14 September

Audience. Discussed the race for the US presidency, where Carter seems still to be leading. We then turned to the underlying reasons for the hostility shown us by the American media. I remarked that the Americans are fools and that their opposition to our arms purchases shows them bowing to Soviet propaganda. If they had any sense they would be crying out for us to buy more not less weapons, since it would increase our dependence on the USA to an even greater extent. 'Quite so', HIM replied. 'Soviet propaganda is remarkably effective and the Americans are even more remarkably stupid. Combine these two factors and you arrive at the present débâcle; every single congressman and pundit acting directly contrary to their own best interests.' ...

Princess Ashraf has again asked the government to pay the expenses of her trip to England, greatly to HIM's annoyance. He instructed me to notify every member of the Imperial family that such impertinent requests to the government will be severely dealt with in future.

This afternoon I received a prominent American journalist named Helen Copley; a supporter of ours. We spent an hour discussing the Information Plan. She suggested we set up a special news agency in the USA, the better to influence public opinion ...

Saturday, 18 September

Audience ... HIM asked me to write to Ardeshir Zahedi, urging him to liaise closely with Israel's embassy in Washington ...

Last Wednesday on HIM's instructions, I cabled General Nassiri in Washington following his prostate operation, notifying him that the Shahanshah had most graciously agreed to pay his medical and travel expenses. Ardeshir Zahedi telephoned yesterday to say that the general had also received money from the PM and that he's now bewildered whether he has HIM to thank for this second payment. 'The PM said nothing about it to me', HIM remarked with a smile.

It seems our PM takes a keen interest in the well-being of the men from Savak! ...

Sunday, 19 September

Audience. HIM declared he felt better today than he's felt for many years ...

Shahriar Shafiq,[1] HIM's nephew by his sister Princess Ashraf, presently an officer in the navy, was at last night's dinner. He and HMQ spent the entire time moaning on about Tehran's chaotic traffic congestion, the incompetence of municipal bureaucracy in Bandar Abbas, and so forth. I told HIM I strongly disapprove of such talk; fair enough if they raised these problems during the day, but they're not appropriate topics for the dinner table and do nothing but damage to HIM's health. Even Hitler spent his evenings listening to music, even at the height of the war. HIM gave a wry smile as if to say such things are beyond his power to change ...

Reported that Danny Chamoun, the son of the former Lebanese Presi-

---

[1] The son of Ahmad Shafiq, an Egyptian, who was the second husband of Princess Ashraf. A graduate of the British Royal Naval College, Dartmouth, Shahriar was regarded as a competent and straight-forward military officer, unaffected by and uninterested in Court life. He was assassinated in Paris in December 1979 amid speculation that the revolutionary regime in Tehran regarded him as a threat.

dent, has asked for an audience in order to pass on a message from his father. 'I'd be ill-advised to receive him in present circumstances', HIM remarked. 'His father has grown old and more than a little mad.' I pointed out that the old man put up a brave resistance to the left-wingers . . . 'Quite so', HIM replied, 'but the determination with which he acted merely proves the degree of his madness.' . . .

Met the Israeli representative after lunch. He predicts the US-presidential elections will be a very close-run affair . . .

Tuesday, 21 September

Audience. HIM was wearing a lounge suit. He had forgotten he was due to receive the Ministers of Labour from various Asian countries and asked whether he should change into something darker. I told him his present clothes were more than suitable and that in any case a change would mean breaking his absolute rule about punctuality.

A few days ago he received an intriguing letter from the US ambassador, congratulating him on the thirty-sixth anniversary of his accession.

[The ambassador, Richard Helms, wrote on 16 September 1976 as follows:]

Your Imperial Majesty,

On the auspicious occasion of the 36th anniversary of your accession to the throne, it is my pleasure and privilege to extend warmest and heartfelt good wishes on behalf of my government, this embassy, Mrs Helms, and myself.

In connection with the celebrations of the 50th anniversary of the Pahlavi dynasty, I have been studying the history of Iran in this century and have been remarkably impressed, as have many other serious students, with the extraordinary metamorphosis which has taken place under the leadership of Reza Shah the Great and Your Imperial Majesty. Not only has progress in all fields been spectacular, but also political and economic stability have been established to a degree that 35 years ago, let alone 50 years ago, would have been unthinkable. Yet you labour tirelessly to make your continuing vision for the country come true. I salute you.

May God go with you, preserve you and guide your hand!

. . . Sought HIM's permission to pay Mrs Diba's expenses for a trip to

Romania. 'By all means', he said, laughing; 'Our dear Mrs Dervish hopes Mrs Aslan's treatment will restore her to the bloom of youth.'[1] ...

Saturday, 25 September
Returned from Birjand last night. Audience ... Reported my discussions with the US ambassador. He's truly devoted to HIM and anxious we succeed in combating anti-Iranian propaganda in the USA ... I refrained from letting him into the secret that we're already taking steps in that direction with the help of the Israelis ...

Monday, 27 September
Flew with HIM to Hamedan. A rapturous reception from the local population. Everyone seemed reasonably well off; very few signs of poverty. Having visited the place with HIM sixteen and then again seven years ago, the physical development of the city came as a revelation ...

In the afternoon we visited an armoured brigade and the Vahdati airbase. They were both superb, especially the airbase which makes one's heart swell with pride at being Iranian. In all they have eighty fully operational Phantoms, besides a whole range of sophisticated missiles and anti-aircraft batteries. HIM spent an hour talking to the commander in the operations room. Like a wrestler about to enter the ring, he was eagerly assessing his enemies' strengths and weaknesses. I was enchanted by the concentration he put into this performance ... and offered up a prayer on behalf of the late General Khatami, the great architect of our air defences ...

Tuesday, 28 September
... In the afternoon HIM arrived in Kermanshah to the most spectacular display of popular enthusiasm I have ever witnessed. Only General Ayadi and I attended Dinner. HIM was much taken with today's welcome, saying: 'It's incredible, but now that living standards have improved it's the mullahs who are most keen to flatter us on our achievements. You should have heard what their spokesmen said to me whilst I was going in to the residence.' I had indeed heard it and been amazed.

[1] Mrs Aslan, a Romanian who claimed to have discovered the secret of eternal youth. Her patients included many foreigners, prominent western politicians amongst them.

Thursday, 30 September

Our tour of Western Iran continues ... Over lunch HIM questioned the continued existence of the Society for Women.[1] 'Now that they've been granted equal rights', he said, 'why do they need this private association? It's a complete waste of time. Its members should simply join the party.' Princess Ashraf, the society's patron, will be most upset by this decision.

... Altogether our trip has been a great success. One positive outcome has been HIM's realization that agriculture needs far more attention and support. What we've done to date is inadequate. The country's farmers are fighting a losing battle ...

Saturday, 2 October

... After lunch accompanied HIM to the Air Force Staff College. The speech he made was of tremendous importance but is not to be reprinted in the newspapers. He remarked that in the past, whenever there had been cases of financial corruption in the airforce, they sprang solely from a desire to carry through our plans at any cost. In these circumstances some degree of waste was inevitable – an indirect criticism of the late General Khatami. But such licence will not be tolerated in future. Referring to the welcoming speech by the college's principal, who expressed a desire to see his school rival the very finest in the world, HIM remarked that their training must match the best elsewhere since they are receiving the world's most advanced equipment. He then drew a comparison between West Germany's thousand aircraft covering a very narrow front and our own mere four hundred which must operate to the north, west and south-east, along a far wider frontier. Since we cannot rival the Germans in numbers, he said, we must make up for it in the skill and training of our pilots ...

Sunday, 3 October

Audience. Passed on a letter I've received from Princess Ashraf, asking me to remind the PM that she is due to receive a balance of $1.5 million paid in her Swiss bank account. HIM gave his permission for the transfer, remarking, 'Write to her all the same, and tell her I've already received her seven-page letter on precisely this same subject. Tell her: my dear lady, if you're so keen to pile up wealth and use my influence to aid your business schemes, then why on earth did you make such a song and dance about

---

[1] Strongly supported, since its inception, by Princess Ashraf, this society was very effective in the promotion of women's rights in Iran.

renouncing your fortune? Have you gone mad? You espouse simplicity yet crave luxury in all things. You even have ambitions to head the UN General Assembly; mere daydreams, fantasies. Why can't you behave like a reasonable woman, like your sister Shams? Write to her in these exact terms. Promise you will?' I assured him his wishes have always been my command.

Monday, 4 October

Audience ... HIM announced he'd laid on a little extra-curricular enter-tainment for this afternoon. I questioned the wisdom of this. The French President was due to arrive at 3 p.m. and the ceremonial would almost certainly keep us tied up for a further hour and a half, after which there would still be dinner to prepare for. Was there really any point in his exhausting himself unnecessarily? 'Speak for yourself', he said ...

Prior to Giscard d'Estaing's arrival, he gave an excellent interview to various Iranian journalists, paying many compliments to HIM. How proud I am of the Shahanshah.

Official banquet at the Niavaran Palace. Again Giscard was lavish in his praise of HIM. However I was upset to note that his speech was actually better than the Shah's. It's hardly surprising since HIM has ordered that his official speeches be shorn of anything that might be construed as literary or high-flown language ...

Sunday, 10 October

Audience. HIM complained that his skin rash is causing him severe discomfort. For my own part, I told him, herpes is making my life unbearable ...

Movassaqi, our ambassador in Jordan, enjoys contacts with Hafiz Assad of Syria via King Hussein and another go-between. He has now requested information about HIM's talks with Giscard insofar as they relate to Assad and the Lebanon. 'Tell him I stood out wholly in support of Assad', HIM said. I remarked that, in Movassaqi's view, Assad has fallen into line with us so far in the hope of material rewards from HIM. 'Out of the question', he replied. 'At least as regards military supplies. However we shall continue to provide what political support we can, despite Sadat's opposition.'

I raised the subject of Lieutenant-General Hashemi Nejad, Adjutant-General to HIM and former Commander of the Imperial Guard, who is up for further promotion. HIM declared he can't be promoted since he is no longer on active service, but I pointed out that this never prevented our promoting at least two other generals who found themselves in the same position. 'But that was in the past', HIM said. I then remarked that Hashemi Nejad is anxious to retain His Majesty's favour. 'Oh no he's not', HIM said. 'Oh yes he is', said I. HIM laughed. 'Whenever I offer this gentleman a job away from Court', he continued, 'he somehow manages to intercede through women, begging to stay close to me and so enjoy the benevolence of my august protection! His wife is lady-in-waiting to Mrs Diba and so has access to HMQ. Tell him he must choose between staying here at Court or taking promotion elsewhere' . . .

Spent two hours this evening with the Minister of Information discussing our poor image abroad. Prepared a report which I shall pass on to HIM. The meeting was attended by MG, our chief coordinator with the Israelis for the Information Plan. However not even the Minister knows about the existence of our scheme . . .

Monday, 11 October
Audience . . . A member of the Royal Family has borrowed $5 million from the First National City Bank of New York . . . but is still refusing to settle debts. 'Send a cable' HIM said. 'Say that they can indulge in as much extravagance as they like but only when they learn to pay their bills.'

Amongst the items of world news I passed on, the BBC have endorsed HIM's views on oil prices in direct contradiction to Simon, the US Treasury Secretary. HIM laughed. 'Now the British have found oil in the North Sea, no wonder they're in favour of price increases', he said.

Later flew to Birjand and am penning these lines seated at my father's old desk in the family house. The whole place unlocks the door to my childhood. I wonder what my father would have made of HIM and the entire royal family paying us a visit here? I'm sure he'd have been overjoyed, but though he received Reza Shah in this very building, I doubt he could have credited such an event. I remember the only gesture he made was to have a special bathroom built for the Shah. In those days no one gave a thought for the Shah's retinue. Now, of course, I've had to take endless pains ensuring that every servant in the royal household has a bathroom all to themselves. What a sign of the change in living standards.

Tuesday, 12–Sunday, 17 October
Their Majesties, the royal children, Princess Fatemeh, the PM, Mrs Diba and fifty others, HMQ's friends, stayed as my guests in Birjand. They all

seemed impressed by the reception I laid on. I thank God for vouchsafing me this opportunity to repay his bounty.

Their Majesties were due to return to Tehran on Saturday morning. HIM left first, but HMQ who was expected to follow two hours later was so pleased with the way I'd entertained them that she accepted my offer to extend her stay for a further twenty-four hours, provided I telephone to obtain HIM's approval. This he granted, much to my delight ...

The whole thing was arranged to mark HMQ's birthday on 14 October, and she even agreed to return for a repeat performance next year. There were goodness knows how many excursions and entertainments, right down to camel and donkey riding. Their Majesties stayed in the main house; the others in splendid tents, equipped with every modern convenience including bathrooms and electric fires. The royal children had theirs pitched in the garden ...

As always HIM couldn't bear to be idle and spent his mornings hard at work ... I passed on a couple of letters from Kissinger. The first was to thank us for financial assistance to the UN Food and Agriculture Organization – FAO. The second contained an extraordinary outpouring of gratitude, prompted by HIM's congratulations to Kissinger following his trip to Africa.

[In this letter of 11 October 1976, Kissinger wrote:]

... It is always a pleasure to be congratulated for one's efforts; but when it comes from a man of your vision and wisdom, it is indeed an honour. ...

... Discussing our image abroad, HIM referred to an interview he gave recently to Mike Wallace of NBC.[1] 'The bloody man's questions were incredibly hostile. He more or less forced me into declaring that the USA is controlled by the Jews and that it's this same influence which has persuaded Carter to oppose our purchasing arms.' ... 'Tell the Israelis', HIM said, 'that the bastard was so malicious I had no choice but to speak my mind. He more or less dragged it out of me.' I reminded him that everyone, the Court press department, our Jewish advisers and myself, had pleaded with him not to receive this man Wallace. Yet he insisted on going ahead and just look where it's led us. 'There's no use wringing our hands', he replied. 'What's done is done. But tell Ardeshir Zahedi that he's not to

[1] See Mike Wallace, *Close Encounters* (New York 1985), pp. 334–5.

arrange interviews with such vultures ever again.' Here too, I pointed out that it's a standing order of our new campaign that no one is to arrange foreign press interviews for HIM. It was for precisely this reason we asked for the Foreign Minister to be admitted to our steering committee. HIM finally approved this last suggestion ...

Monday, 18 October

Audience ... Some time ago HIM's sister, Princess Fatemeh, asked for a 707 army plane to fly her, Mrs Diba and seventy other ladies on pilgrimage to Mashad. Knowing what HIM's reaction would be I avoided reporting the matter whilst we were in Birjand. However last night the Princess telephoned to press her claim and I was forced to raise it at today's audience. HIM was furious. 'Do they suppose the military have nothing better to do', he said, 'than to act as courier to a bunch of redundant old bags in search of God's mercy?' He was so angry that we both kept a tense silence for quite some time. I bitterly regretted having raised the matter.

I asked whether his skin rash was any better. He now believes it was due to the calcium tablets he was taking and has noted a marked improvement since he gave them up. His doctors are due to give him a blood test next week, but he rejected my suggestion that they bring along a dermatologist, saying that the rash is due to some sort of internal reaction not to any problem with his skin.

Reported that Princess Shahnaz has asked for a three-fold increase in salary. 'Has she gone mad?', HIM replied. 'I said raise her salary, not treble it! I'd never be able to justify it to the others. They'd all be clamouring to follow suit.' ... He added that he intends making a tour of inspection of the Tehran barracks next Thursday afternoon. I pointed out that since next Wednesday is a religious holiday, everything will be shut down until the Saturday after.[1] In any case military offices are always closed on Thursday afternoons. He did nothing more than smile by way of reply; in other words warning me to mind my own business ...

There have been municipal elections across the country. Despite being allowed greater licence than normal, people in Tehran seemed utterly indifferent to the whole thing. Of the city's 5 million inhabitants, only about 70,000 bothered to vote. Since the Rastakhiz Party made no attempt to drum up attendance at the polling stations, it only goes to show that nobody's particularly interested in these elections. A worrying sign ...

[1] Thursday and Friday constitute the weekend in Iran.

Sunday, 24 October

... The US ambassador rang to arrange a meeting this morning. He informed me he is to be recalled from Tehran. He intends retiring from the diplomatic service, to go into business ... I was sorry to hear this. He was always honest and straightforward, with a real sense of responsibility.

We talked for a while about the attitude of the US media. I doubt he knows anything of our programme with the Israelis, though he met Yankelovich when the latter was in Tehran and congratulated me on appointing such reliable people to boost our image. He then suggested various improvements, saying that as he was about to leave the diplomatic service he felt at liberty to offer advice. He criticized our failure to respond to Amnesty International and the other organizations protesting against arrests and detentions, remarking that we should spell out to them that we are acting justly, according to local law. To keep silence merely gives the impression that we've eliminated the detainees altogether. I strongly agree with this although I made no comment ... He went on to say that our attempts to raise oil prices can only worsen our standing in the eyes of the American public ...

Presentation of credentials by the ambassadors of Somalia and Mauritania. HIM was most kind to me when he arrived. In front of everyone, the Foreign Minister, the military officers and the Court Chamberlains, he asked how I had got on with my dentist ... a question which put paid to all the rumours about my health which have been circulating at Court. We Iranians are a peculiar people – inclined to believe any rumour, however unfounded ...

Subsequently I was granted an audience to report my discussions with the US ambassador. HIM shares my regret at the man's departure. 'Tell him', he said, 'that the American media seem quite oblivious to the way Iraq and Venezuela are demanding an increase in oil prices of even more than 25 per cent. They're only interested in me and Zaki Yamani. They're determined to portray me as the robber baron, the supporter of price increases, with Yamani cast as the good guy. Nothing could be further from the truth.' ...

Monday, 25 October

Audience. Pointed out to HIM that he has an exceedingly heavy schedule over the next few days ... As it's his birthday everyone is determined to show off by arranging special receptions. Yet he should feel under no obligation to accept so many invitations. He replied that it takes more than a few parties to tire him out, but I told him the same cannot be said for me. I'm utterly exhausted, and my entire body is a mass of boils and sores[1] ... With a face like mine, I asked to be excused from this evening's reception. HIM agreed to my request.

... Reported that ex-Queen Soraya has fallen on hard times and is asking for a monthly allowance of $6,000-$7,000. 'What on earth can she have done with all her money?', HIM said. 'It's not long since you sent her $1.5 million. That father of hers is a dreadful sponger. He takes whatever she has and ruins her chances of enjoying herself. Warn her that this state of affairs cannot go on indefinitely.'

Worked at home all afternoon and evening. I'm plagued by herpes and my genitals have swollen to several times their normal size.

Tuesday, 26 October

Public *Salaam* to mark HIM's birthday. He was in excellent health, and evidently very cheerful ... The US ambassador attended as one of the diplomatic corps, and HIM asked me later whether the man had made any reference to the interview with Mike Wallace. I replied that he'd said absolutely nothing. 'Strange', HIM remarked, 'since I was so outspoken in my criticism of the USA.' I pointed out that he and the ambassador are likely to see eye to eye on such matters since neither of them is exactly enchanted with Washington's recent behaviour. 'Quite so', he said. 'The poor man's been close to the top for the past nine years, yet they reward his loyalty by chucking him out like so much dirty washing.'

In spite of the pain below my belt, I managed to remain standing for the whole five hours without showing any outward sign of discomfort ... The doctors examined me again this evening but they seem just as uncertain of what's wrong as I am.

Thursday, 28 October

Audience ... Reported that Princess Ashraf telephoned last night to complain that my recent reply bore no relation to the request she'd sent HIM.[2] He burst into laughter at this. 'Oh, she's out to confuse you', he said; 'All because you pretended not to have seen her letter to me.'

Last night I also spoke to Professor Safavian in Paris. He seems thoroughly satisfied with HIM's latest blood tests. Even so he recommends

---

[1] Symptoms of the illness that eventually killed him.
[2] See the entry for 3 October 1976.

that there be no reduction in the dosage of medicines. 'But what about this blasted rash?', HIM said. I replied that the doctors seem to regard it as of no significance, just as they ignore the fact that my herpes is driving me mad with pain. 'Something', I said, 'which I've been unable to tell Your Majesty over the past couple of days for fear of causing you embarrassment.' He asked what I meant, but again I declined an explanation. 'I suppose it's something below the belt', he said. I replied that he'd guessed all too correctly, and that even walking has become an agony for me. He laughed at this point, saying I should get it treated. I told him that one of the doctors I met in Switzerland recommended a particular vaccine but warned me the treatment could take up to three years. 'Extraordinary', he remarked. 'Do you know, they've prescribed sedatives to help with this rash of mine, and the things are causing me no end of trouble.' . . .

Saturday, 30 October–Friday, 12 November

Things got so bad on Saturday . . . that I had to fly to Paris the following morning. Spent five days in hospital and feel much better. I'm still weak and the herpes is still uncomfortable but at least the swelling has gone and I've been able to book into a hotel. Invited an attractive young German girl to stay. We've known each other some time, and if nothing else I can at least play backgammon with her . . . My wife is in Tehran, taking care of our grandchildren whilst my daughters are to join me here. I miss her.

Old age is at last beginning to take its toll. I have no alternative but to retire. I must rest, but how can I abandon my beloved Shahanshah? It's a terrible dilemma. I don't flatter myself that I'm indispensable, yet I'm at a loss to know how to break the news to him . . . Even holding a pen is enough to wear me out . . .

Carter has won the presidential election in the USA by a narrow margin. I read the interview he gave to *Playboy*. He seems to be yet another bloody demagogue . . .

Wednesday, 17 November

Returned to Tehran. Not unduly exhausted by the flight . . .

Thursday, 18 November

I had been told that HIM was away at Kish Island for the weekend and so was surprised last night to find his retinue waiting to greet me at the airport. Apparently he went to Kish but was so badly bitten by a dog that he had to return to have stitches.

He received me in his bedroom, sitting in an armchair with his leg propped up on a table. He seemed to be in pain, which saddened me. Reported various matters, and then, despite the kindness he was showing me, asked that I might return home. He refused this request and insisted I stay chatting to him for an hour or so ...

Saturday, 20 November
Audience ... Prince Gholam Reza has asked permission to visit Germany at the invitation of a tractor company. HIM was adamant in his refusal. 'My family don't appreciate the complications that arise from these whims of theirs', he said.

During my absence there's been a correspondence with the USA over oil prices ...

[In a letter dated 29 October 1976 President Ford wrote:]

Your Imperial Majesty,

Your decision not to insist upon an oil price increase at the Bali OPEC meeting in May was an act of statesmanship which was important in determining the outcome of that meeting. Avoidance of an oil price increase is of such great importance to the maintenance of the global economic recovery now under way that I'm writing to request your continued constructive leadership in order to prevent such an increase ...

My deep concern ... is that the favourable trends towards economic recovery will be reversed by the negative inflationary and balance of payments effects of a new increase of the price of oil. Several important industrialized countries which are experiencing economic difficulties and the attendant danger of political instability would encounter still more severe economic problems if faced next year with a new oil price increase ... Thus, the fragile and uneven nature of the global economic recovery requires that responsible nations avoid action which would endanger it.

Secretary Kissinger, in his talks with you last August, noted your concern about the need to maintain close cooperation between our two countries despite the opposition in the Congress and other circles. As the Secretary told you, this Administration is determined to continue to assist your nation in developing its military establishment and meeting its goals for economic development ... I am sure you have been fully informed of the Administration's successful resistance to Congressional attempts to block the sale of F-16 aircraft and other military equipment to Iran. The struggle with certain segments of American opinion on this subject has by no means been won, however, and I fear that there will be further and perhaps greater pressures next year. By working together, we can overcome these pressures and solidify the close relationships between our two countries. However, Iranian support for an OPEC decision to increase the price of oil at this time would play directly into the hands of those who have been attacking our relationship . . .

Given this situation, I believe that the outcome of the December OPEC meeting will have far reaching economic and political consequences . . . I therefore urge Your Imperial Majesty to give these concerns serious and positive consideration in making your decision in this matter.

[In his reply of 1 November 1976, the Shah wrote:]

. . . As you . . . are aware, Iran didn't insist on an oil price increase at the body meeting in May, despite the fact that many members of the Organization had proved that the oil exporting countries had lost a great deal of their purchasing power . . . Our hope in Bali was that the world would recover, and in the meantime, that the Paris conference between North and South would lead to certain meaningful developments in the interests of all . . .

With regard to your reference, Mr President, to the progress achieved by the industrialized countries in controlling inflation, I must point out that this may be the case with the United States of America, the Federal Republic of Germany and Japan. On the other hand we know that the economies of the developed countries of the world are sick and in a precarious state. We are purchasing commodities also from the United Kingdom, France and Italy and we find that their inflation is running very high, sometimes even at the rate of more than 20 per cent. I realize that their balance of payments' situation remains critical but this certainly doesn't justify our committing suicide by paying for their failure or inability to put their house in order by succeeding in making the necessary adjustments in their economy through domestic measures. . . .

You are no doubt fully aware, Mr President, of my deep concern to maintain close cooperation between our two countries. However, if there were any opposition in the Congress and other circles to see Iran prosperous and militarily strong, there are many sources of supply to which we can turn, for our life is not in their hands. If these circles are irresponsible, then it is hopeless, but should they be responsible, they will certainly regret their attitude to my country. Nothing could provoke more reaction in us than this threatening tone from certain circles and their paternalistic attitude.

As you will no doubt agree, Mr President, Iran has always followed a policy of restraint and moderation, but the incredible economic situation of some Western countries is such that history will not forgive us should we deplete our finite and most precious wealth just to allow these countries to continue their politicizing and indecision. Nevertheless, you may rest assured, Mr President, that in the councils of OPEC, Iran has adopted one of the most moderate attitudes ...

In addition HIM has issued a firman, commanding his personal secretariat to review the government's performance. Were I in Hoveyda's shoes I should resign without a second thought.

Sunday, 21 November
Audience ... Discussing various people, the Secretary-General of the Rastakhiz party and his deputy included, HIM remarked that they appear to be unduly pro-American.[1] I replied that I have received no indications of this myself. 'Why is it', HIM continued, 'that Hoveyda is so hostile to strong personalities? The only ones who have managed to keep their places in my government, men like Mansour Rouhani[2] and Houshang Ansari, have done so solely because of my support. Hoveyda would have sacked them long ago had he been able to.' I replied that the PM is a weakling and a bully. What's more, as we both know, he's a eunuch. Even so he's a eunuch who excels at intrigue. 'You may well be right', HIM replied. I'm not at all sure what he meant by this, or why he raised the subject in the first place ... HIM is so great and yet so stealthy that no man can fathom his reasoning. Is he considering a change in government?[3] ...

---

[1] The new Secretary-General was Jamshid Amouzegar and his Deputy, Darioush Homayoun, a leading journalist who a few months later became Minister of Information in Amouzegar's government.

[2] Minister of Water and Power and later of Agriculture; one of the ablest administrators in the country, Rouhani was executed shortly after the revolution in 1979.

[3] The Shah was not in the habit of discussing his future plans with anyone. But in this instance, uncharacteristically, and to Alam's surprise, he made various broad hints over possible changes in the government. In fact, he was already considering removing Hoveyda and appointing him as Court Minister in succession to the ailing Alam. In short the Shah was trying to prepare his faithful friend for a retirement occasioned entirely by illness.

Monday, 22 November

... Met Yankelovich together with the deputy head of the information and press department of Israel's Foreign Ministry. Between them they have drawn up a lengthy report on Iran's image in the western media. Most interesting and yet alarming to discover how little we really knew of the situation. I am pleased that it is I who should have the responsibility of passing the real facts on to HIM.

Thursday, 25 November

Audience. Amongst other things, reported that Princess Shahnaz was expecting to lunch with the Egyptian Vice-President during her trip to Cairo, but at the last moment Sadat himself telephoned to invite both her and the Vice-President to be his guests ...

Remarked that when I bid farewell to HMQ yesterday on her departure for Egypt, I found her surrounded by the usual bunch of ill-mannered dim-wits. It's only to be expected they should turn up in Kish, Nowshahr, Birjand, even in Amman, but really Cairo is another matter altogether. Their Majesties enjoy a special relationship with Egypt which these people can only jeopardize ... 'But what's to be done?', HIM replied. 'HMQ is genuinely attached to them. Even her mother has warned her, several times, yet she was told to mind her own business so harshly she daren't raise the subject ever again.' ...

'Incidentally', he said, 'I don't suppose you've heard about President Tito's latest statement? He's announced that Yugoslavia needs a strong military defence and can no longer rely on the promises of outsiders.' I remarked this seemed very much in line with what HIM has been saying about Iran. 'Precisely', he said. 'We have to alert the Iranian public to this issue. My political testament consists of little else; above all it emphasizes that the army is the very cornerstone of this country's future. The testament needs to be made public.' I replied that it would be better to wait until the Crown Prince's twentieth birthday.

'The other day', HIM continued, 'I was asked by the US ambassador why Amouzegar had been appointed Secretary-General of the Party. I explained that Amouzegar is an excellent administrator; he's not a free-mason, and I can trust him. No one is perfect, of course. Amouzegar also happens to be extremely mean. He's envious of other people's success and over keen to be generous towards his brothers and his family. But then, as I say, nobody is perfect.' ...

Again, later on, I wondered why HIM should have raised these political issues with me. Of course he's always shown me a great deal of favour and we've many times discussed similar problems. But over the past couple of days he's been especially keen to discuss the government, the Secretary-Generalship of the Party and so on ... Is he trying to tell me something? I have to admit I'm baffled.

... Met Yankelovich this afternoon. He'd just been received for two and a half hours, and told me his report on our image abroad irritated HIM ... This was no more than I'd expected. In an attempt to lighten the mood he remarked to HIM that, contrary to the practice of ancient Rome, the bringer of bad tidings no longer has his head lopped off. Apparently HIM was far from amused ...

Friday, 26 November
... Talked for an hour this afternoon with Joseph Kraft, an American journalist who has been a good friend to Iran. He told me the Carter administration is bound to turn against us, as our policies are mutually incompatible. During his election campaign Carter declared it undesirable that there should be any further military build-up in the Middle East; he blamed Iran for the rise in oil prices, and attacked our record on human rights ... I asked Kraft what we might do to overcome this problem. In his opinion, HIM should visit Carter at the White House as soon as possible. In addition we should dismiss our ambassador in Washington; he's too obviously a supporter of the former regime and has turned our embassy into something not far short of the Playboy Club.

I expressed surprise that Carter should be so taken in by the propaganda of our enemies. Our political prisoners are communists, and in this country communist activity is illegal. To say that we deny political liberty is merely to parrot the slogans of our enemies ... As for our re-armament, I presume Carter has sufficient intelligence not to rush to hasty judgments. We're spending so much money on US military supplies that no US government, let alone the arms manufacturers, could afford to deny us ... I added that even if Carter is foolish enough to opt for confrontation, we are not lacking in the means to retaliate. The USA has no monopoly over arms manufacture, and we can always turn to France or Germany, or exchange our gas for Soviet hardware ...

I didn't bother pointing out the extent to which HIM has the support of his nation. The internal situation is sound. The workers and the farmers are content and the middle classes grow richer day by day. Set against this, what does it matter if a few so-called intellectuals express opinions at odds with our own. In any case what do these blasted dissidents hope to gain? Education and the health service are already free. People are allowed a large degree of control over their own affairs. 'Mr Joseph Kraft', I said, 'you are a friend of Iran. But if you have been sent here to bully us, I must tell you bluntly that we give not a damn for other peoples' opinions. You can rest assured HIM has no intention of visiting the USA either in the immediate future or for some time to come.'

Kraft remarked that, though he'd already met the PM and most of the cabinet, no one had spoken to him as harshly as me. I replied I had done no more than express an honest opinion to someone I assumed to be a friend. It was up to him to interpret my words in whatever way he chose. 'Sure', he said, 'but the opinions you express are really those of the Shah.' I replied that having been granted an audience himself he was already in a position to judge how closely my views accord with those of my Shahanshah. I told him, however, that I had been given no prior briefing and that in any case HIM accounts the entire subject as of very little significance. Kraft was amazed at this, remarking that what I had said about HIM visiting the USA was more or less word for word what the Shah himself had told him.

Saturday, 27 November
Audience ... Reported my conversation with Kraft. HIM was pleased with the way I'd handled it. 'How can they ignore the prestige of my country?', he said. 'How can they think of throwing up business worth $4 billion a year; likely to top $50 billion over the coming decade? I only wish the PM and the cabinet had spoken as you did.' He went on to say that we are in the midst of negotiations with the Soviet Minister of Foreign Trade for the supply of Russian long-range artillery. 'And we can turn to Western Europe for tanks and aircraft. Then we shall see how these American gentlemen react.'

Met the Israeli representative after lunch. He told me that Yankelovich is seriously concerned that his report has offended HIM.

Again met Kraft. He claims that the US embassy here is misleading our government in claiming that Carter has no alternative but to fall into line with previous American policy towards Iran. Apparently the senators who were here recently disbelieved the US ambassador's stories about close relations between Iran and Israel. They asked Kraft to check up on the matter. 'And', he said, 'I had to tell them that everything was just as the ambassador told them. Even so it gives you a good idea how much faith our senators put in the word of their own officials.' ...

Sunday, 28 November

Audience ... Described the findings by our press department on Yankelovich's report of American public opinion.[1] HIM almost exploded with rage, saying, 'How can the bastard have dared be so impertinent? His report was based on wholly negative assumptions. It was not his business to question whether the country enjoys political liberty, nor whether torture is employed against political prisoners. He should not concern himself with whether we are contributing to peace in the Middle East.' I replied that the question of peace was entirely valid, and that Yankelovich's other points were all the subject of intense interest in the USA and therefore of relevance to a report on US opinion. He and his associates must be allowed to diagnose the problem if they're to prescribe a remedy ... 'We shall see', said HIM, 'but in my opinion he and his colleagues are being manipulated by the oil companies. They're out to frighten us.' I replied that as far as I can tell there is no evidence to support such an allegation. 'Very well', HIM said more angrily than ever, 'if you're too blind to see what's been going on, then it's pointless my trying to explain it to you.' Again I did my best to point out that it was we ourselves who asked Yankelovich and his firm to study our image in the West, to show us where we were going wrong and to suggest improvements ... But HIM remained silent and I thought it best to change the subject. Even then his sullen mood persisted and he did no more than snap out brief comments on the matters I had to report ...

Wednesday, 1 December

Audience ... Reported that Amnesty International's survey of Iran is extremely hostile. 'Quite so', HIM remarked. 'But Parviz Radji, our ambassador in London, has answered their criticisms very well.' I pointed out that Amnesty's report has received considerable publicity world-wide, but that Radji's remarks merited no more than a brief reference from the BBC. 'Fair enough', he replied, 'you must cable Radji immediately. Tell him if his statement isn't published, then he must bring it out himself via

[1] 'A Study of the Attitudes of the American Public and Leadership Towards Iran', based on interviews with leading figures in American business, politics, the media, etc. The Court's press department worked closely with the American public relations consultants, agreeing with their methods and findings.

advertising space in the newspapers.' I also had to report that West German radio has broadcast criticisms of Savak. This put HIM in a worse mood still ...

Tuesday, 14 December
Audience ... Cautiously and with a great deal of apprehension I submitted Yankelovich's latest report, setting out proposals for the internal structure of our Information Plan. HIM read it through carefully and without any sign of annoyance. He then instructed me to ensure it's implemented. I was not unduly surprised by this. HIM is a complex individual. He knows very well that Yankelovich can be of service in improving our foreign propaganda, particularly given his influence with Carter and the American Jewish community ...

Thursday, 16 December
Audience. Presented a copy of HIM's film interview with the BBC Panorama programme. He sat watching it in rapt attention for a full half hour. 'For once they've avoided playing tricks', he said. 'It can be shown on public release' ...

Friday, 24 December
Spent much of the past ten days confined to bed. The only ray of sunshine was the occasional telephone call from HIM to ask how I was feeling. Managed to forward various reports to him ...

Saturday, 25 December
Audience. HIM very kindly asked after my health ... We then turned to the Information Plan. 'When did I authorize Yankelovich to handle affairs in Western Europe?', he asked. I reminded him that I myself suggested it. 'Never, never will I entrust our entire propaganda programme to the Jews', he retorted ... I get the impression that, ever since Hoveyda was told about our Plan, he's been doing his best to poison HIM's mind against it ...

Sunday, 26 December
Organized a farewell lunch for the US ambassador. Several ministers were there but the PM was too preoccupied with Bhutto's visit to attend. A very friendly occasion. The ambassador wept. I had no idea he could be so human ...

Tuesday, 28 December

Audience. HIM started off in an excellent mood but my report spoiled everything ... I suggested the government is antagonizing the people beyond endurance with its half-baked and senseless proposals. For example, it's not the government's business to decree that shops must open at nine in the morning and close at seven at night. Why should we imitate the European custom? Housewives in Iran go to market early, in order to prepare lunch for the whole family. If the shops don't open until nine, then the poor women simply won't have time to get things ready. 'I've been informed the measure is intended to ease traffic congestion', HIM said; 'And that it's already started to take effect.' I replied that one need only drive onto the streets to see there's been absolutely no improvement. It took a relative of mine nearly three hours simply to get from the city centre to my home. People won't stand for such nonsense, and yet the government lays all responsibility on HIM's shoulders. 'Your Majesty', I said, 'why should you take the blame? It wasn't you who ordered that shopkeepers be deprived of two hours business in the morning and at least another hour at night. It's almost as if Your Majesty were the victim of a conspiracy.'

Submitted a report on prison conditions by the International Commission of Jurists. It's ironic that Princess Ashraf should have invited their representatives to Tehran, and yet still they produce an extremely hostile report. The Princess herself gets no more than a couple of words in grudging recognition. HIM read through a resumé we'd prepared. 'That twin sister of mine', he said, 'has been a lifelong thorn in the flesh. She is vain and she is greedy. Why on earth did she invite these people, knowing they'd say exactly the same as Amnesty International?'[1]

I had intended to raise other matters, the interminable power–cuts, administrative blunders and unjustifiable impositions on the public. But I thought it best not to overburden him with cares ...

Thursday, 30 December

Audience ... Submitted an organizational chart for the International Information Department as envisaged by Yankelovich. HIM took against it and asked why I had inserted the word international in the title, saying he'd told me before that the department should concern itself exclusively with the USA. I explained that, as he could no doubt appreciate, nowadays it's

[1] The Princess was President of the Iranian Society for Human Rights, a fact well known to the Shah who in the past had encouraged her in this endeavour.

impractical to divide initiatives in the USA from our activities in Western Europe. 'I agree there's bound to be an overlap', he said, 'but I'm extremely reluctant to allow the Jews to take over the entire operation. If it were just the USA, then it would be a different matter; there the Jews are potentially very powerful.' I pointed out that by no means everything will be left to Jewish initiative. The question at stake was whether to adopt Yankelovich's management structure. HIM made no comment.

... Showed him an article on the Iranian economy published in *The Guardian*. He was not at all pleased and said, 'The only thing wrong with the economy is the extraordinary rate at which it's growing.' I suggested there are problems all the same. There's a lack of attention to detail, too much papering over the cracks and not enough dedication on behalf of those in charge. He made no attempt to reply.

1977

With the fall in oil exports even the Shah was forced to admit that the economy was in decline, remarking to Alam: 'We're broke. Everything seems doomed to grind to a standstill, and meanwhile many of the programmes we planned ... must be postponed.' (Diaries, 2 January) As Hoveyda commented, the entire country was stalked by a sense of unease (Diaries, 2 February).

The new US President Jimmy Carter and his human rights campaign were distrusted by the Shah. Iran's military tribunals were instructed to revise procedures and to provide better facilities for political detainees. A Red Cross team was invited to tour Iran's prisons and to investigate the treatment of political prisoners. It reported that one in three of prison inmates had been tortured but that such practices had recently been abandoned. As Iran's political élite began to recognize the signs of crisis, so the more independent-minded among them – who to varying degrees might be regarded as dissenters – plucked up the courage to discuss the situation in public. Such meetings – hitherto unthinkable – were grudgingly tolerated by the government. The Shah's description of the dissenters as non-entities (Diaries, 31 May) may appear harsh; those in question were after all the only people openly to criticize Pahlavi rule and to get away with it. With hindsight, however, it turns out to be remarkably prescient. More adept at discourse and theorizing than in the cut and thrust of politics, such groups were swiftly marginalized as the revolution against the Shah's regime spread.

In August Jamshid Amouzegar was appointed prime minister. Alam's illness at last forced his retirement. He was replaced as Court Minister by Amir Abbas Hoveyda.

Saturday, 1 January

Long audience. Submitted a draft of the speech I'm to make at Pahlavi University. It deals mostly with HIM. He suggested various amendments ... and told me I should use the opportunity to deliver a forthright indictment of Saudi Arabia: 'Make it clear that the Saudis have never shown any respect for human rights, either now or in the past. Even a petty burglar faces having one of his hands chopped off. The liberal press in America prefers to ignore all this, although they don't hesitate to blacken the reputation of Iran.' I questioned whether, as a minister of the Imperial Court, it was appropriate for me to go around delivering tirades against a foreign regime. 'I can see no cause for objection', he replied. 'The blasted Saudis have betrayed both us and themselves.' I promised to do as he had instructed and to show him an advance copy of my speech at tomorrow's audience. None the less, I repeated that, as His Majesty's devoted servant, I still considered it inappropriate for me to make the speech he envisages ... 'Not at all!', he snapped back at me. 'We must give them the thrashing they deserve.' ...

Left the palace at one o'clock this afternoon. I was quite worn out and thought that a walk through the snow might revive me. Ended up this evening feeling feverish once again ...

Sunday, 2 January

Despite being very much under the weather, went for my audience at the palace. The snow was falling harder than ever and we only just managed the short drive to the palace ... Expected to find HIM in good spirits, but on the contrary he was sunk in gloom. In answer to my enquiry, he explained, 'We're broke. Everything seems doomed to grind to a standstill, and meanwhile many of the programmes we had planned must be postponed. Oil exports seem likely to fall by as much as 30 per cent, and the recent price rise will do little to compensate. It's not even certain that we can sell oil at the increased price. If our regular customers try to take advantage of our present situation, I may have no alternative but to threaten to blacklist them; perhaps they'll succumb to that sort of intimidation.' I replied that this is by no means the first time we have been faced with a set-back and that he is bound to overcome this one as he has all the others. 'It's going to be very tough', he said before launching into yet another diatribe against Yamani for betraying us ...

I pointed out that the British, Belgians, Dutch and various others are still prepared to make barter arrangements in exchange for oil. 'At least that's something', he said. 'But it's not at all clear how they'd set the price in such a deal. If we sold below the recognized level, it would be a betrayal of OPEC and I'm most reluctant to contemplate any such move. As for your speech against Yamani', he went on, 'you were right; as Court Minister you're in no position to make that sort of attack. You had better forget the whole idea.' . . .

Today's audience saw one great triumph for me; I have been allowed to use my speech to criticize the government in general terms, stressing that whilst HIM is utterly dedicated to this country, the present administration is more concerned to maintain itself in power by the minimum amount of effort. HIM's orders are implemented so ineptly by the government that their outcome is often quite different to their intention. To begin with, HIM was reluctant to let me say this. But I managed to suppress my irritation and remarked that it was up to him whether he wished to accept responsibility for the failings of other people. I told him that he is the boss; but he should think of the dynasty, of the nation, of his son. He himself may hope to transform Iran into the promised land but the government is leading us straight to hell. 'Your Majesty', I said, 'you have achieved things unparalleled in the history of this nation. What a pity if a ruler of your calibre were to be undone by the miserable performance of a bunch of traitors; or, if you prefer it, by a bunch of incompetents. If you're unwilling to have me use my speech to give them the *coup de grâce*, then at least permit me to explain to the public that Your Majesty is in no way to blame for the present disastrous situation.' At this, he at last gave way[1] . . .

Sunday, 16 January

A red letter day, despite the fact that I've been confined to bed for the past fortnight with a slight temperature.

Last night I called a meeting with Yankelovich's associates, to decide how to counter the attacks on us in the US Senate and the media. We agreed that we should not retreat but meet fire with fire . . .

Wrote to HIM this morning to report this decision . . . I added that the principal problem lies in the way the enemy has penetrated our own defences. How else can I describe the way we ourselves have stirred up the people against us by our own shortcomings? . . . Prolonged power-cuts

---

[1] For a year past Alam was convinced that the country was running off course. Even if he could bring himself to acknowledge the Shah's responsibility for this situation, he preferred to spare his master, heaping all the blame upon Hoveyda who throughout a long premiership had ducked any responsibility for the nation's wrongs.

right across the country, occasioning slow-down in industrial output and serious financial losses; dreadful communications; shortages of every essential foodstuff save bread; a total disregard for the public's needs; soaring inflation; the promulgation of new decrees without any preparation or warning – all these things have been brought about either by deliberate sabotage from within or else by the sheer incompetence of a government in thrall to the CIA and other such organizations.[1] It is the government itself which deserves to be regarded as the chief agent of subversion. We have squandered every cent we had only to find ourselves checkmated by a single move from Saudi Arabia. 'Your Majesty', I wrote in conclusion, 'we are now in dire financial peril and must tighten our belts if we are to survive ... As Your Majesty's loyal servant I urge you to take stern action against the traitors and incompetents who have betrayed us. At least if you were to throw these people in gaol it would enable the rest of us to sleep more easily in our beds.' ...

Finally I wrote that to take action now, to attempt a shift in policy, however limited, will restore the position of my beloved Shahanshah to all its former security and majesty. It was with great misgiving that I sealed the envelope ... Normally HIM returns to me whatever letters I send him, but on this occasion I expected him simply to tear it up, which is precisely what he did[2] ...

Paris, 2 February
Spent nearly three weeks of last month confined to bed in Tehran. Torrential rain or snow the entire time. I cannot recall a winter as harsh as this. The one ray of sunshine has been my more or less daily telephone conversations with HIM. Similarly, every day I write to him on matters of current concern ... My other occupation has been to feed the birds seeking sanctuary outside my window.

On one occasion my temperature rose so alarmingly that HIM ordered me to set out for Europe without a moment's delay. But the Air France flight from the Far East to Paris was unable to make its usual stop-over at Tehran due to heavy snow. On HIM's instructions an Iranair Boeing 707 was got ready for me, my wife and my nephew, Parviz. HIM telephoned just before I left. He was so generous, treating me as if he were my doting father, telling me to wrap up warm and not to catch cold ... I was

---

[1] Alam attributed the longevity of Hoveyda's government to unsubstantiated American support.
[2] Always a sign of disagreement or irritation by the Shah.

deeply touched, literally speechless with emotion ... HMQ too has been tremendously kind.

The time I spent at home in bed was torment to me; to know that all around me people are undergoing such hardship and growing so resentful. We have been thwarted over oil prices and the prospect for our future relations with the USA is bleak indeed ...

I was hospitalized the moment we arrived in Paris and since then have been feeling much better. I'm to be discharged tomorrow, though HIM has ordered me to spend at least a month convalescing in the south of France ...

Hoveyda came to see me in hospital, on his way to Morocco. I reported our discussions by letter to HIM as follows:

... Hoveyda confided that he senses an atmosphere of unease in the country, though he can't tell exactly what's at the root of it ... He asked whether I had felt anything along the same lines, and if so whether I could provide a diagnosis or suggest a remedy. I reminded him that for some time now I've been confined to bed and am therefore bound to be a little out of touch. None the less I agreed that there is a mood of discontent amongst the people, far more pronounced than before ... I told him this smouldering resentment seems exceptional, even allowing for the inadequacy and occasional ineptitude of his government in responding to the public's needs.

He asked what was to be done. I told him not to worry unduly; we have a leader who stands firm as a rock in a storm-tossed sea ... If he has any particular problem, I told him, then he should own up to it to Your Majesty, honestly and openly ... If in spite of all Your Majesty's support, he is still unable to overcome his difficulties, I said, he would have to face up to the fact that he has failed in the service he pledged Your Majesty. He agreed ...

[In addition, on 8 February 1977 Alam wrote to the Shah to report a meeting in Paris with Yankelovich, MG and Lubrani, the Israeli representative to Tehran. He enclosed the schedule of press relations activities for the coming year, analysing the steps to be taken to communicate with the media and political circles in the USA. Amongst other matters, it was suggested that MG visit America some time in May, to meet various prominent figures both in and out of government, to dispel the mistrust that had grown up with respect to Iran. For the purpose of this visit it was recommended that MG be granted the title special envoy. He intended to hold discussions with the US State Department, with a view to Iran's removal from the Department's list of countries violating human rights. The plan appears to have been drawn up with considerable professionalism and to have involved Alam and others in a great deal of effort. Even so, it failed to meet with the Shah's approval since he wrote in the margin, by way of reply to Alam: 'Given present proposals, no call to appoint MG special envoy.']

Wednesday, 27 April

Three months convalescence and medical treatment in Europe. Nothing of importance has happened since I was last well enough to keep up with my writing. I have been deprived of the greatest joy of my life; my regular meetings with my beloved Shahanshah. Thank God I am at least partially recovered, though I shall never be quite my old self again. On the telephone and in my letters I have hinted to HIM that he should relieve me of my present responsibilities and either appoint me to a less exacting post or allow me to retire to pass a graceful old age in Birjand.

... I know that I'm not alone in missing our conversation. HIM is not made of steel. Like any human being he needs someone to whom he can open his heart. I can justly claim to have fulfilled that role and to have enjoyed at least 99 per cent of HIM's confidence. I leave out the final 1 per cent, since the Shah is entitled to hold at least something back. No one man can command all his trust. Our audiences used to be so long, so wide-ranging. We spoke of everything under the sun; foreign affairs, domestic politics, problems with family, girls; literally nothing was left out ...

Dreadful portents everywhere, yet Hoveyda disregards them all ... How can ambition make a man so blindly, senselessly arrogant? I don't give a damn what becomes of Hoveyda personally; what bothers me is the dire impact of his actions on my beloved master.

Saturday, 30 April

Last night I flew back to Tehran. Brief audience this morning ... HIM was most kind, asking after every detail of my health ...

Monday, 2 May

Three new ambassadors were due to present their credentials this morning but I obtained leave of absence. HIM was therefore more than a little surprised to run into me as he was walking, in full dress uniform, from his private apartments to the Jahan Nama Palace. I told him I'd come to beg a few minutes to discuss our trip to Mashad and that, meanwhile, I wanted to show him a magnificent rose blossom I'd found in the garden. To the consternation of his entourage and the Imperial Guard, he did as I asked and for a few minutes stood in rapt contemplation of my flower.

Tuesday, 10 May

Audience ... Kermit Roosevelt, a CIA agent involved in the downfall of Dr Mosaddeq in August 1953, plans to publish an account of the coup. I reported that I've now examined the book and found it most undesirable. It portrays HIM as a waverer, forced into various crucial decisions, for example the appointment of General Zahedi as Prime Minister, by pressure from Roosevelt. The man is ... hoping to present himself as a hero. HIM said he had no idea the book contained so much nonsense. He agreed I must try to prevent publication[1] ...

Thursday, 12 May

Audience ... The telephone rang in the midst of our conversation. Clearly it was to report an enormous fire at an oil field somewhere. I was alarmed and, contrary to my usual discretion, asked HIM for details. 'Oh, it's nothing disastrous', he said. 'It's in Saudi Arabia. Why else do you suppose I sat here so relaxed?' I told him he's enjoying an extraordinary spell of luck. First, the cold winter in the USA, then the storms in the Gulf, and now this fire; the Americans are having little success in sabotaging our oil policy ... 'Quite so', he agreed. 'What's more, Carter is beginning to see sense. He's no longer preaching the same old nonsense he did during the election.'

Monday, 16 May

For the past few days I've been in Birjand, cared for by a nurse, my French doctor and his wife ... Apart from feeling unwell, I've had an enjoyable time. The various buildings in the Institute of Higher Learning are progressing well. The whole thing is to be dedicated to the memory of my late father, and I feel confident it will be open before the end of the year ... It's given me something on which to fix my affection, in compensation for all my former loves. I shall do my best to keep my father's memory alive. He did so much for this region ...

[1] See footnote, page 497.

Tuesday, 17 May

Audience ... Last night's 'Letter from America' broadcast on the BBC exposed all Carter's hypocrisy. He came out of it very badly. 'The BBC is supposed to be independent', said HIM. 'Yet it's funded entirely by the government. What a peculiar people the British are.' ... He asked to be shown a transcript of the programme in question.

I asked what he made of the new US Secretary of State Cyrus Vance. 'Oh, he seems reasonable enough', he replied. 'His remarks seem to the point, and he shows some knowledge of Middle Eastern affairs.' ...

Wednesday, 18 May

Audience. At the end of last month HIM and the President of Venezuela sent a joint letter to King Khalid of Saudi Arabia, proposing a compromise formula for a single, universal oil price. The King's reply, which I submitted today, was not at all well received. 'Send a copy of the original joint letter to the leaders of every OPEC country', HIM told me. 'They must appreciate there was never any question of the Venezuelans and myself seeking a secret deal with the Saudis ... King Khalid writes to me as if he were addressing that blind grandson of his. We simply suggested prices remain frozen until next January, yet now he demands the freeze last for the whole of next year.'

Reported that a prominent individual last night passed on an order from HIM, telling me to write to the government to ensure they provide $3 million a year, for office and other expenses. HIM pondered before opening his heart to me. 'Why so much?', he said. 'These people think of nobody except themselves. They certainly don't care a fig for me. ... Everyone is out to tap me for whatever they can get, especially my relatives. If I refused just one of their requests they'd believe I'd ruined them. They cause me so much trouble, and yet nobody seems to realize if I disappear, they themselves would be utterly expendable.' ...

Thursday, 19 May

Audience ... HIM has been annoyed by an article in *Süddeutsche Zeitung* claiming Iran's domestic situation is close to boiling point. I remarked we would simply ignore such comments by outsiders if we were truly confident of stability at home ... 'I have issued instructions for a new initiative', HIM said. 'Debates in the Imperial Commission are to be televised. Any government official who fails in his duties will be punished.'[1]

Passed on Princess Ashraf's proposals to establish the long-awaited State Council, intended to protect the rights of individuals against violations by the government. 'An excuse for providing employment for a few corrupt scoundrels', HIM commented angrily. They'll do nothing but chase after public sympathy. None of them give a damn for the real national interest.'[2] ...

Reported that Lord Chalfont has delivered a splendid defence of our record on human rights. As a result he's been roundly abused by the leftists ...

Referring to his recent meeting with Cyrus Vance, HIM said, 'He seems all right, but more a bureaucrat than a politician.' ... I asked whether the foreign press were correct in claiming that HIM's decision to reduce the sentences passed on a group of terrorists is a direct outcome of Vance's visit here. To my surprise he admitted it was true. This is quite contrary to the stand he's taken in the past, but I refrained from any comment ...

Saturday, 21 May

Audience ... Much to HIM's disgust the new US ambassador, William Sullivan, has issued a statement to Congress, referring to the existence of religious opposition groups here in Iran ... 'Doesn't he realize these people are Islamic Marxists, mere Soviet puppets', HIM said. I replied that, whilst various of them may well be manipulated by the Soviets, or for that matter by Washington, there are others who act solely out of ignorant fanaticism ... HIM remarked that he had no objection to girls wearing scarves at school or university; 'But veils are out of the question ... Tell my private secretariat to inform the government accordingly.' ...

---

[1] According to the Shah's decree of 7 November 1976; the Imperial Commission was set up to monitor the various government agencies. The PM and his cabinet sat as *ex-officio* members, with the Shah's personal private secretary as chairman. Representatives were also co-opted from amongst the workers, farmers, the media, and the national Chambers of Commerce and Industry. The Commission was generally regarded as a further attack by the Shah against parliamentary prerogative, and as a result, met with no enthusiasm. It achieved very little and the broadcasting of its meetings served only to heighten public dissatisfaction by further discrediting the government.

[2] For several years Parliament had enacted a law calling for the creation of a body similar to the French *Conseil d'Etat*, qualified to examine pleas against the government. However the Shah regarded this as an encroachment on his personal authority. He consequently forbade the government to make any provision for it in the national budget, stifling it at birth.

Monday, 23 May

Audience ... Reported a meeting I held yesterday with the British ambassador Sir Anthony Parsons. He is favourably impressed with the new British Foreign Secretary, David Owen, a man in his early thirties. The ambassador has explained to him that it's pointless to accuse Iran of violating human rights. We've granted substantial social improvements to our people over the past few years; a move unprecedented elsewhere in the world. The foreign media judge us from too narrow an angle ...

Referring to Carter's speech of last night, HIM said, 'He's announced he's willing to supply weapons to NATO, Israel, the Philippines, South Korea, Australia and New Zealand without any conditions attached; he didn't so much as mention Iran. Does he suppose that, strategically speaking, Iran is less significant than a country like New Zealand? Perhaps the Americans and the Soviets have devised some scheme to divide the world between themselves.' I replied that this was quite out of the question. The Americans will never abandon us. As for Carter's pronouncements, they're intended merely to impress American public opinion. Like it or not, these idiot Americans are convinced we're violating human rights ...

Sunday, 29 May

Audience ... Discussing the USA, I remarked I'd been impressed by the latest letter HIM received from Carter. It indicates he's slowly starting to see sense. 'He had no choice', HIM said ...

[Writing on 24 May 1977 President Carter, in the warmest terms, thanked the Shah for accepting an invitation to visit Washington the following November.]

HIM remarked that, when he was in the southern suburbs a couple of days ago, he saw thousands of women wearing the veil ... 'These bloody mullahs don't dare admit that Islam and Marxism are at opposite ends of the spectrum', he said. 'Why did Ayatollah Khonsari beat about the bush for such a long time and then, in the end, decide against speaking out?' I replied that they all go in fear of their lives. 'Have they nothing better to think of than saving their own skins?' HIM asked. 'Of course not', I said ...

Tuesday, 31 May

Met the US Chargé d'Affaires who passed on a text of the discussions between Cyrus Vance and Ardeshir Zahedi. He assured me our special relationship with the USA is as strong as ever, stressing that there is no question of our being excluded from the list of countries strategically important to the USA ...

Audience ... Reported my discussions with the American ... 'I'm told', said HIM, 'that various non-entities, the likes of Ali Amini, Allahyar Saleh[1] and Mozaffar Baqa'i,[2] have begun to meet one another in private. Amini has gone so far as to cancel his annual vacation in Europe, saying he's expecting "a hot summer" in Iran.' I replied that such people have got it all wrong. The Americans are not so stupid as to encourage further instability, and at my next meeting with the ambassador I intend to make him realize that the lousy mullahs he's so keen on are playing with fire. 'Make them understand they can't force us to accept a government made up of American fifth columnists', HIM said. 'To do so would involve their mobilizing millions of troops and spending goodness knows how much money. They'd never dare take such a risk here, right next door to the Soviet Union.' I assured him the Americans are already aware of this, though it's only natural they should try to make contact with the opposition. What should concern us most is the well-being of the public at large ... Public opinion has few enough opportunities to express itself. If resentment against the government escalates much further, we might find ourselves in real peril.

Wednesday, 1 June

Audience. HIM in excellent spirits ... He launched into an attack on the spitefulness of the American press ... 'The President and his Secretary of State are keen to make friends with us', he said. 'But what alternative do they have? In a fortnight's time the Red Cross Commissioners who inspected our prisons will publish their report and so put an end to all this nonsense about human rights. Meanwhile I've instructed the military tribunals to alter their procedures and provided additional facilities for

[1] Leader of the Iran party and an important figure within the National Front coalition which nationalized Iran's oil industry under the leadership of Dr Mosaddeq. By the late 1970s he was regarded as one of the grand old men of Iranian politics.

[2] A founder of the National Front, and leader of the Iran Toilers party, Baqa'i broke with Dr Mosaddeq in 1952. None the less he maintained his political independence and was never won over by the Pahlavi regime. Brief spells in prison after 1954 helped his career later on as the storm clouds gathered and politicians not associated with the regime came to the fore.

detainees.' ... I questioned whether all this might not have been done long ago, before Carter entered the White House. He thought for a while but made no reply. I don't think he was pleased by my remark; I probably went too far ...

The weather was so perfect when I came out that I decided to postpone my meeting with the new ambassadors of France and Morocco until this afternoon and went instead to visit my Iranian lover.

I was planning to stay merely for a coffee but once we'd sat down together things turned out quite unexpectedly pleasant. Despite my frailty, I followed Sa'adi's advice:

> The wine is heady; make haste!
> And time is scarce, take all of it you can.
> Who knows if next year's spring
> So sweet, will find you dust and ash or living man.

Saturday, 4 June

Audience ... Asked whether HIM really believes the Red Cross report will be in our favour. 'So Savak tells me', he said. 'But how does Savak know?', I asked. 'Then again', he said, 'the British Foreign Secretary David Owen believes it goes some way towards vindicating us, or so he told Parviz Radji, our ambassador in London. He says that, whilst by no means a whitewash, it will do a great deal to improve our reputation.' I pointed out that this is much less than Savak are claiming. He made no comment.

Wednesday, 8 June

Audience ... Reported that Carter has given an interview to an American magazine, stating he is delighted by the excellent relationship between the USA and Saudi Arabia. 'Quite so', HIM remarked. 'People are always pleased to have a lackey.' I suggested Carter really is doing his best to get on with us. 'I have no cause for complaint', HIM said.

He then told me he had good news. 'I've decided to give up attending my sisters' dinner parties, and to cease inviting that bunch of creeps to the palace. They had begun to get on my nerves. Every time we played bridge or *belote*, and someone laid down a card, some other bloody fool would interrupt to ask a personal favour ... I told HMQ my decision last night. She was not at all pleased.' ... I congratulated him, pointing out that I've been begging him to do this for the past ten years.

Sunday, 11 June

A reception this morning in the gardens of the Niavaran Palace, attended by 500 members of the Association of Scholars and Intellectuals. In theory they're supposed to examine policy problems and submit their findings to the government ... The Association was established at a time when HIM was anxious to provide some sort of balance, other than the Mardom party, to the power of Iran Novin. Its members seem oblivious to the fact they've been made redundant by the introduction of single party politics ...

Audience ... Referring to this morning's reception HIM said, 'I have to cater to the vanity of these people. Not that I don't appreciate their hard work. Their organization should be kept going for the rest of this year.' I said I had no objection to this, although the poor devils clearly don't realize how superfluous they have become. 'What do you mean?', HIM snapped back. I explained my reasoning. He was disconcerted to find that I'd guessed his motives from the very start ...

Sunday, 12 June

Audience ... The Imperial Air Force is at daggers drawn with Iranair over which one of them is responsible for servicing HIM's private jet. I have looked into the matter, and the air force have sent in a report justifying their claim. 'Then they probably deserve to be in charge', HIM said. 'Form a committee and get things sorted out. Maybe the plane ought to be a joint responsibility.'

Monday, 13 June

Audience ... Reported a meeting held yesterday with the ambassador of Somalia. His country's relations with Ethiopia and the Soviets have deteriorated, and he's anxious to get whatever he can from HIM; weapons, money, oil. 'You're sure there's nothing else he wants?', HIM said with a smile. 'Why doesn't he go cap in hand to the Saudis, the footmen of Washington?' I replied I had suggested this myself, but the ambassador said he could put no faith in promises from his Arab brothers. 'What a joke', HIM said. 'As for us, we're busy supplying oil to Syria, although an Iraqi pipeline runs right across their country. We have always kept our word. Tell the ambassador we may be able to meet his requirements in light armaments. I've already got the list of weapons he put in for.'

Went on to describe my meeting with the Chilean ambassador. He suggested HIM might like to visit his country as part of a forthcoming trip to the USA. It would lend moral support to the Chilean government, or so he claimed. 'What a gift to the cartoonists', HIM laughed. 'They could picture me shaking hands with President Pinochet of Chile, both of us dressed as butchers trampling human rights into the dust.' ...

Tuesday, 14 June
... The PM was my guest for lunch ... He claims HIM has set up the Imperial Commission to lull international opinion – to show we still permit an open expression of views despite the absence of multi-party politics. Consequently he has told the members of his cabinet not to take fright. He went on to complain about HMQ's friends and the way they're always trying to force their opinions on him. His real reason for coming to lunch was to shower praise on HIM ... I suppose he feels insecure about his future ...

Wednesday, 15 June
Audience ... Submitted HIM's schedule for the rest of the summer ... and told him I've arranged to have his medical examination take place in Paris, in November. 'Quite unnecessary', he said. 'There's absolutely nothing the matter with me.' I pointed out that it was he who told me to arrange a check-up. 'And now I'm telling you it's no longer necessary', he snapped ...

Passed on an article from *The Times*, under the headline 'In Search of Democracy'. 'Why "in search"?', HIM asked. 'We're made sure people play a role in every level of production. We're on course to creating an economic and hence a true political democracy.' I replied this might well be the case, but the West tends to look for more in a democracy. 'But what has democracy ever done for them?', he said. That was beside the point, I replied. What matters is that they cannot agree with our own definition of democracy.

Friday, 17 June
... Ayatollah Khonsari telephoned to complain that the city of Qom is without water or electricity. I contacted HIM who told me to inform the PM who duly promised to send someone to investigate. I told him that this simply isn't good enough; hunger and thirst are serious matters, not to be glossed over in his usual way ... He grew a little abashed at this and promised to take action.

Chaos is rife. Once again Tehran, my own house included, is being subjected to power-cuts. I was obliged to purchase a small generator, otherwise all the telephones in the house went dead. I had no alternative, but even so feel ashamed that I can shield myself from the sufferings of my fellow countrymen. Meanwhile the PM poses for the newspapers, out shooting dressed in battle fatigues, or donning the peasant costume of a mountain village near Tehran where he has had himself appointed mayor. The whole thing is like a scene from some incredible farce; the PM behaving as if he hasn't a care in the world, kidding himself that the Imperial Commission is an empty gesture, not a judgment on those who have failed ... It terrifies me that one day everything will simply cave in around us. Please God that we may be spared this.

Tuesday, 21 June

Audience ... Asked HIM what he made of William Sullivan, the new US ambassador. 'No hint of the demagogue', he said. 'Strikes me as having his head screwed on.' Reported that he's asked to call on me, but that I've postponed the meeting for a week so that he won't think I'm unduly anxious to see him.

... It has been hinted abroad that Senator McGovern may head some sort of enquiry into Savak's activities in the USA. HIM told me that, when I meet the ambassador, I should remark to him pleasantly that our own Senate has likewise decided to investigate CIA activities in Iran ... Submitted the *Daily Telegraph*'s review of HIM's latest book. I told him it struck me as being favourable. 'What on earth's "favourable" about it?', he snapped back, as soon as he'd read it. I told him to look again at the final paragraph. 'What do you suppose this word "megalomania" means?', he said. 'Greatness', I replied. 'Greatness be damned', he exclaimed. 'Greatness to the point of madness.' I was thoroughly ashamed of myself. I should have read it more carefully, but by then it was too late ...

Wednesday, 22 June

Audience ... HIM remarked that he'd received the British ambassador yesterday afternoon who told him he considers the *Telegraph*'s review outrageous ... 'Why should they want to print such nonsense?', HIM asked ...

Submitted an article on Israel's Likud party published in the *Jordan Times*. 'I presume it's the Americans who brought them to power', HIM said. I pointed out that Israel has free elections. In any event, why on earth should the Americans do such a thing? ...

Bhutto stopped off for an audience with HIM last night, on his way back from Kuwait. I asked whether Bhutto had said any more about the Americans meddling in Pakistan's internal affairs. Apparently he told HIM that various figures at the American embassy are in contact with opposition groups. I remarked that this was only to be expected, and no justification for launching such a tirade against Washington. 'He regrets it himself', HIM said. 'He's anxious to make it up with the USA by whatever means he can.' I expressed misgivings about the future of Pakistan, and above all about that of Bhutto. Even if he wins the next election, the opposition have scented blood. 'I agree', HIM said. 'Just look at the way they've prohibited the honourable sport of horse-racing, on the pretext that Islam forbids any sort of gambling.' In that case, I suggested, Bhutto is merely whistling in the dark. 'He still counts on the army', HIM said. 'The Pakistani officer class is an enlightened group of men. When the chips are down, they may still be able to suppress those who want the country dragged back to the Dark Ages, 500 years ago.' I replied that even if the army manages to crush the opposition, it wouldn't be out of love for Bhutto but in order to establish military rule in his place. HIM made no comment . . .

Sunday, 26 June
Audience . . . Asked about the report by the International Red Cross; their President was granted an audience yesterday. 'It's still confidential and for our eyes only', HIM said. 'But even so it claims that out of 3,000 political prisoners, 900 bear signs of torture. Precisely the same figure was given by the Commission I myself appointed. The report goes on to say that signs of torture have vanished altogether over the past few months.' . . . I told him that in my view this is serious news indeed, and only goes to show that the dissidents had real cause for protest. We can only hope no word of it gets out. 'It's for our eyes only', HIM repeated. 'No one can leak it, save we ourselves.' I pointed out that, nowadays, nothing can be considered secret, and that it's a pity we did nothing to improve prison conditions on our own initiative. He made no attempt to reply . . .

Monday, 27 June
Audience . . . Reported a conversation I had yesterday with the ambassador of Communist China . . . He invited HIM to visit Peking, but I said we would prefer it if the Chinese President came here – his first visit abroad . . . Cuba has issued a warning to the international community, saying that no representative of the Red Cross or Amnesty International will be allowed to enter the country. 'Pass this news on to our embassies', HIM said. 'Next

time Amnesty International or anyone else comes sniffing around, they can tell them to clear off and pick on Cuba for a change ... Andrew Young, the American ambassador at the UN, even had the gall to announce that Cuban military intervention in Africa is proving a positive help to stability.' ...

Tuesday, 28 June

Audience. Reported meeting the US ambassador yesterday. He suggested we inform the American public about recent improvements in the way political prisoners are handled. 'Why can't they do it themselves?', HIM asked. 'Their media should pass on news of what we've been doing.' I replied they have no reason to help us. Indeed, their media claims the improvements are due solely to pressure from Carter.

We then turned to Yankelovich and the Information Plan which HIM rejected ... 'MG craved a role as part-time ambassador in Washington and part-time Foreign Minister', HIM said. 'He wanted Yankelovich made our secret political representative in the USA'. I've long known HIM harboured such ideas, hence my decision in Paris a few months ago to drop the entire affair. Who knows, even I might have fallen under his suspicions ...

As we were talking news came through of an attempt to assassinate Saddam Hussein of Iraq. Apparently he escaped with only a slight scratch to the eye ... I remarked that his death would have been a grave disappointment to us. 'Quite so', HIM replied. 'But for him, there'd have been no compromise over the Shatt al-Arab.' ...

Wednesday, 29 June

... Escorted HMQ to the airport, ostensibly on her way to attend the summer seminar at Aspen, Colorado, though her real reason for going is to establish personal contact with Rosalind Carter, the President's wife ...

Thursday, 30 June

... HIM has issued a decree, announcing that any house or apartment left vacant for three months without good reason can henceforth be rented out by the local authority on the owner's behalf. At the same time the government has been told to compile a register of all unfinished urban developments, so that a timetable may be drawn up for their completion. I'm afraid the only effect of all this will be to halt whatever building work might have gone on in future ... For an economy to grow, the rights of every sector of society should be respected, tenants and landlords ... The power-cuts continue ...

Saturday, 2 July

Welcomed HIM on his return from a two-day tour of Western Iran ... Whilst still at the airport he told me to contact the US ambassador. I was to assure him that Pakistan bears no grudge against his country, but that, as Bhutto's domestic situation is still shaky, he cannot back down from his commitment to nuclear research. To do so would discredit him in the eyes of the public. 'His position is quite different from ours', HIM went on. 'We had no real problem settling our dispute over Bahrain and we found it just as easy to reach agreement over the Hirmand river with Afghanistan. There was no one leaning over our shoulder, criticizing everything we did.' During the helicopter ride back to Saadabad I was lost in thought, sending up a prayer to the Almighty to watch over this irreplaceable Shah of mine, and to preserve him from vanity. It would be a tragedy if such a great leader were to fall victim to the sin of pride ...

On arrival at the palace HIM asked what I thought of his decree on vacant housing. I told him it can only have a negative effect on future development ... Meanwhile the landlords are bound to be harassed by local authorities. 'I'm aware of all that', he replied. 'But the world needs proof that our revolution continues. We must begin building houses on our own initiative, especially for those less well off.'

Senator Eugene McCarthy lunched as my guest, together with the US ambassador and various others. I told the ambassador what HIM had said about Pakistan ... McCarthy has come here from Israel, which he was anxious to discuss ... He cracked several jokes about Walter Mondale and about Carter, who he said lacks any sense of humour. He was also critical of America's domestic situation and the degree to which corruption reigns. It was not until half past four that he left, having consumed a substantial quantity of wine.

I subsequently received the Israeli representative. His Foreign Minister, Moshe Dayan, wants to be received by HIM, to hear his views on the Middle East before Prime Minister Begin sets out for America ... Altogether a very tiring day. I warned HIM this morning that I'm still far from well. My recovery is taking far too long ...

Monday, 4 July

Audience ... Asked whether Moshe Dayan should also meet our Minister of Foreign Affairs. 'Certainly not', said HIM. I remarked that he's also expressed a wish to call on me; we're friends of nearly twenty years standing. Even so, I suggested it might be better if the Israeli representative were told that such a meeting should be avoided if the trip is to remain secret. HIM greeted this idea with considerable enthusiasm. I've always known my place ...

Tuesday, 5 July

Early this morning the news came through of a military *coup d'état* in Pakistan. Bhutto has been arrested, as have various of the opposition leaders ... The US ambassador telephoned subsequently with a list of those who have been detained ... He remarked in passing that a military takeover also seems the likely outcome to the present political deadlock in Turkey.

Audience. 'You should have told the ambassador', HIM said, 'that this only goes to show how democracy is unsuited to certain countries. I've even heard that the Turks are casting envious glances at our system here in Iran.' ... 'How can you hope to build up a nation by fragmenting its politics into opposing camps?', he continued. 'Whatever one group builds, the other will endeavour to destroy.' It appears his cheerfulness owes much to the news from Pakistan and Turkey ...

The King of Spain has written to HIM asking for $10 million on behalf of the party led by his Prime Minister.

[King Juan Carlos' letter is in French. The address and valediction are hand-written. It is dated at Zarzuela, 22 June 1977:]

My dear brother,

To begin with, I wish to say how immensely grateful I am to you for sending your nephew, Prince Shahram, to see me, thus providing me with a speedy response to my appeal at a difficult moment for my country.

I should next like to lay before you an account of the political situation in Spain, and of the development of the campaign by the political parties, before, during and after the [parliamentary] elections.

Forty years of an entirely personal regime have done much that is good for the country, but at the same time left Spain sadly lacking in political structures, so much so as to pose an enormous risk to the strengthening of the monarchy. Following the first six months of the Arias government, which I was likewise obliged to inherit, in July 1976 I appointed a younger, less compromised man, whom I knew well and who enjoyed my full confidence: Adolfo Suarez.

From that moment onwards I vowed to tread in the path of democracy, endeavouring always to be one step ahead of events in order to forestall a situation like that in Portugal which might prove even more dire in this country of mine.

The legalization of the various political parties allowed them to participate freely in the [election] campaign, to elaborate their strategy and to employ every means of mass communication for their propaganda and the presentation of the image of their leaders, at the same time that they secured for themselves solid financial support; the Right, assisted by the Bank of Spain;[1] Socialism by Willy Brandt, Venezuela and the other European Socialists; the Communists by the usual means.

Meanwhile, Premier Suárez, whom I had firmly entrusted with the responsibility of government, could only participate in the election campaign during its final eight days, bereft of the advantages and opportunities which I have explained above, and from which the other political parties were able to profit.

Despite that, alone, and with an organization still hardly formed, financed by short-term loans from certain private individuals, he managed to secure an outright and decisive victory.

At the same time, however, the Socialist party also obtained a higher than expected percentage of the vote; one which poses a serious threat to the country's security and to the stability of the monarchy, since I am reliably informed that their party is Marxist. A certain part of the electorate is unaware of this, voting for them in the belief that through Socialism Spain might receive aid from such major European countries as Germany, or alternatively from countries such as Venezuela, for the revival of the Spanish economy.

For this reason it is imperative that Adolfo Suárez restructure and consolidate the Centrist Political Coalition, so as to create a political

---

[1] The words used are La Banque d'Espagne, but the King almost certainly meant 'The Spanish Banking System' rather than any particular bank.

party for himself which will serve as the mainstay of the monarchy and of the stability of Spain.

For this to be achieved Prime Minister Suarez clearly needs more than ever before whatever assistance is possible, be it from his fellow countrymen or from friendly countries abroad who look to the preservation of Western civilization and of established monarchies.

It is for this reason, my dear brother, that I take the liberty of requesting your support on behalf of the political party of Prime Minister Suarez, at a critical juncture; the municipal elections are to be held within six months, and it is there more than anywhere that we shall put our very future in the balance.

Thus I take the liberty, with all respect, of submitting for your generous consideration the possibility of granting $10,000,000 as your personal contribution to the strengthening of the Spanish monarchy.

Should my request meet with your approval, I take the liberty to recommend a visit to Tehran by my personal friend, Alexis Mardas, who can take receipt of your instructions.

With all my respect and friendship,

Your brother

Juan Carlos

[The Shah's reply to this letter is dated 4 July 1977. It is warmly worded but displays much greater caution than that of the King of Spain: ' ... As for the question to which Your Majesty alluded in his letter, I shall convey my personal thoughts by word of mouth ... ']

Thursday, 7 July
Audience ... 'Tell the PM he's to set aside a substantial allowance for the Kurdish Mullahs', HIM said. 'They have shown themselves true patriots.' ...

Met the German and American doctors who have been asked to examine the Queen Mother. They consider she's in excellent shape for a lady of eighty-six, and have specified a regime of medicines ...

Friday, 8 July
Rested at home. My present state leaves me little alternative. I'm relieved

I was spared a meeting with Dayan. The effort would have brought me out in a fever.

Moshe Dayan himself was received from eleven this morning until one. HIM was reluctant to let the meeting run so late without inviting him to lunch, but I persuaded him our guest would have no cause for complaint.

HMQ has been in New York preparing to deliver a speech. A thousand people demonstrated against her.

Saturday, 9 July

Audience. Told HIM that Professors Jean Bernard and Georges Flandrin will come to examine him tomorrow morning. Jean Bernard is delighted to find him so well and his spleen disorder quite cured. 'But what went wrong in the first place?', HIM asked. I replied that it was due to some sort of blood disease. 'Perhaps it was chronic malaria', he continued. 'No, Your Majesty', I told him. 'Your tablets were deliberately put in a bottle marked anti-malaria pills, so that nobody would realize what was really the matter.'

Talked about the Queen Mother ... 'She's remarkably attached to my sister Shams', he said. 'Every time Shams goes away on a trip, mother falls ill.' Princess Shams is presently in the USA. I suggested it might be best if she goes away less often, particularly since she's always saying how much she dislikes these trips. 'I'm afraid it's some sort of crazy vanity of hers', he replied. 'Swanning around America with her retinue – ten dogs, and twice as many cats.'

Monday, 11 July

Audience ... Sought permission to travel to Europe to rest. HIM was as kind as always, asking after my health.

Wednesday, 3 August

I've now been in France several weeks. This afternoon I went absent without leave in order to call on an attractive lady friend. As Hafez puts it all too well:

> Ah, foolish heart! The pleasure of today,
> Although abandoned, will tomorrow stand
> A surety for the gold you threw away.

Returned home to be told that HIM had several times tried to contact me. I was surprised, as there seemed nothing particularly important for us to discuss ... Did my best to telephone him in Tehran, but all the lines were engaged.

Thursday, 4 August
HIM telephoned. He said he wanted personally to ask me to submit my resignation. Deeply touched by his thoughtfulness ... Sent an official letter of resignation under a covering note, thanking him for all the kindness and attention he has shown me ... Several times I've hinted he should allow me to retire, but somehow he always managed to change the subject. On the telephone today he confided that he intends making major changes in the government.

Saturday, 6 August
Jamshid Amouzegar has been appointed Prime Minister. Hoveyda becomes Minister of Court in my place ... It's one of those puzzles known only to HIM and Hoveyda himself.

As I have written to HIM, I shall go to Birjand as soon as I return home. There I shall stay, unless my condition deteriorates still further:

> The time is drawing near for me to find
> Some quiet tavern; unmaligned,
> With no companion save my cup and book.
> To quit the wiles and tricks of human kind
> And far from hypocrites select a friend
> Pure-hearted, good, and slowly sip my wine.
> Cypress-like, head high, in peace of mind
> To leave this world's cruel rumours far behind.[1]

In the past two months we've backed down over oil prices. We've surrendered to the Saudis, which means in effect to Carter. Oil prices are to remain frozen until the end of next year ...

These diaries must come to an end. There is nothing left for me to write now that I'm cut from my meetings with HIM ...

[1] From Hafez.

Cap d'Antibes, 9 September

I intended to write no more but there are various press cuttings about my resignation I'd like kept here ... just as a record. They have no other use. I'm too weak, and I lack the desire ever to return to official life.

People showed no enthusiasm for Hoveyda's appointment. It's a vital role he's been given ... but it's said the Shah chose badly. If Hoveyda's government were to blame for the present chaos, why promote him still further? ...

My own hopes and regrets lie elsewhere. I am proud to have served the Shahanshah faithfully for thirty-seven years. Never once did I utter a falsehood or consciously mislead him. Lately I felt compelled to speak my mind, but it saddened me. It took away my zest for public affairs but not my loyalty to my great, beloved Shahanshah. I would gladly lay down my life for him, even now:

> Darius, Alexander, their great hullabaloo
> Can be summed up simply in a line or two.
>
> – Hafez

Alam died on 13 April 1978.
Mohammad Reza Shah died on 27 July 1980.

Index

INDEX